12/15

Invisible Ink

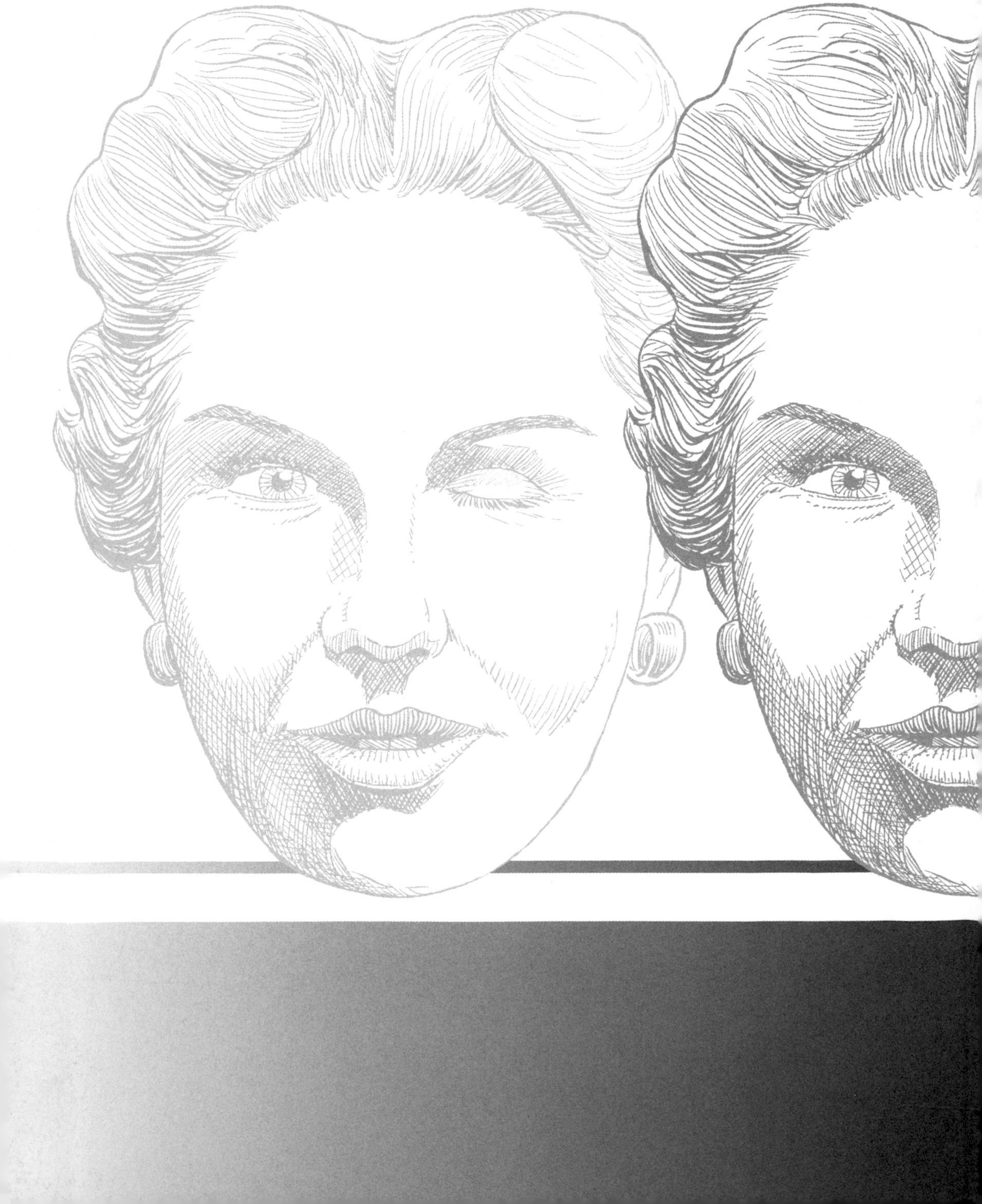

Invisible Ink

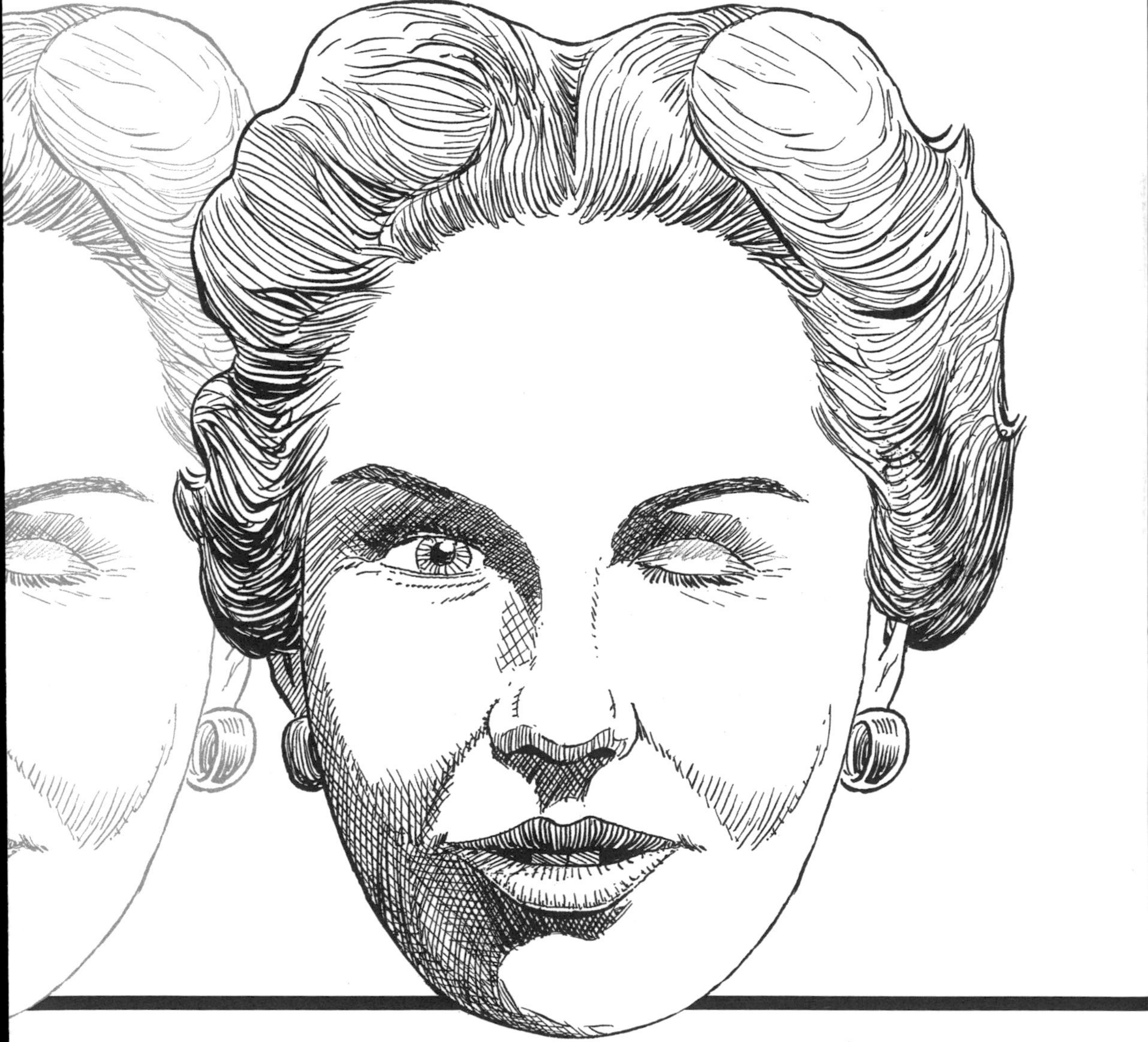

MY MOTHER'S SECRET LOVE AFFAIR WITH A FAMOUS CARTOONIST

a graphic memoir by Bill Griffith

INVISIBLE INK

Library of Congress
Control Number: 2015937719
Invisible Ink, My Mother's Secret
Love Affair with a Famous
Cartoonist, Griffith, Bill p. cm.
ISBN: 978-1-60699-895-3
1. Memoirs 2. Comic books, strips,
etc. 1. Title. PN6727.K28J48
741.5973---DC21 14-23996 CIP

Fantagraphics Books, Inc.
7563 Lake City Way NE,
Seattle WA 98115
www.fantagraphics.com
Call 1-800-657-1100 for a full color
catalog of fine comics publications.

Designed by Bill Griffith
and Keeli McCarthy
Production by Preston White
and Paul Baresh
Associate Publisher: Eric Reynolds
Published by Gary Groth

Printed in Malaysia
First Edition: September 2015
10 9 8 7 6 5 4 3 2 1

For more on Bill Griffith visit:
www.zippythepinhead.com
To contact Bill Griffith:
griffy@zippythepinhead.com

First five lines from "Kaddish" from
Collected Poems 1947–1980 by Allen
Ginsberg copyright © 1959 by Allen
Ginsberg. Reprinted by permission of
HarperCollins Publishers.

"Sit Down You're Rockin' The Boat"
from Guys and Dolls by Frank Loesser
copyright © 1950 (renewed) Frank
Music Corp. All Rights Reserved.
Reprinted by permission of Hal
Leonard Corporation.

Grateful thanks to Diane Noomin for her invaluable editing and overview. I couldn't have done this without her.

All dialogue spoken by my wife, Diane Noomin, on pages 56, 79, 90, 119, 120, 131, 140, 162, 173, 174 and 175, is written by Diane Noomin.

NOTE: All of the drawings in this book are by Bill Griffith. This includes all drawings, cartoons, comics, book and magazine covers by either Lawrence Lariar or any other artist or designer whose work is shown. No art of any kind is reproduced from original sources. It has all been re-drawn.

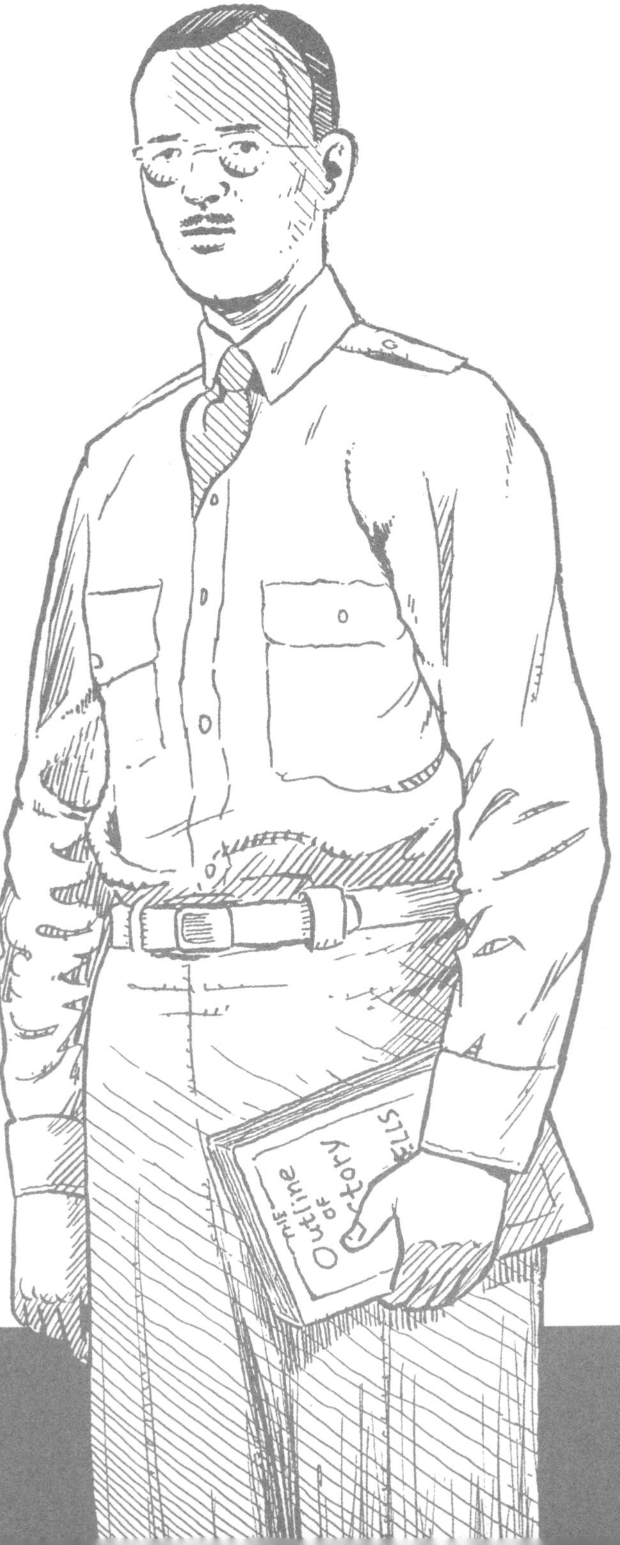
THE Outline of

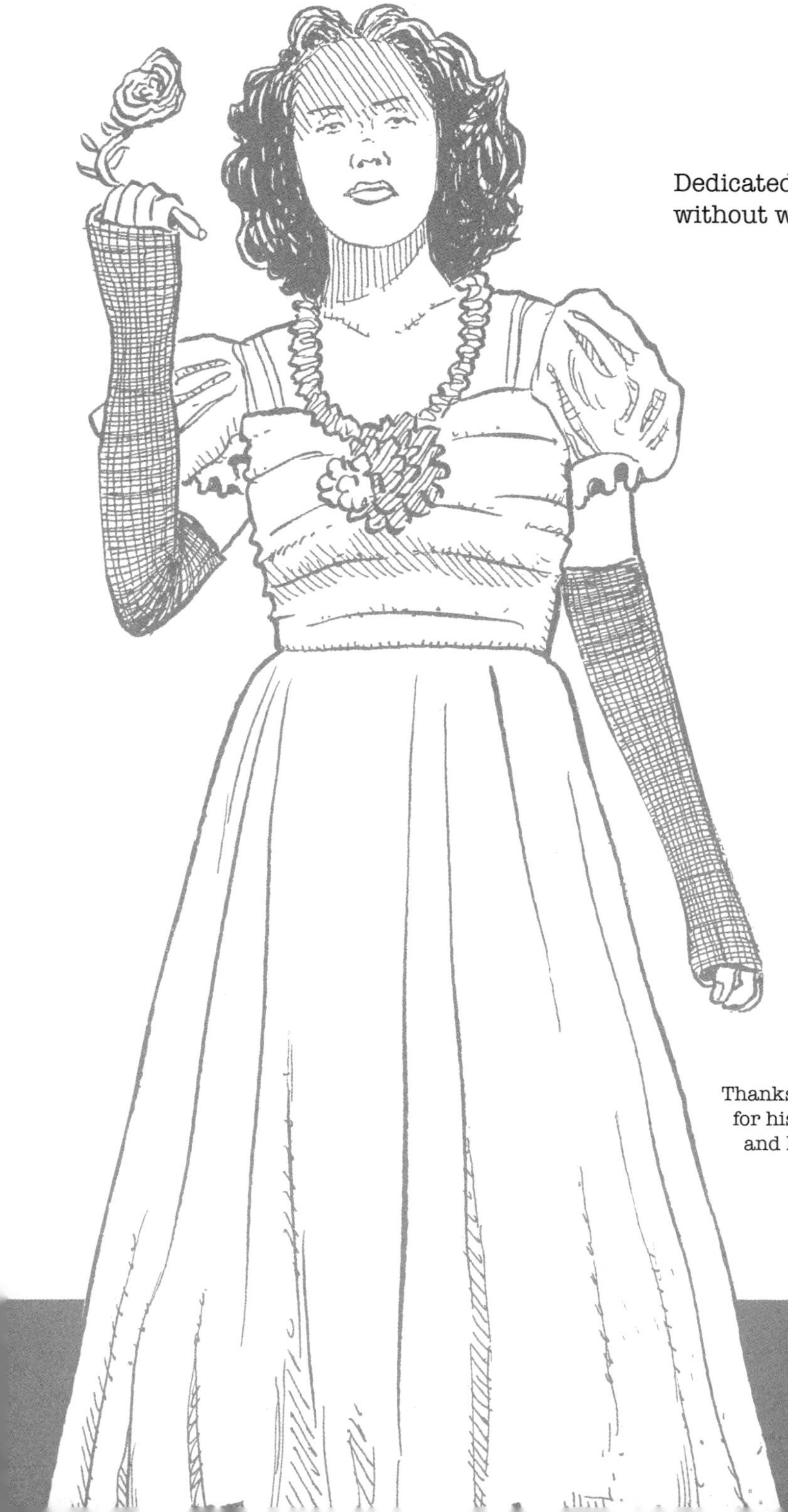

Dedicated to Barbara J. Griffith,
without whom.

Thanks to Alan C. Jackson
for his avuncular affection
and his razor-sharp memory.

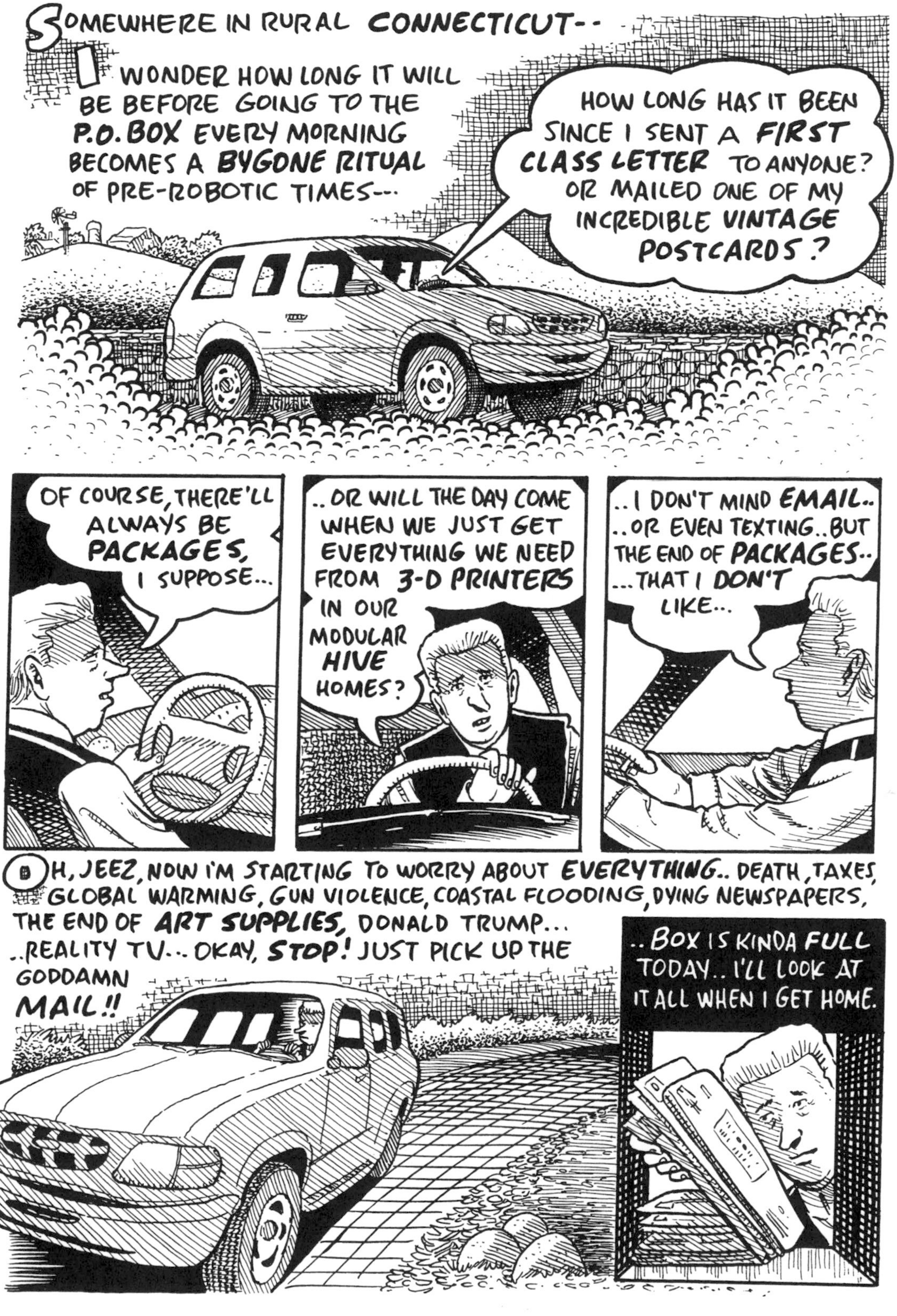
SOMEWHERE IN RURAL CONNECTICUT--
I WONDER HOW LONG IT WILL BE BEFORE GOING TO THE P.O. BOX EVERY MORNING BECOMES A BYGONE RITUAL OF PRE-ROBOTIC TIMES---
HOW LONG HAS IT BEEN SINCE I SENT A FIRST CLASS LETTER TO ANYONE? OR MAILED ONE OF MY INCREDIBLE VINTAGE POSTCARDS?
OF COURSE, THERE'LL ALWAYS BE PACKAGES, I SUPPOSE...
..OR WILL THE DAY COME WHEN WE JUST GET EVERYTHING WE NEED FROM 3-D PRINTERS IN OUR MODULAR HIVE HOMES?
..I DON'T MIND EMAIL.. ..OR EVEN TEXTING..BUT THE END OF PACKAGES.. ...THAT I DON'T LIKE...
OH, JEEZ, NOW I'M STARTING TO WORRY ABOUT EVERYTHING.. DEATH, TAXES, GLOBAL WARMING, GUN VIOLENCE, COASTAL FLOODING, DYING NEWSPAPERS, THE END OF ART SUPPLIES, DONALD TRUMP... ..REALITY TV... OKAY, STOP! JUST PICK UP THE GODDAMN MAIL!!
..BOX IS KINDA FULL TODAY.. I'LL LOOK AT IT ALL WHEN I GET HOME.

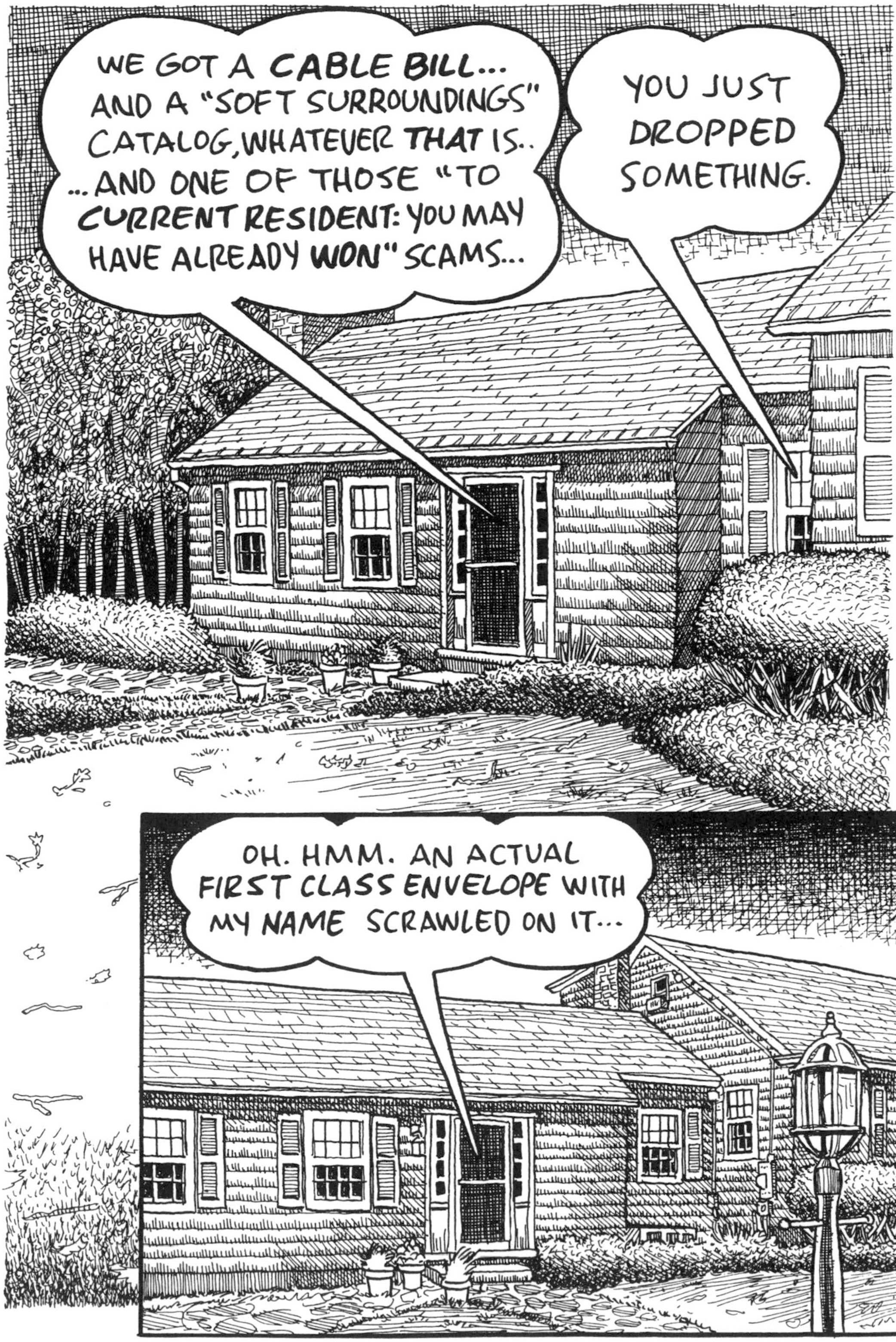
WE GOT A CABLE BILL... AND A "SOFT SURROUNDINGS" CATALOG, WHATEVER THAT IS.. ...AND ONE OF THOSE "TO CURRENT RESIDENT: YOU MAY HAVE ALREADY WON" SCAMS...
YOU JUST DROPPED SOMETHING.
OH. HMM. AN ACTUAL FIRST CLASS ENVELOPE WITH MY NAME SCRAWLED ON IT...

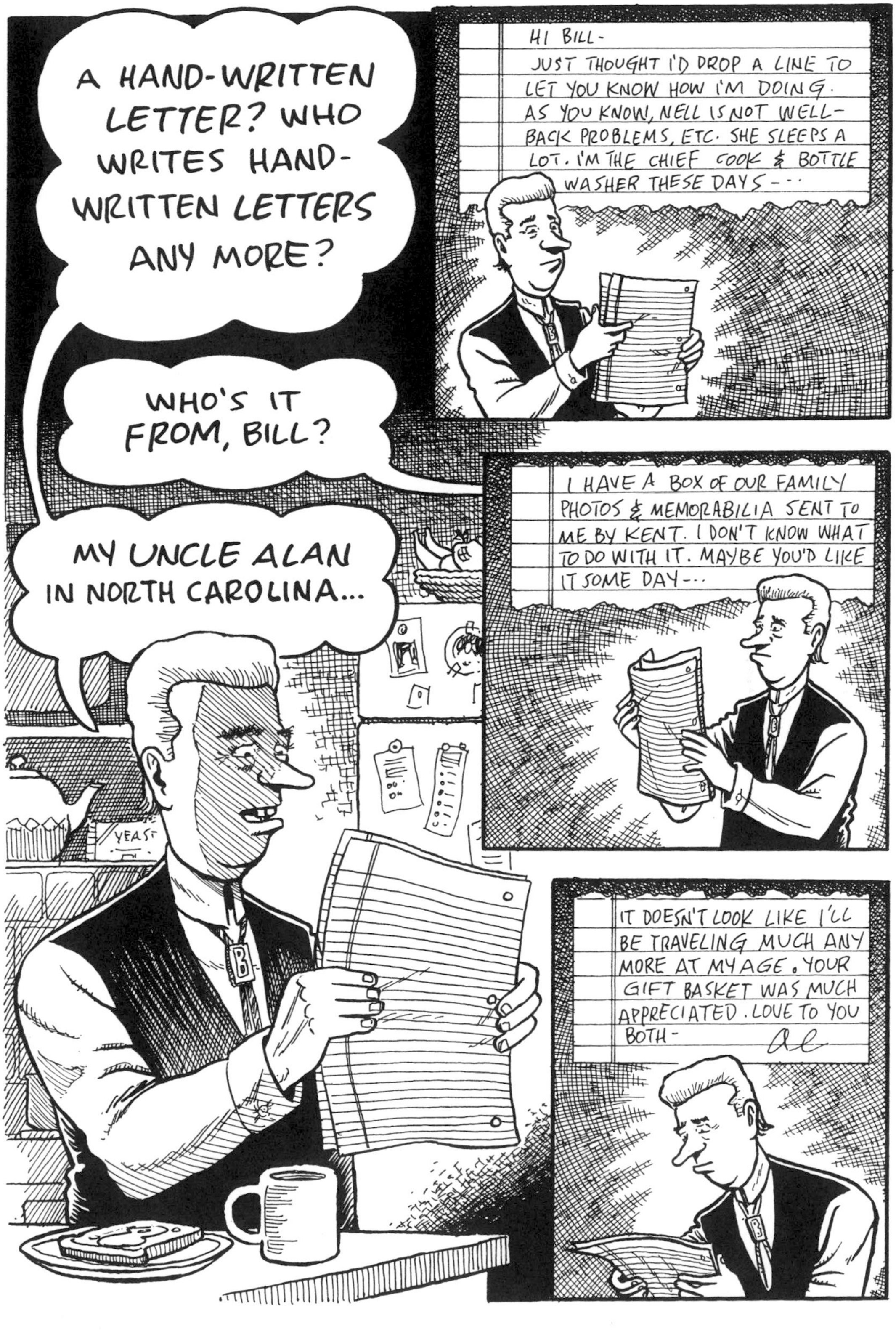
A HAND-WRITTEN LETTER? WHO WRITES HAND-WRITTEN LETTERS ANY MORE?
WHO'S IT FROM, BILL?
MY UNCLE ALAN IN NORTH CAROLINA...
YEAST
HI BILL-
JUST THOUGHT I'D DROP A LINE TO LET YOU KNOW HOW I'M DOING. AS YOU KNOW, NELL IS NOT WELL- BACK PROBLEMS, ETC. SHE SLEEPS A LOT. I'M THE CHIEF COOK & BOTTLE WASHER THESE DAYS---
I HAVE A BOX OF OUR FAMILY PHOTOS & MEMORABILIA SENT TO ME BY KENT. I DON'T KNOW WHAT TO DO WITH IT. MAYBE YOU'D LIKE IT SOME DAY---
IT DOESN'T LOOK LIKE I'LL BE TRAVELING MUCH ANY MORE AT MY AGE. YOUR GIFT BASKET WAS MUCH APPRECIATED. LOVE TO YOU BOTH-
Al

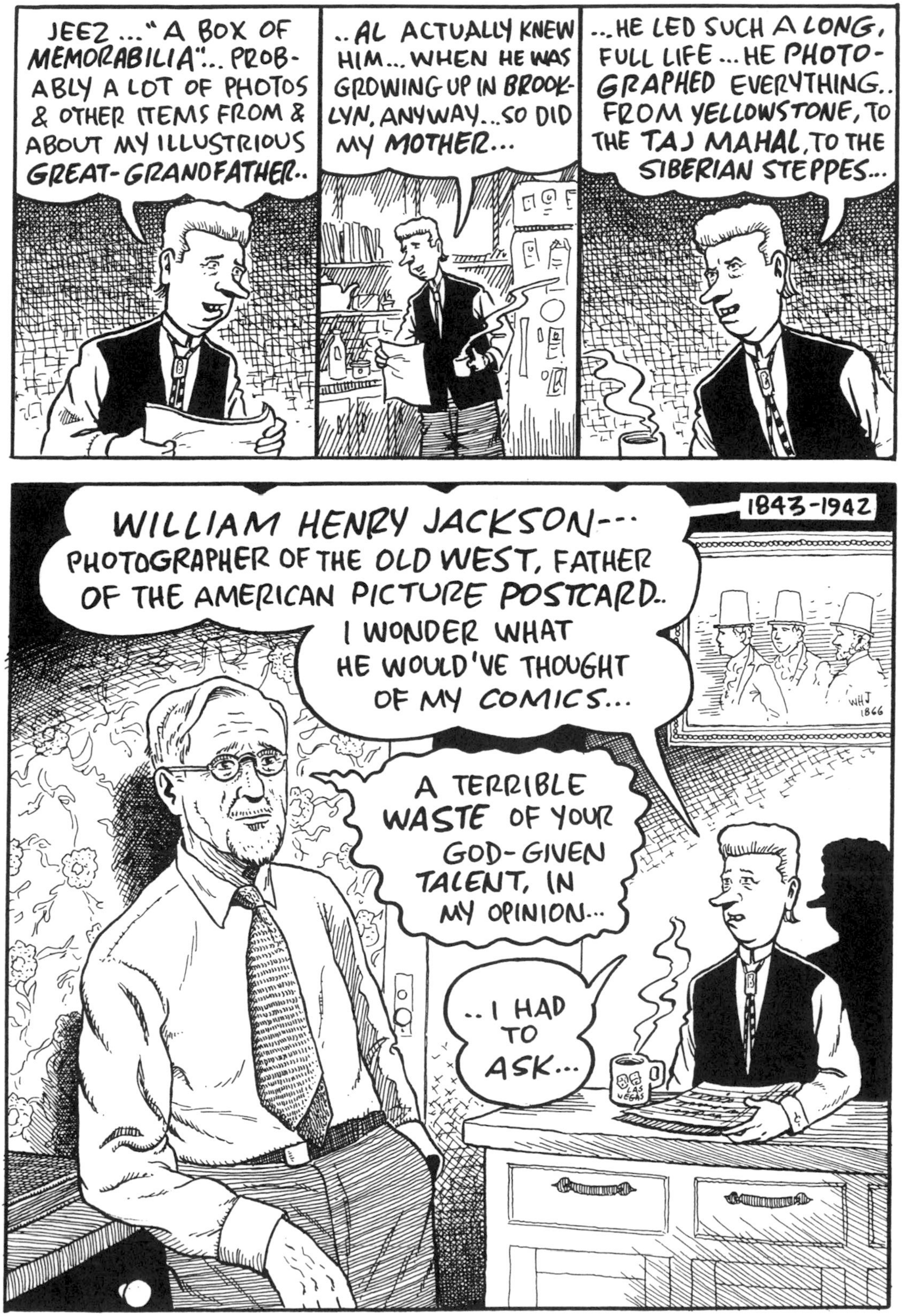
JEEZ ... "A BOX OF MEMORABILIA"... PROBABLY A LOT OF PHOTOS & OTHER ITEMS FROM & ABOUT MY ILLUSTRIOUS GREAT-GRANDFATHER..
..AL ACTUALLY KNEW HIM... WHEN HE WAS GROWING UP IN BROOKLYN, ANYWAY...SO DID MY MOTHER...
...HE LED SUCH A LONG, FULL LIFE ... HE PHOTOGRAPHED EVERYTHING.. FROM YELLOWSTONE, TO THE TAJ MAHAL, TO THE SIBERIAN STEPPES...
WILLIAM HENRY JACKSON--- PHOTOGRAPHER OF THE OLD WEST, FATHER OF THE AMERICAN PICTURE POSTCARD..
1843-1942
I WONDER WHAT HE WOULD'VE THOUGHT OF MY COMICS...
WHJ 1866
A TERRIBLE WASTE OF YOUR GOD-GIVEN TALENT, IN MY OPINION...
..I HAD TO ASK...
LAS VEGAS

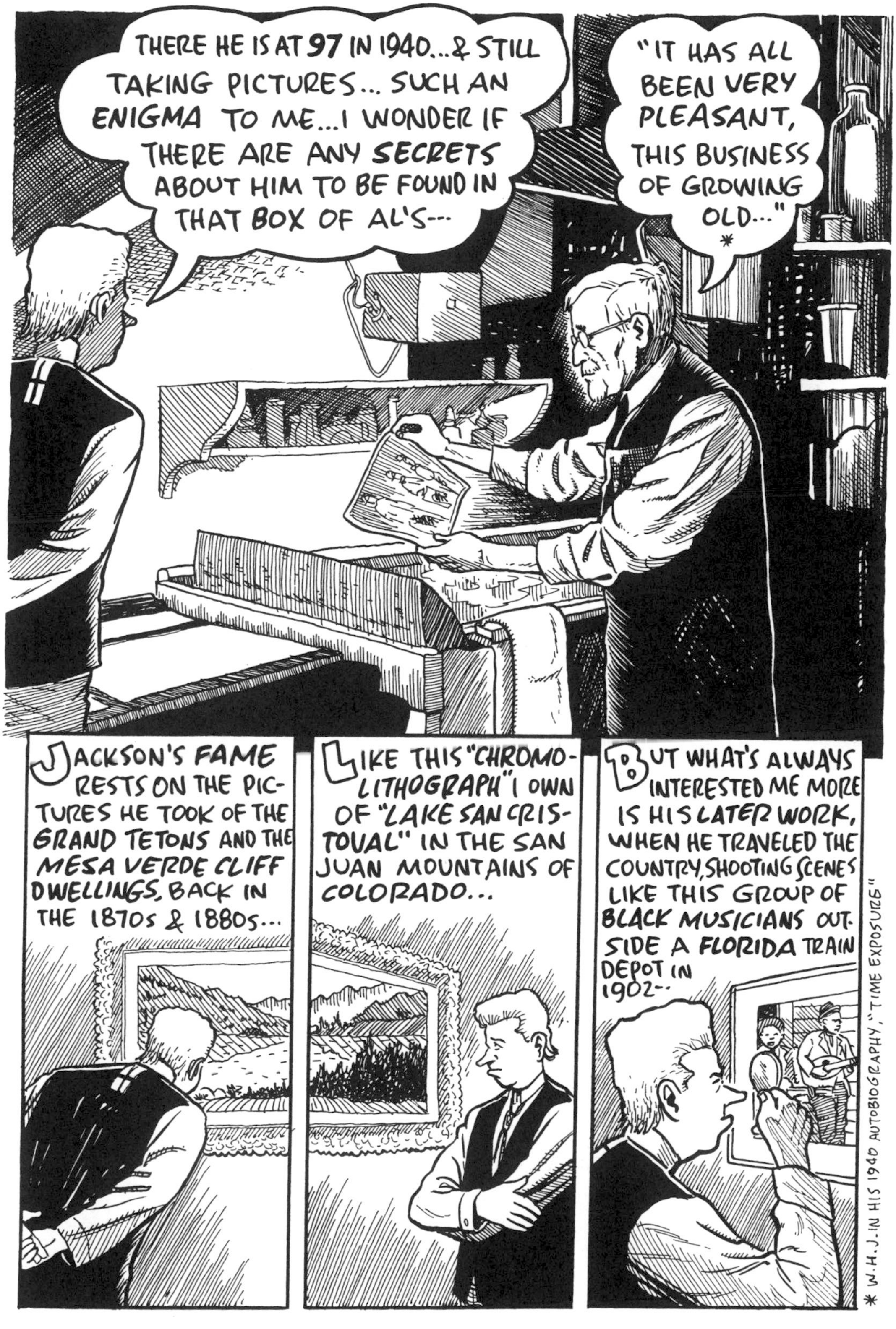
THERE HE IS AT 97 IN 1940...& STILL TAKING PICTURES... SUCH AN ENIGMA TO ME...I WONDER IF THERE ARE ANY SECRETS ABOUT HIM TO BE FOUND IN THAT BOX OF AL'S--
"IT HAS ALL BEEN VERY PLEASANT, THIS BUSINESS OF GROWING OLD..." *
JACKSON'S FAME RESTS ON THE PICTURES HE TOOK OF THE GRAND TETONS AND THE MESA VERDE CLIFF DWELLINGS, BACK IN THE 1870s & 1880s...
LIKE THIS "CHROMO-LITHOGRAPH" I OWN OF "LAKE SAN CRISTOVAL" IN THE SAN JUAN MOUNTAINS OF COLORADO...
BUT WHAT'S ALWAYS INTERESTED ME MORE IS HIS LATER WORK, WHEN HE TRAVELED THE COUNTRY, SHOOTING SCENES LIKE THIS GROUP OF BLACK MUSICIANS OUTSIDE A FLORIDA TRAIN DEPOT IN 1902--
* W.H.J. IN HIS 1940 AUTOBIOGRAPHY, "TIME EXPOSURE"

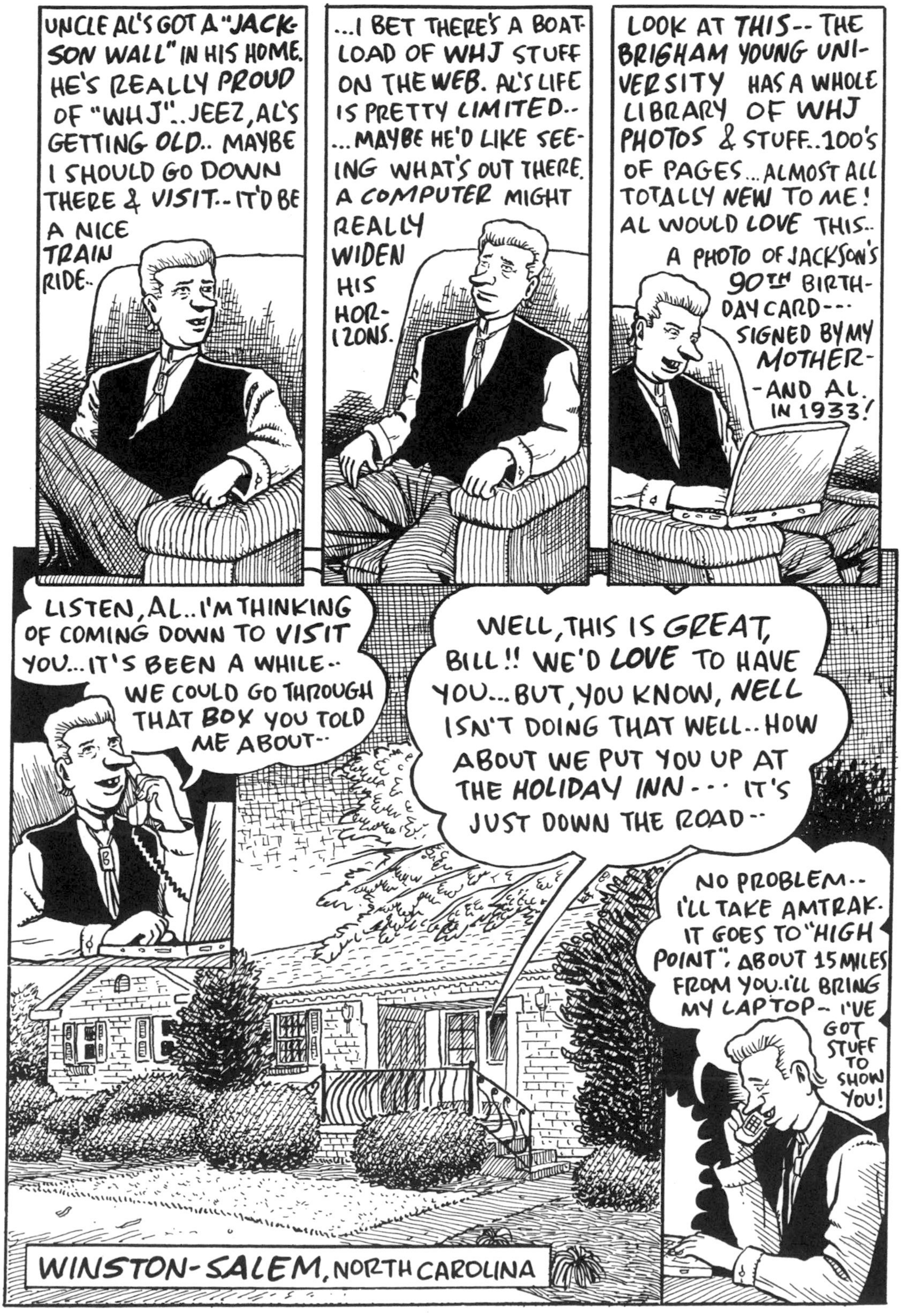
UNCLE AL'S GOT A "JACKSON WALL" IN HIS HOME. HE'S REALLY PROUD OF "WHJ".. JEEZ, AL'S GETTING OLD.. MAYBE I SHOULD GO DOWN THERE & VISIT.- IT'D BE A NICE TRAIN RIDE..
...I BET THERE'S A BOATLOAD OF WHJ STUFF ON THE WEB. AL'S LIFE IS PRETTY LIMITED.. ...MAYBE HE'D LIKE SEEING WHAT'S OUT THERE. A COMPUTER MIGHT REALLY WIDEN HIS HORIZONS.
LOOK AT THIS-- THE BRIGHAM YOUNG UNIVERSITY HAS A WHOLE LIBRARY OF WHJ PHOTOS & STUFF..100'S OF PAGES... ALMOST ALL TOTALLY NEW TO ME! AL WOULD LOVE THIS..
A PHOTO OF JACKSON'S 90TH BIRTHDAY CARD--- SIGNED BY MY MOTHER- -AND AL. IN 1933!
LISTEN, AL.. I'M THINKING OF COMING DOWN TO VISIT YOU... IT'S BEEN A WHILE.. WE COULD GO THROUGH THAT BOX YOU TOLD ME ABOUT..
WELL, THIS IS GREAT, BILL!! WE'D LOVE TO HAVE YOU... BUT, YOU KNOW, NELL ISN'T DOING THAT WELL.. HOW ABOUT WE PUT YOU UP AT THE HOLIDAY INN - - - IT'S JUST DOWN THE ROAD..
NO PROBLEM.. I'LL TAKE AMTRAK. IT GOES TO "HIGH POINT". ABOUT 15 MILES FROM YOU. I'LL BRING MY LAPTOP.. I'VE GOT STUFF TO SHOW YOU!
WINSTON-SALEM, NORTH CAROLINA

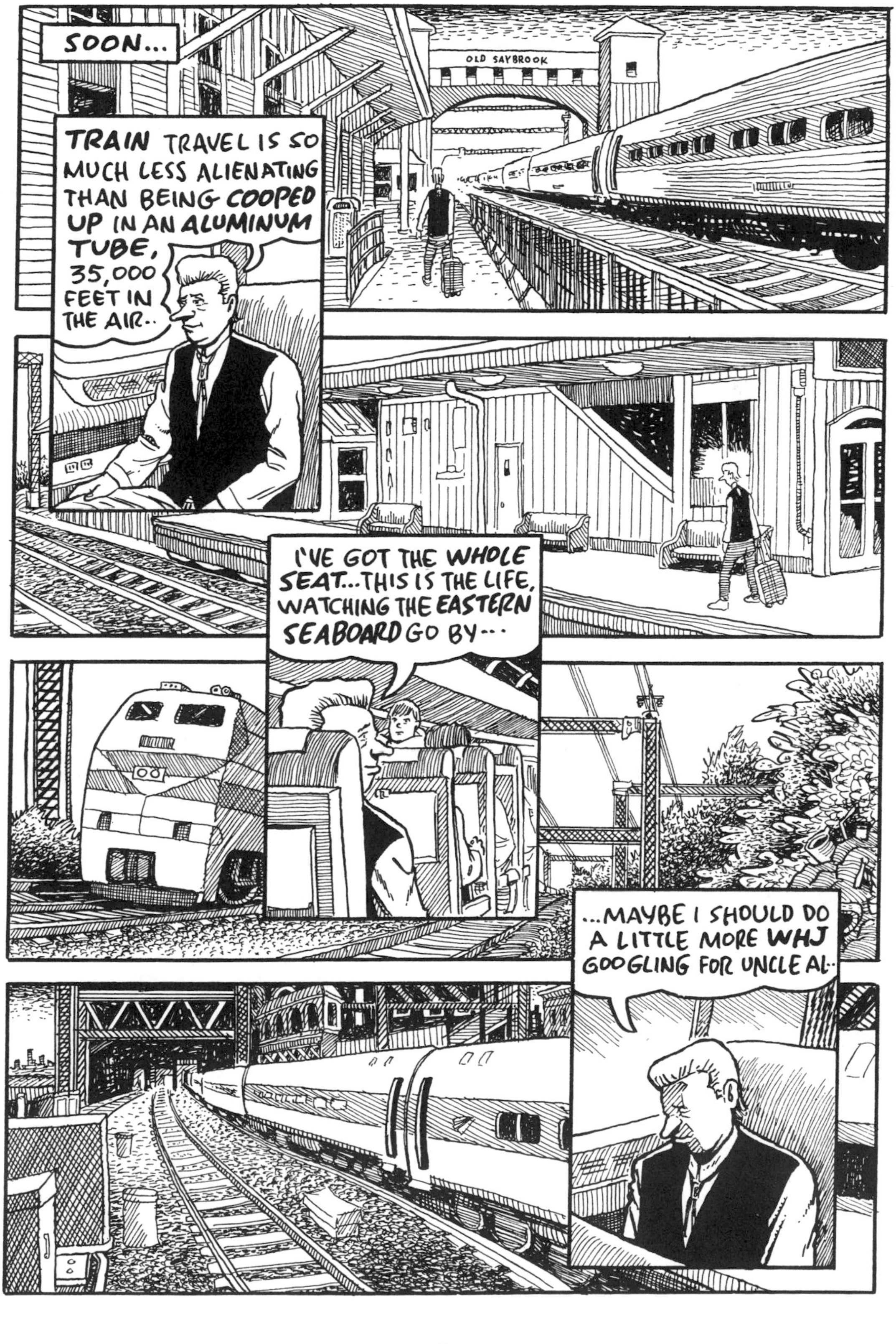
SOON...
OLD SAYBROOK
TRAIN TRAVEL IS SO MUCH LESS ALIENATING THAN BEING COOPED UP IN AN ALUMINUM TUBE, 35,000 FEET IN THE AIR..
I'VE GOT THE WHOLE SEAT...THIS IS THE LIFE, WATCHING THE EASTERN SEABOARD GO BY...
...MAYBE I SHOULD DO A LITTLE MORE WHJ GOOGLING FOR UNCLE AL..

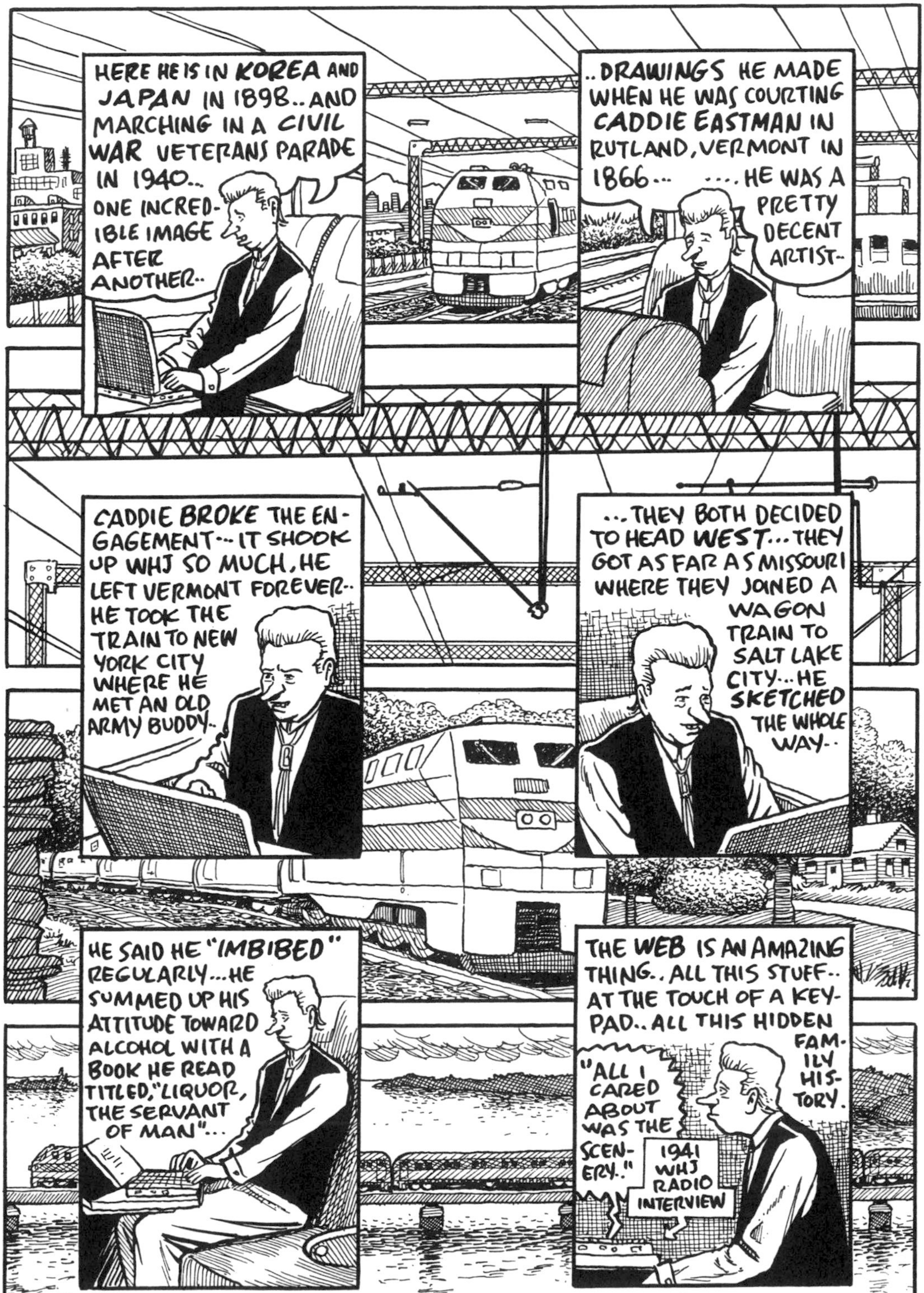
HERE HE IS IN KOREA AND JAPAN IN 1898.. AND MARCHING IN A CIVIL WAR VETERANS PARADE IN 1940.. ONE INCREDIBLE IMAGE AFTER ANOTHER..
..DRAWINGS HE MADE WHEN HE WAS COURTING CADDIE EASTMAN IN RUTLAND, VERMONT IN 1866... ....HE WAS A PRETTY DECENT ARTIST..
CADDIE BROKE THE ENGAGEMENT... IT SHOOK UP WHJ SO MUCH, HE LEFT VERMONT FOREVER.. HE TOOK THE TRAIN TO NEW YORK CITY WHERE HE MET AN OLD ARMY BUDDY..
...THEY BOTH DECIDED TO HEAD WEST... THEY GOT AS FAR AS MISSOURI WHERE THEY JOINED A WAGON TRAIN TO SALT LAKE CITY... HE SKETCHED THE WHOLE WAY..
HE SAID HE "IMBIBED" REGULARLY... HE SUMMED UP HIS ATTITUDE TOWARD ALCOHOL WITH A BOOK HE READ TITLED, "LIQUOR, THE SERVANT OF MAN"...
THE WEB IS AN AMAZING THING.. ALL THIS STUFF.. AT THE TOUCH OF A KEYPAD.. ALL THIS HIDDEN FAMILY HISTORY.
"ALL I CARED ABOUT WAS THE SCENERY."
1941 WHJ RADIO INTERVIEW

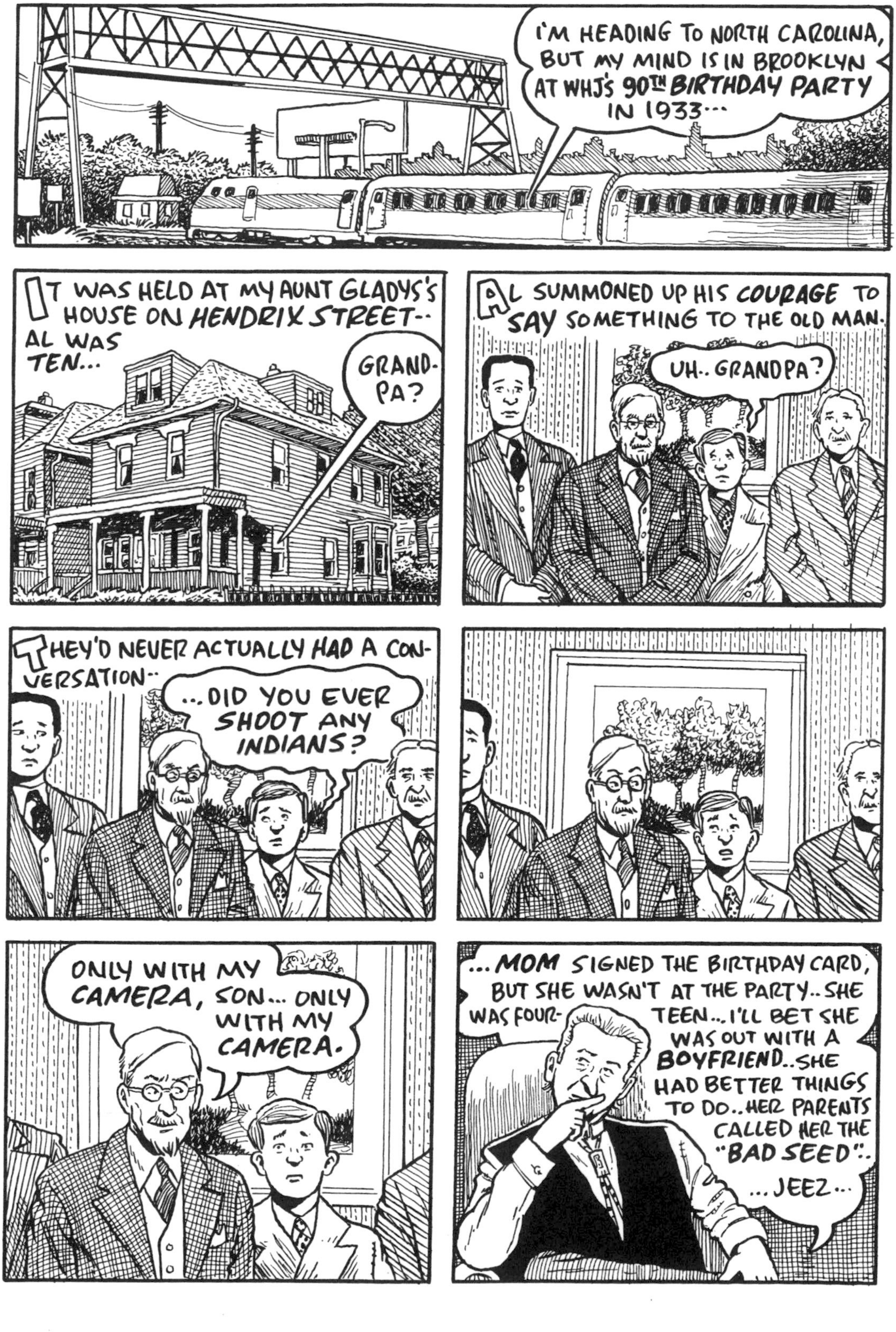
I'M HEADING TO NORTH CAROLINA, BUT MY MIND IS IN BROOKLYN AT WHJ'S 90TH BIRTHDAY PARTY IN 1933...
IT WAS HELD AT MY AUNT GLADYS'S HOUSE ON HENDRIX STREET-- AL WAS TEN...
GRAND-PA?
AL SUMMONED UP HIS COURAGE TO SAY SOMETHING TO THE OLD MAN.
UH.. GRANDPA?
THEY'D NEVER ACTUALLY HAD A CON-VERSATION..
...DID YOU EVER SHOOT ANY INDIANS?
ONLY WITH MY CAMERA, SON... ONLY WITH MY CAMERA.
...MOM SIGNED THE BIRTHDAY CARD, BUT SHE WASN'T AT THE PARTY.. SHE WAS FOUR-TEEN... I'LL BET SHE WAS OUT WITH A BOYFRIEND.. SHE HAD BETTER THINGS TO DO.. HER PARENTS CALLED HER THE "BAD SEED"..
...JEEZ...

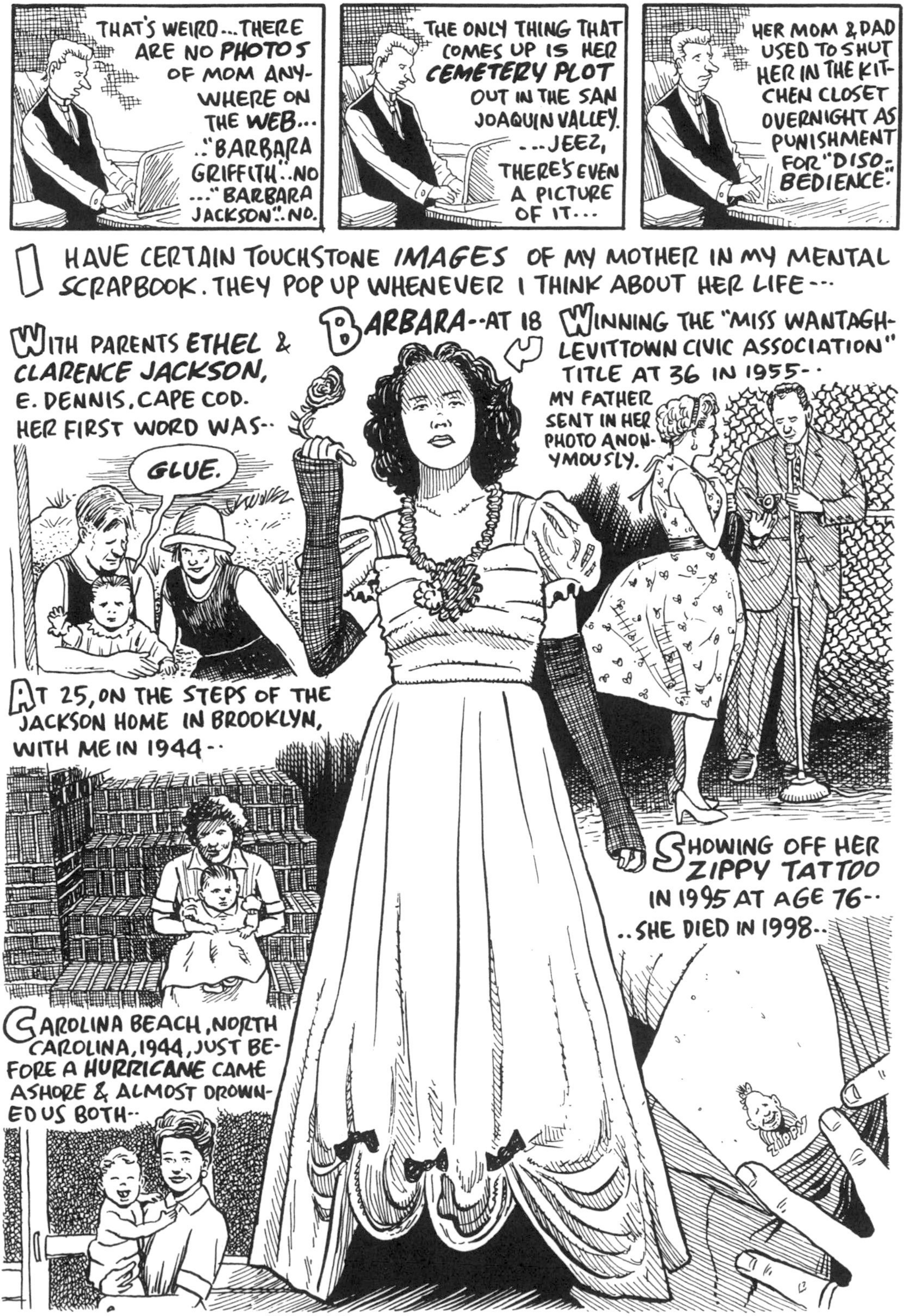
THAT'S WEIRD... THERE ARE NO PHOTOS OF MOM ANYWHERE ON THE WEB... ..."BARBARA GRIFFITH"..NO ..."BARBARA JACKSON"..NO.
THE ONLY THING THAT COMES UP IS HER CEMETERY PLOT OUT IN THE SAN JOAQUIN VALLEY. ...JEEZ, THERE'S EVEN A PICTURE OF IT...
HER MOM & DAD USED TO SHUT HER IN THE KITCHEN CLOSET OVERNIGHT AS PUNISHMENT FOR "DISOBEDIENCE."
I HAVE CERTAIN TOUCHSTONE IMAGES OF MY MOTHER IN MY MENTAL SCRAPBOOK. THEY POP UP WHENEVER I THINK ABOUT HER LIFE...
WITH PARENTS ETHEL & CLARENCE JACKSON, E. DENNIS, CAPE COD. HER FIRST WORD WAS..
GLUE.
BARBARA..AT 18
WINNING THE "MISS WANTAGH-LEVITTOWN CIVIC ASSOCIATION" TITLE AT 36 IN 1955..
MY FATHER SENT IN HER PHOTO ANONYMOUSLY.
AT 25, ON THE STEPS OF THE JACKSON HOME IN BROOKLYN, WITH ME IN 1944..
SHOWING OFF HER ZIPPY TATTOO IN 1995 AT AGE 76.. ..SHE DIED IN 1998..
ZIPPY
CAROLINA BEACH, NORTH CAROLINA, 1944, JUST BEFORE A HURRICANE CAME ASHORE & ALMOST DROWNED US BOTH..

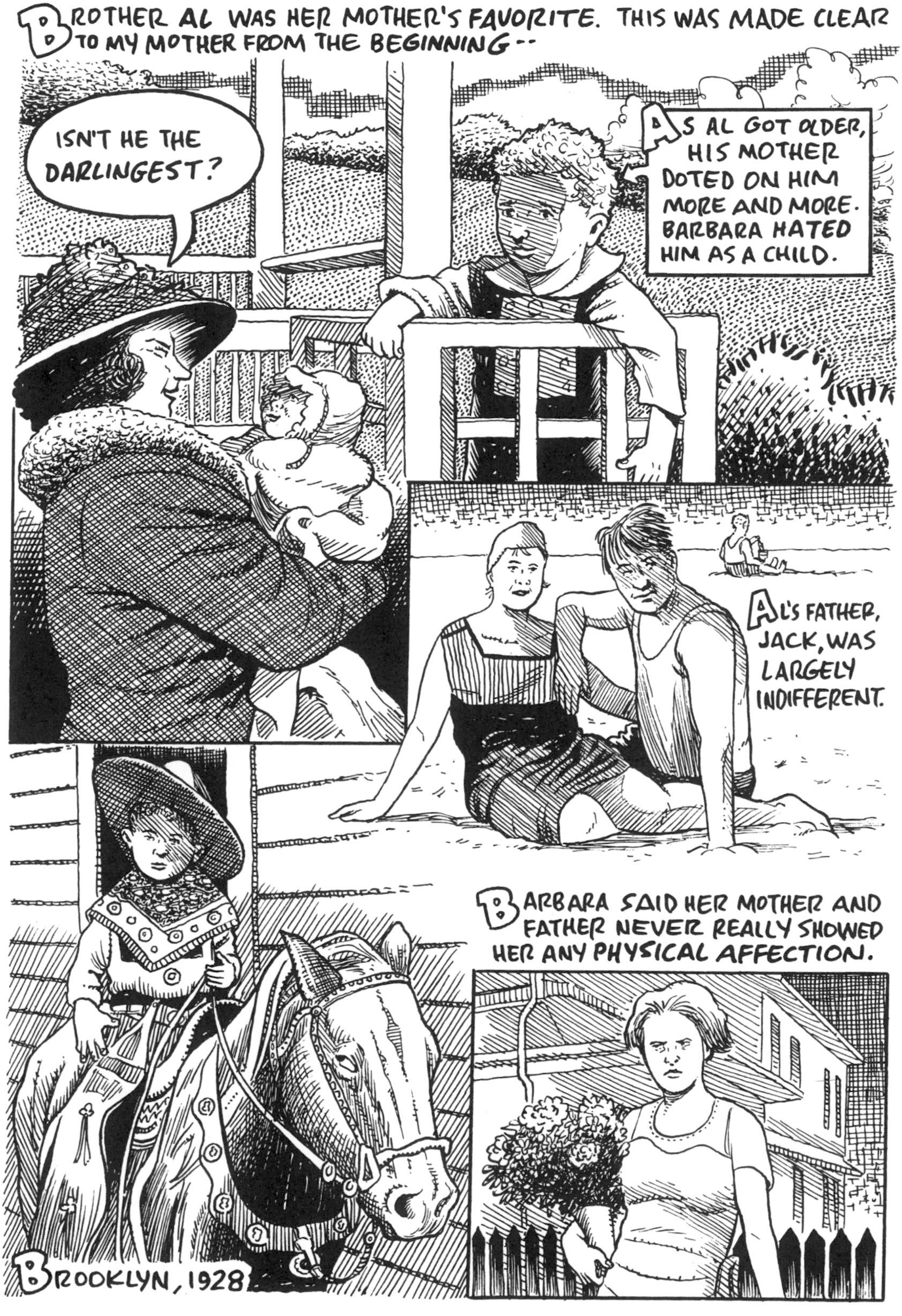
BROTHER AL WAS HER MOTHER'S FAVORITE. THIS WAS MADE CLEAR TO MY MOTHER FROM THE BEGINNING--
ISN'T HE THE DARLINGEST?
AS AL GOT OLDER, HIS MOTHER DOTED ON HIM MORE AND MORE. BARBARA HATED HIM AS A CHILD.
AL'S FATHER, JACK, WAS LARGELY INDIFFERENT.
BROOKLYN, 1928
BARBARA SAID HER MOTHER AND FATHER NEVER REALLY SHOWED HER ANY PHYSICAL AFFECTION.

GOOGLING MY FATHER... NO PHOTOS, EITHER. ...LET'S SEE.. I'LL PUT IN "MANHATTAN". HERE'S SOMETHING..

JUST ONE ENTRY.. IT LISTS HIS CANDIDACY FOR THE NEW YORK STATE ASSEMBLY FROM MANHATTAN'S 3RD DISTRICT IN 1940.

SMACK IN THE MIDDLE OF ROOSEVELT COUNTRY, HE RAN AS A REPUBLICAN. ...WHAT AN OUTSIDER..

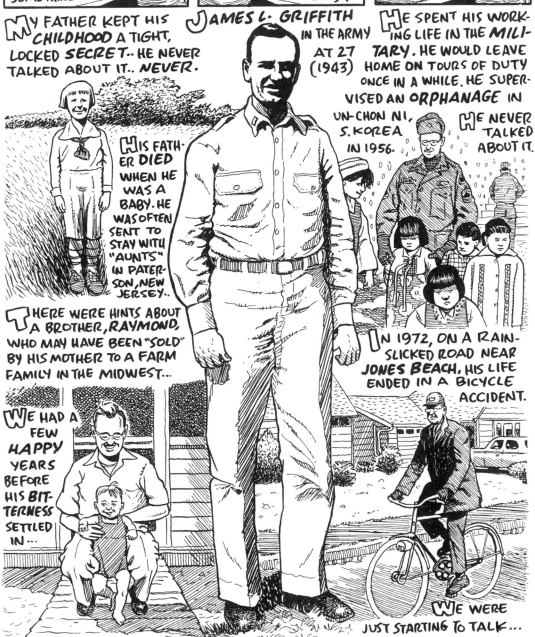

MY FATHER KEPT HIS CHILDHOOD A TIGHT, LOCKED SECRET.. HE NEVER TALKED ABOUT IT.. NEVER.

JAMES L. GRIFFITH IN THE ARMY AT 27 (1943)

HE SPENT HIS WORKING LIFE IN THE MILITARY. HE WOULD LEAVE HOME ON TOURS OF DUTY ONCE IN A WHILE. HE SUPERVISED AN ORPHANAGE IN UN-CHON NI, S. KOREA IN 1956.

HE NEVER TALKED ABOUT IT.

HIS FATHER DIED WHEN HE WAS A BABY. HE WAS OFTEN SENT TO STAY WITH "AUNTS" IN PATERSON, NEW JERSEY..

THERE WERE HINTS ABOUT A BROTHER, RAYMOND, WHO MAY HAVE BEEN "SOLD" BY HIS MOTHER TO A FARM FAMILY IN THE MIDWEST...

IN 1972, ON A RAIN-SLICKED ROAD NEAR JONES BEACH, HIS LIFE ENDED IN A BICYCLE ACCIDENT.

WE HAD A FEW HAPPY YEARS BEFORE HIS BITTERNESS SETTLED IN ...

WE WERE JUST STARTING TO TALK ...

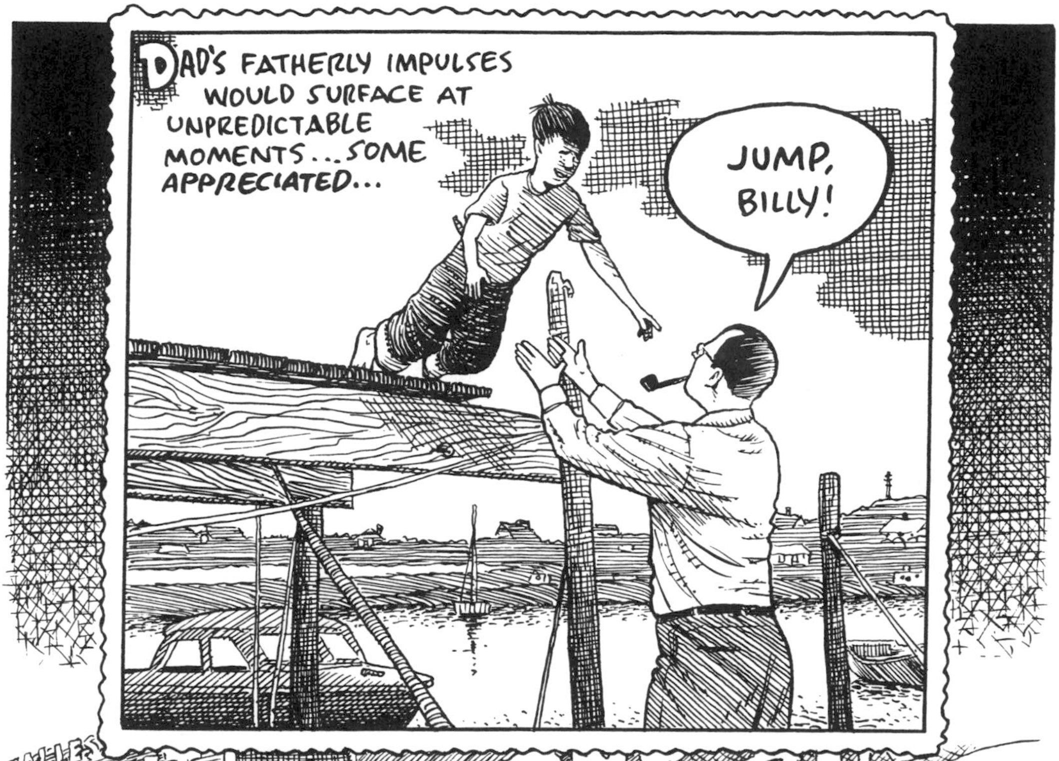
DAD'S FATHERLY IMPULSES WOULD SURFACE AT UNPREDICTABLE MOMENTS... SOME APPRECIATED...
JUMP, BILLY!

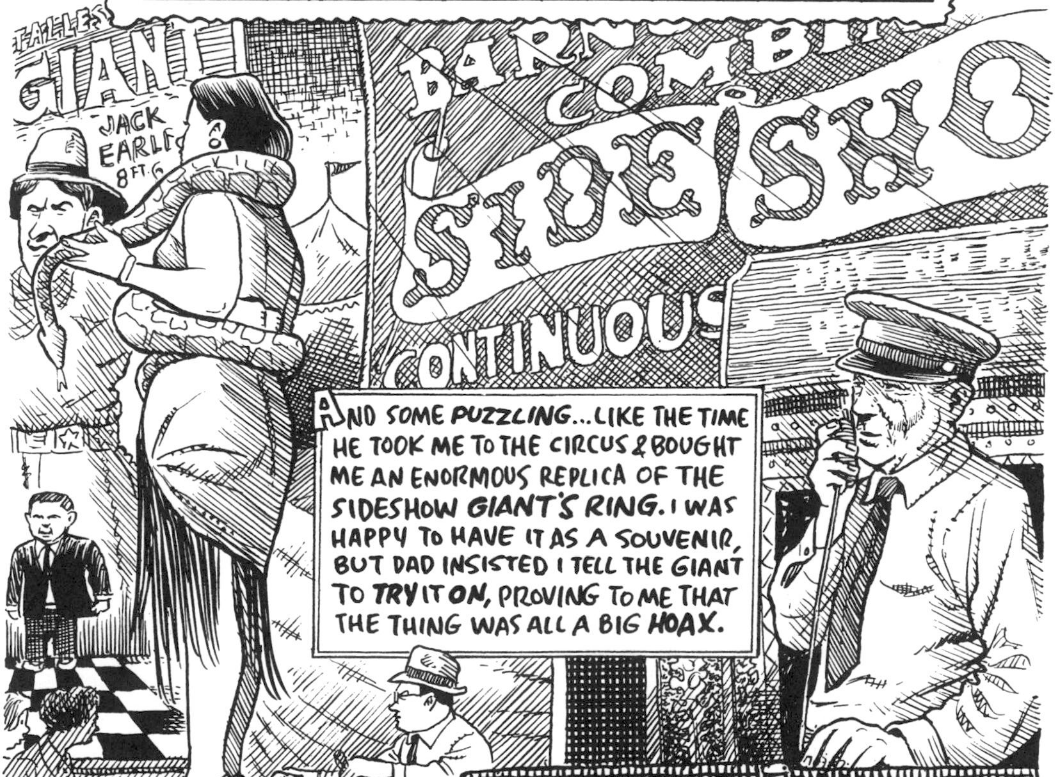
GIANT
JACK EARLE
8 FT. 6
SIDESHO
CONTINUOUS
AND SOME PUZZLING... LIKE THE TIME HE TOOK ME TO THE CIRCUS & BOUGHT ME AN ENORMOUS REPLICA OF THE SIDESHOW GIANT'S RING. I WAS HAPPY TO HAVE IT AS A SOUVENIR, BUT DAD INSISTED I TELL THE GIANT TO TRY IT ON, PROVING TO ME THAT THE THING WAS ALL A BIG HOAX.

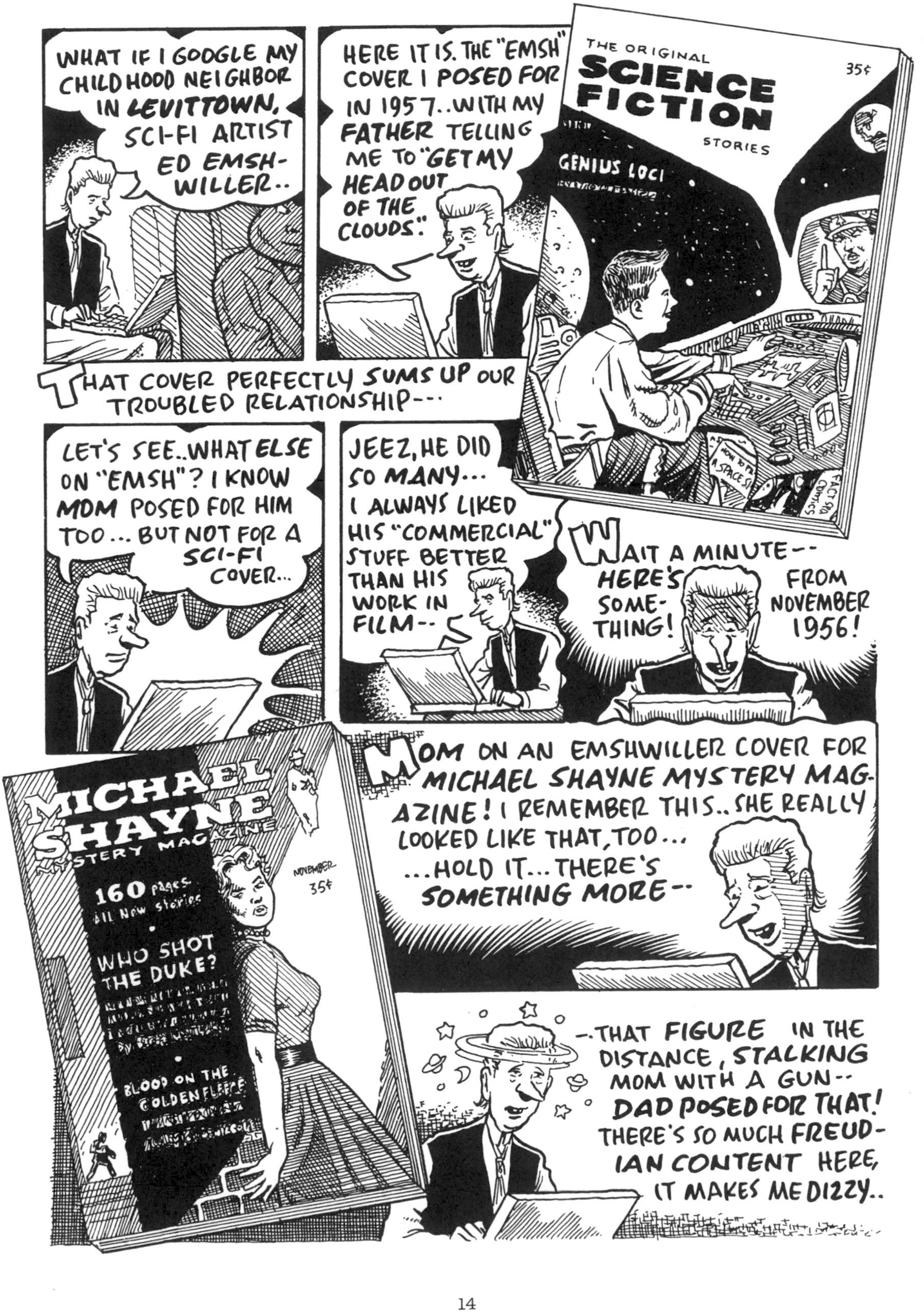

WHAT IF I GOOGLE MY CHILDHOOD NEIGHBOR IN LEVITTOWN, SCI-FI ARTIST ED EMSH-WILLER..
HERE IT IS. THE "EMSH" COVER I POSED FOR IN 1957..WITH MY FATHER TELLING ME TO "GET MY HEAD OUT OF THE CLOUDS."
THE ORIGINAL
SCIENCE FICTION
STORIES
35¢
GENIUS LOCI
THAT COVER PERFECTLY SUMS UP OUR TROUBLED RELATIONSHIP---
LET'S SEE..WHAT ELSE ON "EMSH"? I KNOW MOM POSED FOR HIM TOO... BUT NOT FOR A SCI-FI COVER...
JEEZ, HE DID SO MANY... I ALWAYS LIKED HIS "COMMERCIAL" STUFF BETTER THAN HIS WORK IN FILM--
WAIT A MINUTE--
HERE'S SOME-THING!
FROM NOVEMBER 1956!
MICHAEL SHAYNE MYSTERY MAGAZINE
NOVEMBER
35¢
160 pages All New stories
WHO SHOT THE DUKE?
BLOOD ON THE GOLDEN FLEECE
MOM ON AN EMSHWILLER COVER FOR MICHAEL SHAYNE MYSTERY MAG-AZINE! I REMEMBER THIS.. SHE REALLY LOOKED LIKE THAT, TOO...
...HOLD IT... THERE'S SOMETHING MORE--
--THAT FIGURE IN THE DISTANCE, STALKING MOM WITH A GUN-- DAD POSED FOR THAT! THERE'S SO MUCH FREUD-IAN CONTENT HERE, IT MAKES ME DIZZY..

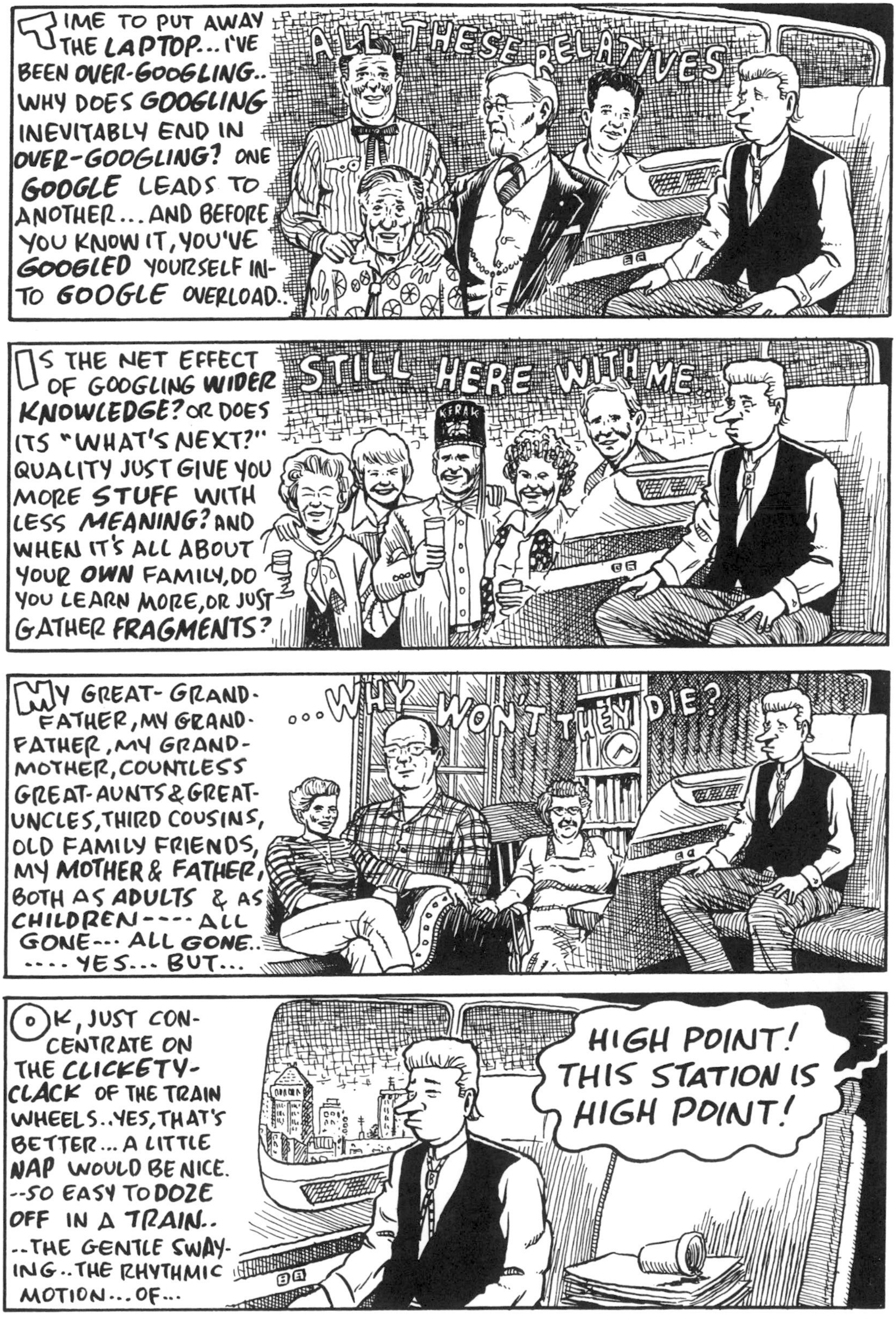
TIME TO PUT AWAY THE LAPTOP... I'VE BEEN OVER-GOOGLING.. WHY DOES GOOGLING INEVITABLY END IN OVER-GOOGLING? ONE GOOGLE LEADS TO ANOTHER... AND BEFORE YOU KNOW IT, YOU'VE GOOGLED YOURSELF IN-TO GOOGLE OVERLOAD..
ALL THESE RELATIVES
IS THE NET EFFECT OF GOOGLING WIDER KNOWLEDGE? OR DOES ITS "WHAT'S NEXT?" QUALITY JUST GIVE YOU MORE STUFF WITH LESS MEANING? AND WHEN IT'S ALL ABOUT YOUR OWN FAMILY, DO YOU LEARN MORE, OR JUST GATHER FRAGMENTS?
STILL HERE WITH ME..
KERAK
MY GREAT-GRAND-FATHER, MY GRAND-FATHER, MY GRAND-MOTHER, COUNTLESS GREAT-AUNTS & GREAT-UNCLES, THIRD COUSINS, OLD FAMILY FRIENDS, MY MOTHER & FATHER, BOTH AS ADULTS & AS CHILDREN---- ALL GONE--- ALL GONE.. .... YES... BUT...
...WHY WON'T THEY DIE?
OK, JUST CON-CENTRATE ON THE CLICKETY-CLACK OF THE TRAIN WHEELS..YES, THAT'S BETTER... A LITTLE NAP WOULD BE NICE. --SO EASY TO DOZE OFF IN A TRAIN.. --THE GENTLE SWAY-ING.. THE RHYTHMIC MOTION... OF...
HIGH POINT! THIS STATION IS HIGH POINT!

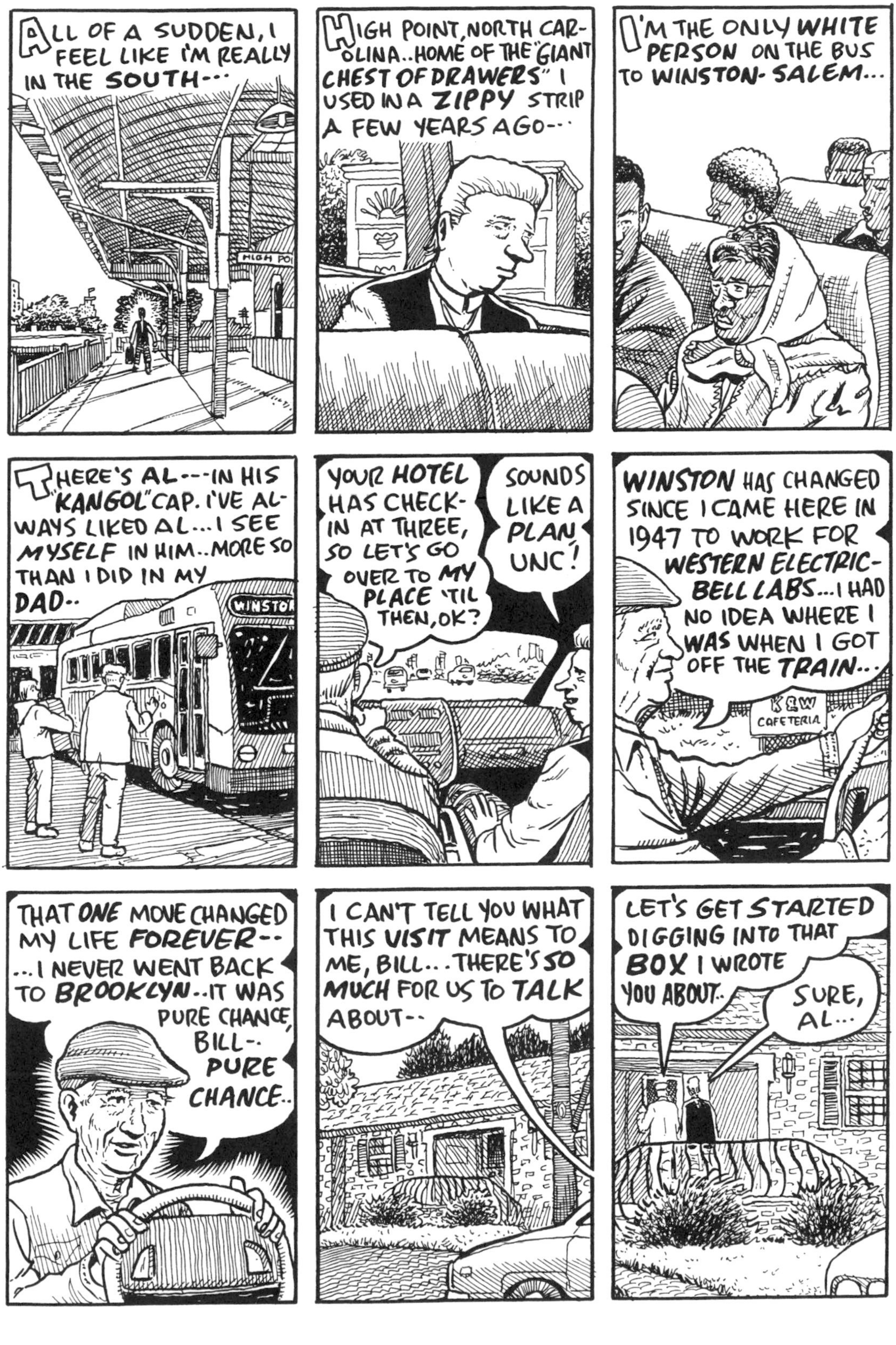
ALL OF A SUDDEN, I FEEL LIKE I'M REALLY IN THE SOUTH---
HIGH PO
HIGH POINT, NORTH CAROLINA.. HOME OF THE "GIANT CHEST OF DRAWERS" I USED IN A ZIPPY STRIP A FEW YEARS AGO---
I'M THE ONLY WHITE PERSON ON THE BUS TO WINSTON-SALEM...
THERE'S AL---IN HIS "KANGOL" CAP. I'VE ALWAYS LIKED AL...I SEE MYSELF IN HIM..MORE SO THAN I DID IN MY DAD..
WINSTON
YOUR HOTEL HAS CHECK-IN AT THREE, SO LET'S GO OVER TO MY PLACE 'TIL THEN, OK?
SOUNDS LIKE A PLAN, UNC!
WINSTON HAS CHANGED SINCE I CAME HERE IN 1947 TO WORK FOR WESTERN ELECTRIC-BELL LABS...I HAD NO IDEA WHERE I WAS WHEN I GOT OFF THE TRAIN...
K&W CAFETERIA
THAT ONE MOVE CHANGED MY LIFE FOREVER-- ...I NEVER WENT BACK TO BROOKLYN..IT WAS PURE CHANCE, BILL-. PURE CHANCE..
I CAN'T TELL YOU WHAT THIS VISIT MEANS TO ME, BILL...THERE'S SO MUCH FOR US TO TALK ABOUT--
LET'S GET STARTED DIGGING INTO THAT BOX I WROTE YOU ABOUT..
SURE, AL...

THERE IT IS...

YOU'RE SURE I'M NOT FORCING THIS STUFF ON YOU..

NO--IT'S **MY** FAMILY, TOO..

KENT--YOU KNOW, BILL'S DAUGHTER-- SHE SENT IT ALL TO ME..

DIDN'T SHE **WANT** IT?

NO...KENT HATED HER FATHER.. I DON'T KNOW WHY..I GUESS SHE'S NOT TOO INTERESTED IN DREDGING UP THE PAST..

PINHEAD

LIGHT ARTIS

FREAK

LIVING WONDERS AND STRANGE PEOPLE FROM EVERY CORNER

MAIN

CIRCUS

"**B**ILL" WAS ANOTHER UNCLE AND A SIDESHOW BARKER IN SAN FRANCISCO BEFORE HE WORKED AT *HARRAH'S CLUB* IN *RENO.* HE LIKED TO TELL JOKES...

RENO
THE BIGGEST LITTLE CITY IN THE WORLD
CLUB
HARRAH'S CLUB
CASINO
SLOTS-O-FUN
CLUB NEVA

HE WAS "SENT AWAY" BY HIS FATHER AS A TEENAGER, BUT THEY RECONCILED AS ADULTS AND BECAME **BEST** FRIENDS. HE WAS MY MOTHER'S **HALF-BROTHER** AND HER FAVOR- ITE RELATIVE-- "BROTHER BILL"--

HAVE YOU HEARD THE ONE ABOUT THE..

17

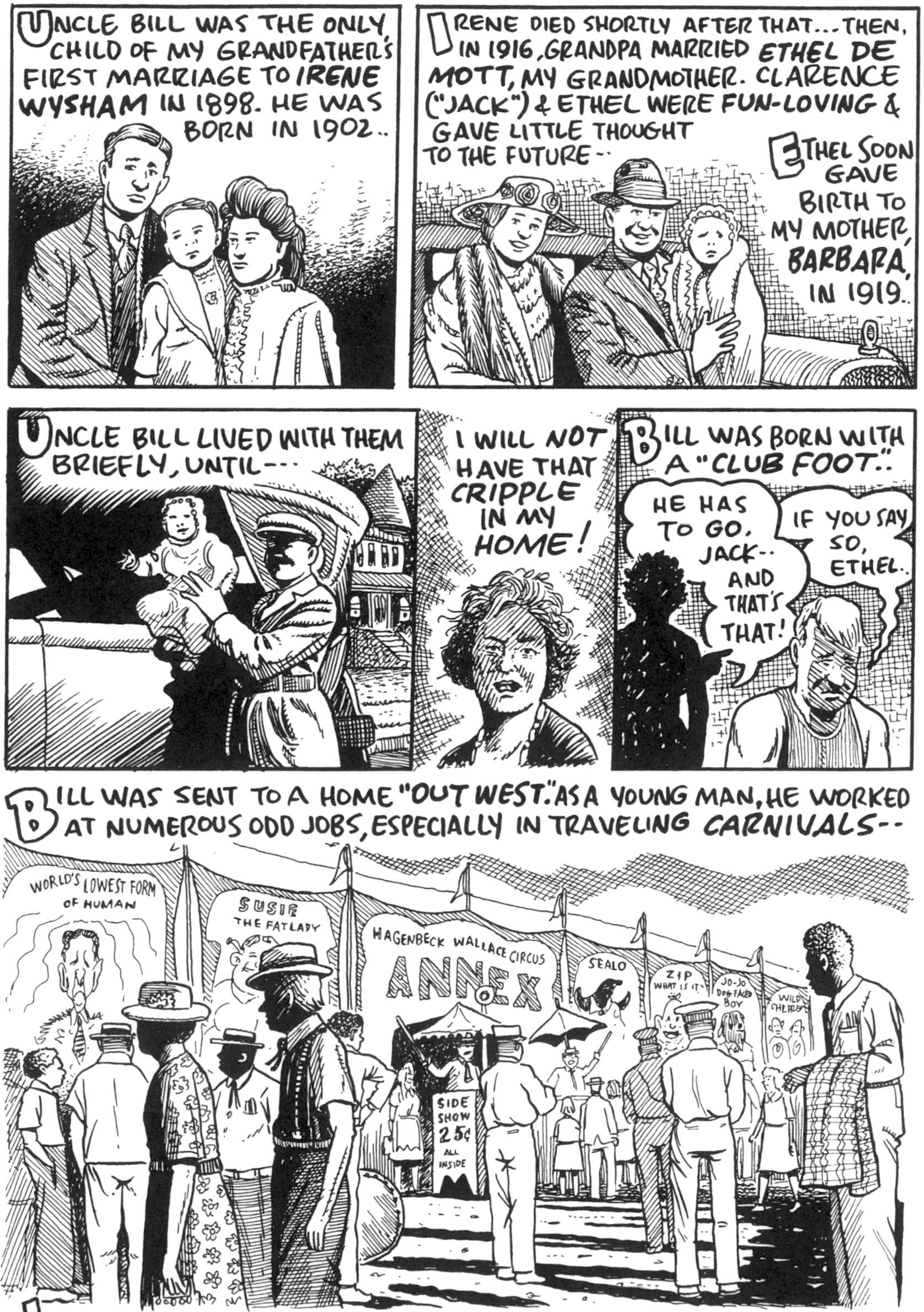
UNCLE BILL WAS THE ONLY CHILD OF MY GRANDFATHER'S FIRST MARRIAGE TO IRENE WYSHAM IN 1898. HE WAS BORN IN 1902..
IRENE DIED SHORTLY AFTER THAT... THEN, IN 1916, GRANDPA MARRIED ETHEL DE MOTT, MY GRANDMOTHER. CLARENCE ("JACK") & ETHEL WERE FUN-LOVING & GAVE LITTLE THOUGHT TO THE FUTURE--
ETHEL SOON GAVE BIRTH TO MY MOTHER, BARBARA, IN 1919..
UNCLE BILL LIVED WITH THEM BRIEFLY, UNTIL---
I WILL NOT HAVE THAT CRIPPLE IN MY HOME!
BILL WAS BORN WITH A "CLUB FOOT."
HE HAS TO GO, JACK.. AND THAT'S THAT!
IF YOU SAY SO, ETHEL..
BILL WAS SENT TO A HOME "OUT WEST." AS A YOUNG MAN, HE WORKED AT NUMEROUS ODD JOBS, ESPECIALLY IN TRAVELING CARNIVALS--
WORLD'S LOWEST FORM OF HUMAN
SUSIE THE FAT LADY
HAGENBECK WALLACE CIRCUS
ANNEX
SEALO
ZIP WHAT IS IT
JO-JO DOG FACED BOY
SIDE SHOW 25¢ ALL INSIDE
JACK & ETHEL PLAYED CARDS, MADE BATHTUB GIN & ENJOYED LIFE IN BROOKLYN.

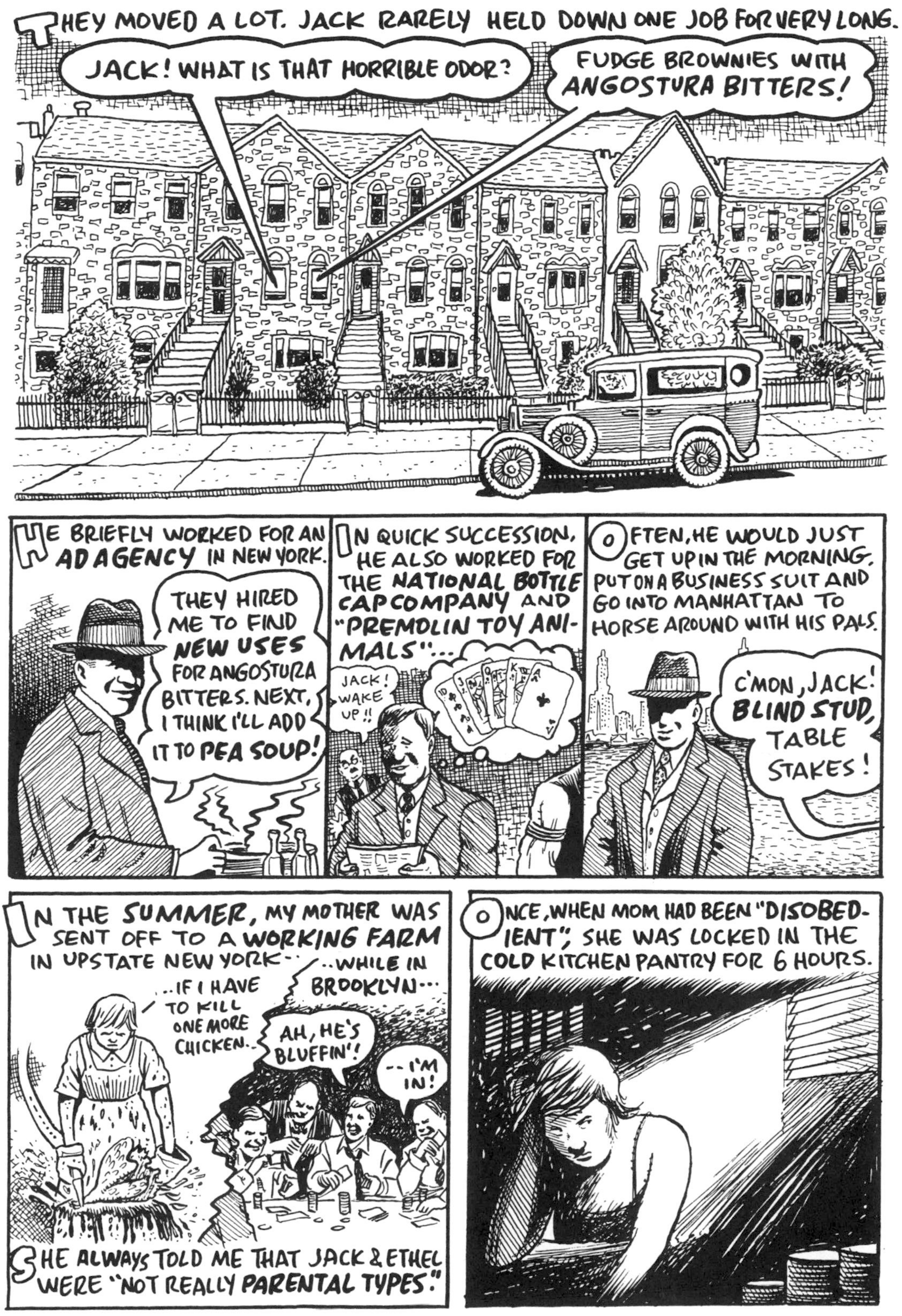
THEY MOVED A LOT. JACK RARELY HELD DOWN ONE JOB FOR VERY LONG.
JACK! WHAT IS THAT HORRIBLE ODOR?
FUDGE BROWNIES WITH ANGOSTURA BITTERS!
HE BRIEFLY WORKED FOR AN AD AGENCY IN NEW YORK.
THEY HIRED ME TO FIND NEW USES FOR ANGOSTURA BITTERS. NEXT, I THINK I'LL ADD IT TO PEA SOUP!
IN QUICK SUCCESSION, HE ALSO WORKED FOR THE NATIONAL BOTTLE CAP COMPANY AND "PREMOLIN TOY ANIMALS"...
JACK! WAKE UP!!
OFTEN, HE WOULD JUST GET UP IN THE MORNING, PUT ON A BUSINESS SUIT AND GO INTO MANHATTAN TO HORSE AROUND WITH HIS PALS.
C'MON, JACK! BLIND STUD, TABLE STAKES!
IN THE SUMMER, MY MOTHER WAS SENT OFF TO A WORKING FARM IN UPSTATE NEW YORK...
...IF I HAVE TO KILL ONE MORE CHICKEN...
...WHILE IN BROOKLYN...
AH, HE'S BLUFFIN'!
--I'M IN!
SHE ALWAYS TOLD ME THAT JACK & ETHEL WERE "NOT REALLY PARENTAL TYPES."
ONCE, WHEN MOM HAD BEEN "DISOBEDIENT", SHE WAS LOCKED IN THE COLD KITCHEN PANTRY FOR 6 HOURS.

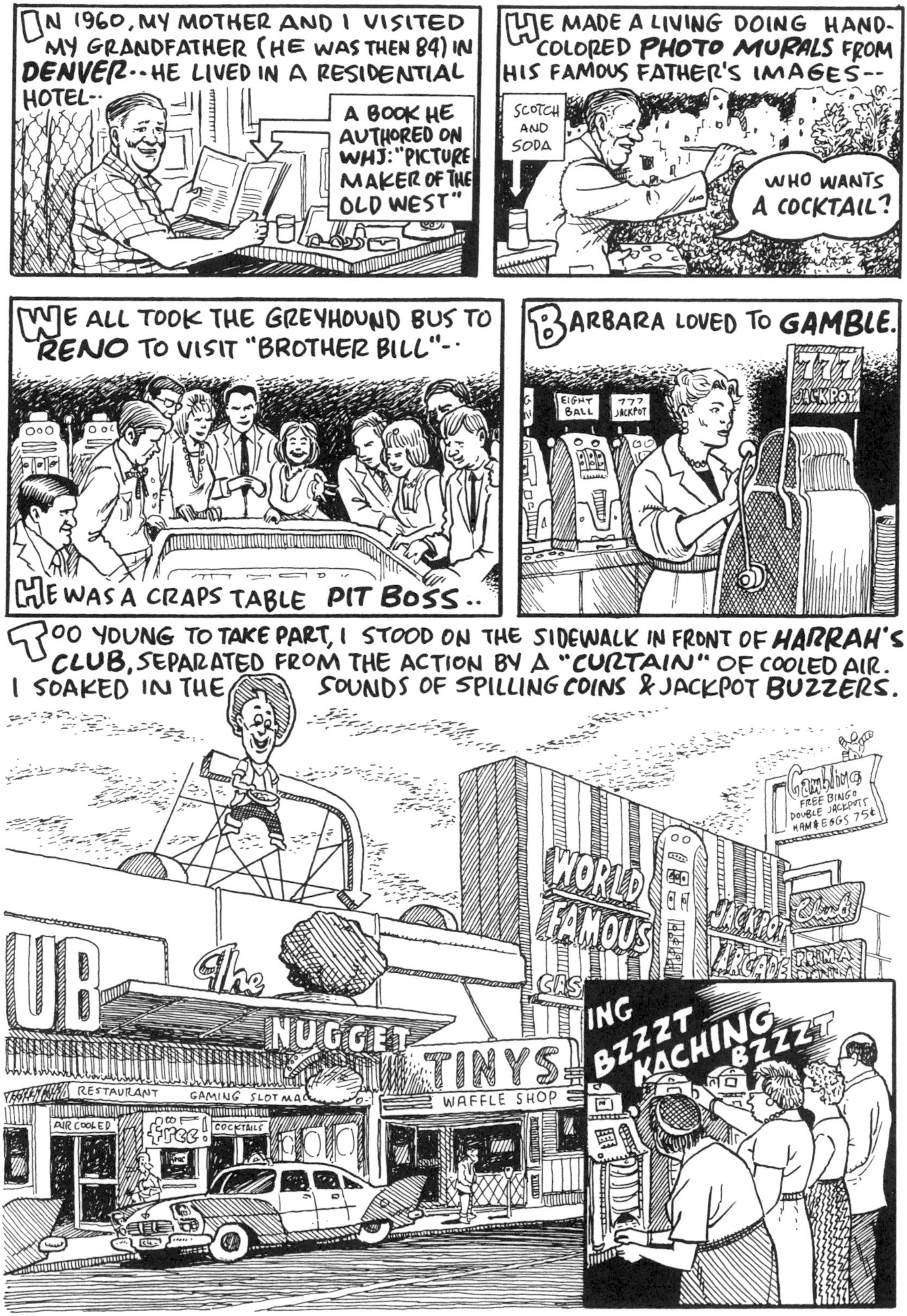
IN 1960, MY MOTHER AND I VISITED MY GRANDFATHER (HE WAS THEN 84) IN DENVER--HE LIVED IN A RESIDENTIAL HOTEL--
A BOOK HE AUTHORED ON WHJ: "PICTURE MAKER OF THE OLD WEST"
HE MADE A LIVING DOING HAND-COLORED PHOTO MURALS FROM HIS FAMOUS FATHER'S IMAGES--
SCOTCH AND SODA
WHO WANTS A COCKTAIL?
WE ALL TOOK THE GREYHOUND BUS TO RENO TO VISIT "BROTHER BILL"--
HE WAS A CRAPS TABLE PIT BOSS..
BARBARA LOVED TO GAMBLE.
EIGHT BALL
777 JACKPOT
777 JACKPOT
TOO YOUNG TO TAKE PART, I STOOD ON THE SIDEWALK IN FRONT OF HARRAH'S CLUB, SEPARATED FROM THE ACTION BY A "CURTAIN" OF COOLED AIR. I SOAKED IN THE SOUNDS OF SPILLING COINS & JACKPOT BUZZERS.
Gambling
FREE BINGO
DOUBLE JACKPOTS
HAM & EGGS 75¢
WORLD FAMOUS
JACKPOT ARCADE
Club
PRIMA
UB
The NUGGET
RESTAURANT
GAMING SLOT MA
AIR COOLED
free!
COCKTAILS
TINYS
WAFFLE SHOP
CAS
ING
BZZZT
KACHING
BZZZT

I WAS SO HYPNOTIZED WATCHING MY MOTHER & GRANDFATHER PUMP NICKELS INTO THE "ONE-ARMED BANDITS", I DIDN'T NOTICE THAT, JUST DOWN THE STREET, **MARILYN MONROE** & **CLARK GABLE** WERE FILMING A LOCATION SCENE FOR "THE MISFITS"...

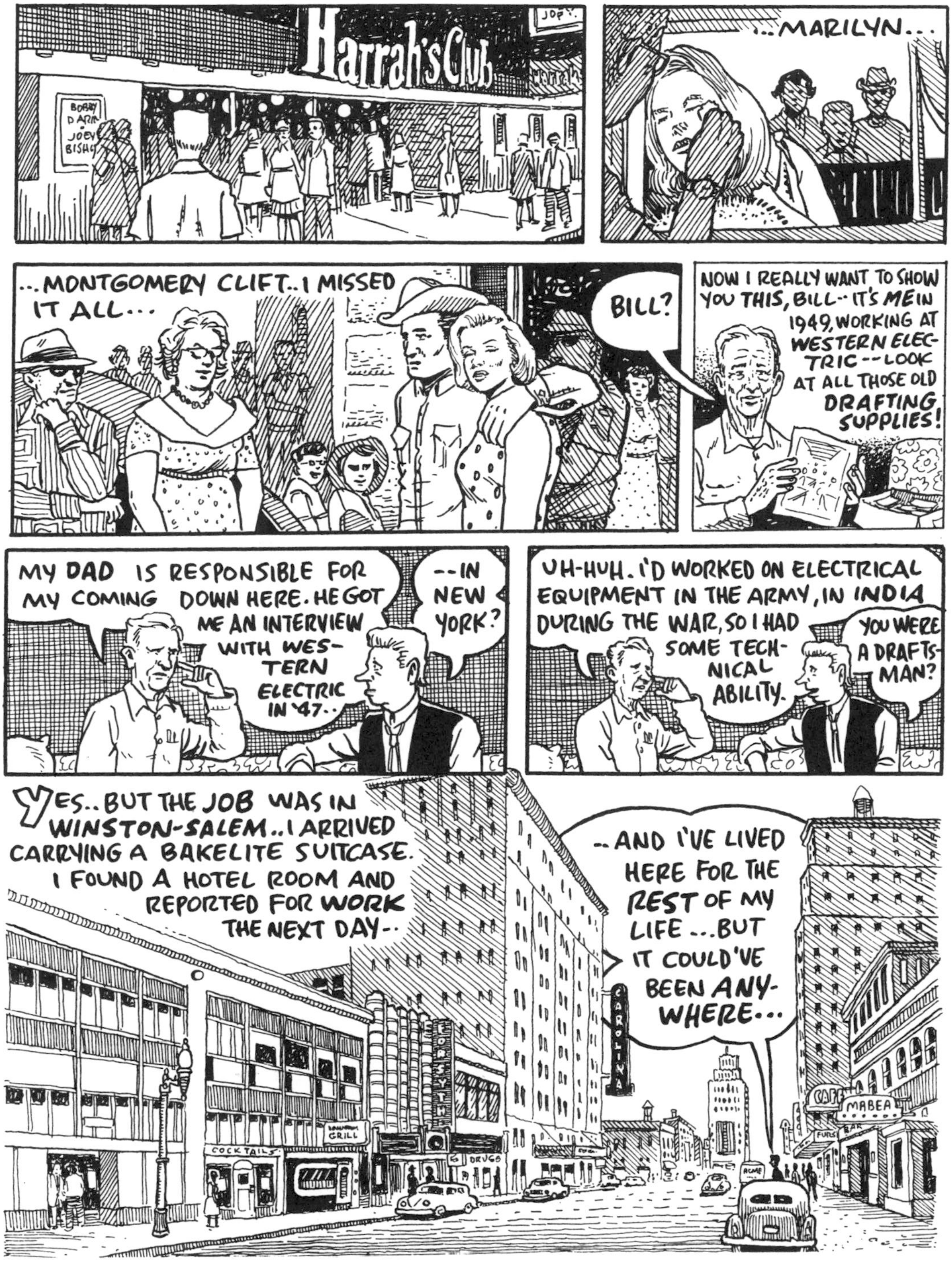

Harrah's Club
...MARILYN...
...MONTGOMERY CLIFT..I MISSED IT ALL...
BILL?
NOW I REALLY WANT TO SHOW YOU **THIS**, BILL-- IT'S **ME** IN 1949, WORKING AT **WESTERN ELECTRIC** -- LOOK AT ALL THOSE OLD **DRAFTING SUPPLIES**!
MY **DAD** IS RESPONSIBLE FOR MY COMING DOWN HERE. HE GOT ME AN INTERVIEW WITH WESTERN ELECTRIC IN '47..
--IN NEW YORK?
UH-HUH. I'D WORKED ON ELECTRICAL EQUIPMENT IN THE ARMY, IN **INDIA** DURING THE WAR, SO I HAD SOME TECHNICAL ABILITY.
YOU WERE A DRAFTSMAN?
YES.. BUT THE **JOB** WAS IN **WINSTON-SALEM**.. I ARRIVED CARRYING A **BAKELITE** SUITCASE. I FOUND A HOTEL ROOM AND REPORTED FOR **WORK** THE NEXT DAY..
--AND I'VE LIVED HERE FOR THE **REST** OF MY LIFE...BUT IT COULD'VE BEEN **ANYWHERE**...
CAROLINA
FORSYTH
COCKTAILS
GRILL
DRUGS
CAFE
MABEA

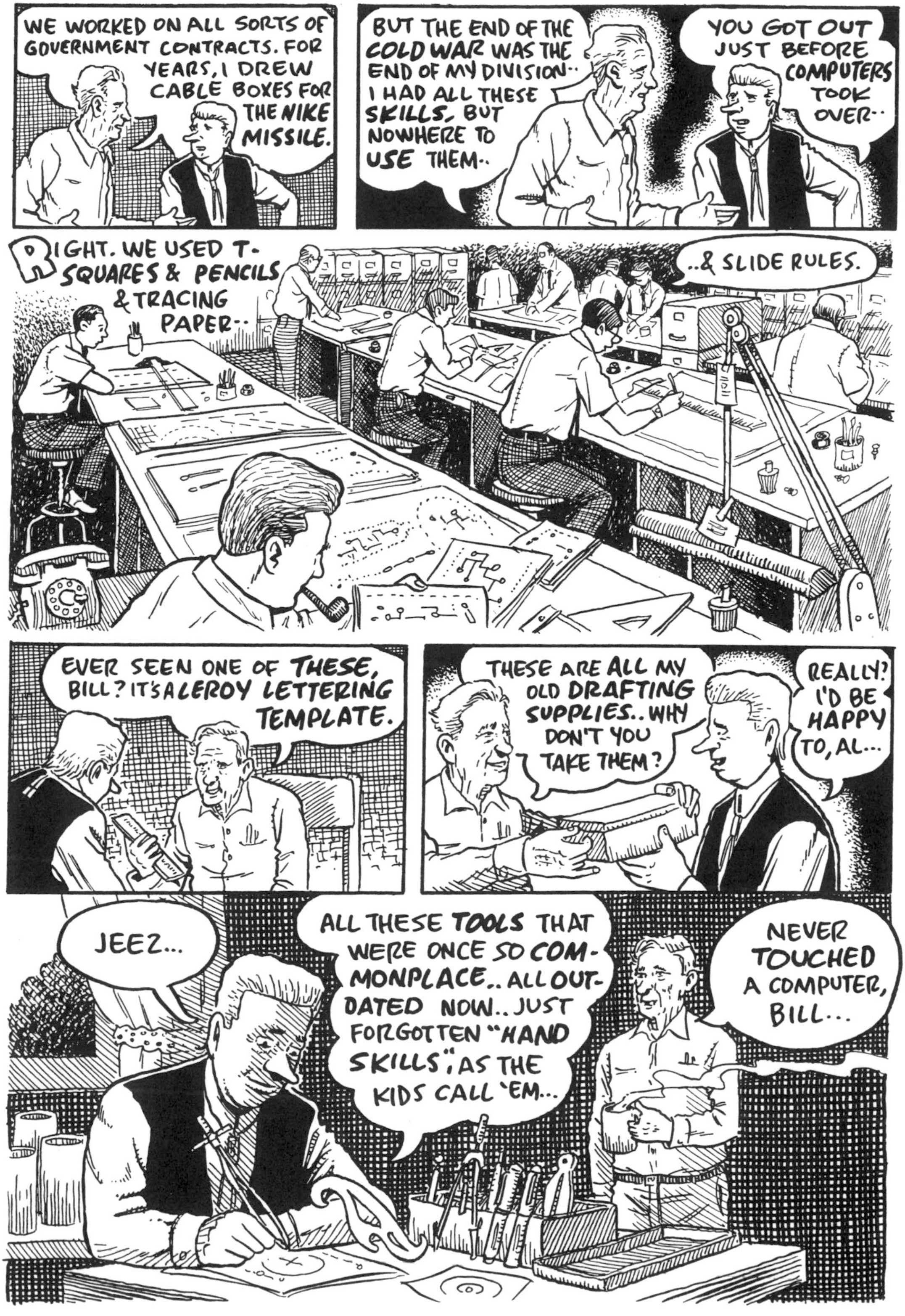
WE WORKED ON ALL SORTS OF GOVERNMENT CONTRACTS. FOR YEARS, I DREW CABLE BOXES FOR THE NIKE MISSILE.
BUT THE END OF THE COLD WAR WAS THE END OF MY DIVISION.. I HAD ALL THESE SKILLS, BUT NOWHERE TO USE THEM..
YOU GOT OUT JUST BEFORE COMPUTERS TOOK OVER..
RIGHT. WE USED T-SQUARES & PENCILS & TRACING PAPER..
..& SLIDE RULES.
EVER SEEN ONE OF THESE, BILL? IT'S A LEROY LETTERING TEMPLATE.
THESE ARE ALL MY OLD DRAFTING SUPPLIES.. WHY DON'T YOU TAKE THEM?
REALLY? I'D BE HAPPY TO, AL...
JEEZ...
ALL THESE TOOLS THAT WERE ONCE SO COMMONPLACE.. ALL OUTDATED NOW.. JUST FORGOTTEN "HAND SKILLS", AS THE KIDS CALL 'EM...
NEVER TOUCHED A COMPUTER, BILL...

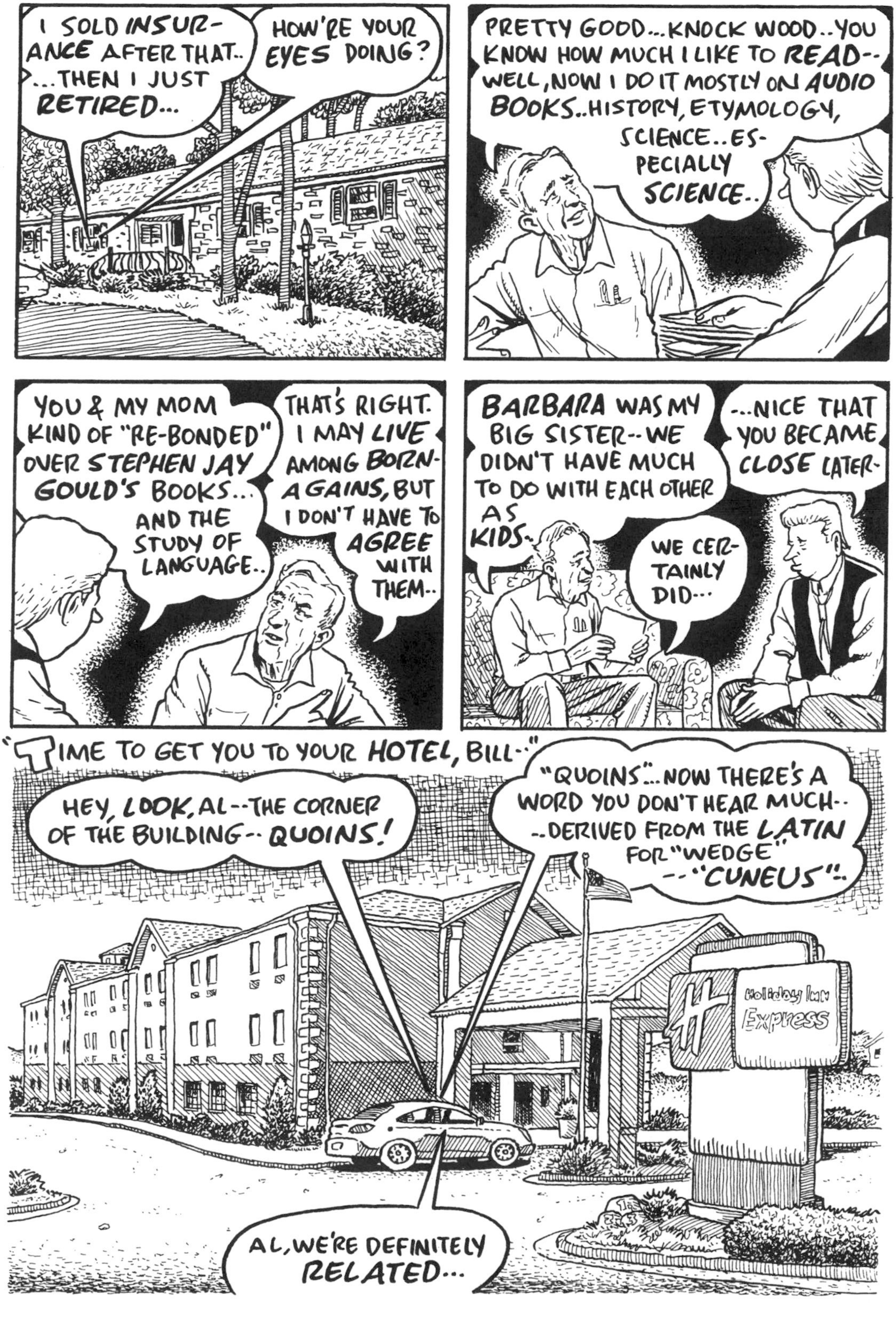
I SOLD INSURANCE AFTER THAT.. ...THEN I JUST RETIRED...
HOW'RE YOUR EYES DOING?
PRETTY GOOD...KNOCK WOOD..YOU KNOW HOW MUCH I LIKE TO READ-- WELL, NOW I DO IT MOSTLY ON AUDIO BOOKS..HISTORY, ETYMOLOGY, SCIENCE..ESPECIALLY SCIENCE..
YOU & MY MOM KIND OF "RE-BONDED" OVER STEPHEN JAY GOULD'S BOOKS... AND THE STUDY OF LANGUAGE..
THAT'S RIGHT. I MAY LIVE AMONG BORN-AGAINS, BUT I DON'T HAVE TO AGREE WITH THEM..
BARBARA WAS MY BIG SISTER--WE DIDN'T HAVE MUCH TO DO WITH EACH OTHER AS KIDS..
...NICE THAT YOU BECAME CLOSE LATER-
WE CERTAINLY DID...
"TIME TO GET YOU TO YOUR HOTEL, BILL.."
HEY, LOOK, AL--THE CORNER OF THE BUILDING--QUOINS!
"QUOINS"...NOW THERE'S A WORD YOU DON'T HEAR MUCH.. ..DERIVED FROM THE LATIN FOR "WEDGE" --"CUNEUS"..
Holiday Inn Express
AL, WE'RE DEFINITELY RELATED...

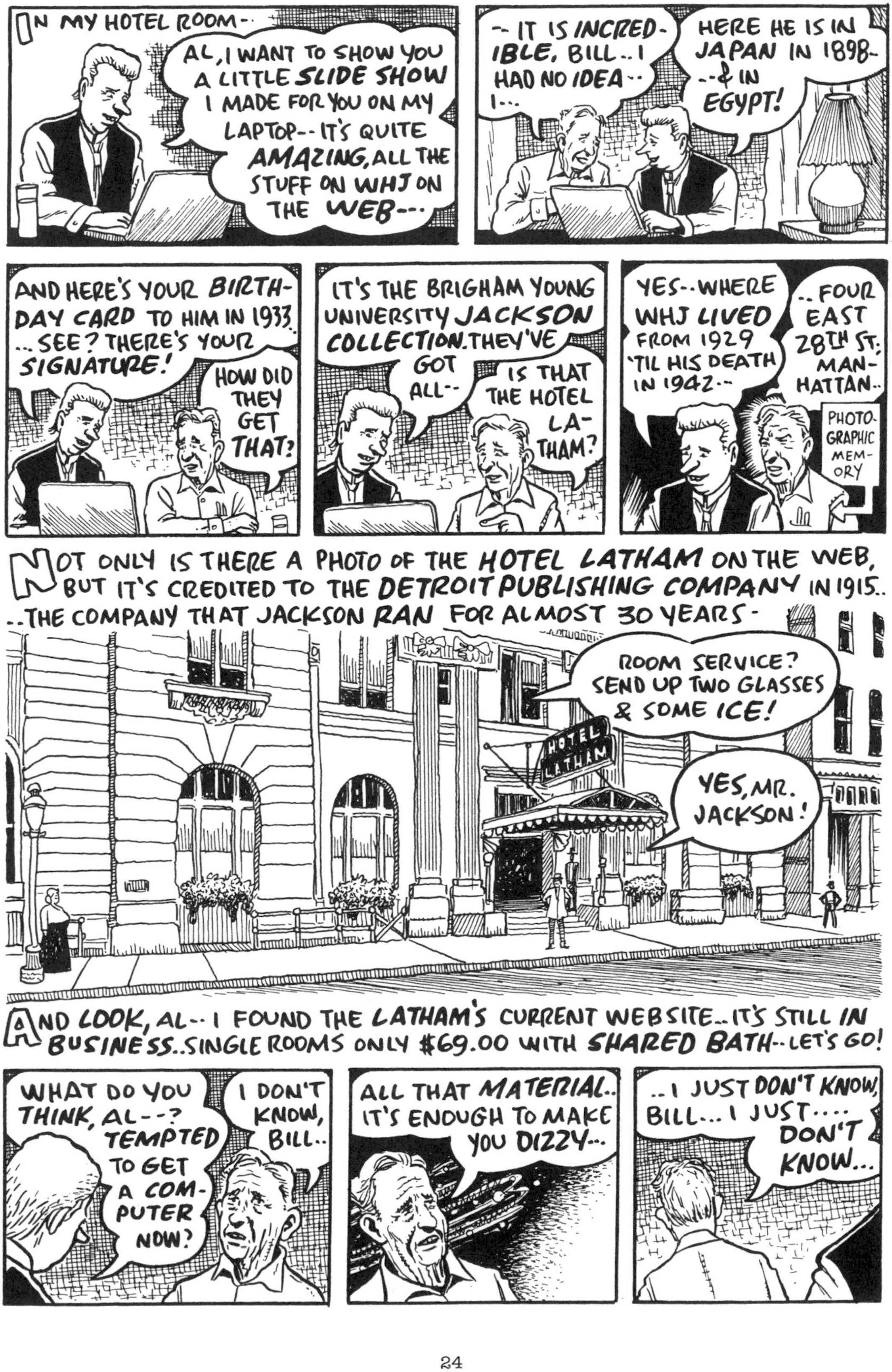
IN MY HOTEL ROOM-.
AL, I WANT TO SHOW YOU A LITTLE SLIDE SHOW I MADE FOR YOU ON MY LAPTOP-- IT'S QUITE AMAZING, ALL THE STUFF ON WHJ ON THE WEB--.
-- IT IS INCREDIBLE, BILL-- I HAD NO IDEA-- I--.
HERE HE IS IN JAPAN IN 1898-- -& IN EGYPT!
AND HERE'S YOUR BIRTHDAY CARD TO HIM IN 1933... SEE? THERE'S YOUR SIGNATURE!
HOW DID THEY GET THAT?
IT'S THE BRIGHAM YOUNG UNIVERSITY JACKSON COLLECTION. THEY'VE GOT ALL--
IS THAT THE HOTEL LATHAM?
YES-- WHERE WHJ LIVED FROM 1929 'TIL HIS DEATH IN 1942--
-- FOUR EAST 28TH ST., MANHATTAN--
PHOTOGRAPHIC MEMORY
NOT ONLY IS THERE A PHOTO OF THE HOTEL LATHAM ON THE WEB, BUT IT'S CREDITED TO THE DETROIT PUBLISHING COMPANY IN 1915--
--THE COMPANY THAT JACKSON RAN FOR ALMOST 30 YEARS-
ROOM SERVICE? SEND UP TWO GLASSES & SOME ICE!
HOTEL LATHAM
YES, MR. JACKSON!
AND LOOK, AL-- I FOUND THE LATHAM'S CURRENT WEBSITE-- IT'S STILL IN BUSINESS--SINGLE ROOMS ONLY $69.00 WITH SHARED BATH--LET'S GO!
WHAT DO YOU THINK, AL--? TEMPTED TO GET A COMPUTER NOW?
I DON'T KNOW, BILL--
ALL THAT MATERIAL-- IT'S ENOUGH TO MAKE YOU DIZZY--
--I JUST DON'T KNOW, BILL... I JUST.... DON'T KNOW...

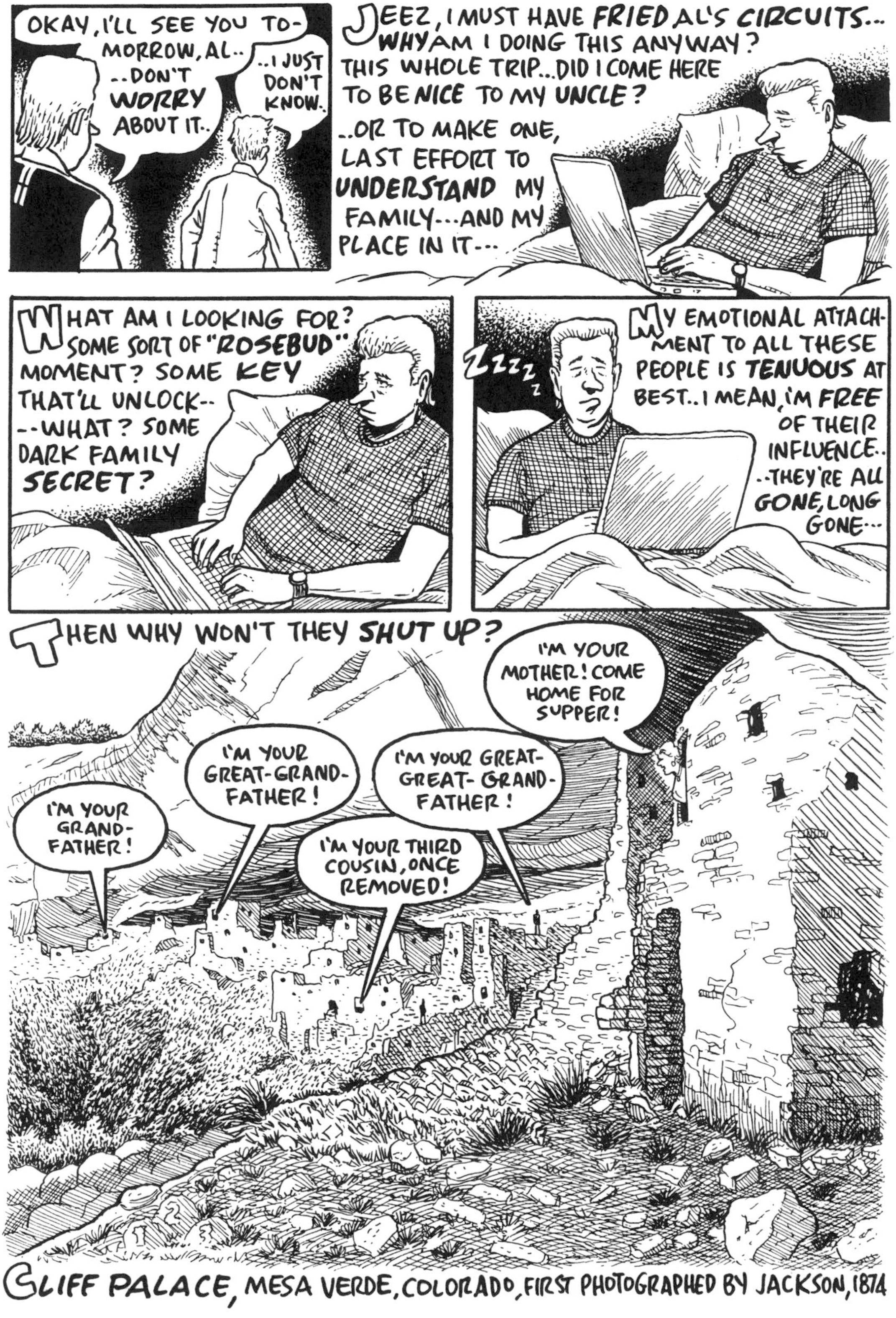
OKAY, I'LL SEE YOU TO-MORROW, AL.. ..DON'T WORRY ABOUT IT..
..I JUST DON'T KNOW..
JEEZ, I MUST HAVE FRIED AL'S CIRCUITS... WHY AM I DOING THIS ANYWAY? THIS WHOLE TRIP...DID I COME HERE TO BE NICE TO MY UNCLE?
..OR TO MAKE ONE, LAST EFFORT TO UNDERSTAND MY FAMILY...AND MY PLACE IN IT...
WHAT AM I LOOKING FOR? SOME SORT OF "ROSEBUD" MOMENT? SOME KEY THAT'LL UNLOCK-- --WHAT? SOME DARK FAMILY SECRET?
ZZZZ
MY EMOTIONAL ATTACH-MENT TO ALL THESE PEOPLE IS TENUOUS AT BEST..I MEAN, I'M FREE OF THEIR INFLUENCE.. ..THEY'RE ALL GONE, LONG GONE...
THEN WHY WON'T THEY SHUT UP?
I'M YOUR MOTHER! COME HOME FOR SUPPER!
I'M YOUR GREAT-GRAND-FATHER!
I'M YOUR GREAT-GREAT-GRAND-FATHER!
I'M YOUR GRAND-FATHER!
I'M YOUR THIRD COUSIN, ONCE REMOVED!
CLIFF PALACE, MESA VERDE, COLORADO, FIRST PHOTOGRAPHED BY JACKSON, 1874

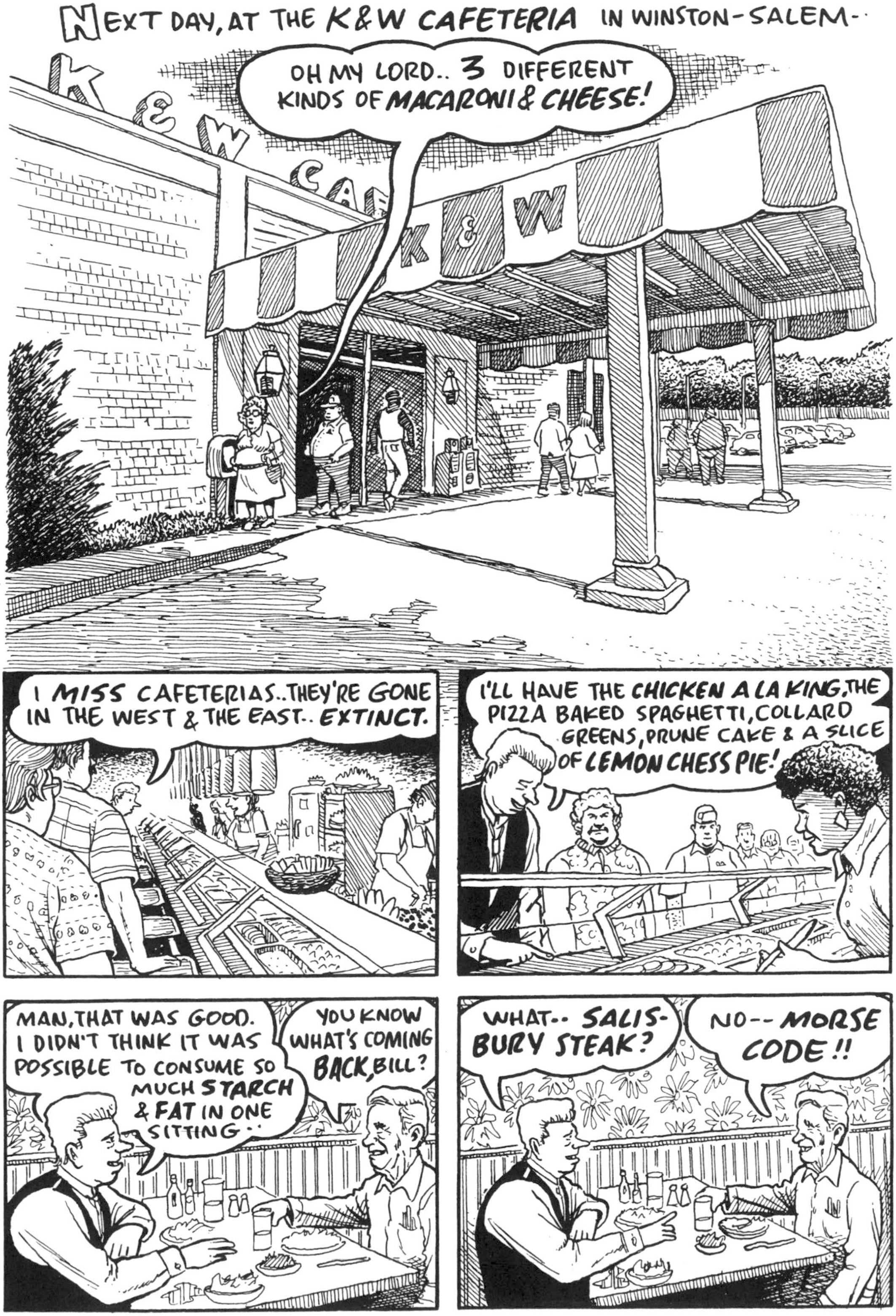
NEXT DAY, AT THE K&W CAFETERIA IN WINSTON-SALEM..
OH MY LORD.. 3 DIFFERENT KINDS OF MACARONI & CHEESE!
K&W CAFE
K&W
I MISS CAFETERIAS..THEY'RE GONE IN THE WEST & THE EAST.. EXTINCT.
I'LL HAVE THE CHICKEN A LA KING, THE PIZZA BAKED SPAGHETTI, COLLARD GREENS, PRUNE CAKE & A SLICE OF LEMON CHESS PIE!
MAN, THAT WAS GOOD. I DIDN'T THINK IT WAS POSSIBLE TO CONSUME SO MUCH STARCH & FAT IN ONE SITTING..
YOU KNOW WHAT'S COMING BACK, BILL?
WHAT.. SALISBURY STEAK?
NO-- MORSE CODE!!

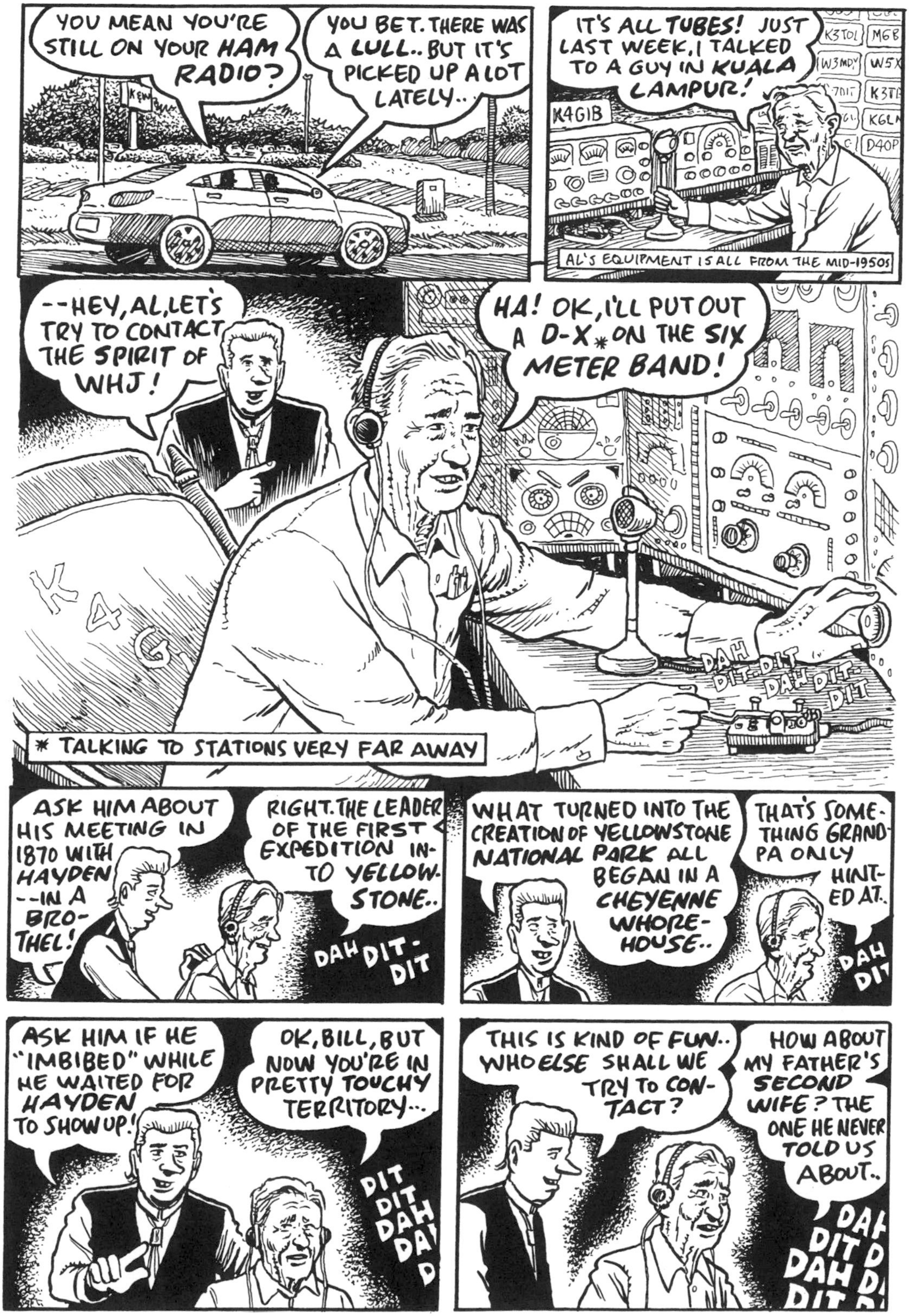
YOU MEAN YOU'RE STILL ON YOUR HAM RADIO?
YOU BET. THERE WAS A LULL.. BUT IT'S PICKED UP A LOT LATELY..
IT'S ALL TUBES! JUST LAST WEEK, I TALKED TO A GUY IN KUALA LAMPUR!
K4GIB
K3TOL
M6B
W3MDY
W5X
K3T
KGL
D40P
AL'S EQUIPMENT IS ALL FROM THE MID-1950s
--HEY, AL, LET'S TRY TO CONTACT THE SPIRIT OF WHJ!
HA! OK, I'LL PUT OUT A D-X* ON THE SIX METER BAND!
K 4 G
DAH DIT-DIT DAH DIT-DIT
* TALKING TO STATIONS VERY FAR AWAY
ASK HIM ABOUT HIS MEETING IN 1870 WITH HAYDEN --IN A BROTHEL!
RIGHT. THE LEADER OF THE FIRST EXPEDITION INTO YELLOWSTONE..
DAH DIT-DIT
WHAT TURNED INTO THE CREATION OF YELLOWSTONE NATIONAL PARK ALL BEGAN IN A CHEYENNE WHOREHOUSE..
THAT'S SOMETHING GRANDPA ONLY HINTED AT..
DAH DI
ASK HIM IF HE "IMBIBED" WHILE HE WAITED FOR HAYDEN TO SHOW UP!
OK, BILL, BUT NOW YOU'RE IN PRETTY TOUCHY TERRITORY...
DIT DIT DAH DAH D
THIS IS KIND OF FUN.. WHO ELSE SHALL WE TRY TO CONTACT?
HOW ABOUT MY FATHER'S SECOND WIFE? THE ONE HE NEVER TOLD US ABOUT..
DAH DIT DAH DIT

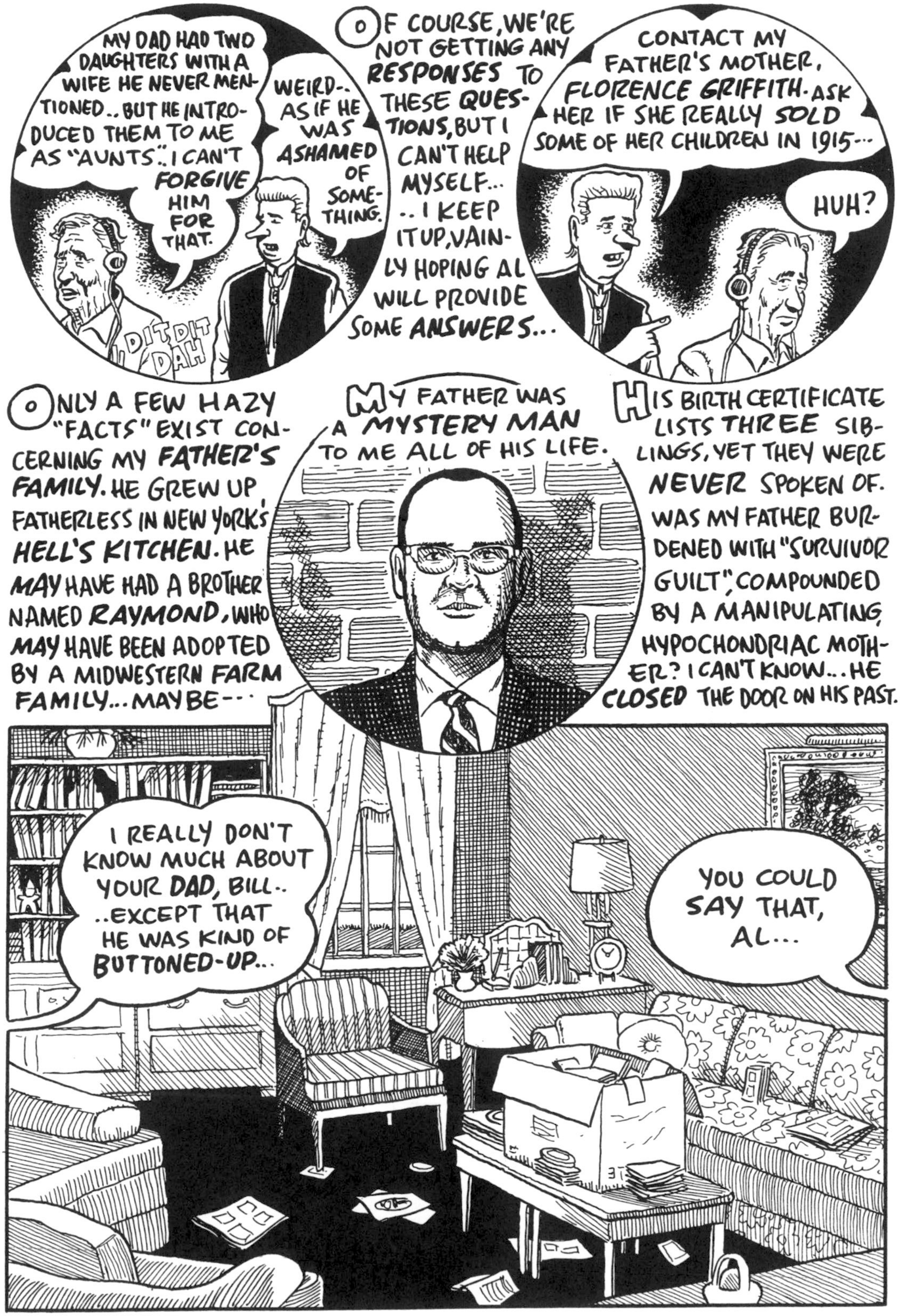
MY DAD HAD TWO DAUGHTERS WITH A WIFE HE NEVER MENTIONED.. BUT HE INTRODUCED THEM TO ME AS "AUNTS".. I CAN'T FORGIVE HIM FOR THAT.
WEIRD-- AS IF HE WAS ASHAMED OF SOMETHING.
DIT DIT DAH
OF COURSE, WE'RE NOT GETTING ANY RESPONSES TO THESE QUESTIONS, BUT I CAN'T HELP MYSELF... ..I KEEP IT UP, VAINLY HOPING AL WILL PROVIDE SOME ANSWERS...
CONTACT MY FATHER'S MOTHER, FLORENCE GRIFFITH. ASK HER IF SHE REALLY SOLD SOME OF HER CHILDREN IN 1915...
HUH?
ONLY A FEW HAZY "FACTS" EXIST CONCERNING MY FATHER'S FAMILY. HE GREW UP FATHERLESS IN NEW YORK'S HELL'S KITCHEN. HE MAY HAVE HAD A BROTHER NAMED RAYMOND, WHO MAY HAVE BEEN ADOPTED BY A MIDWESTERN FARM FAMILY... MAYBE--
MY FATHER WAS A MYSTERY MAN TO ME ALL OF HIS LIFE.
HIS BIRTH CERTIFICATE LISTS THREE SIBLINGS, YET THEY WERE NEVER SPOKEN OF. WAS MY FATHER BURDENED WITH "SURVIVOR GUILT", COMPOUNDED BY A MANIPULATING, HYPOCHONDRIAC MOTHER? I CAN'T KNOW... HE CLOSED THE DOOR ON HIS PAST.
I REALLY DON'T KNOW MUCH ABOUT YOUR DAD, BILL.. ..EXCEPT THAT HE WAS KIND OF BUTTONED-UP...
YOU COULD SAY THAT, AL...

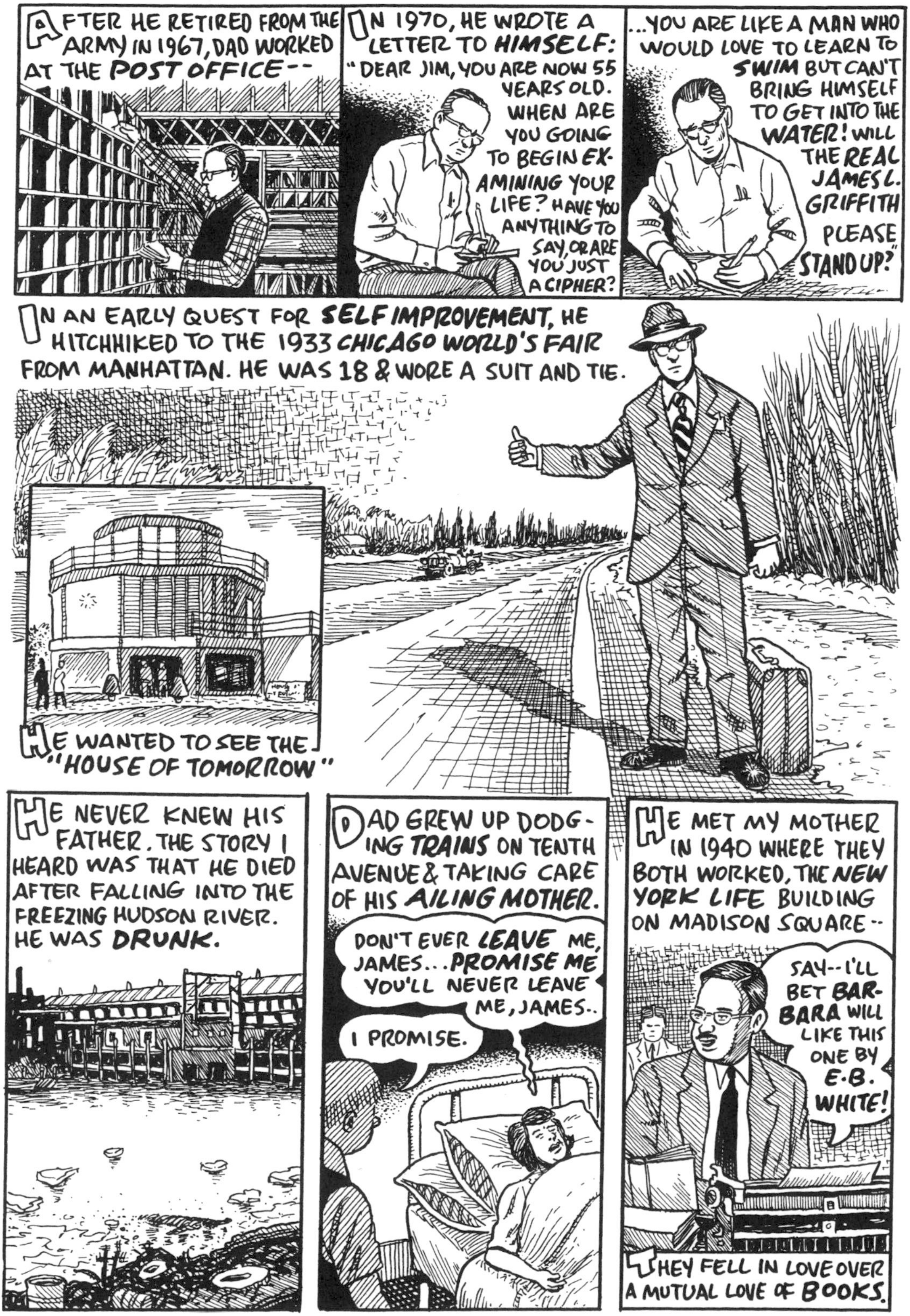
AFTER HE RETIRED FROM THE ARMY IN 1967, DAD WORKED AT THE POST OFFICE--
IN 1970, HE WROTE A LETTER TO HIMSELF: "DEAR JIM, YOU ARE NOW 55 YEARS OLD. WHEN ARE YOU GOING TO BEGIN EX-AMINING YOUR LIFE? HAVE YOU ANYTHING TO SAY, OR ARE YOU JUST A CIPHER?
...YOU ARE LIKE A MAN WHO WOULD LOVE TO LEARN TO SWIM BUT CAN'T BRING HIMSELF TO GET INTO THE WATER! WILL THE REAL JAMES L. GRIFFITH PLEASE STAND UP?"
IN AN EARLY QUEST FOR SELF IMPROVEMENT, HE HITCHHIKED TO THE 1933 CHICAGO WORLD'S FAIR FROM MANHATTAN. HE WAS 18 & WORE A SUIT AND TIE.
HE WANTED TO SEE THE "HOUSE OF TOMORROW"
HE NEVER KNEW HIS FATHER. THE STORY I HEARD WAS THAT HE DIED AFTER FALLING INTO THE FREEZING HUDSON RIVER. HE WAS DRUNK.
DAD GREW UP DODG-ING TRAINS ON TENTH AVENUE & TAKING CARE OF HIS AILING MOTHER.
DON'T EVER LEAVE ME, JAMES... PROMISE ME YOU'LL NEVER LEAVE ME, JAMES..
I PROMISE.
HE MET MY MOTHER IN 1940 WHERE THEY BOTH WORKED, THE NEW YORK LIFE BUILDING ON MADISON SQUARE--
SAY--I'LL BET BAR-BARA WILL LIKE THIS ONE BY E.B. WHITE!
THEY FELL IN LOVE OVER A MUTUAL LOVE OF BOOKS.

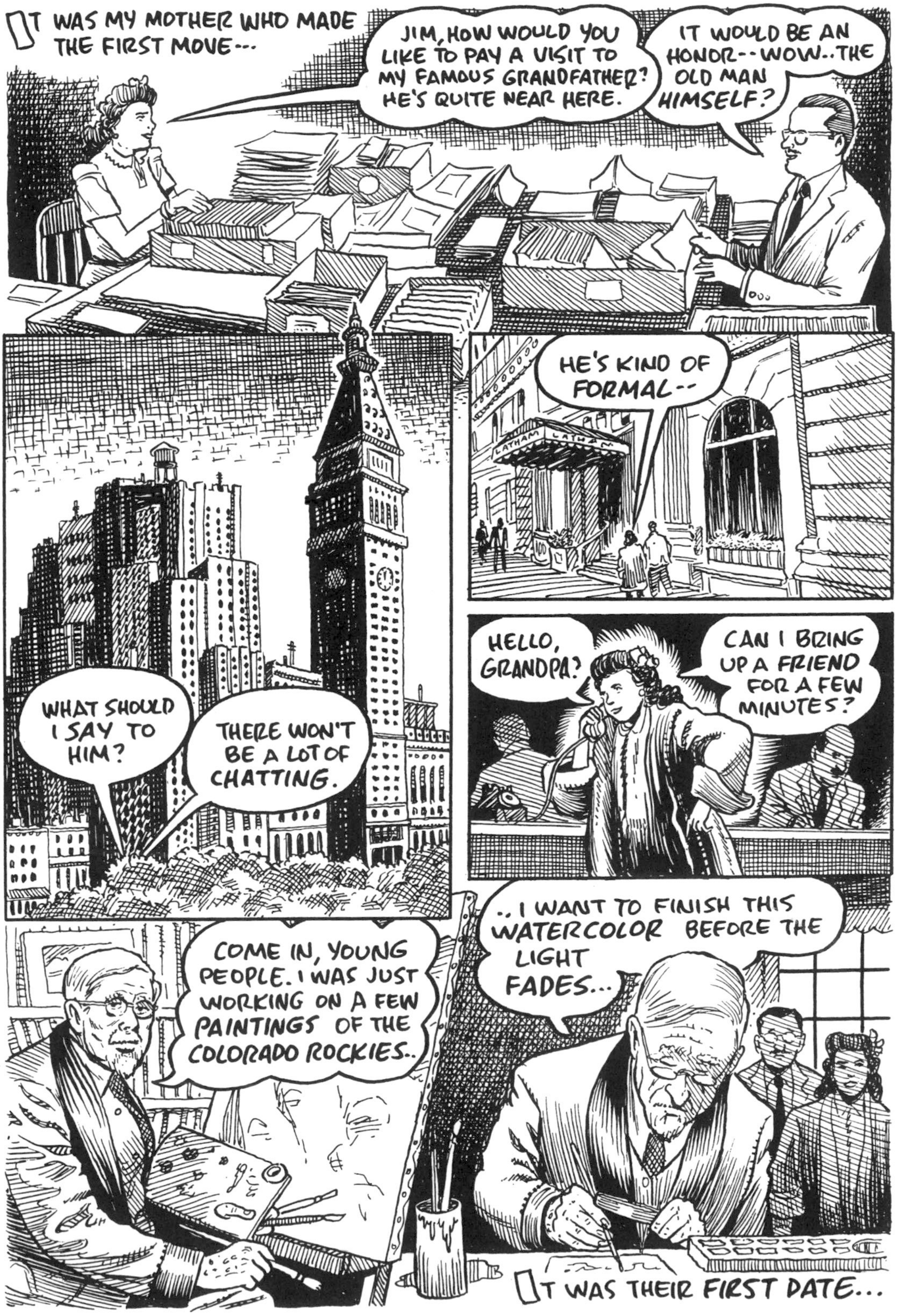
IT WAS MY MOTHER WHO MADE THE FIRST MOVE---
JIM, HOW WOULD YOU LIKE TO PAY A VISIT TO MY FAMOUS GRANDFATHER? HE'S QUITE NEAR HERE.
IT WOULD BE AN HONOR--WOW..THE OLD MAN HIMSELF?
WHAT SHOULD I SAY TO HIM?
THERE WON'T BE A LOT OF CHATTING.
HE'S KIND OF FORMAL--
LATHAM
HELLO, GRANDPA?
CAN I BRING UP A FRIEND FOR A FEW MINUTES?
COME IN, YOUNG PEOPLE. I WAS JUST WORKING ON A FEW PAINTINGS OF THE COLORADO ROCKIES..
..I WANT TO FINISH THIS WATERCOLOR BEFORE THE LIGHT FADES...
IT WAS THEIR FIRST DATE...

I SEARCHED CENSUS RECORDS FOR DAD AND CAME UP WITH HIS **ADDRESS** IN 1925-- **315 W. 20TH STREET**... HIS **MOTHER'S** OCCUPATION WAS LISTED AS "**ADVERTISING**" AND A **SIBLING** LIVING WITH HIM, ***HARRIET***, WAS LISTED AS IN "**ILL HEALTH**". DAD ***NEVER*** MENTIONED ***HARRIET***--- NEVER...

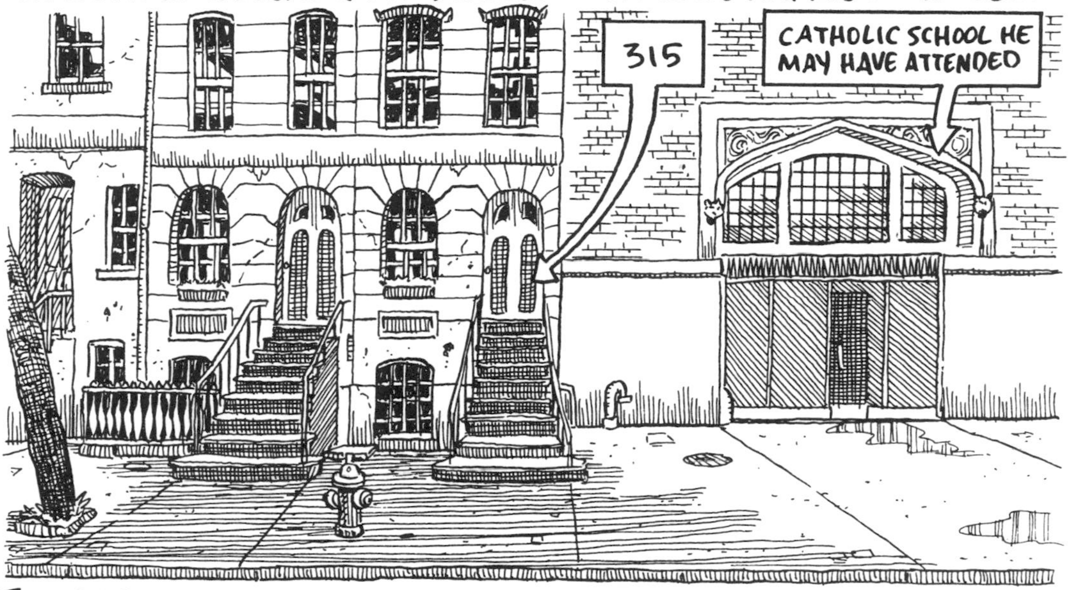

315
CATHOLIC SCHOOL HE MAY HAVE ATTENDED

IN 1958, HE WAS A CONTESTANT ON THE POPULAR TV QUIZ SHOW, "***TIC-TAC-DOUGH***", HOSTED BY **JACK BARRY**--

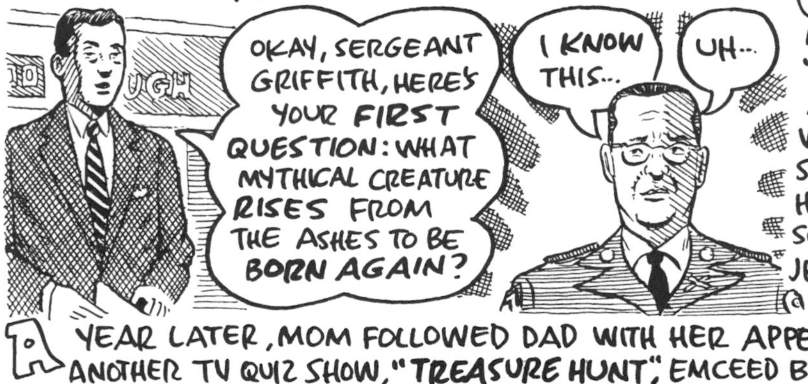

OKAY, SERGEANT GRIFFITH, HERE'S YOUR **FIRST** QUESTION: WHAT MYTHICAL CREATURE **RISES** FROM THE ASHES TO BE **BORN AGAIN**?
I KNOW THIS...
UH...

WATCHING AT HOME, MY MOTHER SCREAMED, "**THE PHOENIX!**" AT THE TV, BUT DAD WAS ALREADY **OFF** THE SHOW. ON THE WAY HOME, HE **PAWNED** HIS CONSOLATION PRIZE, A 21 JEWEL BULOVA WATCH.

A YEAR LATER, MOM FOLLOWED DAD WITH HER APPEARANCES ON ANOTHER TV QUIZ SHOW, "**TREASURE HUNT**", EMCEED BY **JAN MURRAY**.

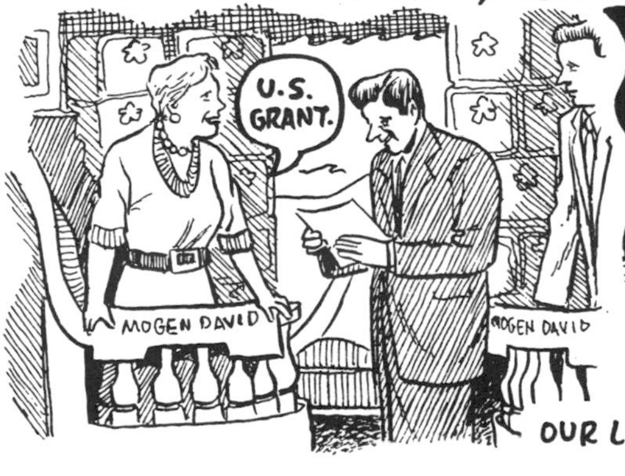

U.S. GRANT.
MOGEN DAVID
MOGEN DAVID

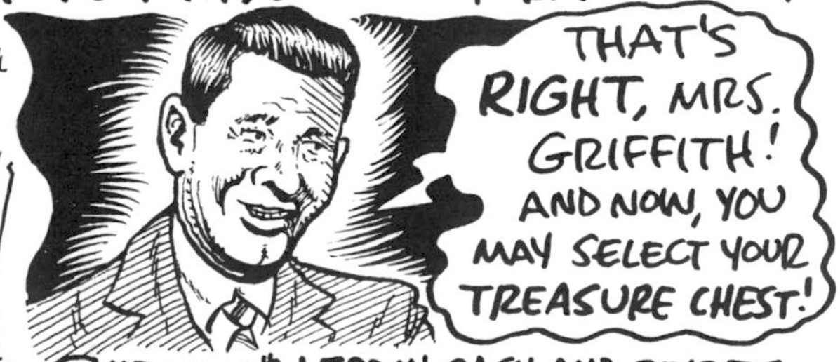

THAT'S **RIGHT**, MRS. GRIFFITH! AND NOW, YOU MAY SELECT YOUR **TREASURE CHEST**!

SHE WON $ 1,300 IN CASH AND PRIZES WORTH $ 1,890.. THE "COLONIAL LIVING ROOM SET" SHE WAS AWARDED SAT IN OUR **LEVITTOWN** HOME FOR YEARS AFTERWARD.

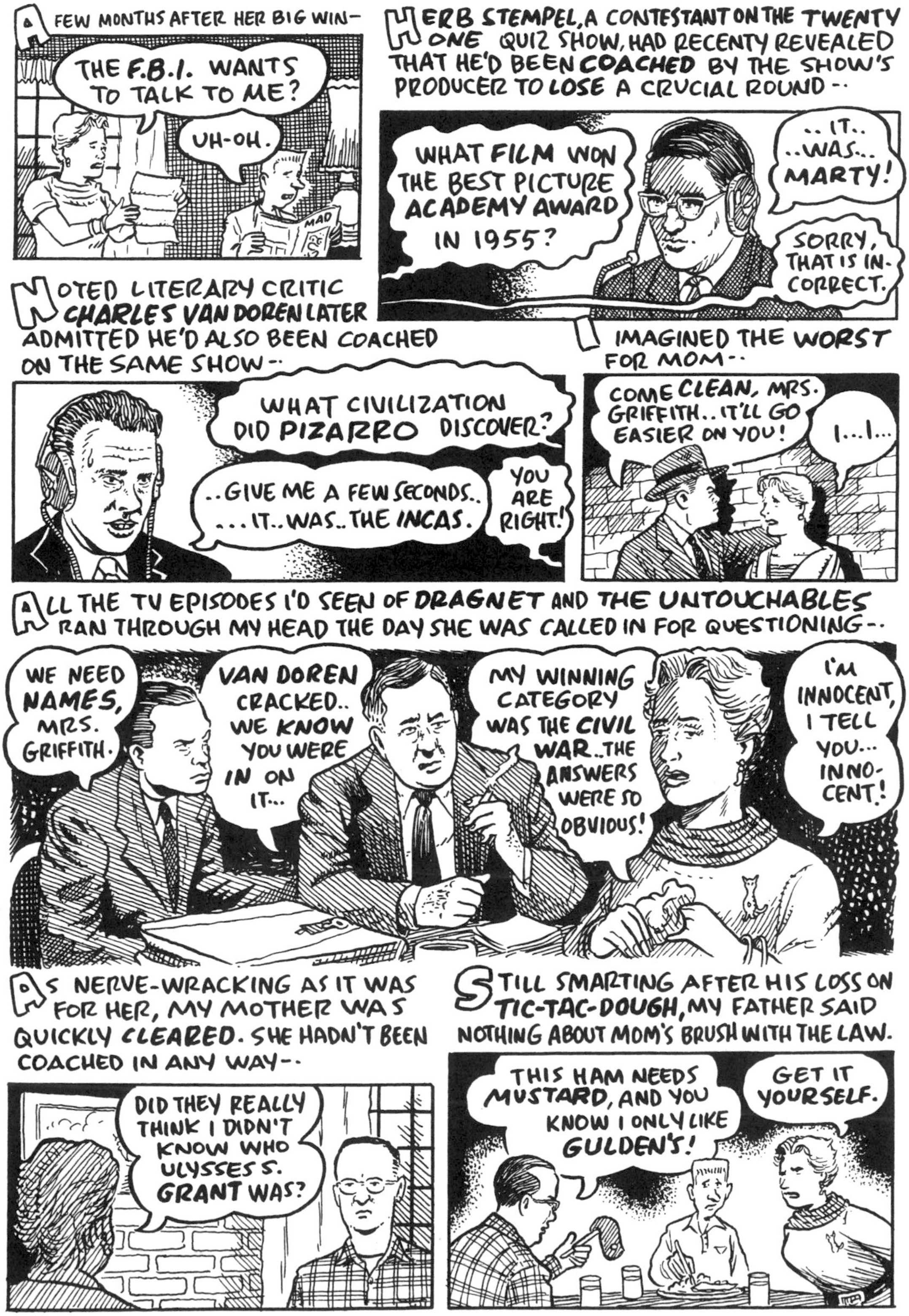
A FEW MONTHS AFTER HER BIG WIN–
THE F.B.I. WANTS TO TALK TO ME?
UH-OH.
MAD
HERB STEMPEL, A CONTESTANT ON THE TWENTY ONE QUIZ SHOW, HAD RECENTY REVEALED THAT HE'D BEEN COACHED BY THE SHOW'S PRODUCER TO LOSE A CRUCIAL ROUND--
WHAT FILM WON THE BEST PICTURE ACADEMY AWARD IN 1955?
.. IT.. ..WAS... MARTY!
SORRY, THAT IS IN-CORRECT.
NOTED LITERARY CRITIC CHARLES VAN DOREN LATER ADMITTED HE'D ALSO BEEN COACHED ON THE SAME SHOW--
WHAT CIVILIZATION DID PIZARRO DISCOVER?
..GIVE ME A FEW SECONDS.. ... IT.. WAS.. THE INCAS.
YOU ARE RIGHT!
I IMAGINED THE WORST FOR MOM--
COME CLEAN, MRS. GRIFFITH... IT'LL GO EASIER ON YOU!
I...I...
ALL THE TV EPISODES I'D SEEN OF DRAGNET AND THE UNTOUCHABLES RAN THROUGH MY HEAD THE DAY SHE WAS CALLED IN FOR QUESTIONING--.
WE NEED NAMES, MRS. GRIFFITH.
VAN DOREN CRACKED.. WE KNOW YOU WERE IN ON IT...
MY WINNING CATEGORY WAS THE CIVIL WAR..THE ANSWERS WERE SO OBVIOUS!
I'M INNOCENT, I TELL YOU... INNO-CENT!
AS NERVE-WRACKING AS IT WAS FOR HER, MY MOTHER WAS QUICKLY CLEARED. SHE HADN'T BEEN COACHED IN ANY WAY--
DID THEY REALLY THINK I DIDN'T KNOW WHO ULYSSES S. GRANT WAS?
STILL SMARTING AFTER HIS LOSS ON TIC-TAC-DOUGH, MY FATHER SAID NOTHING ABOUT MOM'S BRUSH WITH THE LAW.
THIS HAM NEEDS MUSTARD, AND YOU KNOW I ONLY LIKE GULDEN'S!
GET IT YOURSELF.

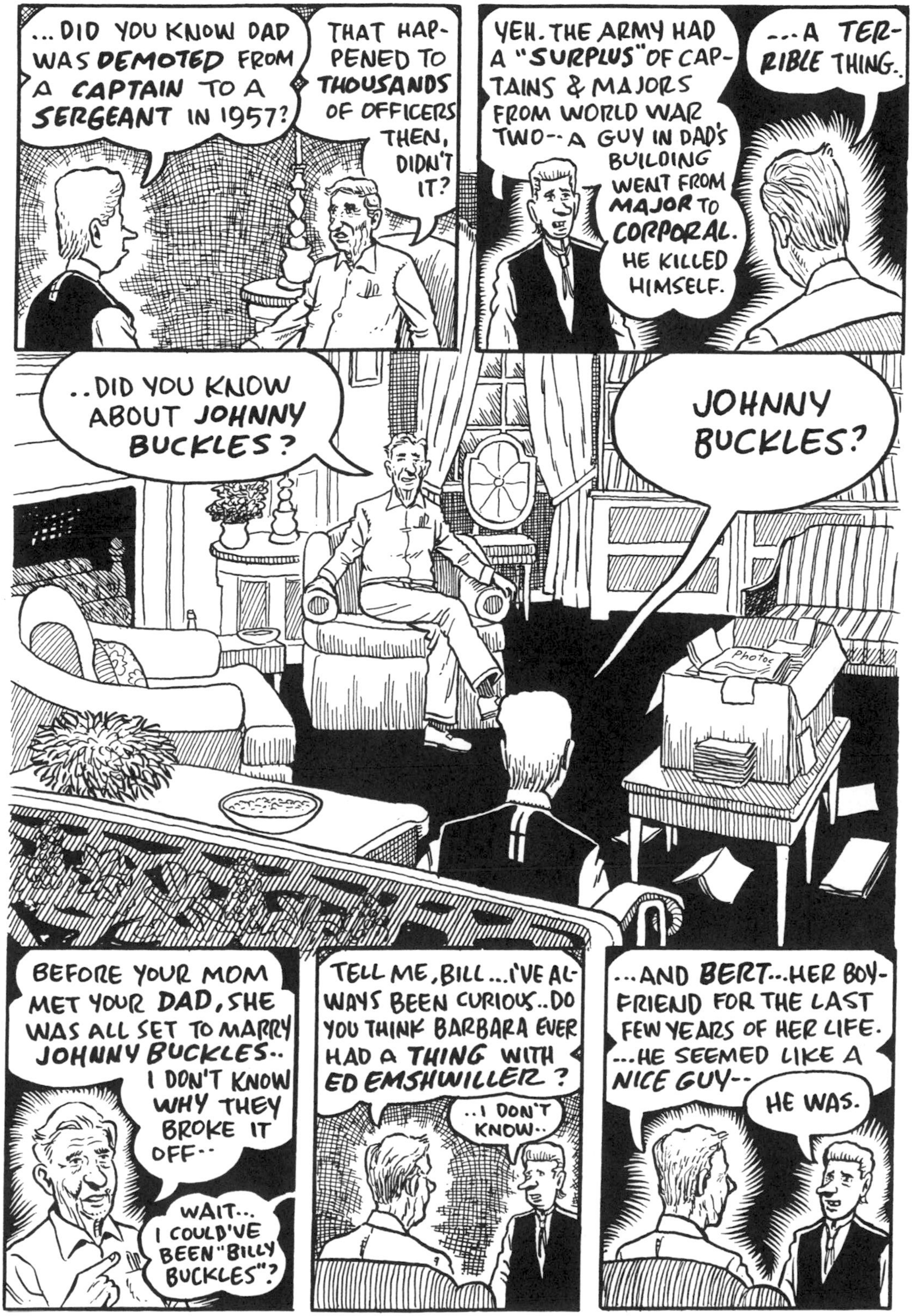
...DID YOU KNOW DAD WAS DEMOTED FROM A CAPTAIN TO A SERGEANT IN 1957?
THAT HAPPENED TO THOUSANDS OF OFFICERS THEN, DIDN'T IT?
YEH. THE ARMY HAD A "SURPLUS" OF CAPTAINS & MAJORS FROM WORLD WAR TWO-- A GUY IN DAD'S BUILDING WENT FROM MAJOR TO CORPORAL. HE KILLED HIMSELF.
--A TERRIBLE THING..
..DID YOU KNOW ABOUT JOHNNY BUCKLES?
JOHNNY BUCKLES?
Photos
BEFORE YOUR MOM MET YOUR DAD, SHE WAS ALL SET TO MARRY JOHNNY BUCKLES.. I DON'T KNOW WHY THEY BROKE IT OFF--
WAIT... I COULD'VE BEEN "BILLY BUCKLES"?
TELL ME, BILL...I'VE ALWAYS BEEN CURIOUS..DO YOU THINK BARBARA EVER HAD A THING WITH ED EMSHWILLER?
..I DON'T KNOW..
...AND BERT...HER BOYFRIEND FOR THE LAST FEW YEARS OF HER LIFE. ...HE SEEMED LIKE A NICE GUY--
HE WAS.

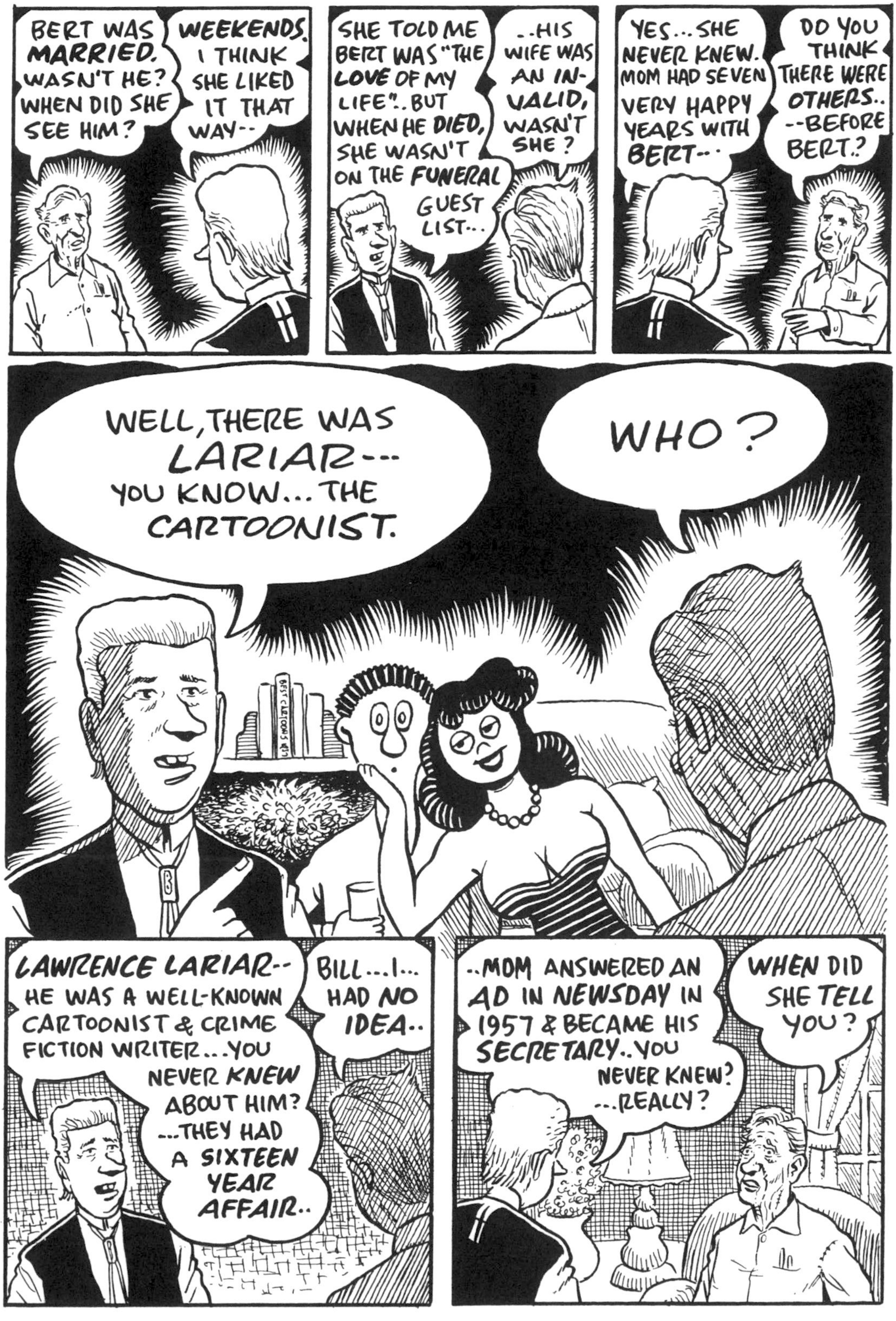
BERT WAS MARRIED. WASN'T HE? WHEN DID SHE SEE HIM?
WEEKENDS. I THINK SHE LIKED IT THAT WAY--
SHE TOLD ME BERT WAS "THE LOVE OF MY LIFE".. BUT WHEN HE DIED, SHE WASN'T ON THE FUNERAL GUEST LIST...
..HIS WIFE WAS AN IN-VALID, WASN'T SHE?
YES... SHE NEVER KNEW. MOM HAD SEVEN VERY HAPPY YEARS WITH BERT--.
DO YOU THINK THERE WERE OTHERS.. --BEFORE BERT.?
WELL, THERE WAS LARIAR--- YOU KNOW... THE CARTOONIST.
WHO?
BEST CARTOONS
LAWRENCE LARIAR-- HE WAS A WELL-KNOWN CARTOONIST & CRIME FICTION WRITER...YOU NEVER KNEW ABOUT HIM? ...THEY HAD A SIXTEEN YEAR AFFAIR..
BILL...I... HAD NO IDEA..
..MOM ANSWERED AN AD IN NEWSDAY IN 1957 & BECAME HIS SECRETARY..YOU NEVER KNEW? ...REALLY?
WHEN DID SHE TELL YOU?

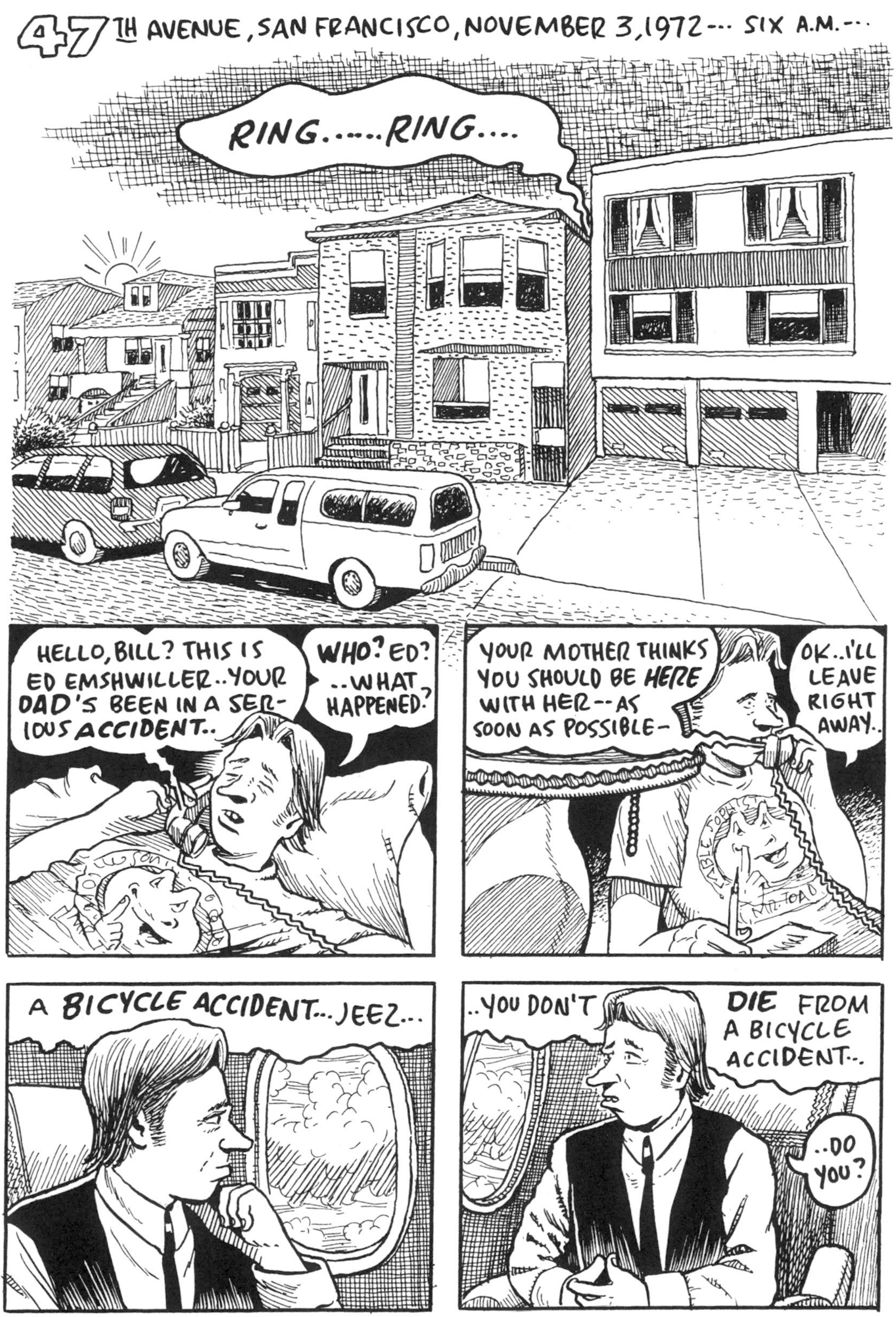
47TH AVENUE, SAN FRANCISCO, NOVEMBER 3, 1972--- SIX A.M.---
RING......RING....
HELLO, BILL? THIS IS ED EMSHWILLER..YOUR DAD'S BEEN IN A SERIOUS ACCIDENT..
WHO? ED? ..WHAT HAPPENED?
YOUR MOTHER THINKS YOU SHOULD BE HERE WITH HER--AS SOON AS POSSIBLE-
OK..I'LL LEAVE RIGHT AWAY..
A BICYCLE ACCIDENT...JEEZ...
..YOU DON'T DIE FROM A BICYCLE ACCIDENT...
..DO YOU?

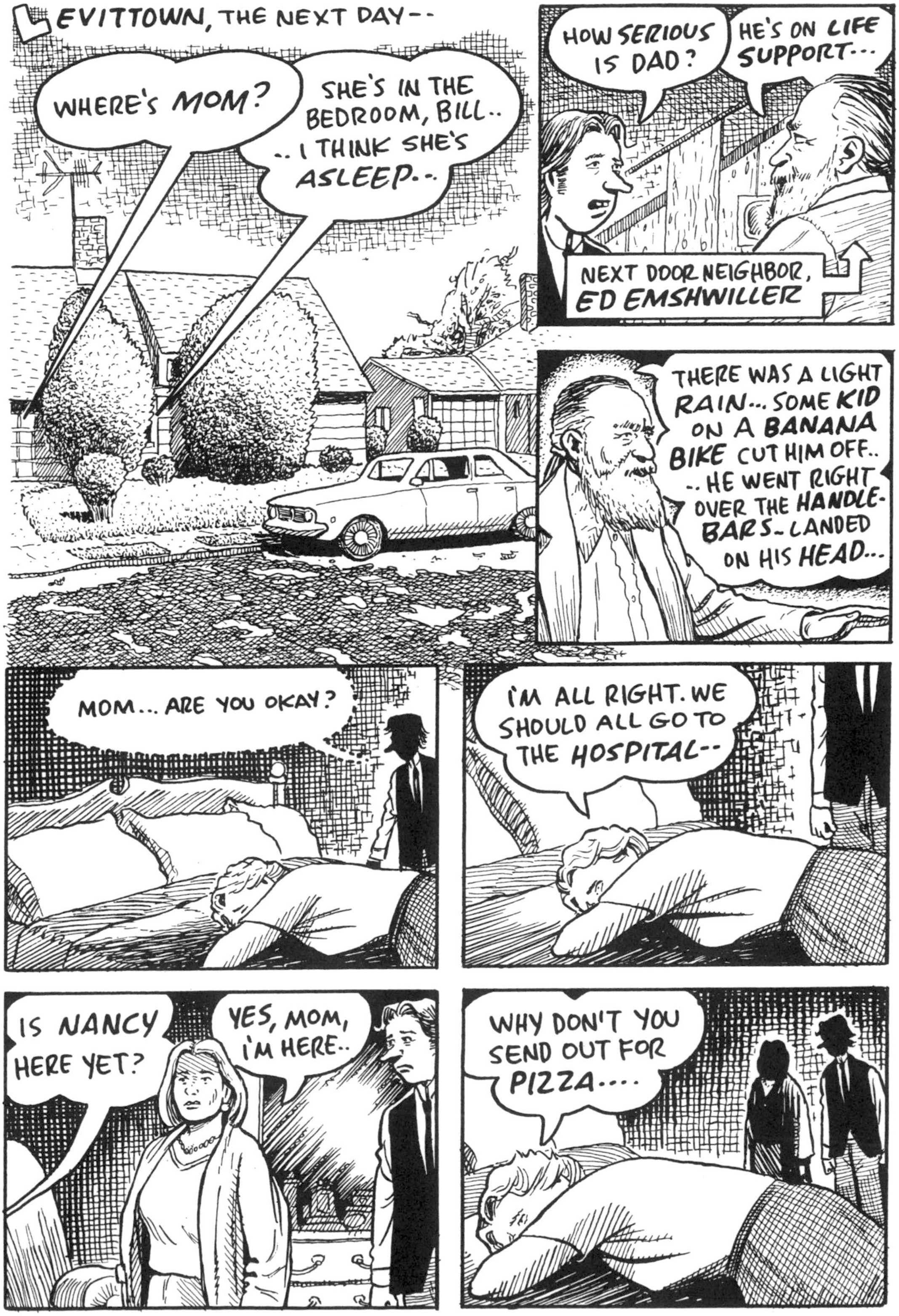
LEVITTOWN, THE NEXT DAY--
WHERE'S MOM?
SHE'S IN THE BEDROOM, BILL.. ..I THINK SHE'S ASLEEP..
HOW SERIOUS IS DAD?
HE'S ON LIFE SUPPORT...
NEXT DOOR NEIGHBOR, ED EMSHWILLER
THERE WAS A LIGHT RAIN... SOME KID ON A BANANA BIKE CUT HIM OFF.. ..HE WENT RIGHT OVER THE HANDLE-BARS.. LANDED ON HIS HEAD...
MOM... ARE YOU OKAY?
I'M ALL RIGHT. WE SHOULD ALL GO TO THE HOSPITAL--
IS NANCY HERE YET?
YES, MOM, I'M HERE..
WHY DON'T YOU SEND OUT FOR PIZZA....

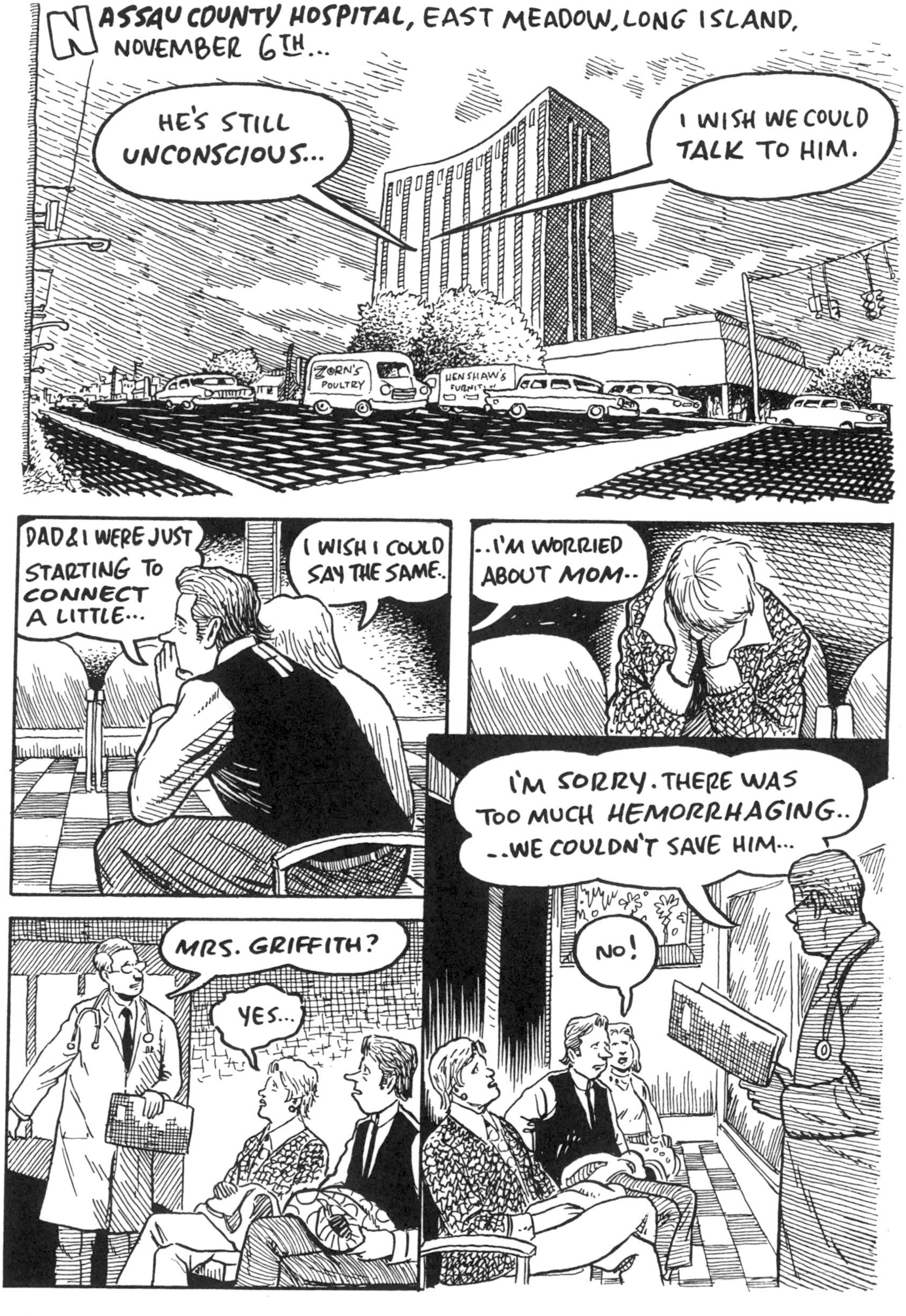
NASSAU COUNTY HOSPITAL, EAST MEADOW, LONG ISLAND, NOVEMBER 6TH...
HE'S STILL UNCONSCIOUS...
I WISH WE COULD TALK TO HIM.
ZORN'S POULTRY
HENSHAW'S FURNIT...
DAD & I WERE JUST STARTING TO CONNECT A LITTLE...
I WISH I COULD SAY THE SAME..
..I'M WORRIED ABOUT MOM..
MRS. GRIFFITH?
YES...
I'M SORRY. THERE WAS TOO MUCH HEMORRHAGING..
..WE COULDN'T SAVE HIM...
NO!

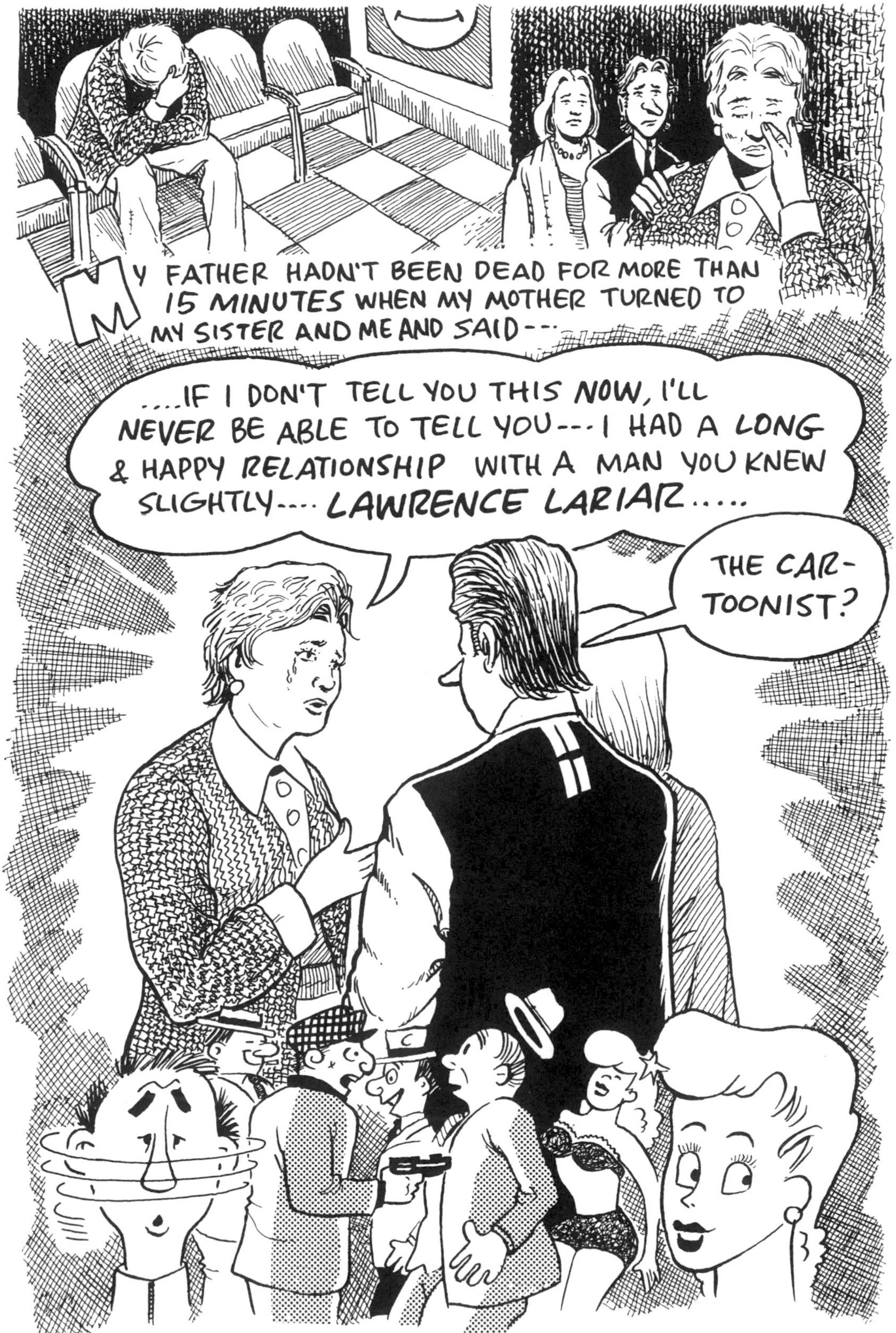
MY FATHER HADN'T BEEN DEAD FOR MORE THAN 15 MINUTES WHEN MY MOTHER TURNED TO MY SISTER AND ME AND SAID---
....IF I DON'T TELL YOU THIS NOW, I'LL NEVER BE ABLE TO TELL YOU---I HAD A LONG & HAPPY RELATIONSHIP WITH A MAN YOU KNEW SLIGHTLY.... LAWRENCE LARIAR.....
THE CAR-TOONIST?

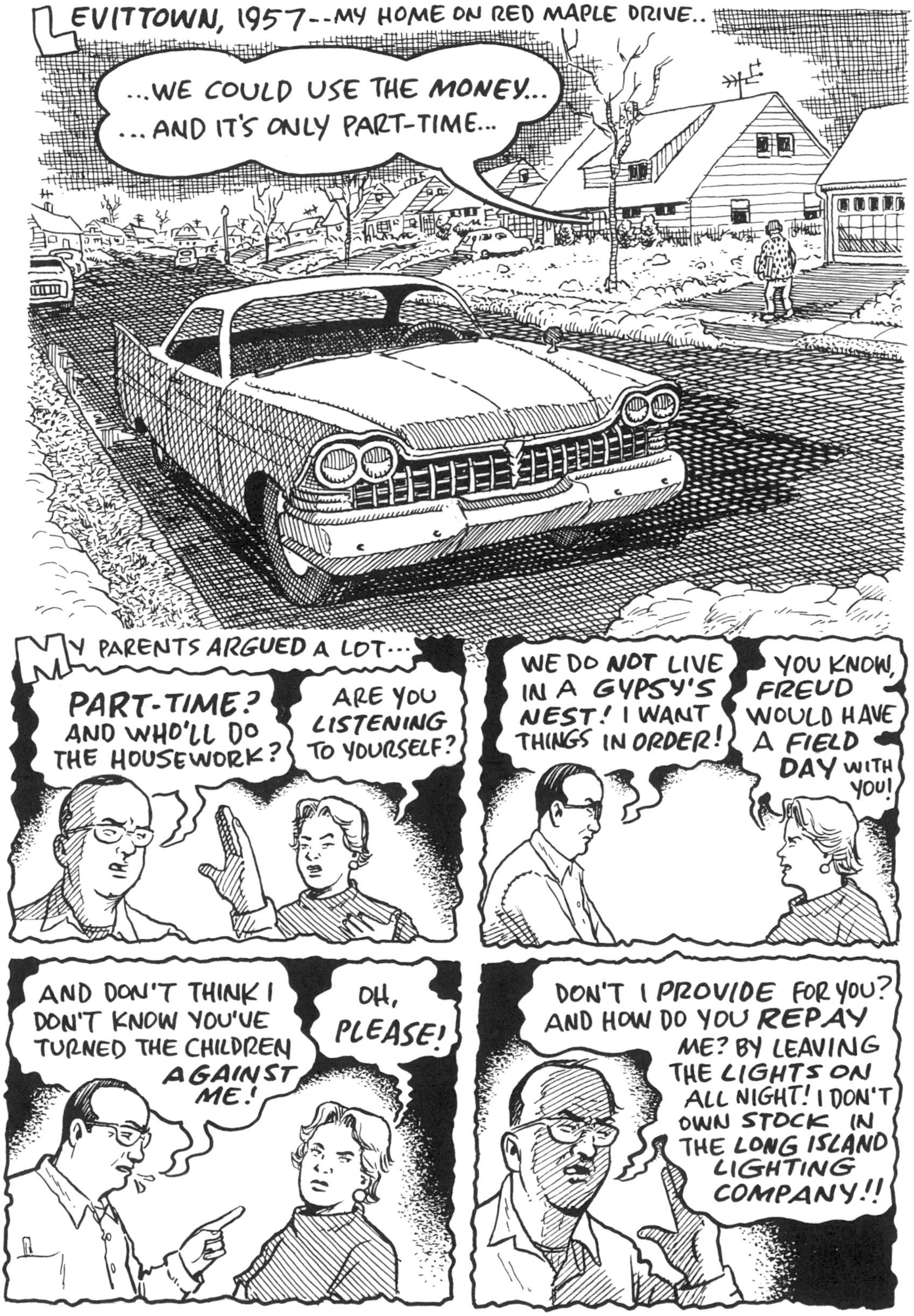
LEVITTOWN, 1957--MY HOME ON RED MAPLE DRIVE..
...WE COULD USE THE MONEY... ...AND IT'S ONLY PART-TIME...
MY PARENTS ARGUED A LOT...
PART-TIME? AND WHO'LL DO THE HOUSEWORK?
ARE YOU LISTENING TO YOURSELF?
WE DO NOT LIVE IN A GYPSY'S NEST! I WANT THINGS IN ORDER!
YOU KNOW, FREUD WOULD HAVE A FIELD DAY WITH YOU!
AND DON'T THINK I DON'T KNOW YOU'VE TURNED THE CHILDREN AGAINST ME!
OH, PLEASE!
DON'T I PROVIDE FOR YOU? AND HOW DO YOU REPAY ME? BY LEAVING THE LIGHTS ON ALL NIGHT! I DON'T OWN STOCK IN THE LONG ISLAND LIGHTING COMPANY!!

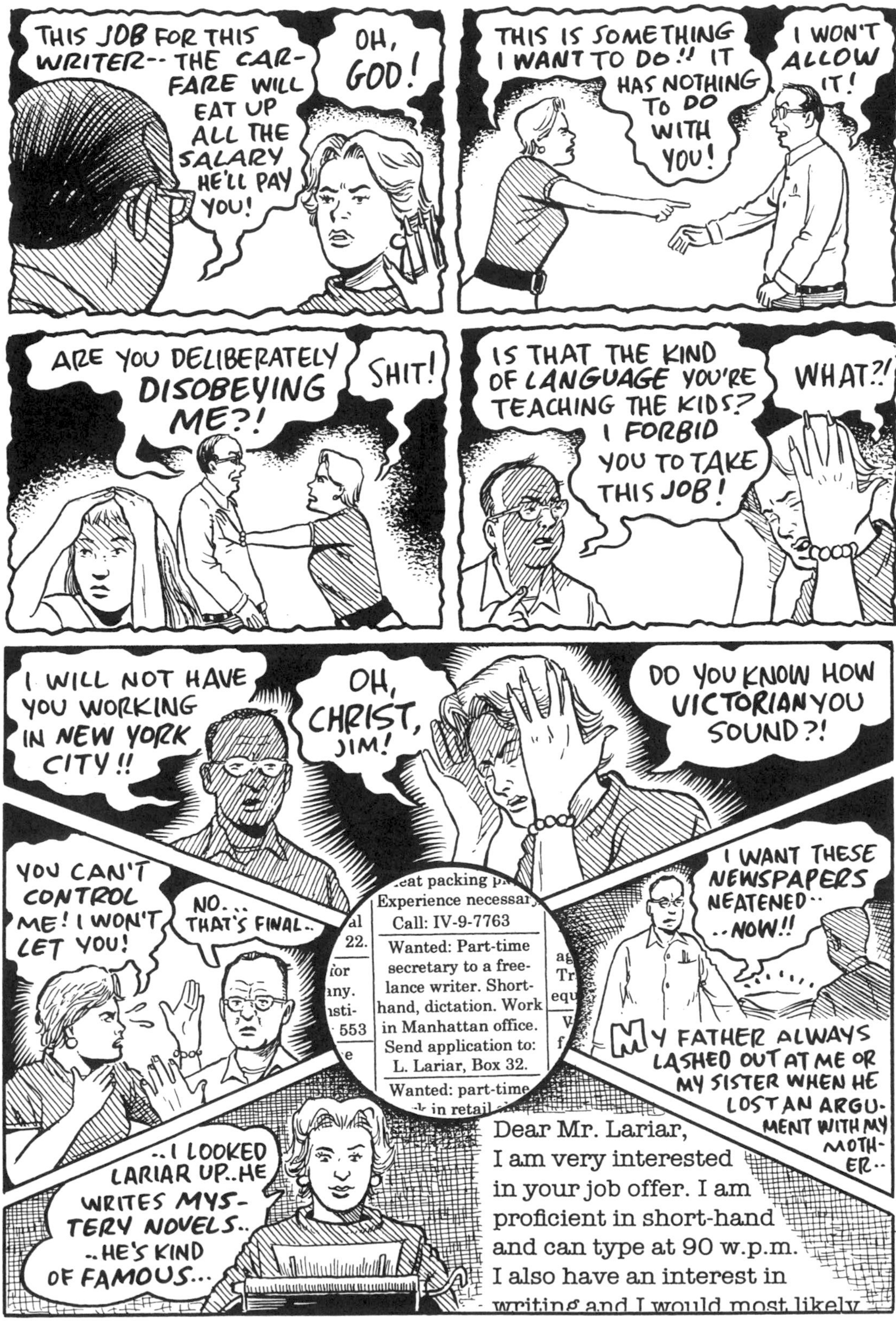
THIS JOB FOR THIS WRITER-- THE CAR-FARE WILL EAT UP ALL THE SALARY HE'LL PAY YOU!
OH, GOD!
THIS IS SOMETHING I WANT TO DO!! IT HAS NOTHING TO DO WITH YOU!
I WON'T ALLOW IT!
ARE YOU DELIBERATELY DISOBEYING ME?!
SHIT!
IS THAT THE KIND OF LANGUAGE YOU'RE TEACHING THE KIDS? I FORBID YOU TO TAKE THIS JOB!
WHAT?!
I WILL NOT HAVE YOU WORKING IN NEW YORK CITY!!
OH, CHRIST, JIM!
DO YOU KNOW HOW VICTORIAN YOU SOUND?!
YOU CAN'T CONTROL ME! I WON'T LET YOU!
NO... THAT'S FINAL..
Experience necessary
Call: IV-9-7763
Wanted: Part-time secretary to a free-lance writer. Short-hand, dictation. Work in Manhattan office. Send application to: L. Lariar, Box 32.
Wanted: part-time
I WANT THESE NEWSPAPERS NEATENED.. ..NOW!!
MY FATHER ALWAYS LASHED OUT AT ME OR MY SISTER WHEN HE LOST AN ARGUMENT WITH MY MOTHER..
..I LOOKED LARIAR UP..HE WRITES MYSTERY NOVELS.. ..HE'S KIND OF FAMOUS...
Dear Mr. Lariar,
I am very interested in your job offer. I am proficient in short-hand and can type at 90 w.p.m. I also have an interest in

THIS WAS THE SAME TIME THE ARMY SUDDENLY DEMOTED MY FATHER. IT WAS EXPLAINED AS A "BUDGET-CUTTING MEASURE." IT WAS ALSO THE YEAR I BECAME OBSESSED WITH THE "SERGEANT BILKO" TV SHOW---

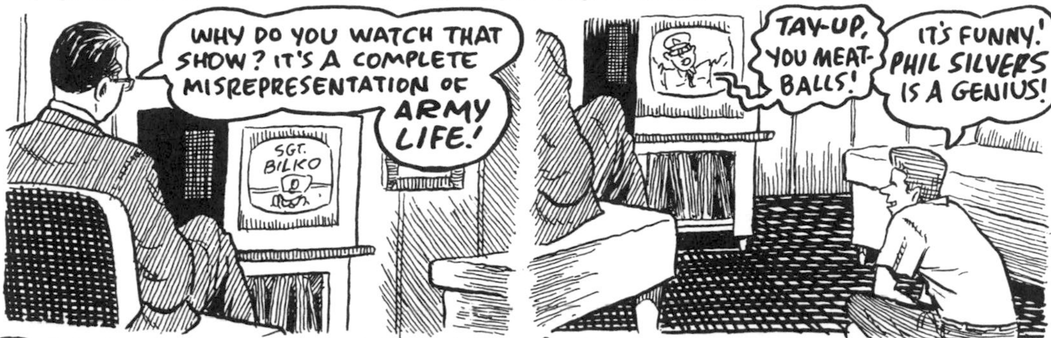
WHY DO YOU WATCH THAT SHOW? IT'S A COMPLETE MISREPRESENTATION OF ARMY LIFE!
SGT. BILKO
TAY-UP, YOU MEAT-BALLS!
IT'S FUNNY! PHIL SILVERS IS A GENIUS!

DAD HANDED IN HIS RESIGNATION & SPENT A FRUITLESS YEAR LOOKING FOR OTHER WORK. IN THE END, HE RETURNED TO THE ARMY, THIS TIME WITH THE LOWER RANK OF MASTER SERGEANT...HE FELT HUMILIATED.

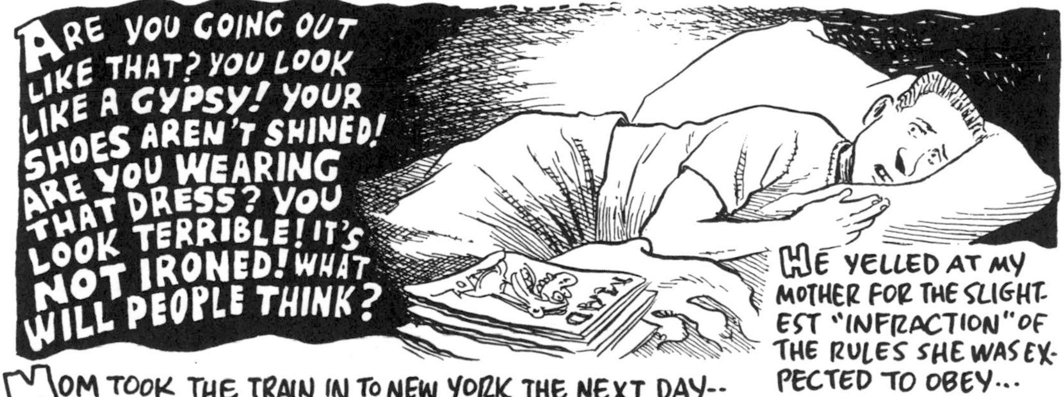
ARE YOU GOING OUT LIKE THAT? YOU LOOK LIKE A GYPSY! YOUR SHOES AREN'T SHINED! ARE YOU WEARING THAT DRESS? YOU LOOK TERRIBLE! IT'S NOT IRONED! WHAT WILL PEOPLE THINK?
MAD
HE YELLED AT MY MOTHER FOR THE SLIGHT-EST "INFRACTION" OF THE RULES SHE WAS EX-PECTED TO OBEY...

MOM TOOK THE TRAIN IN TO NEW YORK THE NEXT DAY--

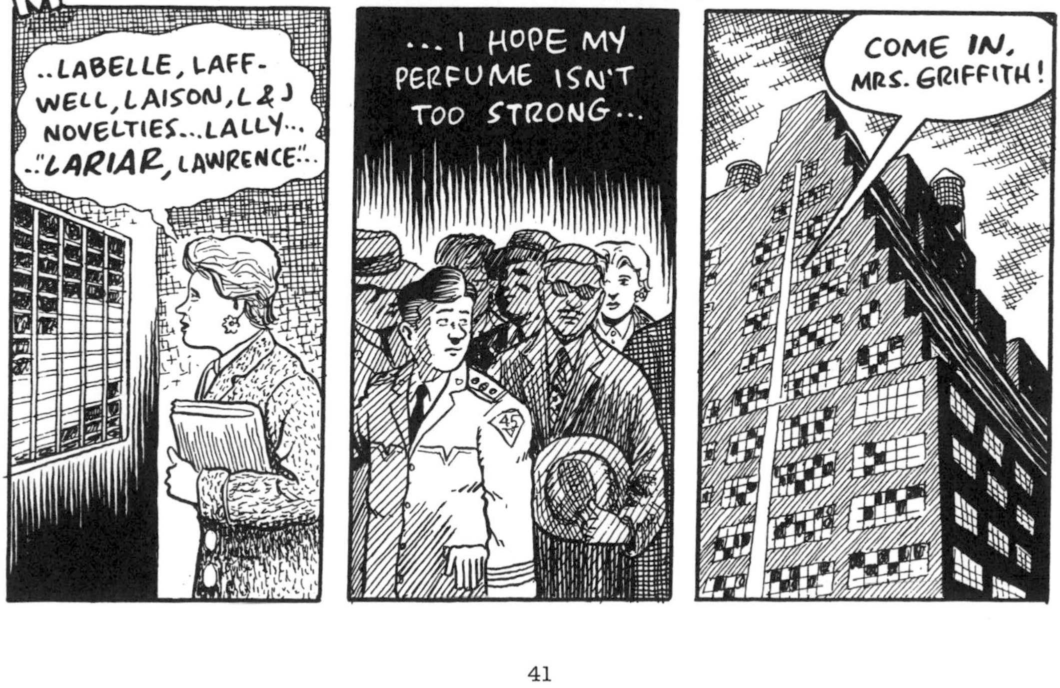
..LABELLE, LAFF-WELL, LAISON, L&J NOVELTIES...LALLY... .."LARIAR, LAWRENCE"..
... I HOPE MY PERFUME ISN'T TOO STRONG...
45
COME IN, MRS. GRIFFITH!

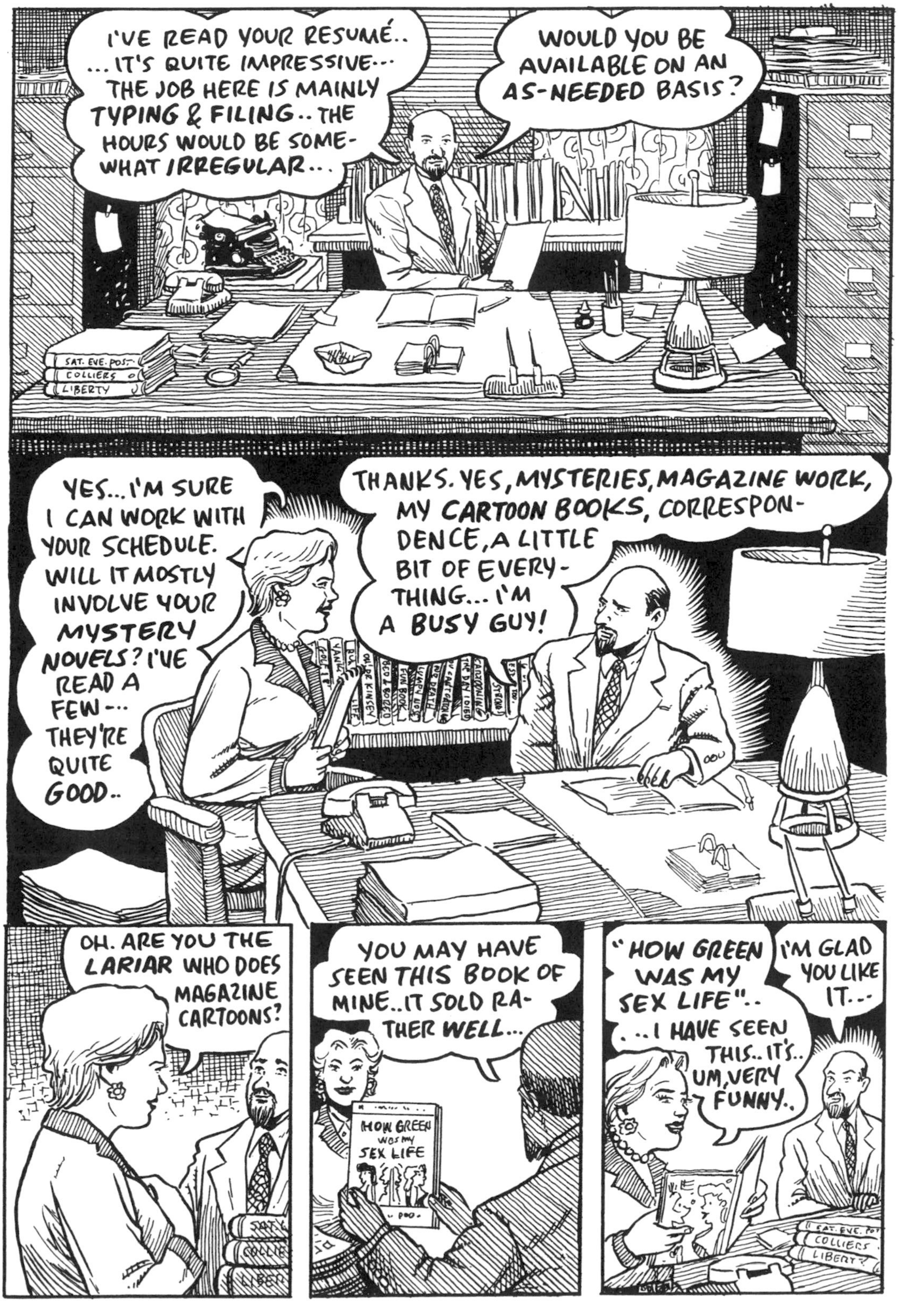
I'VE READ YOUR RESUMÉ.. ...IT'S QUITE IMPRESSIVE... THE JOB HERE IS MAINLY TYPING & FILING.. THE HOURS WOULD BE SOMEWHAT IRREGULAR...
WOULD YOU BE AVAILABLE ON AN AS-NEEDED BASIS?
SAT. EVE. POST
COLLIERS
LIBERTY
YES... I'M SURE I CAN WORK WITH YOUR SCHEDULE. WILL IT MOSTLY INVOLVE YOUR MYSTERY NOVELS? I'VE READ A FEW... THEY'RE QUITE GOOD..
THANKS. YES, MYSTERIES, MAGAZINE WORK, MY CARTOON BOOKS, CORRESPONDENCE, A LITTLE BIT OF EVERYTHING... I'M A BUSY GUY!
OH. ARE YOU THE LARIAR WHO DOES MAGAZINE CARTOONS?
YOU MAY HAVE SEEN THIS BOOK OF MINE.. IT SOLD RATHER WELL...
HOW GREEN WAS MY SEX LIFE
"HOW GREEN WAS MY SEX LIFE".. ...I HAVE SEEN THIS.. IT'S.. UM, VERY FUNNY..
I'M GLAD YOU LIKE IT...
SAT. EVE. POST
COLLIERS
LIBERTY

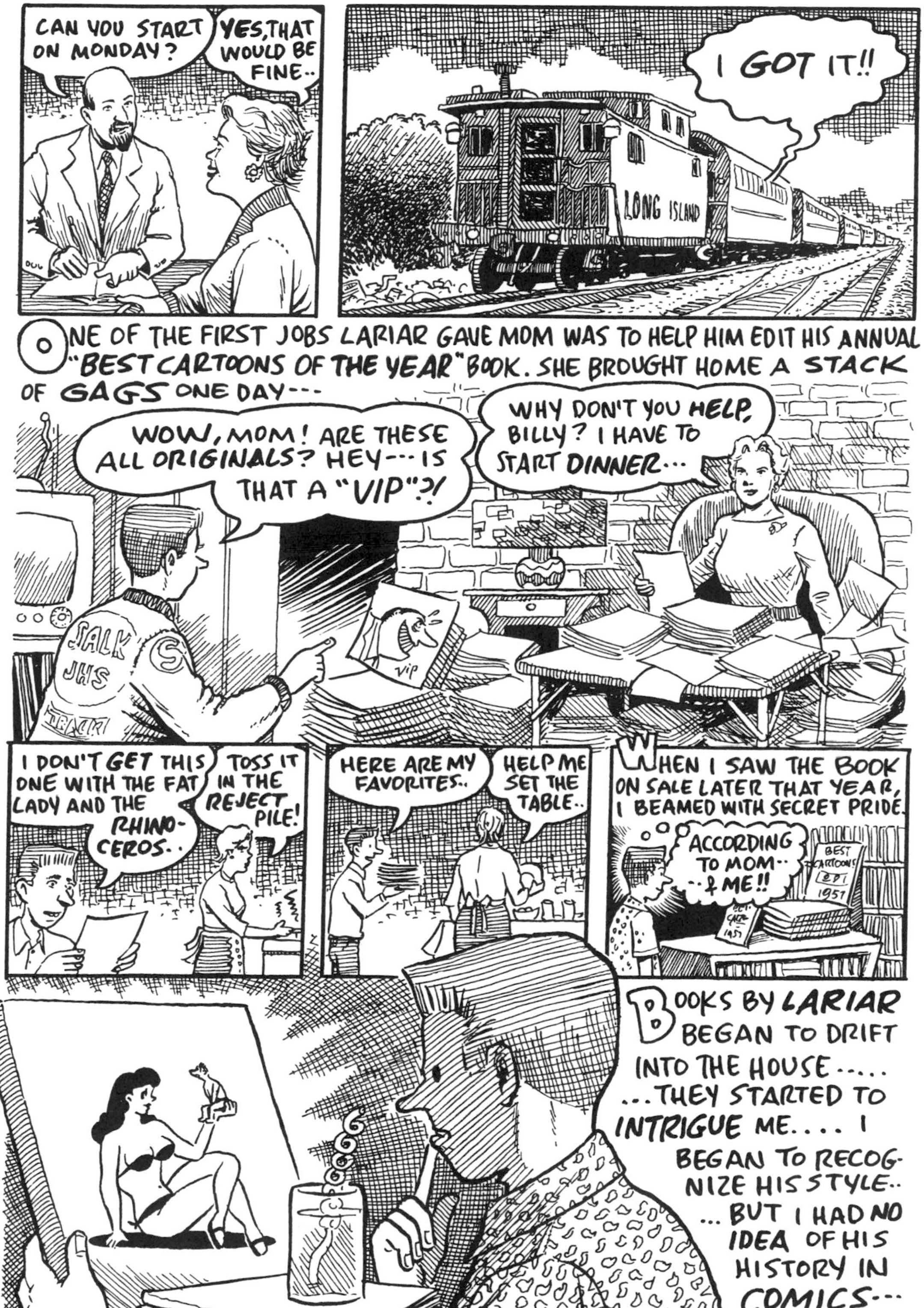
CAN YOU START ON MONDAY?
YES, THAT WOULD BE FINE..
I GOT IT!!
LONG ISLAND
ONE OF THE FIRST JOBS LARIAR GAVE MOM WAS TO HELP HIM EDIT HIS ANNUAL "BEST CARTOONS OF THE YEAR" BOOK. SHE BROUGHT HOME A STACK OF GAGS ONE DAY---
WOW, MOM! ARE THESE ALL ORIGINALS? HEY--- IS THAT A "VIP"?!
WHY DON'T YOU HELP, BILLY? I HAVE TO START DINNER...
SALK JHS
VIP
I DON'T GET THIS ONE WITH THE FAT LADY AND THE RHINOCEROS..
TOSS IT IN THE REJECT PILE!
HERE ARE MY FAVORITES..
HELP ME SET THE TABLE..
WHEN I SAW THE BOOK ON SALE LATER THAT YEAR, I BEAMED WITH SECRET PRIDE.
ACCORDING TO MOM.. ..& ME!!
BEST CARTOONS 1957
BOOKS BY LARIAR BEGAN TO DRIFT INTO THE HOUSE..... ...THEY STARTED TO INTRIGUE ME.... I BEGAN TO RECOGNIZE HIS STYLE.. ...BUT I HAD NO IDEA OF HIS HISTORY IN COMICS---

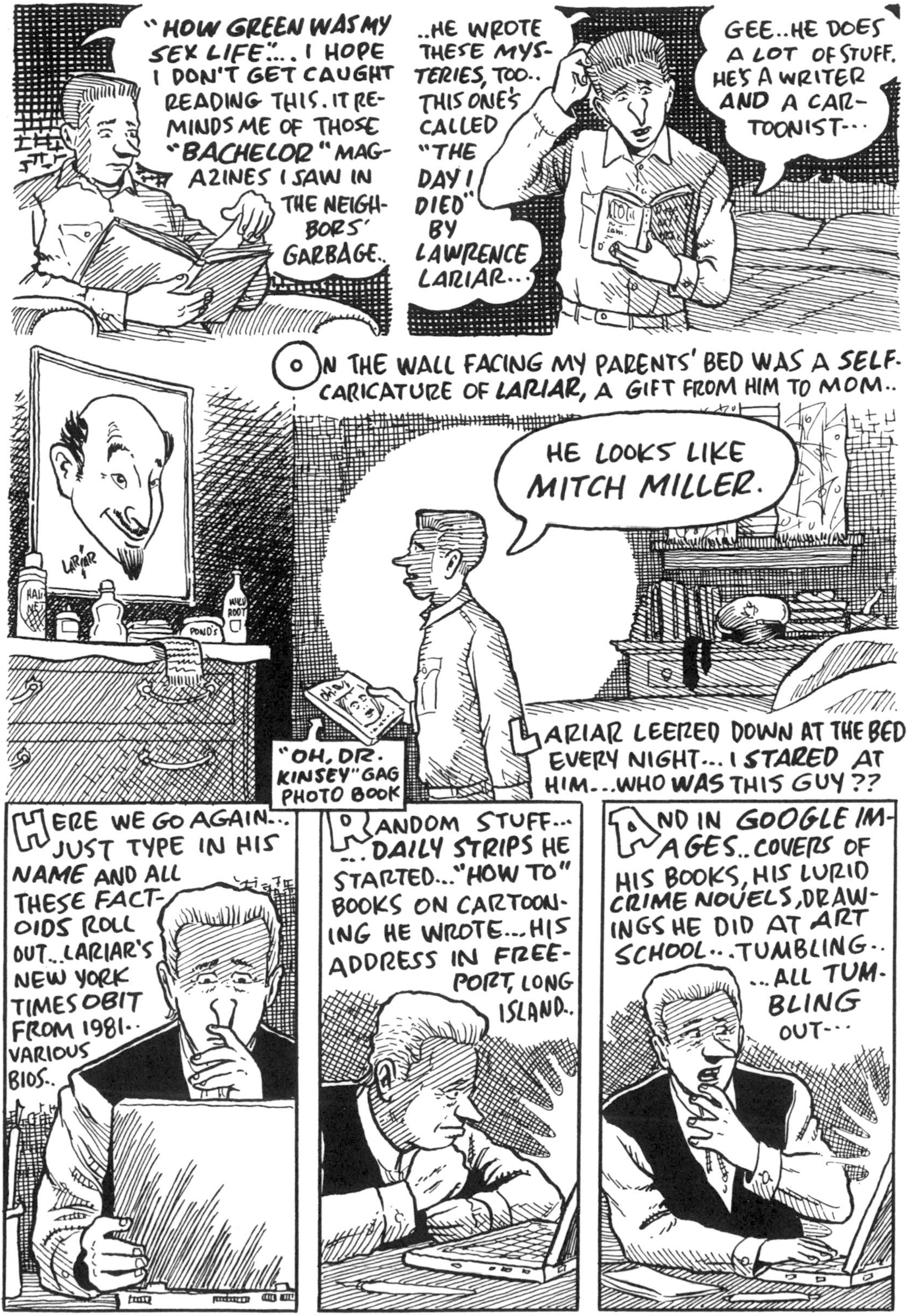
"HOW GREEN WAS MY SEX LIFE"... I HOPE I DON'T GET CAUGHT READING THIS. IT REMINDS ME OF THOSE "BACHELOR" MAGAZINES I SAW IN THE NEIGHBORS' GARBAGE..
..HE WROTE THESE MYSTERIES, TOO.. THIS ONE'S CALLED "THE DAY I DIED" BY LAWRENCE LARIAR...
GEE..HE DOES A LOT OF STUFF. HE'S A WRITER AND A CARTOONIST...
ON THE WALL FACING MY PARENTS' BED WAS A SELF-CARICATURE OF LARIAR, A GIFT FROM HIM TO MOM..
HE LOOKS LIKE MITCH MILLER.
LARIAR
POND'S
"OH, DR. KINSEY" GAG PHOTO BOOK
LARIAR LEERED DOWN AT THE BED EVERY NIGHT... I STARED AT HIM...WHO WAS THIS GUY??
HERE WE GO AGAIN... JUST TYPE IN HIS NAME AND ALL THESE FACTOIDS ROLL OUT...LARIAR'S NEW YORK TIMES OBIT FROM 1981.. VARIOUS BIOS..
RANDOM STUFF... ...DAILY STRIPS HE STARTED..."HOW TO" BOOKS ON CARTOONING HE WROTE...HIS ADDRESS IN FREEPORT, LONG ISLAND..
AND IN GOOGLE IMAGES..COVERS OF HIS BOOKS, HIS LURID CRIME NOVELS, DRAWINGS HE DID AT ART SCHOOL...TUMBLING.. ...ALL TUMBLING OUT...

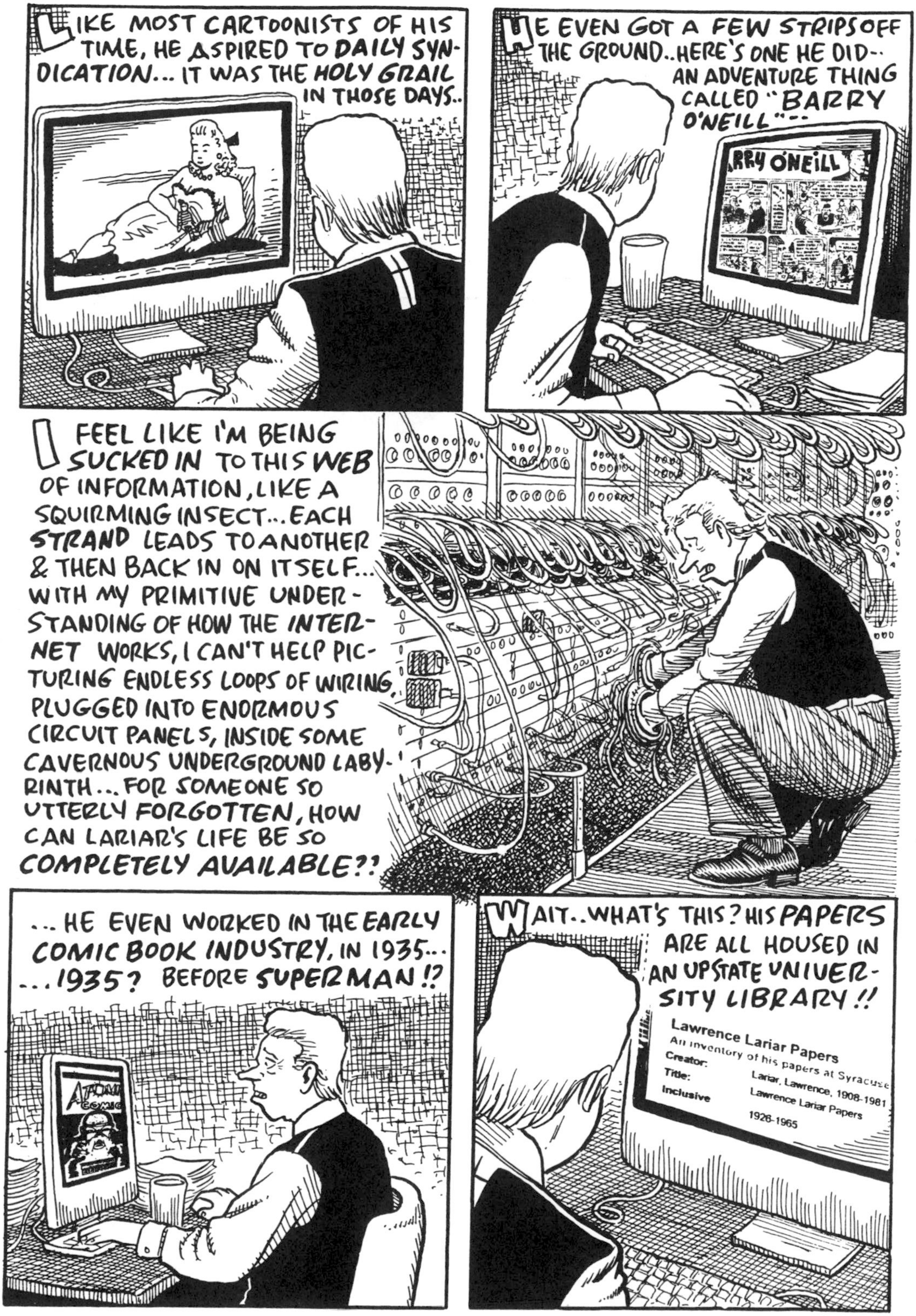
LIKE MOST CARTOONISTS OF HIS TIME, HE ASPIRED TO DAILY SYNDICATION... IT WAS THE HOLY GRAIL IN THOSE DAYS..
HE EVEN GOT A FEW STRIPS OFF THE GROUND.. HERE'S ONE HE DID-- AN ADVENTURE THING CALLED "BARRY O'NEILL"--
RRY O'NEILL
I FEEL LIKE I'M BEING SUCKED IN TO THIS WEB OF INFORMATION, LIKE A SQUIRMING INSECT... EACH STRAND LEADS TO ANOTHER & THEN BACK IN ON ITSELF... WITH MY PRIMITIVE UNDERSTANDING OF HOW THE INTERNET WORKS, I CAN'T HELP PICTURING ENDLESS LOOPS OF WIRING, PLUGGED INTO ENORMOUS CIRCUIT PANELS, INSIDE SOME CAVERNOUS UNDERGROUND LABYRINTH... FOR SOMEONE SO UTTERLY FORGOTTEN, HOW CAN LARIAR'S LIFE BE SO COMPLETELY AVAILABLE?!
...HE EVEN WORKED IN THE EARLY COMIC BOOK INDUSTRY, IN 1935... ...1935? BEFORE SUPERMAN!?
WAIT.. WHAT'S THIS? HIS PAPERS ARE ALL HOUSED IN AN UPSTATE UNIVERSITY LIBRARY!!
Lawrence Lariar Papers
An inventory of his papers at Syracuse
Creator: Lariar, Lawrence, 1908-1981
Title: Lawrence Lariar Papers
Inclusive 1926-1965

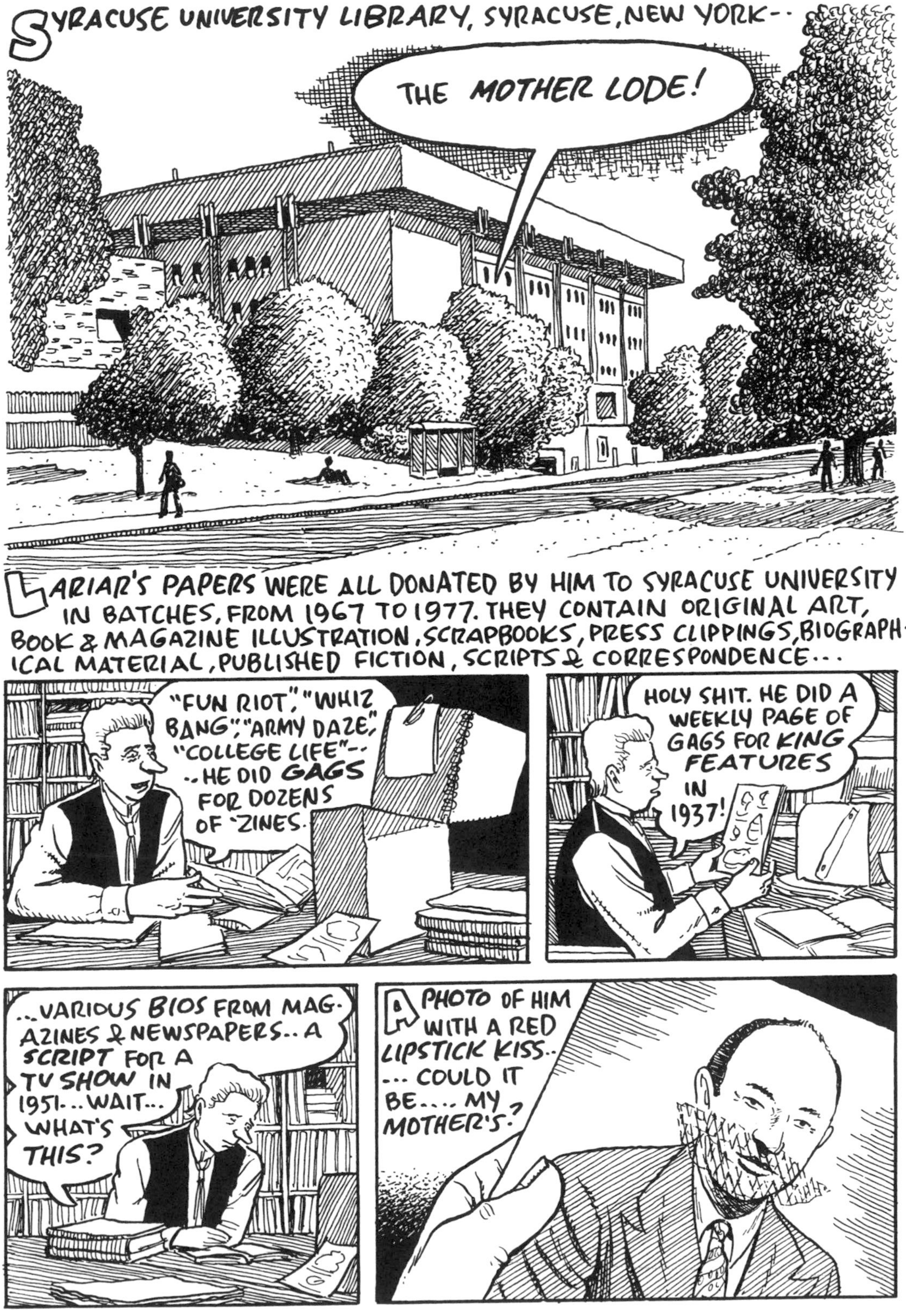
SYRACUSE UNIVERSITY LIBRARY, SYRACUSE, NEW YORK--
THE MOTHER LODE!
LARIAR'S PAPERS WERE ALL DONATED BY HIM TO SYRACUSE UNIVERSITY IN BATCHES, FROM 1967 TO 1977. THEY CONTAIN ORIGINAL ART, BOOK & MAGAZINE ILLUSTRATION, SCRAPBOOKS, PRESS CLIPPINGS, BIOGRAPHICAL MATERIAL, PUBLISHED FICTION, SCRIPTS & CORRESPONDENCE...
"FUN RIOT," "WHIZ BANG," "ARMY DAZE," "COLLEGE LIFE"-- ..HE DID GAGS FOR DOZENS OF 'ZINES.
HOLY SHIT. HE DID A WEEKLY PAGE OF GAGS FOR KING FEATURES IN 1937!
...VARIOUS BIOS FROM MAGAZINES & NEWSPAPERS.. A SCRIPT FOR A TV SHOW IN 1951...WAIT... WHAT'S THIS?
A PHOTO OF HIM WITH A RED LIPSTICK KISS.. ...COULD IT BE.... MY MOTHER'S?

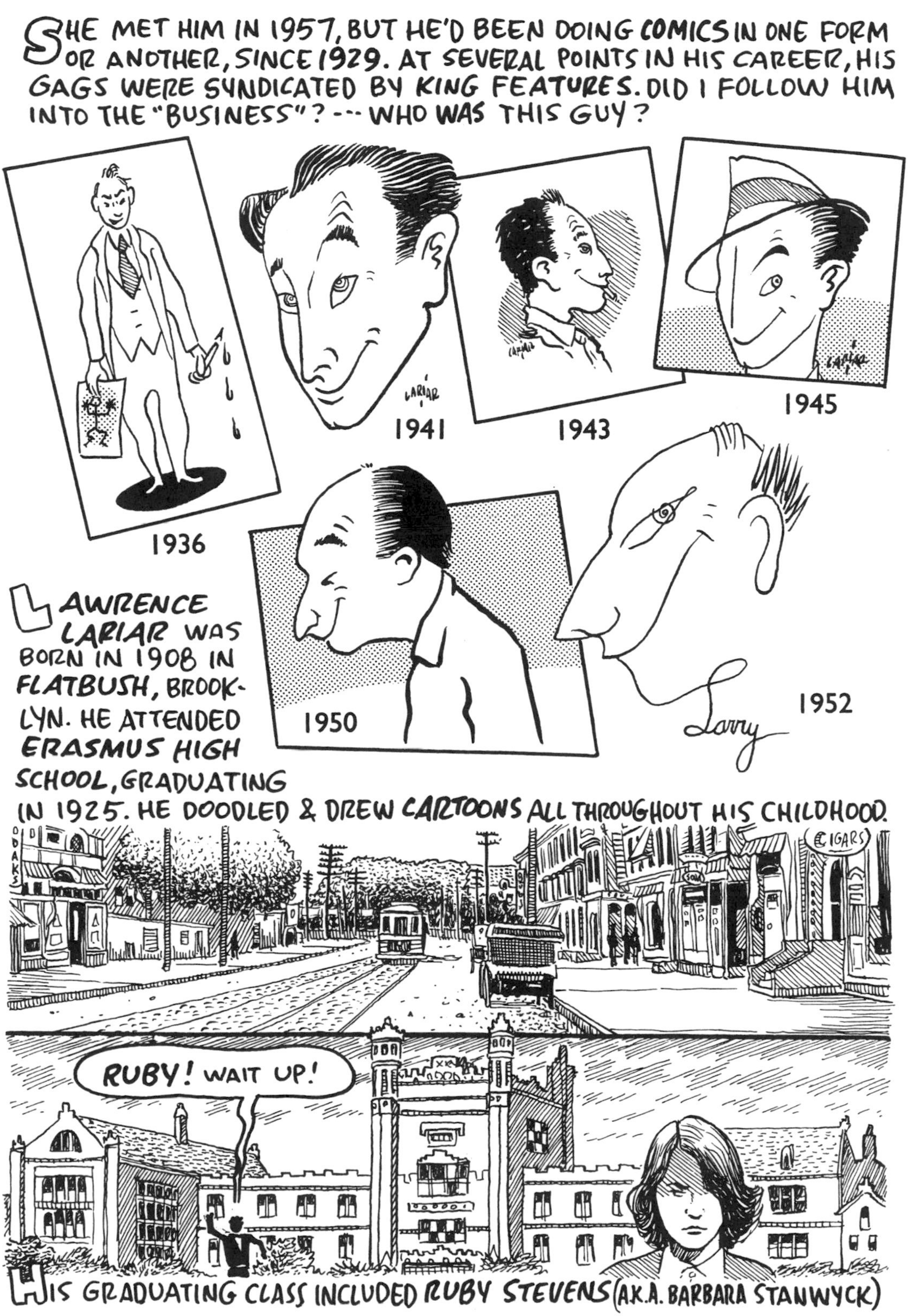
SHE MET HIM IN 1957, BUT HE'D BEEN DOING COMICS IN ONE FORM OR ANOTHER, SINCE 1929. AT SEVERAL POINTS IN HIS CAREER, HIS GAGS WERE SYNDICATED BY KING FEATURES. DID I FOLLOW HIM INTO THE "BUSINESS"? --- WHO WAS THIS GUY?
1936
LARIAR
1941
LARIAR
1943
LARIAR
1945
1950
Larry
1952
LAWRENCE LARIAR WAS BORN IN 1908 IN FLATBUSH, BROOKLYN. HE ATTENDED ERASMUS HIGH SCHOOL, GRADUATING IN 1925. HE DOODLED & DREW CARTOONS ALL THROUGHOUT HIS CHILDHOOD.
CIGARS
RUBY! WAIT UP!
HIS GRADUATING CLASS INCLUDED RUBY STEVENS (A.K.A. BARBARA STANWYCK)

FROM 1926 TO 1929, LARIAR TOOK CLASSES AT THE NEW YORK SCHOOL FOR FINE AND APPLIED ARTS, FORMERLY THE CHASE SCHOOL, WHERE NORMAN ROCKWELL & EDWARD HOPPER WERE ONCE ENROLLED--

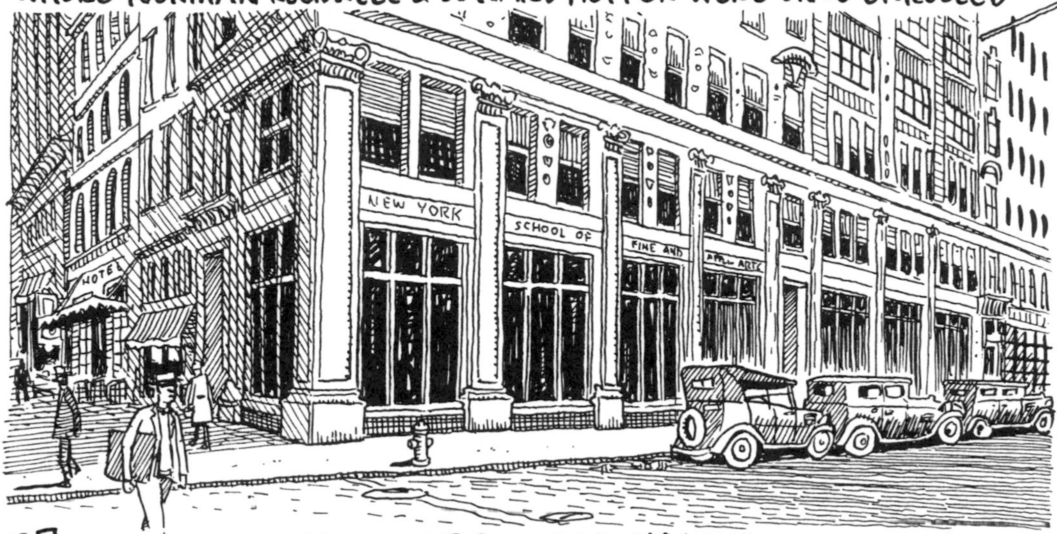
NEW YORK
SCHOOL OF
FINE AND
HOTEL

HE ALSO ATTENDED THE ART STUDENTS LEAGUE, WHERE HE DREW FROM THE MODEL. LARIAR MET TWO OTHER ARTISTS AT THIS TIME, ADOLPH SCHUS & JACK ARTHUR. THEY BECAME FRIENDS--

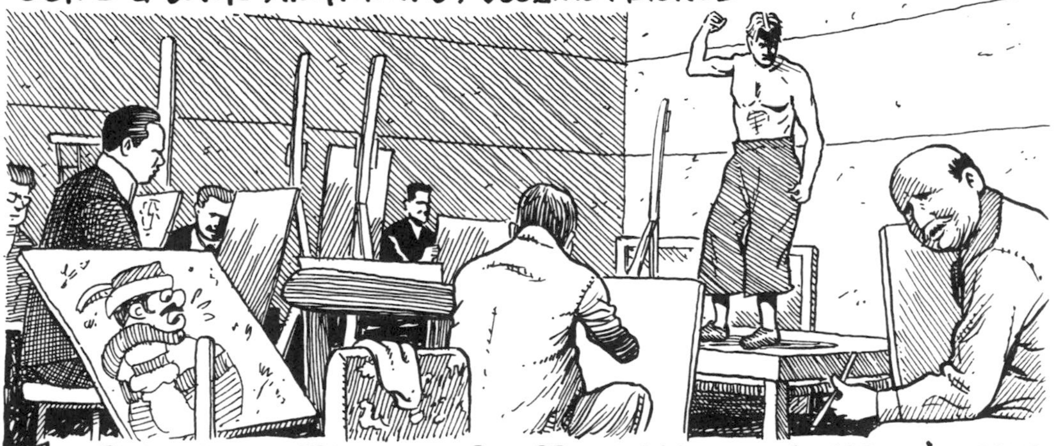

TOGETHER THE THREE SET UP SHOP IN A FLAT ON MANHATTAN'S UPPER EAST SIDE TO SELL GAGS & ILLUSTRATIONS TO LOCAL MAGAZINES. IT WAS CALLED THE LAWRENCE COMPANY..."COLLEGE LIFE" WAS AN EARLY CLIENT---

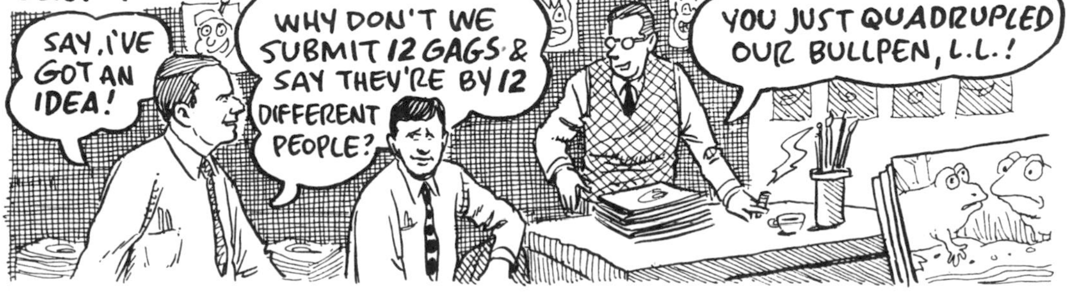
SAY, I'VE GOT AN IDEA!
WHY DON'T WE SUBMIT 12 GAGS & SAY THEY'RE BY 12 DIFFERENT PEOPLE?
YOU JUST QUADRUPLED OUR BULLPEN, L.L.!

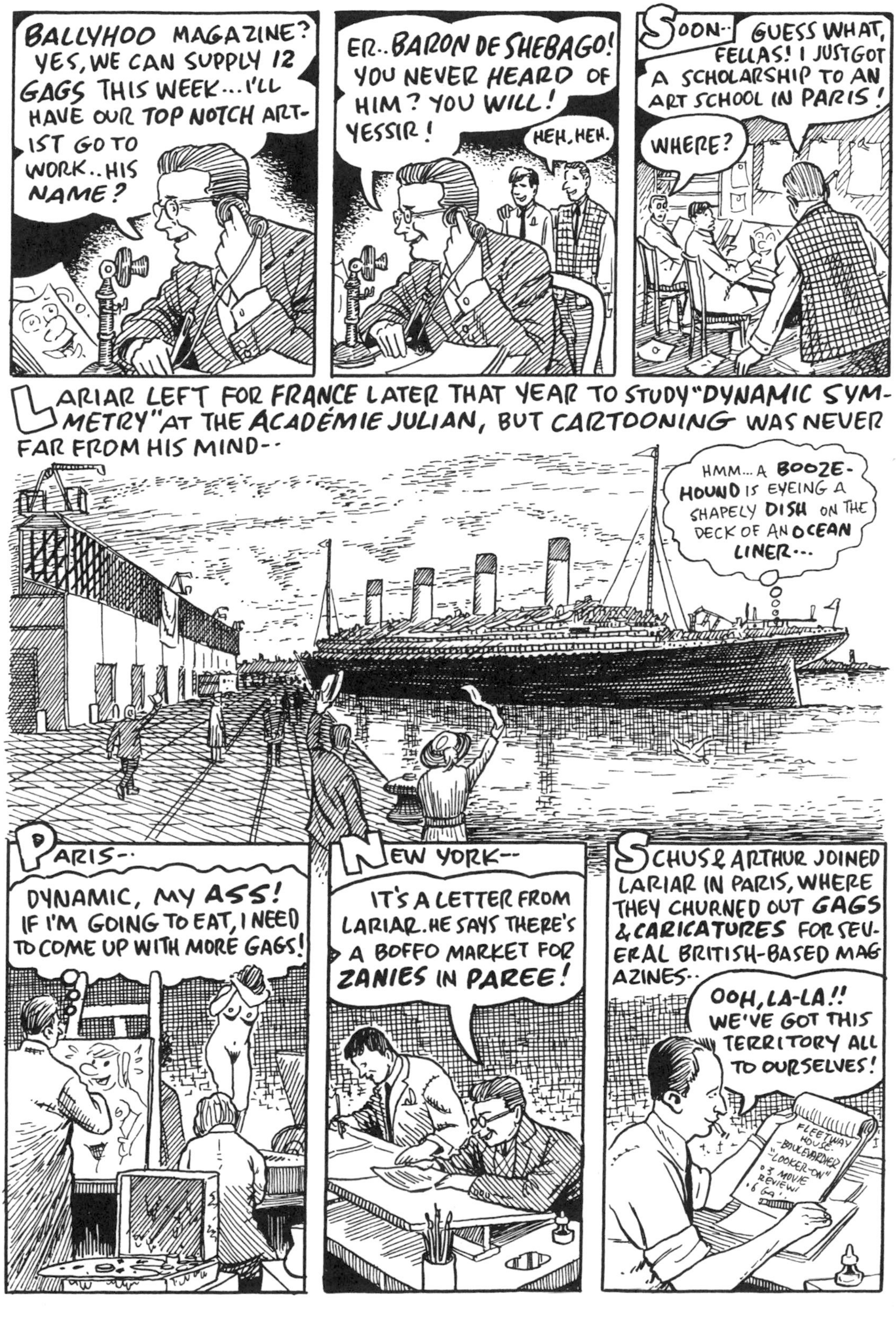
BALLYHOO MAGAZINE? YES, WE CAN SUPPLY 12 GAGS THIS WEEK... I'LL HAVE OUR TOP NOTCH ARTIST GO TO WORK.. HIS NAME?
ER.. BARON DE SHEBAGO! YOU NEVER HEARD OF HIM? YOU WILL! YESSIR!
HEH, HEH.
SOON..
GUESS WHAT, FELLAS! I JUST GOT A SCHOLARSHIP TO AN ART SCHOOL IN PARIS!
WHERE?
LARIAR LEFT FOR FRANCE LATER THAT YEAR TO STUDY "DYNAMIC SYMMETRY" AT THE ACADÉMIE JULIAN, BUT CARTOONING WAS NEVER FAR FROM HIS MIND--
HMM... A BOOZE-HOUND IS EYEING A SHAPELY DISH ON THE DECK OF AN OCEAN LINER...
PARIS--
DYNAMIC, MY ASS! IF I'M GOING TO EAT, I NEED TO COME UP WITH MORE GAGS!
NEW YORK--
IT'S A LETTER FROM LARIAR. HE SAYS THERE'S A BOFFO MARKET FOR ZANIES IN PAREE!
SCHUS & ARTHUR JOINED LARIAR IN PARIS, WHERE THEY CHURNED OUT GAGS & CARICATURES FOR SEVERAL BRITISH-BASED MAGAZINES..
OOH, LA-LA!! WE'VE GOT THIS TERRITORY ALL TO OURSELVES!
FLEETWAY HOUSE
-BOULEVARDIER
-"LOOKER-ON"
3 MOVIE REVIEW
6 GA

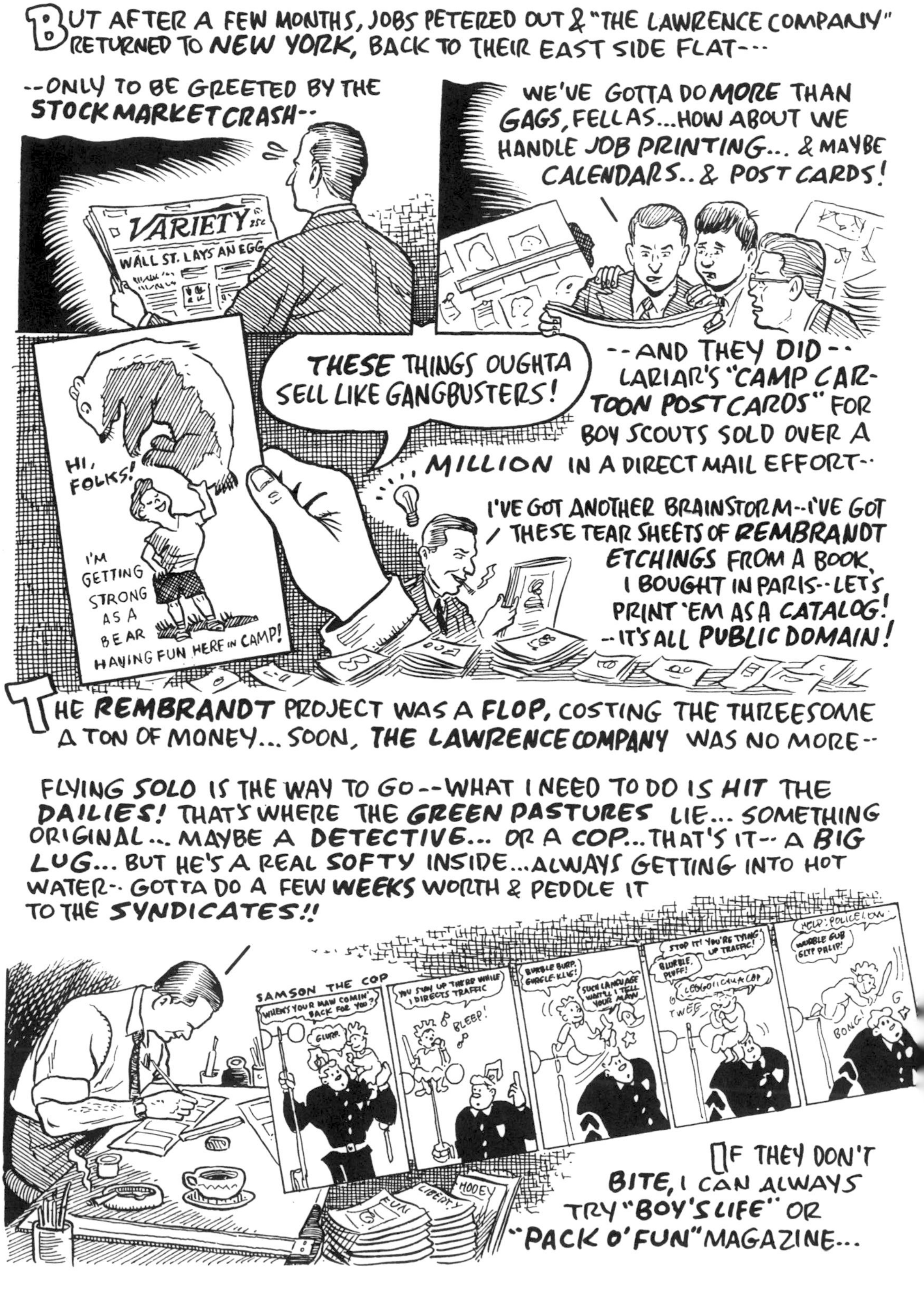
BUT AFTER A FEW MONTHS, JOBS PETERED OUT & "THE LAWRENCE COMPANY" RETURNED TO NEW YORK, BACK TO THEIR EAST SIDE FLAT---
--ONLY TO BE GREETED BY THE STOCK MARKET CRASH--
VARIETY
WALL ST. LAYS AN EGG
WE'VE GOTTA DO MORE THAN GAGS, FELLAS...HOW ABOUT WE HANDLE JOB PRINTING... & MAYBE CALENDARS..& POST CARDS!
HI, FOLKS!
I'M GETTING STRONG AS A BEAR HAVING FUN HERE IN CAMP!
THESE THINGS OUGHTA SELL LIKE GANGBUSTERS!
--AND THEY DID-- LARIAR'S "CAMP CARTOON POSTCARDS" FOR BOY SCOUTS SOLD OVER A MILLION IN A DIRECT MAIL EFFORT--
I'VE GOT ANOTHER BRAINSTORM--I'VE GOT THESE TEAR SHEETS OF REMBRANDT ETCHINGS FROM A BOOK I BOUGHT IN PARIS--LET'S PRINT 'EM AS A CATALOG! --IT'S ALL PUBLIC DOMAIN!
THE REMBRANDT PROJECT WAS A FLOP, COSTING THE THREESOME A TON OF MONEY... SOON, THE LAWRENCE COMPANY WAS NO MORE--
FLYING SOLO IS THE WAY TO GO--WHAT I NEED TO DO IS HIT THE DAILIES! THAT'S WHERE THE GREEN PASTURES LIE... SOMETHING ORIGINAL... MAYBE A DETECTIVE... OR A COP...THAT'S IT-- A BIG LUG... BUT HE'S A REAL SOFTY INSIDE...ALWAYS GETTING INTO HOT WATER-- GOTTA DO A FEW WEEKS WORTH & PEDDLE IT TO THE SYNDICATES!!
SAMSON THE COP
WHEN'S YOUR MAW COMIN' BACK FOR YOU?
GLURP.
YOU STAY UP THERE WHILE I DIRECTS TRAFFIC
BLEEP!
BURBLE BURP. GURGLE-KLUG!
SUCH LANGUAGE WAIT'LL I TELL YOUR MAW
STOP IT! YOU'RE TYING UP TRAFFIC!
BLURBLE, PLUFF!
TWEE
HELP! POLICE! OW
WURBLE GUB GLYP PHLIP!
BONG!
IF THEY DON'T BITE, I CAN ALWAYS TRY "BOY'S LIFE" OR "PACK O' FUN" MAGAZINE...
LIBERTY
HOOEY
FUN

"SAMSON THE COP" NEVER SAW SYNDICATION, BUT THAT DIDN'T STOP LARIAR FROM TRYING AGAIN-- AND AGAIN-- NOTABLY WITH "BARRY O'NEILL", AN ADVENTURE SERIES PITTING HIS ALL-AMERICAN HERO AGAINST A FU MANCHU-LIKE MASTERMIND NAMED FANG GOW..

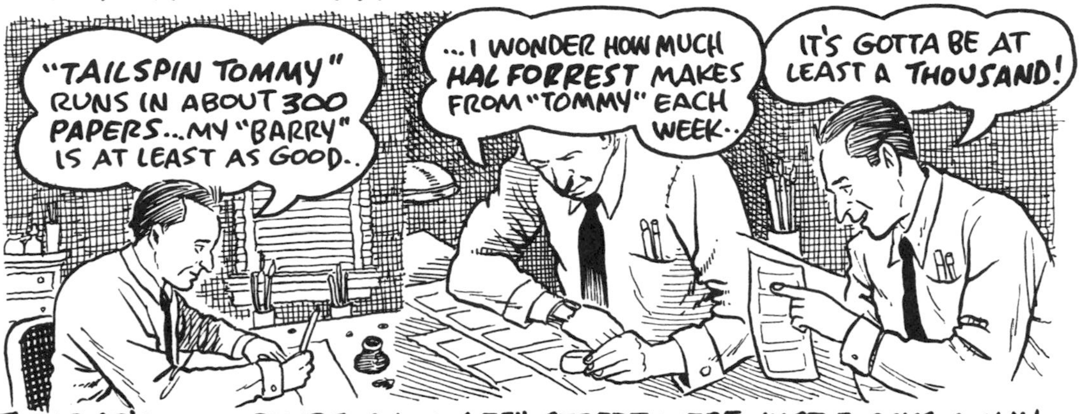
"TAILSPIN TOMMY" RUNS IN ABOUT 300 PAPERS...MY "BARRY" IS AT LEAST AS GOOD..
...I WONDER HOW MUCH HAL FORREST MAKES FROM "TOMMY" EACH WEEK..
IT'S GOTTA BE AT LEAST A THOUSAND!

LARIAR'S NEW OFFICES ON W. 45TH STREET WERE JUST BLOCKS AWAY FROM THE HEADQUARTERS OF A DOZEN NEW COMIC BOOK PUBLISHERS--

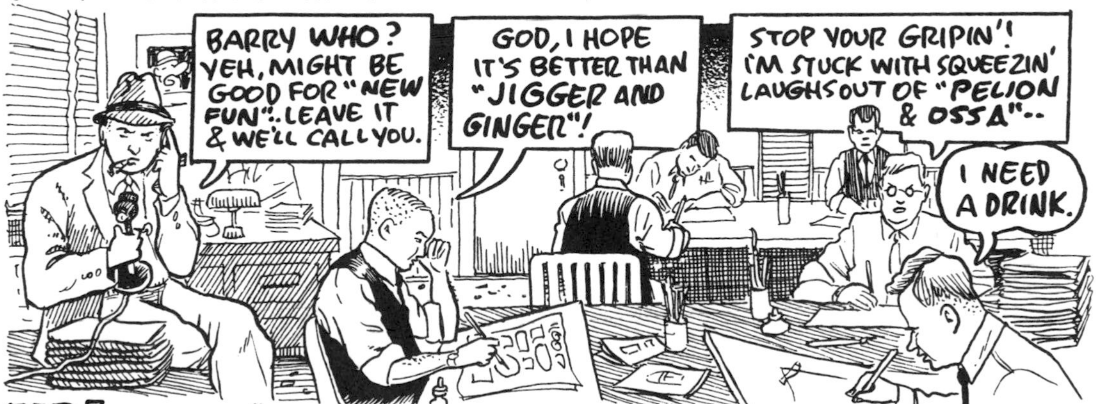
BARRY WHO? YEH, MIGHT BE GOOD FOR "NEW FUN"..LEAVE IT & WE'LL CALL YOU.
GOD, I HOPE IT'S BETTER THAN "JIGGER AND GINGER"!
STOP YOUR GRIPIN'! I'M STUCK WITH SQUEEZIN' LAUGHS OUT OF "PELION & OSSA"..
I NEED A DRINK.

"NEW FUN" WAS THE FIRST TITLE FROM NATIONAL PERIODICAL PUBLICATIONS IN 1934.. IT LATER BECAME DC COMICS.

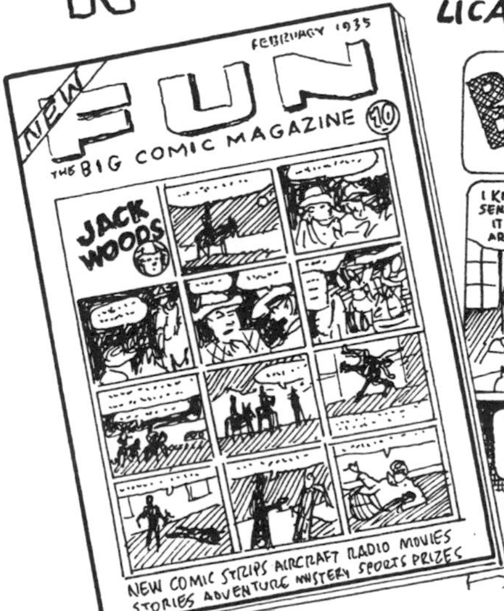
FEBRUARY 1935
NEW FUN
THE BIG COMIC MAGAZINE
10¢
JACK WOODS
NEW COMIC STRIPS AIRCRAFT RADIO MOVIES STORIES ADVENTURE MYSTERY SPORTS PRIZES

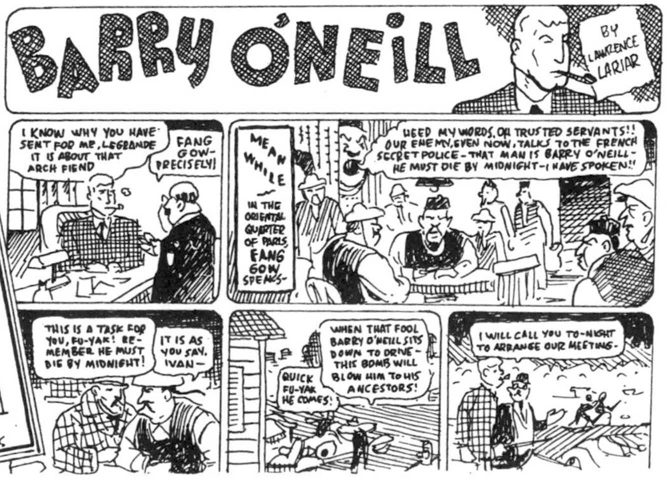
BARRY O'NEILL
BY LAWRENCE LARIAR
I KNOW WHY YOU HAVE SENT FOR ME, LEGRANDE IT IS ABOUT THAT ARCH FIEND
FANG GOW- PRECISELY!
MEANWHILE - IN THE ORIENTAL QUARTER OF PARIS, FANG GOW SPEAKS-
HEED MY WORDS, OH TRUSTED SERVANTS!! OUR ENEMY, EVEN NOW, TALKS TO THE FRENCH SECRET POLICE - THAT MAN IS BARRY O'NEILL - HE MUST DIE BY MIDNIGHT - I HAVE SPOKEN!!
THIS IS A TASK FOR YOU, FU-YAK! REMEMBER HE MUST DIE BY MIDNIGHT!
IT IS AS YOU SAY, IVAN-
WHEN THAT FOOL BARRY O'NEILL SITS DOWN TO DRIVE - THIS BOMB WILL BLOW HIM TO HIS ANCESTORS!
QUICK FU-YAK HE COMES!
I WILL CALL YOU TO-NIGHT TO ARRANGE OUR MEETING-

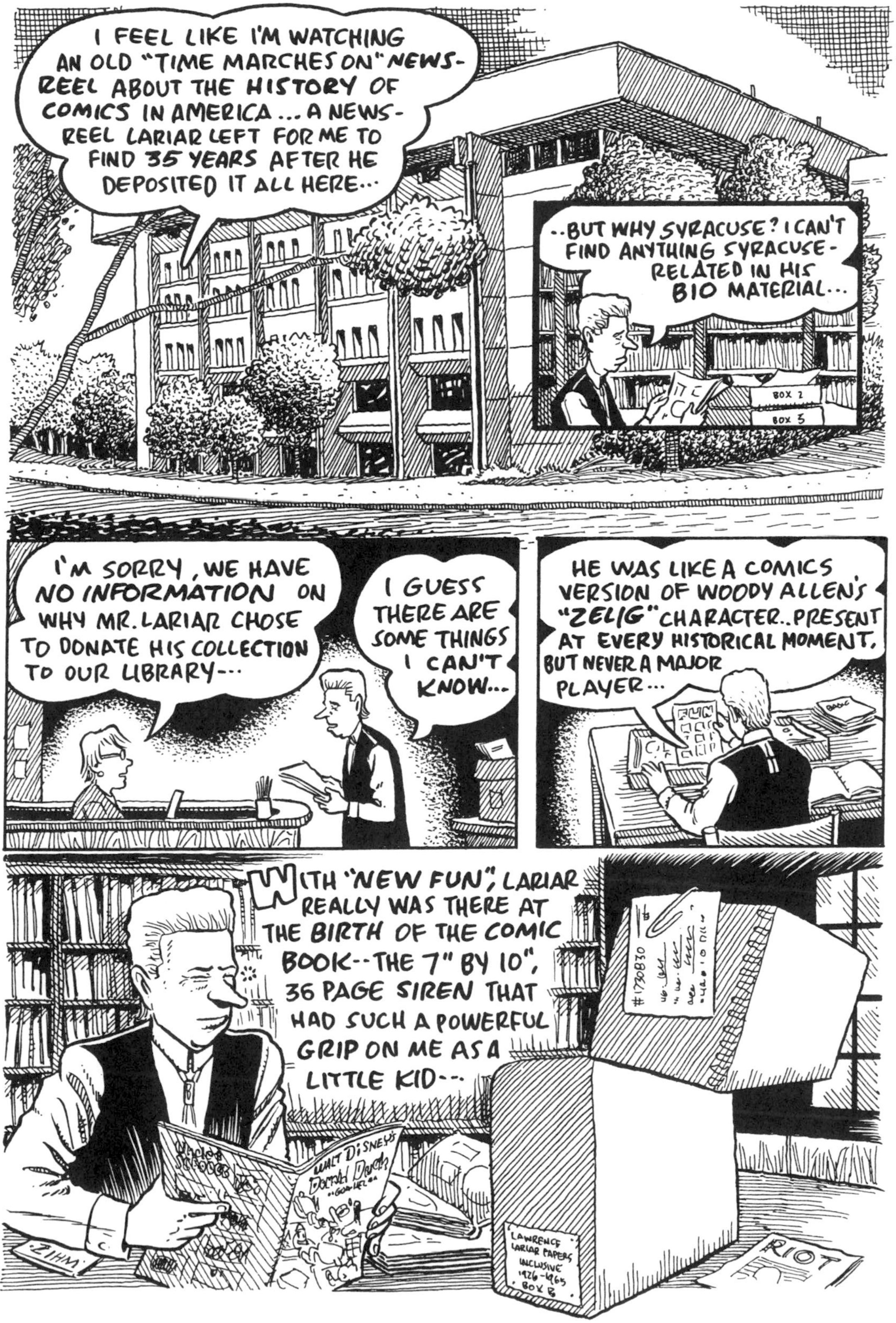
I FEEL LIKE I'M WATCHING AN OLD "TIME MARCHES ON" NEWS-REEL ABOUT THE HISTORY OF COMICS IN AMERICA ... A NEWS-REEL LARIAR LEFT FOR ME TO FIND 35 YEARS AFTER HE DEPOSITED IT ALL HERE...
..BUT WHY SYRACUSE? I CAN'T FIND ANYTHING SYRACUSE-RELATED IN HIS BIO MATERIAL...
BOX 2
BOX 3
I'M SORRY, WE HAVE NO INFORMATION ON WHY MR. LARIAR CHOSE TO DONATE HIS COLLECTION TO OUR LIBRARY...
I GUESS THERE ARE SOME THINGS I CAN'T KNOW...
HE WAS LIKE A COMICS VERSION OF WOODY ALLEN'S "ZELIG" CHARACTER.. PRESENT AT EVERY HISTORICAL MOMENT, BUT NEVER A MAJOR PLAYER...
FUN
WITH "NEW FUN", LARIAR REALLY WAS THERE AT THE BIRTH OF THE COMIC BOOK--THE 7" BY 10", 36 PAGE SIREN THAT HAD SUCH A POWERFUL GRIP ON ME AS A LITTLE KID--
WALT DISNEY'S Donald Duck
LAWRENCE LARIAR PAPERS INCLUSIVE 1926-1965 BOX B
RIOT

NEW FUN WAS ALSO THE FIRST COMIC BOOK TO PUBLISH **ALL NEW MATERIAL**. ISSUE NUMBER SIX SAW THE DEBUTS OF **JERRY SIEGEL & JOE SHUSTER**, THE FUTURE CREATORS OF **SUPERMAN**. WHEN LARIAR BROUGHT IN HIS LATEST **BARRY O'NEILL** PAGES, SIEGEL & SHUSTER WERE BUSY AT WORK ON A **SWASHBUCKLER** SERIES CALLED **"HENRI DUVAL"**--

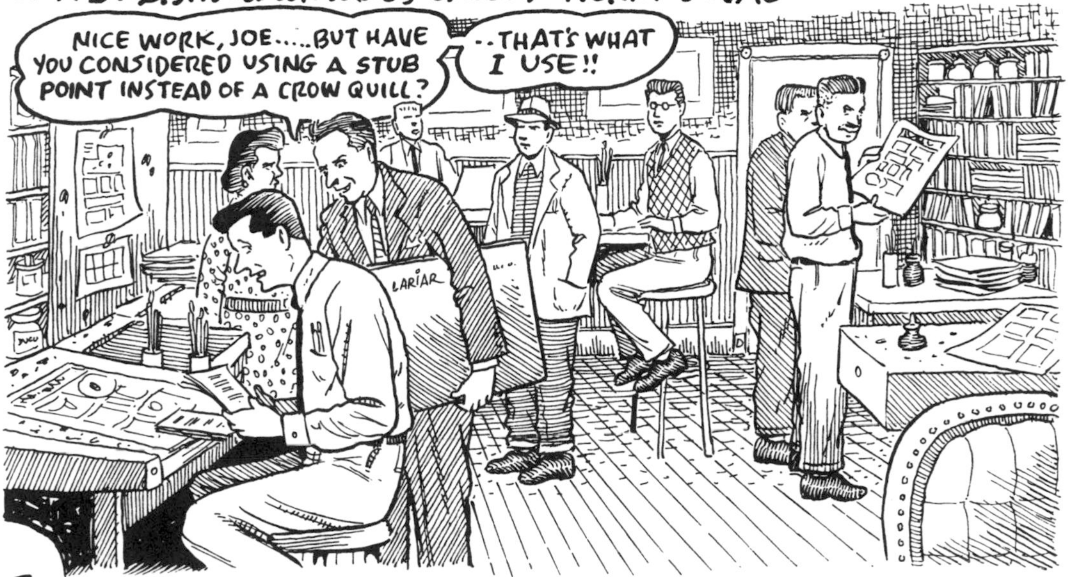
NICE WORK, JOE.....BUT HAVE YOU CONSIDERED USING A STUB POINT INSTEAD OF A CROW QUILL?
--THAT'S WHAT I USE!!
LARIAR

LARIAR CONTINUED TO PLUG AWAY AT **DAILY STRIP IDEAS**. LATER IN 1934, HE SOLD **"INSPECTOR KEENE OF SCOTLAND YARD"** TO **YOUNG AMERICA** MAGAZINE, BUT IT NEVER WENT INTO SYNDICATION--

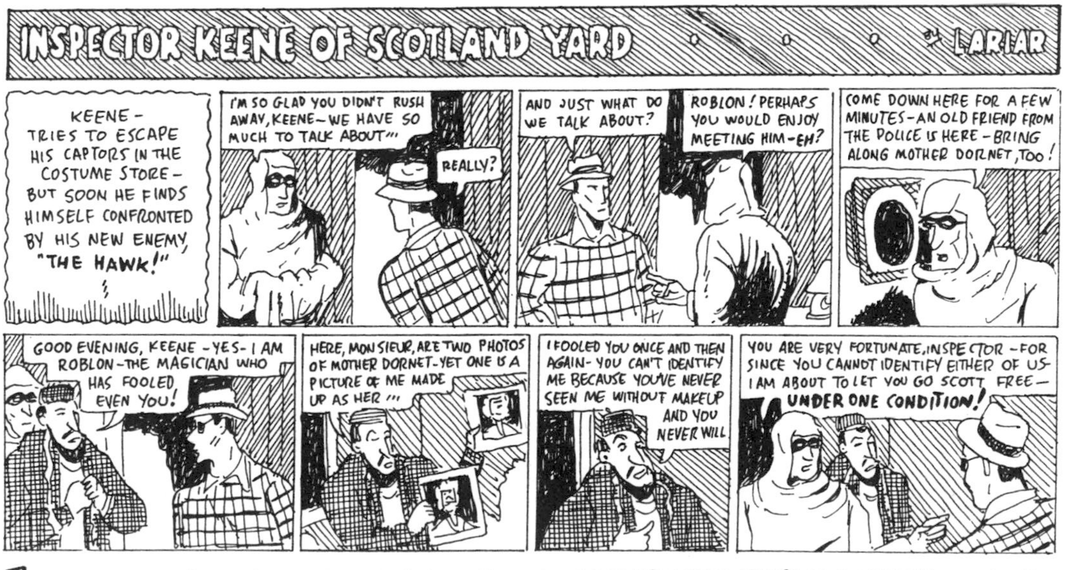
INSPECTOR KEENE OF SCOTLAND YARD
BY LARIAR
KEENE - TRIES TO ESCAPE HIS CAPTORS IN THE COSTUME STORE - BUT SOON HE FINDS HIMSELF CONFRONTED BY HIS NEW ENEMY, "THE HAWK!"
I'M SO GLAD YOU DIDN'T RUSH AWAY, KEENE - WE HAVE SO MUCH TO TALK ABOUT'''
REALLY?
AND JUST WHAT DO WE TALK ABOUT?
ROBLON! PERHAPS YOU WOULD ENJOY MEETING HIM - EH?
COME DOWN HERE FOR A FEW MINUTES - AN OLD FRIEND FROM THE POLICE IS HERE - BRING ALONG MOTHER DORNET, TOO!
GOOD EVENING, KEENE - YES - I AM ROBLON - THE MAGICIAN WHO HAS FOOLED EVEN YOU!
HERE, MONSIEUR, ARE TWO PHOTOS OF MOTHER DORNET - YET ONE IS A PICTURE OF ME MADE UP AS HER '''
I FOOLED YOU ONCE AND THEN AGAIN - YOU CAN'T IDENTIFY ME BECAUSE YOU'VE NEVER SEEN ME WITHOUT MAKEUP AND YOU NEVER WILL
YOU ARE VERY FORTUNATE, INSPECTOR - FOR SINCE YOU CANNOT IDENTIFY EITHER OF US - I AM ABOUT TO LET YOU GO SCOTT FREE - UNDER ONE CONDITION!

IT WAS ALSO AROUND THIS TIME THAT LARIAR MET **SUSAN MAYER**, WHO BECAME HIS **AGENT**..THEY WORKED IN THE SAME BUILDING. **MAYER** HAS BEEN CALLED THE **FIRST** CARTOONIST'S AGENT. SHE ALSO WORKED AS A **GAG WRITER** ON HER OWN. THEY WERE MARRIED IN 1935---

LARIAR TEMPORARILY ABANDONED HIS QUEST FOR A DAILY STRIP. AS THE 1930S WORE ON, HE CONTRIBUTED **GAGS** TO A WIDE VARIETY OF MAGAZINES, INCLUDING **CLOWN, HOOEY, JUDGE, COLLIER'S, SATURDAY EVENING POST** AND **KEN**, FOR WHICH HE PENNED **ANTI-HITLER** CARTOONS.

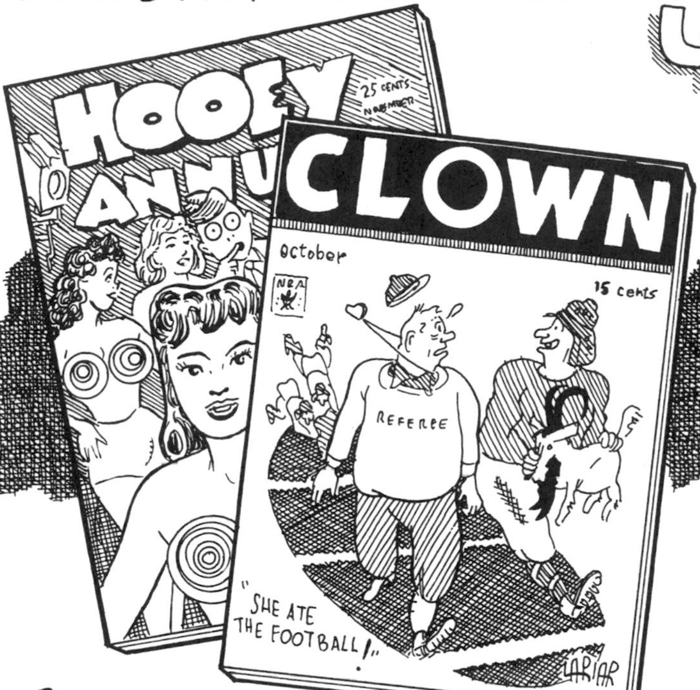
HOOEY
ANNU
25 CENTS
CLOWN
October
NRA
15 cents
REFEREE
"SHE ATE THE FOOTBALL!"
LARIAR

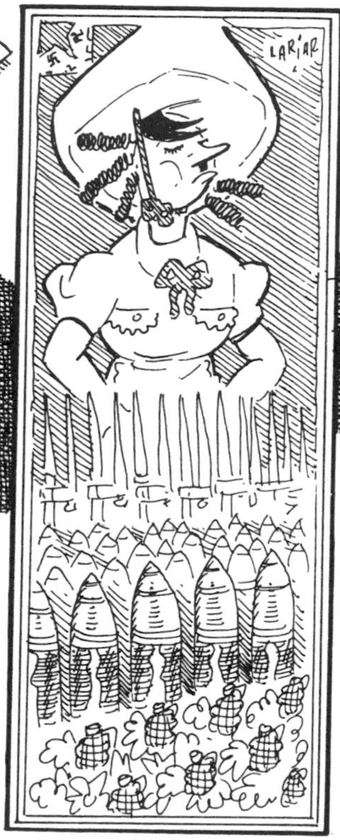
LARIAR

HE DID A SUNDAY NEWSPAPER PAGE OF GAGS FOR **KING FEATURES** IN 1937--

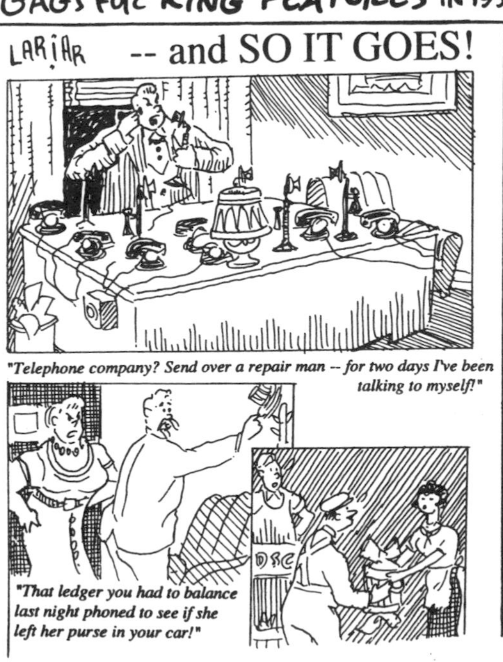
LARIAR -- and SO IT GOES!
"Telephone company? Send over a repair man -- for two days I've been talking to myself!"
"That ledger you had to balance last night phoned to see if she left her purse in your car!"

THEN, IN 1938, HE TOOK A **DISNEY** "APTITUDE TEST" AND TRAVELED TO **LOS ANGELES** TO WORK ON DISNEY'S ANIMATED FEATURE, **"FANTASIA"**--

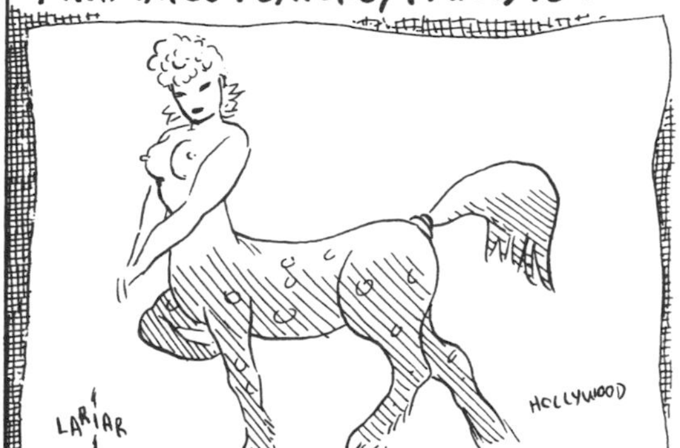
LARIAR
HOLLYWOOD

UNHAPPY AS JUST A COG IN THE DISNEY MACHINE, HE QUIT THE JOB AND RETURNED TO **NEW YORK** IN 1939.

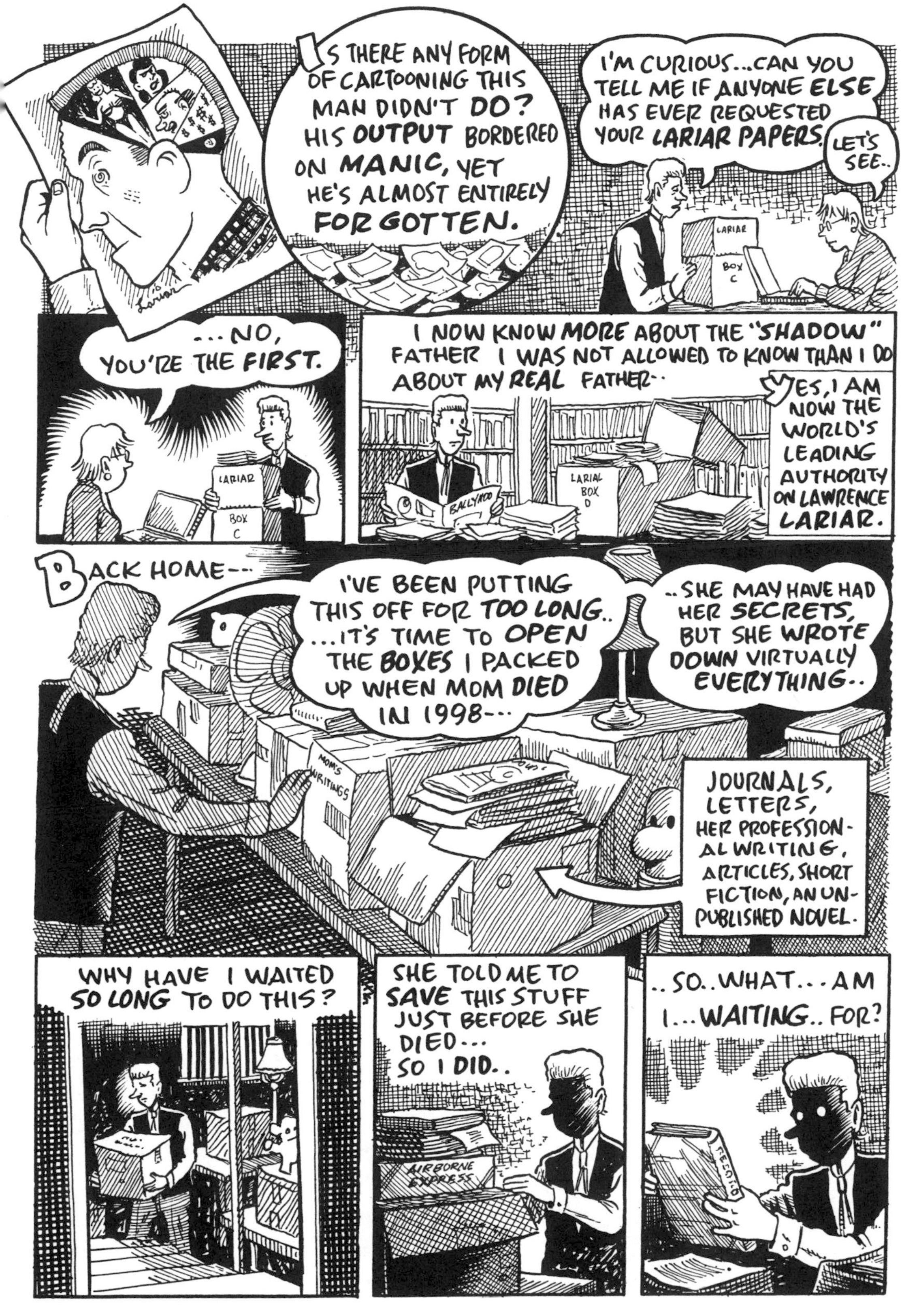

Lariar
IS THERE ANY FORM OF CARTOONING THIS MAN DIDN'T DO? HIS OUTPUT BORDERED ON MANIC, YET HE'S ALMOST ENTIRELY FORGOTTEN.
I'M CURIOUS...CAN YOU TELL ME IF ANYONE ELSE HAS EVER REQUESTED YOUR LARIAR PAPERS.
LET'S SEE..
LARIAR BOX C
...NO, YOU'RE THE FIRST.
LARIAR BOX C
I NOW KNOW MORE ABOUT THE "SHADOW" FATHER I WAS NOT ALLOWED TO KNOW THAN I DO ABOUT MY REAL FATHER..
BALLYHOO
LARIAL BOX D
YES, I AM NOW THE WORLD'S LEADING AUTHORITY ON LAWRENCE LARIAR.
BACK HOME--
I'VE BEEN PUTTING THIS OFF FOR TOO LONG.. ...IT'S TIME TO OPEN THE BOXES I PACKED UP WHEN MOM DIED IN 1998--
..SHE MAY HAVE HAD HER SECRETS, BUT SHE WROTE DOWN VIRTUALLY EVERYTHING..
MOM'S WRITINGS
JOURNALS, LETTERS, HER PROFESSIONAL WRITING, ARTICLES, SHORT FICTION, AN UNPUBLISHED NOVEL.
WHY HAVE I WAITED SO LONG TO DO THIS?
SHE TOLD ME TO SAVE THIS STUFF JUST BEFORE SHE DIED... SO I DID..
AIRBORNE EXPRESS
..SO..WHAT...AM I...WAITING..FOR?

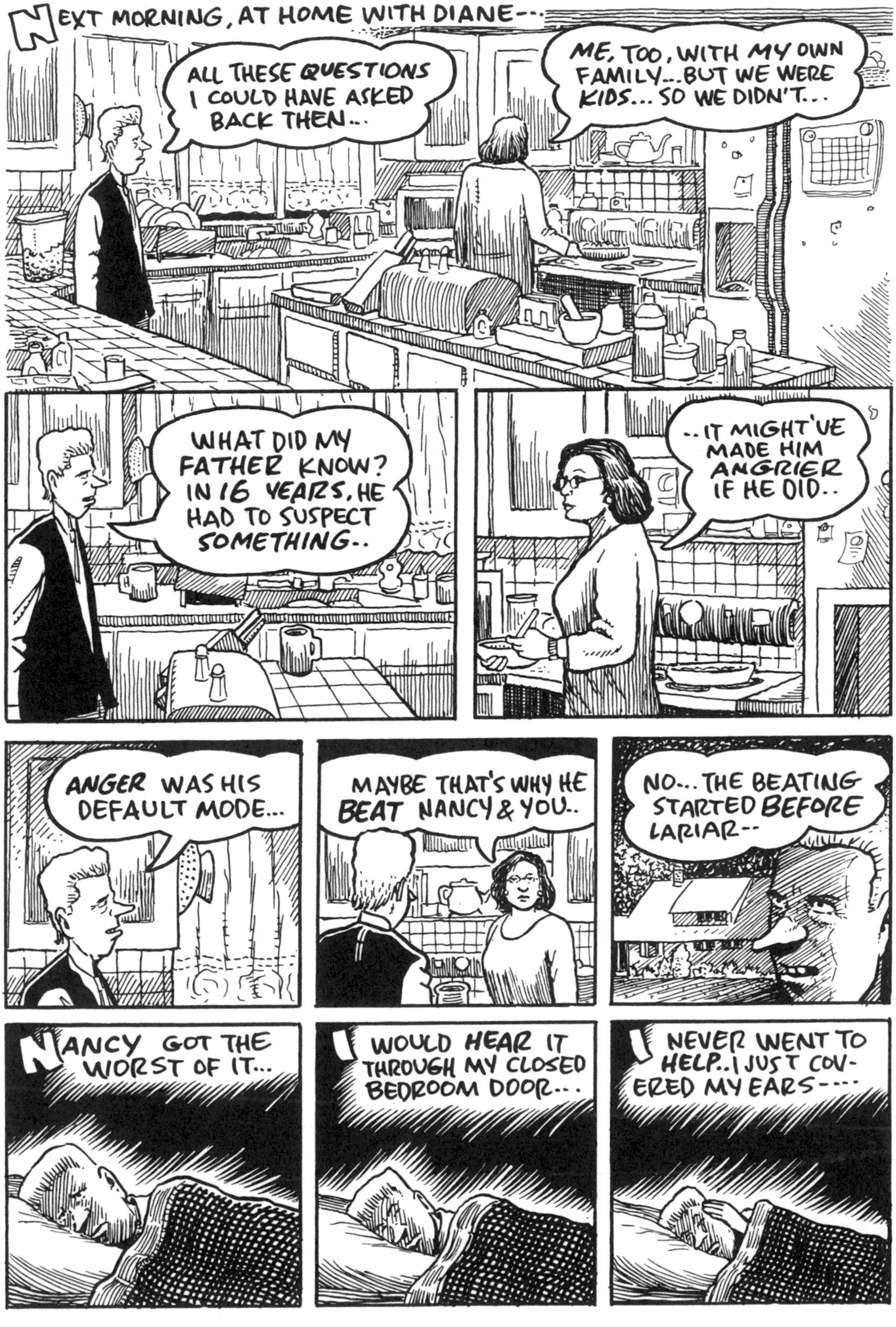
NEXT MORNING, AT HOME WITH DIANE---
ALL THESE QUESTIONS I COULD HAVE ASKED BACK THEN...
ME, TOO, WITH MY OWN FAMILY...BUT WE WERE KIDS... SO WE DIDN'T...
WHAT DID MY FATHER KNOW? IN 16 YEARS, HE HAD TO SUSPECT SOMETHING..
..IT MIGHT'VE MADE HIM ANGRIER IF HE DID..
ANGER WAS HIS DEFAULT MODE...
MAYBE THAT'S WHY HE BEAT NANCY & YOU..
NO... THE BEATING STARTED BEFORE LARIAR--
NANCY GOT THE WORST OF IT...
I WOULD HEAR IT THROUGH MY CLOSED BEDROOM DOOR...
I NEVER WENT TO HELP..I JUST COVERED MY EARS----

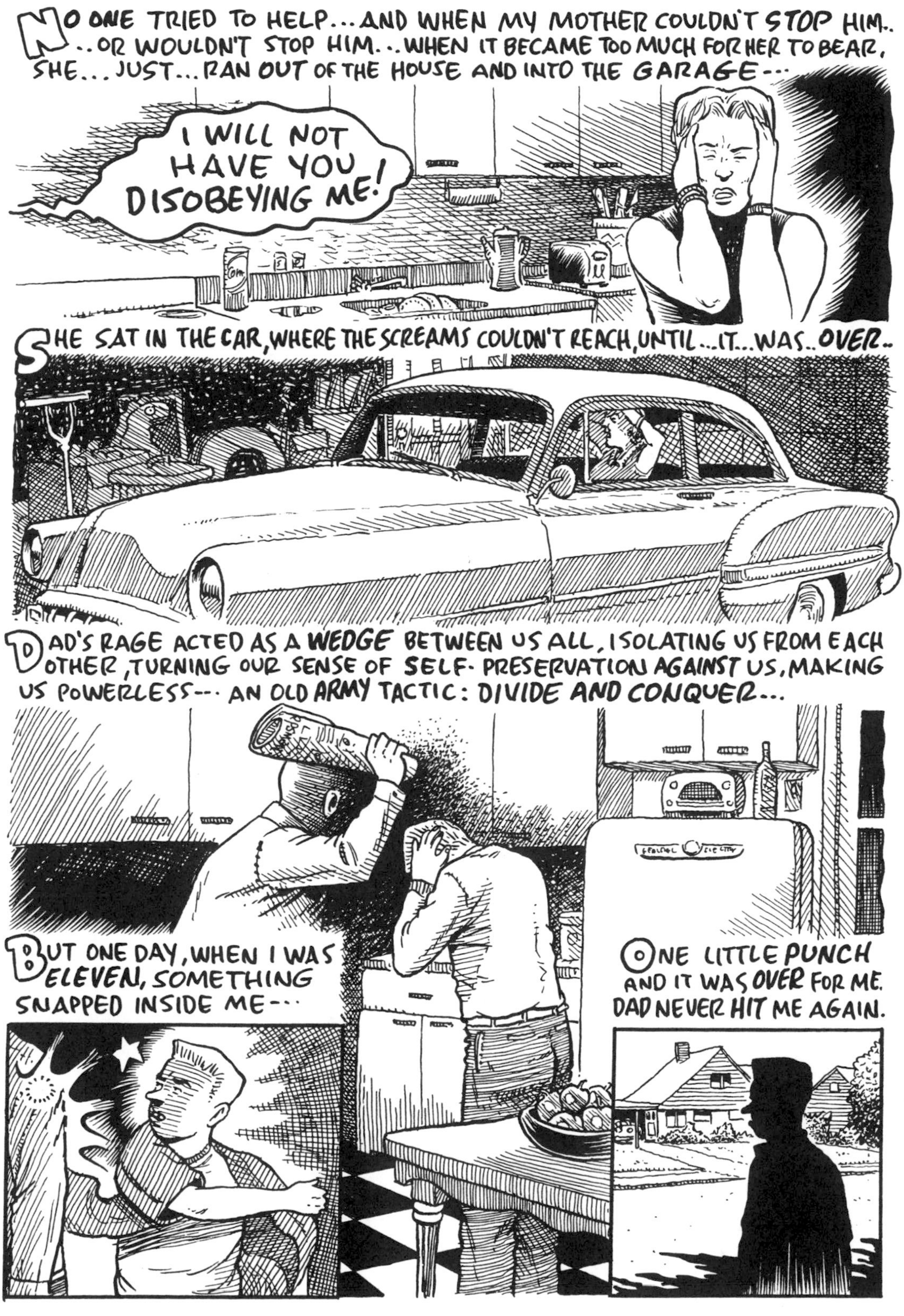
NO ONE TRIED TO HELP... AND WHEN MY MOTHER COULDN'T STOP HIM.. ..OR WOULDN'T STOP HIM...WHEN IT BECAME TOO MUCH FOR HER TO BEAR, SHE... JUST... RAN OUT OF THE HOUSE AND INTO THE GARAGE---
I WILL NOT HAVE YOU DISOBEYING ME!
SHE SAT IN THE CAR, WHERE THE SCREAMS COULDN'T REACH, UNTIL...IT...WAS..OVER..
DAD'S RAGE ACTED AS A WEDGE BETWEEN US ALL, ISOLATING US FROM EACH OTHER, TURNING OUR SENSE OF SELF-PRESERVATION AGAINST US, MAKING US POWERLESS--- AN OLD ARMY TACTIC: DIVIDE AND CONQUER...
BUT ONE DAY, WHEN I WAS ELEVEN, SOMETHING SNAPPED INSIDE ME---
ONE LITTLE PUNCH AND IT WAS OVER FOR ME. DAD NEVER HIT ME AGAIN.

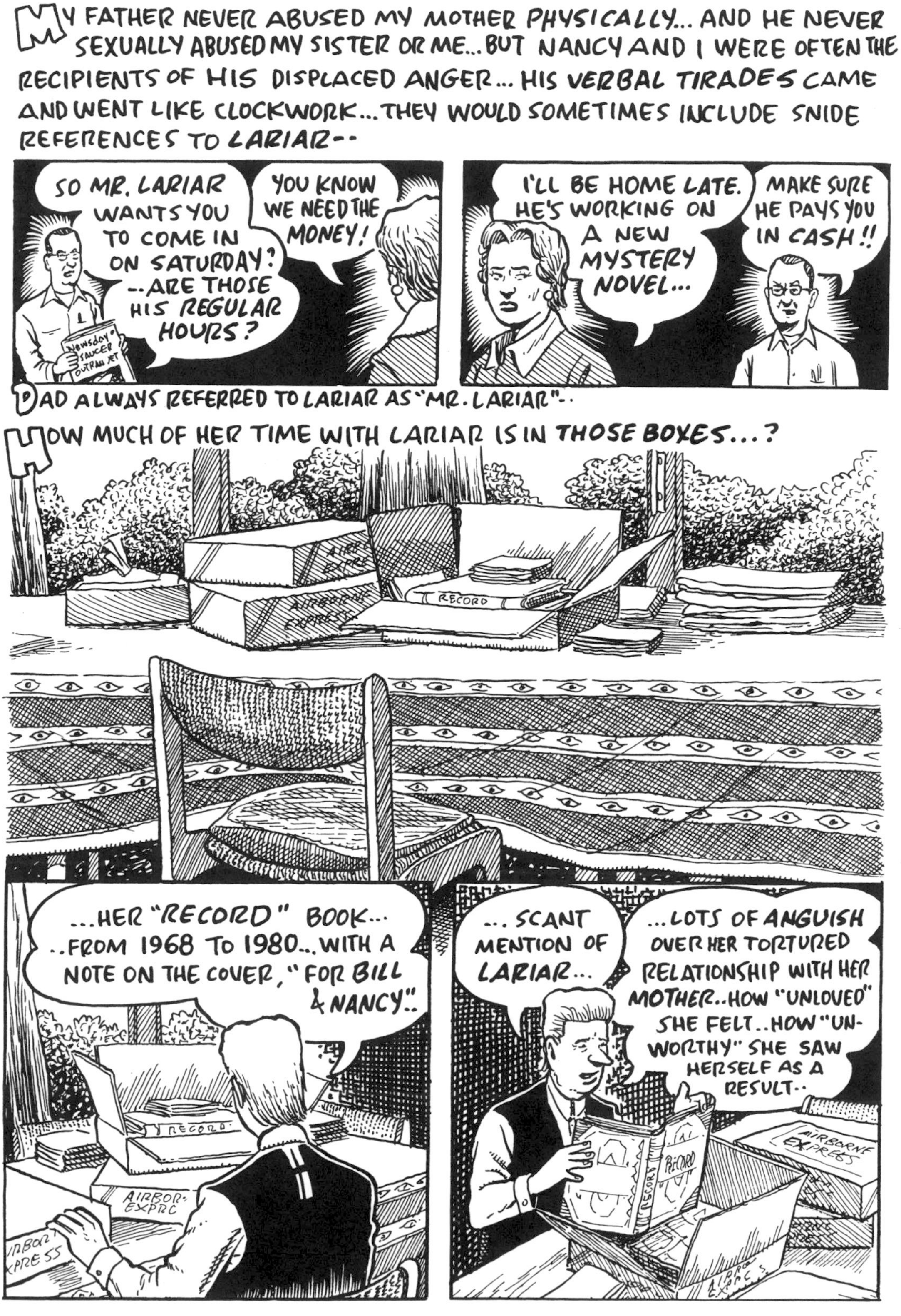
MY FATHER NEVER ABUSED MY MOTHER PHYSICALLY... AND HE NEVER SEXUALLY ABUSED MY SISTER OR ME...BUT NANCY AND I WERE OFTEN THE RECIPIENTS OF HIS DISPLACED ANGER... HIS VERBAL TIRADES CAME AND WENT LIKE CLOCKWORK...THEY WOULD SOMETIMES INCLUDE SNIDE REFERENCES TO LARIAR--
SO MR. LARIAR WANTS YOU TO COME IN ON SATURDAY? --ARE THOSE HIS REGULAR HOURS?
YOU KNOW WE NEED THE MONEY!
I'LL BE HOME LATE. HE'S WORKING ON A NEW MYSTERY NOVEL...
MAKE SURE HE PAYS YOU IN CASH!!
DAD ALWAYS REFERRED TO LARIAR AS "MR. LARIAR"..
HOW MUCH OF HER TIME WITH LARIAR IS IN THOSE BOXES...?
RECORD
...HER "RECORD" BOOK... ..FROM 1968 TO 1980...WITH A NOTE ON THE COVER, "FOR BILL & NANCY"..
...SCANT MENTION OF LARIAR...
...LOTS OF ANGUISH OVER HER TORTURED RELATIONSHIP WITH HER MOTHER..HOW "UNLOVED" SHE FELT..HOW "UNWORTHY" SHE SAW HERSELF AS A RESULT..
AIRBORNE EXPRESS
RECORD

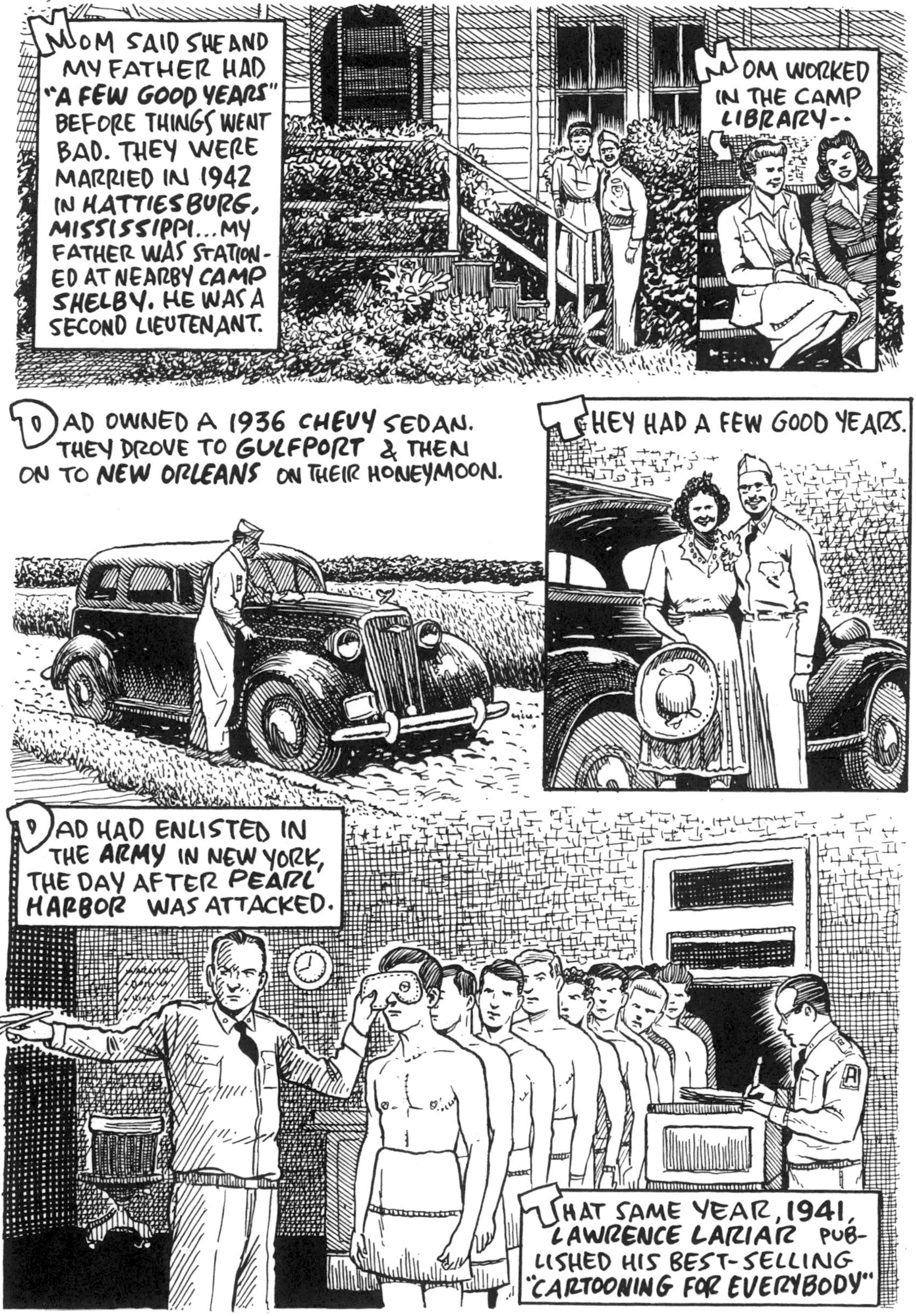
MOM SAID SHE AND MY FATHER HAD "A FEW GOOD YEARS" BEFORE THINGS WENT BAD. THEY WERE MARRIED IN 1942 IN HATTIESBURG, MISSISSIPPI... MY FATHER WAS STATIONED AT NEARBY CAMP SHELBY. HE WAS A SECOND LIEUTENANT.
MOM WORKED IN THE CAMP LIBRARY--
DAD OWNED A 1936 CHEVY SEDAN. THEY DROVE TO GULFPORT & THEN ON TO NEW ORLEANS ON THEIR HONEYMOON.
THEY HAD A FEW GOOD YEARS.
DAD HAD ENLISTED IN THE ARMY IN NEW YORK, THE DAY AFTER PEARL HARBOR WAS ATTACKED.
THAT SAME YEAR, 1941, LAWRENCE LARIAR PUBLISHED HIS BEST-SELLING "CARTOONING FOR EVERYBODY"

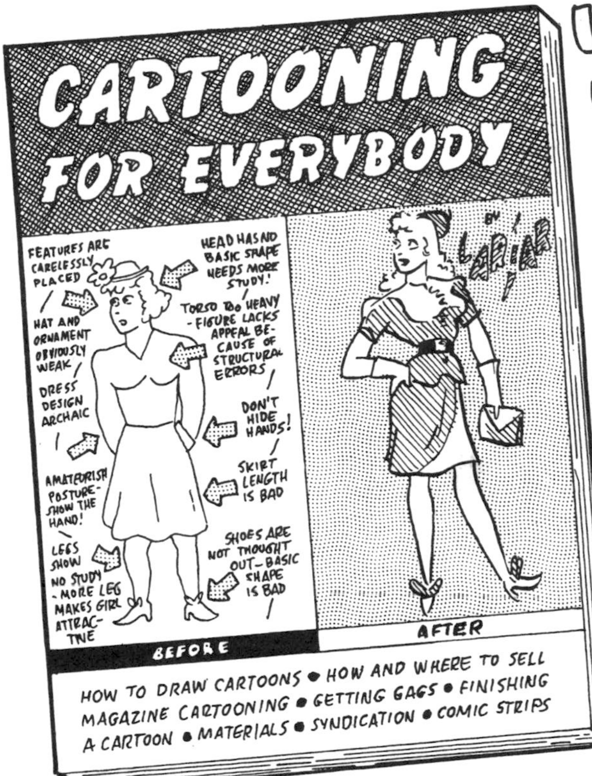
CARTOONING FOR EVERYBODY
FEATURES ARE CARELESSLY PLACED
HAT AND ORNAMENT OBVIOUSLY WEAK
DRESS DESIGN ARCHAIC
AMATEURISH POSTURE-SHOW THE HAND!
LEGS SHOW NO STUDY - MORE LEG MAKES GIRL ATTRACTIVE
HEAD HAS NO BASIC SHAPE NEEDS MORE STUDY!
TORSO TOO HEAVY - FIGURE LACKS APPEAL BECAUSE OF STRUCTURAL ERRORS
DON'T HIDE HANDS!
SKIRT LENGTH IS BAD
SHOES ARE NOT THOUGHT OUT-BASIC SHAPE IS BAD
BEFORE
AFTER
HOW TO DRAW CARTOONS • HOW AND WHERE TO SELL MAGAZINE CARTOONING • GETTING GAGS • FINISHING A CARTOON • MATERIALS • SYNDICATION • COMIC STRIPS

IN HIS FIRST "HOW TO" CARTOON BOOK, LARIAR SAYS "CARTOONISTS, IN THE MAIN, ARE **SIMPLE** SOULS, MOVED TO **SIMPLE** EXPRESSION OF **SIMPLE** IDEAS", BUT HE GOES ON TO ADD, "THE GREATEST MASTER OF THE **CARTOONING ART** WAS **HONORÉ DAUMIER**. --- STUDY **DAUMIER**!"

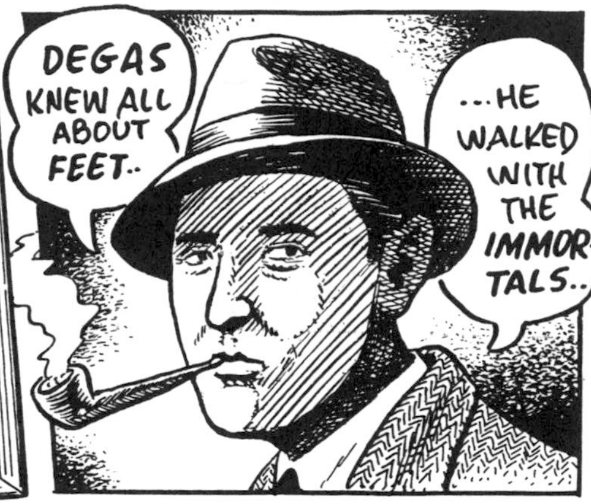
DEGAS KNEW ALL ABOUT FEET..
...HE WALKED WITH THE IMMORTALS..

LARIAR HAD AN INTELLECTUAL'S APPRECIATION FOR ART, BUT HIS AIM IN COMICS WAS ALWAYS TO **SATISFY** THE **MARKET** & **MAKE THE SALE**. EVERYTHING IN COMIC ART, HE TAUGHT, WAS BASED ON **THE DOODLE**...

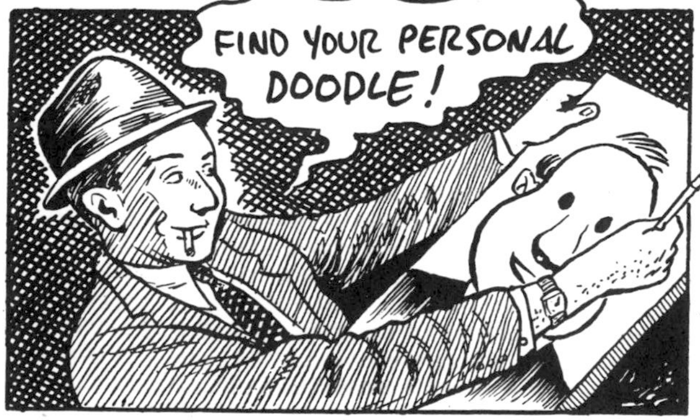
FIND YOUR **PERSONAL** DOODLE!

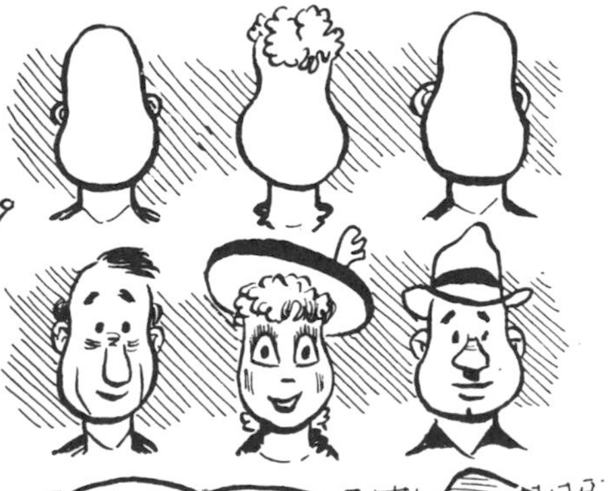

"THE MODERN CARTOONIST NEEDN'T BE A MASTER PEN AND INK CRAFTSMAN TO SELL HIS WORK... **CROSS-HATCHING** IS RAPIDLY DISAPPEARING FROM THE COMIC BUSINESS. THERE IS A SMALL DEMAND FOR THE **CROSS-HATCH SYSTEM** IN CERTAIN COMIC STRIPS, BUT THE MORE **MODERN** COMIC ARTISTS FORGOT ABOUT THE **CROSS-HATCH** LONG AGO."

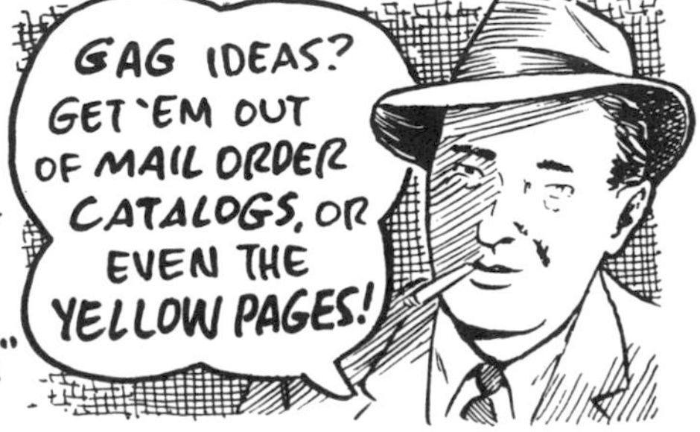
GAG IDEAS? GET 'EM OUT OF MAIL ORDER CATALOGS, OR EVEN THE YELLOW PAGES!

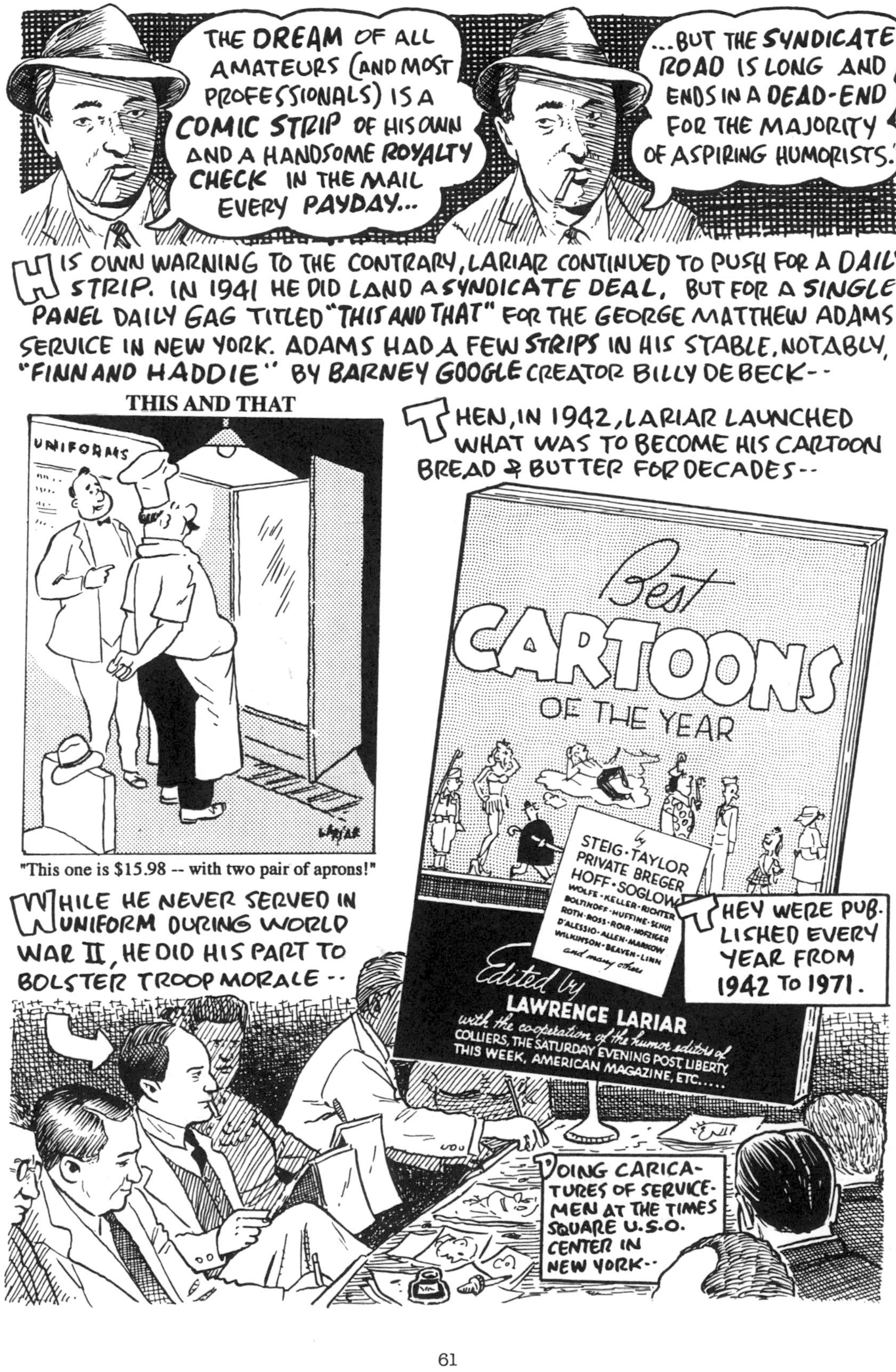
THE DREAM OF ALL AMATEURS (AND MOST PROFESSIONALS) IS A COMIC STRIP OF HIS OWN AND A HANDSOME ROYALTY CHECK IN THE MAIL EVERY PAYDAY...
...BUT THE SYNDICATE ROAD IS LONG AND ENDS IN A DEAD-END FOR THE MAJORITY OF ASPIRING HUMORISTS."
HIS OWN WARNING TO THE CONTRARY, LARIAR CONTINUED TO PUSH FOR A DAILY STRIP. IN 1941 HE DID LAND A SYNDICATE DEAL, BUT FOR A SINGLE PANEL DAILY GAG TITLED "THIS AND THAT" FOR THE GEORGE MATTHEW ADAMS SERVICE IN NEW YORK. ADAMS HAD A FEW STRIPS IN HIS STABLE, NOTABLY, "FINN AND HADDIE" BY BARNEY GOOGLE CREATOR BILLY DE BECK--
THIS AND THAT
UNIFORMS
LARIAR
"This one is $15.98 -- with two pair of aprons!"
THEN, IN 1942, LARIAR LAUNCHED WHAT WAS TO BECOME HIS CARTOON BREAD & BUTTER FOR DECADES--
Best CARTOONS OF THE YEAR
by STEIG·TAYLOR PRIVATE BREGER HOFF·SOGLOW
WOLFE·KELLER·RICHTER BOLTINOFF·HUFFINE·SCHUS ROTH·ROSS·ROIR·HOFZIGER D'ALESSIO·ALLEN·MARKOW WILKINSON·BEAVEN·LINN
and many others
Edited by LAWRENCE LARIAR
with the cooperation of the humor editors of COLLIERS, THE SATURDAY EVENING POST, LIBERTY, THIS WEEK, AMERICAN MAGAZINE, ETC.....
THEY WERE PUBLISHED EVERY YEAR FROM 1942 TO 1971.
WHILE HE NEVER SERVED IN UNIFORM DURING WORLD WAR II, HE DID HIS PART TO BOLSTER TROOP MORALE--
DOING CARICATURES OF SERVICEMEN AT THE TIMES SQUARE U.S.O. CENTER IN NEW YORK--

IN 1943, LARIAR PUBLISHED HIS FIRST MYSTERY NOVEL, "DEATH PAINTS THE PICTURE", FOLLOWED IN THE NEXT FEW YEARS BY THREE OTHERS---

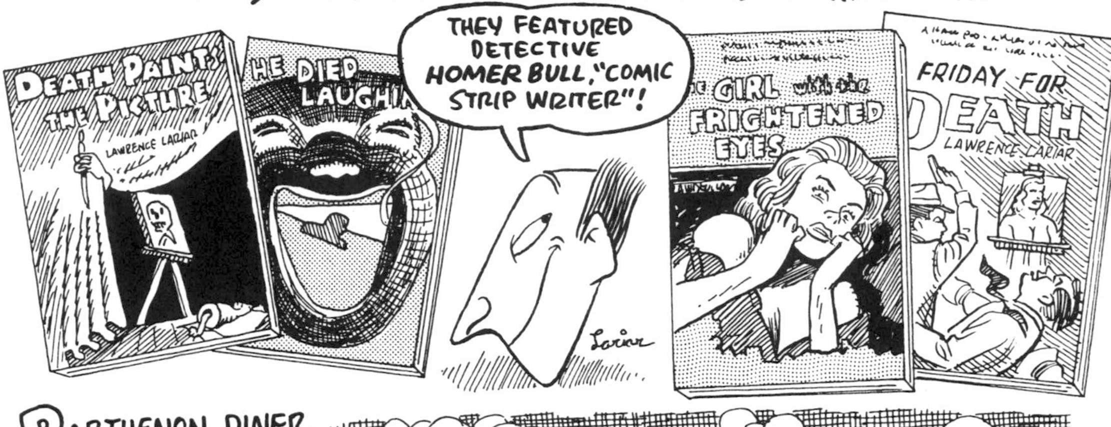

DEATH PAINTS THE PICTURE
LAWRENCE LARIAR
HE DIED LAUGHING
THEY FEATURED DETECTIVE HOMER BULL, "COMIC STRIP WRITER"!
Lariar
GIRL with the FRIGHTENED EYES
FRIDAY FOR DEATH
LAWRENCE LARIAR

PARTHENON DINER, OLD SAYBROOK, CONNECTICUT

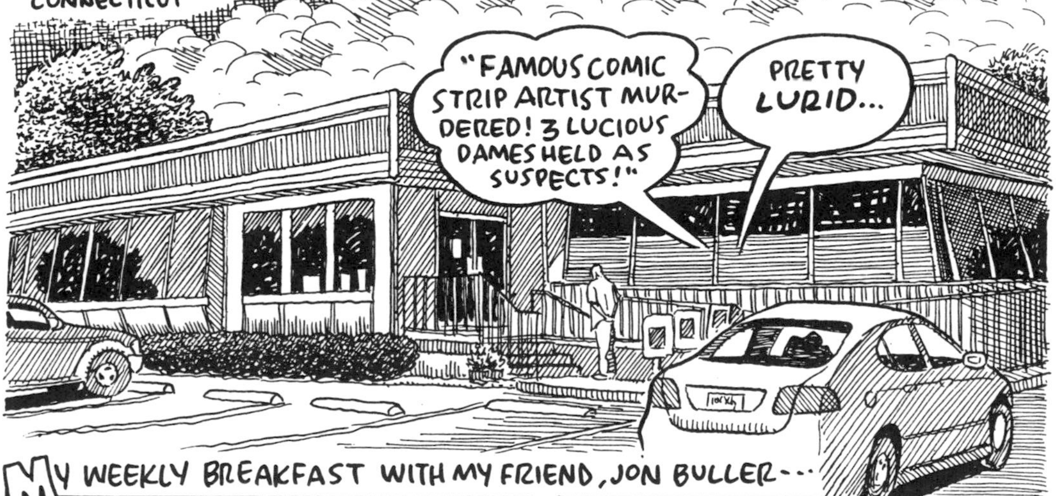

"FAMOUS COMIC STRIP ARTIST MURDERED! 3 LUCIOUS DAMES HELD AS SUSPECTS!"
PRETTY LURID...

MY WEEKLY BREAKFAST WITH MY FRIEND, JON BULLER---

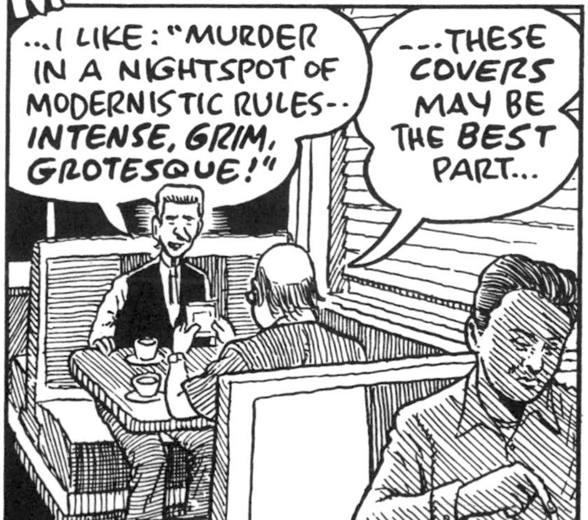

...I LIKE: "MURDER IN A NIGHTSPOT OF MODERNISTIC RULES-- INTENSE, GRIM, GROTESQUE!"
---THESE COVERS MAY BE THE BEST PART...

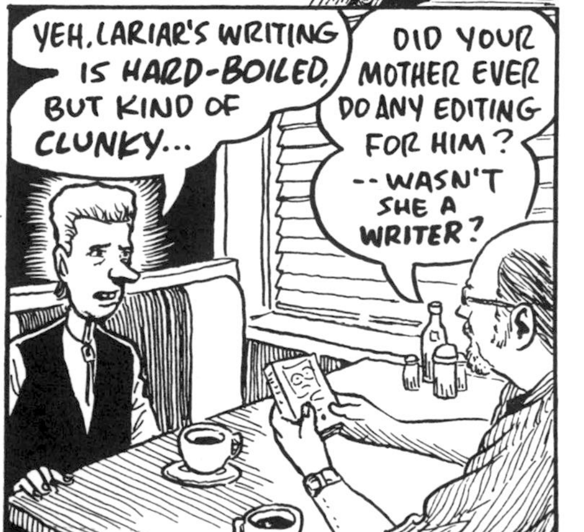

YEH, LARIAR'S WRITING IS HARD-BOILED, BUT KIND OF CLUNKY...
DID YOUR MOTHER EVER DO ANY EDITING FOR HIM? --WASN'T SHE A WRITER?

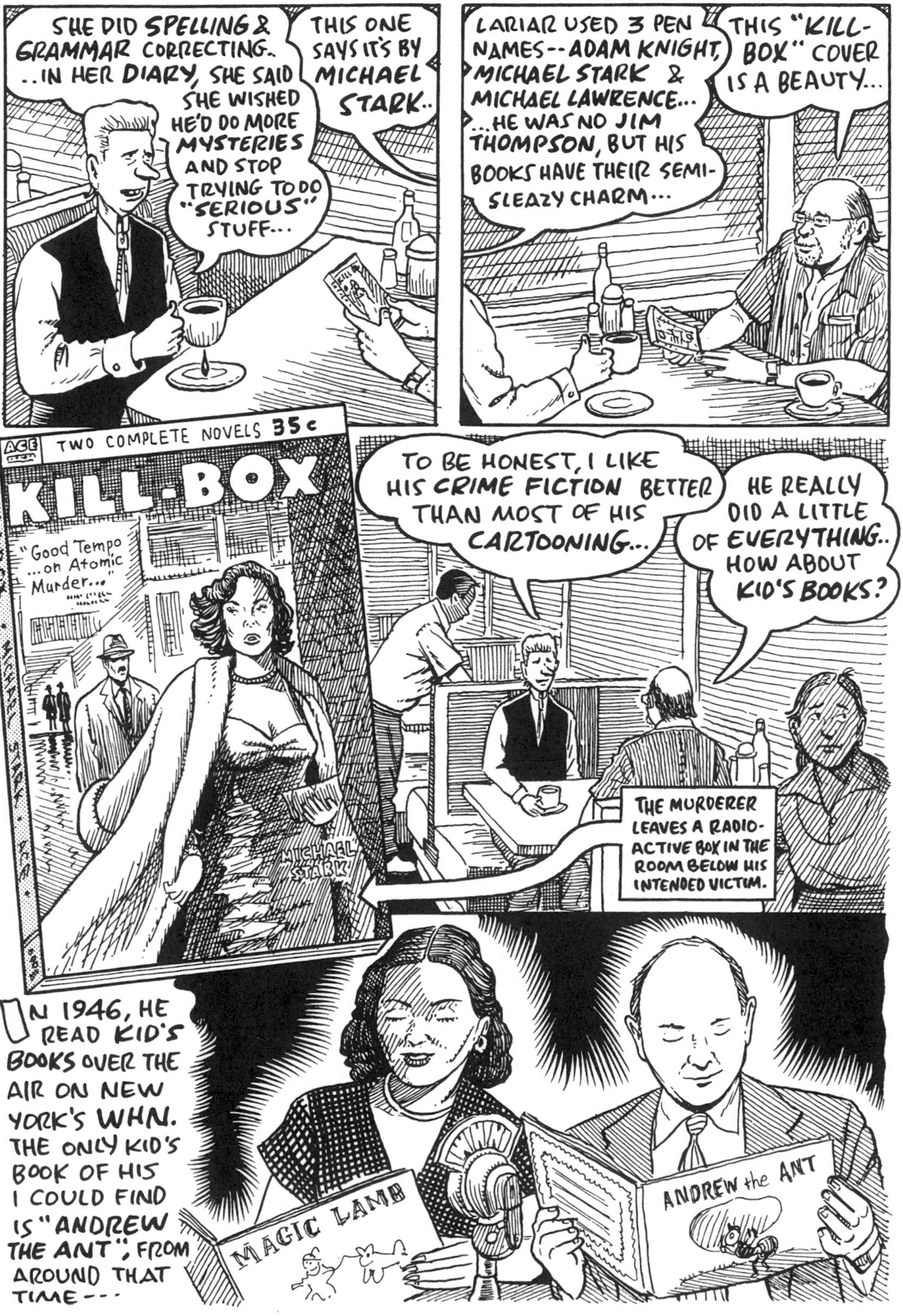

SHE DID SPELLING & GRAMMAR CORRECTING.. ..IN HER DIARY, SHE SAID SHE WISHED HE'D DO MORE MYSTERIES AND STOP TRYING TO DO "SERIOUS" STUFF...
THIS ONE SAYS IT'S BY MICHAEL STARK..
LARIAR USED 3 PEN NAMES--ADAM KNIGHT, MICHAEL STARK & MICHAEL LAWRENCE... ...HE WAS NO JIM THOMPSON, BUT HIS BOOKS HAVE THEIR SEMI-SLEAZY CHARM...
THIS "KILL-BOX" COVER IS A BEAUTY...
ACE
TWO COMPLETE NOVELS 35c
KILL-BOX
"Good Tempo ...on Atomic Murder..."
MICHAEL STARK
TO BE HONEST, I LIKE HIS CRIME FICTION BETTER THAN MOST OF HIS CARTOONING...
HE REALLY DID A LITTLE OF EVERYTHING.. HOW ABOUT KID'S BOOKS?
THE MURDERER LEAVES A RADIO-ACTIVE BOX IN THE ROOM BELOW HIS INTENDED VICTIM.
IN 1946, HE READ KID'S BOOKS OVER THE AIR ON NEW YORK'S WHN. THE ONLY KID'S BOOK OF HIS I COULD FIND IS "ANDREW THE ANT", FROM AROUND THAT TIME---
MAGIC LAMB
ANDREW the ANT

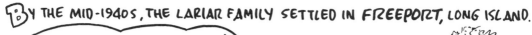
By THE MID-1940S, THE LARIAR FAMILY SETTLED IN **FREEPORT**, LONG ISLAND.

LOOK AT THIS REVIEW, SUZIE! "LARIAR HAS FASHIONED QUITE A NEAT PLOT, BUT BEST FEATURE OF THE YARN IS ITS PICTURE OF THE BOHEMIAN WORLD OF THE COMIC STRIP ARTIST."

HEY, I'VE GOT ANOTHER IDEA!

LARIAR CHURNED OUT MORE **MYSTERIES** WHILE ALSO HOLDING DOWN A JOB AS CARTOON EDITOR OF LIBERTY MAGAZINE, WHERE HIS TWO-PAGE STRIP, "THE THROPP FAMILY," APPEARED WEEKLY. LARIAR WROTE THE ONGOING STORY, WHILE DON KOMISAROW & LOU FINE DID THE DRAWING ---

I GET IT, PRINCE. WE SELL HIPPLEBY 15,000 DIAPERS, DUMP THE REST ON THE HICKS AND THEN SCRAM. MEET YOU HERE AT THE TURNPIKE INN AFTER THE PANIC!

WHAT WERE YOU DOING AT THAT WINDOW, OZZIE?

EXERCISING MY CRANIAL PROCLIVITY, PATER, ON A LITTLE PUZZLE. WHEN I FIT THE PIECES TOGETHER, THE RESULTS MAY RIVAL THE ATOMIC BOMB!

AS IF HE WASN'T BUSY ENOUGH, HIS "BARRY O'NEILL" CHARACTER WAS REVIVED FOR ATOMIC COMICS FROM GREEN PUBLISHING COMPANY IN CHICAGO IN 1946-

DANGER? — HERE? IT'S AS QUIET AS A GRAVEYARD!

"Barry O'Neill": Written by Lariar, art by Leo E. O'Mealia

ALSO IN THIS EARLY COMIC, SIEGEL & SHUSTER'S "SANDY KEAN & THE RADIO SQUAD."

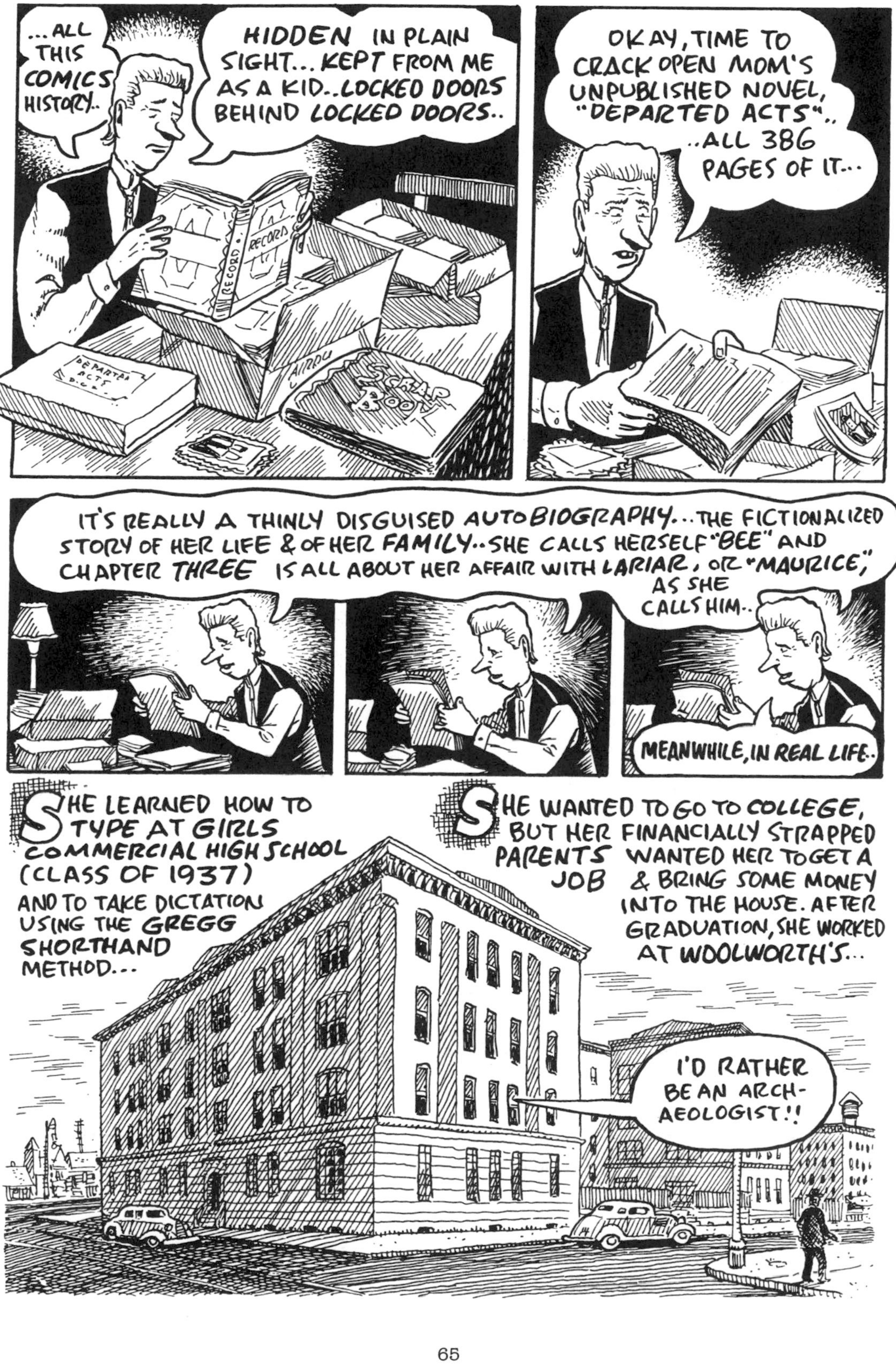
...ALL THIS COMICS HISTORY..
HIDDEN IN PLAIN SIGHT... KEPT FROM ME AS A KID..LOCKED DOORS BEHIND LOCKED DOORS..
RECORD
RECORD
DEPARTED ACTS
SCRAP BOOK
OKAY, TIME TO CRACK OPEN MOM'S UNPUBLISHED NOVEL, "DEPARTED ACTS".. ..ALL 386 PAGES OF IT...
IT'S REALLY A THINLY DISGUISED AUTOBIOGRAPHY...THE FICTIONALIZED STORY OF HER LIFE & OF HER FAMILY..SHE CALLS HERSELF "BEE" AND CHAPTER THREE IS ALL ABOUT HER AFFAIR WITH LARIAR, OR "MAURICE," AS SHE CALLS HIM..
MEANWHILE, IN REAL LIFE..
SHE LEARNED HOW TO TYPE AT GIRLS COMMERCIAL HIGH SCHOOL (CLASS OF 1937) AND TO TAKE DICTATION USING THE GREGG SHORTHAND METHOD...
SHE WANTED TO GO TO COLLEGE, BUT HER FINANCIALLY STRAPPED PARENTS WANTED HER TO GET A JOB & BRING SOME MONEY INTO THE HOUSE. AFTER GRADUATION, SHE WORKED AT WOOLWORTH'S...
I'D RATHER BE AN ARCH-AEOLOGIST!!

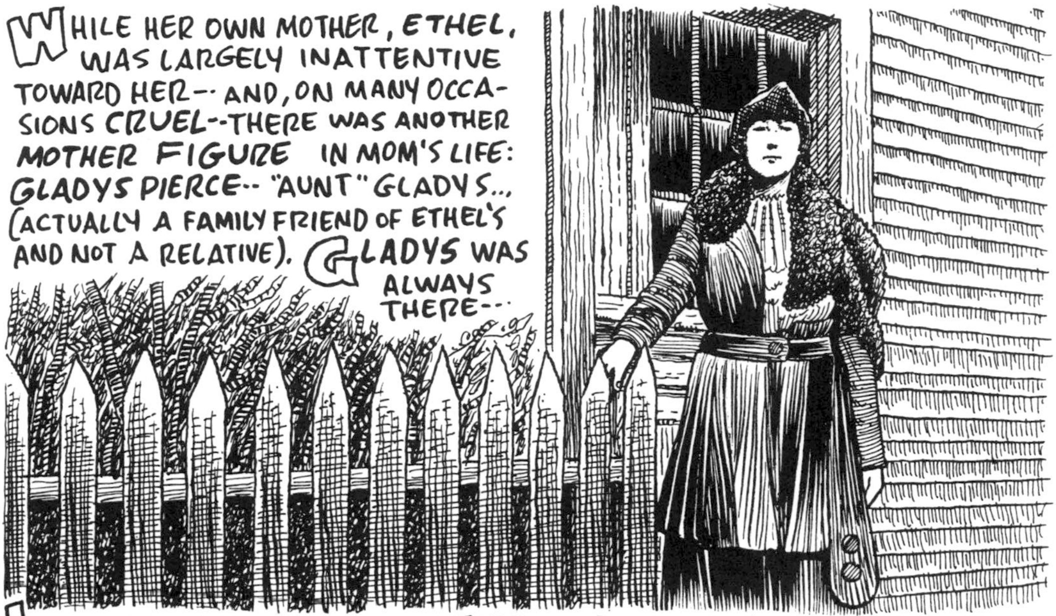
WHILE HER OWN MOTHER, ETHEL, WAS LARGELY INATTENTIVE TOWARD HER-- AND, ON MANY OCCASIONS CRUEL--THERE WAS ANOTHER MOTHER FIGURE IN MOM'S LIFE: GLADYS PIERCE-- "AUNT" GLADYS..., (ACTUALLY A FAMILY FRIEND OF ETHEL'S AND NOT A RELATIVE). GLADYS WAS ALWAYS THERE--

IN EFFECT, ETHEL HANDED MY MOTHER OVER TO GLADYS... WHO REMAINED SINGLE ALL HER LIFE-- AS DID HER 3 SISTERS, ALMA, MARJORIE & MILLICENT

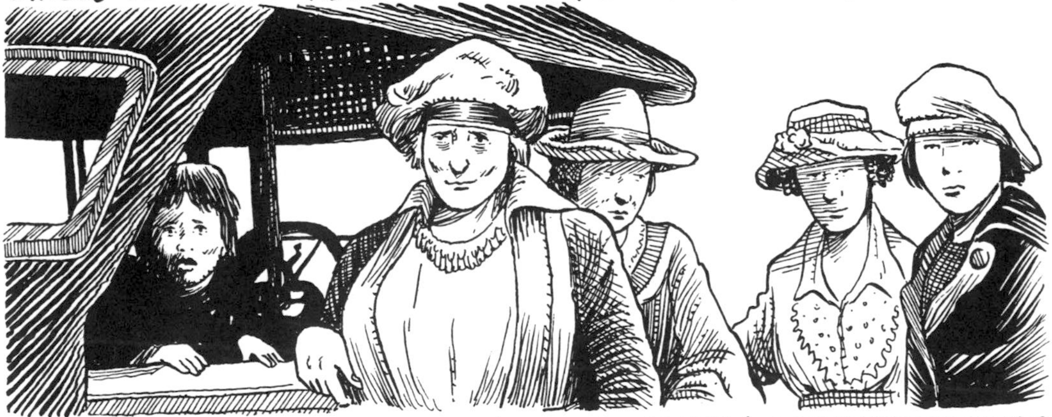

LATER, WHEN MY MOTHER HAD MY SISTER, NANCY, THE PATTERN WAS REPEATED... GLADYS BECAME A "SECOND MOTHER" TO NANCY IN TURN.

GLADYS OWNED A HOUSE ON CAPE COD, WHICH MY FAMILY FREQUENTLY VISITED. THE HOUSE, ACROSS FROM A BEAUTIFUL BEACH, WAS THE REWARD GLADYS OFFERED TO GET THE THINGS SHE WANTED, BOTH PRACTICAL AND EMOTIONAL---

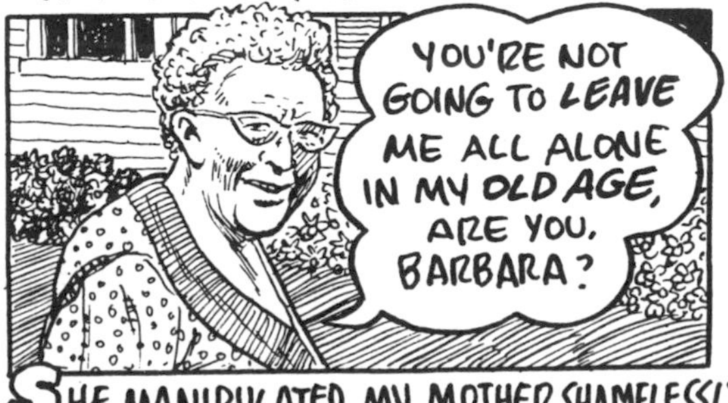
YOU'RE NOT GOING TO LEAVE ME ALL ALONE IN MY OLD AGE, ARE YOU, BARBARA?

SHE MANIPULATED MY MOTHER SHAMELESSLY.

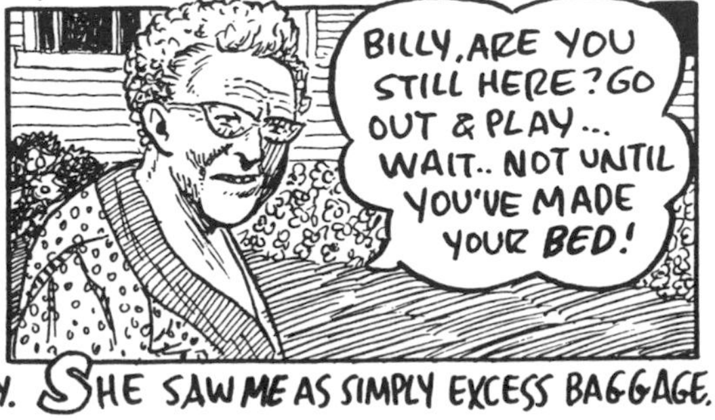
BILLY, ARE YOU STILL HERE? GO OUT & PLAY... WAIT.. NOT UNTIL YOU'VE MADE YOUR BED!

SHE SAW ME AS SIMPLY EXCESS BAGGAGE.

GLADYS REGULARLY ASKED MOM TO COME UP TO THE CAPE HOUSE AND "HELP OUT". THESE VISITS BECAME MORE FREQUENT AS GLADYS GOT OLDER--- FROM MY MOTHER'S JOURNAL, NOVEMBER 15, 1968:

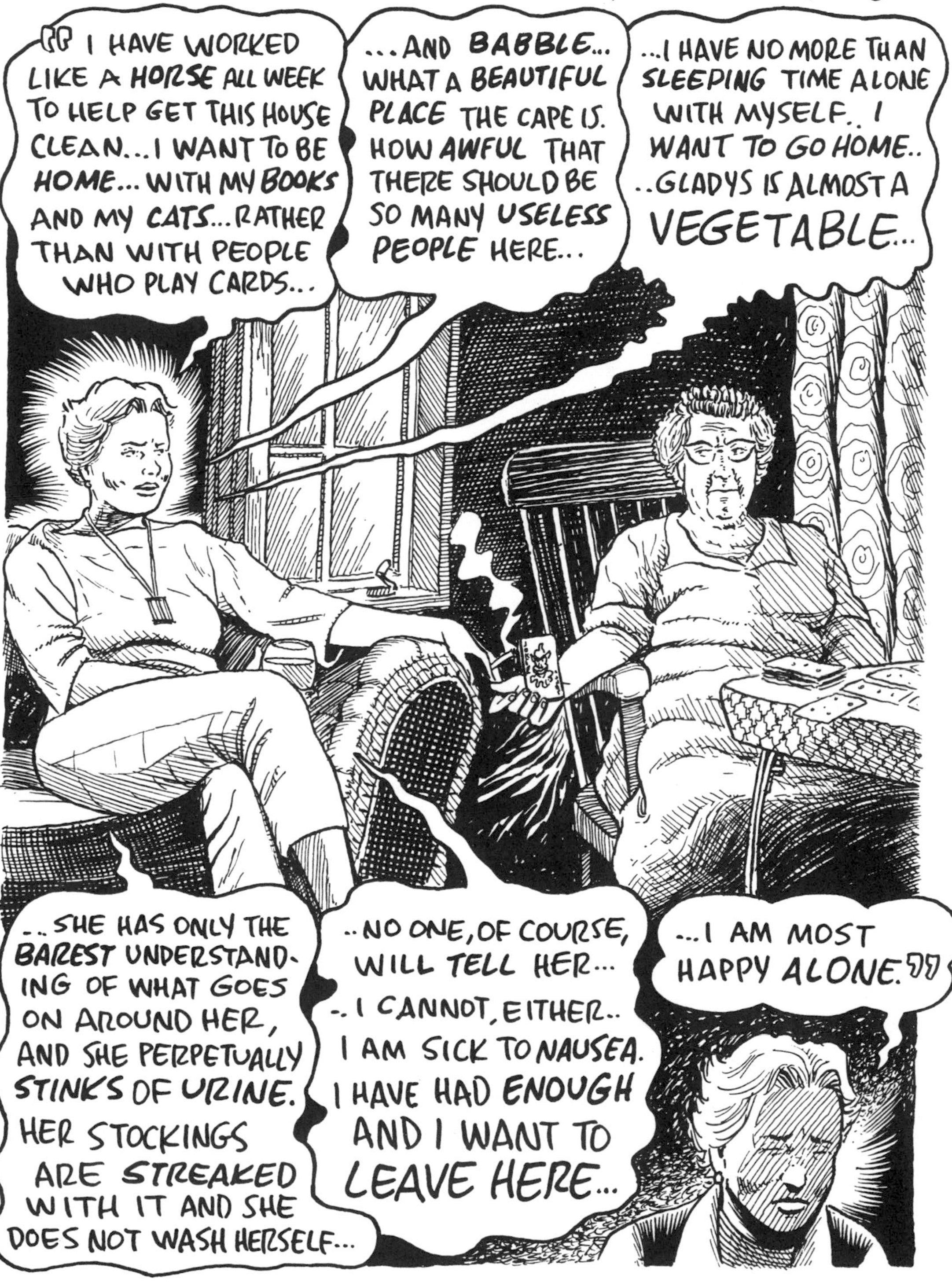
"I HAVE WORKED LIKE A HORSE ALL WEEK TO HELP GET THIS HOUSE CLEAN... I WANT TO BE HOME... WITH MY BOOKS AND MY CATS... RATHER THAN WITH PEOPLE WHO PLAY CARDS...
...AND BABBLE... WHAT A BEAUTIFUL PLACE THE CAPE IS. HOW AWFUL THAT THERE SHOULD BE SO MANY USELESS PEOPLE HERE...
...I HAVE NO MORE THAN SLEEPING TIME ALONE WITH MYSELF.. I WANT TO GO HOME.. ..GLADYS IS ALMOST A VEGETABLE...
...SHE HAS ONLY THE BAREST UNDERSTANDING OF WHAT GOES ON AROUND HER, AND SHE PERPETUALLY STINKS OF URINE. HER STOCKINGS ARE STREAKED WITH IT AND SHE DOES NOT WASH HERSELF...
..NO ONE, OF COURSE, WILL TELL HER... ..I CANNOT, EITHER.. I AM SICK TO NAUSEA. I HAVE HAD ENOUGH AND I WANT TO LEAVE HERE...
...I AM MOST HAPPY ALONE."

ALTHOUGH SHE PROMISED THE CAPE HOUSE TO MY MOTHER & THEN TO NANCY, IN THE END, GLADYS LEFT IT TO HER CHURCH---HER NEPHEW CONTESTED THE WILL AND EVENTUALLY WON HIS CLAIM TO THE PROPERTY---

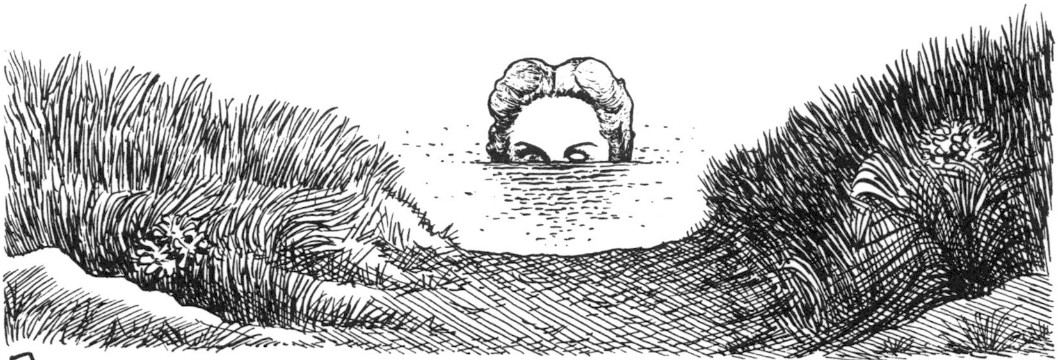

AFTER WWII, OUR FAMILY LIVED JUST DOWN THE STREET FROM GLADYS IN BROOKLYN... SHE WAS A STEADY PRESENCE IN OUR LIVES... THEN...

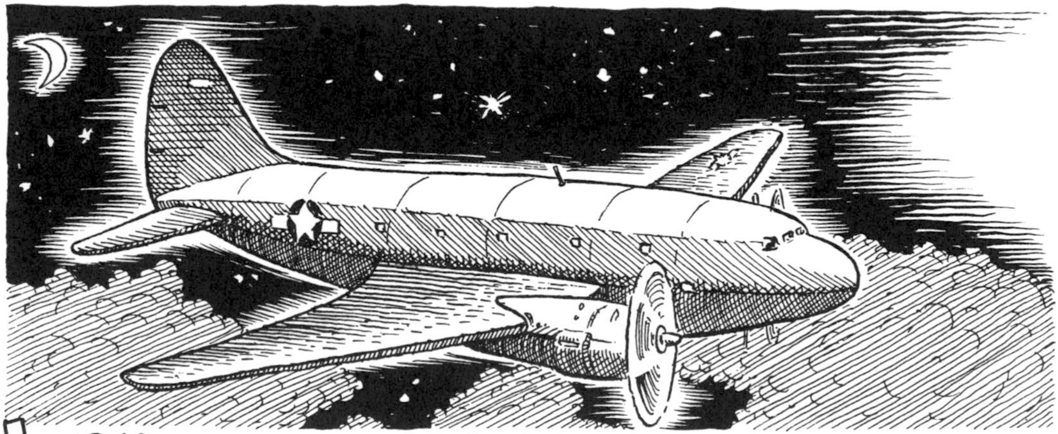

IN 1949, MY FATHER WAS DEPLOYED TO OCCUPIED GERMANY. HE TOOK US ALL WITH HIM. WE LIVED IN BOMBED-OUT FRANKFURT, WHERE I PLAYED "WAR" WITH FRIENDS IN THE RUBBLE BEHIND OUR ARMY HOUSING---

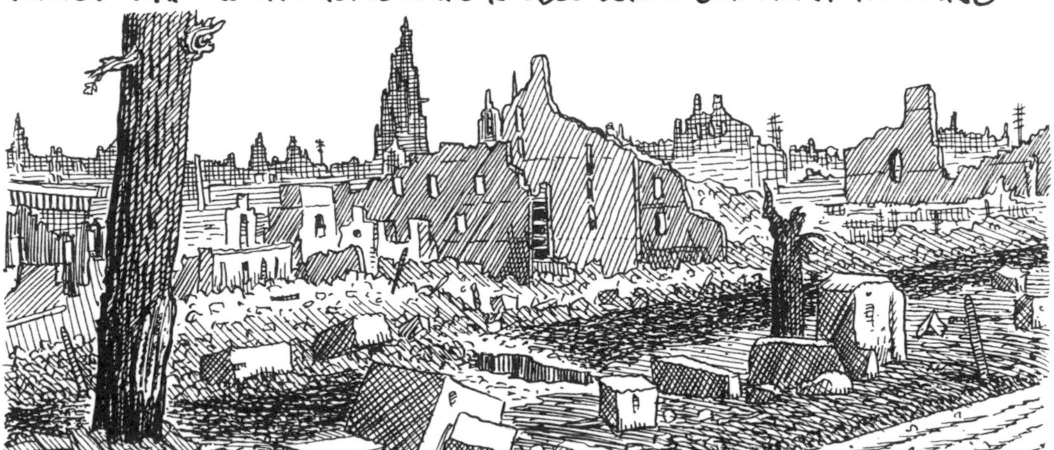

WHILE MY FATHER TOOK INVENTORY OF STOLEN **NAZI LOOT** IN CASTLES ON THE **RHINE**, MOM TOOK **PIANO LESSONS** AND LEARNED **GERMAN**--

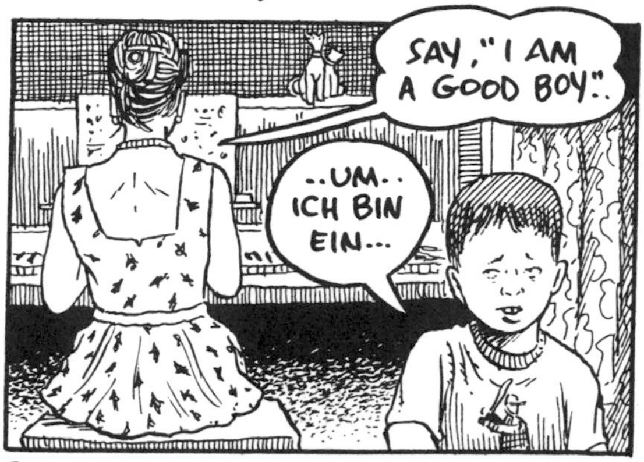

SAY, "I AM A GOOD BOY".
..UM.. ICH BIN EIN...

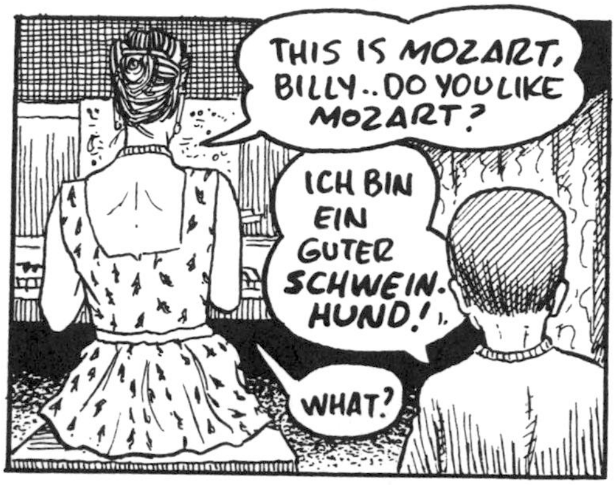

THIS IS MOZART, BILLY.. DO YOU LIKE MOZART?
ICH BIN EIN GUTER SCHWEINHUND!
WHAT?

I SPOKE ENOUGH **GERMAN** TO PLAY WITH THE NEIGHBOR KIDS, BUT ALL I'VE RETAINED IS:

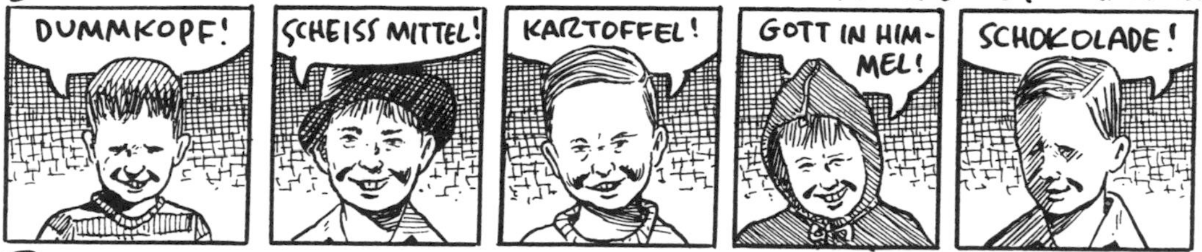

DUMMKOPF!
SCHEISS MITTEL!
KARTOFFEL!
GOTT IN HIMMEL!
SCHOKOLADE!

BACK **HOME**, WE LIVED BRIEFLY WITH **AUNT GLADYS** IN **BROOKLYN**, THEN, IN 1951, WE MOVED TO **LEVITTOWN**. MY MOTHER GOT A JOB AS A SECRETARY IN A **REAL ESTATE OFFICE** ON HEMPSTEAD TURNPIKE--

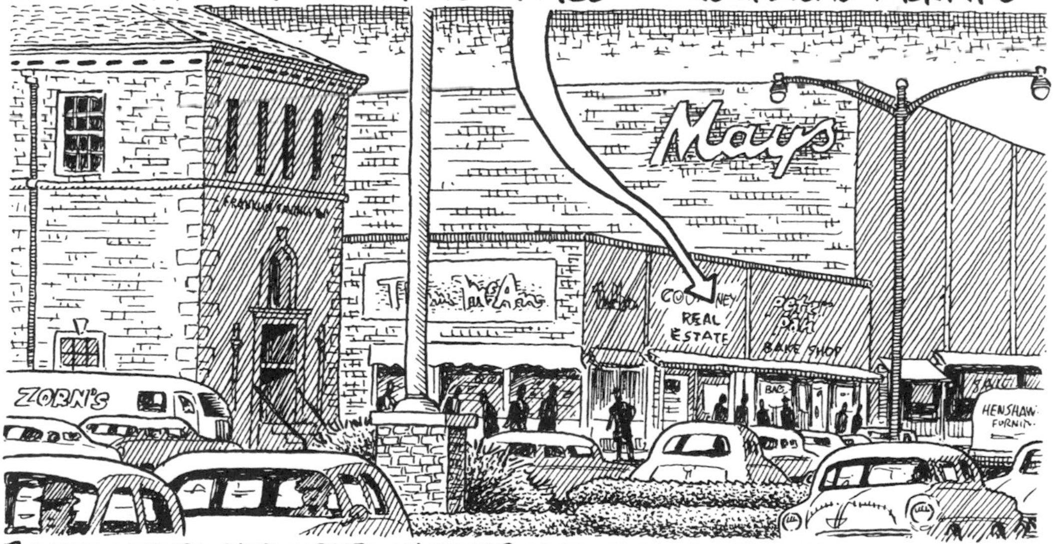

Mays
REAL ESTATE
BAKE SHOP
ZORN'S
HENSHAW

IN HER UNPUBLISHED **NOVEL**, MY MOTHER DESCRIBES LIFE IN THE OFFICE AND THE FOUR (FICTIONAL) **SALESMEN** WHO WORKED THERE--

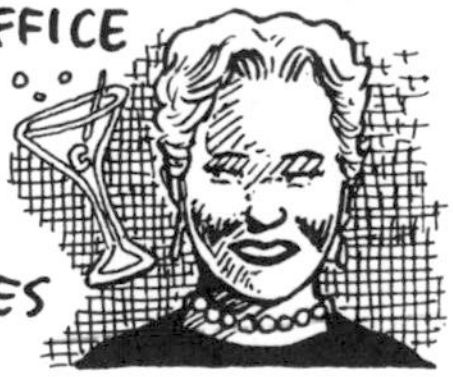

"ANDY PACELLO, ON THE MAKE AS ALWAYS, HAD TO BE DISCOURAGED NOW AND THEN, BUT HE TOOK IT GOOD-NATUREDLY... THE SPUR OF THE MOMENT INVITATION, THE MEANINGLESS BAR TALK, THE CARELESS FLIRTING EXCHANGES SEEMED TO REPAY ANDY FOR THE MONEY HE SPENT."

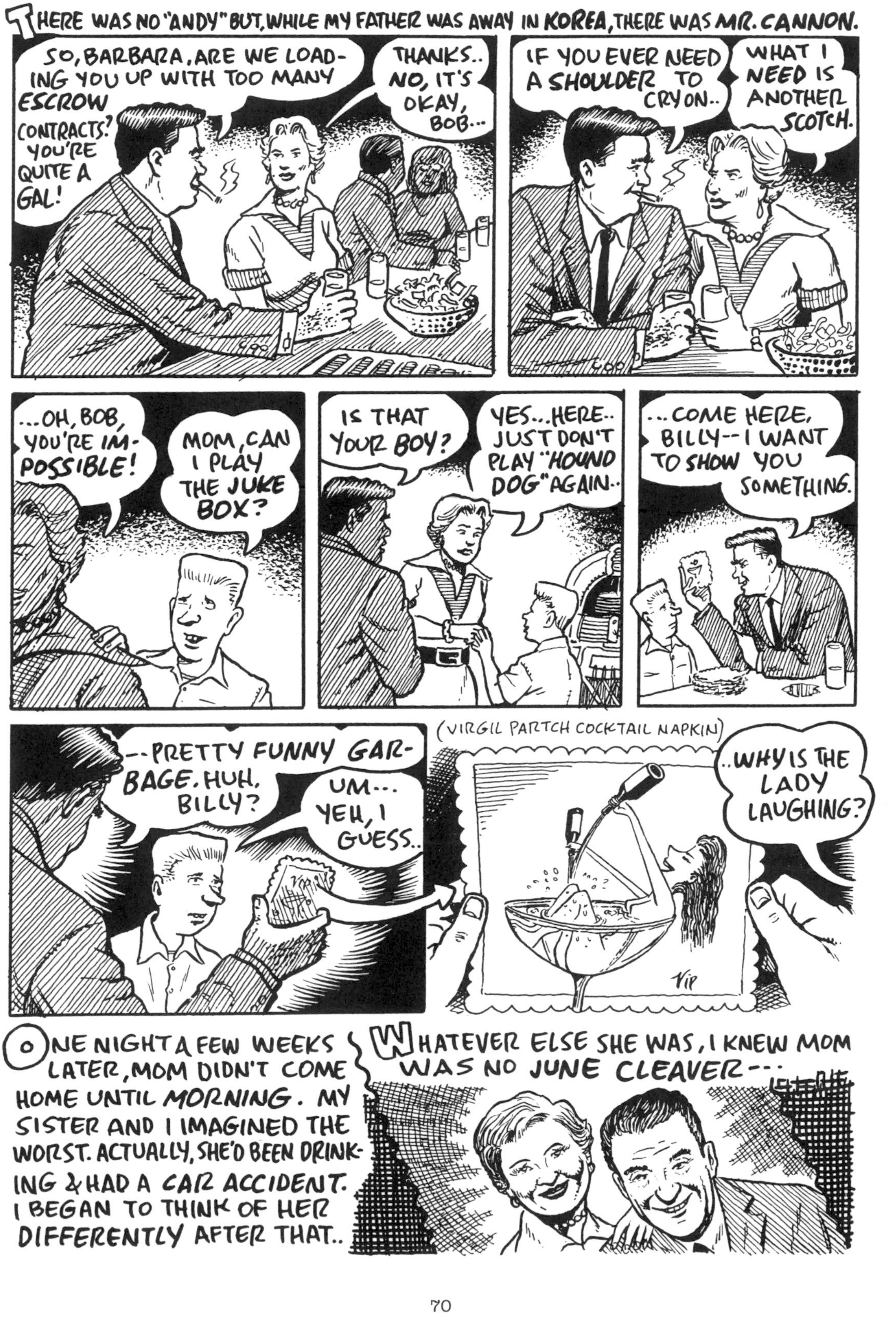
THERE WAS NO "ANDY" BUT, WHILE MY FATHER WAS AWAY IN KOREA, THERE WAS MR. CANNON.
SO, BARBARA, ARE WE LOADING YOU UP WITH TOO MANY ESCROW CONTRACTS? YOU'RE QUITE A GAL!
THANKS.. NO, IT'S OKAY, BOB...
IF YOU EVER NEED A SHOULDER TO CRY ON..
WHAT I NEED IS ANOTHER SCOTCH.
...OH, BOB, YOU'RE IMPOSSIBLE!
MOM, CAN I PLAY THE JUKE BOX?
IS THAT YOUR BOY?
YES...HERE.. JUST DON'T PLAY "HOUND DOG" AGAIN..
...COME HERE, BILLY-- I WANT TO SHOW YOU SOMETHING.
--PRETTY FUNNY GARBAGE, HUH, BILLY?
UM... YEH, I GUESS..
(VIRGIL PARTCH COCKTAIL NAPKIN)
..WHY IS THE LADY LAUGHING?
ONE NIGHT A FEW WEEKS LATER, MOM DIDN'T COME HOME UNTIL MORNING. MY SISTER AND I IMAGINED THE WORST. ACTUALLY, SHE'D BEEN DRINKING & HAD A CAR ACCIDENT. I BEGAN TO THINK OF HER DIFFERENTLY AFTER THAT..
WHATEVER ELSE SHE WAS, I KNEW MOM WAS NO JUNE CLEAVER--.

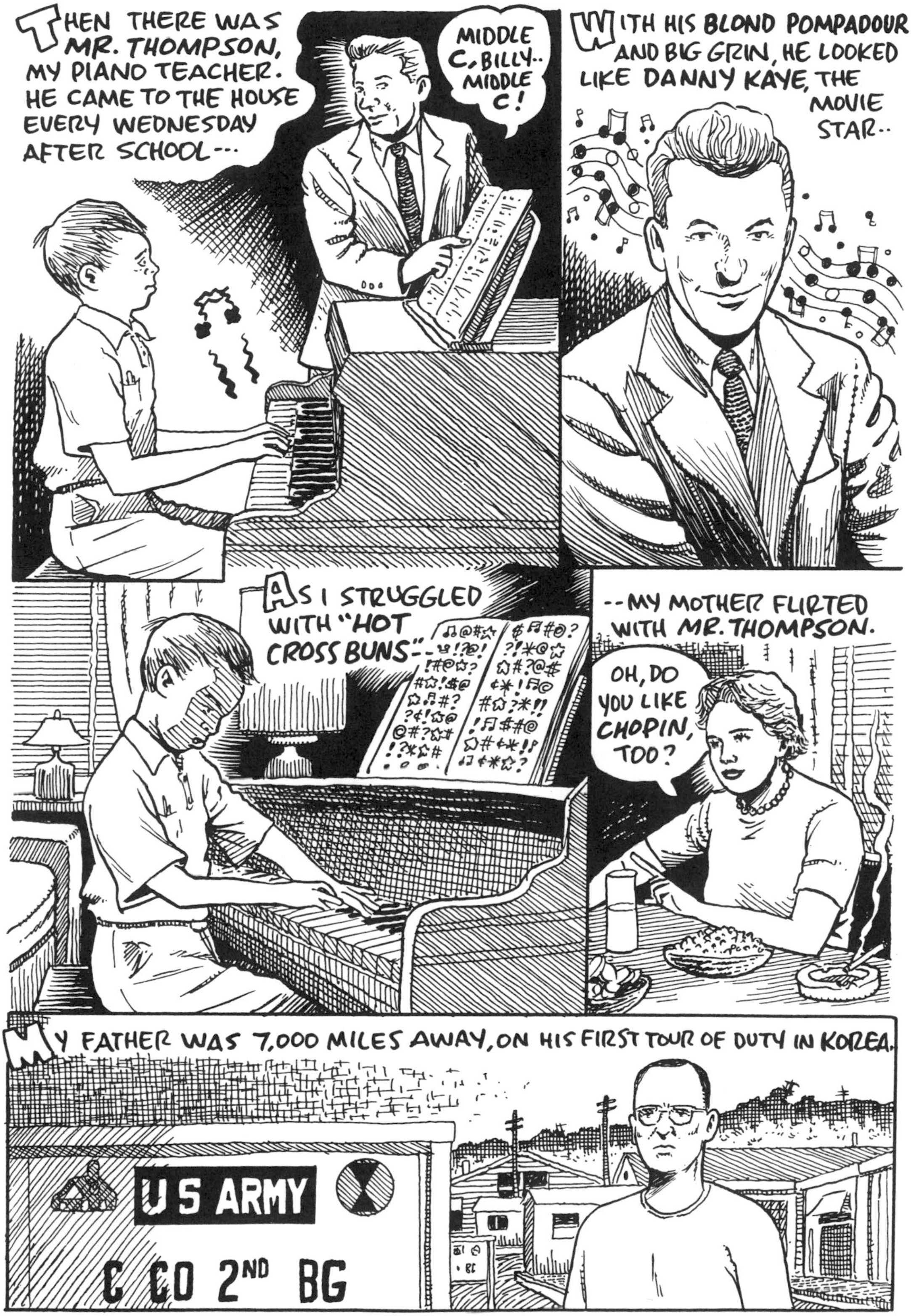
THEN THERE WAS MR. THOMPSON, MY PIANO TEACHER. HE CAME TO THE HOUSE EVERY WEDNESDAY AFTER SCHOOL---
MIDDLE C, BILLY.. MIDDLE C!
WITH HIS BLOND POMPADOUR AND BIG GRIN, HE LOOKED LIKE DANNY KAYE, THE MOVIE STAR..
AS I STRUGGLED WITH "HOT CROSS BUNS"--
--MY MOTHER FLIRTED WITH MR. THOMPSON.
OH, DO YOU LIKE CHOPIN, TOO?
MY FATHER WAS 7,000 MILES AWAY, ON HIS FIRST TOUR OF DUTY IN KOREA.
US ARMY
C CO 2ND BG

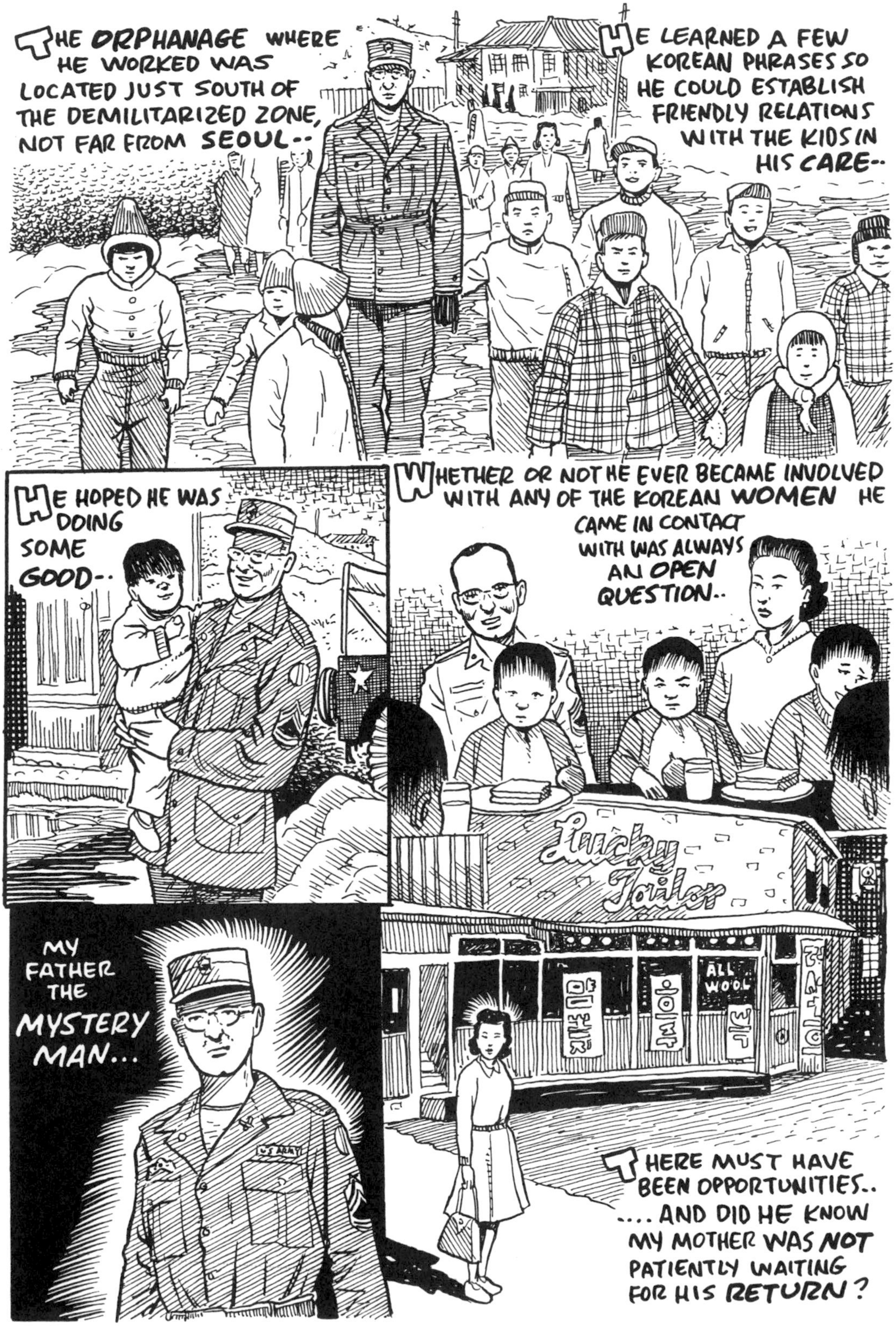
THE ORPHANAGE WHERE HE WORKED WAS LOCATED JUST SOUTH OF THE DEMILITARIZED ZONE, NOT FAR FROM SEOUL--
HE LEARNED A FEW KOREAN PHRASES SO HE COULD ESTABLISH FRIENDLY RELATIONS WITH THE KIDS IN HIS CARE--
HE HOPED HE WAS DOING SOME GOOD--
WHETHER OR NOT HE EVER BECAME INVOLVED WITH ANY OF THE KOREAN WOMEN HE CAME IN CONTACT WITH WAS ALWAYS AN OPEN QUESTION..
Lucky Tailor
ALL WOOL
MY FATHER THE MYSTERY MAN...
U.S. ARMY
THERE MUST HAVE BEEN OPPORTUNITIES..
.... AND DID HE KNOW MY MOTHER WAS NOT PATIENTLY WAITING FOR HIS RETURN?

DAD DID TWO TOURS OF DUTY IN KOREA. DURING HIS FIRST DEPLOYMENT, HE WAS GONE FOR ABOUT A **YEAR**.

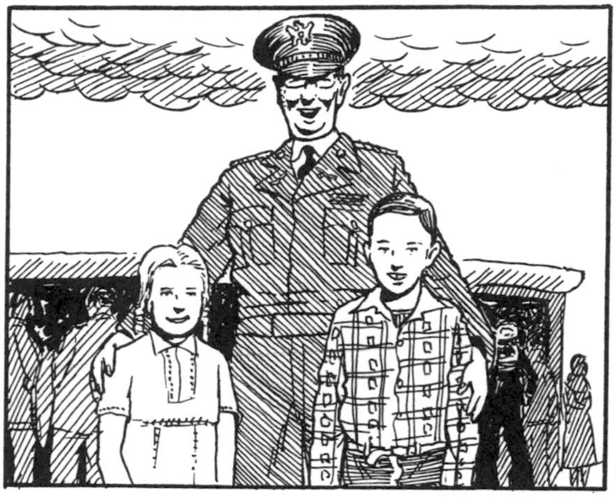

MOM FORMED A **WRITERS GROUP**.. A FEW OF HER **SHORT STORIES** WERE PUBLISHED IN **SCI-FI MAGAZINES**..

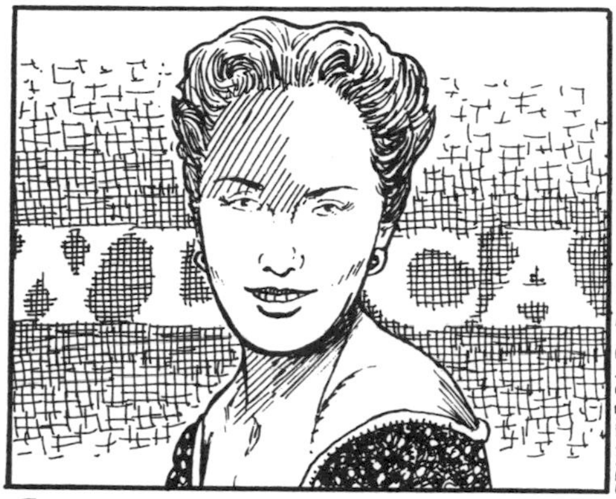

FROM THE PHOTO THAT WON HER THE TITLE "MISS WANTAGH-LEVITTOWN CIVIC ASSOCIATION".

THE GROUP MET EVERY MONTH.

I COULD HEAR LOUD DISCUSSIONS ABOUT **NABOKOV** AND **PROUST** & **MICKEY SPILLANE** FROM MY UPSTAIRS BEDROOM..

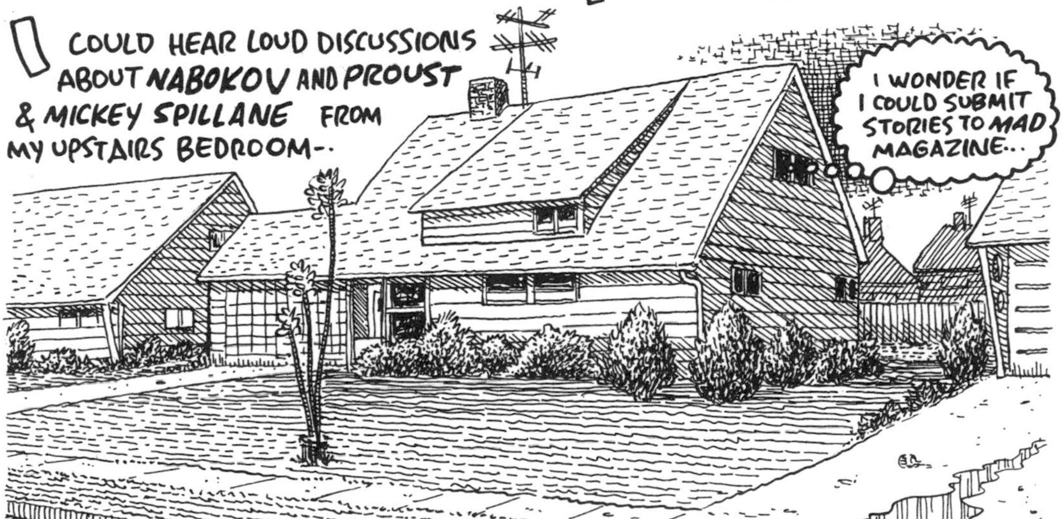
I WONDER IF I COULD SUBMIT STORIES TO MAD MAGAZINE..

IN THE MIDST OF A BLAND, EISENHOWER-ERA SUBURBIA, MY MOTHER GATHERED AROUND HER THE OTHER EIGHT INTELLECTUALS IN **LEVITTOWN** AND ARGUED THE LITERARY MERITS OF GRAHAM GREENE'S "THE QUIET AMERICAN" VERSUS CURRENT BEST-SELLERS LIKE "**AUNTIE MAME**"--

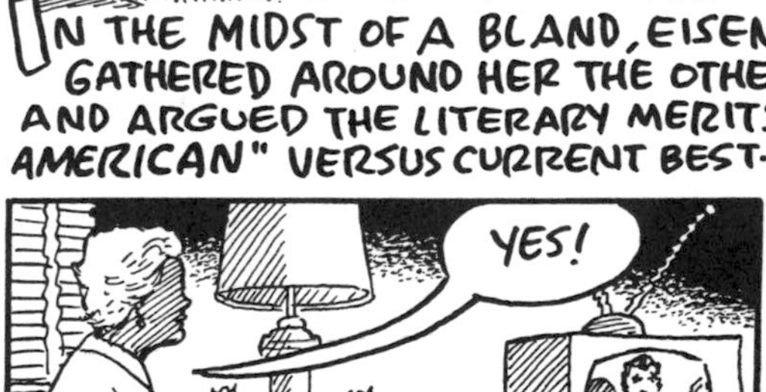
YES!

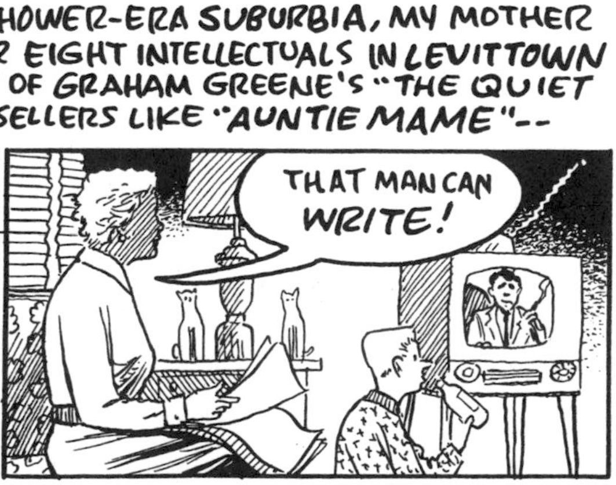
THAT MAN CAN WRITE!

SHE LOVED **ROD SERLING** & NEVER MISSED AN EPISODE OF "**THE TWILIGHT ZONE**."

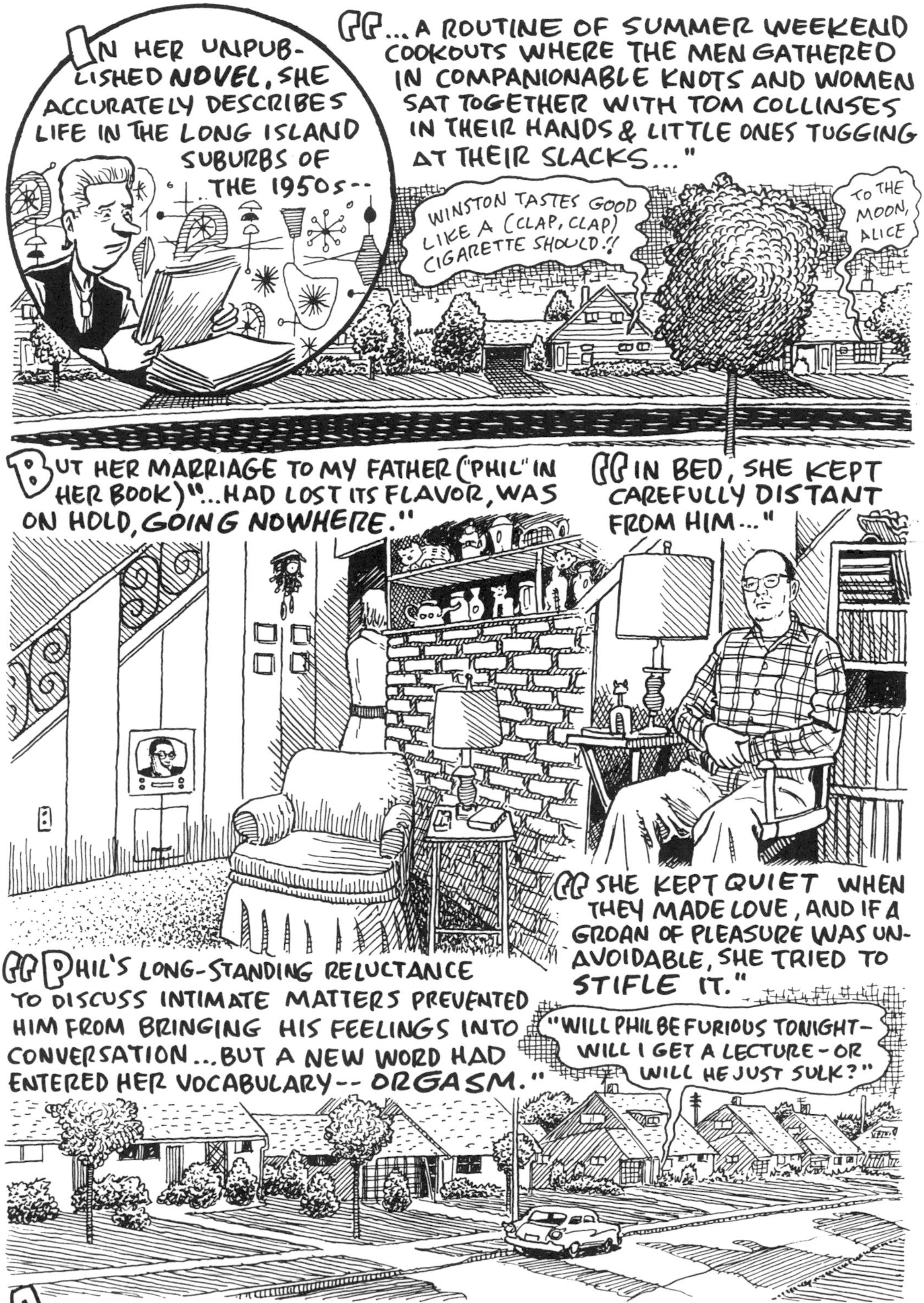
IN HER UNPUBLISHED NOVEL, SHE ACCURATELY DESCRIBES LIFE IN THE LONG ISLAND SUBURBS OF THE 1950s--
"...A ROUTINE OF SUMMER WEEKEND COOKOUTS WHERE THE MEN GATHERED IN COMPANIONABLE KNOTS AND WOMEN SAT TOGETHER WITH TOM COLLINSES IN THEIR HANDS & LITTLE ONES TUGGING AT THEIR SLACKS..."
WINSTON TASTES GOOD LIKE A (CLAP, CLAP) CIGARETTE SHOULD!!
TO THE MOON, ALICE
BUT HER MARRIAGE TO MY FATHER ("PHIL" IN HER BOOK) "...HAD LOST ITS FLAVOR, WAS ON HOLD, GOING NOWHERE."
"IN BED, SHE KEPT CAREFULLY DISTANT FROM HIM..."
"SHE KEPT QUIET WHEN THEY MADE LOVE, AND IF A GROAN OF PLEASURE WAS UNAVOIDABLE, SHE TRIED TO STIFLE IT."
"PHIL'S LONG-STANDING RELUCTANCE TO DISCUSS INTIMATE MATTERS PREVENTED HIM FROM BRINGING HIS FEELINGS INTO CONVERSATION... BUT A NEW WORD HAD ENTERED HER VOCABULARY-- ORGASM."
"WILL PHIL BE FURIOUS TONIGHT-- WILL I GET A LECTURE-- OR WILL HE JUST SULK?"
A FEW TOWNS AWAY, HER FUTURE LOVER PLUGGED AWAY AT HIS HECTIC CAREER..

THE LATE 1940s AND EARLY 1950s WERE A BUSIER-THAN-EVER TIME FOR LARIAR. IN ADDITION TO STINTS IN RADIO (HE WROTE SCRIPTS FOR THE "COLONEL STOOPNAGLE" AND "ROCKY KING, DETECTIVE" SHOWS), HE KEPT AFTER THE "HOLY GRAIL", HIS OWN DAILY NEWSPAPER STRIP---

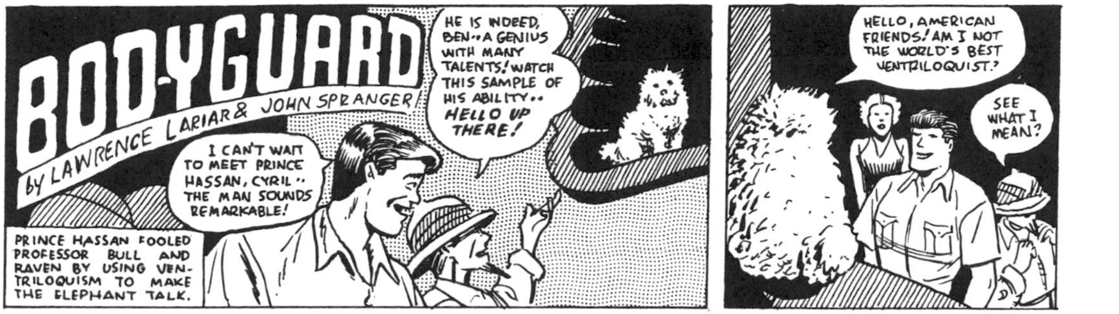
BODYGUARD
by LAWRENCE LARIAR & JOHN SPRANGER
PRINCE HASSAN FOOLED PROFESSOR BULL AND RAVEN BY USING VENTRILOQUISM TO MAKE THE ELEPHANT TALK.
I CAN'T WAIT TO MEET PRINCE HASSAN, CYRIL.. THE MAN SOUNDS REMARKABLE!
HE IS INDEED, BEN.. A GENIUS WITH MANY TALENTS! WATCH THIS SAMPLE OF HIS ABILITY.. HELLO UP THERE!
HELLO, AMERICAN FRIENDS! AM I NOT THE WORLD'S BEST VENTRILOQUIST?
SEE WHAT I MEAN?

HE LANDED A HARD-WON DEAL WITH THE NEW YORK HERALD TRIBUNE SYNDICATE FOR "THE BODYGUARD" IN 1949. JOHN SPRANGER, WHO WENT ON TO DO "THE SAINT", DID THE DRAWING...THE STRIP STRUGGLED...

IN AN ATTEMPT TO REVIVE FLAGGING SALES, LARIAR CHANGED THE TITLE TO "BEN FRIDAY", THE STRIP'S DASHING ADVENTURER/PROTAGONIST. A SIDEKICK CHARACTER, "PRINCE HASSAN", TOOK ON A MORE PROMINENT ROLE. THE "PRINCE" WAS DESCRIBED IN SYNDICATE PROMOS AS A KID WITH "AN EINSTEIN MIND" WHO SPOKE IN AN AMALGAM OF STAGE HINDU & GEE-WHIZ-ALL-AMERICAN-BOY. THE STRIP AGAIN FALTERED.

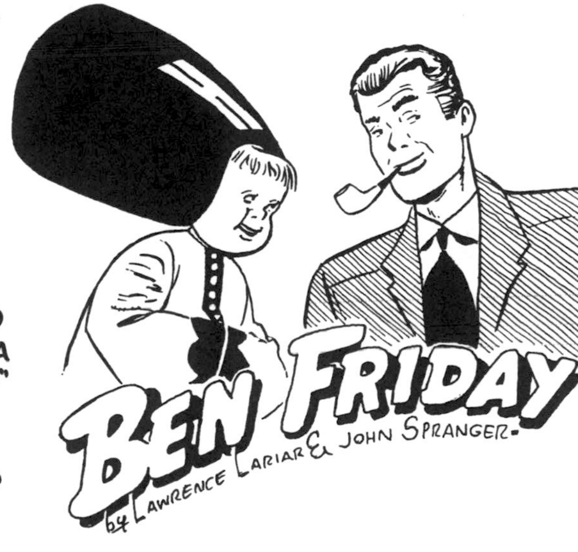
BEN FRIDAY
by LAWRENCE LARIAR & JOHN SPRANGER

FROM THE BEN FRIDAY SALES PITCH TO NEWSPAPER EDITORS--

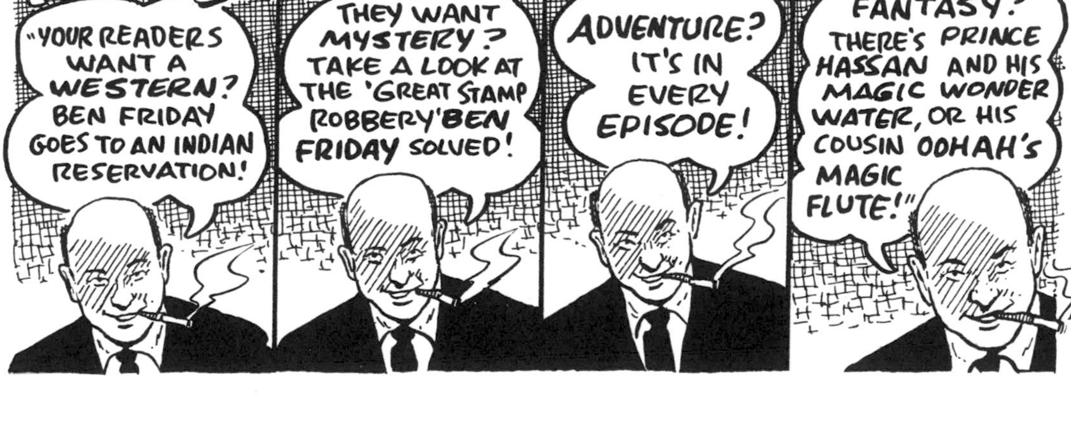
"YOUR READERS WANT A WESTERN? BEN FRIDAY GOES TO AN INDIAN RESERVATION!
THEY WANT MYSTERY? TAKE A LOOK AT THE 'GREAT STAMP ROBBERY' BEN FRIDAY SOLVED!
ADVENTURE? IT'S IN EVERY EPISODE!
FANTASY? THERE'S PRINCE HASSAN AND HIS MAGIC WONDER WATER, OR HIS COUSIN OOHAH'S MAGIC FLUTE!"

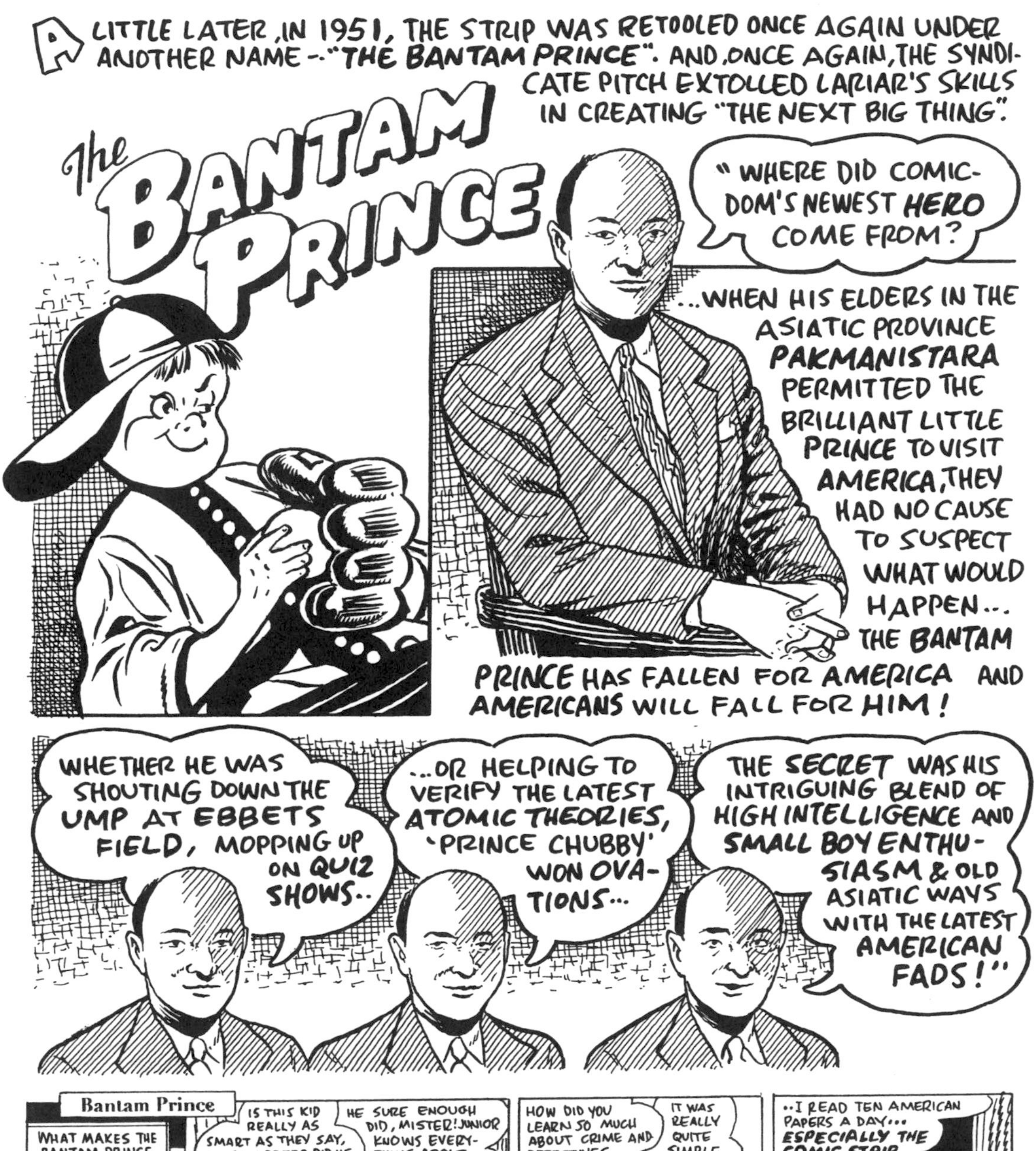
A LITTLE LATER, IN 1951, THE STRIP WAS RETOOLED ONCE AGAIN UNDER ANOTHER NAME -- "THE BANTAM PRINCE". AND, ONCE AGAIN, THE SYNDICATE PITCH EXTOLLED LARIAR'S SKILLS IN CREATING "THE NEXT BIG THING".
The BANTAM PRINCE
" WHERE DID COMIC-DOM'S NEWEST HERO COME FROM?
...WHEN HIS ELDERS IN THE ASIATIC PROVINCE PAKMANISTARA PERMITTED THE BRILLIANT LITTLE PRINCE TO VISIT AMERICA, THEY HAD NO CAUSE TO SUSPECT WHAT WOULD HAPPEN... THE BANTAM PRINCE HAS FALLEN FOR AMERICA AND AMERICANS WILL FALL FOR HIM!
WHETHER HE WAS SHOUTING DOWN THE UMP AT EBBETS FIELD, MOPPING UP ON QUIZ SHOWS..
...OR HELPING TO VERIFY THE LATEST ATOMIC THEORIES, 'PRINCE CHUBBY' WON OVATIONS...
THE SECRET WAS HIS INTRIGUING BLEND OF HIGH INTELLIGENCE AND SMALL BOY ENTHUSIASM & OLD ASIATIC WAYS WITH THE LATEST AMERICAN FADS!"
Bantam Prince
WHAT MAKES THE BANTAM PRINCE TICK? HOW CAN A SEVEN YEAR OLD BOY KNOW SO MUCH ABOUT DETECTION?
IS THIS KID REALLY AS SMART AS THEY SAY, MISS WUPPER? DID HE REALLY CATCH TWO ART SWINDLERS?
HE SURE ENOUGH DID, MISTER! JUNIOR KNOWS EVERYTHING ABOUT CRIMINAL STUFF! ASK HIM YOURSELF!
2-27
Copyright, 1951, New York Herald Tribune Inc.
LARIAR & SPRANGER
HOW DID YOU LEARN SO MUCH ABOUT CRIME AND DETECTIVES, PRINCE?
IT WAS REALLY QUITE SIMPLE, SAHIB! YOU SEE...
..I READ TEN AMERICAN PAPERS A DAY... ESPECIALLY THE COMIC STRIP SECTIONS!
ANOTHER ARTIST WAS BROUGHT ON BOARD LATER THAT YEAR -- CARL PFEUFFER. PFEUFFER HAD A LONG CAREER IN COMICS, INCLUDING WORK ON MARVEL COMICS' "SUB-MARINER" AND, LATER, SOFT-CORE BONDAGE ILLUSTRATION. THE "PRINCE" ENDED ITS RUN IN 1954.

THE EARLY 1950S ALSO SAW THE PUBLICATION OF TWO "**HOW TO**" BOOKS ON CARTOONING BY LARIAR WHO, BY THEN, WAS ALSO RUNNING THE "**PROFESSIONAL SCHOOL OF CARTOONING**", A CORRESPONDENCE COURSE HE STARTED. ONE OF THE INSTRUCTORS WAS HIS OLD STUDIO-MATE, **ADOLPH SCHUS**. THE COURSE CONSISTED OF **45 LESSONS** PLUS CRITICISM BY "NINE FAMOUS AMERCAN PROFESSIONAL CARTOONISTS."

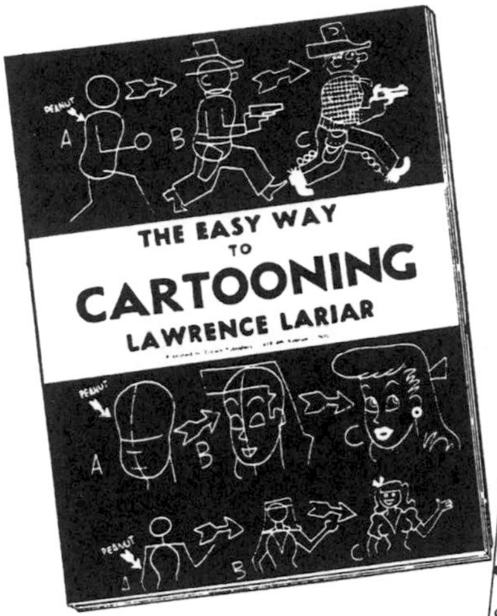

PEANUT
A
B
C
THE EASY WAY TO
CARTOONING
LAWRENCE LARIAR

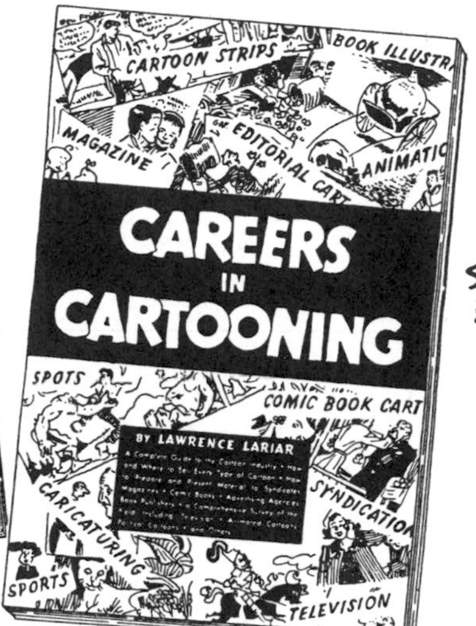

CARTOON STRIPS
BOOK ILLUSTR
MAGAZINE
EDITORIAL CART
ANIMATIO
CAREERS IN CARTOONING
SPOTS
COMIC BOOK CART
BY LAWRENCE LARIAR
CARICATURING
SYNDICATION
SPORTS
TELEVISION

LARIAR WAS LISTED AS THE ***EXECUTIVE DIRECTOR*** OF THE SCHOOL, BUT HE ALSO SENT OUT PERSONAL, DETAILED CRITIQUES TO MANY WOULD-BE CARTOONISTS... INCLUDED IN THE SCHOOL'S PROMOTIONAL MATERIALS WERE "HOW TO'S" ON THE THREE ***ESSENTIALS***--

1. HOW TO DRAW **FEAR**.

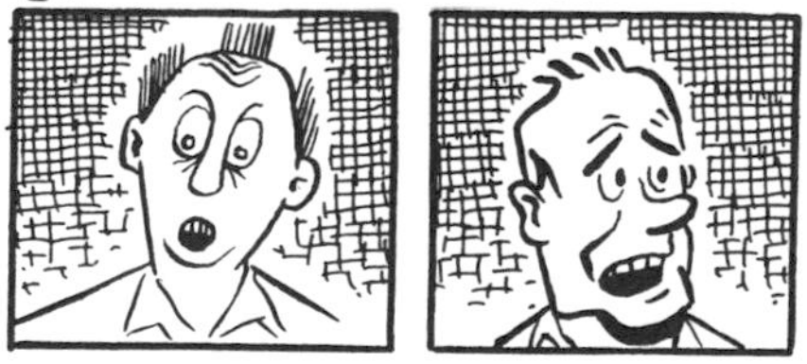

2. HOW TO DRAW **JOY**.

3. HOW TO DRAW ***GIRLS***.

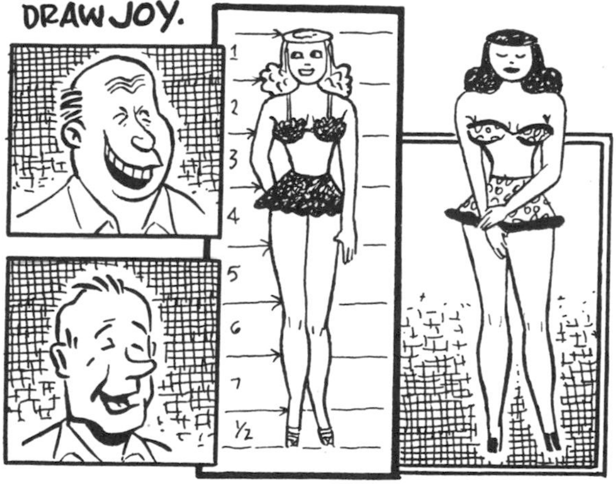

1
2
3
4
5
6
7
1/2

IN "***CAREERS IN CARTOONING***", LARIAR LAYS OUT A LIST OF **TABOOS** FOR ASPIRING CARTOONISTS TO ***AVOID***--

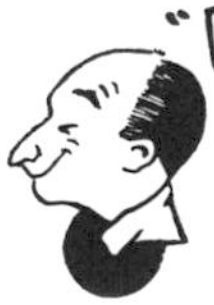

"NEVER RIDICULE THE NEGRO RACE. SUCH CARICATURES ARE USUALLY CREATED TO PROMOTE PREJUDICE AND HATE.

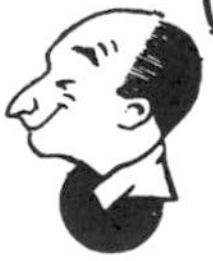

KANGAROO POUCH GAGS. THIS BEAST SHOULD BE BURIED IN THE CLICHE DEPARTMENT.

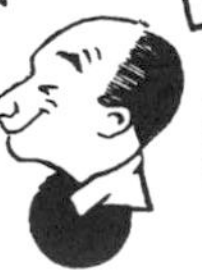

NAPOLEON IN THE MADHOUSE. MOST MENTAL VICTIMS HAVE GIVEN THIS UP IN FAVOR OF MORE MODERN FIXATIONS.

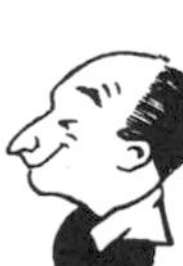

NEVER SUBMIT OVER-SEXY CARTOONS. THERE WILL ALWAYS BE A MARKET FOR CUTE GIRLS BUT THERE IS A LIMIT TO THE CARTOONING OF NUDITY.

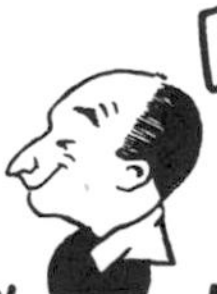

HINDUS WHO FLY MAGIC CARPETS. ...BEATEN TO DEATH BY ALL MANNER OF ARTISTS, FAMOUS & INFAMOUS.

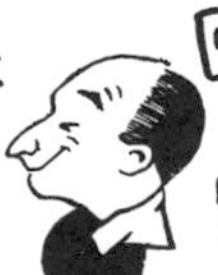

DESERT ISLANDS. POSSIBILITIES OF FINDING SOMETHING NEW & FUNNY ON A RAFT OR DESERT ISLAND ARE NIL."

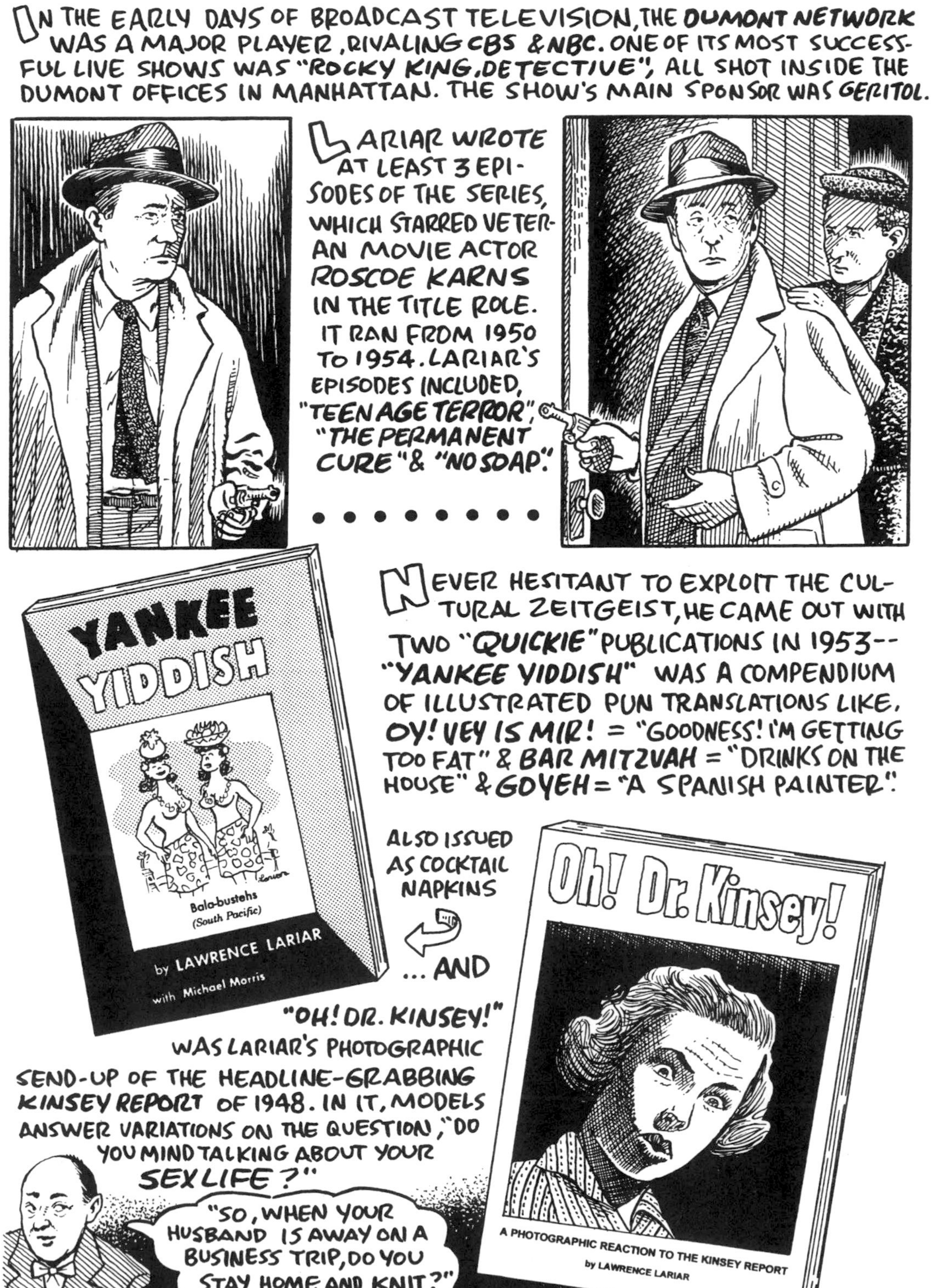
IN THE EARLY DAYS OF BROADCAST TELEVISION, THE DUMONT NETWORK WAS A MAJOR PLAYER, RIVALING CBS & NBC. ONE OF ITS MOST SUCCESSFUL LIVE SHOWS WAS "ROCKY KING, DETECTIVE", ALL SHOT INSIDE THE DUMONT OFFICES IN MANHATTAN. THE SHOW'S MAIN SPONSOR WAS GERITOL.
LARIAR WROTE AT LEAST 3 EPISODES OF THE SERIES, WHICH STARRED VETERAN MOVIE ACTOR ROSCOE KARNS IN THE TITLE ROLE. IT RAN FROM 1950 TO 1954. LARIAR'S EPISODES INCLUDED, "TEEN AGE TERROR", "THE PERMANENT CURE" & "NO SOAP".
C
YANKEE YIDDISH
Bala-bustehs
(South Pacific)
by LAWRENCE LARIAR
with Michael Morris
NEVER HESITANT TO EXPLOIT THE CULTURAL ZEITGEIST, HE CAME OUT WITH TWO "QUICKIE" PUBLICATIONS IN 1953-- "YANKEE YIDDISH" WAS A COMPENDIUM OF ILLUSTRATED PUN TRANSLATIONS LIKE, OY! VEY IS MIR! = "GOODNESS! I'M GETTING TOO FAT" & BAR MITZVAH = "DRINKS ON THE HOUSE" & GOYEH = "A SPANISH PAINTER".
ALSO ISSUED AS COCKTAIL NAPKINS
...AND
Oh! Dr. Kinsey!
A PHOTOGRAPHIC REACTION TO THE KINSEY REPORT
by LAWRENCE LARIAR
"OH! DR. KINSEY!" WAS LARIAR'S PHOTOGRAPHIC SEND-UP OF THE HEADLINE-GRABBING KINSEY REPORT OF 1948. IN IT, MODELS ANSWER VARIATIONS ON THE QUESTION, "DO YOU MIND TALKING ABOUT YOUR SEX LIFE?"
"SO, WHEN YOUR HUSBAND IS AWAY ON A BUSINESS TRIP, DO YOU STAY HOME AND KNIT?"

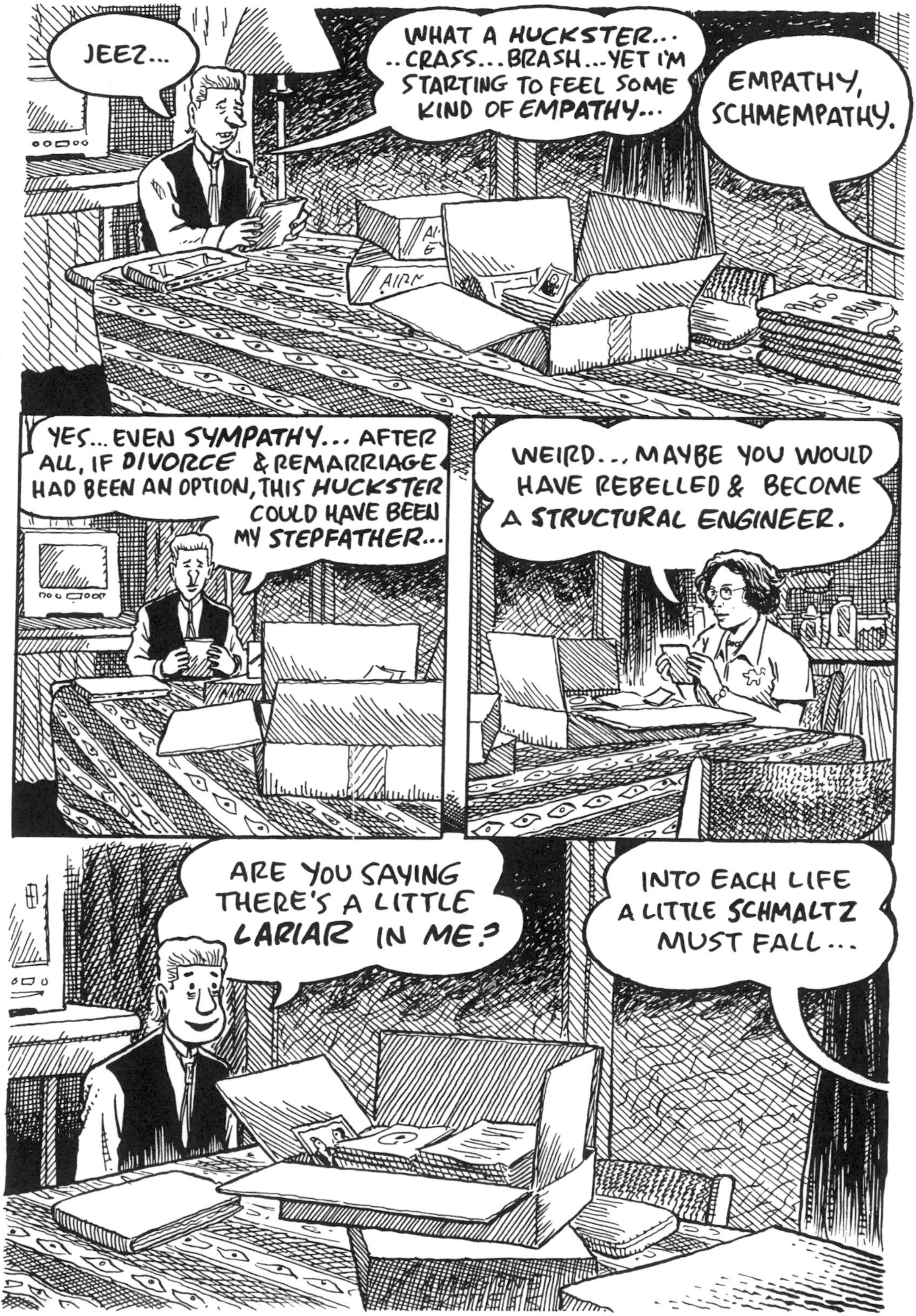
JEEZ...
WHAT A HUCKSTER... ..CRASS...BRASH...YET I'M STARTING TO FEEL SOME KIND OF EMPATHY...
EMPATHY, SCHMEMPATHY.
YES...EVEN SYMPATHY... AFTER ALL, IF DIVORCE & REMARRIAGE HAD BEEN AN OPTION, THIS HUCKSTER COULD HAVE BEEN MY STEPFATHER...
WEIRD..., MAYBE YOU WOULD HAVE REBELLED & BECOME A STRUCTURAL ENGINEER.
ARE YOU SAYING THERE'S A LITTLE LARIAR IN ME?
INTO EACH LIFE A LITTLE SCHMALTZ MUST FALL...

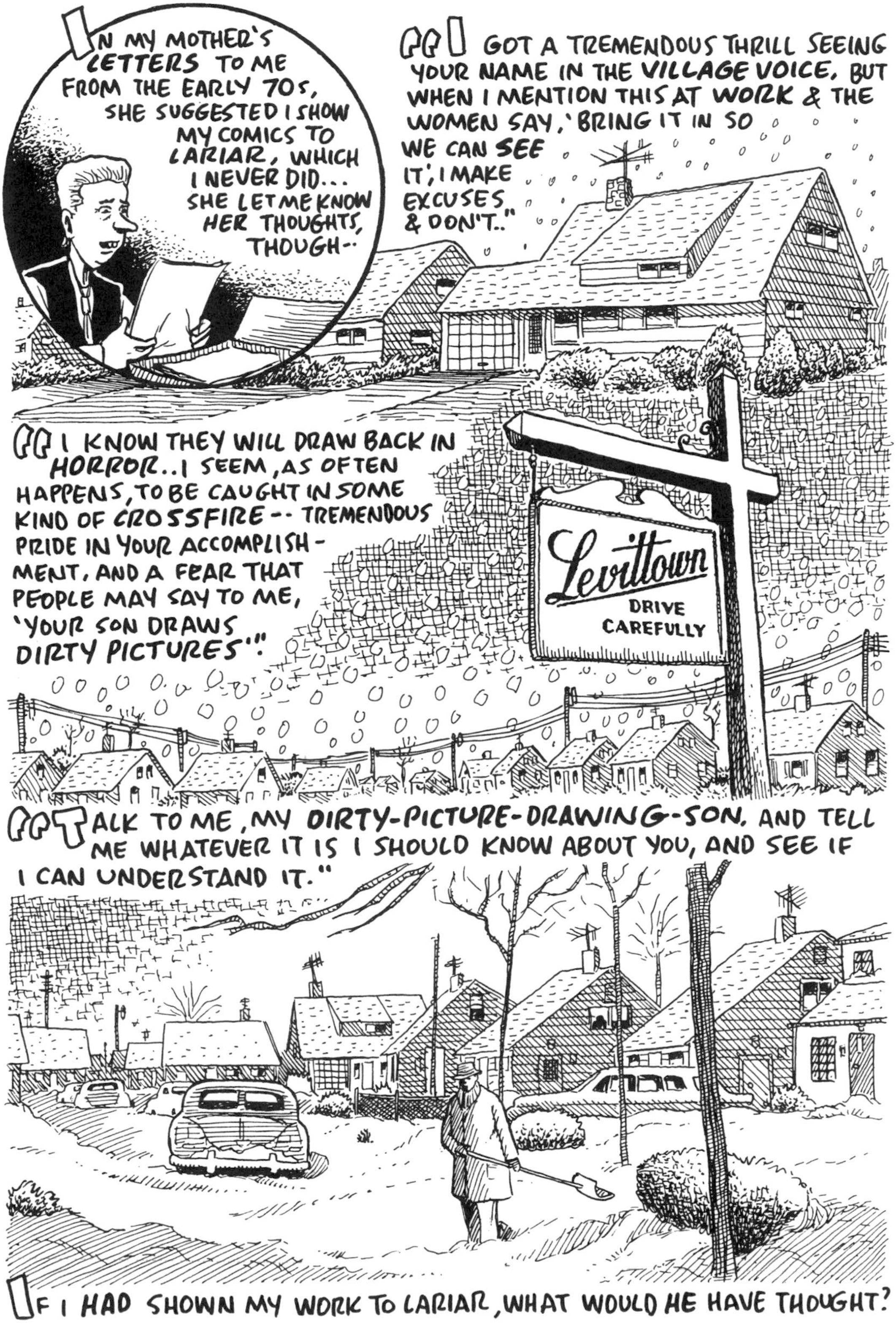
In my mother's letters to me from the early 70s, she suggested I show my comics to Lariar, which I never did... she let me know her thoughts, though--
"I got a tremendous thrill seeing your name in the Village Voice. But when I mention this at work & the women say, 'Bring it in so we can see it', I make excuses & don't.."
"I know they will draw back in horror.. I seem, as often happens, to be caught in some kind of crossfire -- tremendous pride in your accomplishment, and a fear that people may say to me, 'Your son draws dirty pictures'."
Levittown
DRIVE CAREFULLY
"Talk to me, my dirty-picture-drawing-son, and tell me whatever it is I should know about you, and see if I can understand it."
If I had shown my work to Lariar, what would he have thought?

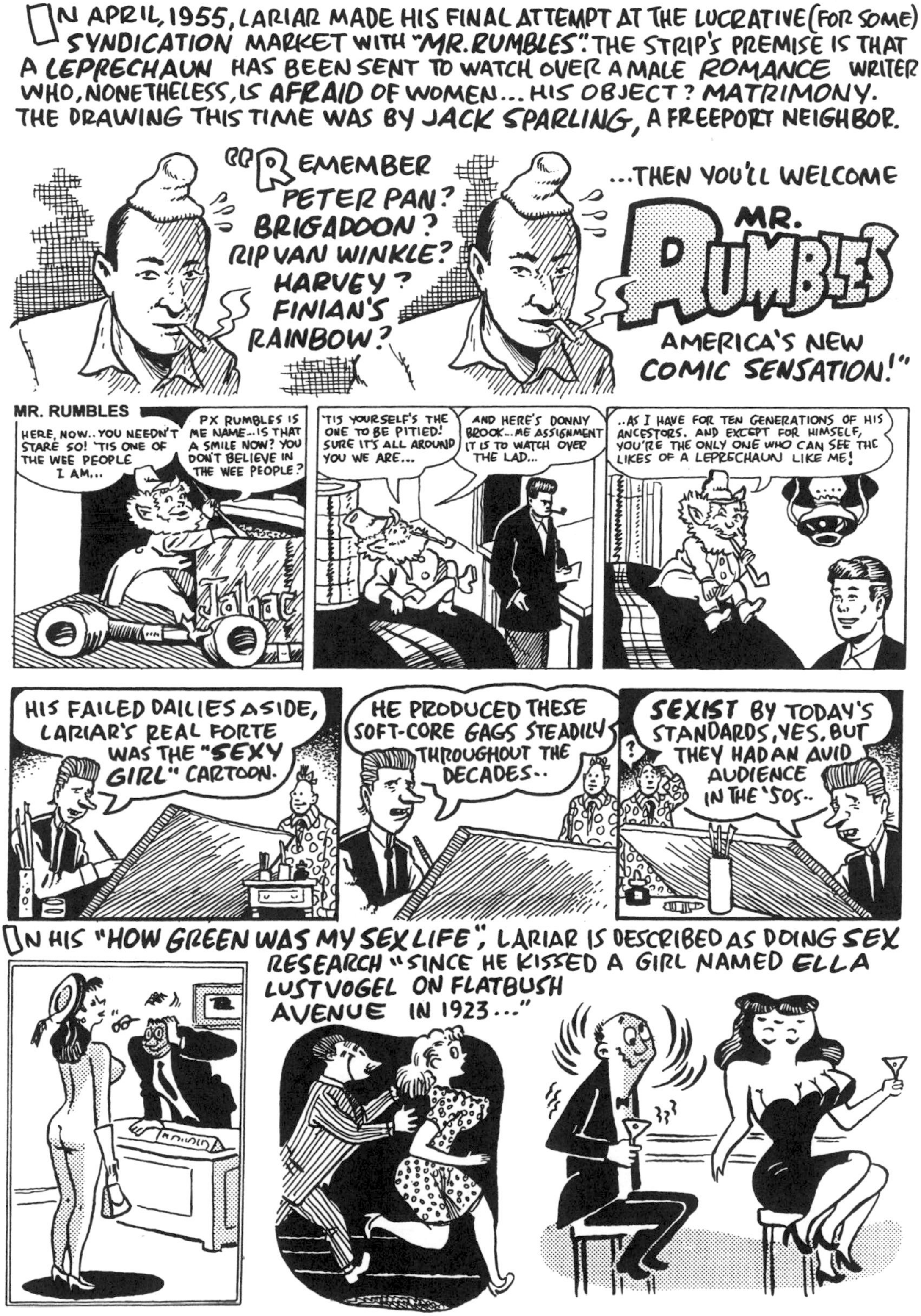
IN APRIL, 1955, LARIAR MADE HIS FINAL ATTEMPT AT THE LUCRATIVE (FOR SOME) SYNDICATION MARKET WITH "MR. RUMBLES". THE STRIP'S PREMISE IS THAT A LEPRECHAUN HAS BEEN SENT TO WATCH OVER A MALE ROMANCE WRITER WHO, NONETHELESS, IS AFRAID OF WOMEN... HIS OBJECT? MATRIMONY. THE DRAWING THIS TIME WAS BY JACK SPARLING, A FREEPORT NEIGHBOR.
"REMEMBER PETER PAN? BRIGADOON? RIP VAN WINKLE? HARVEY? FINIAN'S RAINBOW?
...THEN YOU'LL WELCOME MR. RUMBLES AMERICA'S NEW COMIC SENSATION!"
MR. RUMBLES
HERE, NOW.. YOU NEEDN'T STARE SO! 'TIS ONE OF THE WEE PEOPLE I AM...
PX RUMBLES IS ME NAME...IS THAT A SMILE NOW? YOU DON'T BELIEVE IN THE WEE PEOPLE?
TABAC
'TIS YOURSELF'S THE ONE TO BE PITIED! SURE IT'S ALL AROUND YOU WE ARE...
AND HERE'S DONNY BROOK...ME ASSIGNMENT IT IS TO WATCH OVER THE LAD...
..AS I HAVE FOR TEN GENERATIONS OF HIS ANCESTORS. AND EXCEPT FOR HIMSELF, YOU'RE THE ONLY ONE WHO CAN SEE THE LIKES OF A LEPRECHAUN LIKE ME!
HIS FAILED DAILIES ASIDE, LARIAR'S REAL FORTE WAS THE "SEXY GIRL" CARTOON.
HE PRODUCED THESE SOFT-CORE GAGS STEADILY THROUGHOUT THE DECADES..
SEXIST BY TODAY'S STANDARDS, YES. BUT THEY HAD AN AVID AUDIENCE IN THE '50s..
IN HIS "HOW GREEN WAS MY SEX LIFE", LARIAR IS DESCRIBED AS DOING SEX RESEARCH "SINCE HE KISSED A GIRL NAMED ELLA LUSTVOGEL ON FLATBUSH AVENUE IN 1923..."

HE EDITED A SERIES OF THEMED CARTOON COLLECTIONS ("YOU'VE GOT ME IN STITCHES", "YOU'VE GOT ME IN THE NURSERY", "YOU'VE GOT ME FROM 9 TO 5") BUT ALSO MANAGED TO FIND TIME TO PRODUCE A FLOCK OF *SOLO* EFFORTS--PARODIES OF THE *GUIDE BOOKS* & *HOW TO BOOKS* POPULAR AMONG THE *SUBURBANITES* OF POST-WAR AMERICA--

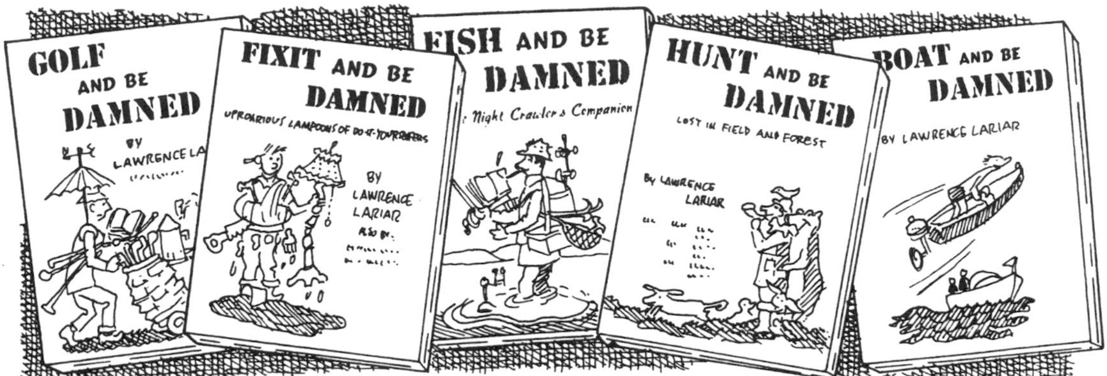
GOLF AND BE DAMNED
BY LAWRENCE LA
FIXIT AND BE DAMNED
UPROARIOUS LAMPOONS OF DO-IT-YOURSELFERS
BY LAWRENCE LARIAR
AND BE DAMNED
Night Crawler's Companion
HUNT AND BE DAMNED
LOST IN FIELD AND FOREST
BY LAWRENCE LARIAR
BOAT AND BE DAMNED
BY LAWRENCE LARIAR

THEN, IN 1956, SHORTLY BEFORE MY MOTHER BEGAN HER JOB AS HIS *SECRETARY*, LARIAR PUBLISHED "*THE REAL LOW-DOWN*", A RACY SPOOF, PURPORTING TO TELL *SALESMEN* HOW TO IMPROVE THEIR PROSPECTS---

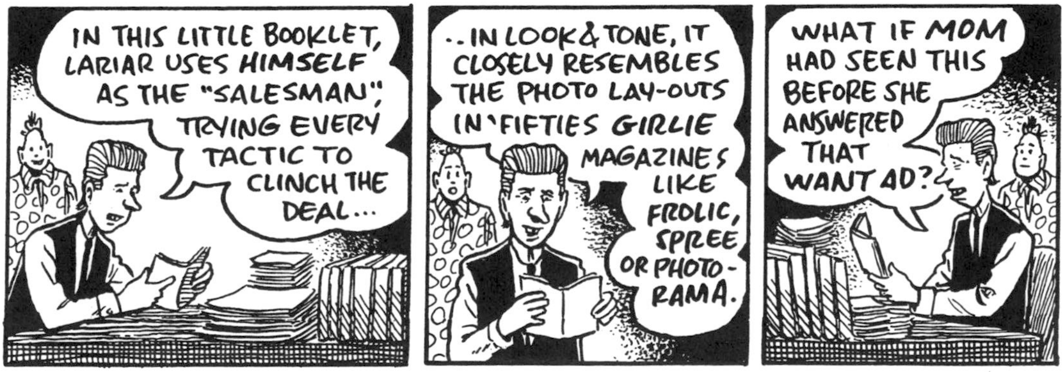
IN THIS LITTLE BOOKLET, LARIAR USES HIMSELF AS THE "SALESMAN", TRYING EVERY TACTIC TO CLINCH THE DEAL...
..IN LOOK & TONE, IT CLOSELY RESEMBLES THE PHOTO LAY-OUTS IN 'FIFTIES GIRLIE MAGAZINES LIKE FROLIC, SPREE OR PHOTO-RAMA.
WHAT IF MOM HAD SEEN THIS BEFORE SHE ANSWERED THAT WANT AD?

THE BOOKLET *WINKS, NODS* & *LEERS* AT ALL THE RAUNCHY OPPORTUNITIES A SALESMAN FINDS TO "NOT HURRY HOME TO CINCINNATI."

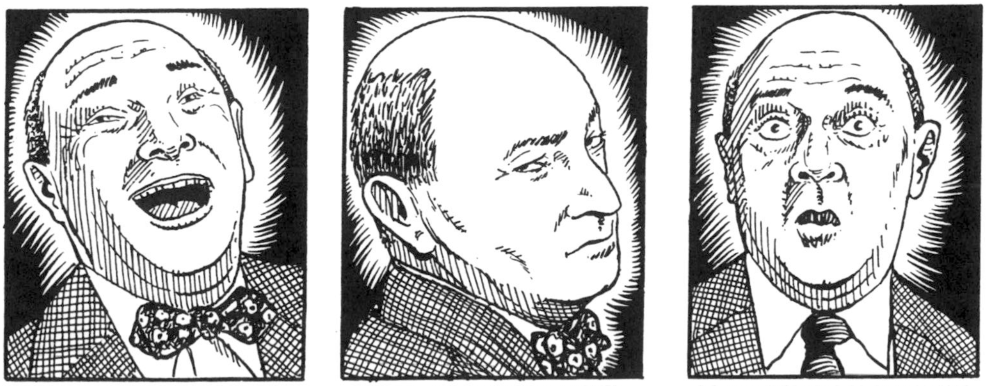

DO YOU FEEL BLUE WHEN YOU LEAVE YOUR WIFE TO GO ON THE ROAD?

WOULDN'T YOU BE MUCH HAPPIER IF YOU TOOK YOUR WIFE WITH YOU TO THE NEXT SALES CONVENTION?

DO YOU EVER STOP TO THINK WHAT YOUR WIFE MAY BE DOING WHEN YOU'RE AWAY ON A SELLING TRIP?

LARIAR'S INNER SHOWMAN IS IN FULL FLOWER HERE--HE COMES CLOSE TO TURNING HIMSELF INTO A CARTOON CHARACTER IN ITS 48 PAGES.

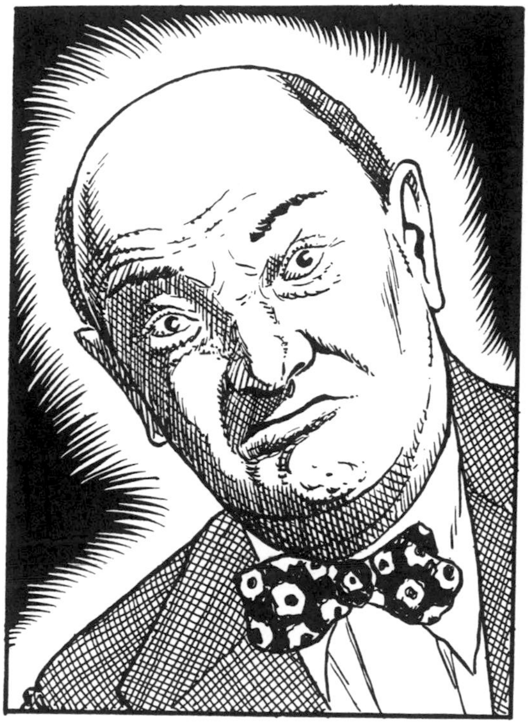

HOW DOES IT FEEL TO BE A SALESMAN?

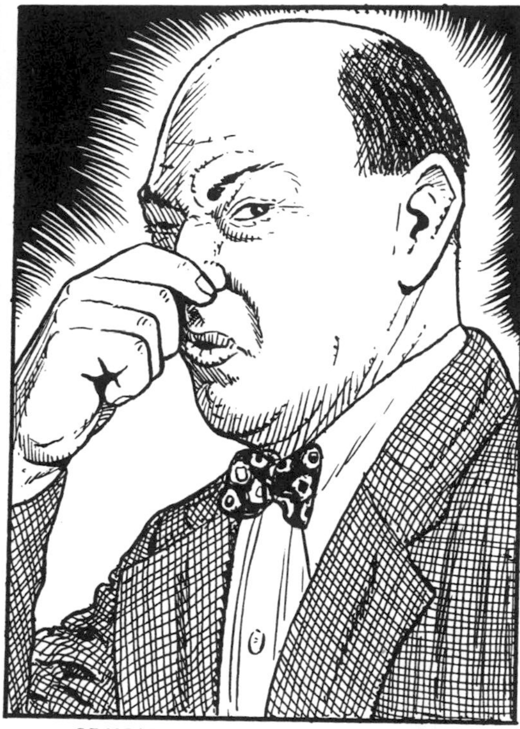

BE HONEST NOW . . . WHAT DO YOU REALLY THINK OF SALES MANAGERS?

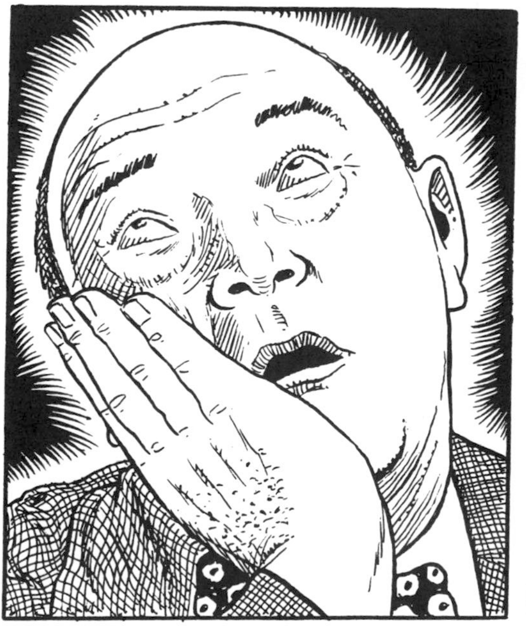

WHEN YOU WANT TO MEET A COMPETITOR'S LOWER PRICE, WHAT DOES YOUR COMPANY SAY?

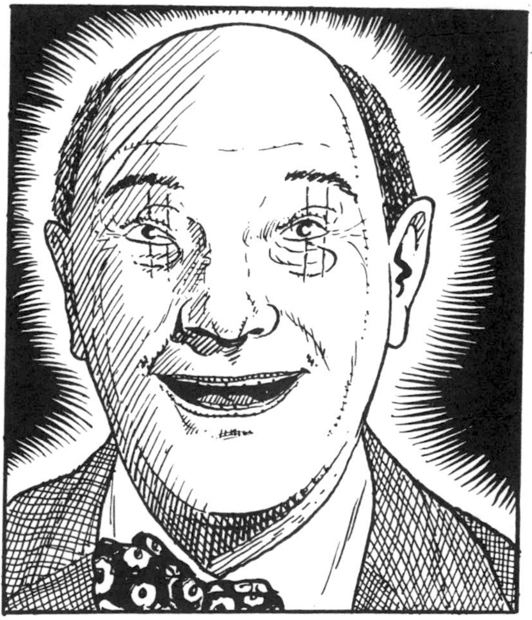

IF SELLING'S SO TOUGH, WHY DO YOU STICK TO IT?

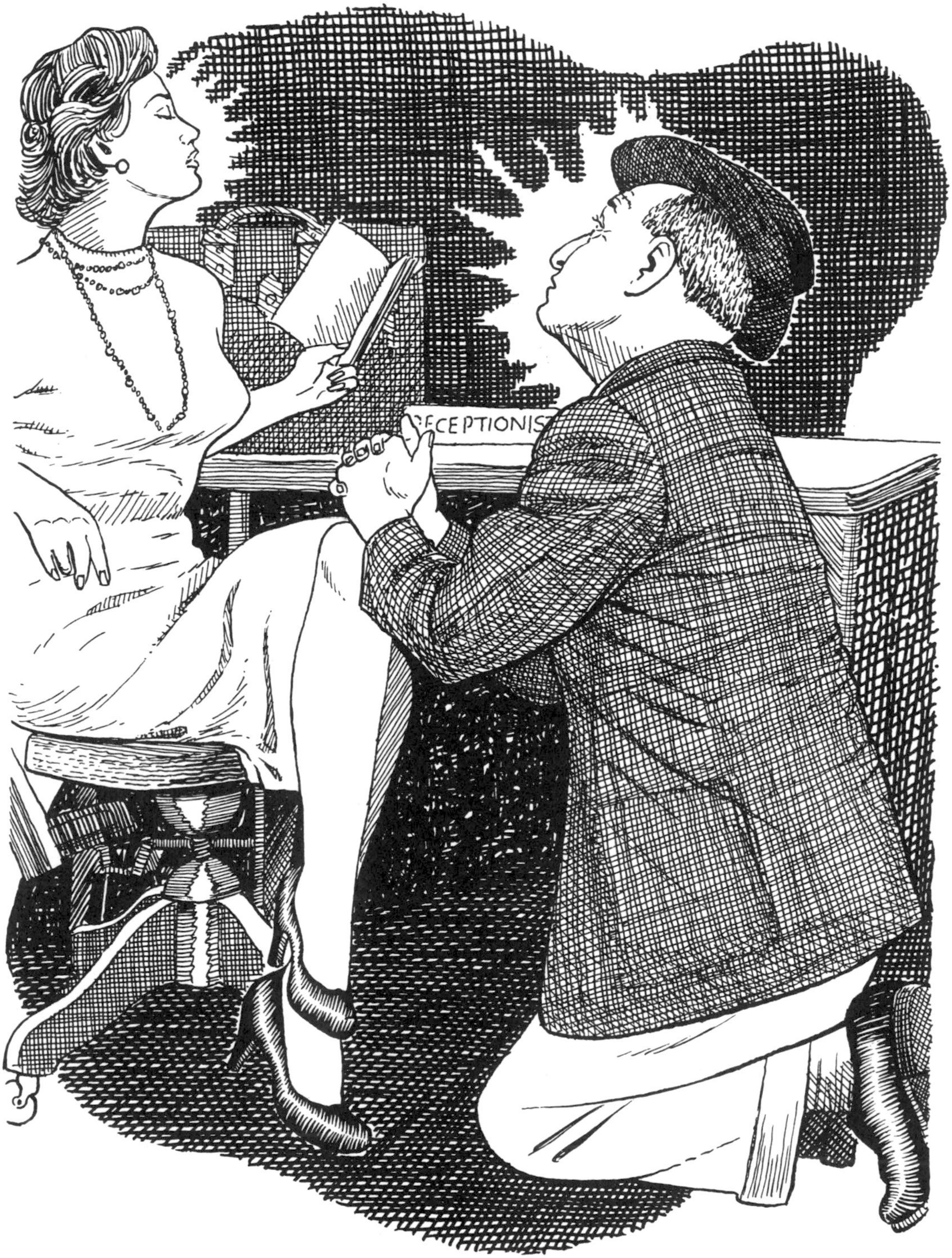
RECEPTIONIST

WHAT'S YOUR BEST APPROACH FOR
GETTING PAST THE GIRL
IN THE OUTER OFFICE?

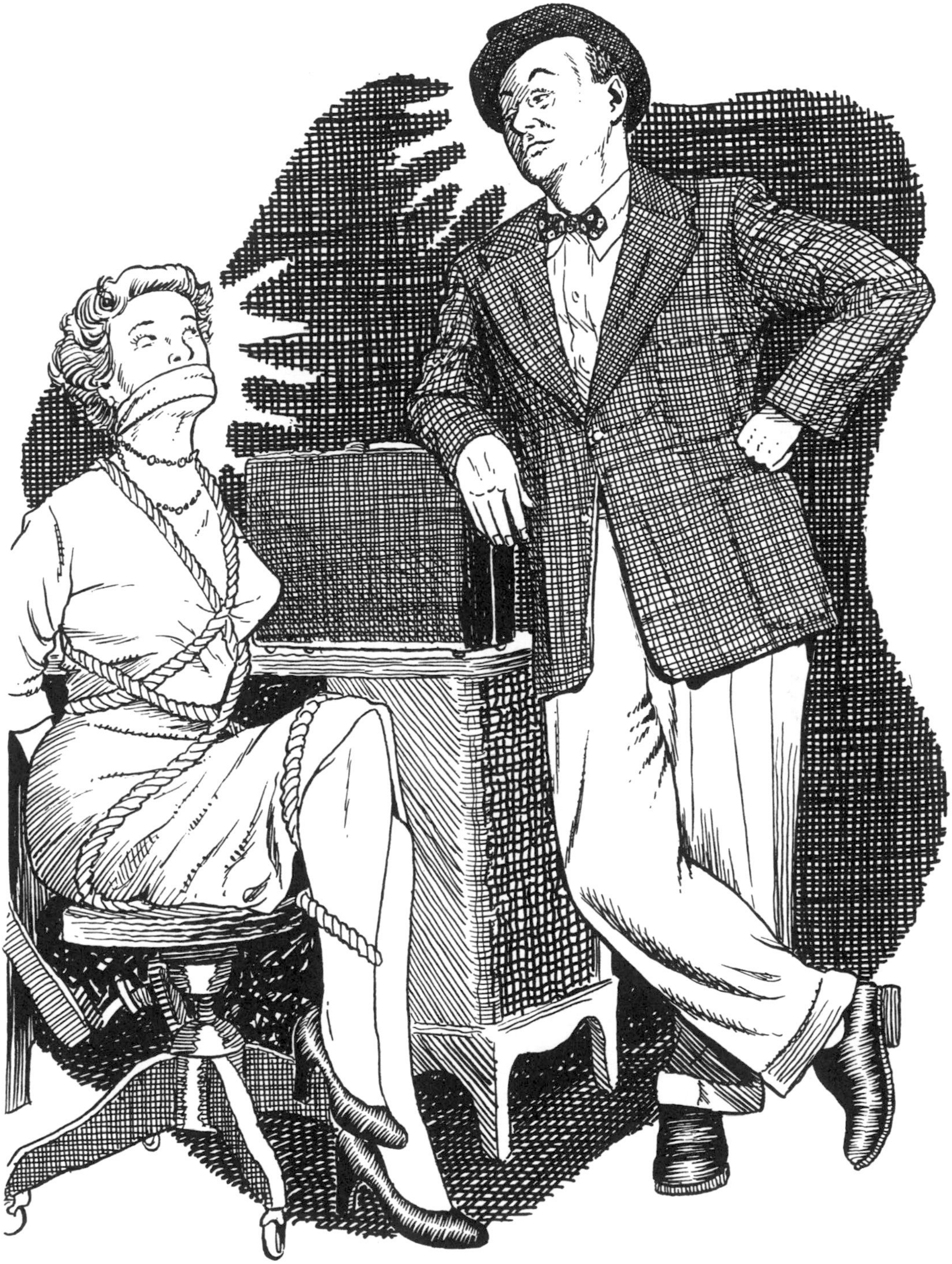

IF THAT FAILS, CAN YOU SUGGEST ANOTHER METHOD FOR GETTING IN?

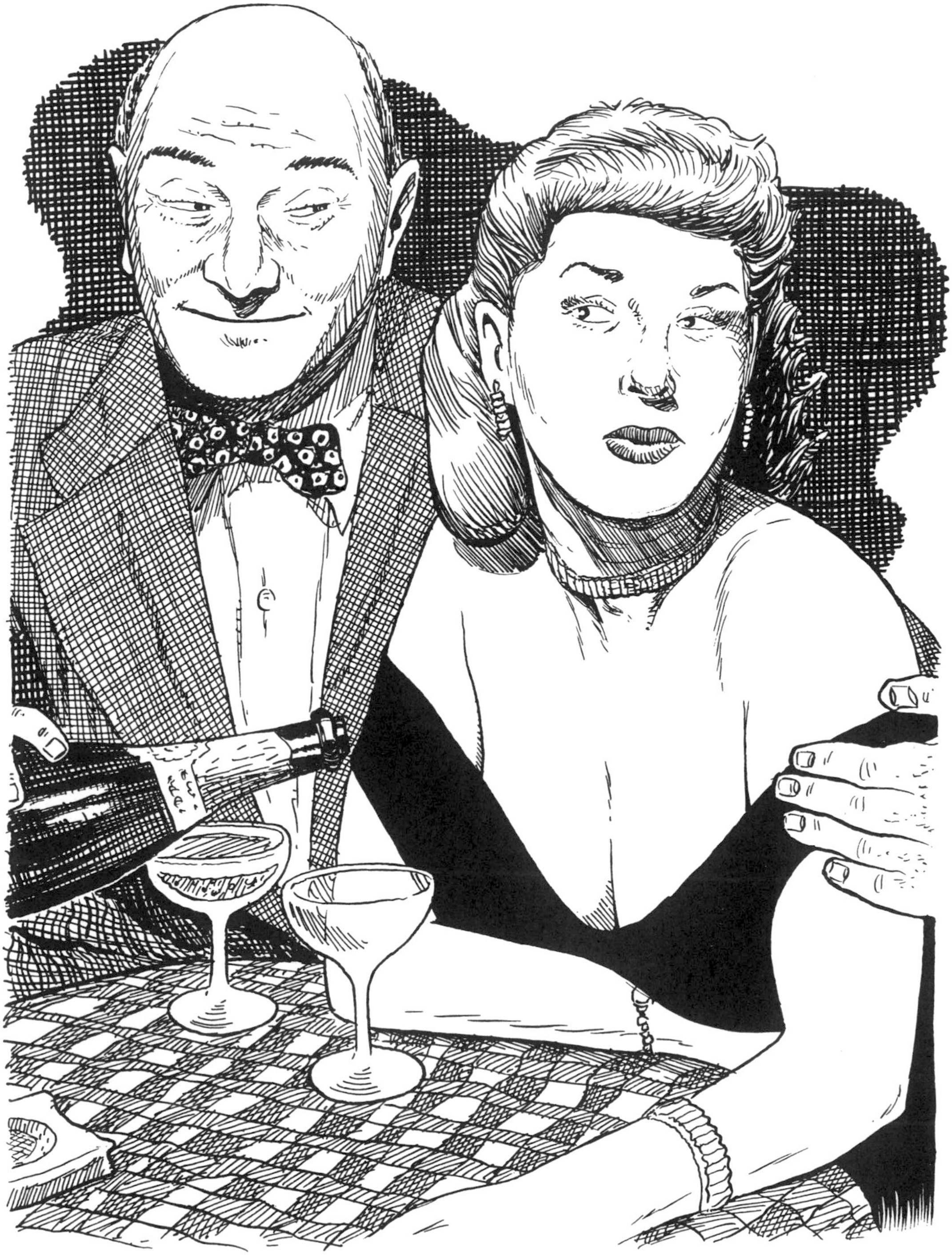

WHAT'S THE MOST EFFECTIVE WAY
TO WARM UP A COLD PROSPECT?

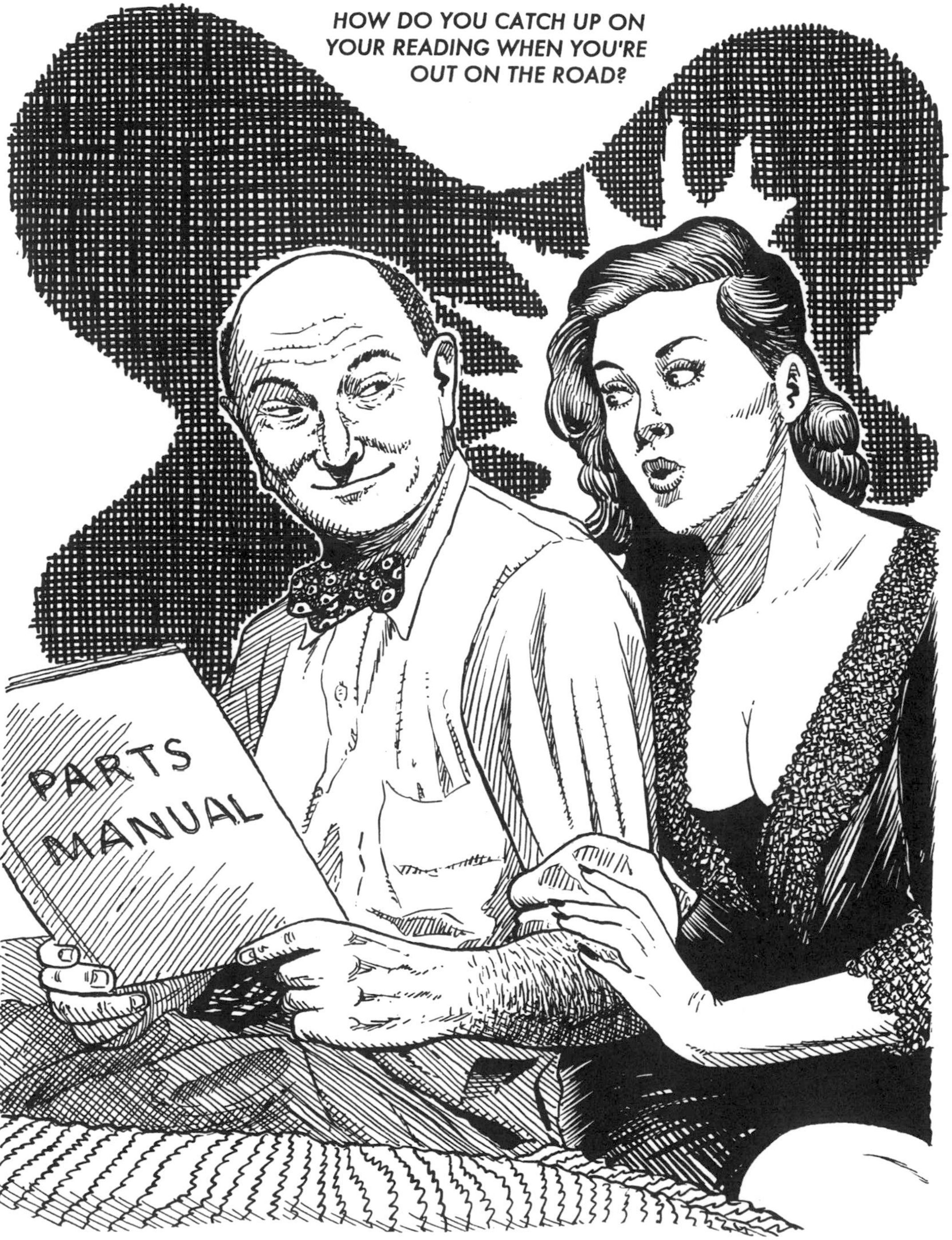
HOW DO YOU CATCH UP ON YOUR READING WHEN YOU'RE OUT ON THE ROAD?
PARTS MANUAL

THESE BAWDY IMAGES, STAGED & SCRIPTED, STILL FUNCTION AS A KIND OF PORTRAIT OF LARIAR THE MAN. I CRINGE & LAUGH AT THEM... BUT *HERE* HE IS... IN ALL HIS BURLESQUE LECHERY... NOT LARIAR THE GO-GETTER... NOT LARIAR THE WRITER... OR THE CARTOONIST... BUT THE MAN MY MOTHER LOVED?

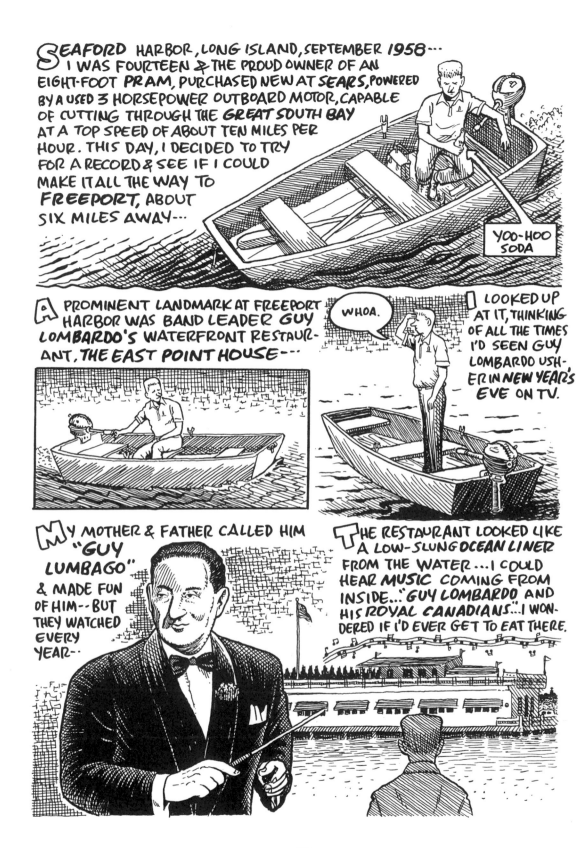

SEAFORD HARBOR, LONG ISLAND, SEPTEMBER 1958... I WAS FOURTEEN & THE PROUD OWNER OF AN EIGHT-FOOT *PRAM*, PURCHASED NEW AT *SEARS*, POWERED BY A USED 3 HORSEPOWER OUTBOARD MOTOR, CAPABLE OF CUTTING THROUGH THE *GREAT SOUTH BAY* AT A TOP SPEED OF ABOUT TEN MILES PER HOUR. THIS DAY, I DECIDED TO TRY FOR A RECORD & SEE IF I COULD MAKE IT ALL THE WAY TO *FREEPORT*, ABOUT SIX MILES AWAY...

YOO-HOO SODA

A PROMINENT LANDMARK AT FREEPORT HARBOR WAS BAND LEADER *GUY LOMBARDO'S* WATERFRONT RESTAURANT, *THE EAST POINT HOUSE*---

WHOA.

I LOOKED UP AT IT, THINKING OF ALL THE TIMES I'D SEEN GUY LOMBARDO USHER IN NEW YEAR'S EVE ON TV.

MY MOTHER & FATHER CALLED HIM "GUY LUMBAGO" & MADE FUN OF HIM-- BUT THEY WATCHED EVERY YEAR--

THE RESTAURANT LOOKED LIKE A LOW-SLUNG *OCEAN LINER* FROM THE WATER... I COULD HEAR *MUSIC* COMING FROM INSIDE..."GUY LOMBARDO AND HIS *ROYAL CANADIANS*"... I WONDERED IF I'D EVER GET TO EAT THERE.

88

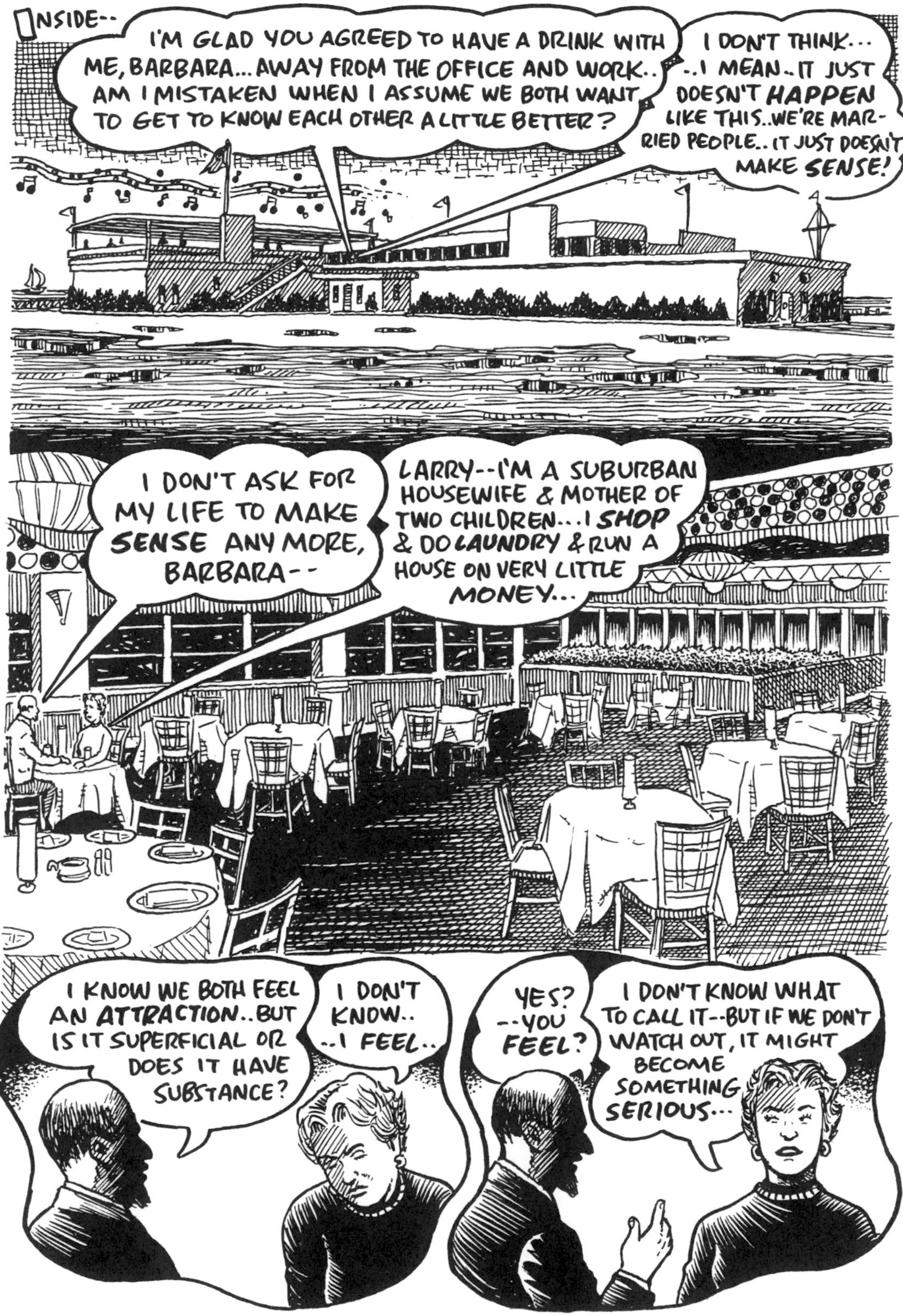
INSIDE--
I'M GLAD YOU AGREED TO HAVE A DRINK WITH ME, BARBARA... AWAY FROM THE OFFICE AND WORK.. AM I MISTAKEN WHEN I ASSUME WE BOTH WANT TO GET TO KNOW EACH OTHER A LITTLE BETTER?
I DON'T THINK... ..I MEAN.. IT JUST DOESN'T HAPPEN LIKE THIS..WE'RE MARRIED PEOPLE.. IT JUST DOESN'T MAKE SENSE!
I DON'T ASK FOR MY LIFE TO MAKE SENSE ANY MORE, BARBARA--
LARRY--I'M A SUBURBAN HOUSEWIFE & MOTHER OF TWO CHILDREN...I SHOP & DO LAUNDRY & RUN A HOUSE ON VERY LITTLE MONEY...
I KNOW WE BOTH FEEL AN ATTRACTION..BUT IS IT SUPERFICIAL OR DOES IT HAVE SUBSTANCE?
I DON'T KNOW.. ..I FEEL..
YES? --YOU FEEL?
I DON'T KNOW WHAT TO CALL IT--BUT IF WE DON'T WATCH OUT, IT MIGHT BECOME SOMETHING SERIOUS...

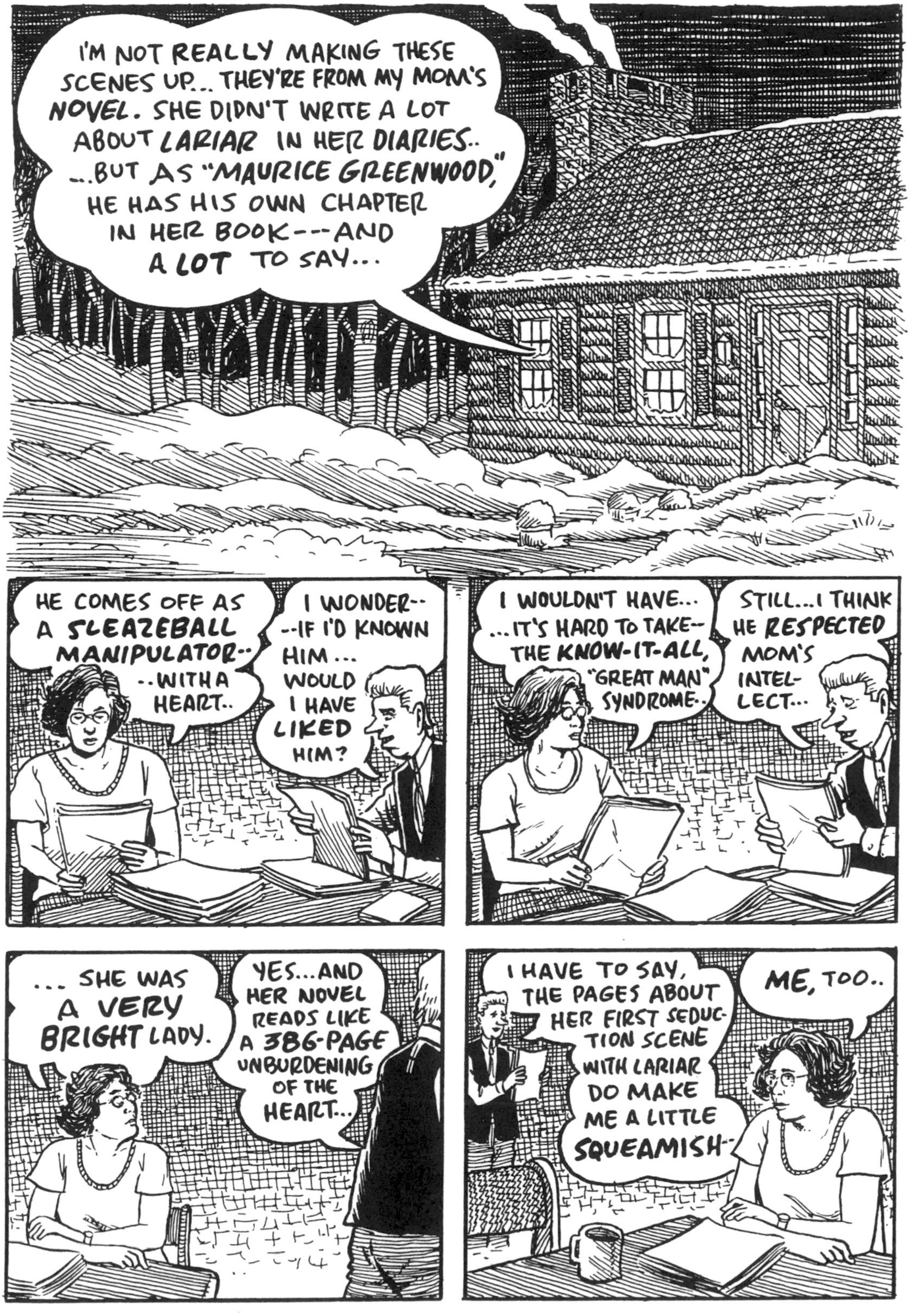
I'M NOT REALLY MAKING THESE SCENES UP... THEY'RE FROM MY MOM'S NOVEL. SHE DIDN'T WRITE A LOT ABOUT LARIAR IN HER DIARIES.. ...BUT AS "MAURICE GREENWOOD," HE HAS HIS OWN CHAPTER IN HER BOOK---AND A LOT TO SAY...
HE COMES OFF AS A SLEAZEBALL MANIPULATOR-- --WITH A HEART..
I WONDER-- --IF I'D KNOWN HIM... WOULD I HAVE LIKED HIM?
I WOULDN'T HAVE... ...IT'S HARD TO TAKE-- THE KNOW-IT-ALL, "GREAT MAN" SYNDROME..
STILL...I THINK HE RESPECTED MOM'S INTEL-LECT...
... SHE WAS A VERY BRIGHT LADY.
YES...AND HER NOVEL READS LIKE A 386-PAGE UNBURDENING OF THE HEART...
I HAVE TO SAY, THE PAGES ABOUT HER FIRST SEDUC-TION SCENE WITH LARIAR DO MAKE ME A LITTLE SQUEAMISH--
ME, TOO..

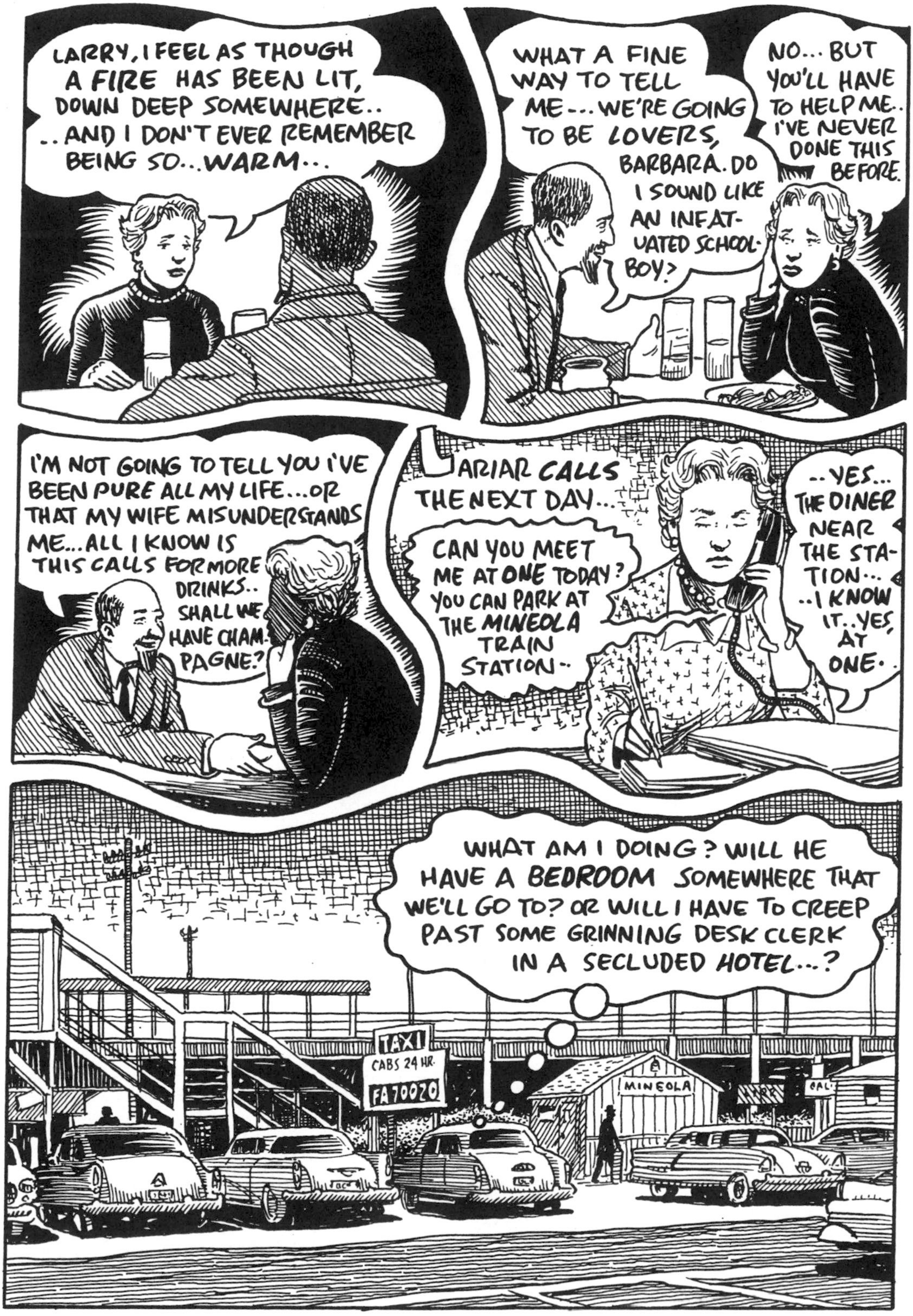

LARRY, I FEEL AS THOUGH A FIRE HAS BEEN LIT, DOWN DEEP SOMEWHERE.. ..AND I DON'T EVER REMEMBER BEING SO...WARM...
WHAT A FINE WAY TO TELL ME... WE'RE GOING TO BE LOVERS, BARBARA. DO I SOUND LIKE AN INFATUATED SCHOOLBOY?
NO... BUT YOU'LL HAVE TO HELP ME.. I'VE NEVER DONE THIS BEFORE.
I'M NOT GOING TO TELL YOU I'VE BEEN PURE ALL MY LIFE...OR THAT MY WIFE MISUNDERSTANDS ME...ALL I KNOW IS THIS CALLS FOR MORE DRINKS.. SHALL WE HAVE CHAMPAGNE?
LARIAR CALLS THE NEXT DAY...
CAN YOU MEET ME AT ONE TODAY? YOU CAN PARK AT THE MINEOLA TRAIN STATION.
..YES... THE DINER NEAR THE STATION... ..I KNOW IT..YES, AT ONE..
WHAT AM I DOING? WILL HE HAVE A BEDROOM SOMEWHERE THAT WE'LL GO TO? OR WILL I HAVE TO CREEP PAST SOME GRINNING DESK CLERK IN A SECLUDED HOTEL...?
TAXI
CABS 24 HR.
FA 70020
MINEOLA

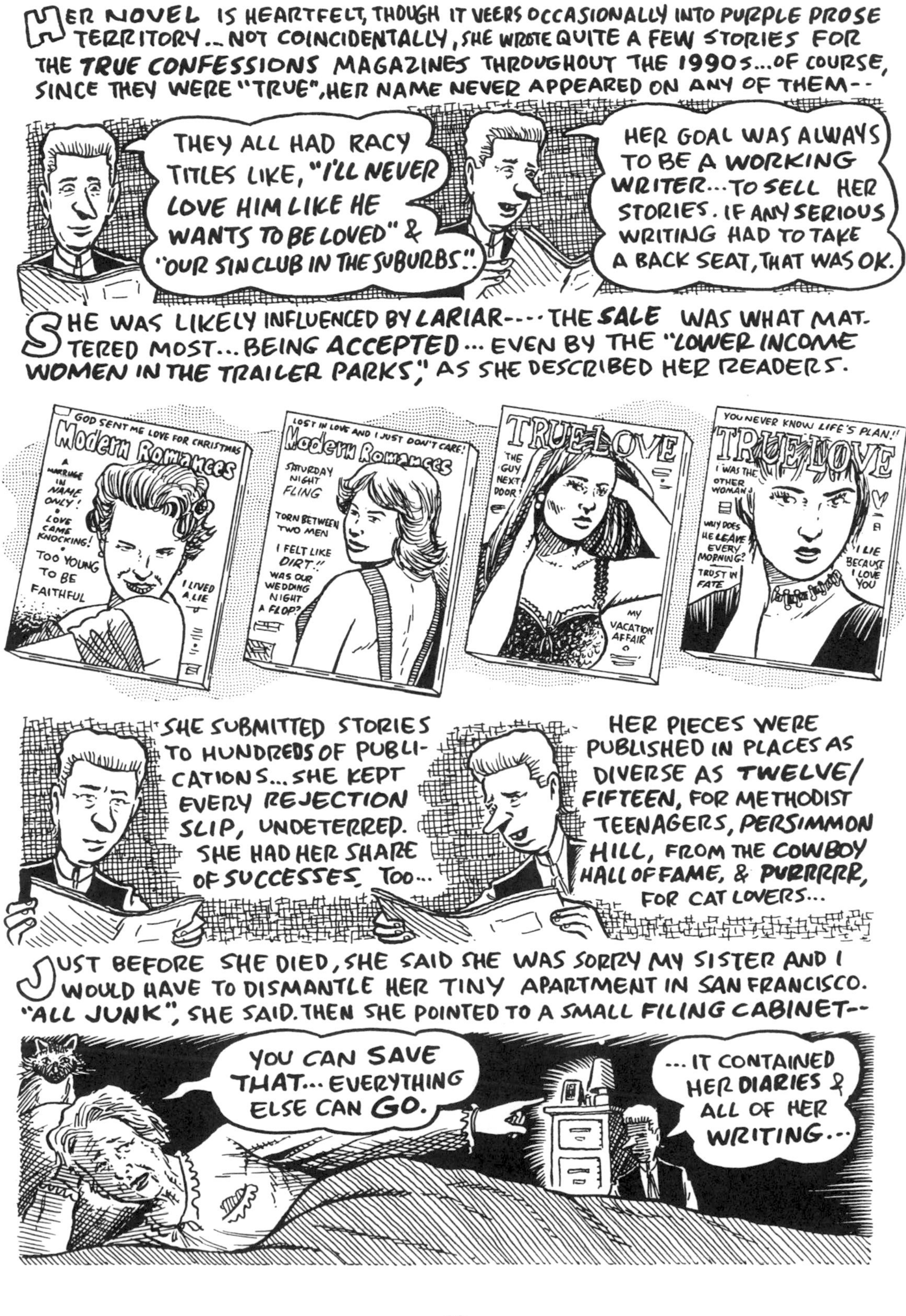
HER NOVEL IS HEARTFELT, THOUGH IT VEERS OCCASIONALLY INTO PURPLE PROSE TERRITORY... NOT COINCIDENTALLY, SHE WROTE QUITE A FEW STORIES FOR THE TRUE CONFESSIONS MAGAZINES THROUGHOUT THE 1990s... OF COURSE, SINCE THEY WERE "TRUE", HER NAME NEVER APPEARED ON ANY OF THEM--
THEY ALL HAD RACY TITLES LIKE, "I'LL NEVER LOVE HIM LIKE HE WANTS TO BE LOVED" & "OUR SIN CLUB IN THE SUBURBS".
HER GOAL WAS ALWAYS TO BE A WORKING WRITER... TO SELL HER STORIES. IF ANY SERIOUS WRITING HAD TO TAKE A BACK SEAT, THAT WAS OK.
SHE WAS LIKELY INFLUENCED BY LARIAR---- THE SALE WAS WHAT MATTERED MOST... BEING ACCEPTED... EVEN BY THE "LOWER INCOME WOMEN IN THE TRAILER PARKS," AS SHE DESCRIBED HER READERS.
GOD SENT ME LOVE FOR CHRISTMAS
Modern Romances
A MARRIAGE IN NAME ONLY!
LOVE CAME KNOCKING!
TOO YOUNG TO BE FAITHFUL
I LIVED A LIE
LOST IN LOVE AND I JUST DON'T CARE!
Modern Romances
SATURDAY NIGHT FLING
TORN BETWEEN TWO MEN
I FELT LIKE DIRT!!
WAS OUR WEDDING NIGHT A FLOP?
TRUE LOVE
THE GUY NEXT DOOR
MY VACATION AFFAIR
YOU NEVER KNOW LIFE'S PLAN!!
TRUE LOVE
I WAS THE OTHER WOMAN
WHY DOES HE LEAVE EVERY MORNING?
TRUST IN FATE
I LIE BECAUSE I LOVE YOU
SHE SUBMITTED STORIES TO HUNDREDS OF PUBLICATIONS... SHE KEPT EVERY REJECTION SLIP, UNDETERRED. SHE HAD HER SHARE OF SUCCESSES, TOO...
HER PIECES WERE PUBLISHED IN PLACES AS DIVERSE AS TWELVE/FIFTEEN, FOR METHODIST TEENAGERS, PERSIMMON HILL, FROM THE COWBOY HALL OF FAME, & PURRRRR, FOR CAT LOVERS...
JUST BEFORE SHE DIED, SHE SAID SHE WAS SORRY MY SISTER AND I WOULD HAVE TO DISMANTLE HER TINY APARTMENT IN SAN FRANCISCO. "ALL JUNK", SHE SAID. THEN SHE POINTED TO A SMALL FILING CABINET--
YOU CAN SAVE THAT... EVERYTHING ELSE CAN GO.
...IT CONTAINED HER DIARIES & ALL OF HER WRITING...

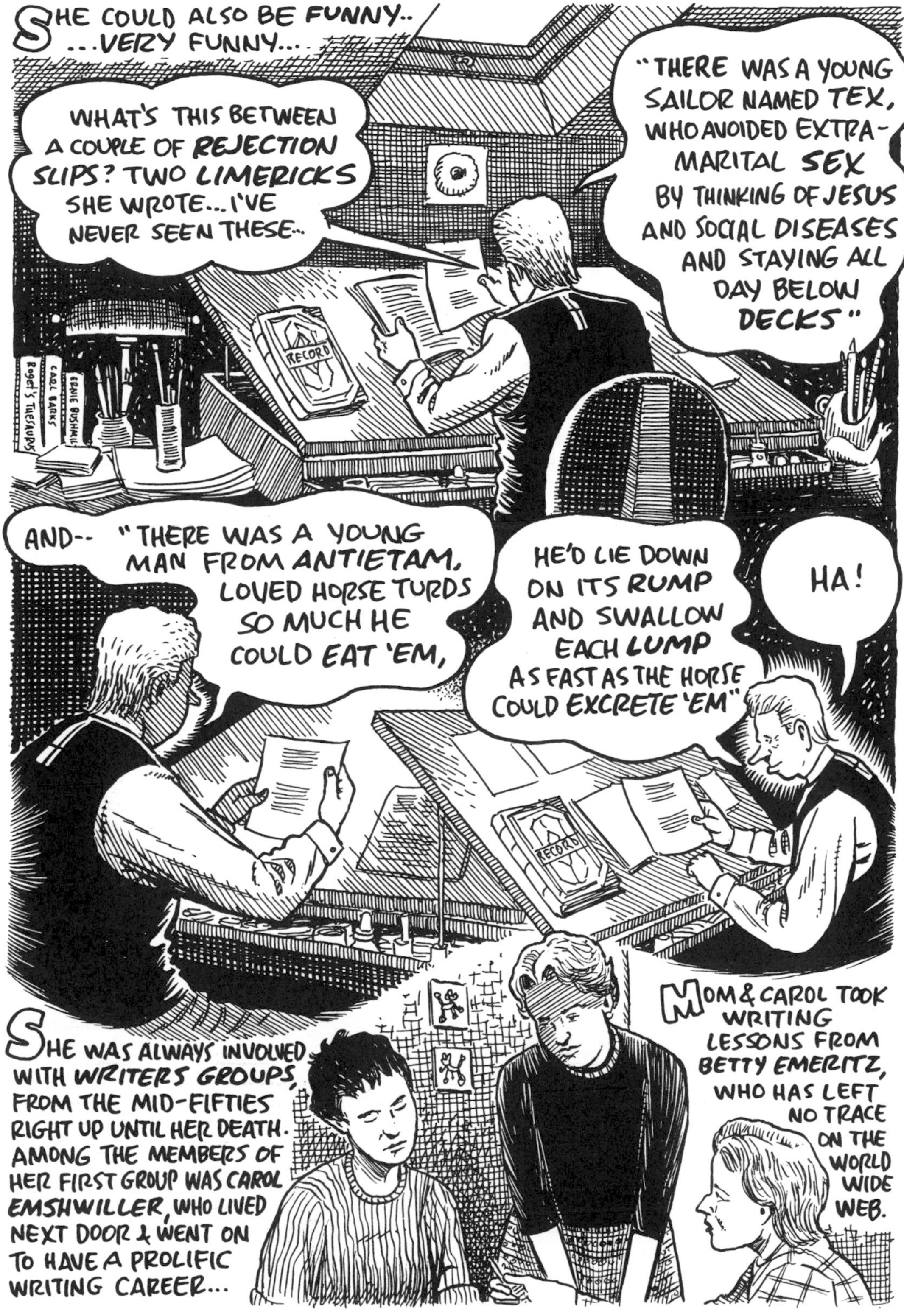
SHE COULD ALSO BE FUNNY.. ...VERY FUNNY...
WHAT'S THIS BETWEEN A COUPLE OF REJECTION SLIPS? TWO LIMERICKS SHE WROTE... I'VE NEVER SEEN THESE..
"THERE WAS A YOUNG SAILOR NAMED TEX, WHO AVOIDED EXTRA-MARITAL SEX BY THINKING OF JESUS AND SOCIAL DISEASES AND STAYING ALL DAY BELOW DECKS"
RECORD
ROGET'S THESAURUS
CARL BARKS
ERNIE BUSHMILLER
AND-- "THERE WAS A YOUNG MAN FROM ANTIETAM, LOVED HORSE TURDS SO MUCH HE COULD EAT 'EM,
HE'D LIE DOWN ON ITS RUMP AND SWALLOW EACH LUMP AS FAST AS THE HORSE COULD EXCRETE 'EM"
HA!
RECORD
SHE WAS ALWAYS INVOLVED WITH WRITERS GROUPS, FROM THE MID-FIFTIES RIGHT UP UNTIL HER DEATH. AMONG THE MEMBERS OF HER FIRST GROUP WAS CAROL EMSHWILLER, WHO LIVED NEXT DOOR & WENT ON TO HAVE A PROLIFIC WRITING CAREER...
MOM & CAROL TOOK WRITING LESSONS FROM BETTY EMERITZ, WHO HAS LEFT NO TRACE ON THE WORLD WIDE WEB.

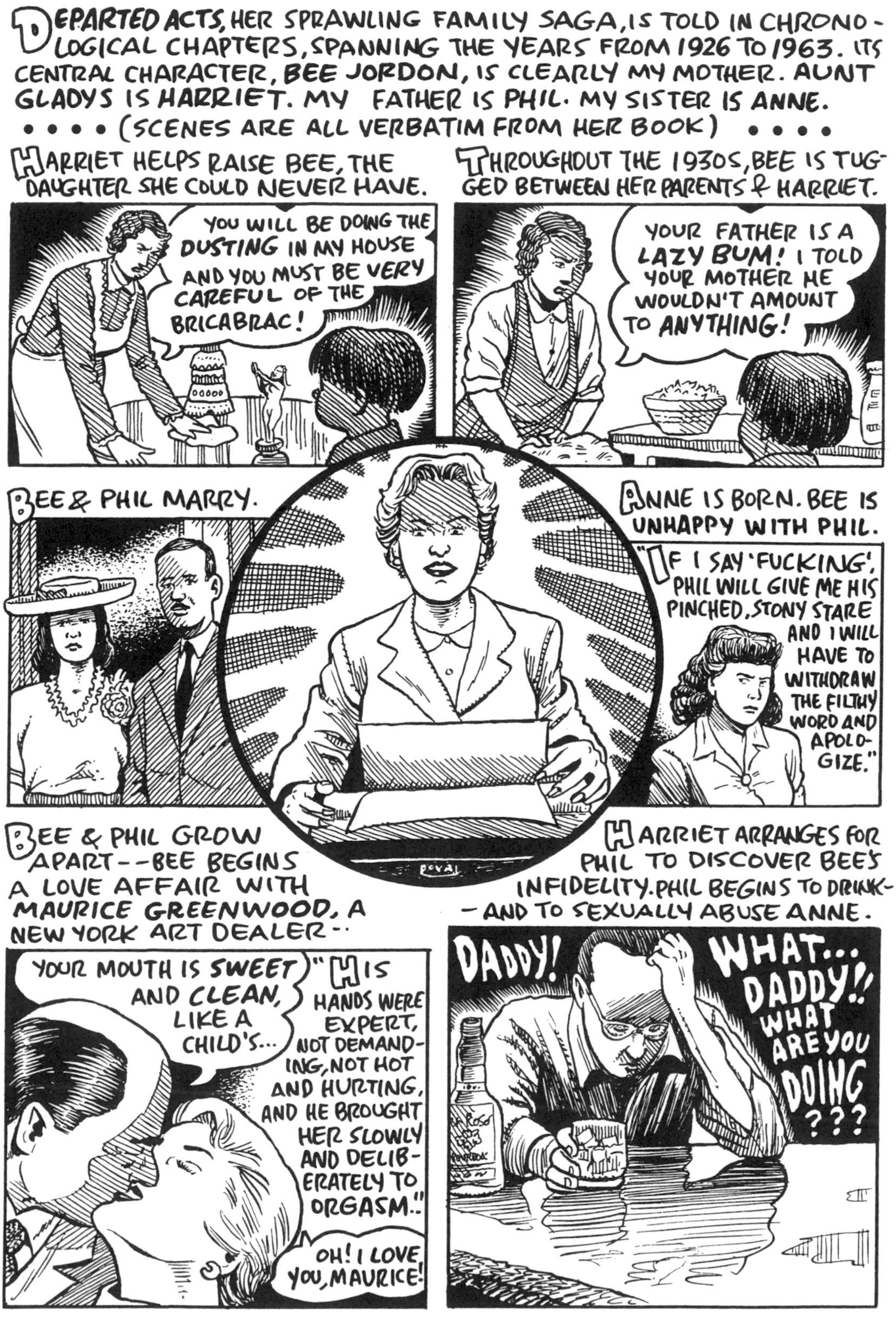
DEPARTED ACTS, HER SPRAWLING FAMILY SAGA, IS TOLD IN CHRONOLOGICAL CHAPTERS, SPANNING THE YEARS FROM 1926 TO 1963. ITS CENTRAL CHARACTER, BEE JORDON, IS CLEARLY MY MOTHER. AUNT GLADYS IS HARRIET. MY FATHER IS PHIL. MY SISTER IS ANNE.
• • • • (SCENES ARE ALL VERBATIM FROM HER BOOK) • • • •
HARRIET HELPS RAISE BEE, THE DAUGHTER SHE COULD NEVER HAVE.
YOU WILL BE DOING THE DUSTING IN MY HOUSE AND YOU MUST BE VERY CAREFUL OF THE BRICABRAC!
THROUGHOUT THE 1930S, BEE IS TUGGED BETWEEN HER PARENTS & HARRIET.
YOUR FATHER IS A LAZY BUM! I TOLD YOUR MOTHER HE WOULDN'T AMOUNT TO ANYTHING!
BEE & PHIL MARRY.
ROYAL
ANNE IS BORN. BEE IS UNHAPPY WITH PHIL.
"IF I SAY 'FUCKING', PHIL WILL GIVE ME HIS PINCHED, STONY STARE AND I WILL HAVE TO WITHDRAW THE FILTHY WORD AND APOLOGIZE."
BEE & PHIL GROW APART--BEE BEGINS A LOVE AFFAIR WITH MAURICE GREENWOOD, A NEW YORK ART DEALER--
YOUR MOUTH IS SWEET AND CLEAN, LIKE A CHILD'S...
"HIS HANDS WERE EXPERT, NOT DEMANDING, NOT HOT AND HURTING, AND HE BROUGHT HER SLOWLY AND DELIBERATELY TO ORGASM."
OH! I LOVE YOU, MAURICE!
HARRIET ARRANGES FOR PHIL TO DISCOVER BEE'S INFIDELITY. PHIL BEGINS TO DRINK--AND TO SEXUALLY ABUSE ANNE.
DADDY!
WHAT... DADDY!! WHAT ARE YOU DOING???

THE BOOK'S TITLE IS DERIVED FROM A POEM BY EMILY DICKINSON:

Remorse is memory awake,
Her companies astir,
A presence of departed acts
At window and at door.

Its past set down before the soul,
And lighted with a match,
Perusal to facilitate
Of its condensed despatch.

Remorse is cureless, the disease
Not even God can heal:
For 'tis his institution,
The complement of Hell.

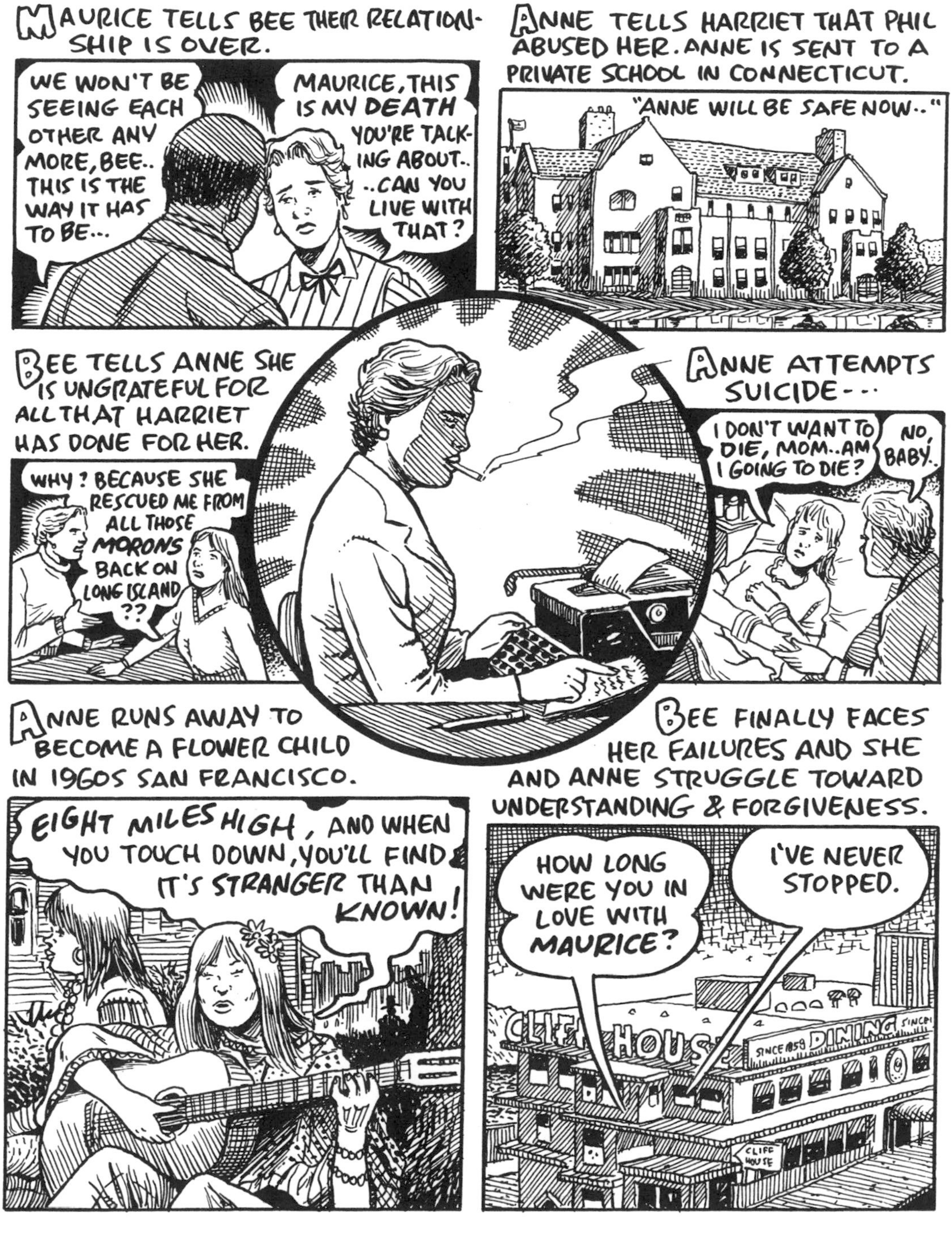
MAURICE TELLS BEE THEIR RELATIONSHIP IS OVER.
WE WON'T BE SEEING EACH OTHER ANY MORE, BEE.. THIS IS THE WAY IT HAS TO BE...
MAURICE, THIS IS MY DEATH YOU'RE TALKING ABOUT.. ..CAN YOU LIVE WITH THAT?
ANNE TELLS HARRIET THAT PHIL ABUSED HER. ANNE IS SENT TO A PRIVATE SCHOOL IN CONNECTICUT.
"ANNE WILL BE SAFE NOW.."
BEE TELLS ANNE SHE IS UNGRATEFUL FOR ALL THAT HARRIET HAS DONE FOR HER.
WHY? BECAUSE SHE RESCUED ME FROM ALL THOSE MORONS BACK ON LONG ISLAND??
ANNE ATTEMPTS SUICIDE---
I DON'T WANT TO DIE, MOM..AM I GOING TO DIE?
NO, BABY.
ANNE RUNS AWAY TO BECOME A FLOWER CHILD IN 1960S SAN FRANCISCO.
EIGHT MILES HIGH, AND WHEN YOU TOUCH DOWN, YOU'LL FIND IT'S STRANGER THAN KNOWN!
BEE FINALLY FACES HER FAILURES AND SHE AND ANNE STRUGGLE TOWARD UNDERSTANDING & FORGIVENESS.
HOW LONG WERE YOU IN LOVE WITH MAURICE?
I'VE NEVER STOPPED.
CLIFF HOUSE
SINCE 1859 DINING
CLIFF HOUSE

MAURICE GREENWOOD ENTERED BEE'S LIFE IN 1950. LAWRENCE LARIAR ENTERED MY MOTHER'S LIFE IN 1957. MAURICE OWNED AN ART GALLERY IN NEW YORK. LARIAR WAS A CARTOONIST AND CRIME FICTION WRITER WITH AN OFFICE IN NEW YORK. THE FACTS DON'T ALWAYS EQUATE, BUT THE UNDERLYING TRUTHS DO---

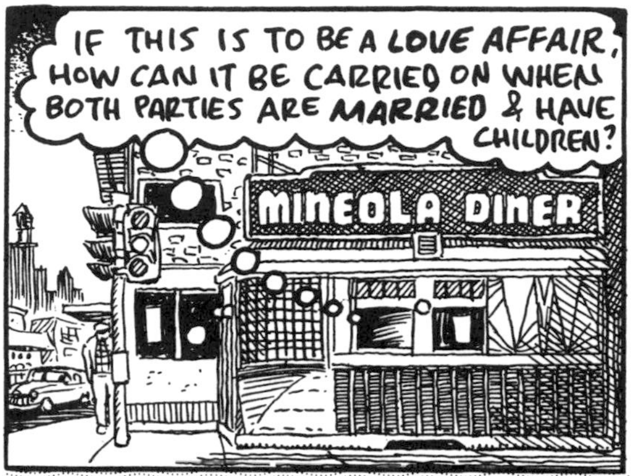

IF THIS IS TO BE A LOVE AFFAIR, HOW CAN IT BE CARRIED ON WHEN BOTH PARTIES ARE MARRIED & HAVE CHILDREN?
MINEOLA DINER

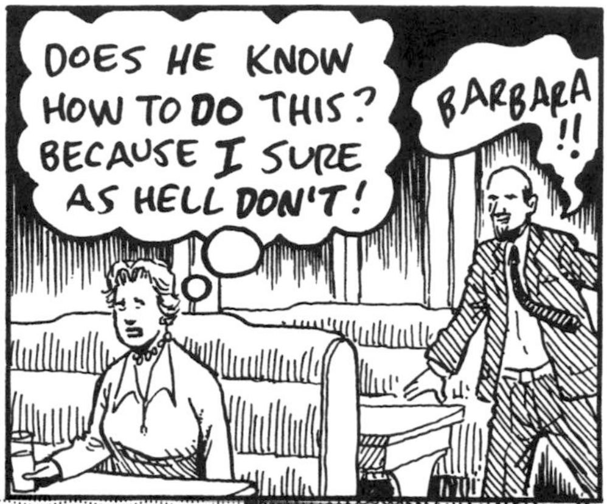

DOES HE KNOW HOW TO DO THIS? BECAUSE I SURE AS HELL DON'T!
BARBARA!!

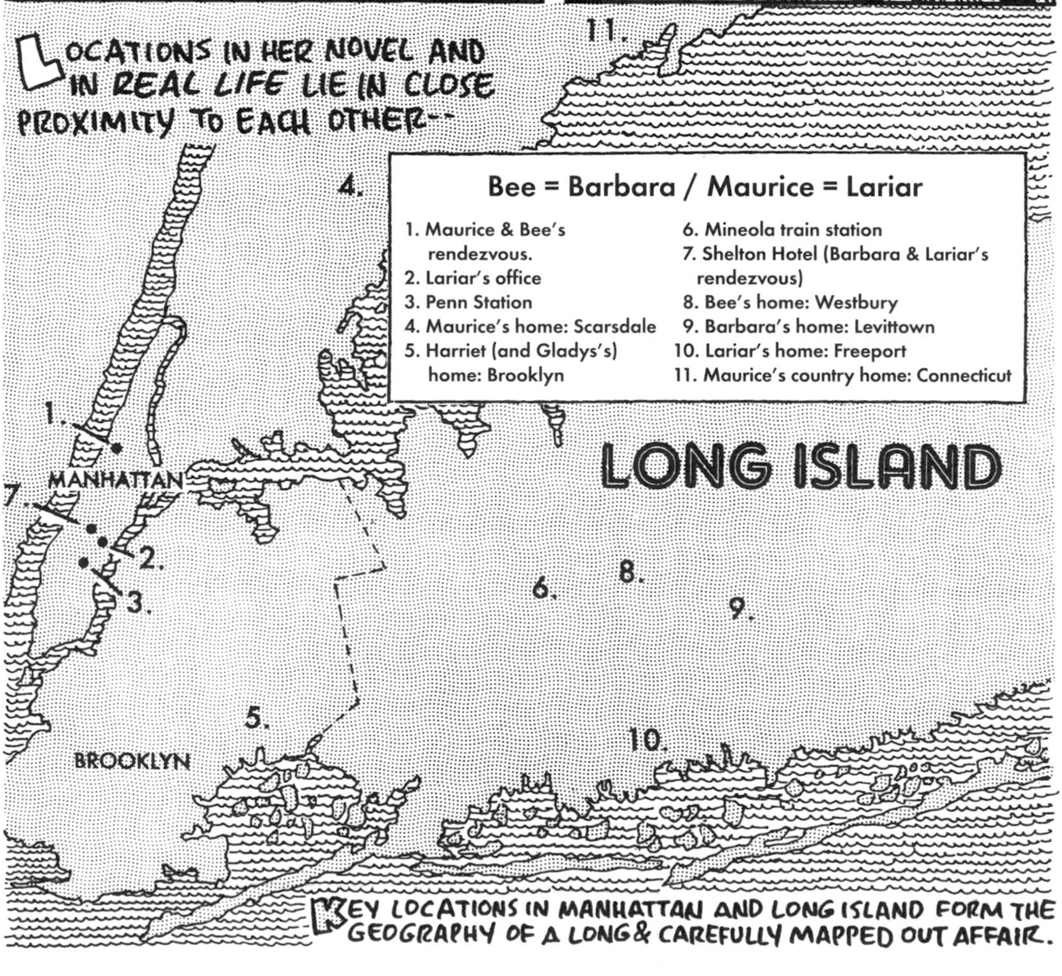

LOCATIONS IN HER NOVEL AND IN REAL LIFE LIE IN CLOSE PROXIMITY TO EACH OTHER--
Bee = Barbara / Maurice = Lariar
1. Maurice & Bee's rendezvous.
2. Lariar's office
3. Penn Station
4. Maurice's home: Scarsdale
5. Harriet (and Gladys's) home: Brooklyn
6. Mineola train station
7. Shelton Hotel (Barbara & Lariar's rendezvous)
8. Bee's home: Westbury
9. Barbara's home: Levittown
10. Lariar's home: Freeport
11. Maurice's country home: Connecticut
11.
4.
1.
MANHATTAN
7.
2.
3.
LONG ISLAND
8.
6.
9.
5.
BROOKLYN
10.
KEY LOCATIONS IN MANHATTAN AND LONG ISLAND FORM THE GEOGRAPHY OF A LONG & CAREFULLY MAPPED OUT AFFAIR.

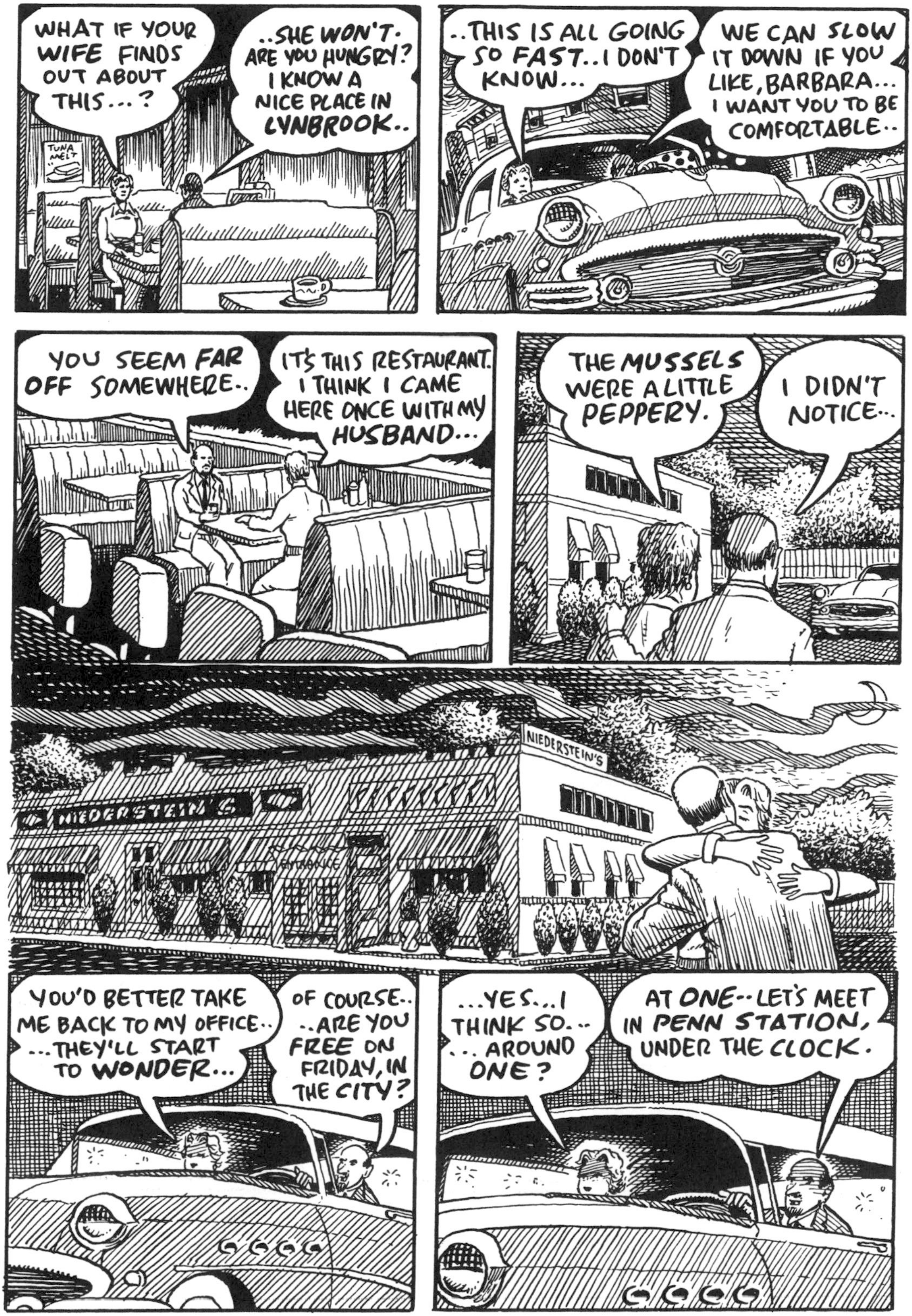

WHAT IF YOUR WIFE FINDS OUT ABOUT THIS...?
TUNA MELT
..SHE WON'T. ARE YOU HUNGRY? I KNOW A NICE PLACE IN LYNBROOK..
..THIS IS ALL GOING SO FAST..I DON'T KNOW...
WE CAN SLOW IT DOWN IF YOU LIKE, BARBARA... I WANT YOU TO BE COMFORTABLE..
YOU SEEM FAR OFF SOMEWHERE..
IT'S THIS RESTAURANT. I THINK I CAME HERE ONCE WITH MY HUSBAND...
THE MUSSELS WERE A LITTLE PEPPERY.
I DIDN'T NOTICE...
NIEDERSTEIN'S
NIEDERSTEIN'S
ENTRANCE
YOU'D BETTER TAKE ME BACK TO MY OFFICE.. ...THEY'LL START TO WONDER...
OF COURSE.. ..ARE YOU FREE ON FRIDAY, IN THE CITY?
...YES...I THINK SO.. ...AROUND ONE?
AT ONE--LET'S MEET IN PENN STATION, UNDER THE CLOCK.

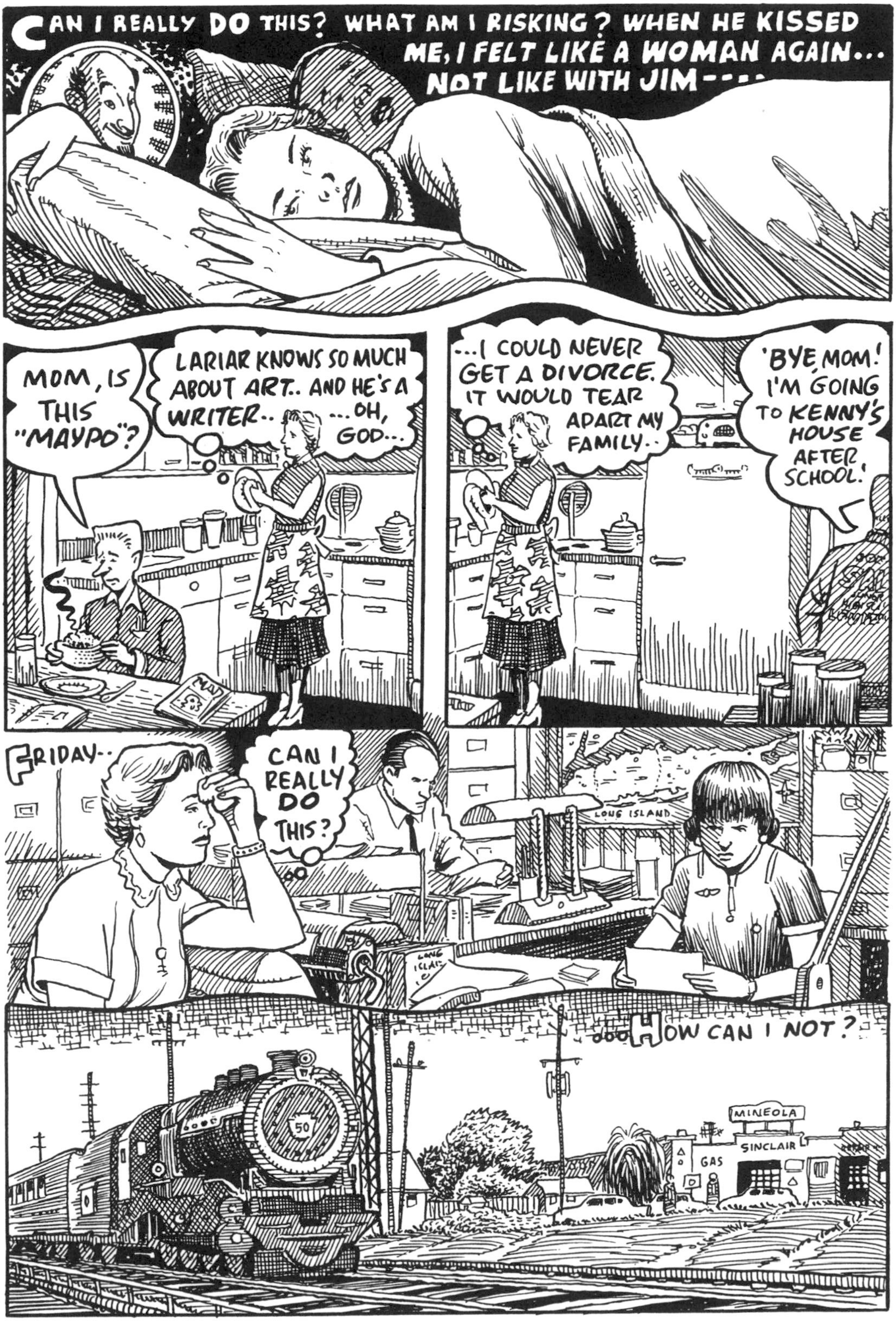
CAN I REALLY DO THIS? WHAT AM I RISKING? WHEN HE KISSED ME, I FELT LIKE A WOMAN AGAIN... NOT LIKE WITH JIM----
MOM, IS THIS "MAYPO"?
LARIAR KNOWS SO MUCH ABOUT ART.. AND HE'S A WRITER.. ...OH, GOD...
...I COULD NEVER GET A DIVORCE. IT WOULD TEAR APART MY FAMILY..
'BYE, MOM! I'M GOING TO KENNY'S HOUSE AFTER SCHOOL.'
FRIDAY..
CAN I REALLY DO THIS?
LONG ISLAND
...HOW CAN I NOT?
MINEOLA
SINCLAIR
GAS

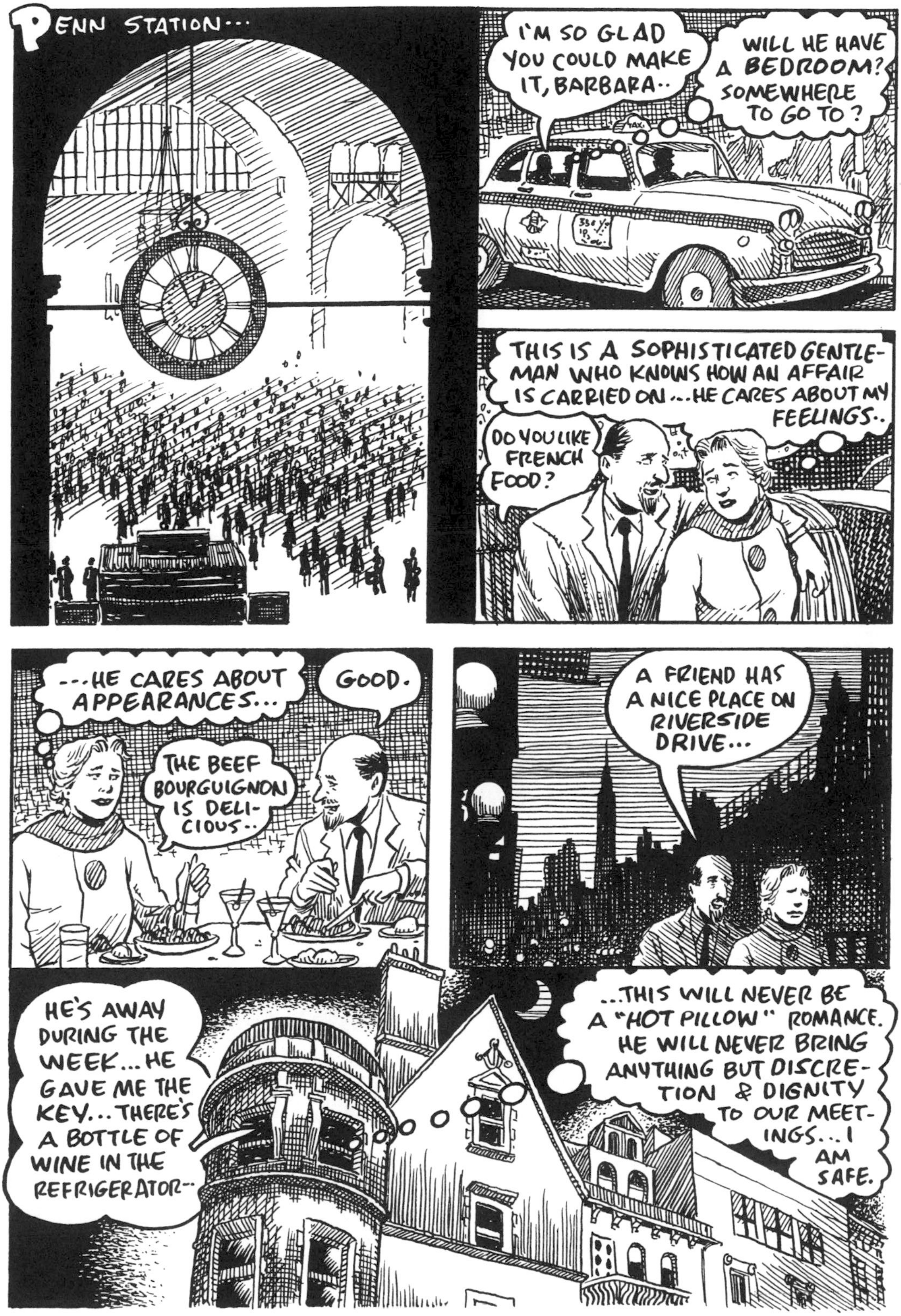
PENN STATION...
I'M SO GLAD YOU COULD MAKE IT, BARBARA..
WILL HE HAVE A BEDROOM? SOMEWHERE TO GO TO?
TAXI
THIS IS A SOPHISTICATED GENTLEMAN WHO KNOWS HOW AN AFFAIR IS CARRIED ON...HE CARES ABOUT MY FEELINGS..
DO YOU LIKE FRENCH FOOD?
...HE CARES ABOUT APPEARANCES...
GOOD.
THE BEEF BOURGUIGNON IS DELICIOUS..
A FRIEND HAS A NICE PLACE ON RIVERSIDE DRIVE...
HE'S AWAY DURING THE WEEK...HE GAVE ME THE KEY...THERE'S A BOTTLE OF WINE IN THE REFRIGERATOR--
...THIS WILL NEVER BE A "HOT PILLOW" ROMANCE. HE WILL NEVER BRING ANYTHING BUT DISCRETION & DIGNITY TO OUR MEETINGS...I AM SAFE.

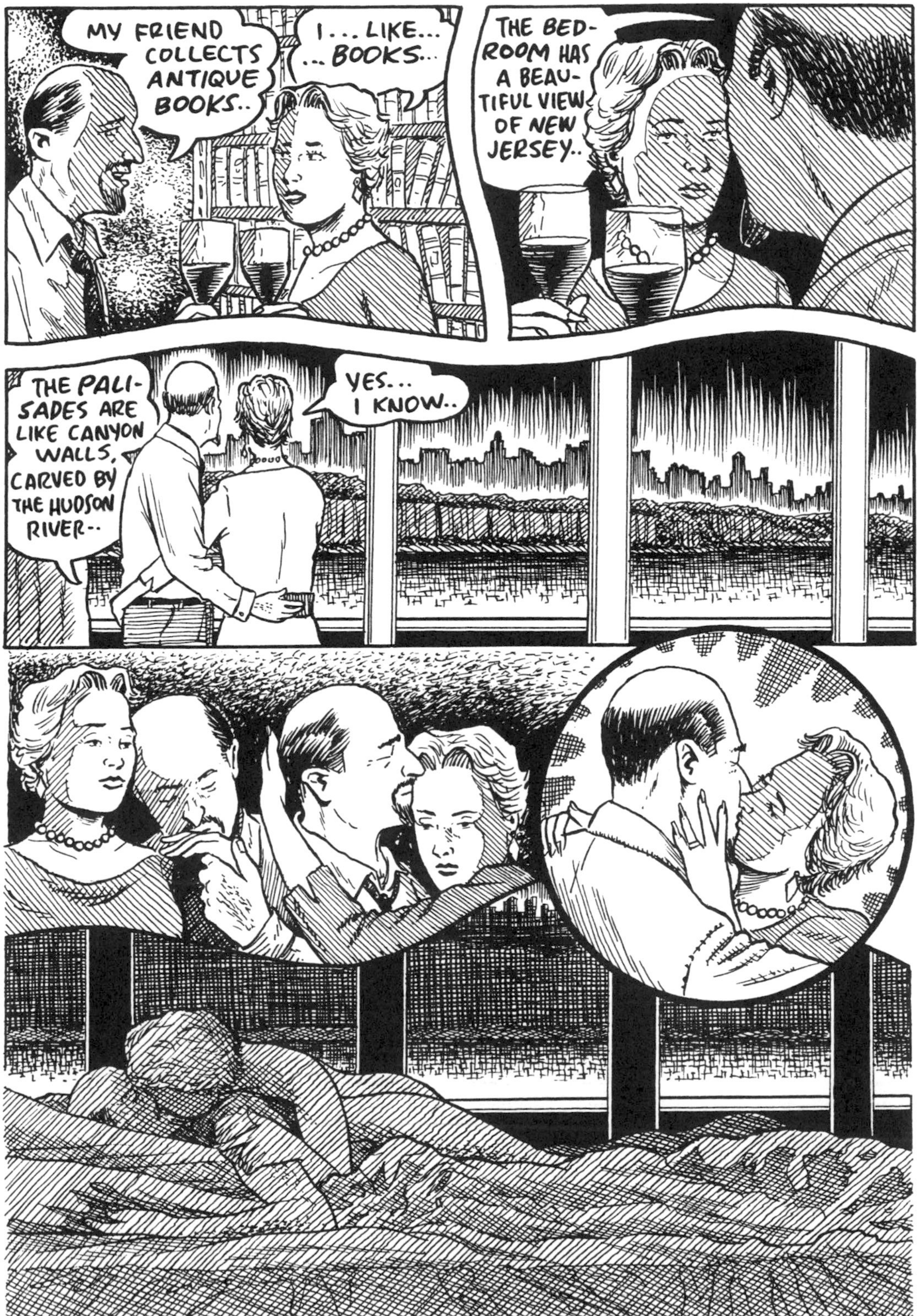

MY FRIEND COLLECTS ANTIQUE BOOKS..
I... LIKE... ...BOOKS...
THE BED-ROOM HAS A BEAU-TIFUL VIEW OF NEW JERSEY..
THE PALI-SADES ARE LIKE CANYON WALLS, CARVED BY THE HUDSON RIVER..
YES... I KNOW..

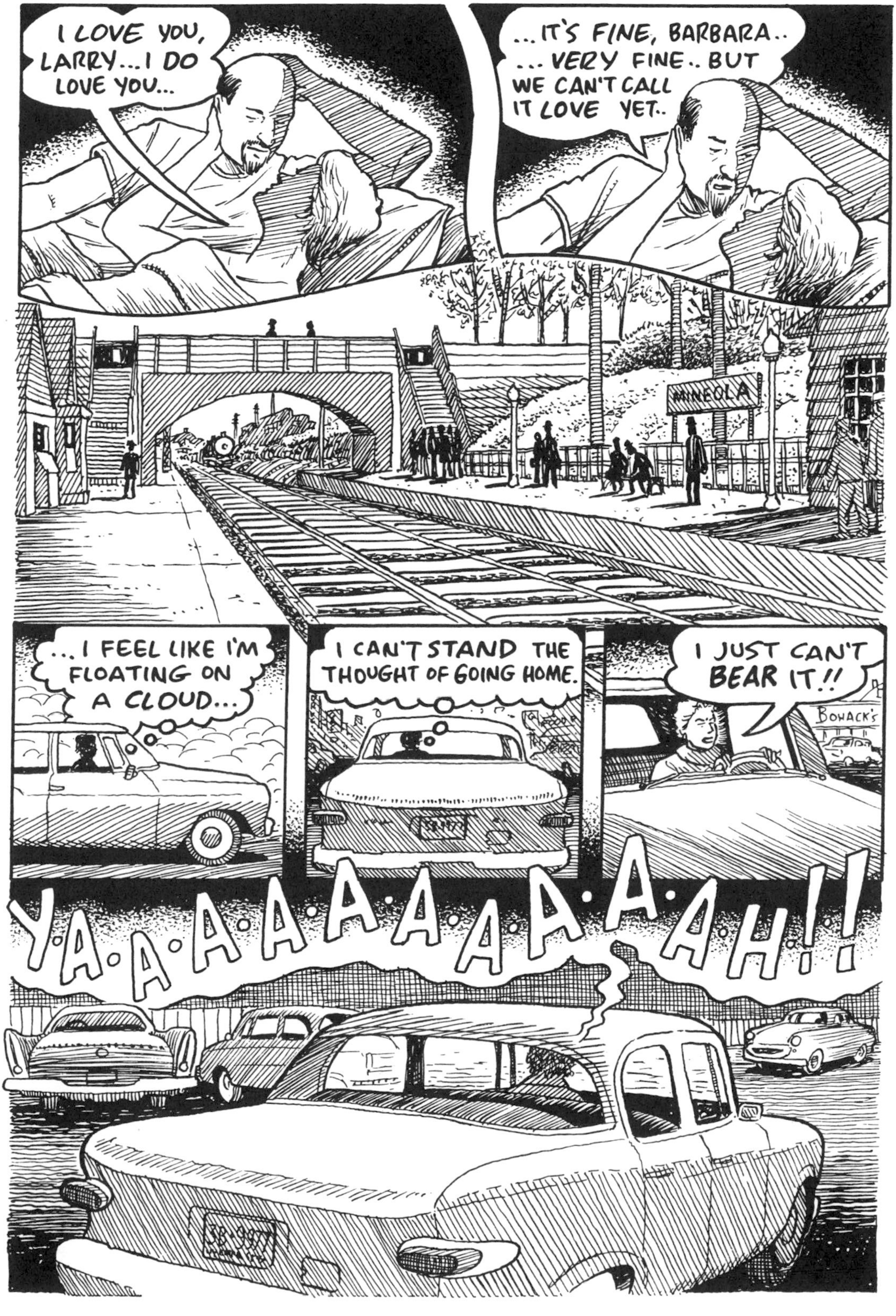
I LOVE YOU, LARRY...I DO LOVE YOU...
...IT'S FINE, BARBARA.. ...VERY FINE.. BUT WE CAN'T CALL IT LOVE YET..
MINEOLA
...I FEEL LIKE I'M FLOATING ON A CLOUD...
I CAN'T STAND THE THOUGHT OF GOING HOME.
I JUST CAN'T BEAR IT!!
BOHACK'S
YA-A-A-A-A-A-A-A-A-A-AH!!

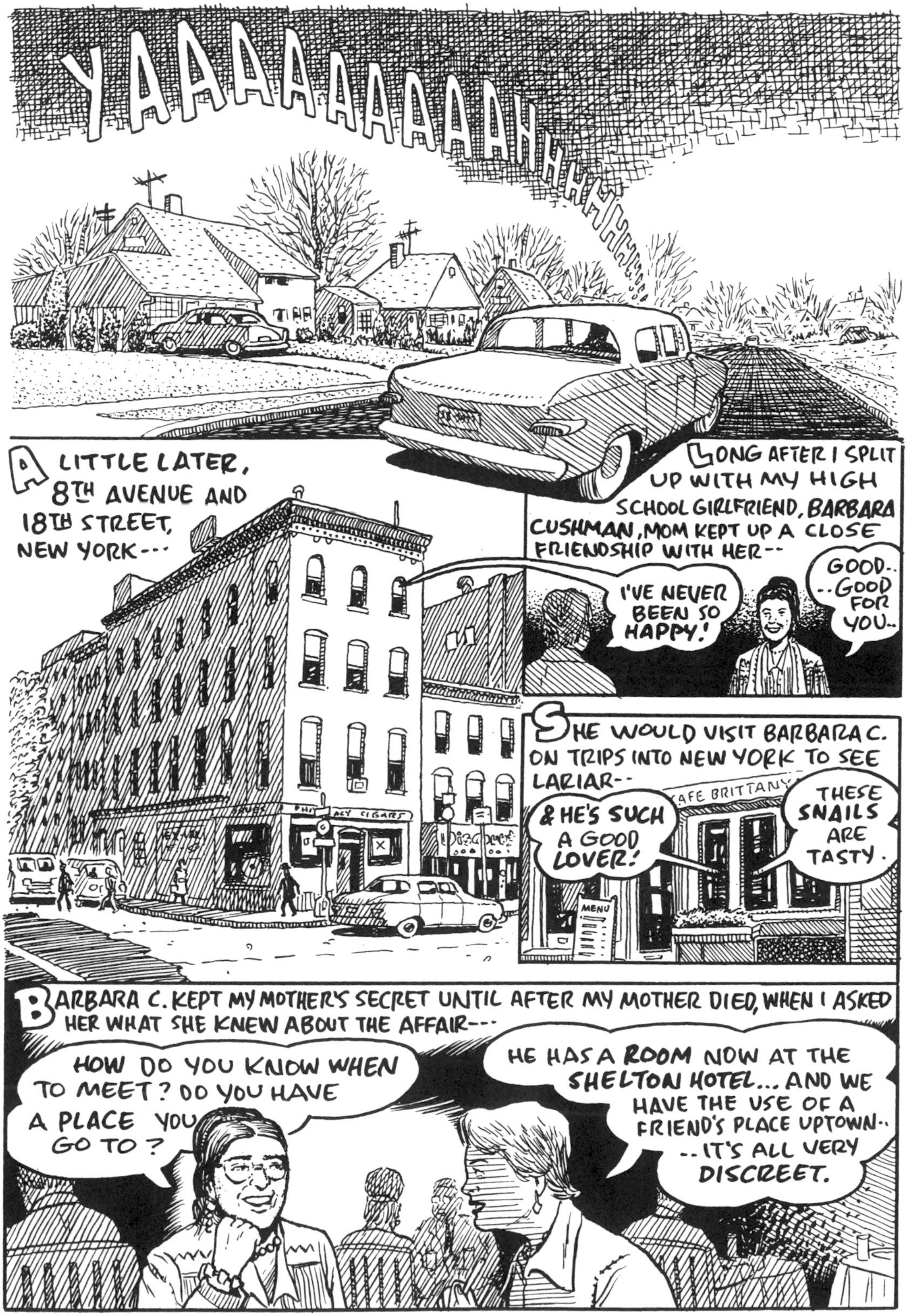
YAAAAAAAAAAHHHHHHHH
A LITTLE LATER, 8TH AVENUE AND 18TH STREET, NEW YORK---
LONG AFTER I SPLIT UP WITH MY HIGH SCHOOL GIRLFRIEND, BARBARA CUSHMAN, MOM KEPT UP A CLOSE FRIENDSHIP WITH HER--
I'VE NEVER BEEN SO HAPPY!
GOOD.. ..GOOD FOR YOU..
SHE WOULD VISIT BARBARA C. ON TRIPS INTO NEW YORK TO SEE LARIAR--
CAFE BRITTANY
& HE'S SUCH A GOOD LOVER!
THESE SNAILS ARE TASTY.
MENU
BARBARA C. KEPT MY MOTHER'S SECRET UNTIL AFTER MY MOTHER DIED, WHEN I ASKED HER WHAT SHE KNEW ABOUT THE AFFAIR---
HOW DO YOU KNOW WHEN TO MEET? DO YOU HAVE A PLACE YOU GO TO?
HE HAS A ROOM NOW AT THE SHELTON HOTEL... AND WE HAVE THE USE OF A FRIEND'S PLACE UPTOWN.. ..IT'S ALL VERY DISCREET.

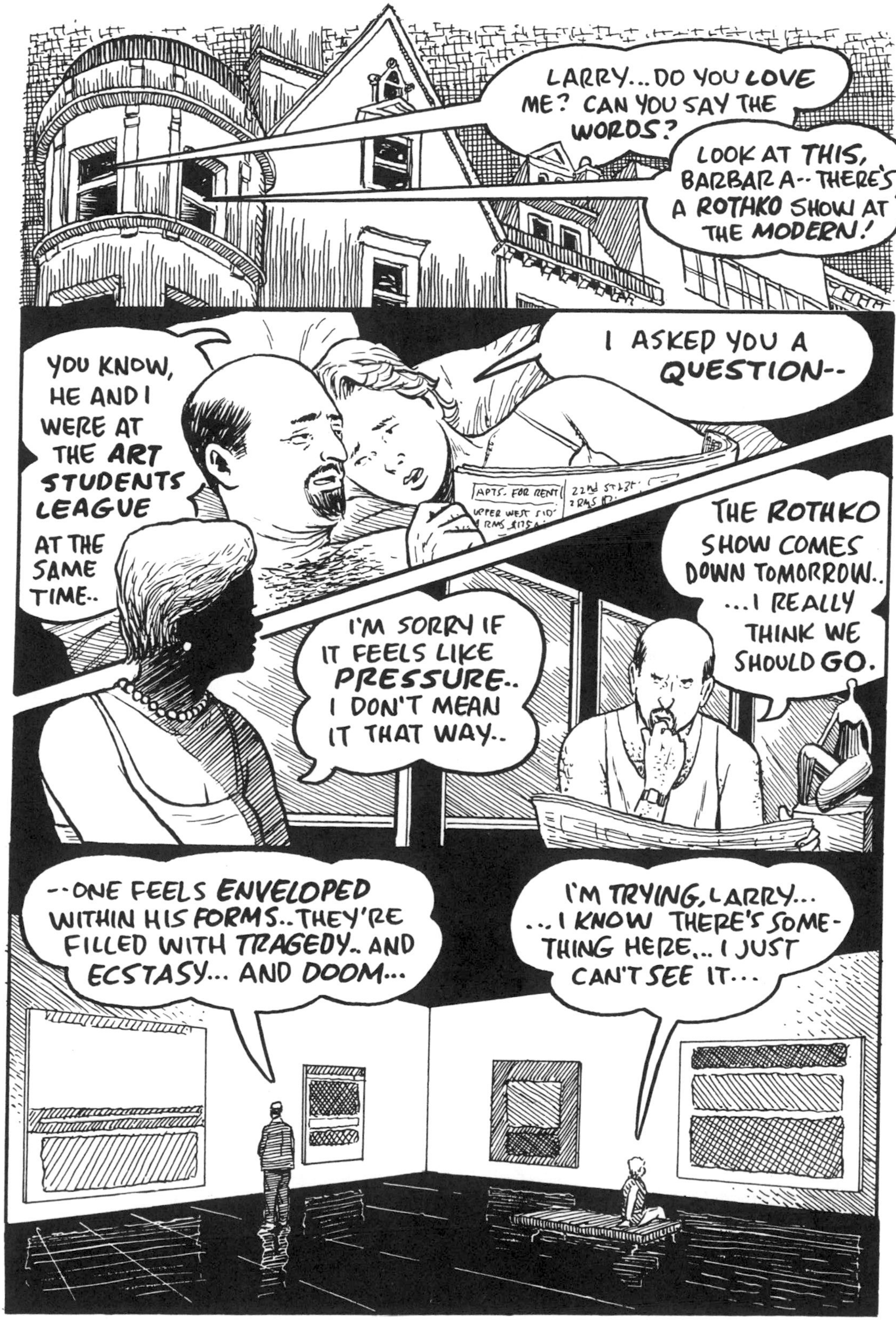
LARRY... DO YOU LOVE ME? CAN YOU SAY THE WORDS?
LOOK AT THIS, BARBARA-- THERE'S A ROTHKO SHOW AT THE MODERN!
YOU KNOW, HE AND I WERE AT THE ART STUDENTS LEAGUE AT THE SAME TIME..
I ASKED YOU A QUESTION--
APTS. FOR RENT
THE ROTHKO SHOW COMES DOWN TOMORROW.. ...I REALLY THINK WE SHOULD GO.
I'M SORRY IF IT FEELS LIKE PRESSURE.. I DON'T MEAN IT THAT WAY..
--ONE FEELS ENVELOPED WITHIN HIS FORMS.. THEY'RE FILLED WITH TRAGEDY.. AND ECSTASY... AND DOOM...
I'M TRYING, LARRY... ...I KNOW THERE'S SOMETHING HERE... I JUST CAN'T SEE IT...

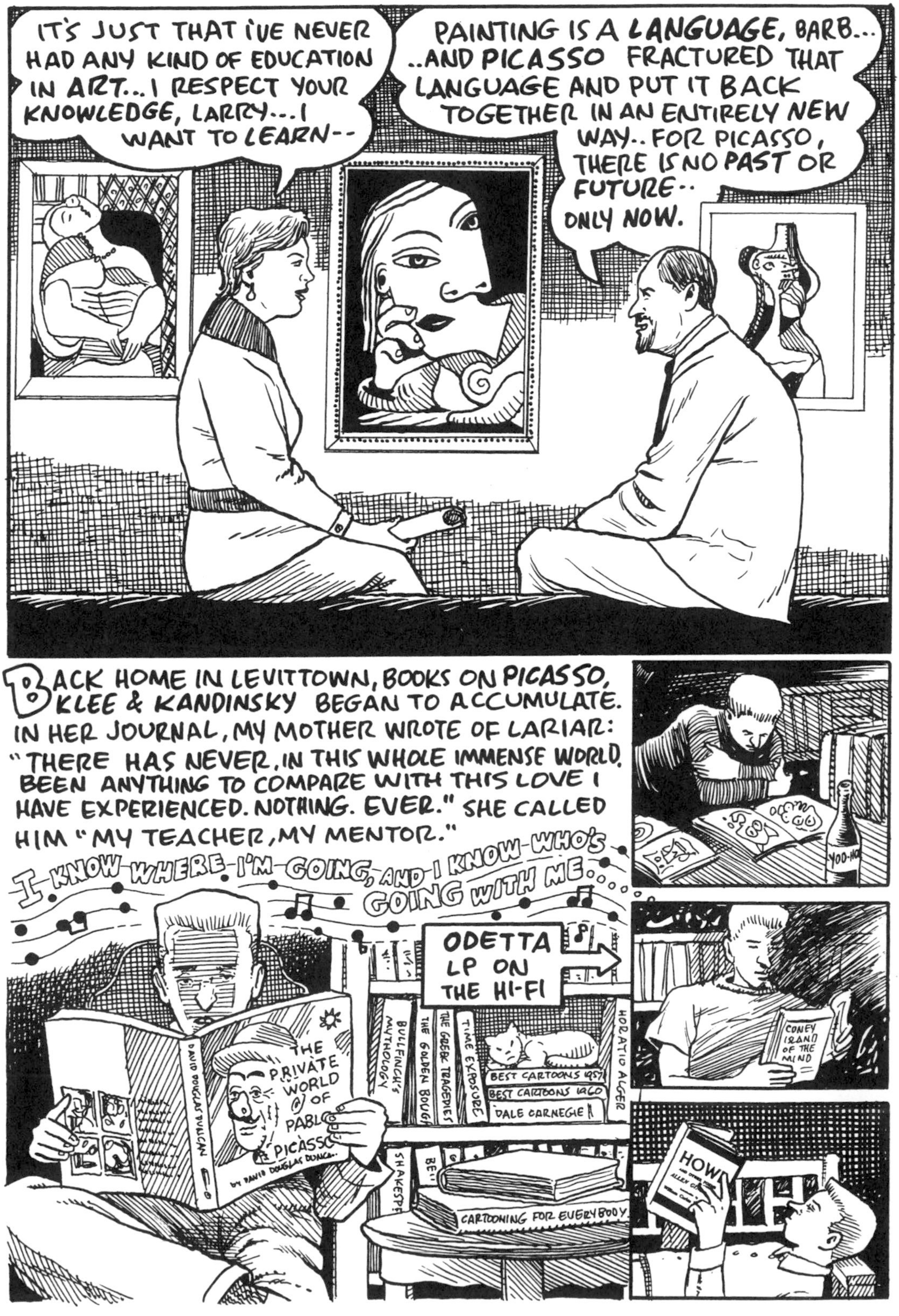
IT'S JUST THAT I'VE NEVER HAD ANY KIND OF EDUCATION IN ART... I RESPECT YOUR KNOWLEDGE, LARRY... I WANT TO LEARN--
PAINTING IS A LANGUAGE, BARB... ...AND PICASSO FRACTURED THAT LANGUAGE AND PUT IT BACK TOGETHER IN AN ENTIRELY NEW WAY.. FOR PICASSO, THERE IS NO PAST OR FUTURE.. ONLY NOW.
BACK HOME IN LEVITTOWN, BOOKS ON PICASSO, KLEE & KANDINSKY BEGAN TO ACCUMULATE. IN HER JOURNAL, MY MOTHER WROTE OF LARIAR: "THERE HAS NEVER, IN THIS WHOLE IMMENSE WORLD, BEEN ANYTHING TO COMPARE WITH THIS LOVE I HAVE EXPERIENCED. NOTHING. EVER." SHE CALLED HIM "MY TEACHER, MY MENTOR."
YOO-HOO
I KNOW WHERE I'M GOING, AND I KNOW WHO'S GOING WITH ME...
ODETTA LP ON THE HI-FI
DAVID DOUGLAS DUNCAN
THE PRIVATE WORLD OF PABLO PICASSO
BY DAVID DOUGLAS DUNCA...
BULLFINCH'S MYTHOLOGY
THE GOLDEN BOUGH
THE GREEK TRAGEDIES
TIME EXPOSURE
BEST CARTOONS 1959
BEST CARTOONS 1960
DALE CARNEGIE
HORATIO ALGER
SHAKESP
CARTOONING FOR EVERYBODY
CONEY ISLAND OF THE MIND
HOWL

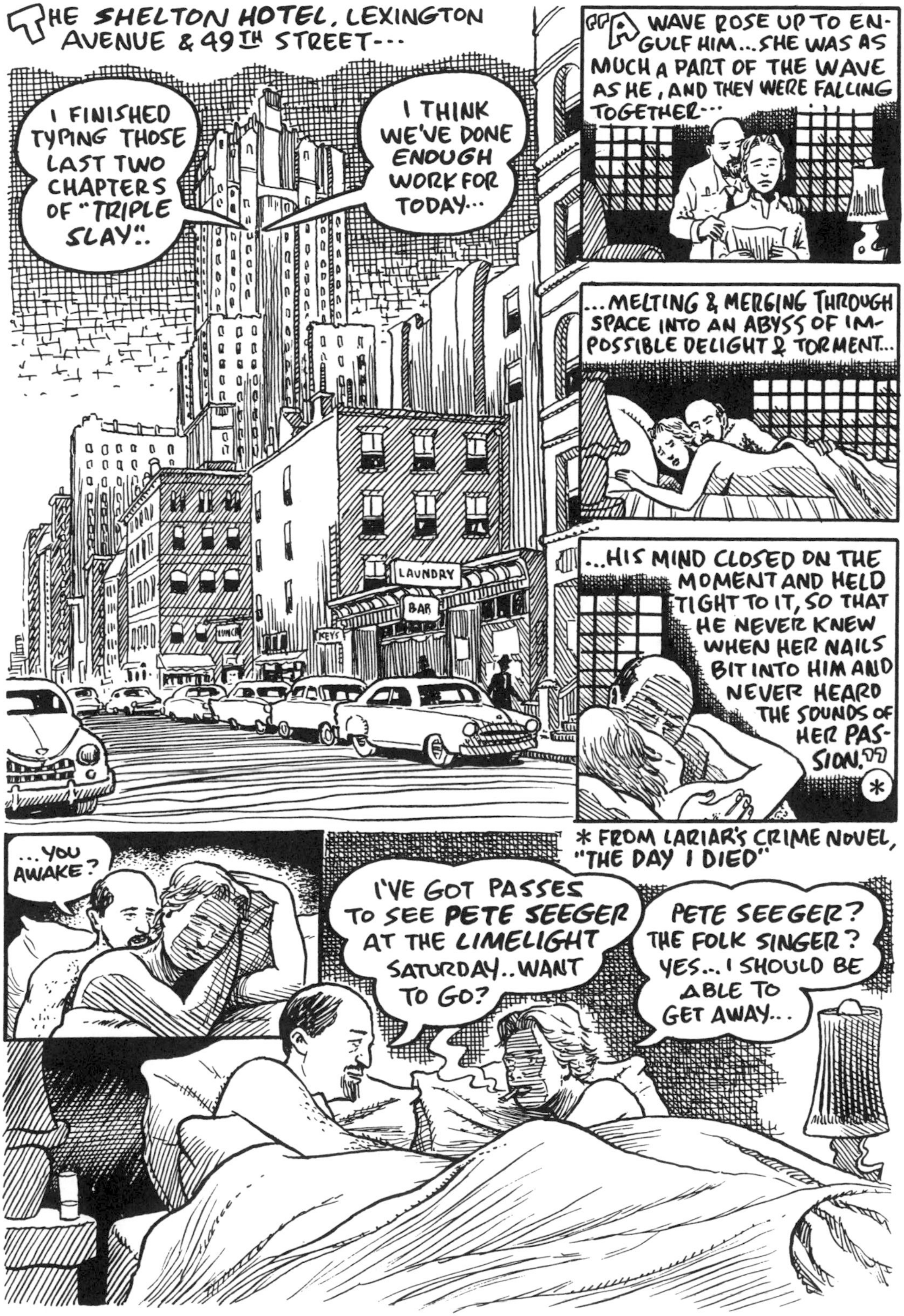
THE SHELTON HOTEL, LEXINGTON AVENUE & 49TH STREET---
I FINISHED TYPING THOSE LAST TWO CHAPTERS OF "TRIPLE SLAY"..
I THINK WE'VE DONE ENOUGH WORK FOR TODAY...
LAUNDRY
BAR
KEYS
"A WAVE ROSE UP TO ENGULF HIM... SHE WAS AS MUCH A PART OF THE WAVE AS HE, AND THEY WERE FALLING TOGETHER---
...MELTING & MERGING THROUGH SPACE INTO AN ABYSS OF IMPOSSIBLE DELIGHT & TORMENT...
...HIS MIND CLOSED ON THE MOMENT AND HELD TIGHT TO IT, SO THAT HE NEVER KNEW WHEN HER NAILS BIT INTO HIM AND NEVER HEARD THE SOUNDS OF HER PASSION." *
* FROM LARIAR'S CRIME NOVEL, "THE DAY I DIED"
...YOU AWAKE?
I'VE GOT PASSES TO SEE PETE SEEGER AT THE LIMELIGHT SATURDAY.. WANT TO GO?
PETE SEEGER? THE FOLK SINGER? YES... I SHOULD BE ABLE TO GET AWAY...

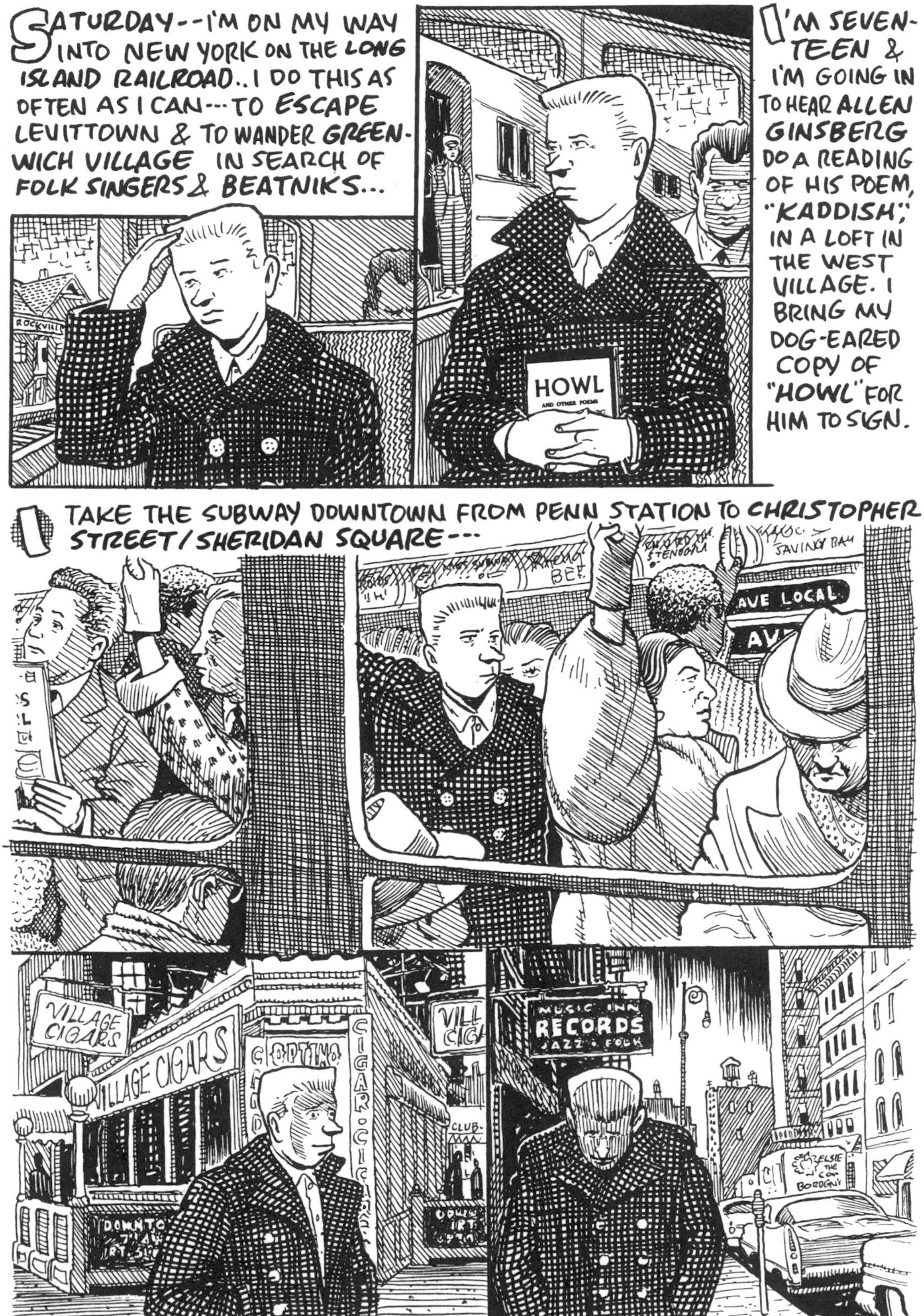
SATURDAY--I'M ON MY WAY INTO NEW YORK ON THE LONG ISLAND RAILROAD.. I DO THIS AS OFTEN AS I CAN--- TO ESCAPE LEVITTOWN & TO WANDER GREENWICH VILLAGE IN SEARCH OF FOLK SINGERS & BEATNIKS...
I'M SEVENTEEN & I'M GOING IN TO HEAR ALLEN GINSBERG DO A READING OF HIS POEM, "KADDISH," IN A LOFT IN THE WEST VILLAGE. I BRING MY DOG-EARED COPY OF "HOWL" FOR HIM TO SIGN.
HOWL
AND OTHER POEMS
I TAKE THE SUBWAY DOWNTOWN FROM PENN STATION TO CHRISTOPHER STREET/SHERIDAN SQUARE---
AVE LOCAL
VILLAGE CIGARS
VILLAGE CIGARS
CIGAR
CLUB
MUSIC INN
RECORDS
JAZZ & FOLK

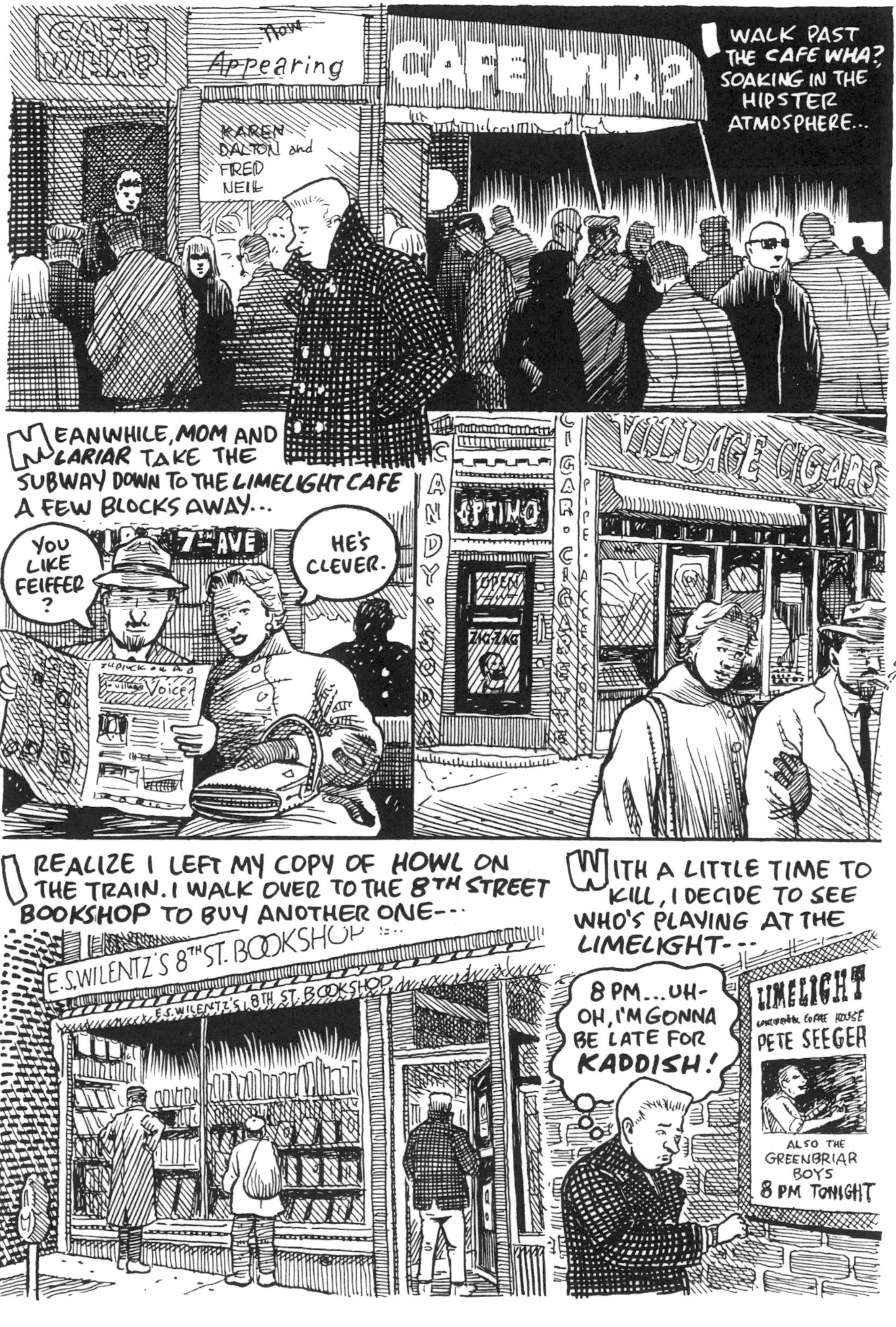
CAFE WHA?
Now Appearing
KAREN DALTON and FRED NEIL
CAFE WHA?
I WALK PAST THE CAFE WHA? SOAKING IN THE HIPSTER ATMOSPHERE...
MEANWHILE, MOM AND LARIAR TAKE THE SUBWAY DOWN TO THE LIMELIGHT CAFE A FEW BLOCKS AWAY...
7TH AVE
YOU LIKE FEIFFER?
HE'S CLEVER.
Village Voice
CANDY SODA
CIGARS CIGARETTES
PIPE ACCESSORIES
OPTIMO
OPEN
ZIG-ZAG
VILLAGE CIGARS
I REALIZE I LEFT MY COPY OF HOWL ON THE TRAIN. I WALK OVER TO THE 8TH STREET BOOKSHOP TO BUY ANOTHER ONE---
E.S. WILENTZ'S 8TH ST. BOOKSHOP
E.S. WILENTZ'S 8TH ST. BOOKSHOP
WITH A LITTLE TIME TO KILL, I DECIDE TO SEE WHO'S PLAYING AT THE LIMELIGHT---
8 PM...UH-OH, I'M GONNA BE LATE FOR KADDISH!
LIMELIGHT
CONTINENTAL COFFEE HOUSE
PETE SEEGER
ALSO THE GREENBRIAR BOYS
8 PM TONIGHT

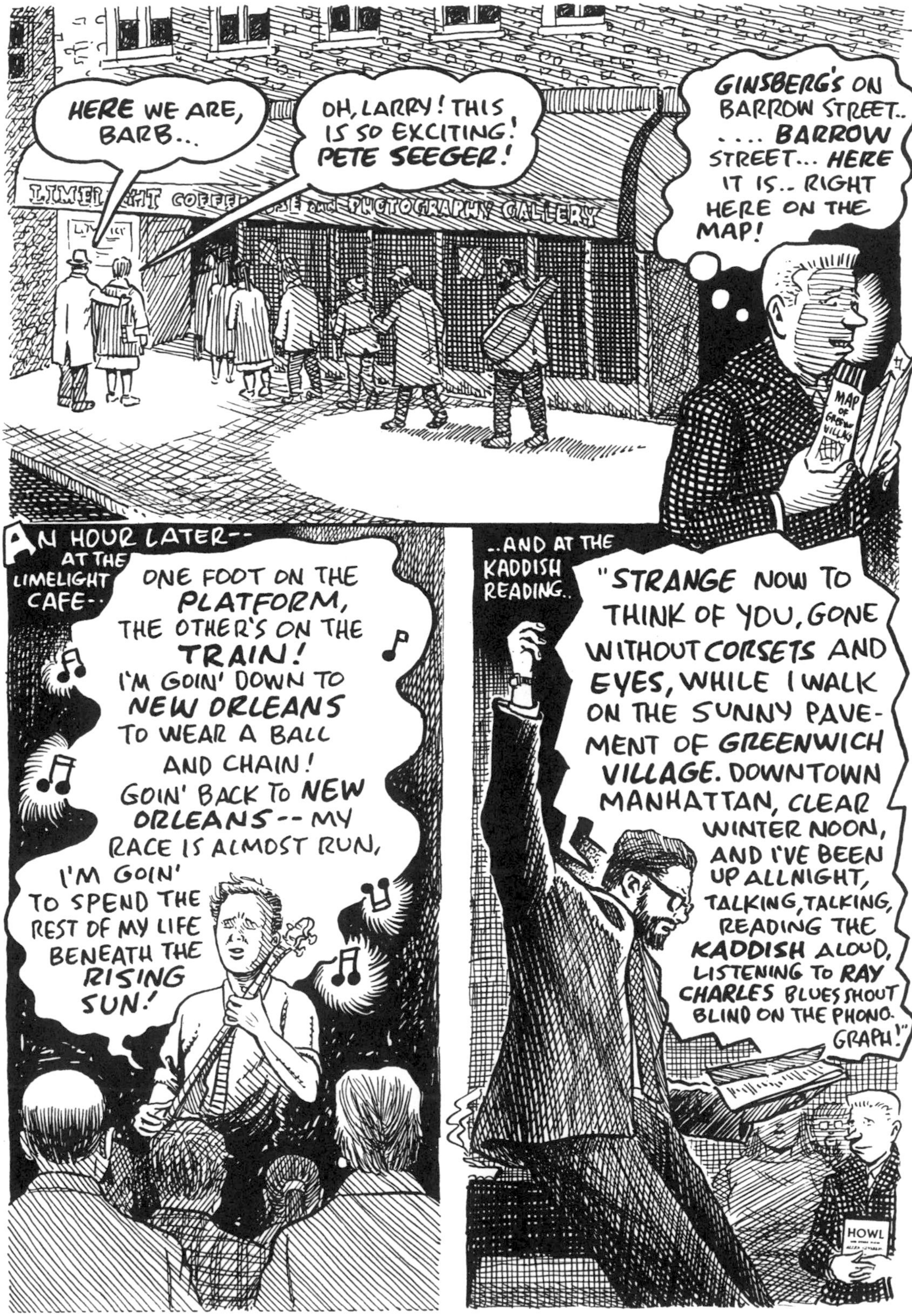
HERE WE ARE, BARB...
OH, LARRY! THIS IS SO EXCITING! PETE SEEGER!
PHOTOGRAPHY GALLERY
GINSBERG'S ON BARROW STREET.. .... BARROW STREET... HERE IT IS.. RIGHT HERE ON THE MAP!
AN HOUR LATER-- AT THE LIMELIGHT CAFE--
ONE FOOT ON THE PLATFORM, THE OTHER'S ON THE TRAIN! I'M GOIN' DOWN TO NEW ORLEANS TO WEAR A BALL AND CHAIN! GOIN' BACK TO NEW ORLEANS -- MY RACE IS ALMOST RUN, I'M GOIN' TO SPEND THE REST OF MY LIFE BENEATH THE RISING SUN!
..AND AT THE KADDISH READING..
"STRANGE NOW TO THINK OF YOU, GONE WITHOUT CORSETS AND EYES, WHILE I WALK ON THE SUNNY PAVEMENT OF GREENWICH VILLAGE. DOWNTOWN MANHATTAN, CLEAR WINTER NOON, AND I'VE BEEN UP ALLNIGHT, TALKING, TALKING, READING THE KADDISH ALOUD, LISTENING TO RAY CHARLES BLUES SHOUT BLIND ON THE PHONOGRAPH!"
HOWL

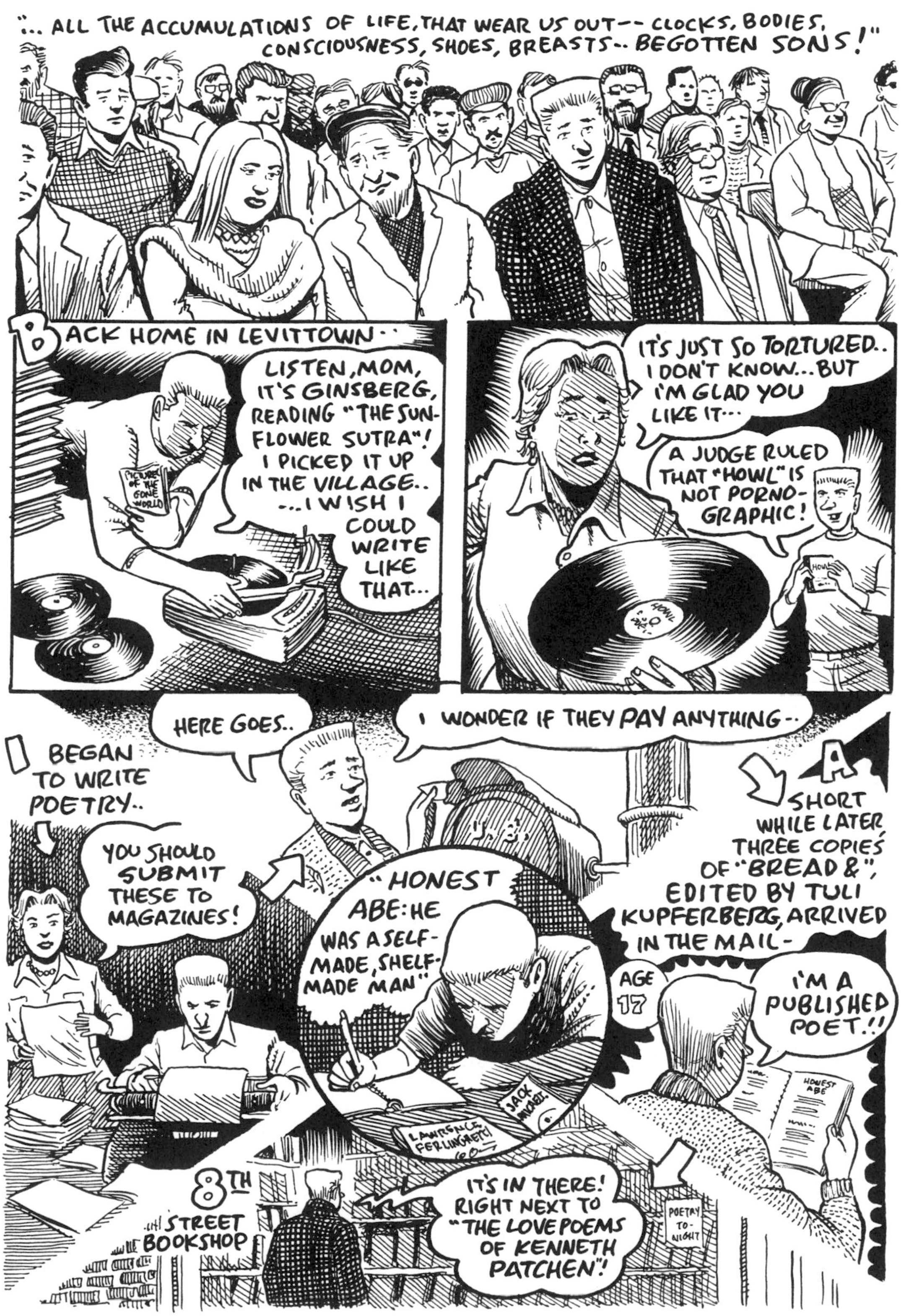
"... ALL THE ACCUMULATIONS OF LIFE, THAT WEAR US OUT -- CLOCKS, BODIES, CONSCIOUSNESS, SHOES, BREASTS -- BEGOTTEN SONS!"
BACK HOME IN LEVITTOWN..
LISTEN, MOM, IT'S GINSBERG, READING "THE SUNFLOWER SUTRA"! I PICKED IT UP IN THE VILLAGE.. ...I WISH I COULD WRITE LIKE THAT...
PICTURES OF THE GONE WORLD
IT'S JUST SO TORTURED.. I DON'T KNOW... BUT I'M GLAD YOU LIKE IT...
A JUDGE RULED THAT "HOWL" IS NOT PORNOGRAPHIC!
HOWL
I BEGAN TO WRITE POETRY..
YOU SHOULD SUBMIT THESE TO MAGAZINES!
HERE GOES..
I WONDER IF THEY PAY ANYTHING..
"HONEST ABE: HE WAS A SELF-MADE, SHELF-MADE MAN"
LAWRENCE FERLINGHETTI
JACK MICHELINE
A SHORT WHILE LATER, THREE COPIES OF "BREAD &", EDITED BY TULI KUPFERBERG, ARRIVED IN THE MAIL-
AGE 17
I'M A PUBLISHED POET.!!
HONEST ABE
8TH STREET BOOKSHOP
IT'S IN THERE! RIGHT NEXT TO "THE LOVE POEMS OF KENNETH PATCHEN"!
POETRY TO-NIGHT

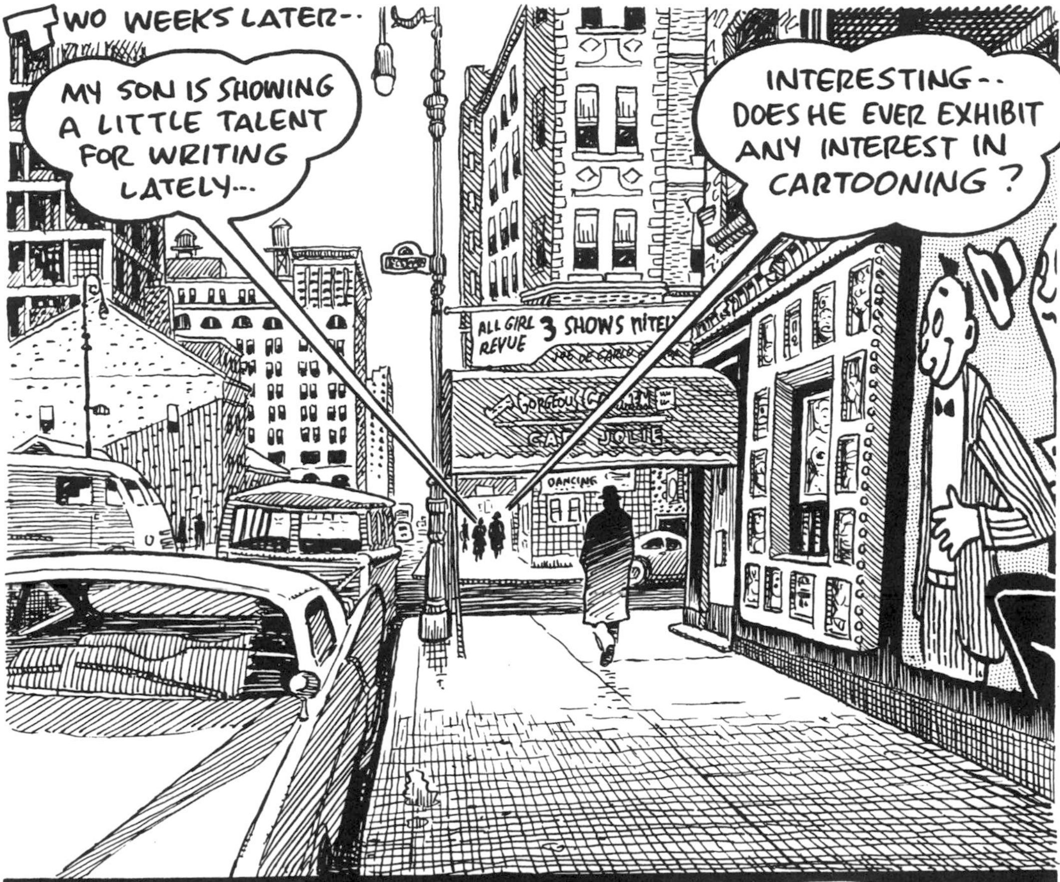
TWO WEEKS LATER--
MY SON IS SHOWING A LITTLE TALENT FOR WRITING LATELY...
INTERESTING-- DOES HE EVER EXHIBIT ANY INTEREST IN CARTOONING?
ALL GIRL REVUE 3 SHOWS NITELY
CAFE JOLIE
DANCING
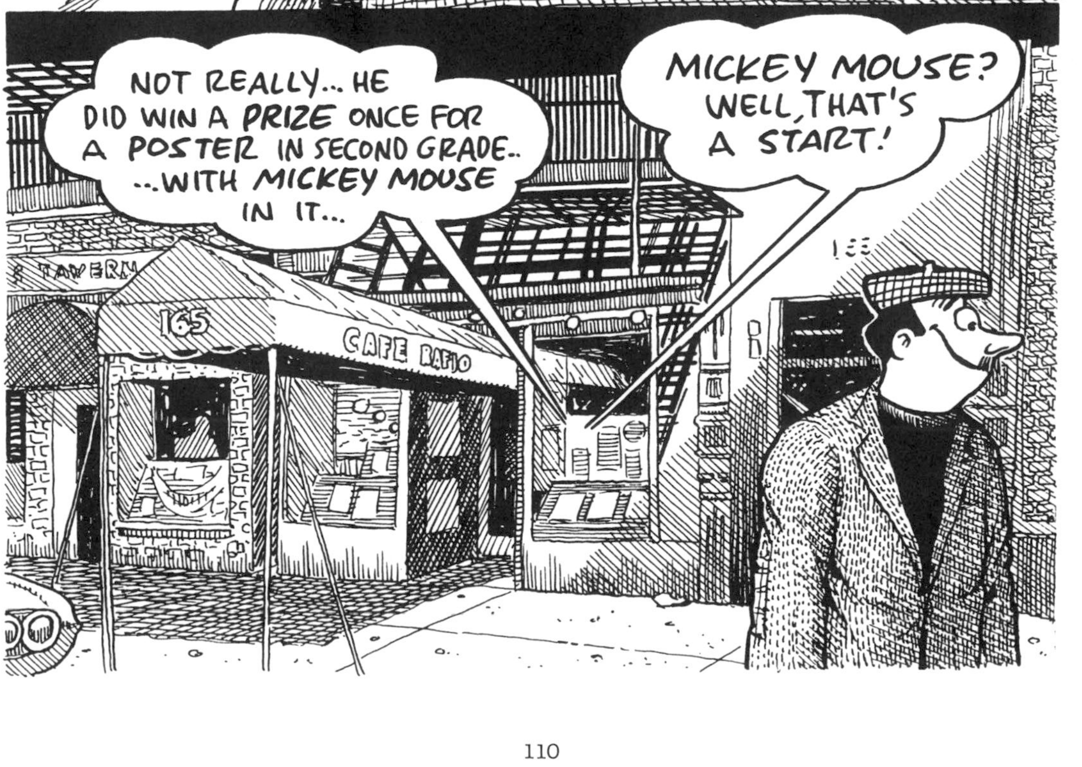
NOT REALLY... HE DID WIN A PRIZE ONCE FOR A POSTER IN SECOND GRADE.. ...WITH MICKEY MOUSE IN IT...
MICKEY MOUSE? WELL, THAT'S A START!
TAVERN
165
CAFE RAFIO

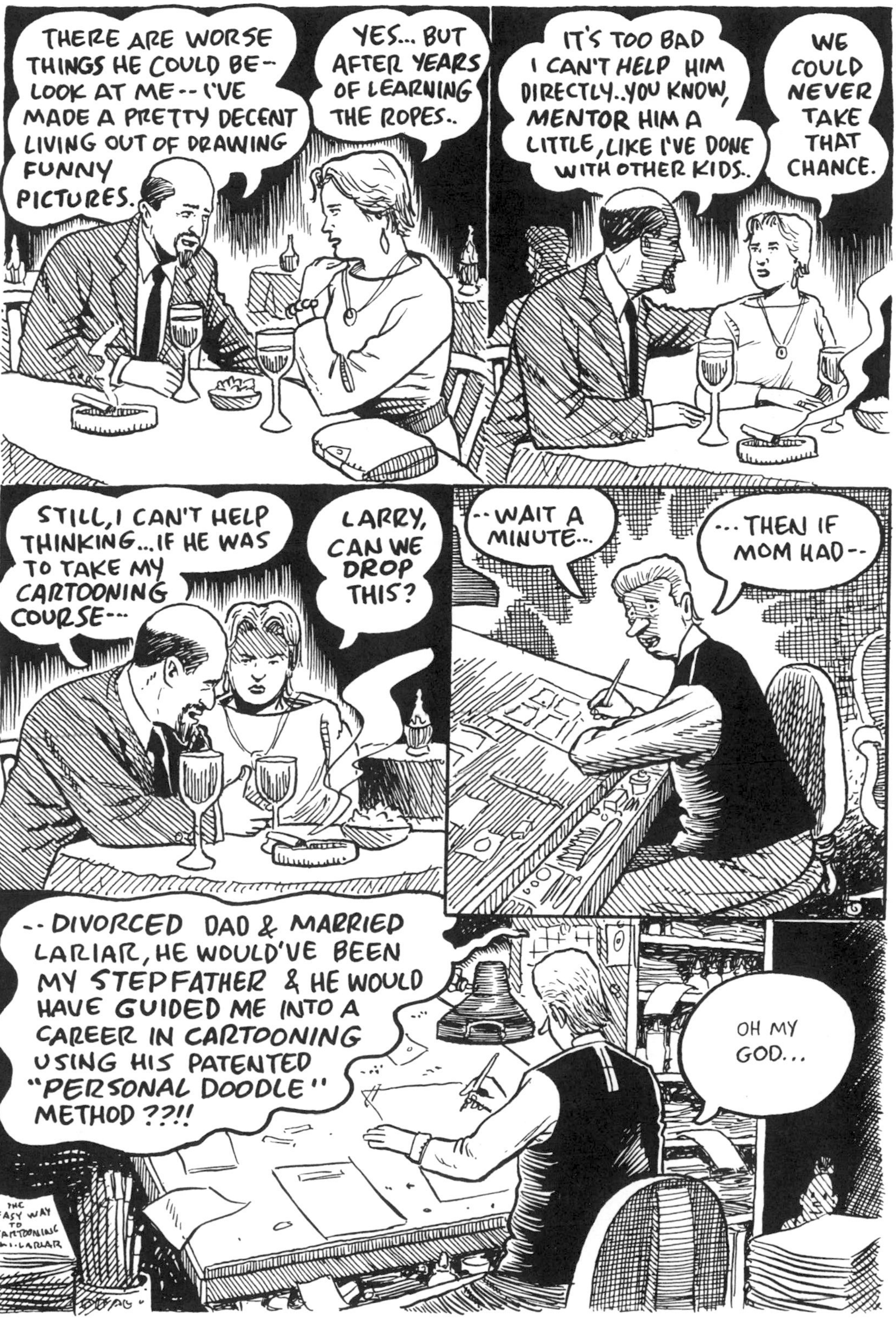
THERE ARE WORSE THINGS HE COULD BE-- LOOK AT ME-- I'VE MADE A PRETTY DECENT LIVING OUT OF DRAWING FUNNY PICTURES.
YES... BUT AFTER YEARS OF LEARNING THE ROPES..
IT'S TOO BAD I CAN'T HELP HIM DIRECTLY..YOU KNOW, MENTOR HIM A LITTLE, LIKE I'VE DONE WITH OTHER KIDS..
WE COULD NEVER TAKE THAT CHANCE.
STILL, I CAN'T HELP THINKING...IF HE WAS TO TAKE MY CARTOONING COURSE---
LARRY, CAN WE DROP THIS?
--WAIT A MINUTE...
--THEN IF MOM HAD--
--DIVORCED DAD & MARRIED LARIAR, HE WOULD'VE BEEN MY STEPFATHER & HE WOULD HAVE GUIDED ME INTO A CAREER IN CARTOONING USING HIS PATENTED "PERSONAL DOODLE" METHOD ??!!
OH MY GOD...

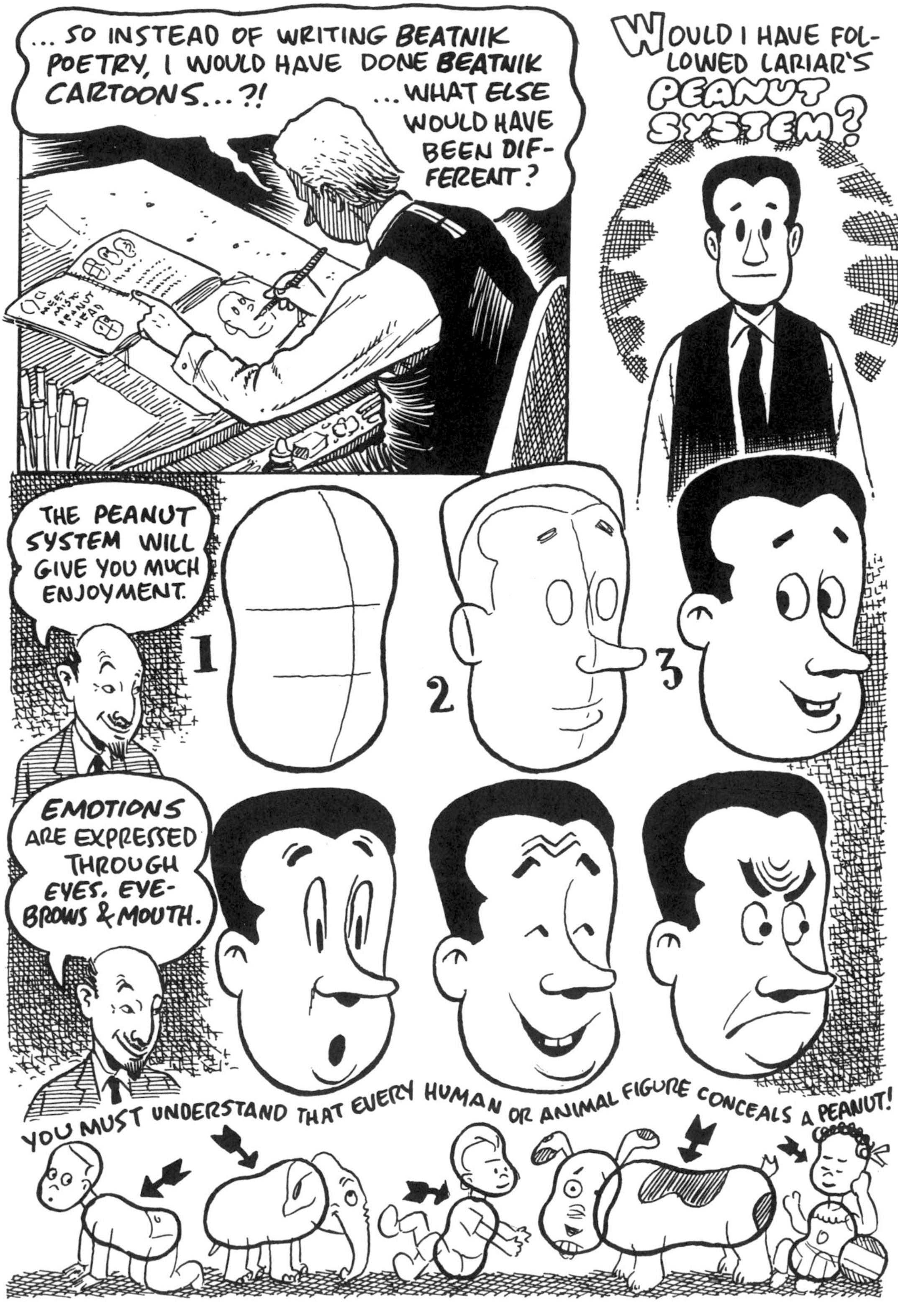
... SO INSTEAD OF WRITING BEATNIK POETRY, I WOULD HAVE DONE BEATNIK CARTOONS...?!
...WHAT ELSE WOULD HAVE BEEN DIFFERENT?
MEET MISTER PEANUT HEAD
WOULD I HAVE FOLLOWED LARIAR'S PEANUT SYSTEM?
THE PEANUT SYSTEM WILL GIVE YOU MUCH ENJOYMENT.
1
2
3
EMOTIONS ARE EXPRESSED THROUGH EYES, EYEBROWS & MOUTH.
YOU MUST UNDERSTAND THAT EVERY HUMAN OR ANIMAL FIGURE CONCEALS A PEANUT!

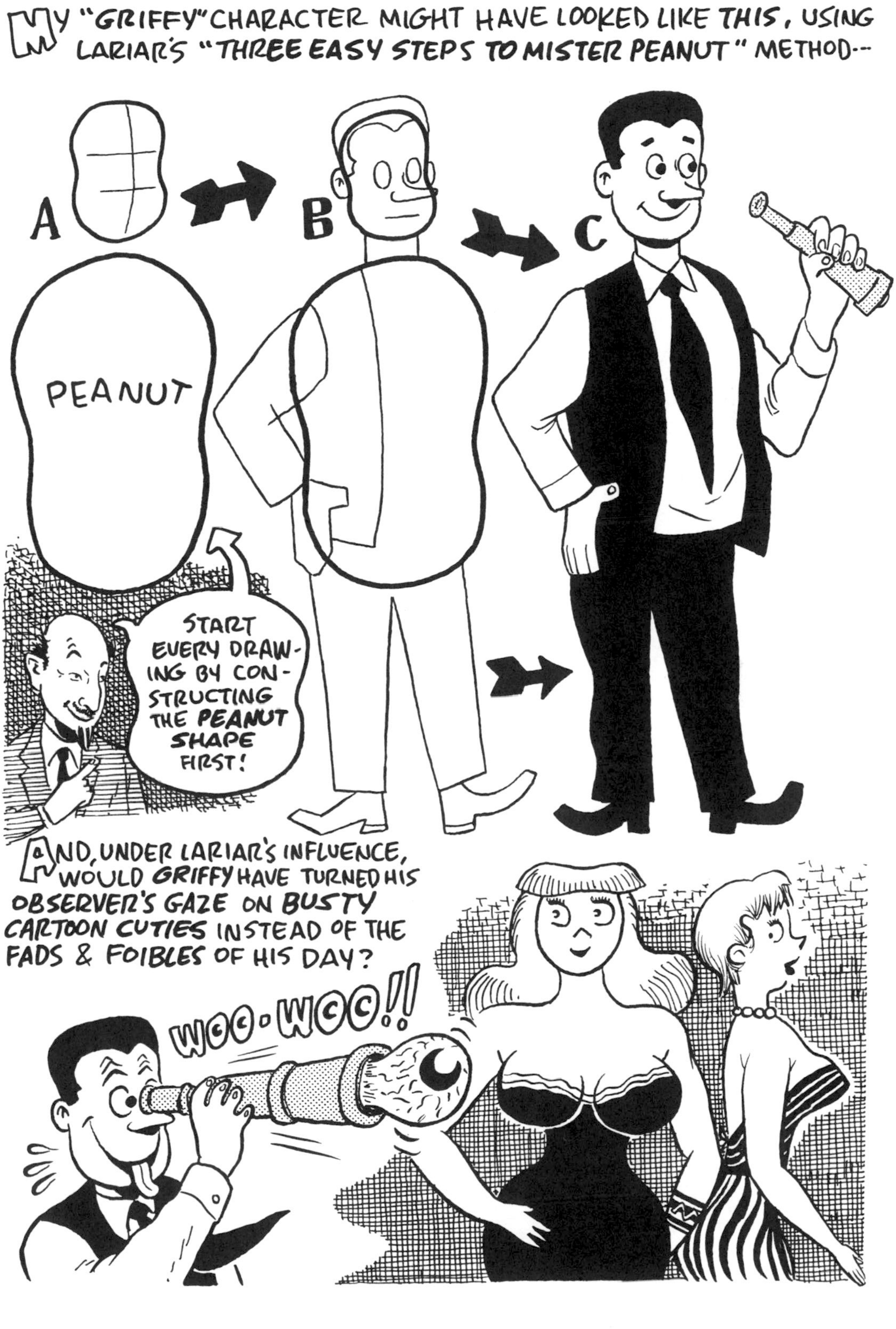
MY "GRIFFY" CHARACTER MIGHT HAVE LOOKED LIKE THIS, USING LARIAR'S "THREE EASY STEPS TO MISTER PEANUT" METHOD--
A
B
C
PEANUT
START EVERY DRAWING BY CONSTRUCTING THE PEANUT SHAPE FIRST!
AND, UNDER LARIAR'S INFLUENCE, WOULD GRIFFY HAVE TURNED HIS OBSERVER'S GAZE ON BUSTY CARTOON CUTIES INSTEAD OF THE FADS & FOIBLES OF HIS DAY?
WOO-WOO!!

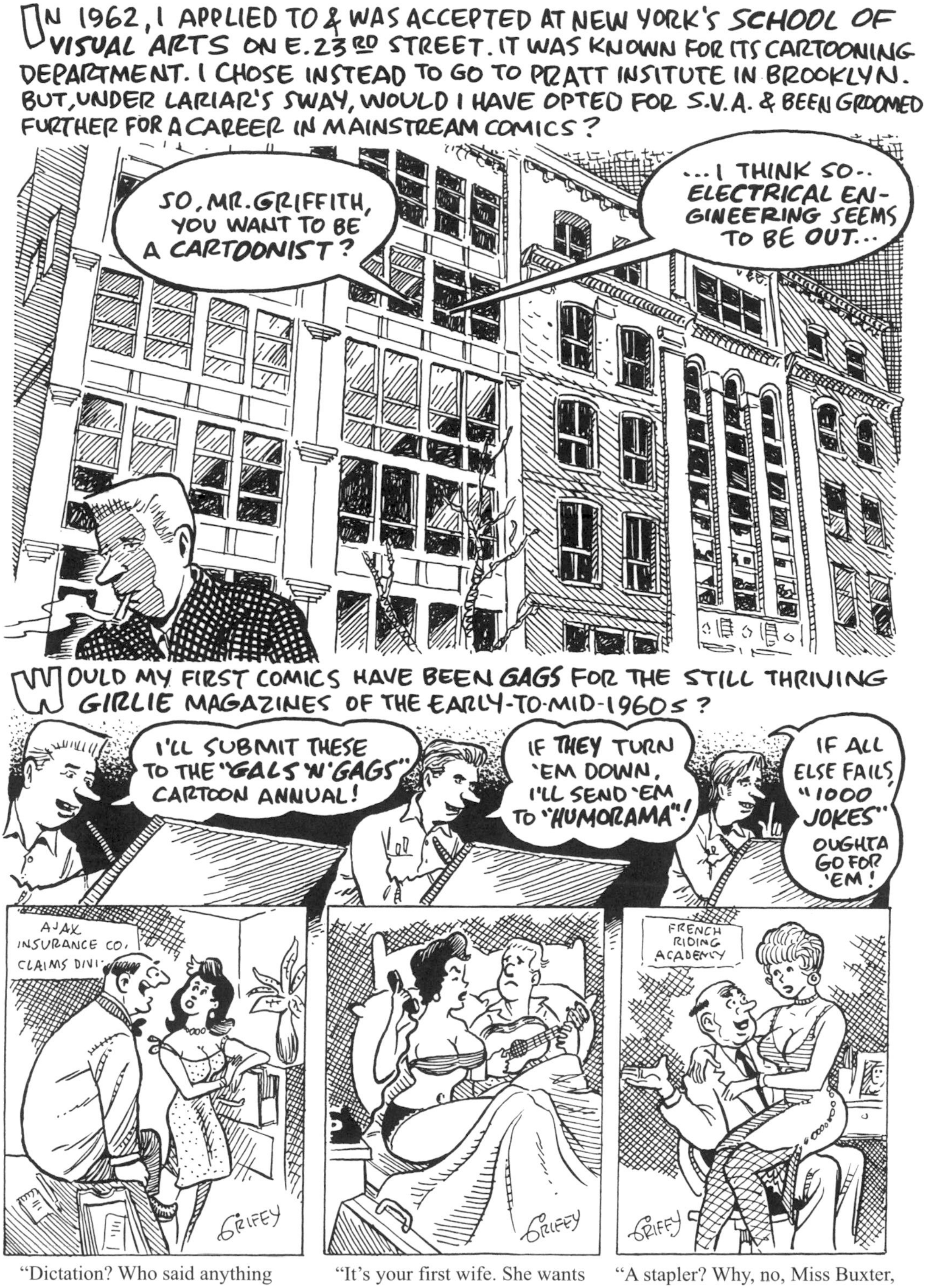
IN 1962, I APPLIED TO & WAS ACCEPTED AT NEW YORK'S SCHOOL OF VISUAL ARTS ON E. 23RD STREET. IT WAS KNOWN FOR ITS CARTOONING DEPARTMENT. I CHOSE INSTEAD TO GO TO PRATT INSITUTE IN BROOKLYN. BUT, UNDER LARIAR'S SWAY, WOULD I HAVE OPTED FOR S.V.A. & BEEN GROOMED FURTHER FOR A CAREER IN MAINSTREAM COMICS?
SO, MR. GRIFFITH, YOU WANT TO BE A CARTOONIST?
...I THINK SO.. ELECTRICAL ENGINEERING SEEMS TO BE OUT...
WOULD MY FIRST COMICS HAVE BEEN GAGS FOR THE STILL THRIVING GIRLIE MAGAZINES OF THE EARLY-TO-MID-1960s?
I'LL SUBMIT THESE TO THE "GALS 'N' GAGS" CARTOON ANNUAL!
IF THEY TURN 'EM DOWN, I'LL SEND 'EM TO "HUMORAMA"!
IF ALL ELSE FAILS, "1000 JOKES" OUGHTA GO FOR 'EM!
AJAX INSURANCE CO. CLAIMS DIV.
GRIFFY
GRIFFY
FRENCH RIDING ACADEMY
GRIFFY

"Dictation? Who said anything about dictation?"

"It's your first wife. She wants her ukulele back."

"A stapler? Why, no, Miss Buxter, I'm just glad to see you!"

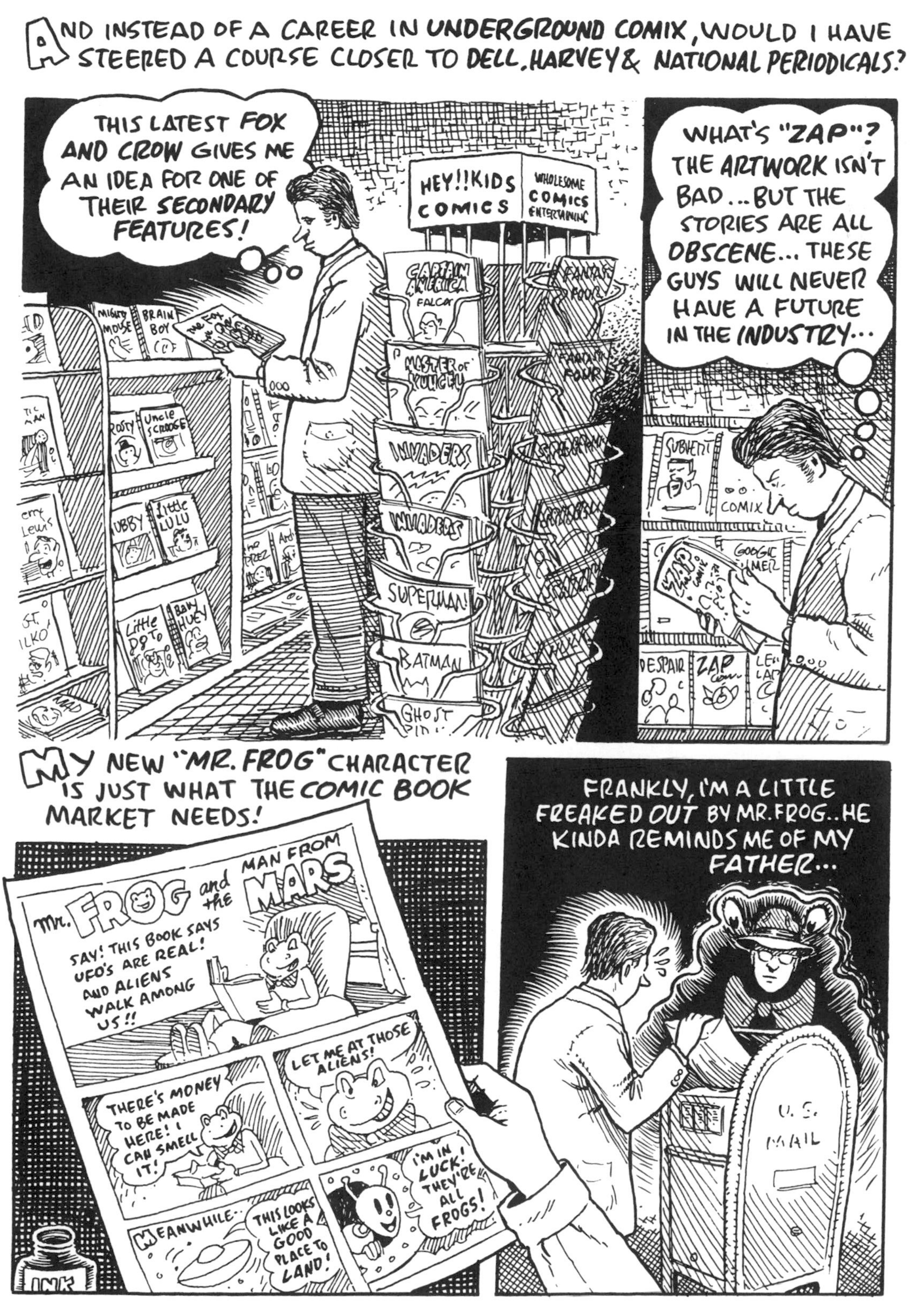
AND INSTEAD OF A CAREER IN UNDERGROUND COMIX, WOULD I HAVE STEERED A COURSE CLOSER TO DELL, HARVEY & NATIONAL PERIODICALS?
THIS LATEST FOX AND CROW GIVES ME AN IDEA FOR ONE OF THEIR SECONDARY FEATURES!
HEY!! KIDS COMICS
WHOLESOME COMICS ENTERTAINING
WHAT'S "ZAP"? THE ARTWORK ISN'T BAD... BUT THE STORIES ARE ALL OBSCENE... THESE GUYS WILL NEVER HAVE A FUTURE IN THE INDUSTRY...
MY NEW "MR. FROG" CHARACTER IS JUST WHAT THE COMIC BOOK MARKET NEEDS!
MR. FROG and the MAN FROM MARS
SAY! THIS BOOK SAYS UFO'S ARE REAL! AND ALIENS WALK AMONG US!!
THERE'S MONEY TO BE MADE HERE! I CAN SMELL IT!
LET ME AT THOSE ALIENS!
MEANWHILE...
THIS LOOKS LIKE A GOOD PLACE TO LAND!
I'M IN LUCK! THEY'RE ALL FROGS!
INK
FRANKLY, I'M A LITTLE FREAKED OUT BY MR. FROG.. HE KINDA REMINDS ME OF MY FATHER...
U.S. MAIL

AND ZIPPY? WHAT IF I HAD CREATED ZIPPY WITH A MORE COMMERCIAL PURPOSE -- MORE OUT OF A DESIRE TO PLEASE THE **MOST** PEOPLE? EVEN TO THE POINT OF **RETOOLING** HIM AS EACH NEW SYNDICATE DEAL FIZZLED?

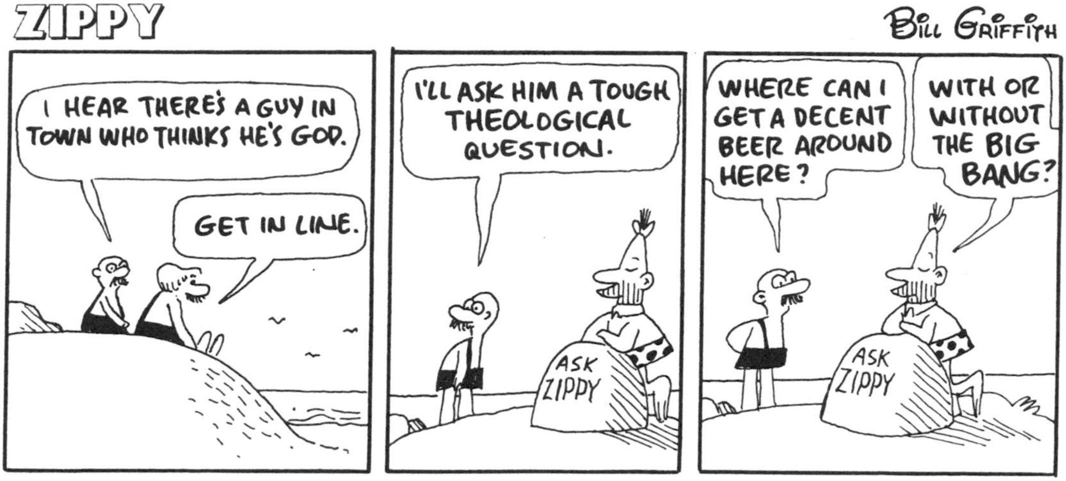
ZIPPY
BILL GRIFFITH
I HEAR THERE'S A GUY IN TOWN WHO THINKS HE'S GOD.
GET IN LINE.
I'LL ASK HIM A TOUGH THEOLOGICAL QUESTION.
ASK ZIPPY
WHERE CAN I GET A DECENT BEER AROUND HERE?
WITH OR WITHOUT THE BIG BANG?
ASK ZIPPY

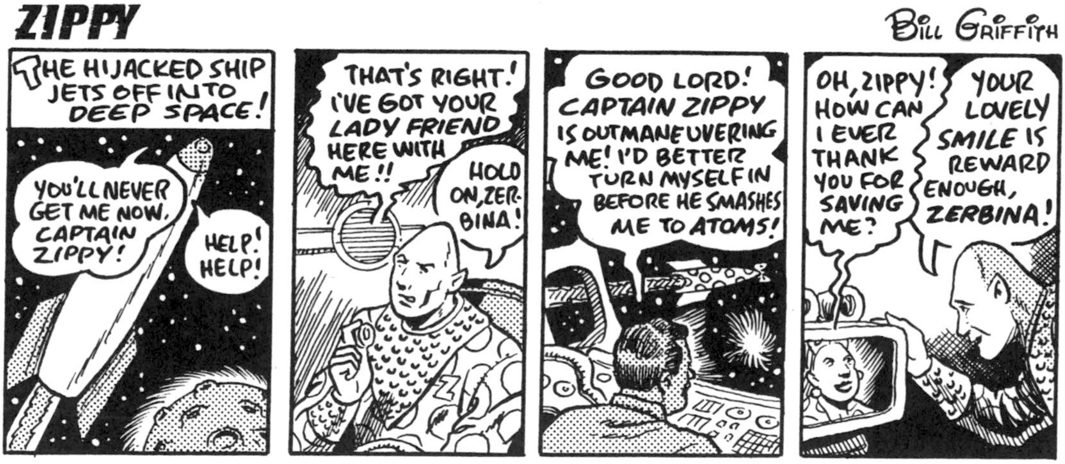
ZIPPY
BILL GRIFFITH
THE HIJACKED SHIP JETS OFF INTO DEEP SPACE!
YOU'LL NEVER GET ME NOW, CAPTAIN ZIPPY!
HELP! HELP!
THAT'S RIGHT! I'VE GOT YOUR LADY FRIEND HERE WITH ME!!
HOLD ON, ZERBINA!
GOOD LORD! CAPTAIN ZIPPY IS OUTMANEUVERING ME! I'D BETTER TURN MYSELF IN BEFORE HE SMASHES ME TO ATOMS!
OH, ZIPPY! HOW CAN I EVER THANK YOU FOR SAVING ME?
YOUR LOVELY SMILE IS REWARD ENOUGH, ZERBINA!

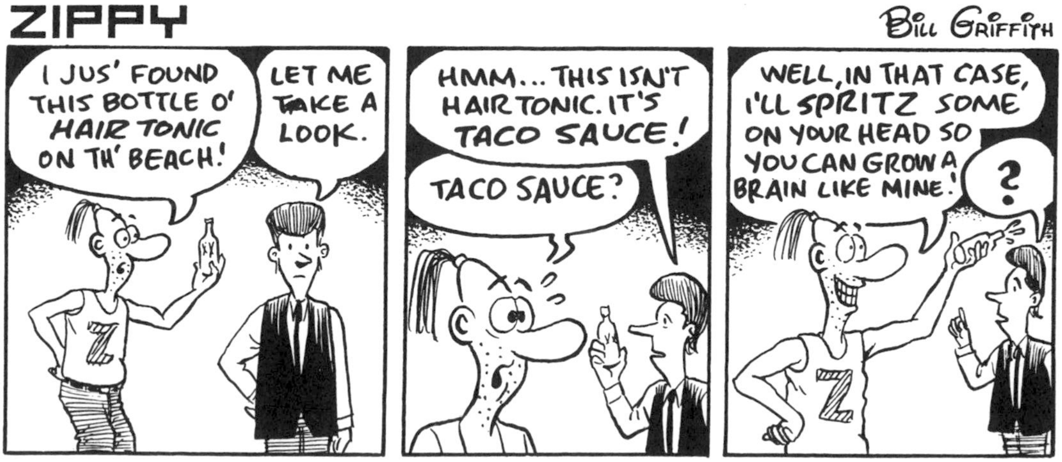
ZIPPY
BILL GRIFFITH
I JUS' FOUND THIS BOTTLE O' HAIR TONIC ON TH' BEACH!
LET ME TAKE A LOOK.
HMM... THIS ISN'T HAIR TONIC. IT'S TACO SAUCE!
TACO SAUCE?
WELL, IN THAT CASE, I'LL SPRITZ SOME ON YOUR HEAD SO YOU CAN GROW A BRAIN LIKE MINE!
?

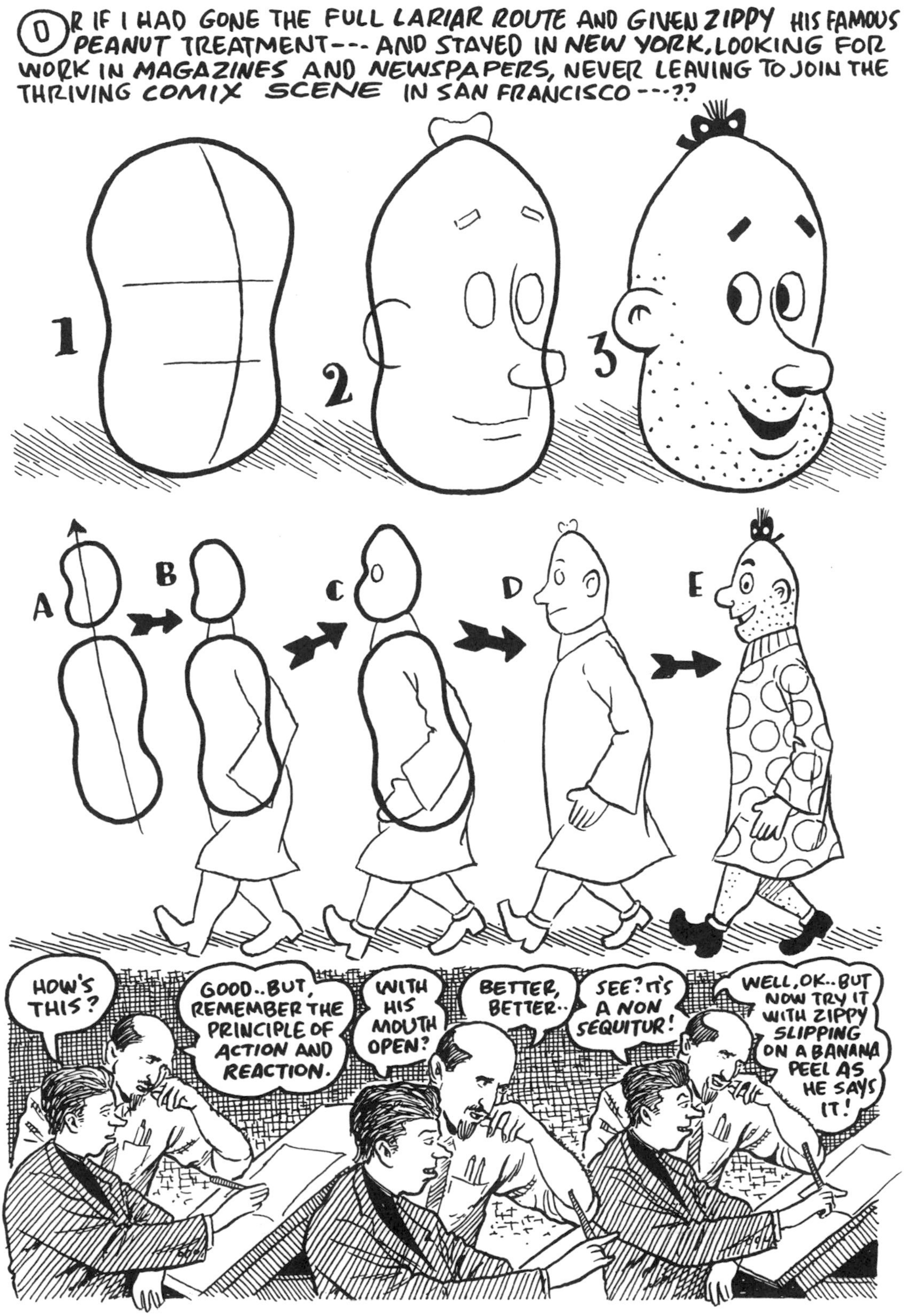
OR IF I HAD GONE THE FULL LARIAR ROUTE AND GIVEN ZIPPY HIS FAMOUS PEANUT TREATMENT--- AND STAYED IN NEW YORK, LOOKING FOR WORK IN MAGAZINES AND NEWSPAPERS, NEVER LEAVING TO JOIN THE THRIVING COMIX SCENE IN SAN FRANCISCO---??
1
2
3
A
B
C
D
E
HOW'S THIS?
GOOD..BUT, REMEMBER THE PRINCIPLE OF ACTION AND REACTION.
WITH HIS MOUTH OPEN?
BETTER, BETTER..
SEE? IT'S A NON SEQUITUR!
WELL, OK..BUT NOW TRY IT WITH ZIPPY SLIPPING ON A BANANA PEEL AS HE SAYS IT!

AND, WITH LARIAR'S HELP AND MENTORING, MIGHT I HAVE EVENTUALLY CREATED A MODESTLY SUCCESSFUL, LONG-RUNNING DAILY CALLED --- "ZIPZ"?

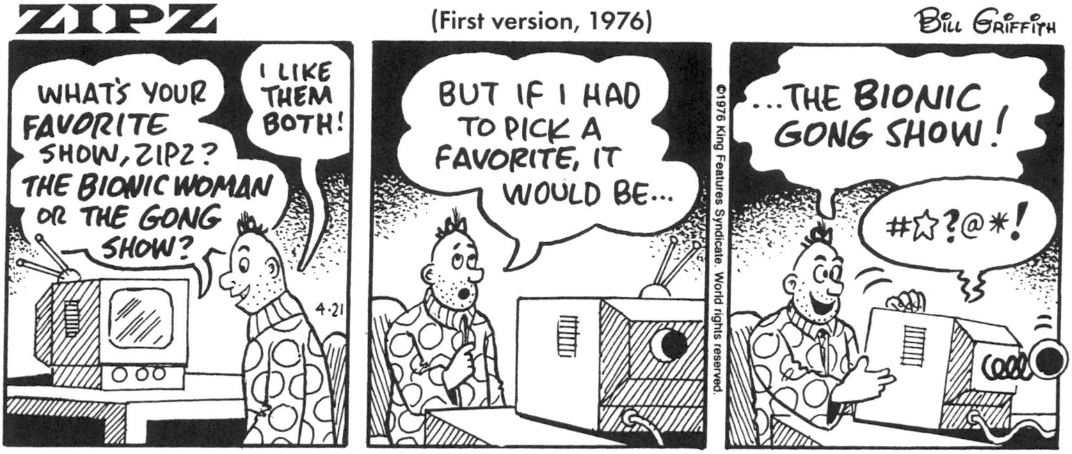
ZIPZ
(First version, 1976)
BILL GRIFFITH
WHAT'S YOUR FAVORITE SHOW, ZIPZ? THE BIONIC WOMAN OR THE GONG SHOW?
I LIKE THEM BOTH!
4·21
BUT IF I HAD TO PICK A FAVORITE, IT WOULD BE...
©1976 King Features Syndicate. World rights reserved.
...THE BIONIC GONG SHOW!
#☆?@*!

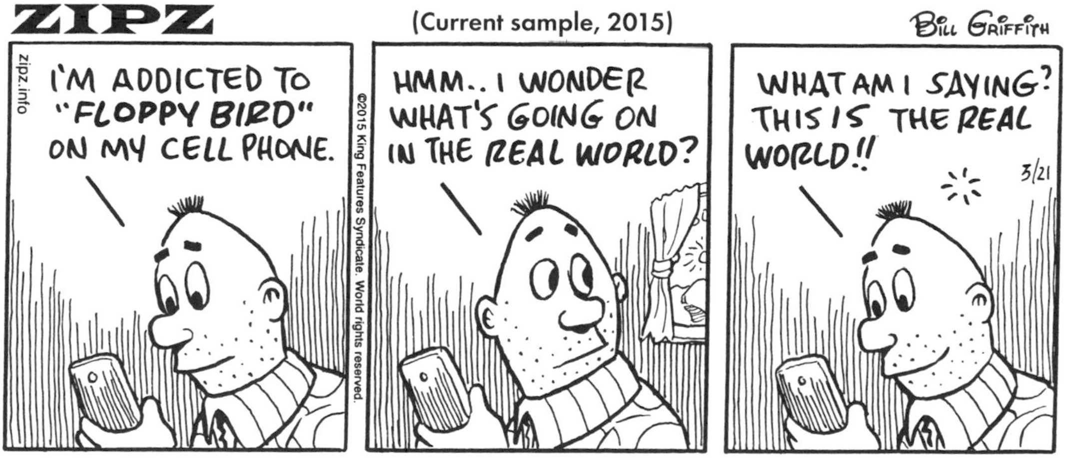
ZIPZ
(Current sample, 2015)
BILL GRIFFITH
zipz.info
I'M ADDICTED TO "FLOPPY BIRD" ON MY CELL PHONE.
©2015 King Features Syndicate. World rights reserved.
HMM.. I WONDER WHAT'S GOING ON IN THE REAL WORLD?
WHAT AM I SAYING? THIS IS THE REAL WORLD!!
3/21

THEN, LIKE HIM, WOULD I HAVE CHURNED OUT OTHER COMICS, ALWAYS AFTER THE "SALE"... ALWAYS COURTING THE ELUSIVE "MASS MARKET"?

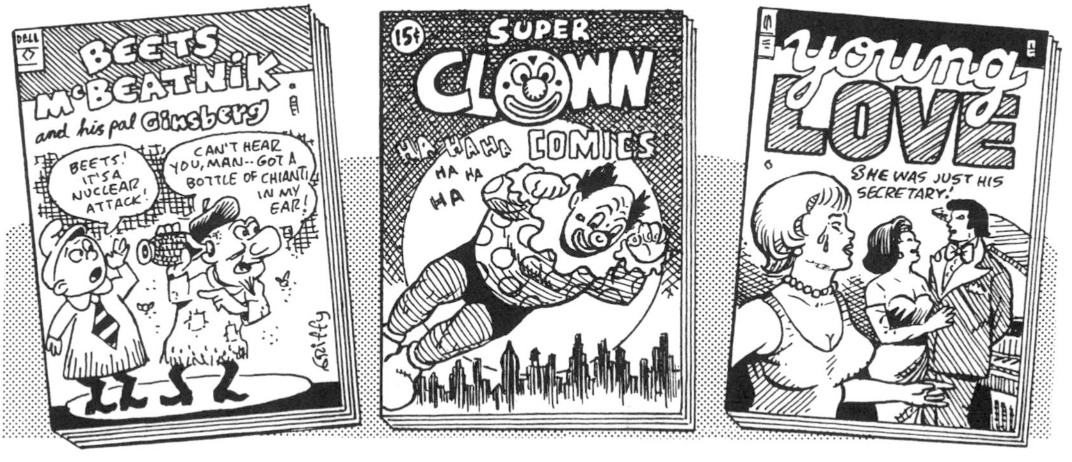
DELL
BEETS McBEATNIK
and his pal Ginsberg
BEETS! IT'S A NUCLEAR ATTACK!
CAN'T HEAR YOU, MAN-- GOT A BOTTLE OF CHIANTI IN MY EAR!
Griffy
15¢
SUPER CLOWN COMICS
HA HA HA HA
HA HA
HA
young LOVE
SHE WAS JUST HIS SECRETARY!

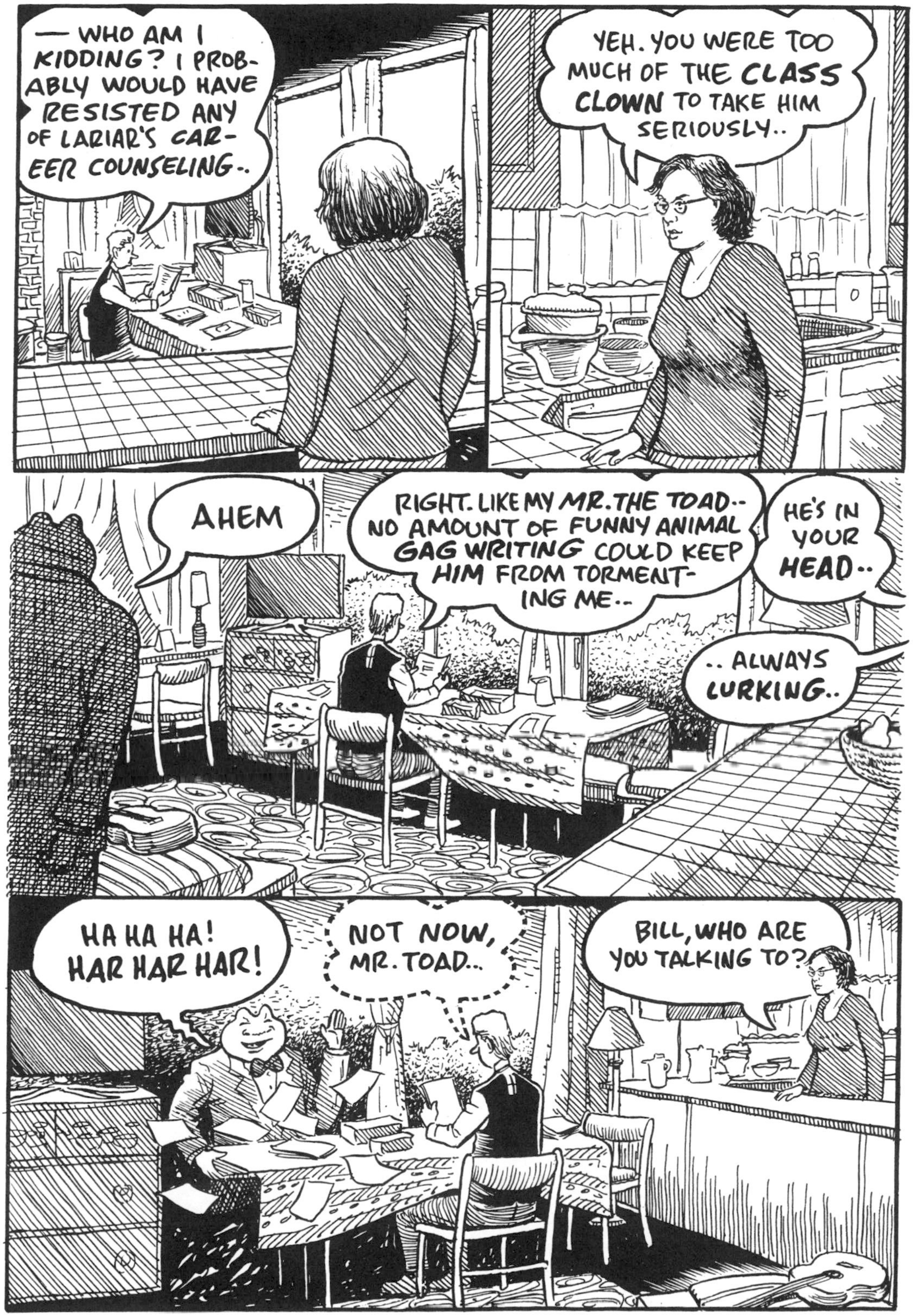
— WHO AM I KIDDING? I PROBABLY WOULD HAVE RESISTED ANY OF LARIAR'S CAREER COUNSELING..
YEH. YOU WERE TOO MUCH OF THE CLASS CLOWN TO TAKE HIM SERIOUSLY..
AHEM
RIGHT. LIKE MY MR. THE TOAD.. NO AMOUNT OF FUNNY ANIMAL GAG WRITING COULD KEEP HIM FROM TORMENTING ME..
HE'S IN YOUR HEAD..
.. ALWAYS LURKING..
HA HA HA! HAR HAR HAR!
NOT NOW, MR. TOAD..
BILL, WHO ARE YOU TALKING TO?

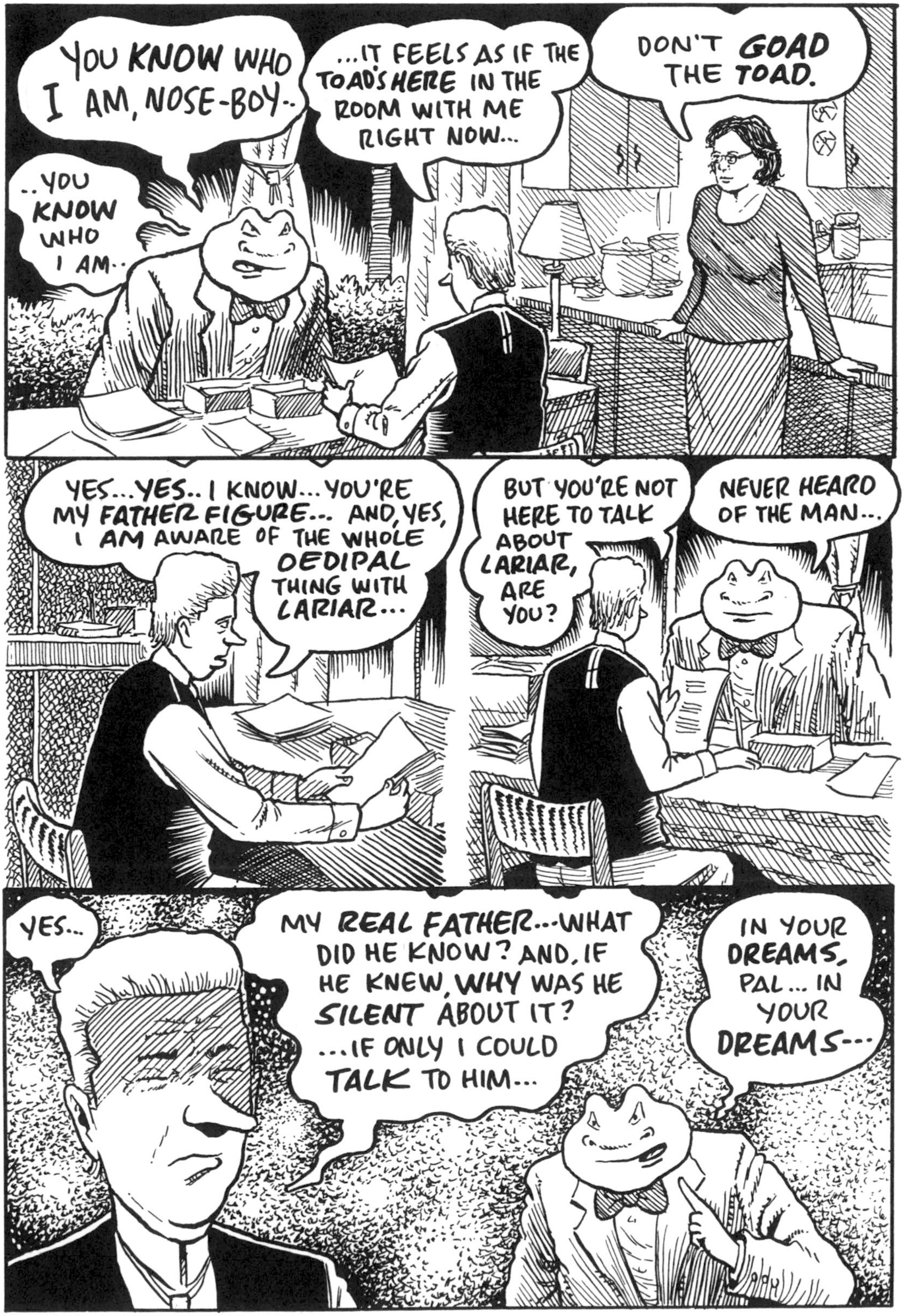
YOU KNOW WHO I AM, NOSE-BOY..
..YOU KNOW WHO I AM..
...IT FEELS AS IF THE TOAD'S HERE IN THE ROOM WITH ME RIGHT NOW...
DON'T GOAD THE TOAD.
YES...YES..I KNOW...YOU'RE MY FATHER FIGURE... AND, YES, I AM AWARE OF THE WHOLE OEDIPAL THING WITH LARIAR...
BUT YOU'RE NOT HERE TO TALK ABOUT LARIAR, ARE YOU?
NEVER HEARD OF THE MAN...
YES...
MY REAL FATHER...WHAT DID HE KNOW? AND, IF HE KNEW, WHY WAS HE SILENT ABOUT IT? ...IF ONLY I COULD TALK TO HIM...
IN YOUR DREAMS, PAL... IN YOUR DREAMS...

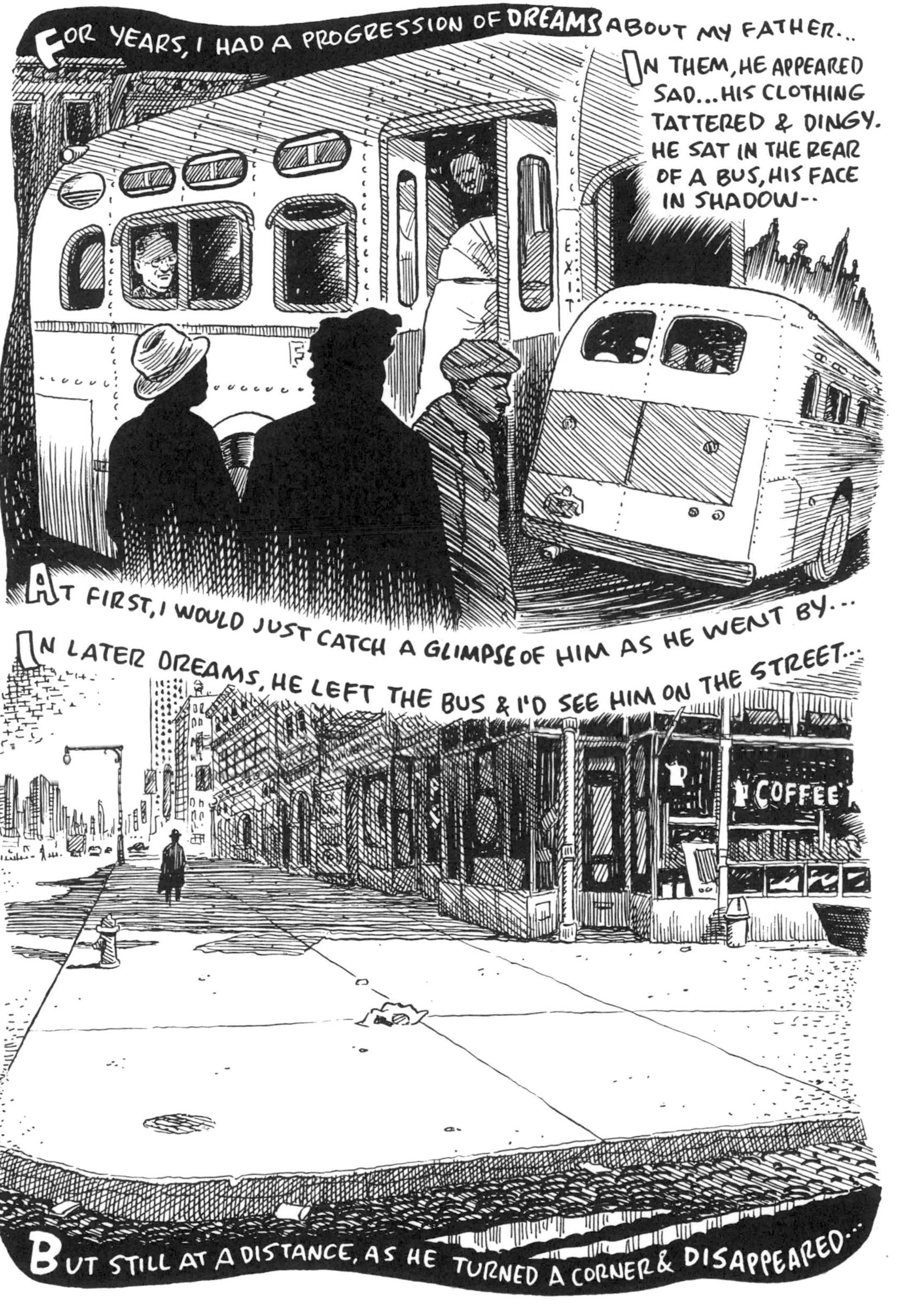
FOR YEARS, I HAD A PROGRESSION OF DREAMS ABOUT MY FATHER...
IN THEM, HE APPEARED SAD...HIS CLOTHING TATTERED & DINGY. HE SAT IN THE REAR OF A BUS, HIS FACE IN SHADOW--
EXIT
AT FIRST, I WOULD JUST CATCH A GLIMPSE OF HIM AS HE WENT BY...
IN LATER DREAMS, HE LEFT THE BUS & I'D SEE HIM ON THE STREET...
COFFEE
BUT STILL AT A DISTANCE, AS HE TURNED A CORNER & DISAPPEARED...

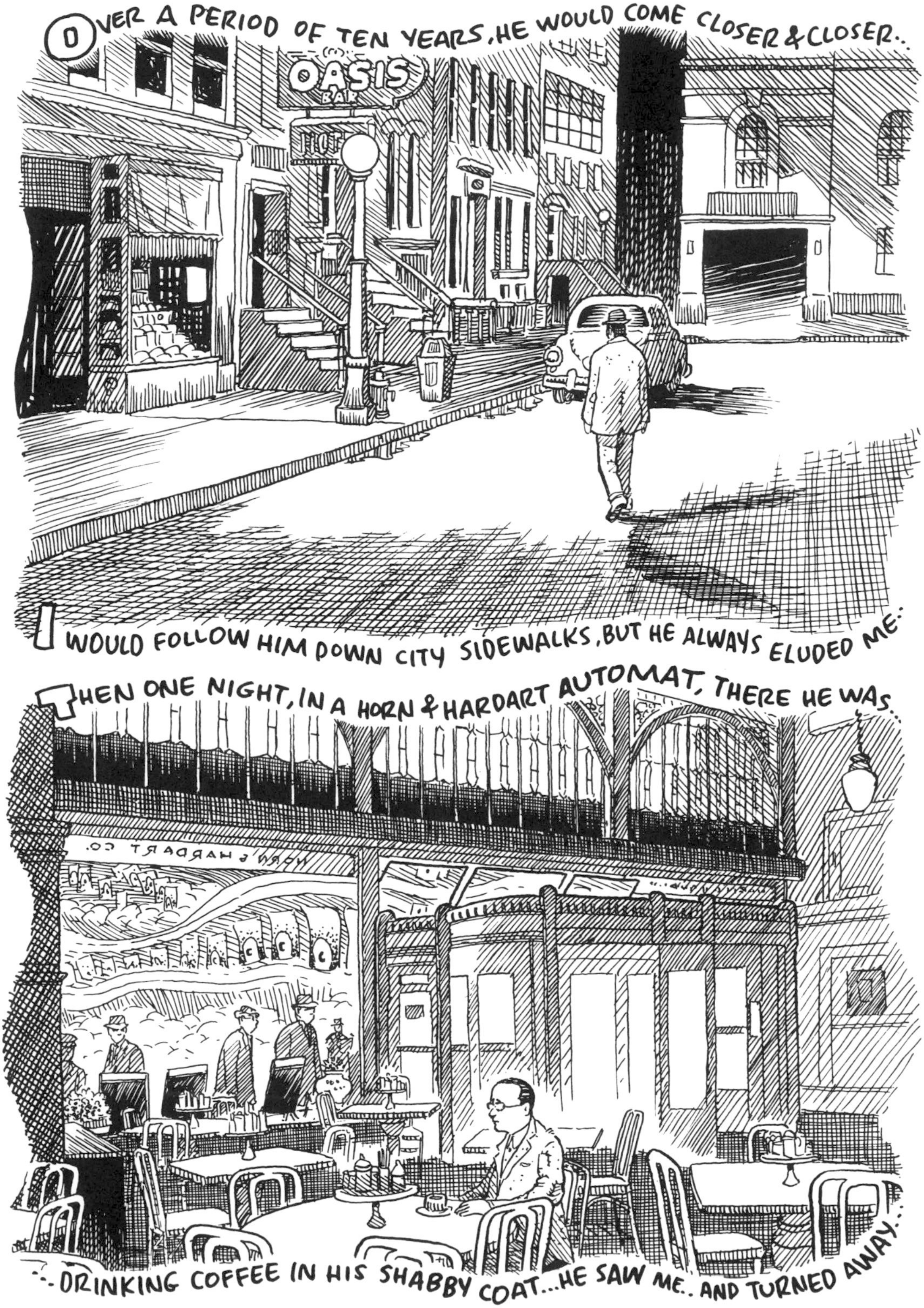
OVER A PERIOD OF TEN YEARS, HE WOULD COME CLOSER & CLOSER..
OASIS
I WOULD FOLLOW HIM DOWN CITY SIDEWALKS, BUT HE ALWAYS ELUDED ME..
THEN ONE NIGHT, IN A HORN & HARDART AUTOMAT, THERE HE WAS..
..DRINKING COFFEE IN HIS SHABBY COAT...HE SAW ME.. AND TURNED AWAY..

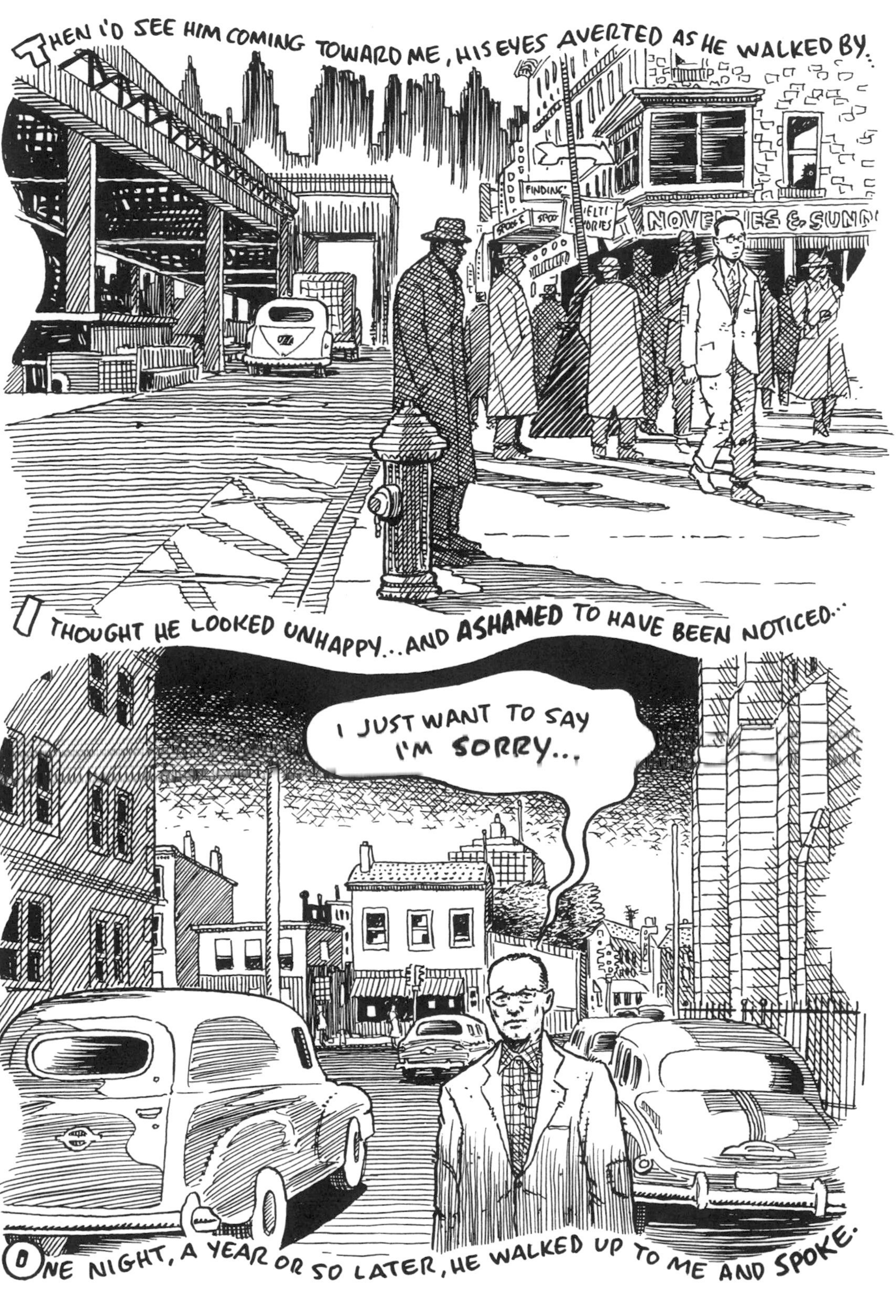
THEN I'D SEE HIM COMING TOWARD ME, HIS EYES AVERTED AS HE WALKED BY...
FINDING
I THOUGHT HE LOOKED UNHAPPY... AND ASHAMED TO HAVE BEEN NOTICED...
I JUST WANT TO SAY I'M SORRY...
ONE NIGHT, A YEAR OR SO LATER, HE WALKED UP TO ME AND SPOKE.

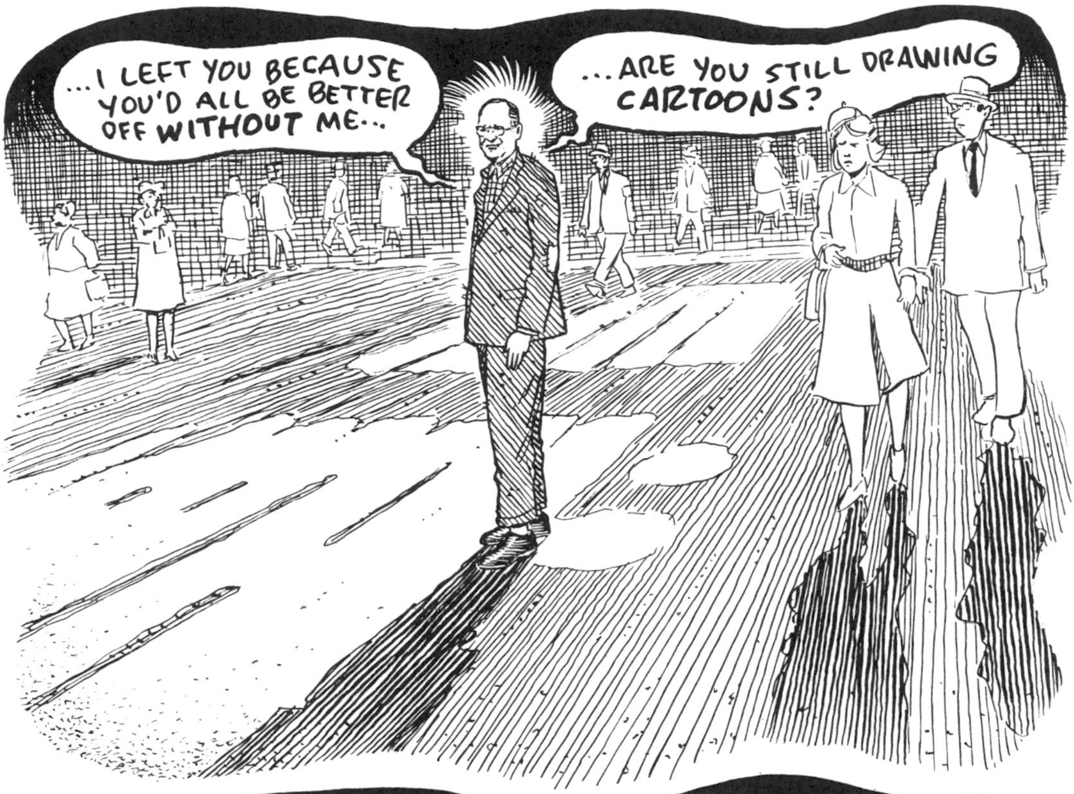
...I LEFT YOU BECAUSE YOU'D ALL BE BETTER OFF WITHOUT ME...
...ARE YOU STILL DRAWING CARTOONS?

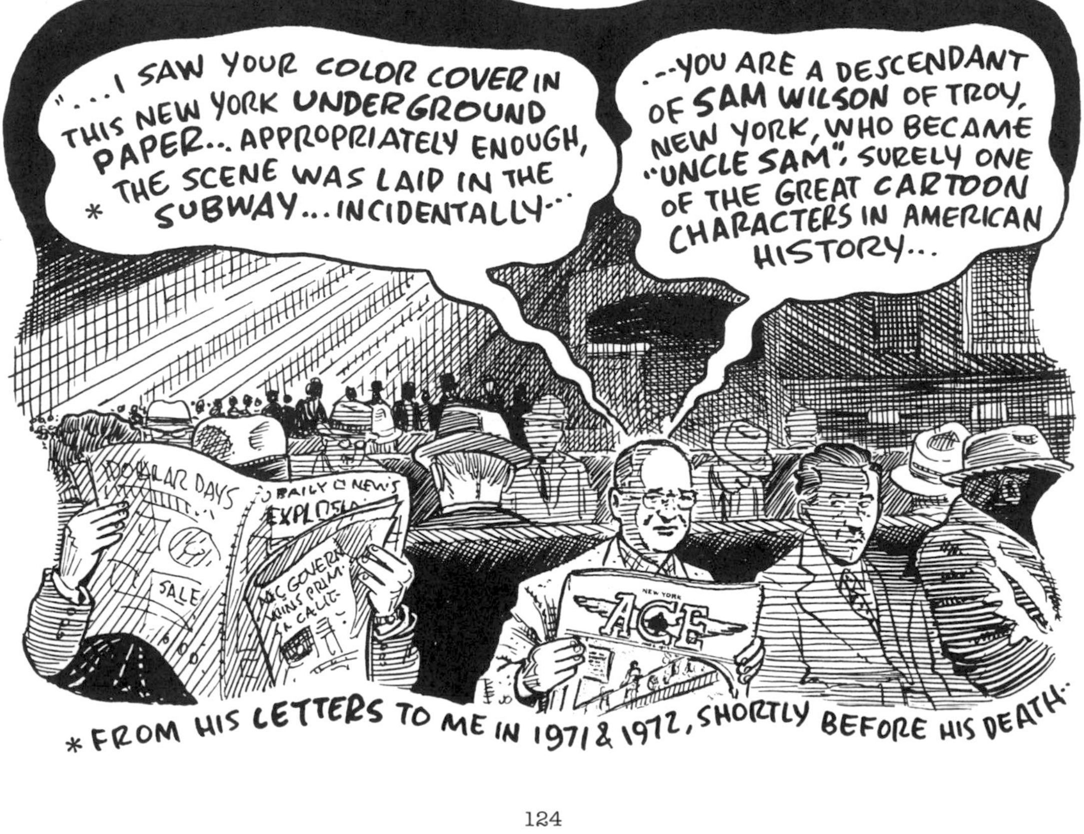
"...I SAW YOUR COLOR COVER IN THIS NEW YORK UNDERGROUND PAPER... APPROPRIATELY ENOUGH, THE SCENE WAS LAID IN THE * SUBWAY... INCIDENTALLY...
...YOU ARE A DESCENDANT OF SAM WILSON OF TROY, NEW YORK, WHO BECAME "UNCLE SAM", SURELY ONE OF THE GREAT CARTOON CHARACTERS IN AMERICAN HISTORY...
DOLLAR DAYS
SALE
DAILY NEWS
NEW YORK
ACE

* FROM HIS LETTERS TO ME IN 1971 & 1972, SHORTLY BEFORE HIS DEATH.

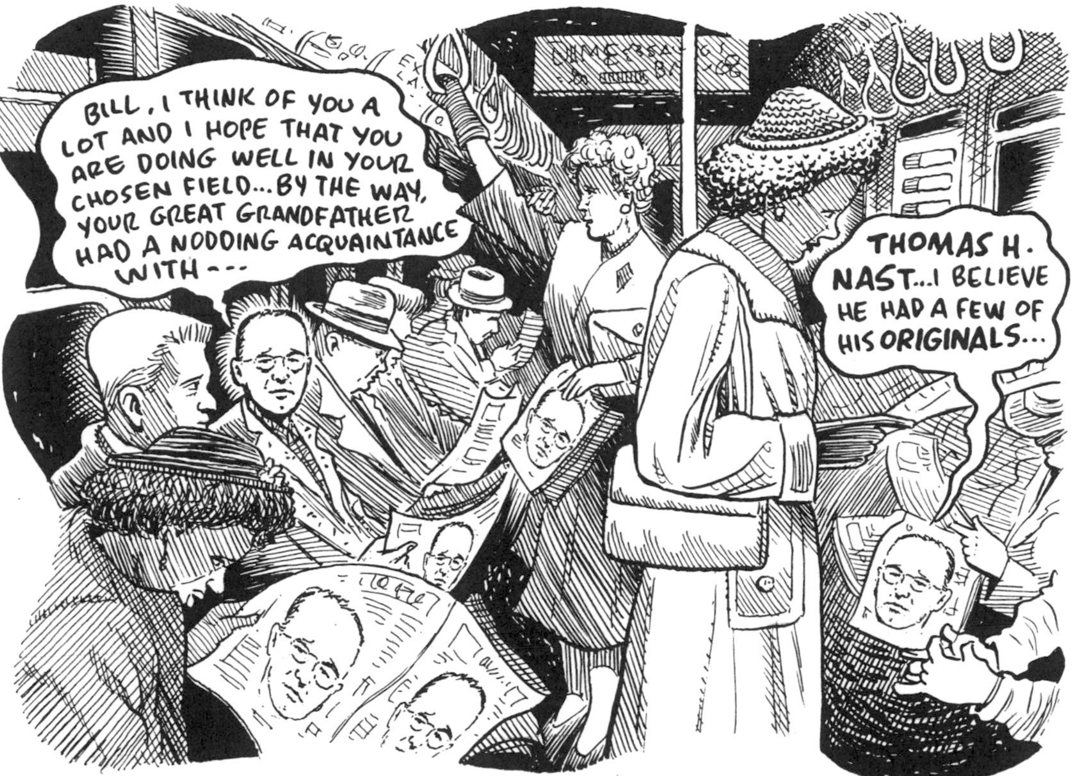
BILL, I THINK OF YOU A LOT AND I HOPE THAT YOU ARE DOING WELL IN YOUR CHOSEN FIELD... BY THE WAY, YOUR GREAT GRANDFATHER HAD A NODDING ACQUAINTANCE WITH---
THOMAS H. NAST... I BELIEVE HE HAD A FEW OF HIS ORIGINALS...

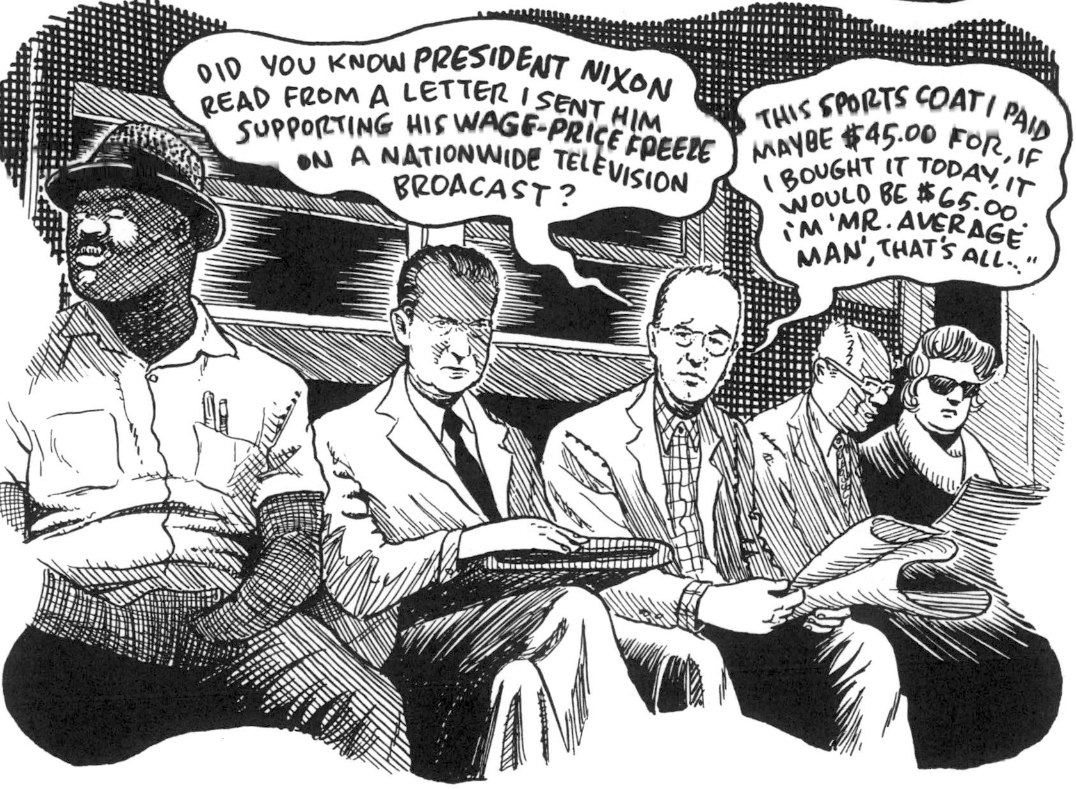
DID YOU KNOW PRESIDENT NIXON READ FROM A LETTER I SENT HIM SUPPORTING HIS WAGE-PRICE FREEZE ON A NATIONWIDE TELEVISION BROACAST?
THIS SPORTS COAT I PAID MAYBE $45.00 FOR, IF I BOUGHT IT TODAY, IT WOULD BE $65.00. I'M 'MR. AVERAGE MAN', THAT'S ALL..."

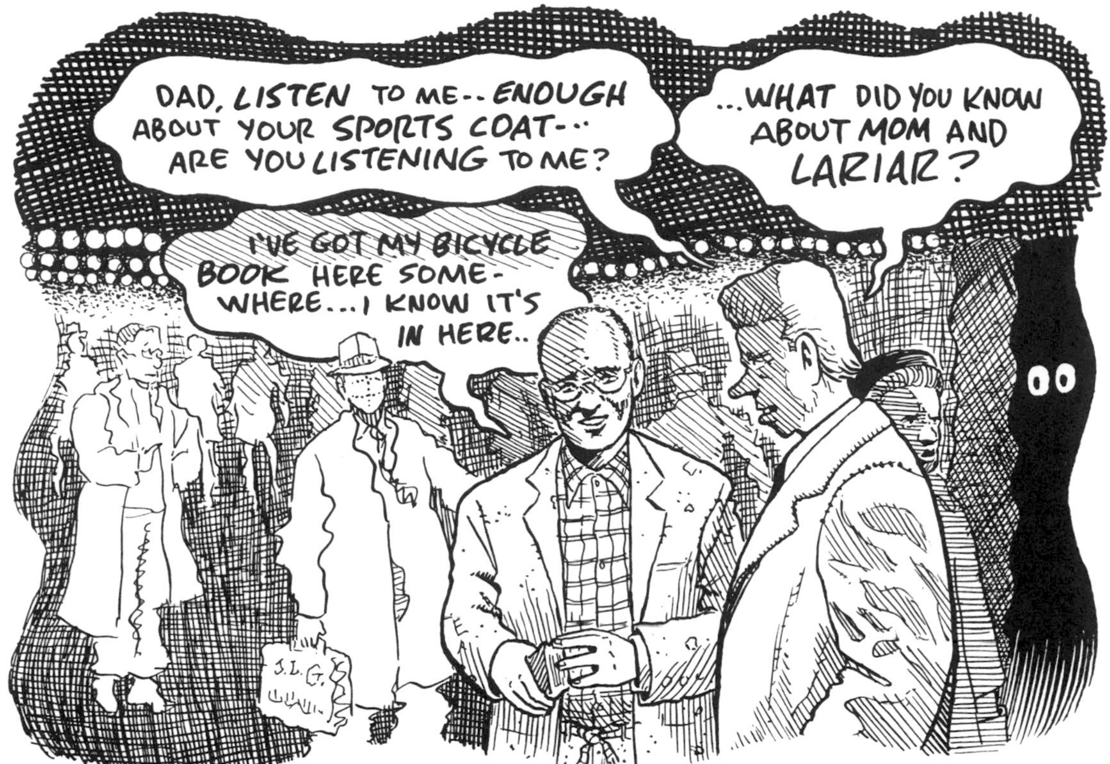
DAD, LISTEN TO ME-- ENOUGH ABOUT YOUR SPORTS COAT-- ARE YOU LISTENING TO ME?
...WHAT DID YOU KNOW ABOUT MOM AND LARIAR?
I'VE GOT MY BICYCLE BOOK HERE SOME-WHERE... I KNOW IT'S IN HERE..
J.L.G.

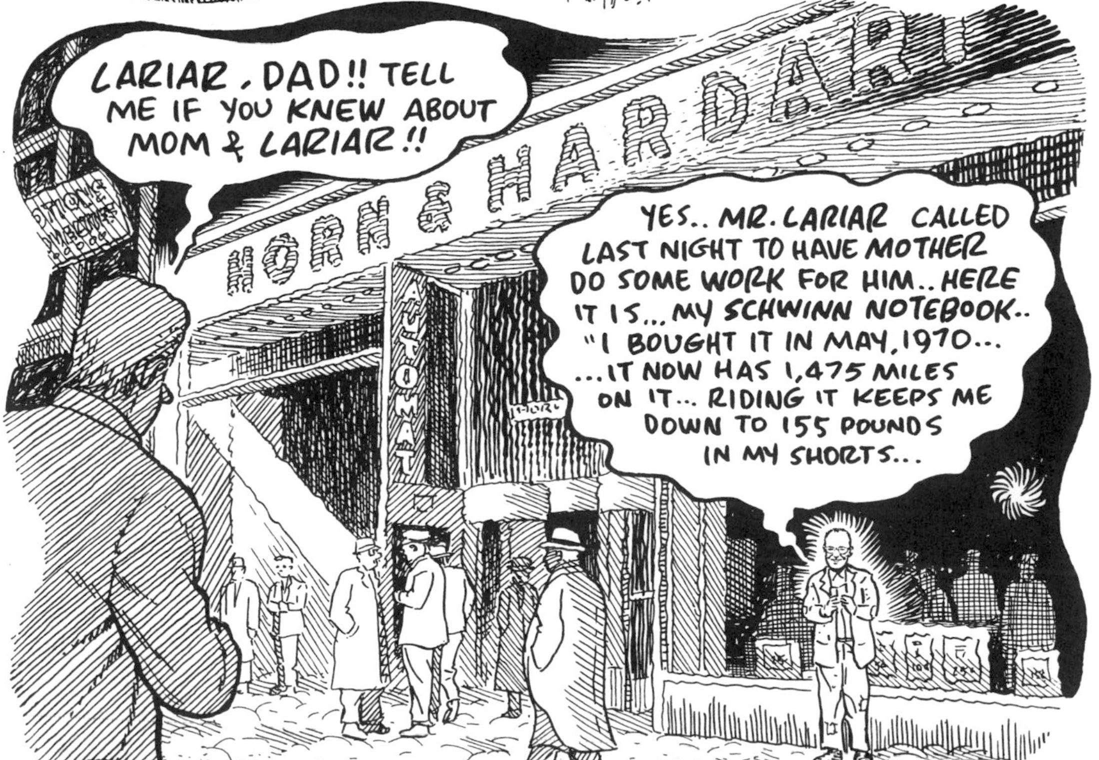
LARIAR, DAD!! TELL ME IF YOU KNEW ABOUT MOM & LARIAR!!
AUTOMAT
YES.. MR. LARIAR CALLED LAST NIGHT TO HAVE MOTHER DO SOME WORK FOR HIM.. HERE IT IS... MY SCHWINN NOTEBOOK.. "I BOUGHT IT IN MAY, 1970... ...IT NOW HAS 1,475 MILES ON IT... RIDING IT KEEPS ME DOWN TO 155 POUNDS IN MY SHORTS...

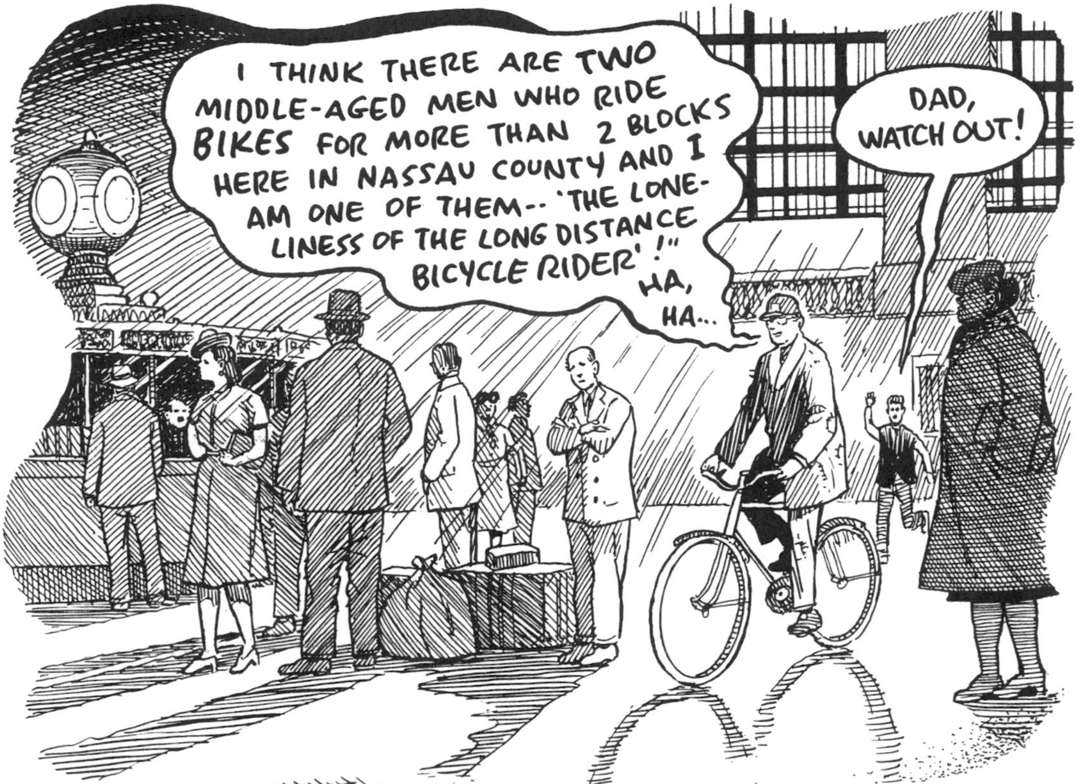
I THINK THERE ARE TWO MIDDLE-AGED MEN WHO RIDE BIKES FOR MORE THAN 2 BLOCKS HERE IN NASSAU COUNTY AND I AM ONE OF THEM-- 'THE LONELINESS OF THE LONG DISTANCE BICYCLE RIDER'!" HA, HA...
DAD, WATCH OUT!

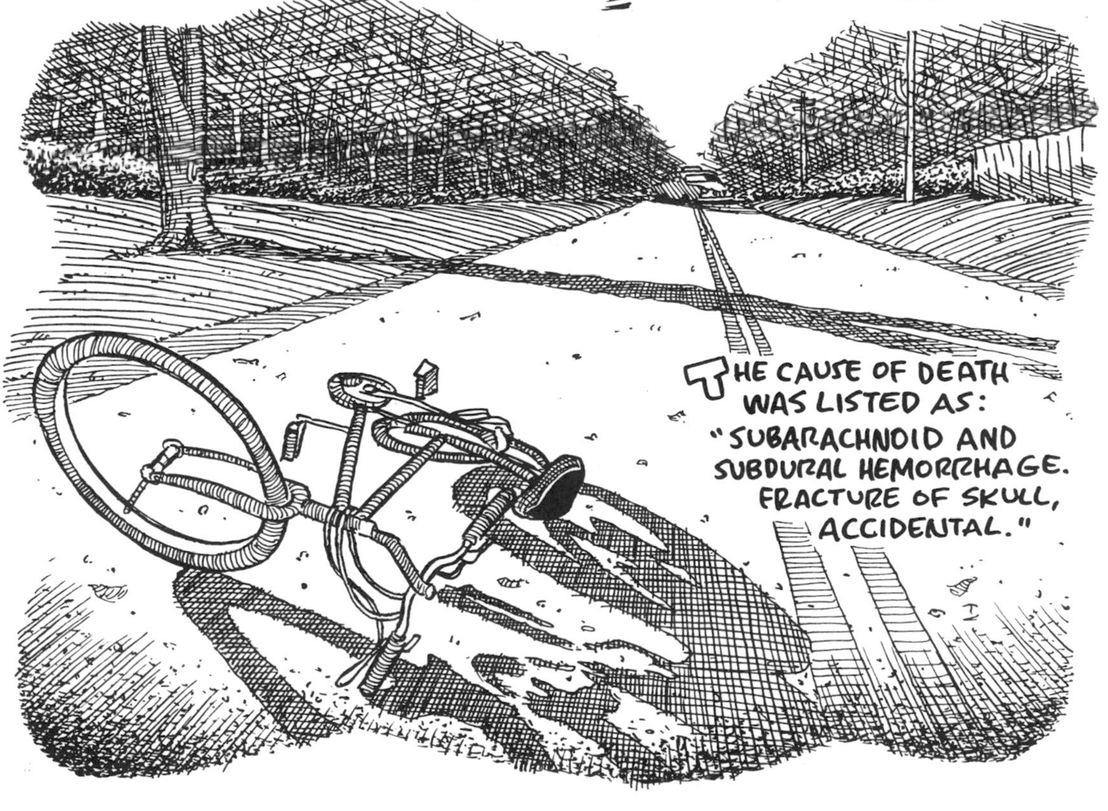
THE CAUSE OF DEATH WAS LISTED AS: "SUBARACHNOID AND SUBDURAL HEMORRHAGE. FRACTURE OF SKULL, ACCIDENTAL."

WHILE MY FATHER MIGHT HAVE SUSPECTED THE AFFAIR--OVER A SPAN OF SIXTEEN LONG YEARS--"PHIL", HIS FICTIONAL COUNTERPART IN MY MOTHER'S NOVEL, NOT ONLY HAD HIS SUSPICIONS, HE ACTED ON THEM. IN THE NOVEL, *HARRIET* TELLS PHIL BEE IS CHEATING ON HIM....

"...HE HAD TO FIND OUT."

HARRIET SAYS BEE USES HER HOUSE IN BROOKLYN AS THEIR LOVE NEST...

"THIS IS A WILD GOOSE CHASE. NOTHING TO WORRY ABOUT--I TRUST HER--SHE WOULDN'T DO SUCH A THING."

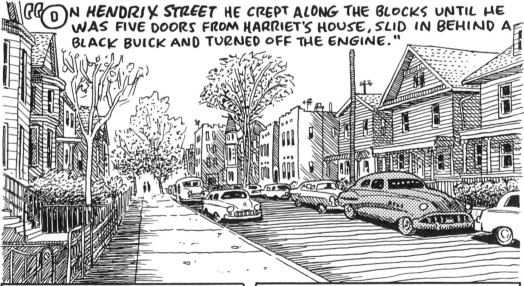

"ON HENDRIX STREET HE CREPT ALONG THE BLOCKS UNTIL HE WAS FIVE DOORS FROM HARRIET'S HOUSE, SLID IN BEHIND A BLACK BUICK AND TURNED OFF THE ENGINE."

"HE PREPARED HIMSELF TO WAIT, LEANING BACK, EYES ON THE REAR VIEW MIRROR..."

"AT 2:15 BEE'S VW PULLED UP TO THE CURB IN FRONT OF HARRIET'S GATE AND SHE GOT OUT, ALONE."

128

" AT THE FRONT DOOR SOMETHING CAUGHT HER ATTENTION..."

" SHE WATCHED AS AN MG CAME TO A STOP BEHIND HER CAR."

" A MAN IN A GRAY RAINCOAT GOT OUT AND WENT THROUGH HARRIET'S GATE. BEE WAITED..."

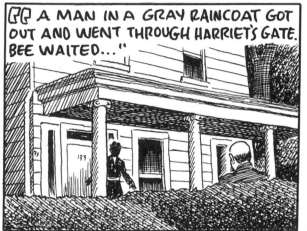

" THEY KISSED & WENT IN."

" PHIL SAT AND STARED AT THE CLOSED DOOR... IT COULD BE HOURS BEFORE THEY CAME OUT. HOURS OF SWEATY GROPING AT EACH OTHER... HOURS OF GASPING AND MOANING AND -- BODIES RUBBING TOGETHER, LEGS TANGLED, ARMS CLUTCHING, LIPS --- LIPS ---"

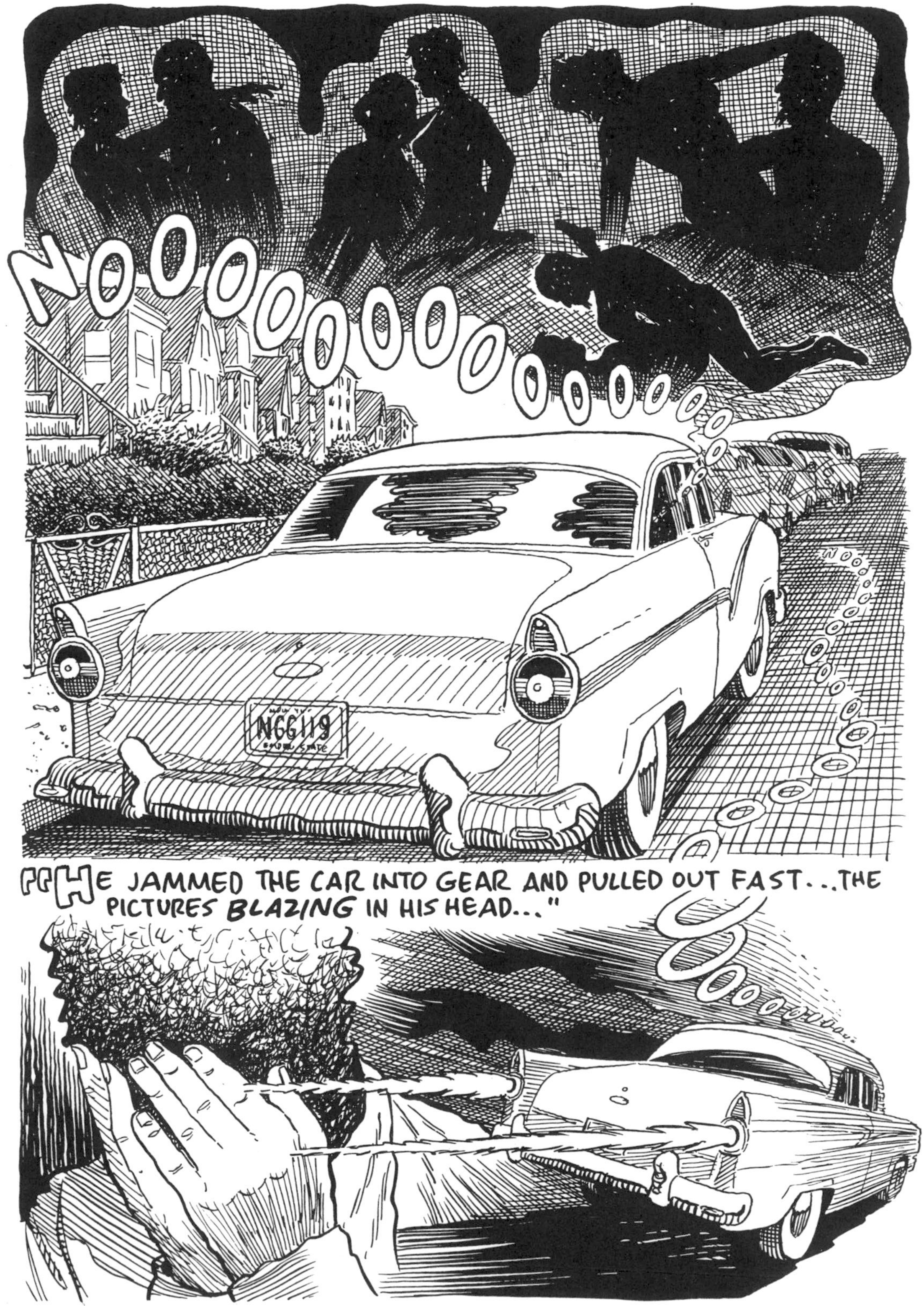
NOOOOOOOOOOOOOOOOO
NG6119
"HE JAMMED THE CAR INTO GEAR AND PULLED OUT FAST...THE PICTURES BLAZING IN HIS HEAD..."

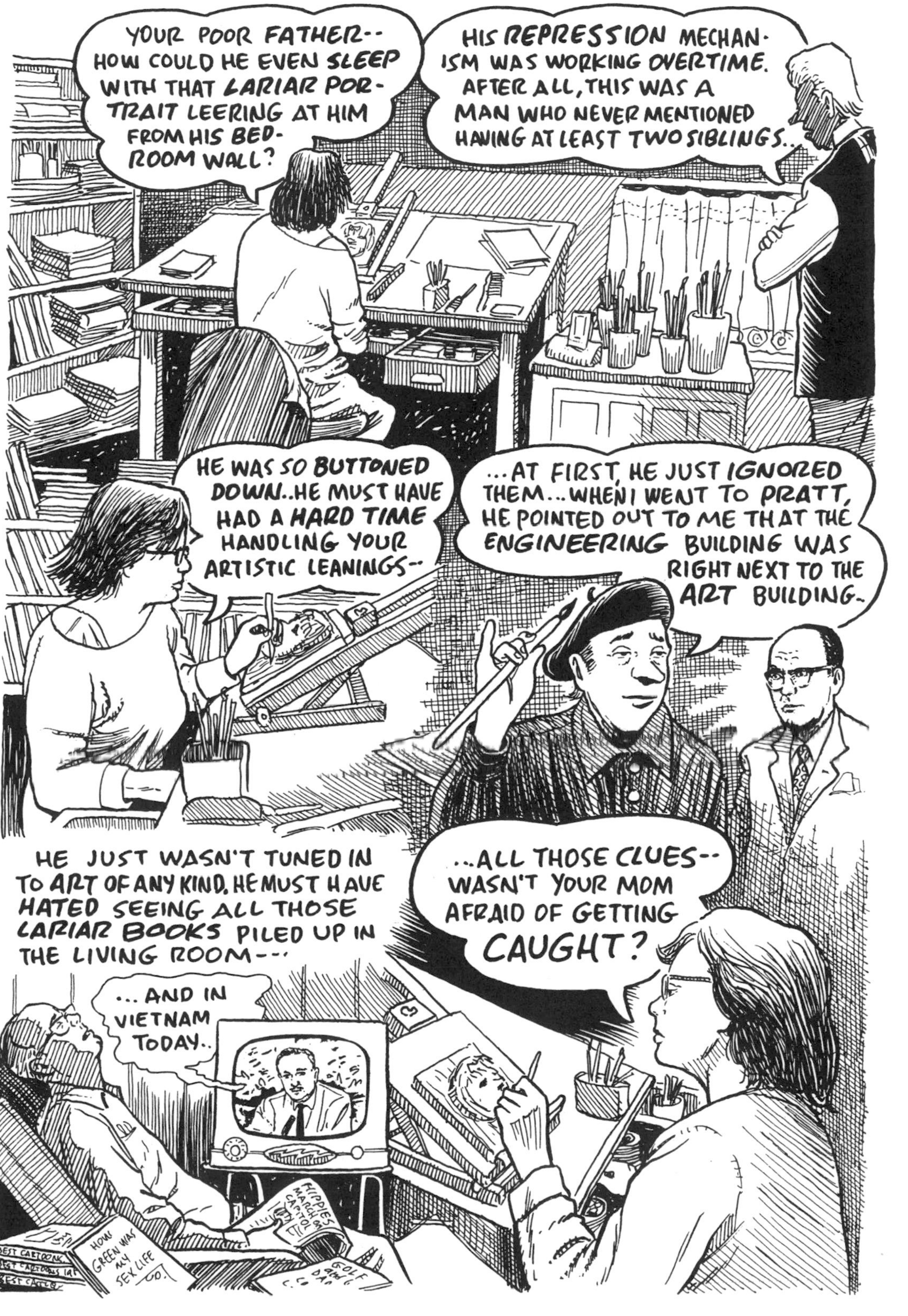
YOUR POOR FATHER-- HOW COULD HE EVEN SLEEP WITH THAT LARIAR PORTRAIT LEERING AT HIM FROM HIS BEDROOM WALL?
HIS REPRESSION MECHANISM WAS WORKING OVERTIME. AFTER ALL, THIS WAS A MAN WHO NEVER MENTIONED HAVING AT LEAST TWO SIBLINGS...
HE WAS SO BUTTONED DOWN..HE MUST HAVE HAD A HARD TIME HANDLING YOUR ARTISTIC LEANINGS--
...AT FIRST, HE JUST IGNORED THEM... WHEN I WENT TO PRATT, HE POINTED OUT TO ME THAT THE ENGINEERING BUILDING WAS RIGHT NEXT TO THE ART BUILDING..
HE JUST WASN'T TUNED IN TO ART OF ANY KIND. HE MUST HAVE HATED SEEING ALL THOSE LARIAR BOOKS PILED UP IN THE LIVING ROOM--.
...ALL THOSE CLUES-- WASN'T YOUR MOM AFRAID OF GETTING CAUGHT?
...AND IN VIETNAM TODAY..

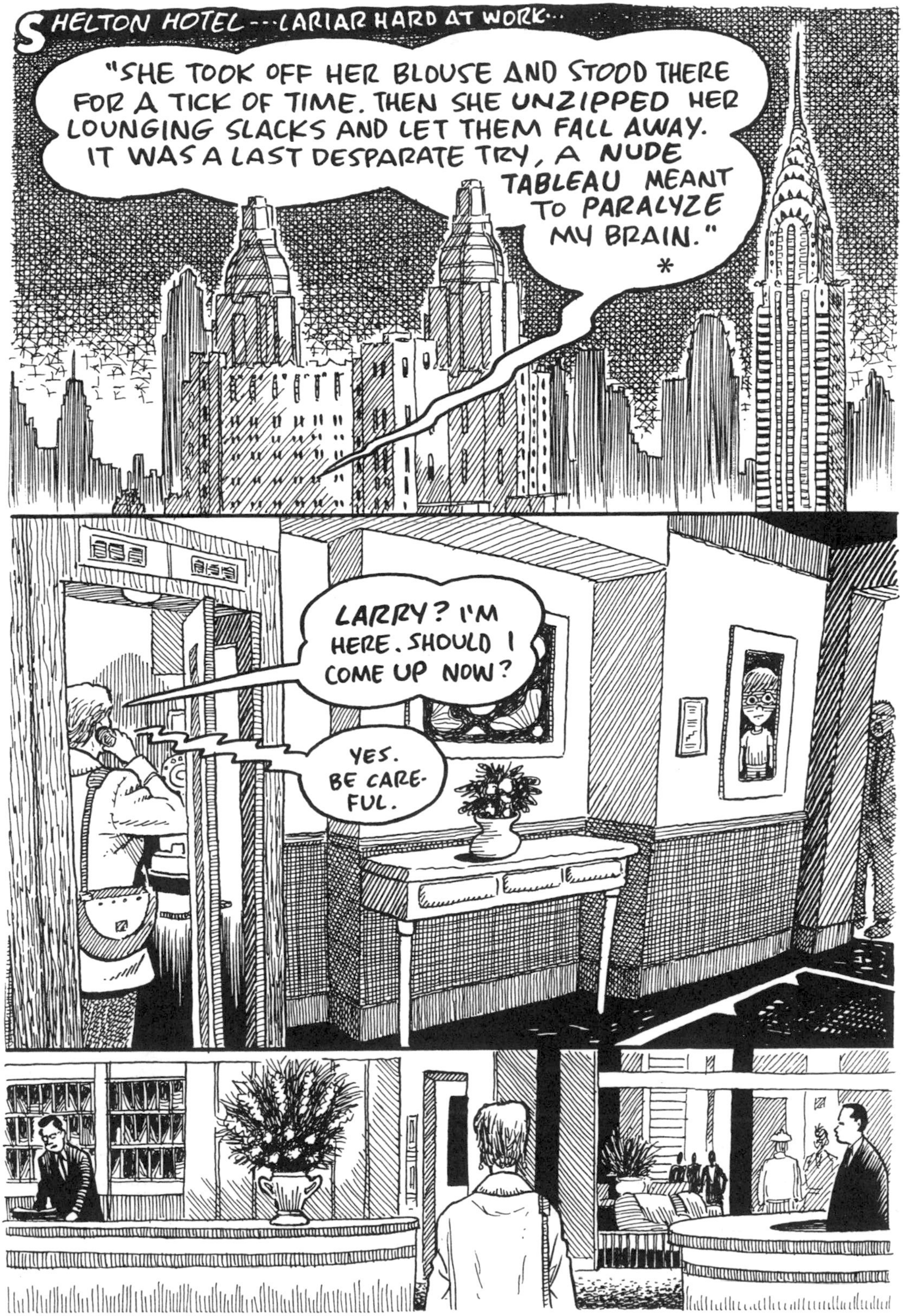
SHELTON HOTEL---LARIAR HARD AT WORK...
"SHE TOOK OFF HER BLOUSE AND STOOD THERE FOR A TICK OF TIME. THEN SHE UNZIPPED HER LOUNGING SLACKS AND LET THEM FALL AWAY. IT WAS A LAST DESPARATE TRY, A NUDE TABLEAU MEANT TO PARALYZE MY BRAIN." *
LARRY? I'M HERE. SHOULD I COME UP NOW?
YES. BE CARE-FUL.

* FROM LARIAR'S CRIME NOVEL, "YOU CAN'T CATCH ME"

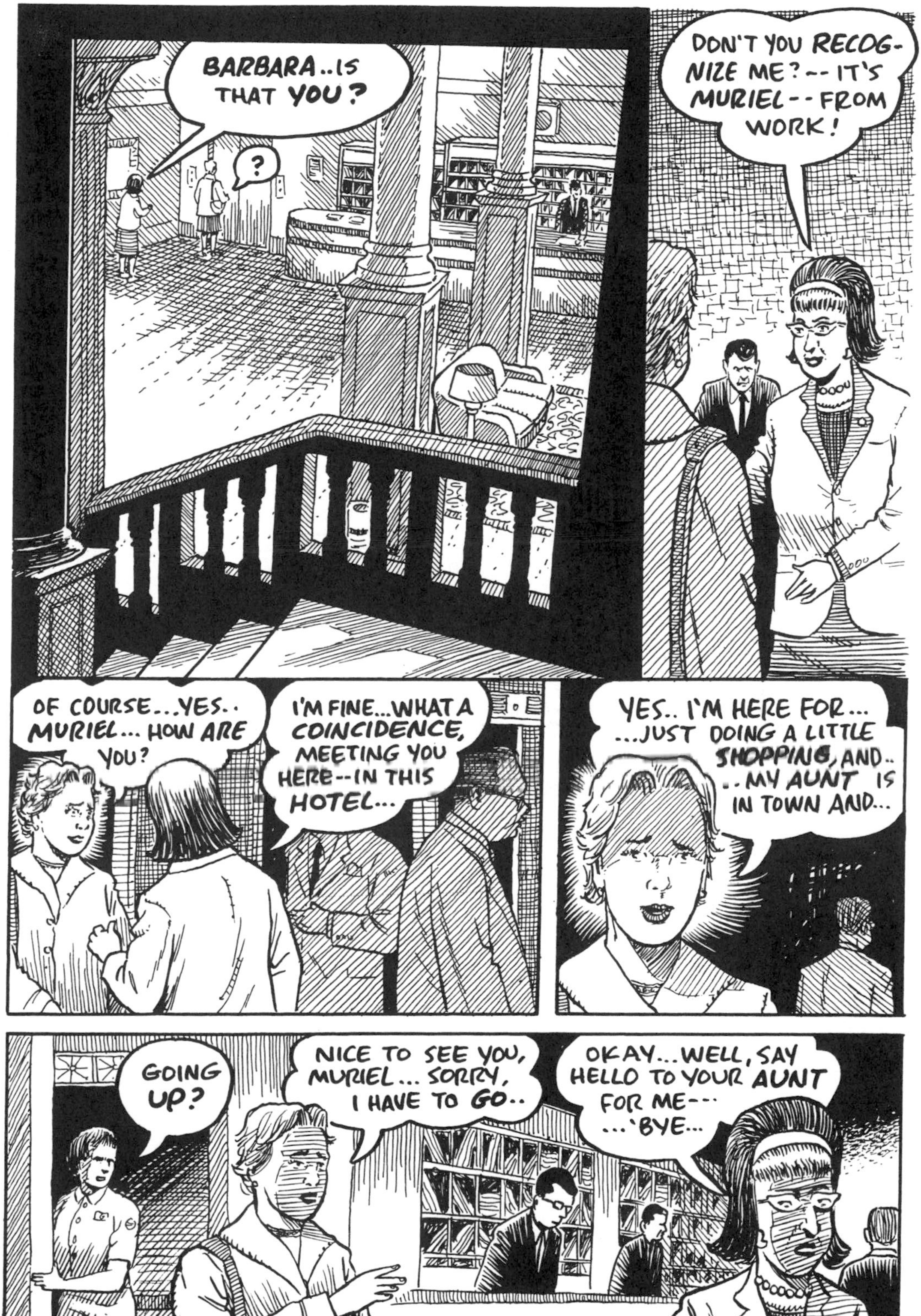
BARBARA..IS THAT YOU?
?
DON'T YOU RECOGNIZE ME?-- IT'S MURIEL--FROM WORK!
OF COURSE...YES.. MURIEL... HOW ARE YOU?
I'M FINE...WHAT A COINCIDENCE, MEETING YOU HERE--IN THIS HOTEL...
YES.. I'M HERE FOR... ...JUST DOING A LITTLE SHOPPING, AND.. ..MY AUNT IS IN TOWN AND...
GOING UP?
NICE TO SEE YOU, MURIEL... SORRY, I HAVE TO GO..
OKAY...WELL, SAY HELLO TO YOUR AUNT FOR ME--- ...'BYE...

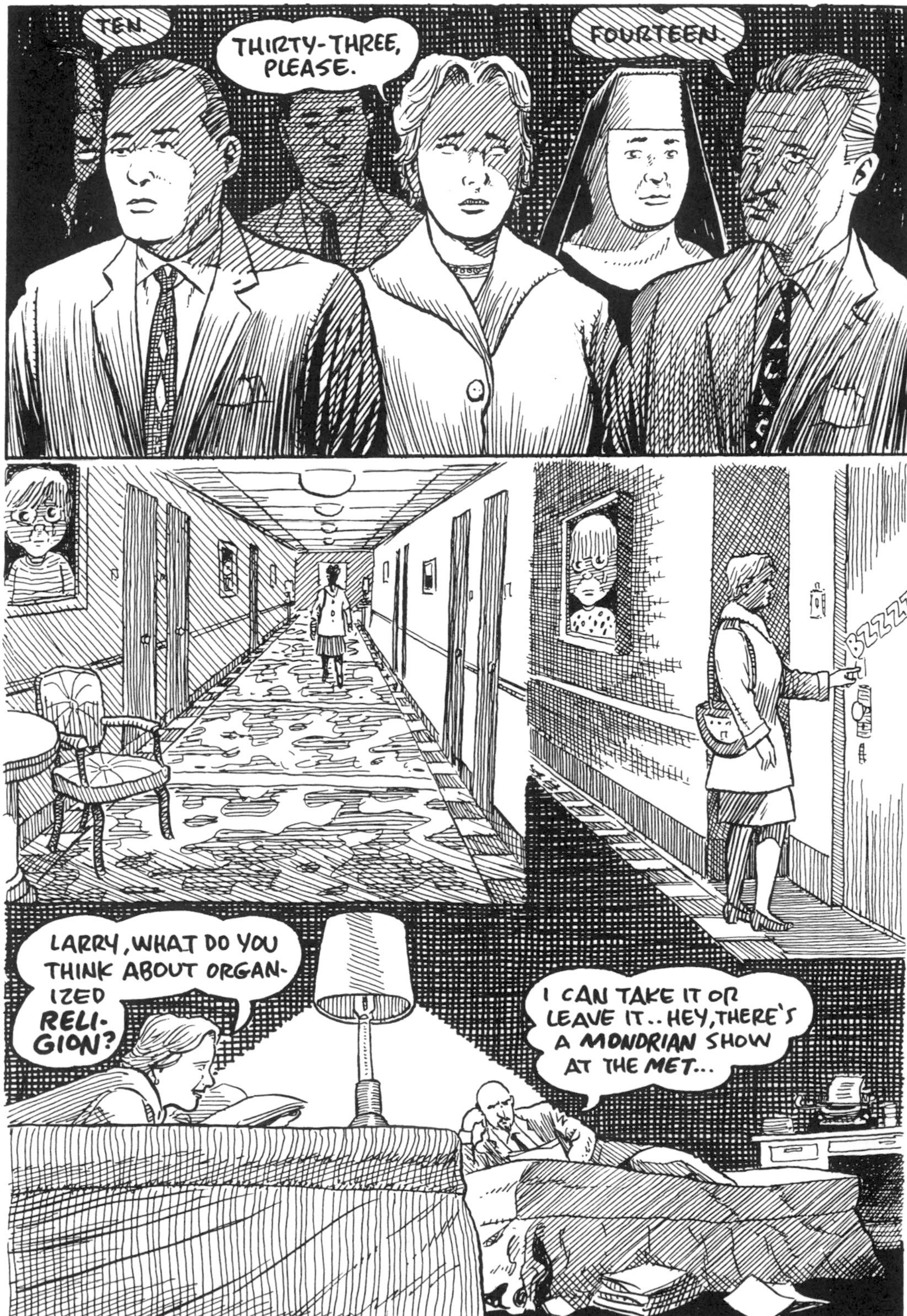
TEN.
THIRTY-THREE, PLEASE.
FOURTEEN.
BZZZZT!
LARRY, WHAT DO YOU THINK ABOUT ORGAN-IZED RELI-GION?
I CAN TAKE IT OR LEAVE IT.. HEY, THERE'S A MONDRIAN SHOW AT THE MET...

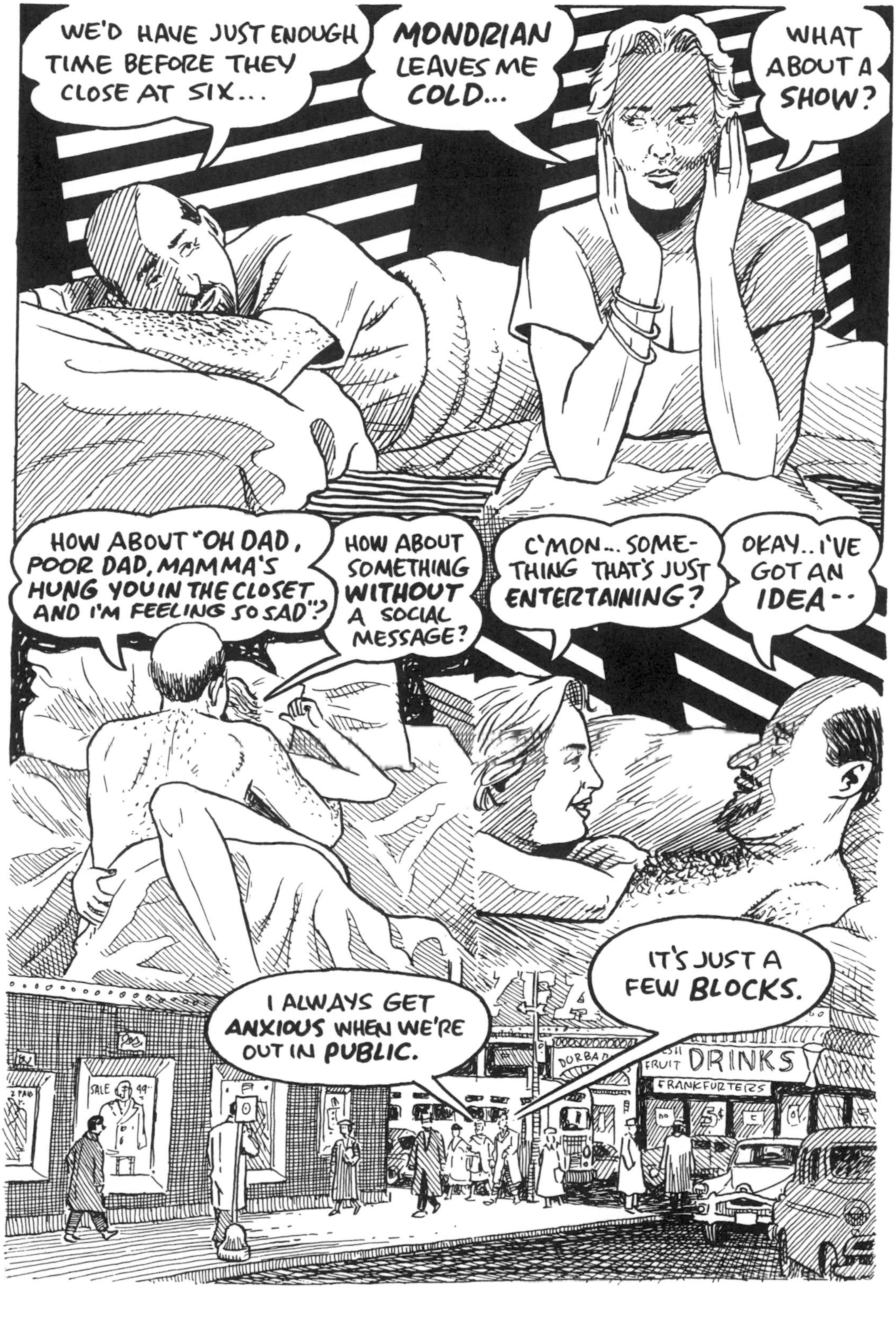
WE'D HAVE JUST ENOUGH TIME BEFORE THEY CLOSE AT SIX...
MONDRIAN LEAVES ME COLD...
WHAT ABOUT A SHOW?
HOW ABOUT "OH DAD, POOR DAD, MAMMA'S HUNG YOU IN THE CLOSET AND I'M FEELING SO SAD"?
HOW ABOUT SOMETHING WITHOUT A SOCIAL MESSAGE?
C'MON... SOMETHING THAT'S JUST ENTERTAINING?
OKAY.. I'VE GOT AN IDEA--
I ALWAYS GET ANXIOUS WHEN WE'RE OUT IN PUBLIC.
IT'S JUST A FEW BLOCKS.
DRINKS
FRANKFURTERS

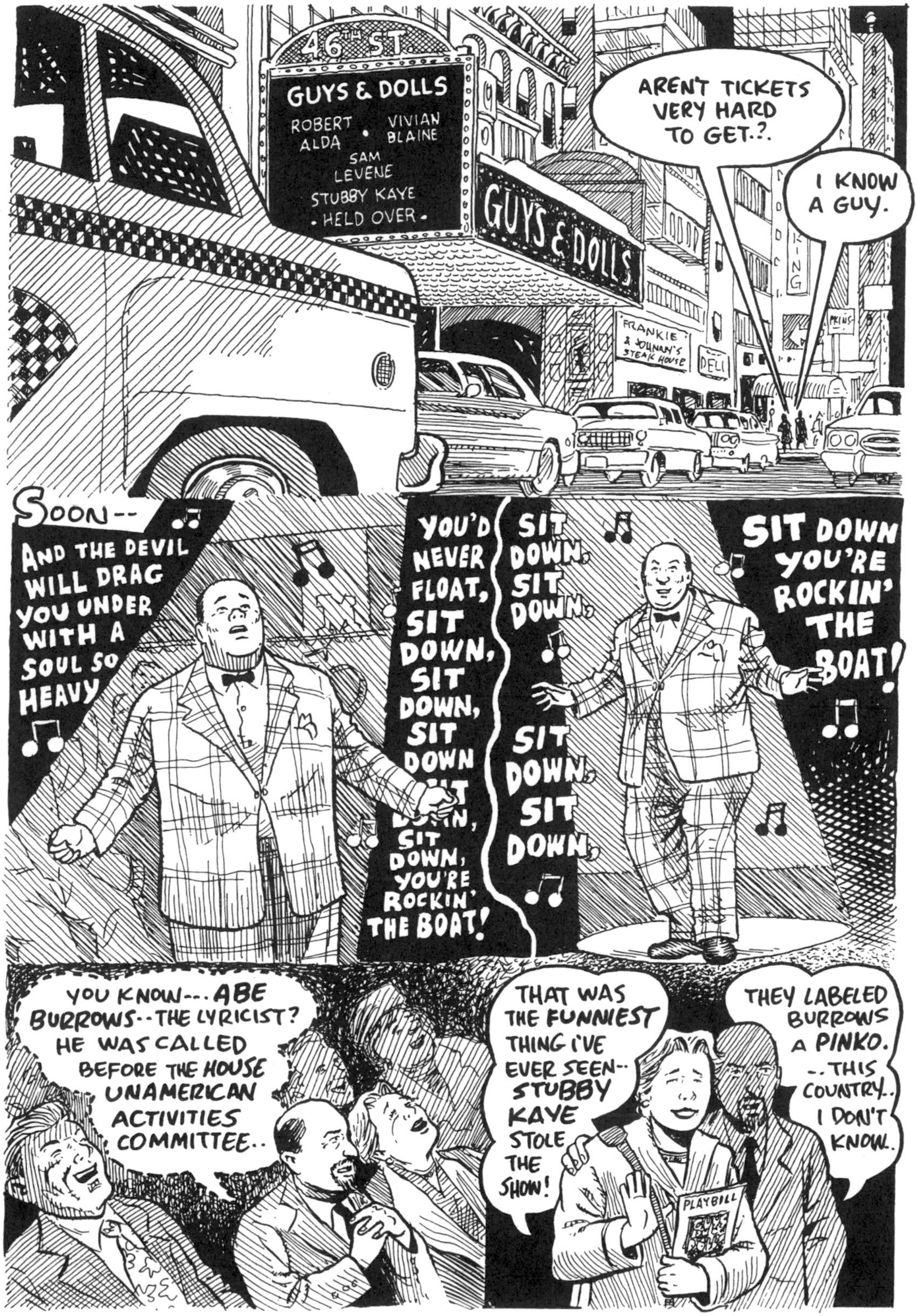
46TH ST.
GUYS & DOLLS
ROBERT ALDA • VIVIAN BLAINE
SAM LEVENE
STUBBY KAYE
• HELD OVER •
GUYS & DOLLS
FRANKIE & JOHNNY'S STEAK HOUSE
DELI
AREN'T TICKETS VERY HARD TO GET..?.
I KNOW A GUY.
SOON--
AND THE DEVIL WILL DRAG YOU UNDER WITH A SOUL SO HEAVY
YOU'D NEVER FLOAT, SIT DOWN, SIT DOWN, SIT DOWN SIT DOWN, SIT DOWN, YOU'RE ROCKIN' THE BOAT!
SIT DOWN, SIT DOWN, SIT DOWN, SIT DOWN,
SIT DOWN YOU'RE ROCKIN' THE BOAT!
YOU KNOW---. ABE BURROWS--THE LYRICIST? HE WAS CALLED BEFORE THE HOUSE UNAMERICAN ACTIVITIES COMMITTEE..
THAT WAS THE FUNNIEST THING I'VE EVER SEEN-- STUBBY KAYE STOLE THE SHOW!
THEY LABELED BURROWS A PINKO. --THIS COUNTRY.. I DON'T KNOW.
PLAYBILL

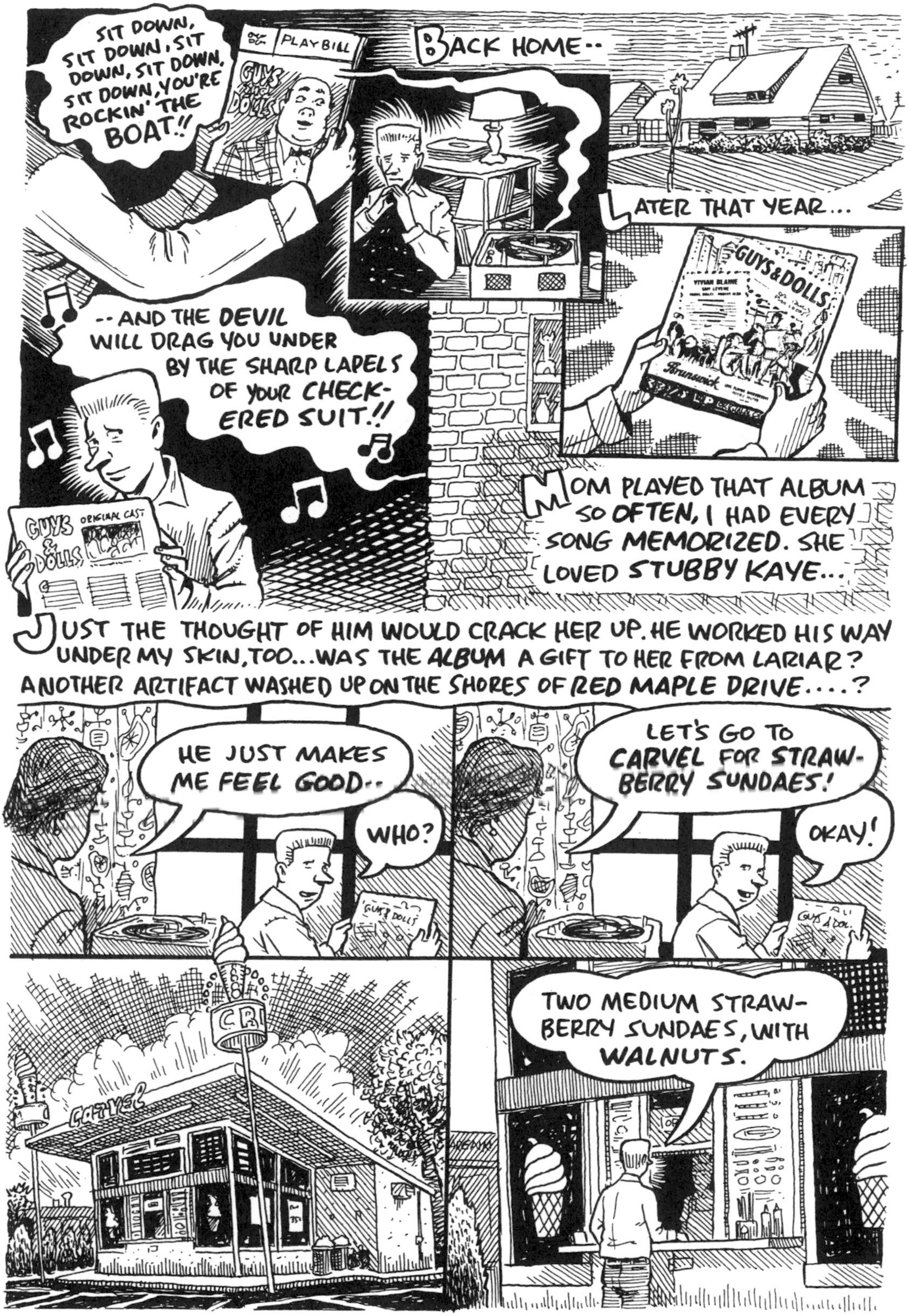

SIT DOWN, SIT DOWN, SIT DOWN, SIT DOWN, SIT DOWN, YOU'RE ROCKIN' THE BOAT!!
PLAYBILL
GUYS AND DOLLS
BACK HOME..
LATER THAT YEAR...
GUYS & DOLLS
Brunswick
--AND THE DEVIL WILL DRAG YOU UNDER BY THE SHARP LAPELS OF YOUR CHECKERED SUIT!!
GUYS & DOLLS ORIGINAL CAST
MOM PLAYED THAT ALBUM SO OFTEN, I HAD EVERY SONG MEMORIZED. SHE LOVED STUBBY KAYE...
JUST THE THOUGHT OF HIM WOULD CRACK HER UP. HE WORKED HIS WAY UNDER MY SKIN, TOO...WAS THE ALBUM A GIFT TO HER FROM LARIAR? ANOTHER ARTIFACT WASHED UP ON THE SHORES OF RED MAPLE DRIVE....?
HE JUST MAKES ME FEEL GOOD..
WHO?
GUYS & DOLLS
LET'S GO TO CARVEL FOR STRAWBERRY SUNDAES!
OKAY!
CARVEL
TWO MEDIUM STRAWBERRY SUNDAES, WITH WALNUTS.

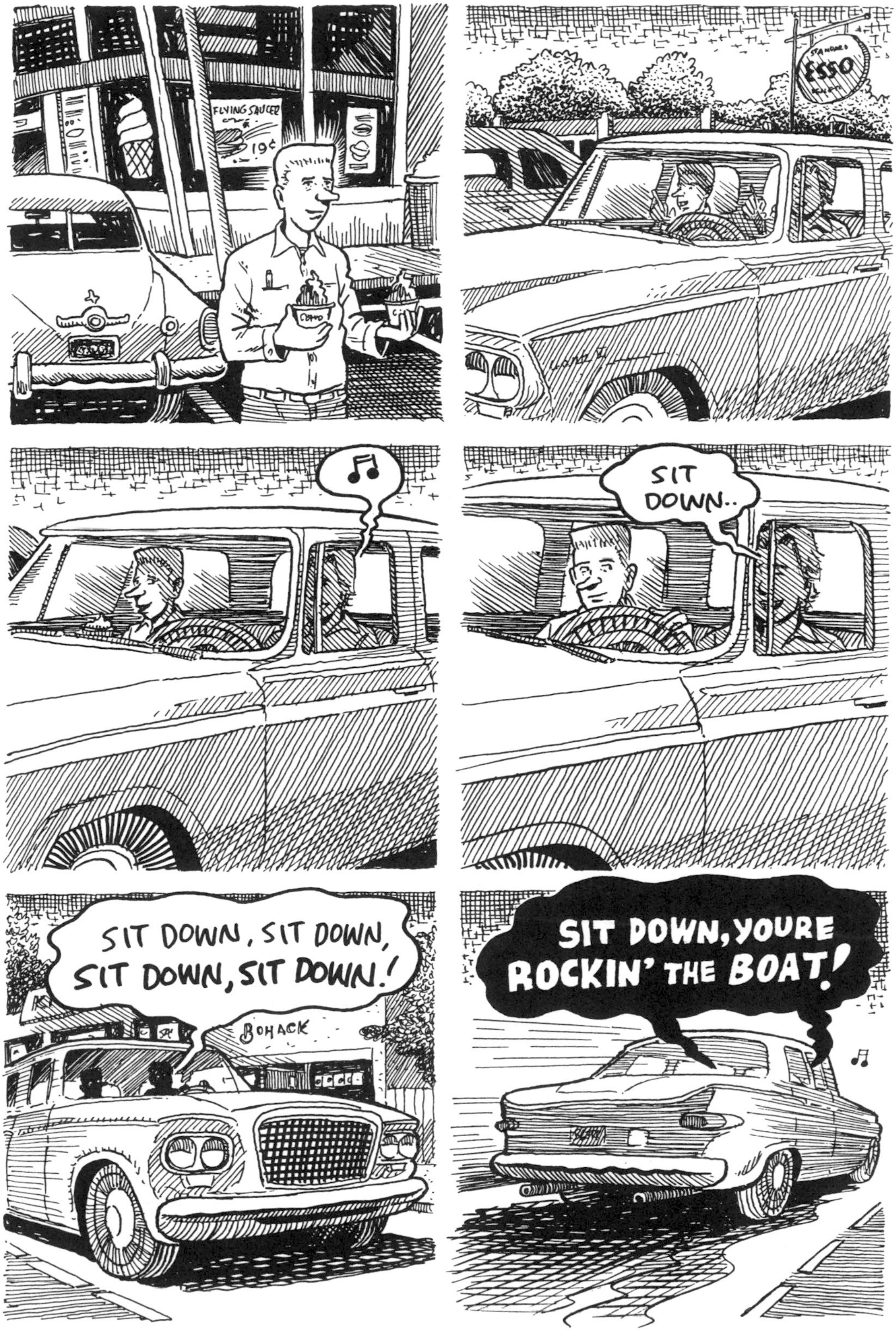
FLYING SAUCER
19¢
STANDARD
ESSO
SIT DOWN..
SIT DOWN, SIT DOWN,
SIT DOWN, SIT DOWN!
BOHACK
SIT DOWN, YOURE
ROCKIN' THE BOAT!

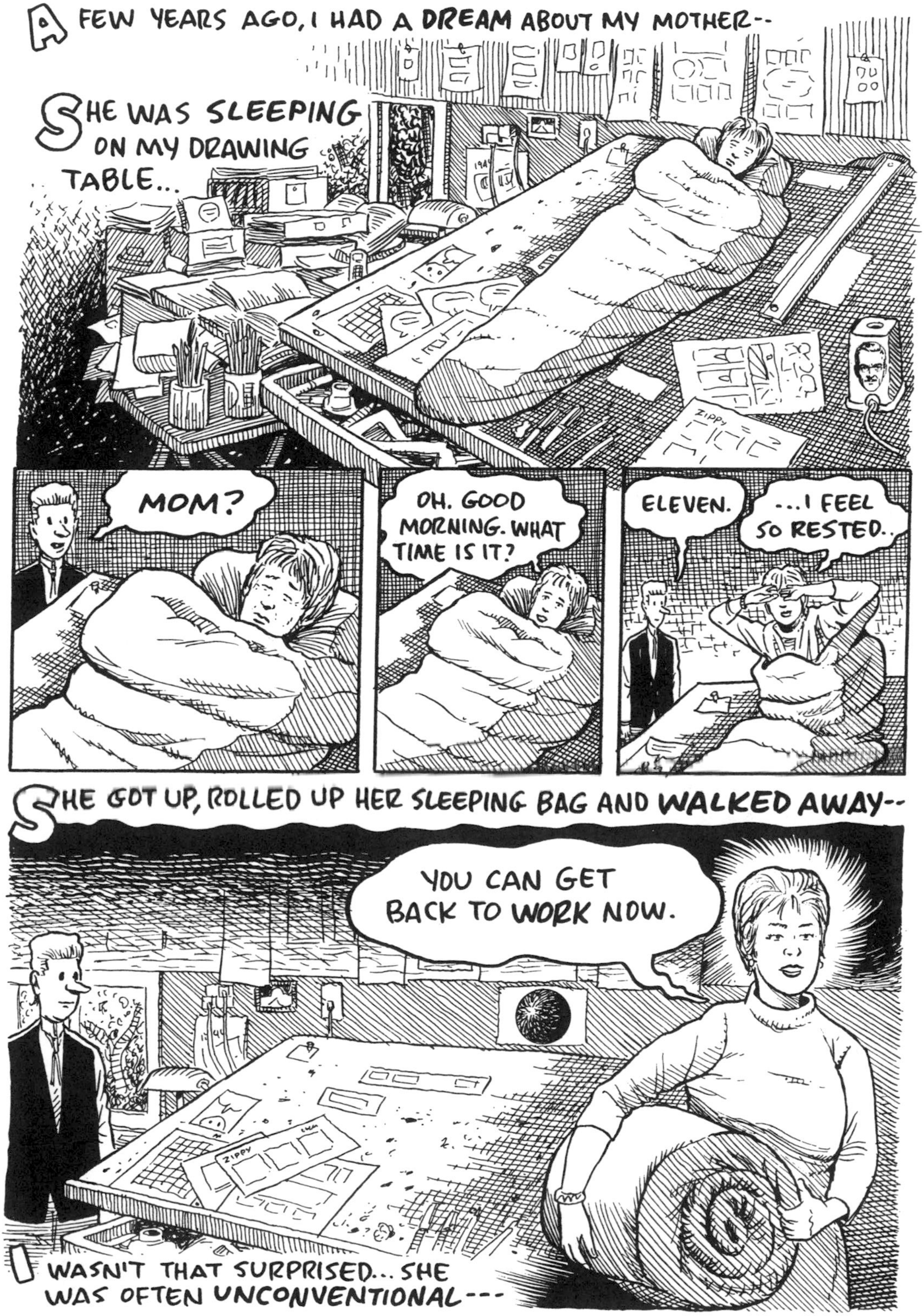
A FEW YEARS AGO, I HAD A DREAM ABOUT MY MOTHER--
SHE WAS SLEEPING ON MY DRAWING TABLE...
MOM?
OH. GOOD MORNING. WHAT TIME IS IT?
ELEVEN.
...I FEEL SO RESTED..
SHE GOT UP, ROLLED UP HER SLEEPING BAG AND WALKED AWAY--
YOU CAN GET BACK TO WORK NOW.
I WASN'T THAT SURPRISED... SHE WAS OFTEN UNCONVENTIONAL---

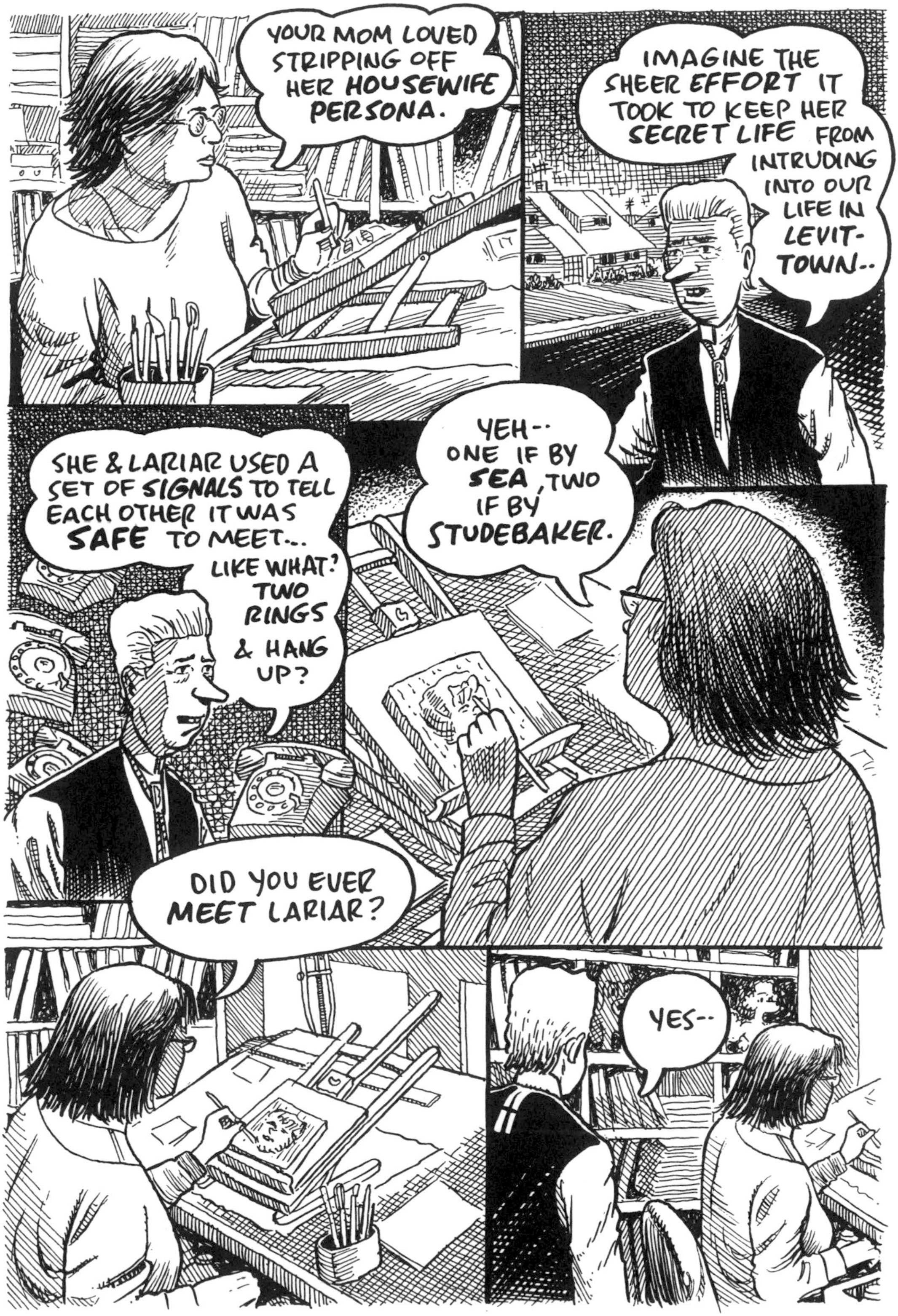
YOUR MOM LOVED STRIPPING OFF HER HOUSEWIFE PERSONA.
IMAGINE THE SHEER EFFORT IT TOOK TO KEEP HER SECRET LIFE FROM INTRUDING INTO OUR LIFE IN LEVIT-TOWN..
SHE & LARIAR USED A SET OF SIGNALS TO TELL EACH OTHER IT WAS SAFE TO MEET...
LIKE WHAT? TWO RINGS & HANG UP?
YEH-- ONE IF BY SEA, TWO IF BY STUDEBAKER.
DID YOU EVER MEET LARIAR?
YES--

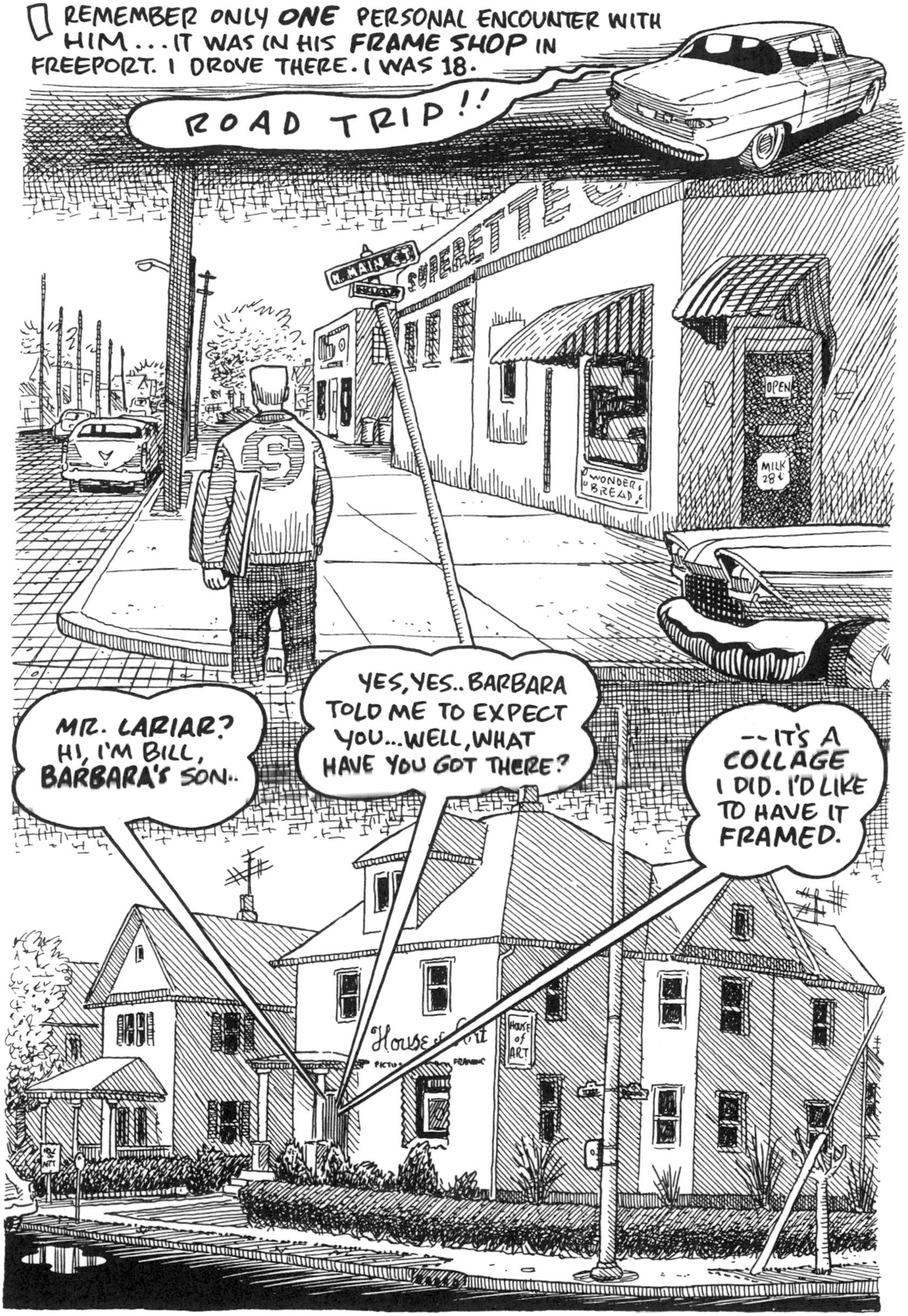
I REMEMBER ONLY ONE PERSONAL ENCOUNTER WITH HIM... IT WAS IN HIS FRAME SHOP IN FREEPORT. I DROVE THERE. I WAS 18.
ROAD TRIP!!
MAIN ST
SUPERETTE
OPEN
MILK 28¢
WONDER BREAD
MR. LARIAR? HI, I'M BILL, BARBARA'S SON..
YES, YES.. BARBARA TOLD ME TO EXPECT YOU... WELL, WHAT HAVE YOU GOT THERE?
-- IT'S A COLLAGE I DID. I'D LIKE TO HAVE IT FRAMED.
HOUSE of ART

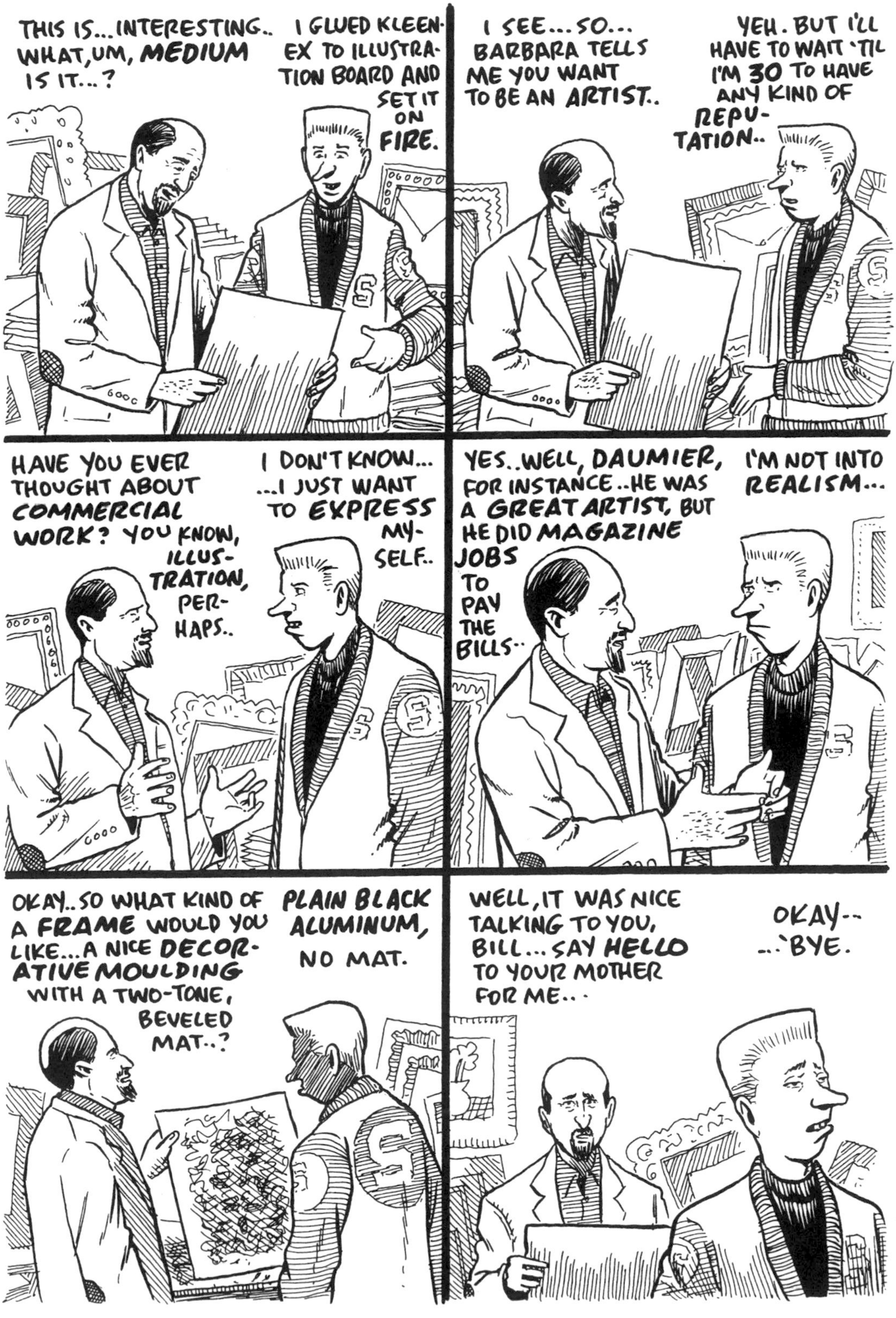
THIS IS... INTERESTING.. WHAT, UM, MEDIUM IS IT...?
I GLUED KLEENEX TO ILLUSTRATION BOARD AND SET IT ON FIRE.
I SEE... SO... BARBARA TELLS ME YOU WANT TO BE AN ARTIST..
YEH. BUT I'LL HAVE TO WAIT 'TIL I'M 30 TO HAVE ANY KIND OF REPUTATION..
HAVE YOU EVER THOUGHT ABOUT COMMERCIAL WORK? YOU KNOW, ILLUSTRATION, PERHAPS..
I DON'T KNOW... ...I JUST WANT TO EXPRESS MYSELF..
YES..WELL, DAUMIER, FOR INSTANCE..HE WAS A GREAT ARTIST, BUT HE DID MAGAZINE JOBS TO PAY THE BILLS..
I'M NOT INTO REALISM...
OKAY..SO WHAT KIND OF A FRAME WOULD YOU LIKE...A NICE DECORATIVE MOULDING WITH A TWO-TONE, BEVELED MAT..?
PLAIN BLACK ALUMINUM, NO MAT.
WELL, IT WAS NICE TALKING TO YOU, BILL... SAY HELLO TO YOUR MOTHER FOR ME...
OKAY-- ..`BYE.

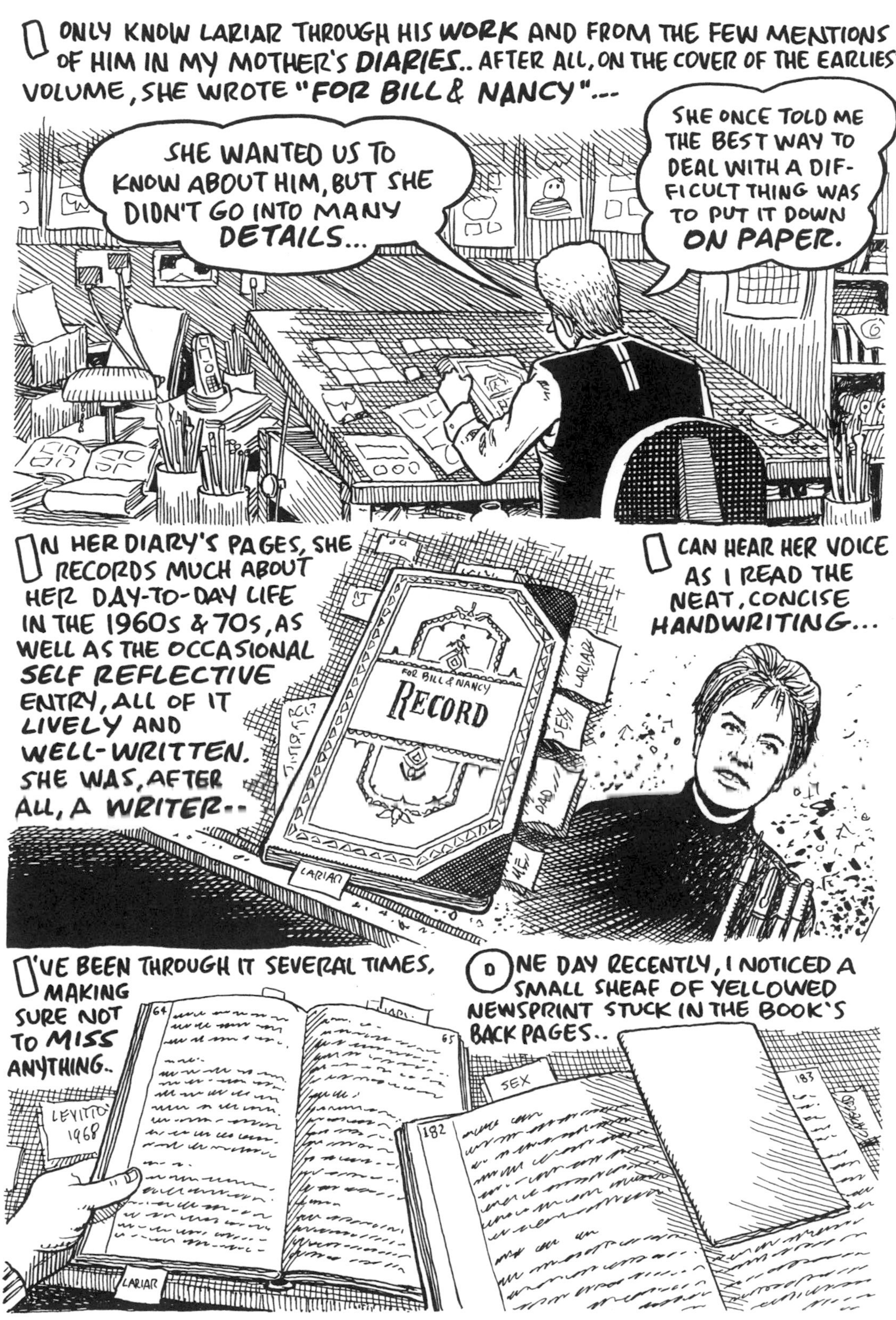
I ONLY KNOW LARIAR THROUGH HIS WORK AND FROM THE FEW MENTIONS OF HIM IN MY MOTHER'S DIARIES.. AFTER ALL, ON THE COVER OF THE EARLIEST VOLUME, SHE WROTE "FOR BILL & NANCY"...
SHE WANTED US TO KNOW ABOUT HIM, BUT SHE DIDN'T GO INTO MANY DETAILS...
SHE ONCE TOLD ME THE BEST WAY TO DEAL WITH A DIFFICULT THING WAS TO PUT IT DOWN ON PAPER.
IN HER DIARY'S PAGES, SHE RECORDS MUCH ABOUT HER DAY-TO-DAY LIFE IN THE 1960s & 70s, AS WELL AS THE OCCASIONAL SELF REFLECTIVE ENTRY, ALL OF IT LIVELY AND WELL-WRITTEN. SHE WAS, AFTER ALL, A WRITER..
FOR BILL & NANCY
RECORD
LARIAR
SEX
DAD
LARIAR
I CAN HEAR HER VOICE AS I READ THE NEAT, CONCISE HANDWRITING...
I'VE BEEN THROUGH IT SEVERAL TIMES, MAKING SURE NOT TO MISS ANYTHING..
64
65
LEVITTO 1968
LARIAR
ONE DAY RECENTLY, I NOTICED A SMALL SHEAF OF YELLOWED NEWSPRINT STUCK IN THE BOOK'S BACK PAGES..
SEX
182
183

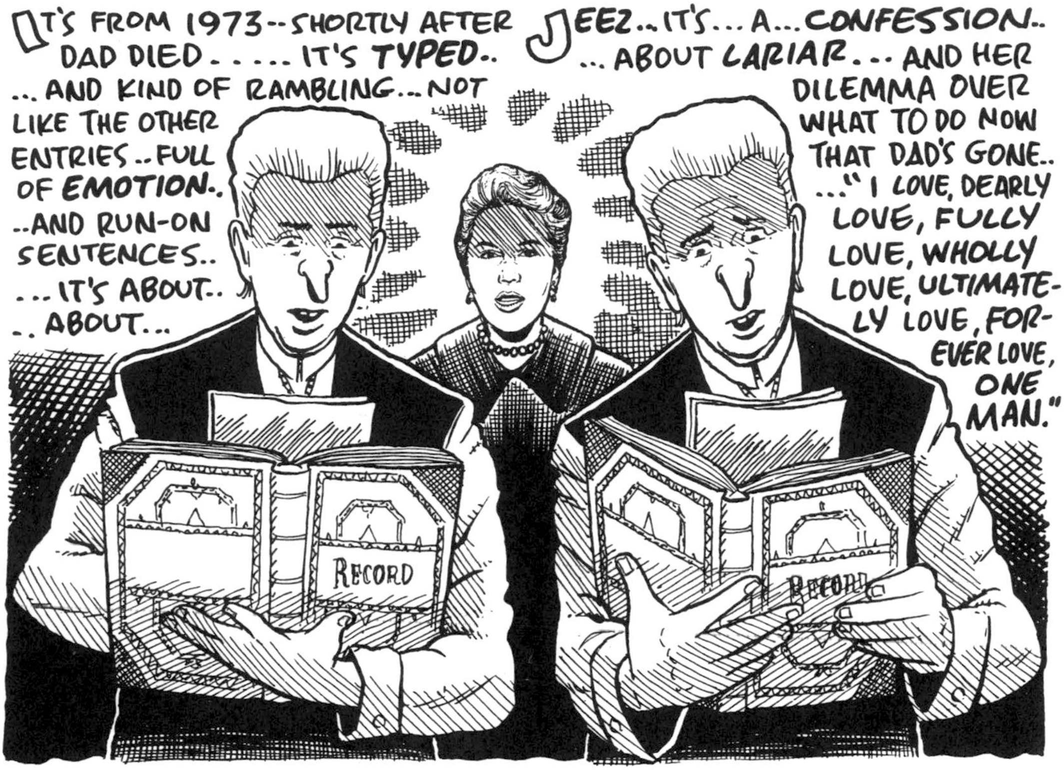
IT'S FROM 1973--SHORTLY AFTER DAD DIED.....IT'S TYPED.. ...AND KIND OF RAMBLING...NOT LIKE THE OTHER ENTRIES..FULL OF EMOTION.. ..AND RUN-ON SENTENCES.. ...IT'S ABOUT.. ..ABOUT...
JEEZ..IT'S...A...CONFESSION.. ...ABOUT LARIAR...AND HER DILEMMA OVER WHAT TO DO NOW THAT DAD'S GONE.. ..."I LOVE, DEARLY LOVE, FULLY LOVE, WHOLLY LOVE, ULTIMATELY LOVE, FOREVER LOVE, ONE MAN."
RECORD
RECORD

I love, dearly love, fully love, wholly love, ultimately love, forever love, one man. From far back I have dearly loved, fully loved, etc.,,,,, one man. Like more than half of my life with my husband. Like everytthing good I have done about my children has come from this one whole, full, ultimate, forever loved man. Like all I have ever done good about myself has come from the same source....

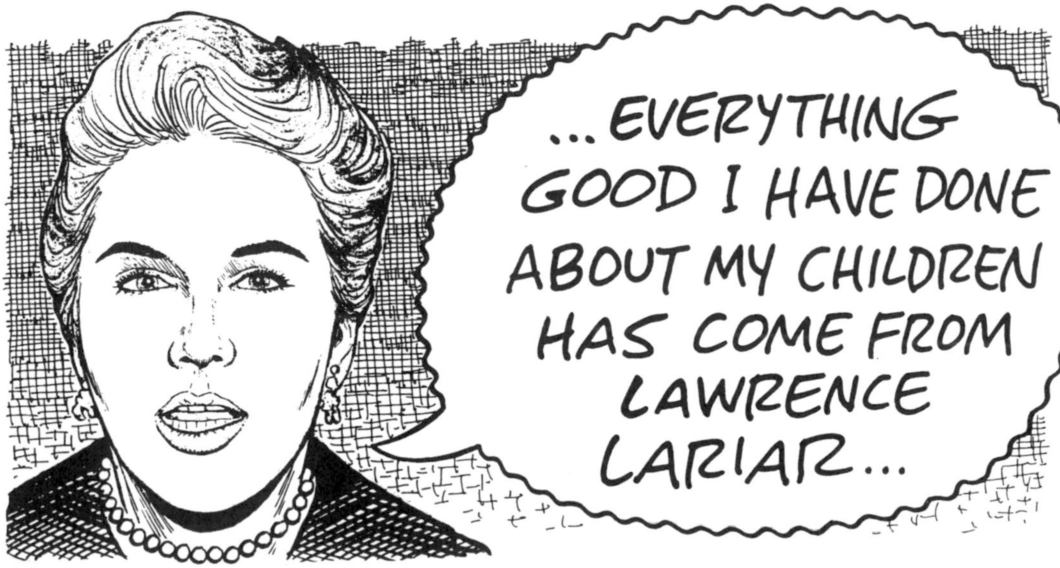
...EVERYTHING GOOD I HAVE DONE ABOUT MY CHILDREN HAS COME FROM LAWRENCE LARIAR...

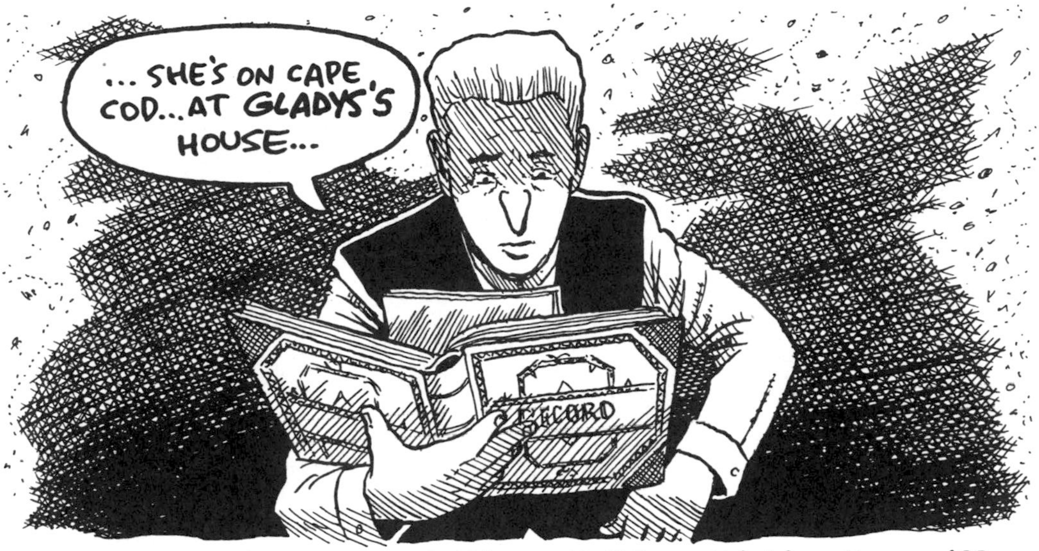
...SHE'S ON CAPE COD...AT GLADYS'S HOUSE...

I come here, having suspended this good thing, thinking there will be compensations, things that will fill up the time until I can go back to him. Thinking I can manufacture things to fill up this interim. And for a while this happens. But it is all made up. It is not real, it is fashioned. So I arrive at a dilemma.

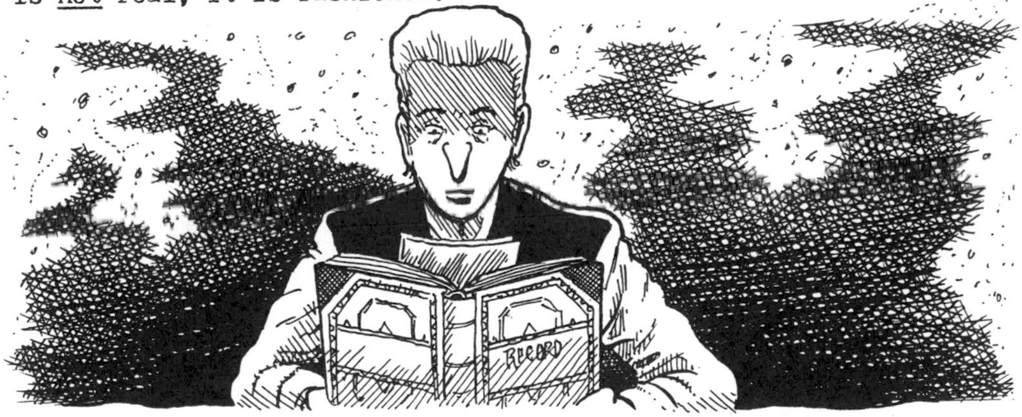

We are separated. For the first time in sixteen years, we are separated, apart, not-with, not-near -- unbearably not-together. There is correspondence, naturally. Little notes, verses even (being writers, both of us, and kind of sentimental at heart) and voluminous letters, going back to the beginning, like ".....remember when we had the place in the city......remember the deli-dinners of chicken, onions in sour cream, french bread, washed down with a good french wine....remember the tiny little shower where we soaped each other and laughed until we almost slipped on the bar of soap and broke a few bones....remember, remember, remember......"

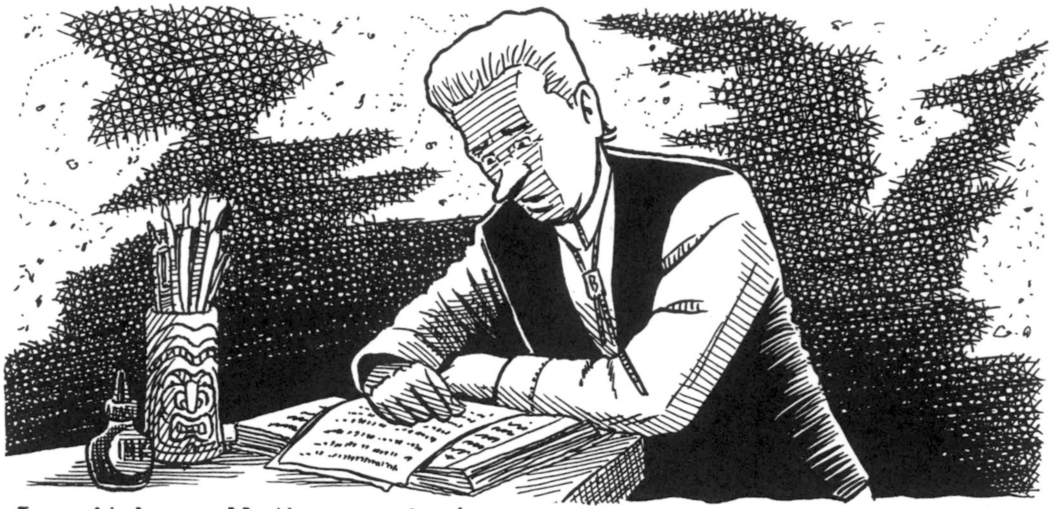

I can't bear all the remembering......the contrast between then and now is too poignant, too intense. There has never, in this whole immense world, been anything to compare with this love I have experienced. Nothing. Ever. I am created by it, I exist only because of it. It has been constant, never diminishing, only growing. New every time we have come together. Of such magnificence that I am unable to find words for it.

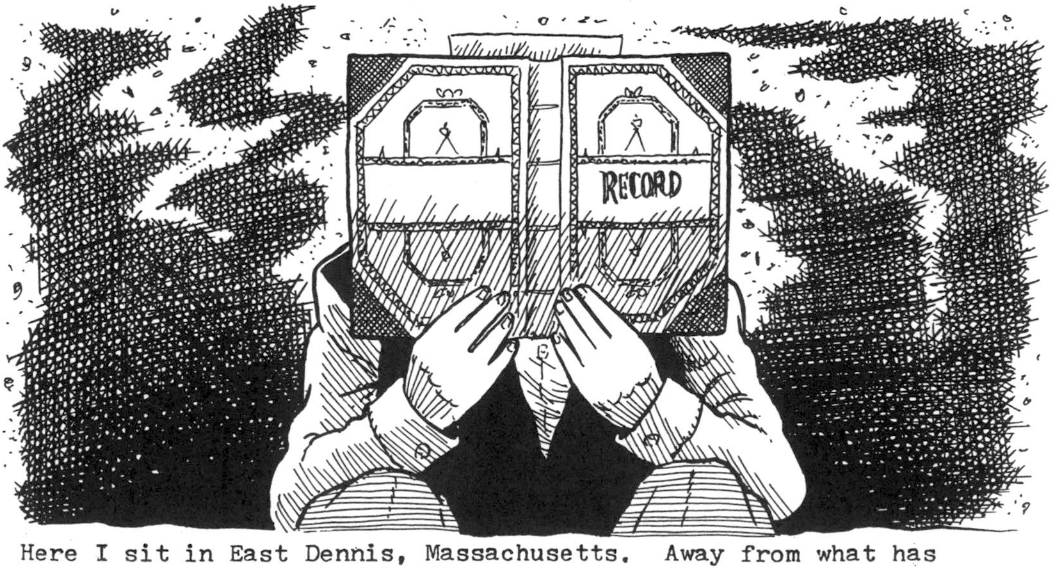
RECORD

Here I sit in East Dennis, Massachusetts. Away from what has nourished me for sixteen years. I am not unhappy, but on the other hand, I am desolate. I am deprived. I ache. He is not within reach, except by telephone, which lacks something. I make a file of his letters, tacking the ones he illustrates up onto the wall next to my dresser. I look at them for minutes and sometimes hours. I am desolate. I am alone. I ache.

And look who shows up, for God's holy catholic sake.

An old friend, a man I knew, have known, know.....a nice kind
of person, warm, troubled perhaps, unsure. And of all incredible
things, going through a situation similar to mine. All-of-a-sudden
one-ness, where two-ness had existed for over 30 years .
There is, quite naturally, a certain comradeship established.
From my end of it, there's a little of the feeling of having
adopted an orphan, I suppose. He has always seemed so self-
denigrating, so quick to see slight intended.

From his end of it, things start too fast, too intense ---
he confesses all kinds of past unhappiness and the pitiful
fact that his wife (due to illness, probably, but he also
hints there were other reasons) hadn't slept with him in
over seven years -- the classic story, but nonetheless sorrowful.

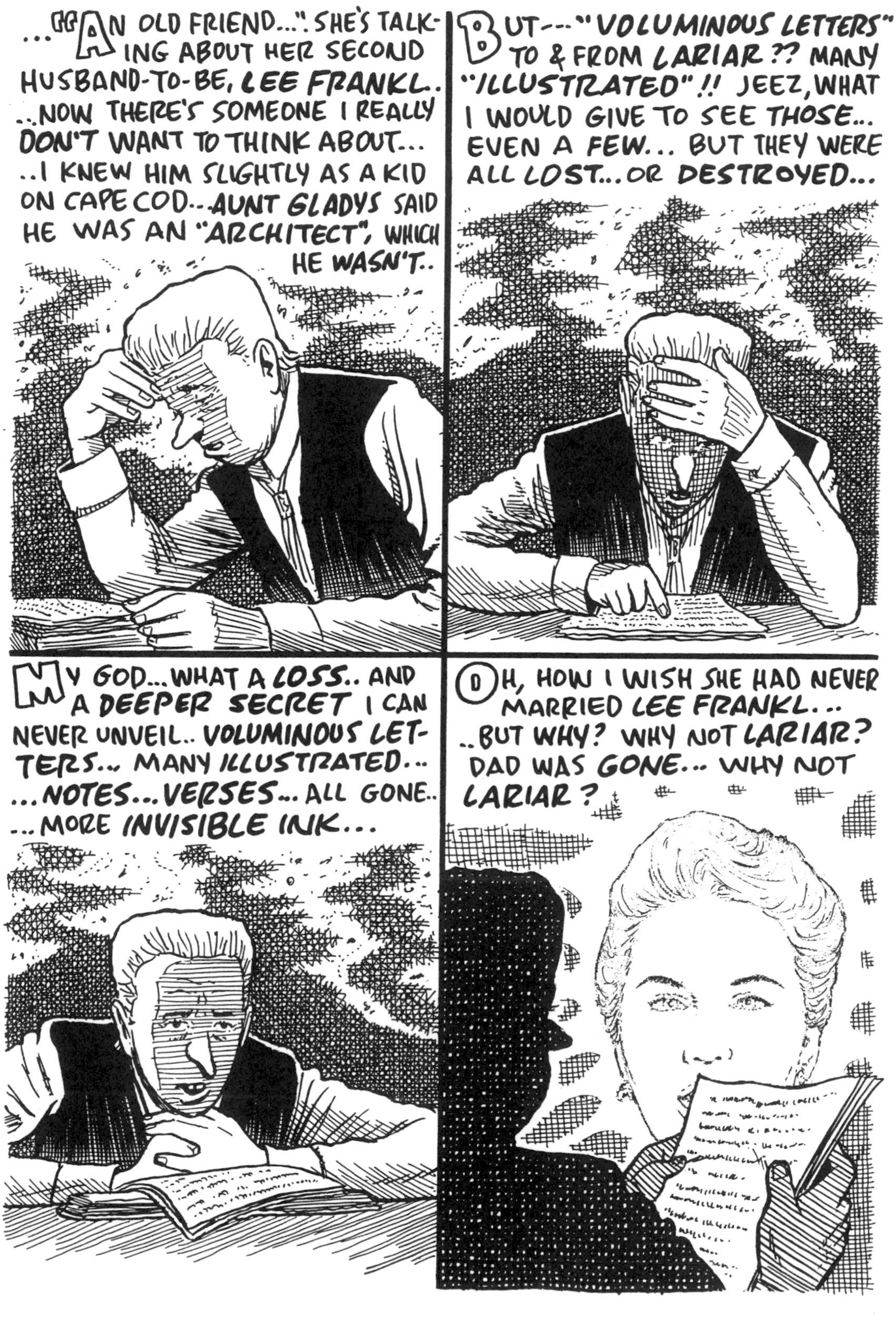
..."AN OLD FRIEND...". SHE'S TALKING ABOUT HER SECOND HUSBAND-TO-BE, LEE FRANKL.. ..NOW THERE'S SOMEONE I REALLY DON'T WANT TO THINK ABOUT... ..I KNEW HIM SLIGHTLY AS A KID ON CAPE COD...AUNT GLADYS SAID HE WAS AN "ARCHITECT", WHICH HE WASN'T..
BUT---"VOLUMINOUS LETTERS" TO & FROM LARIAR?? MANY "ILLUSTRATED"!! JEEZ, WHAT I WOULD GIVE TO SEE THOSE... EVEN A FEW... BUT THEY WERE ALL LOST...OR DESTROYED...
MY GOD...WHAT A LOSS.. AND A DEEPER SECRET I CAN NEVER UNVEIL.. VOLUMINOUS LETTERS... MANY ILLUSTRATED... ...NOTES...VERSES...ALL GONE.. ...MORE INVISIBLE INK...
OH, HOW I WISH SHE HAD NEVER MARRIED LEE FRANKL... ..BUT WHY? WHY NOT LARIAR? DAD WAS GONE... WHY NOT LARIAR?

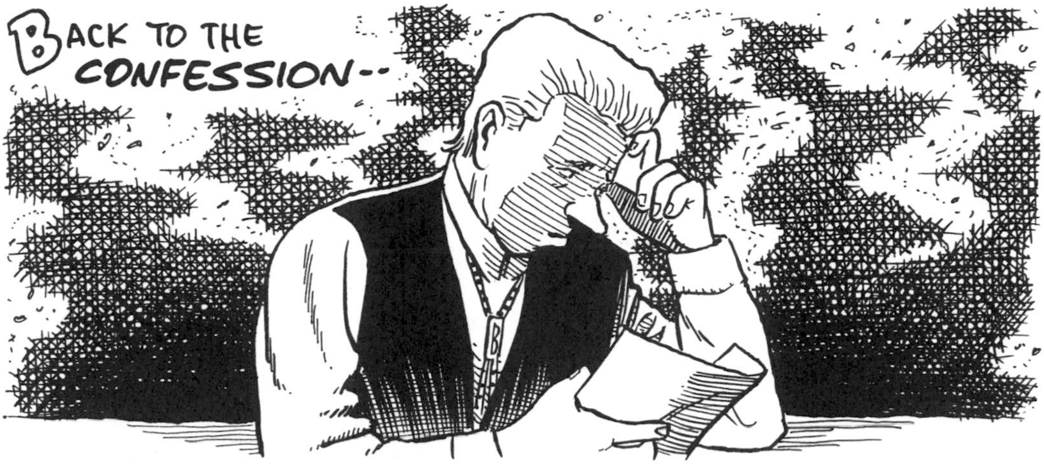
BACK TO THE CONFESSION--

Then the acknowledgment (as if I didn't know) that he had leched for me for years. Ugh. He says the wrong things at the wrong time in the wrong way, and I find it all not very funny but not deeply tragic either, and try to think of myself and my own present deprivations -- which is a mistake, since almost by themselves my eyes begin to wander in his direction, driven by the aforementioned feeling of deprivation and a real, honest-to-god groin ache which I have never (in sixteen glorious years) ever learned to deny.

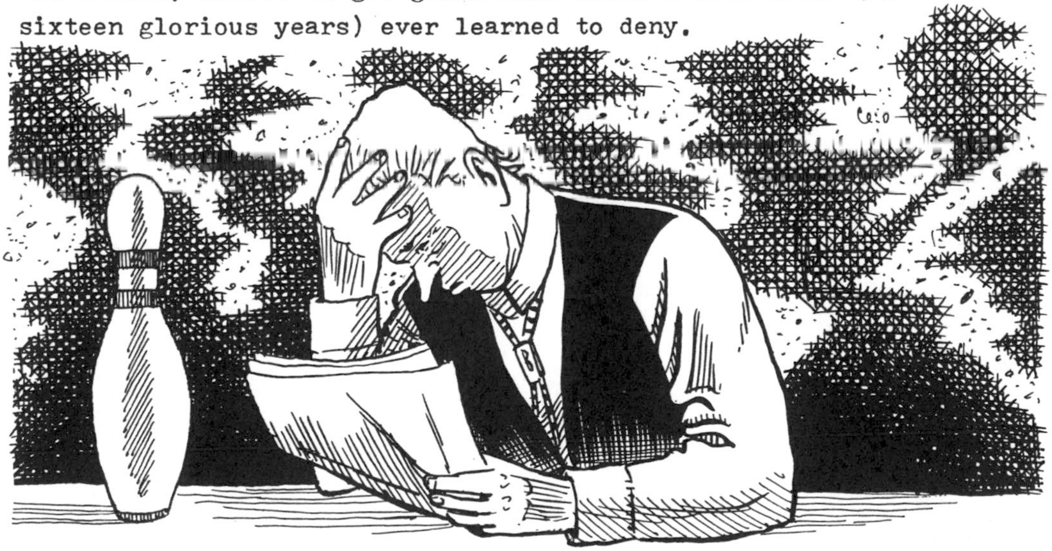

Now comes what appears to be (since I'm not all that sure it is) the clincher. He begins to call for me at odd times during the day and take me on long out-in-the-country or down-the-beach walks, and I don't mean around here -- but fabulous places in the Conservation areas, like Crow Pasture, Sandy Neck, Chapin Beach-- with a promise of other similar delights.

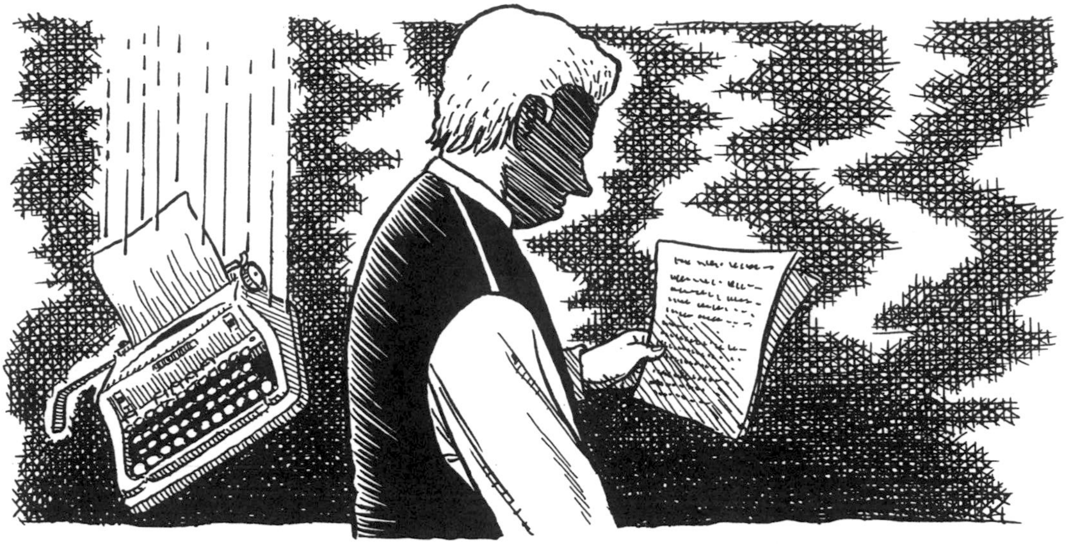

He takes me through a swamp - a cold, black and white, cypress filled,tangled soggy area, where the moss is brilliant green and treacherous, the only thing of color visible. I hold on to his trench coat, slipping and sliding behind him, he crashes through a beaver burrow and we both go down, come up muddy and laughing hysterically, two lunatics who could have broken half a dozen legs -- and something like friendship begins to develop. I am given tracts to read on local politics (again, ugh)..... but also he can't pass a book store without buying me something wonderful to read.... I make a scrumptious lasagne dinner for six of us over at his place, and when the others go home I go to bed with him.

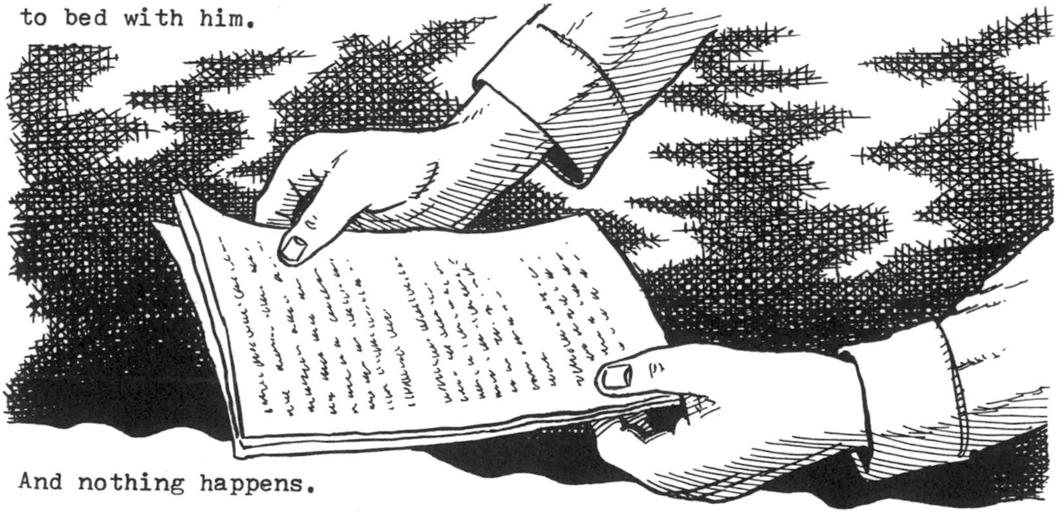

And nothing happens.

It's like shaking hands with a friend who's dropped by for a chat. He's delirious. I'm unmoved.

OKAY.. DAD IS DEAD... SHE'S UP AT THE *CAPE* A FEW MONTHS LATER... TO TAKE A BREAK... ...TO CARE FOR *AUNT GLADYS*... TO THINK ABOUT *LARIAR* AND WHAT MIGHT BE *NEXT*... SHE CLEARLY DOES NOT *LOVE* — OR PARTICULARY *LIKE* — LEE FRANKL... BUT HE'S *PERSISTENT*.. SHE STILL SEES LARIAR... SO *WHAT* DOES THIS NEW MAN REPRESENT TO HER...?

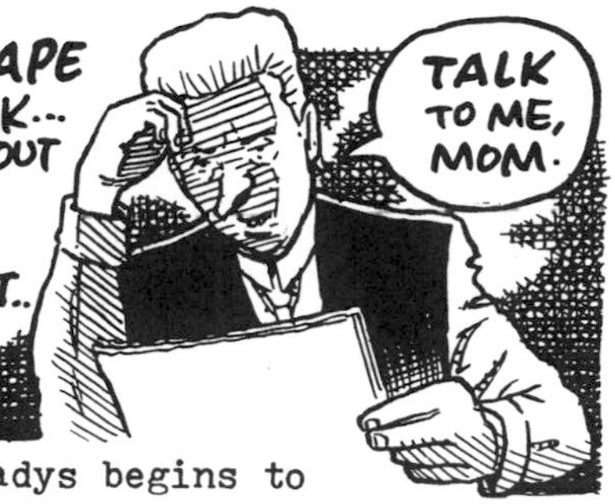
TALK TO ME, MOM.

But the friendship grows, becomes firm. Gladys begins to suspect I'm planning to marry and abandon her. I assure her it's the last thing from my mind. It is. I want to be absolutely unencumbered.

The next time, I plan it better. I set a stage, I refuse the third drink, I don't eat a rich meal, I bathe in your delicious body-lotion-bath stuff, making sure I smell nice. I buy a ridiculously expensive post-orgasm garment, probably a negligee -- and slippers. I wash my hair in Ivory, because <u>that</u> also smells nice.

And nothing happens. Shit, I say.

And again, nothing happens. I am still waiting.

Now, back to the dilemma.

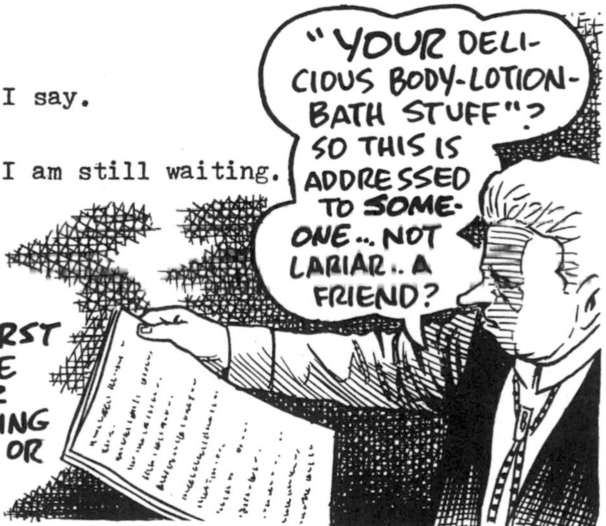
"YOUR DELICIOUS BODY-LOTION-BATH STUFF"? SO THIS IS ADDRESSED TO SOMEONE... NOT LARIAR.. A FRIEND?

SHE'S STILL IN LOVE WITH LARIAR... BUT, FOR THE *FIRST TIME* IN SIXTEEN YEARS, SHE GOES TO BED WITH *ANOTHER MAN*... IS THIS THE BEGINNING OF HER *BREAK-UP* WITH LARIAR OR IS *MARRIAGE* WITH HIM NOW A POSSIBILITY?

The few previous separations Larry and I have had have been terribly painful for him. He sees me in other beds, meeting other men in out-of-the-way places, doing things with them I have done with him.....he goes into neurotic shock when I go away for a few weeks .... We both know about this from the beginning. I live with it, always doing all I can to relieve his mind. And in sixteen years, I have never looked in another direction.

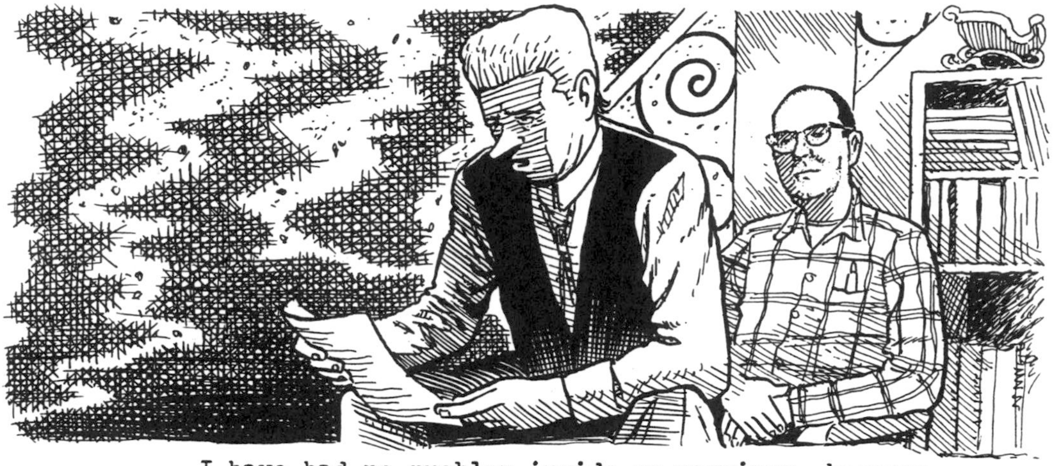

I have had no problem inside my marriage, because the sexual demands made upon me were minimal and easily satisfied. And through all these years I have come to depend upon a steady, sure, perfect, wonderful and deep satisfaction of everything I have ever wanted from a man. Sex? Spectacular, incredible, -- words fail me. And no separations for more than 3 weeks. How could I have understood what this kind of separation would do to me? I had become [redacted] without knowing it utterly dependent upon this relationship to provide everything I needed.

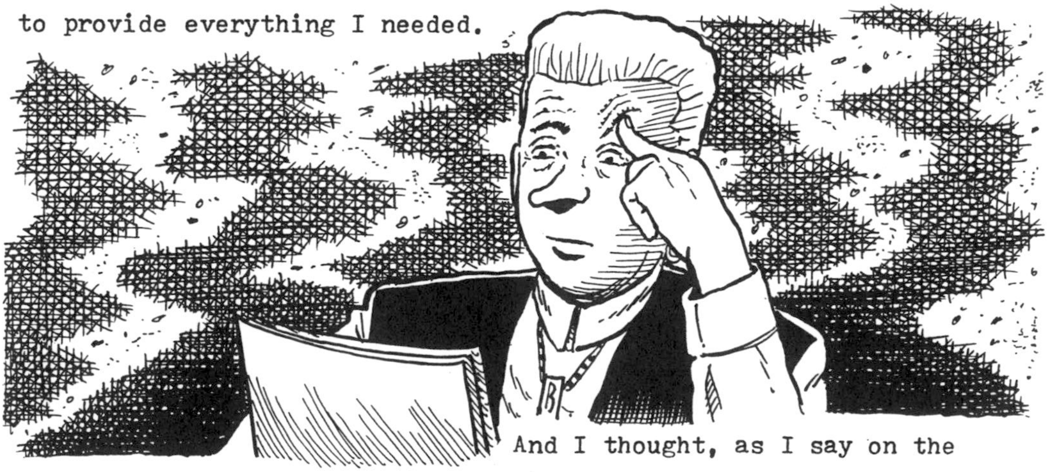

And I thought, as I say on the first page, that I could fill up the time required with little bits of busyness, and just patiently wait until it was over and I could go back to him. But I see that I had no way to prepare myself, and with such satisfactions regular and full, their absence sent me up the wall.

Now I begin to feel this limbo-land closing in. I cannot feel guilty-unto-suicide over having done what I had to.....but somehow I feel I <u>should</u> feel guilty-unto-suicide, for having done the awful thing my love always feared I would do, out of his own neurosis. But I exist in my unreal world, not guilty, not enjoying, only missing and aching for what I left down there on Long Island.

I walk away from <u>this</u> man here, get up and get dressed and go home from him, and he's a friend for whom I've done a favor, since it really didn't require much from me. He is lit up like Coney Island.....joyous, happy, content even when I tell him I don't feel any love for him, only friendship and the fun we have together. I don't tell him about my love. What point?

Now a question or two, maybe you can see an answer to.

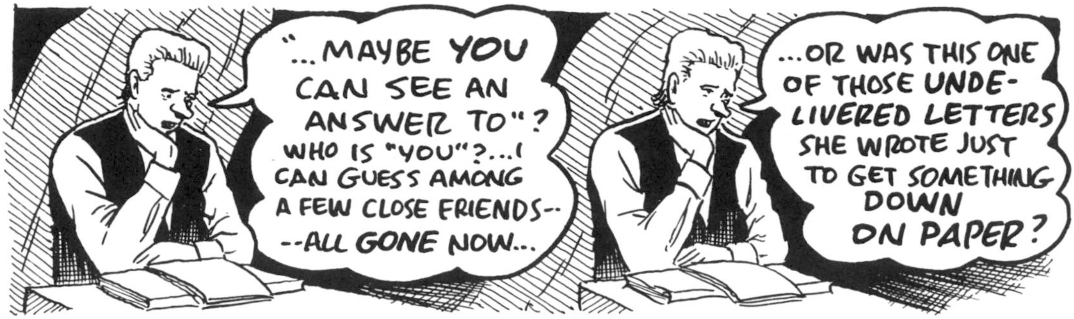
"...MAYBE YOU CAN SEE AN ANSWER TO"? WHO IS "YOU"?...I CAN GUESS AMONG A FEW CLOSE FRIENDS-- --ALL GONE NOW...
...OR WAS THIS ONE OF THOSE UNDELIVERED LETTERS SHE WROTE JUST TO GET SOMETHING DOWN ON PAPER?

Suppose this bed-trip should turn out to be a lot better than its first few attempts? Suppose I should begin to feel that it's more than a handshake? Add that to the fun in the swamp, and what happens?

From out of whatever hole I have dug myself into in this limbo-land, I shout "I shall never until I die love another man - there is only my first, true love, and I can never know another in the same way!"

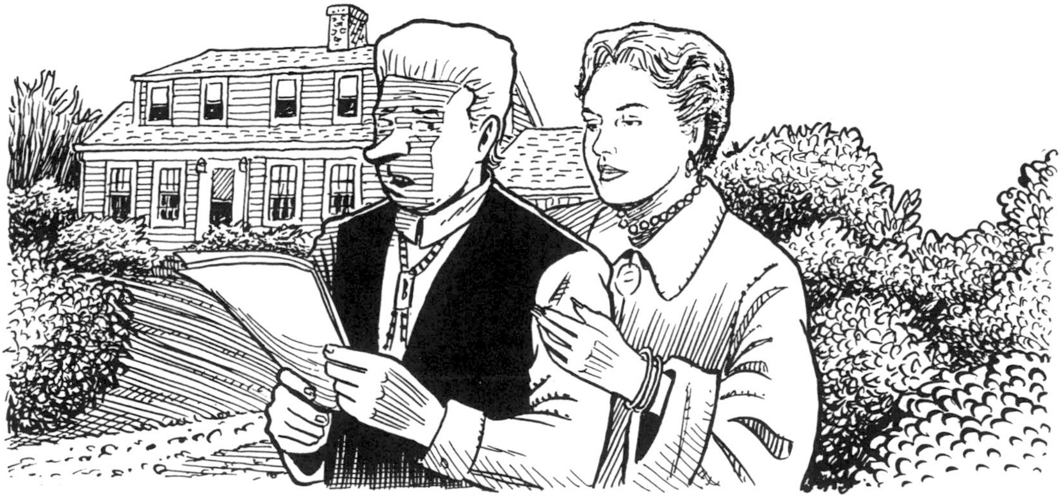

I wait, here in East Dennis, for the once-a-month trip back home. We plan at least two whole days together.....and they are wonderful, as always. We do something special, like a fancy restaurant, a drive somewhere. We go to a plush motel, dress up, have dinner. Then this whole scene drops away...I am where I want to be, doing what I want to do more than anything else.

What in Christ's name is wrong with me?

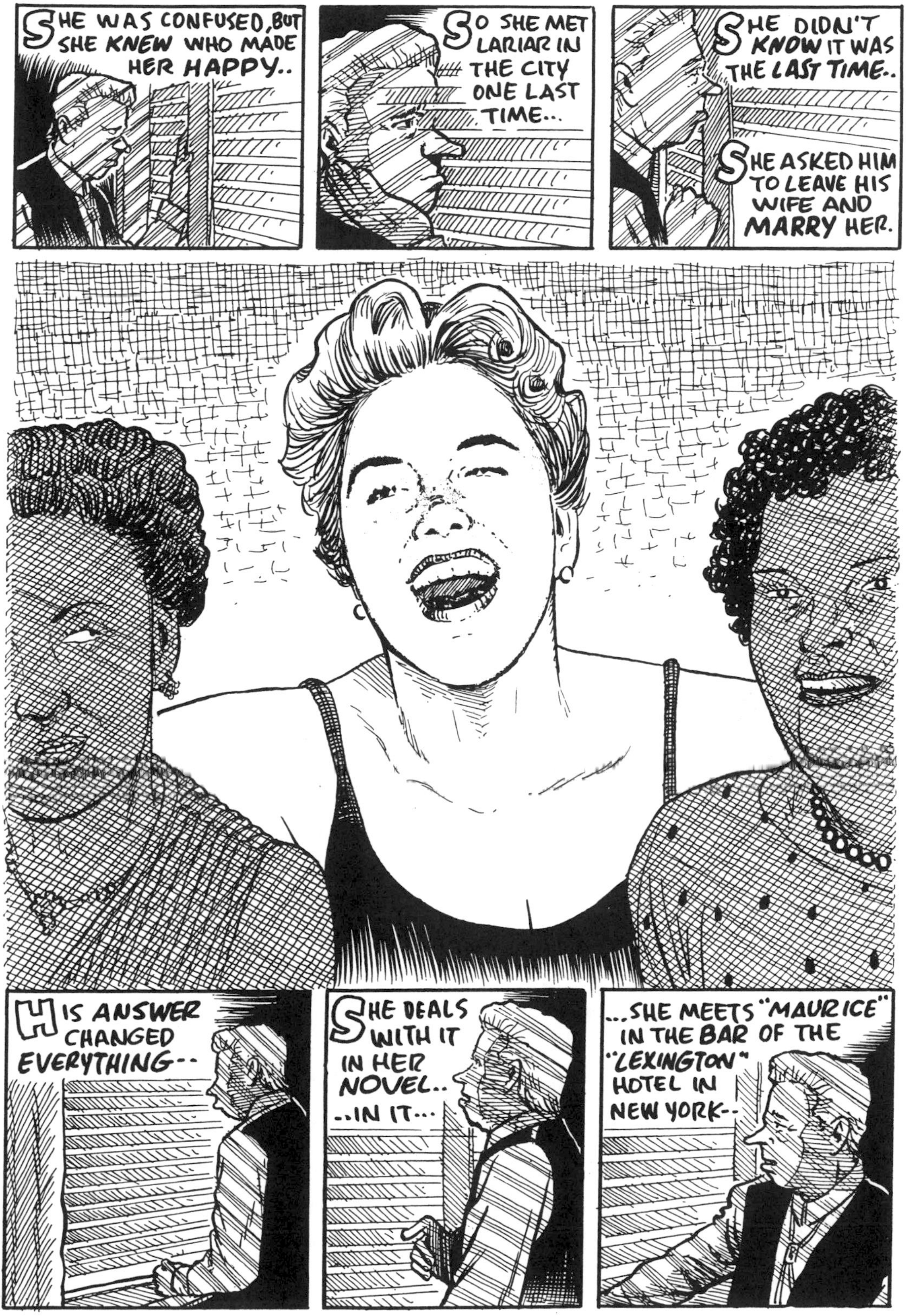

SHE WAS CONFUSED, BUT SHE KNEW WHO MADE HER HAPPY..
SO SHE MET LARIAR IN THE CITY ONE LAST TIME...
SHE DIDN'T KNOW IT WAS THE LAST TIME..
SHE ASKED HIM TO LEAVE HIS WIFE AND MARRY HER.
HIS ANSWER CHANGED EVERYTHING--
SHE DEALS WITH IT IN HER NOVEL.. ..IN IT...
...SHE MEETS "MAURICE" IN THE BAR OF THE "LEXINGTON" HOTEL IN NEW YORK--

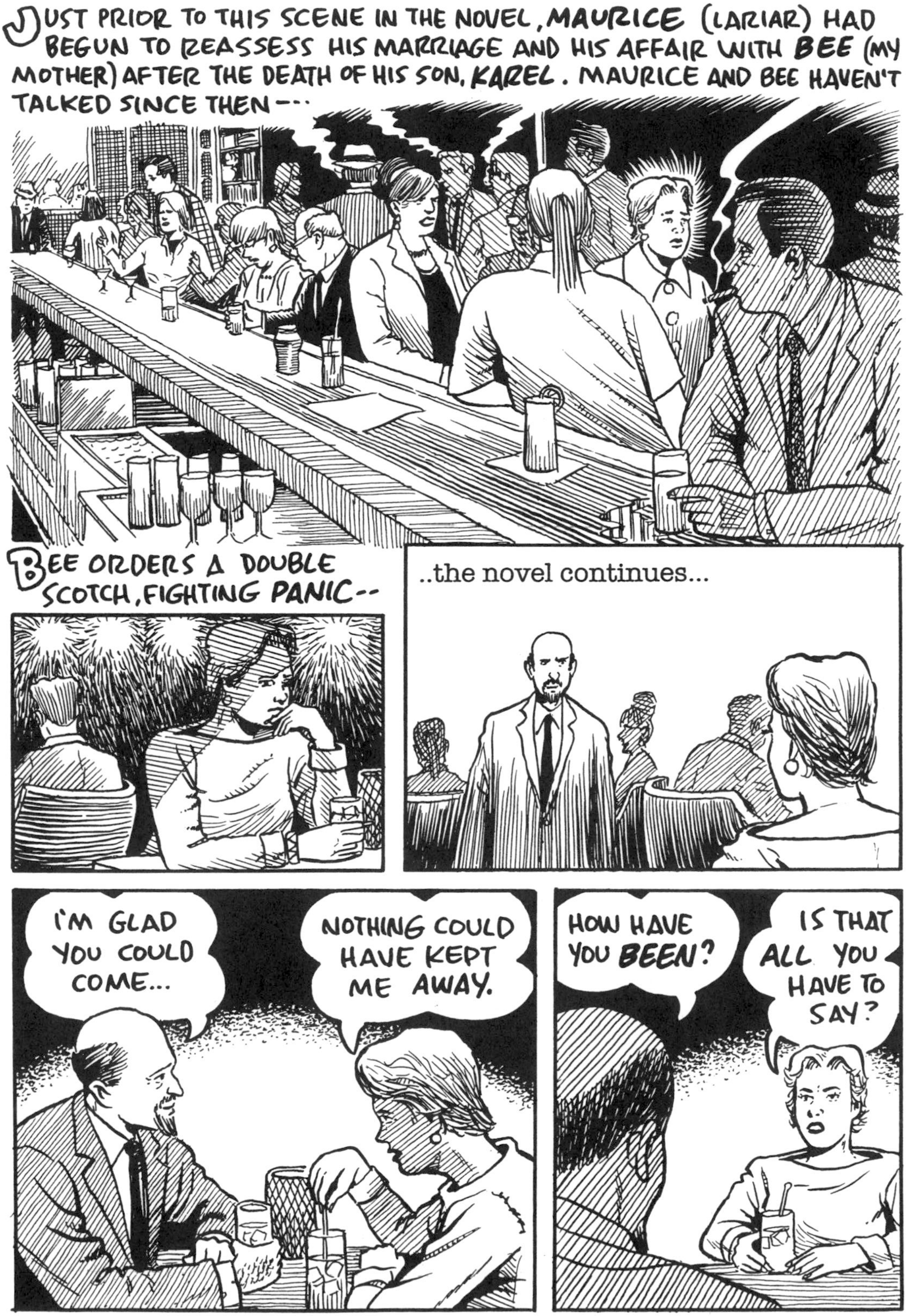
JUST PRIOR TO THIS SCENE IN THE NOVEL, MAURICE (LARIAR) HAD BEGUN TO REASSESS HIS MARRIAGE AND HIS AFFAIR WITH BEE (MY MOTHER) AFTER THE DEATH OF HIS SON, KAREL. MAURICE AND BEE HAVEN'T TALKED SINCE THEN---
BEE ORDERS A DOUBLE SCOTCH, FIGHTING PANIC--
..the novel continues...
I'M GLAD YOU COULD COME...
NOTHING COULD HAVE KEPT ME AWAY.
HOW HAVE YOU BEEN?
IS THAT ALL YOU HAVE TO SAY?

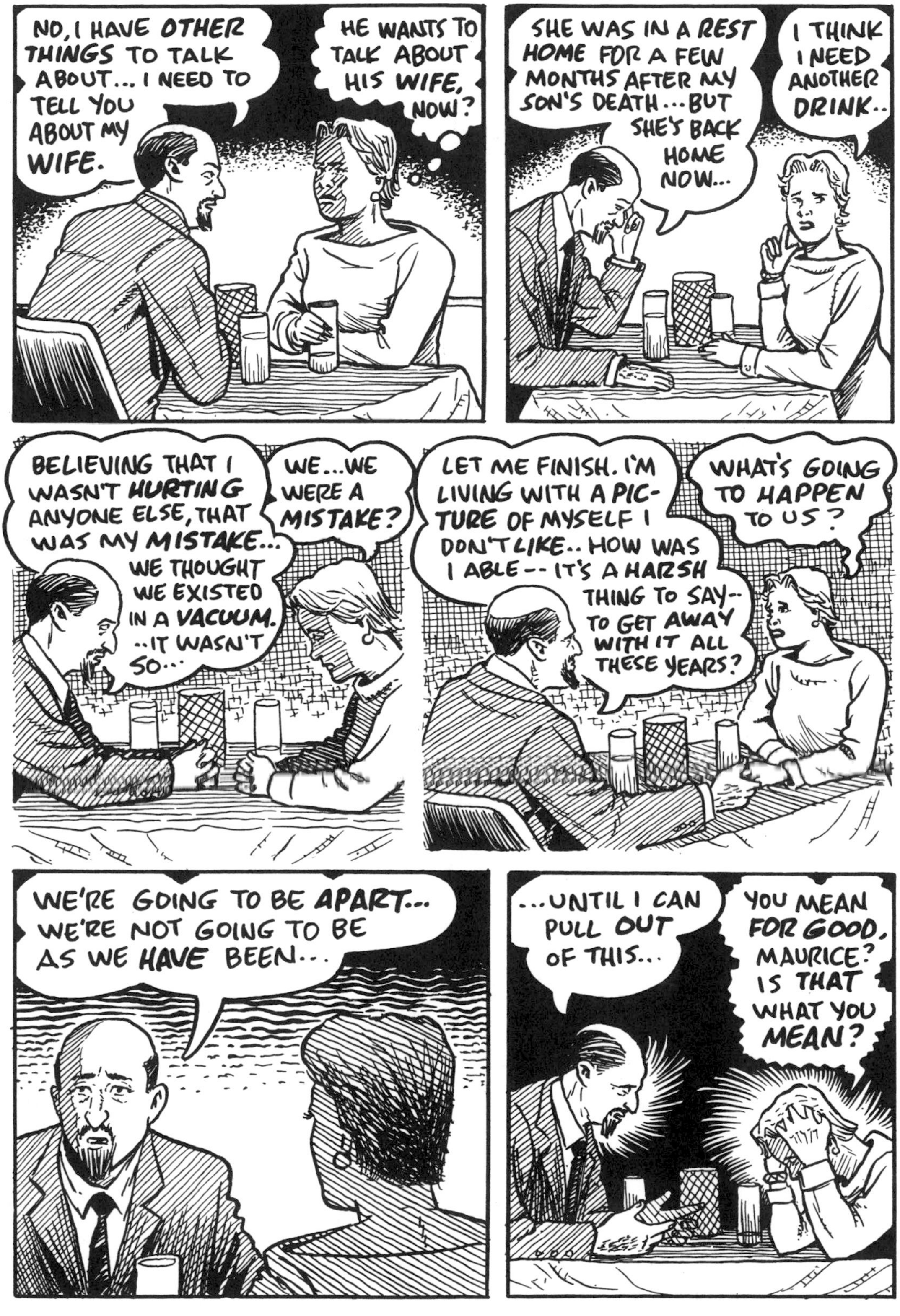
NO, I HAVE OTHER THINGS TO TALK ABOUT... I NEED TO TELL YOU ABOUT MY WIFE.
HE WANTS TO TALK ABOUT HIS WIFE, NOW?
SHE WAS IN A REST HOME FOR A FEW MONTHS AFTER MY SON'S DEATH... BUT SHE'S BACK HOME NOW...
I THINK I NEED ANOTHER DRINK..
BELIEVING THAT I WASN'T HURTING ANYONE ELSE, THAT WAS MY MISTAKE... WE THOUGHT WE EXISTED IN A VACUUM. ..IT WASN'T SO...
WE...WE WERE A MISTAKE?
LET ME FINISH. I'M LIVING WITH A PICTURE OF MYSELF I DON'T LIKE.. HOW WAS I ABLE -- IT'S A HARSH THING TO SAY-- TO GET AWAY WITH IT ALL THESE YEARS?
WHAT'S GOING TO HAPPEN TO US?
WE'RE GOING TO BE APART... WE'RE NOT GOING TO BE AS WE HAVE BEEN...
...UNTIL I CAN PULL OUT OF THIS...
YOU MEAN FOR GOOD, MAURICE? IS THAT WHAT YOU MEAN?

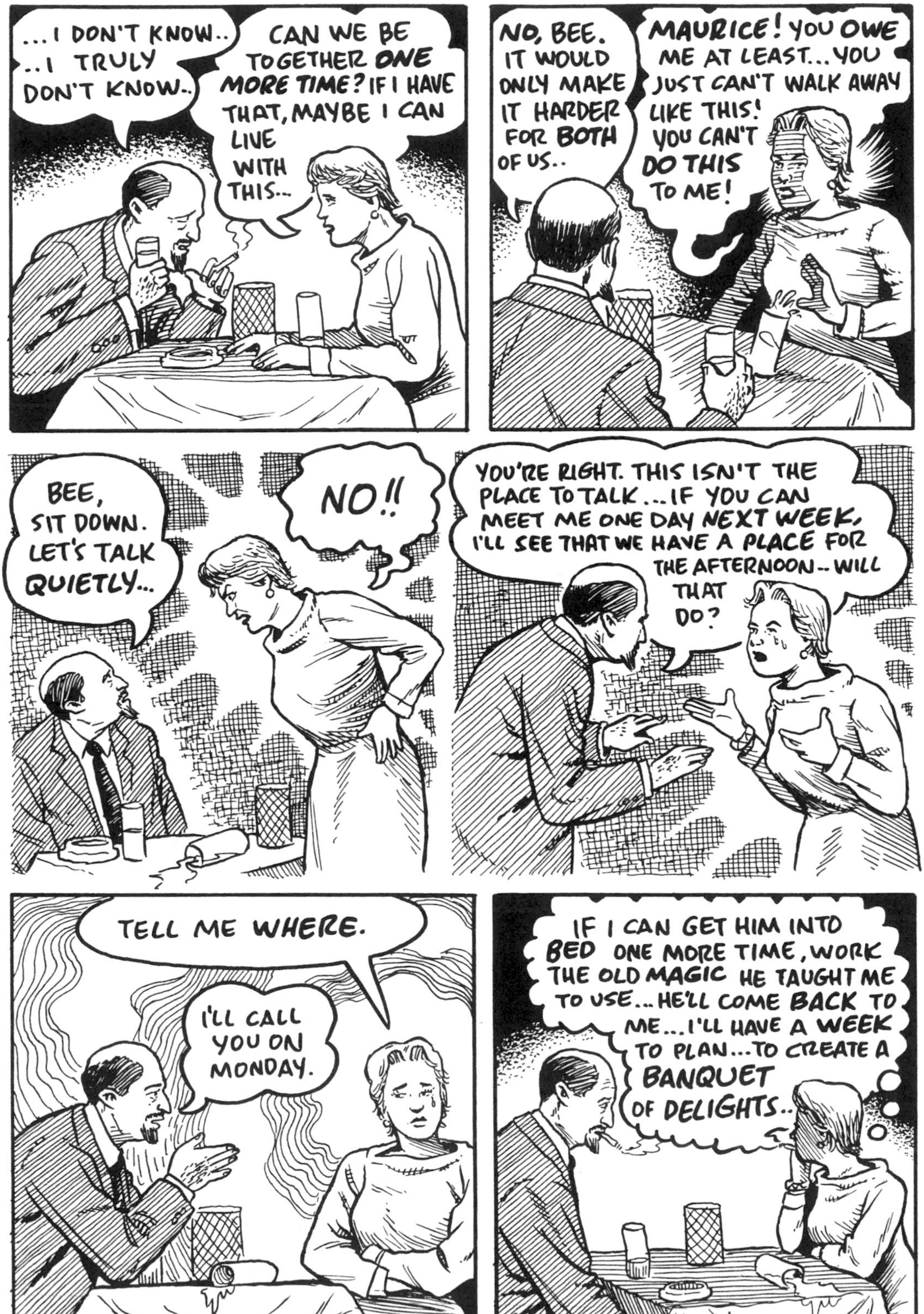
...I DON'T KNOW.. ..I TRULY DON'T KNOW..
CAN WE BE TOGETHER ONE MORE TIME? IF I HAVE THAT, MAYBE I CAN LIVE WITH THIS...
NO, BEE. IT WOULD ONLY MAKE IT HARDER FOR BOTH OF US..
MAURICE! YOU OWE ME AT LEAST... YOU JUST CAN'T WALK AWAY LIKE THIS! YOU CAN'T DO THIS TO ME!
BEE, SIT DOWN. LET'S TALK QUIETLY...
NO!!
YOU'RE RIGHT. THIS ISN'T THE PLACE TO TALK... IF YOU CAN MEET ME ONE DAY NEXT WEEK, I'LL SEE THAT WE HAVE A PLACE FOR THE AFTERNOON-- WILL THAT DO?
TELL ME WHERE.
I'LL CALL YOU ON MONDAY.
IF I CAN GET HIM INTO BED ONE MORE TIME, WORK THE OLD MAGIC HE TAUGHT ME TO USE... HE'LL COME BACK TO ME... I'LL HAVE A WEEK TO PLAN... TO CREATE A BANQUET OF DELIGHTS..

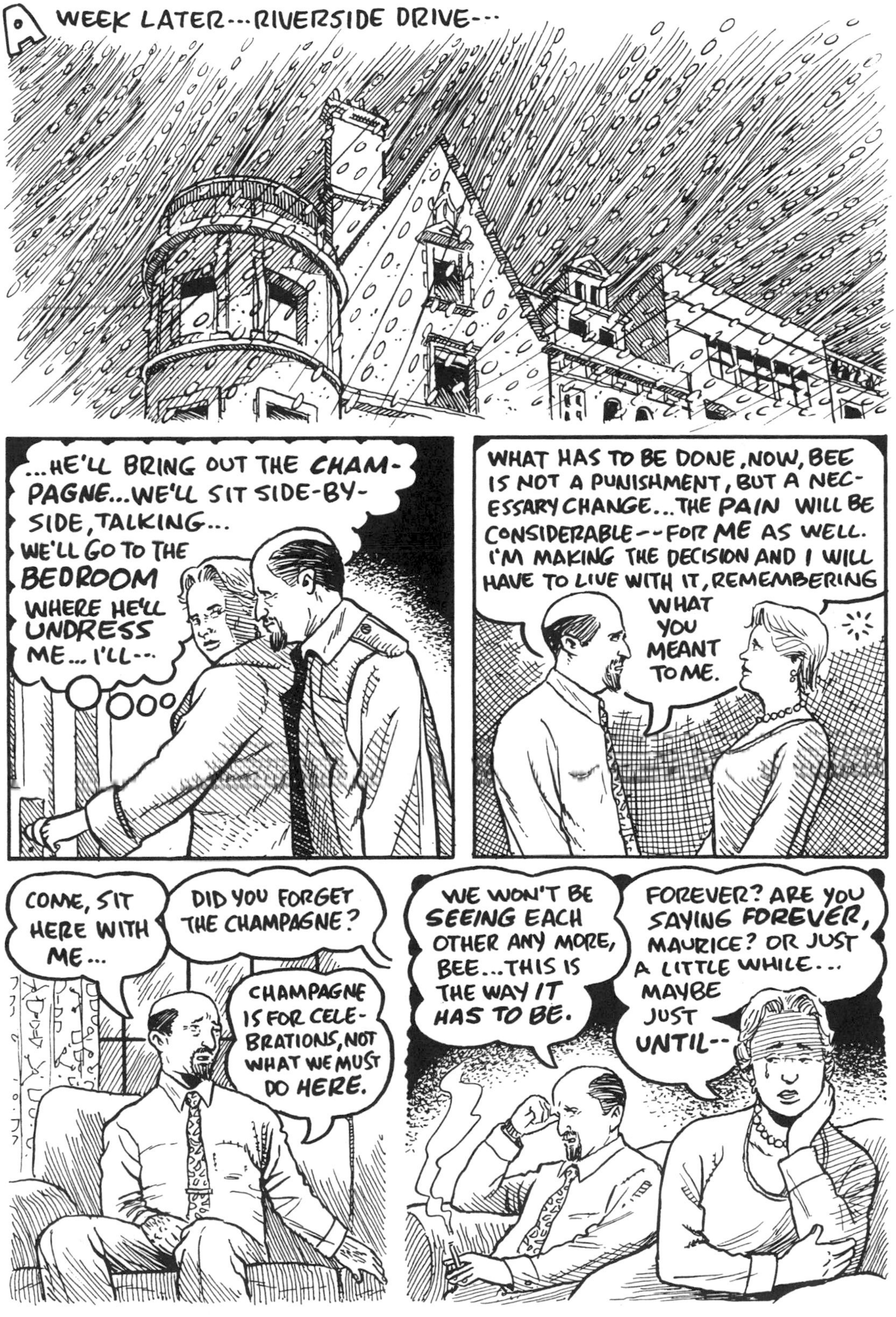
A WEEK LATER---RIVERSIDE DRIVE---
...HE'LL BRING OUT THE CHAMPAGNE...WE'LL SIT SIDE-BY-SIDE, TALKING... WE'LL GO TO THE BEDROOM WHERE HE'LL UNDRESS ME... I'LL--
WHAT HAS TO BE DONE, NOW, BEE IS NOT A PUNISHMENT, BUT A NECESSARY CHANGE... THE PAIN WILL BE CONSIDERABLE--FOR ME AS WELL. I'M MAKING THE DECISION AND I WILL HAVE TO LIVE WITH IT, REMEMBERING WHAT YOU MEANT TO ME.
COME, SIT HERE WITH ME...
DID YOU FORGET THE CHAMPAGNE?
CHAMPAGNE IS FOR CELEBRATIONS, NOT WHAT WE MUST DO HERE.
WE WON'T BE SEEING EACH OTHER ANY MORE, BEE... THIS IS THE WAY IT HAS TO BE.
FOREVER? ARE YOU SAYING FOREVER, MAURICE? OR JUST A LITTLE WHILE... MAYBE JUST UNTIL--

NO, BEE, I WON'T SAY **FOREVER**, BUT I DON'T KNOW IF WE CAN BE **TOGETHER** THE WAY WE WERE.

..HE LOOKS AWFUL.. HIS FACE IS WHITE, SO PINCHED. THIS IS HAPPENING TO **ME**, NOT TO HIM.. WHY SHOULD HE LOOK SO **MISER-ABLE**?

MAURICE, THIS IS **MY DEATH** YOU'RE TALKING ABOUT.. CAN YOU **LIVE** WITH THAT? CAN **YOU**?

DON'T **DO** THIS! IT'S **NOT** YOUR **DEATH**! DON'T MAKE THIS INTO A DAMNED **SOAP OPERA**!

WE **KNEW** FROM THE BEGINNING IT WOULD NEVER BE **MORE** THAN IT **WAS**...

SO THAT'S IT--- YOU'RE **LEAVING** ME...I NEVER **COUNTED** ALL THAT MUCH, DID I? JUST FILLED A ONCE-IN-A-WHILE NEED, NOT THE **REAL THING**...

DON'T LET THESE BE THE LAST WORDS BETWEEN US, I BEG YOU, BEE..YOU KNOW WHAT I **FEEL** FOR YOU, WHAT I'VE **ALWAYS** FELT.. DON'T SAY IT DOESN'T MATTER.

WHAT DO YOU FEEL FOR ME, MAURICE? YOU'VE NEVER SAID I LOVE YOU BEE, I LOVE YOU THE WAY YOU LOVE ME! YOU NEVER HAD THE GUTS TO SAY IT AND NOW, WHEN IT'S ALL OVER AND I ASK YOU

I LOVE YOU, BEE. I LOVE YOU DEARLY AND PROBABLY WON'T EVER STOP. I LOVE YOU IN WAYS I'VE NEVER LOVED ANOTHER WOMAN.
HIS WORDS ARE LIKE A CURTAIN COMING DOWN.
BEE'S ANGER DISSOLVES

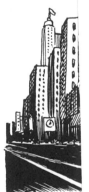

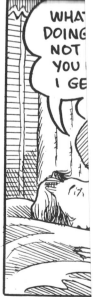

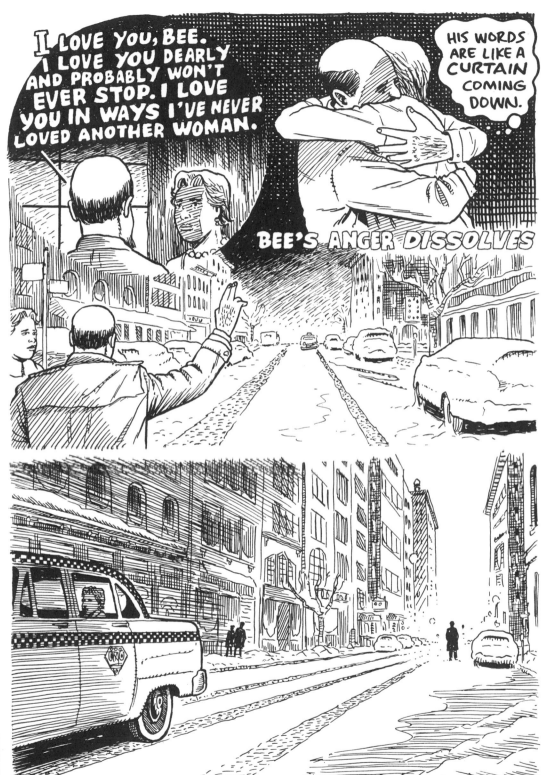

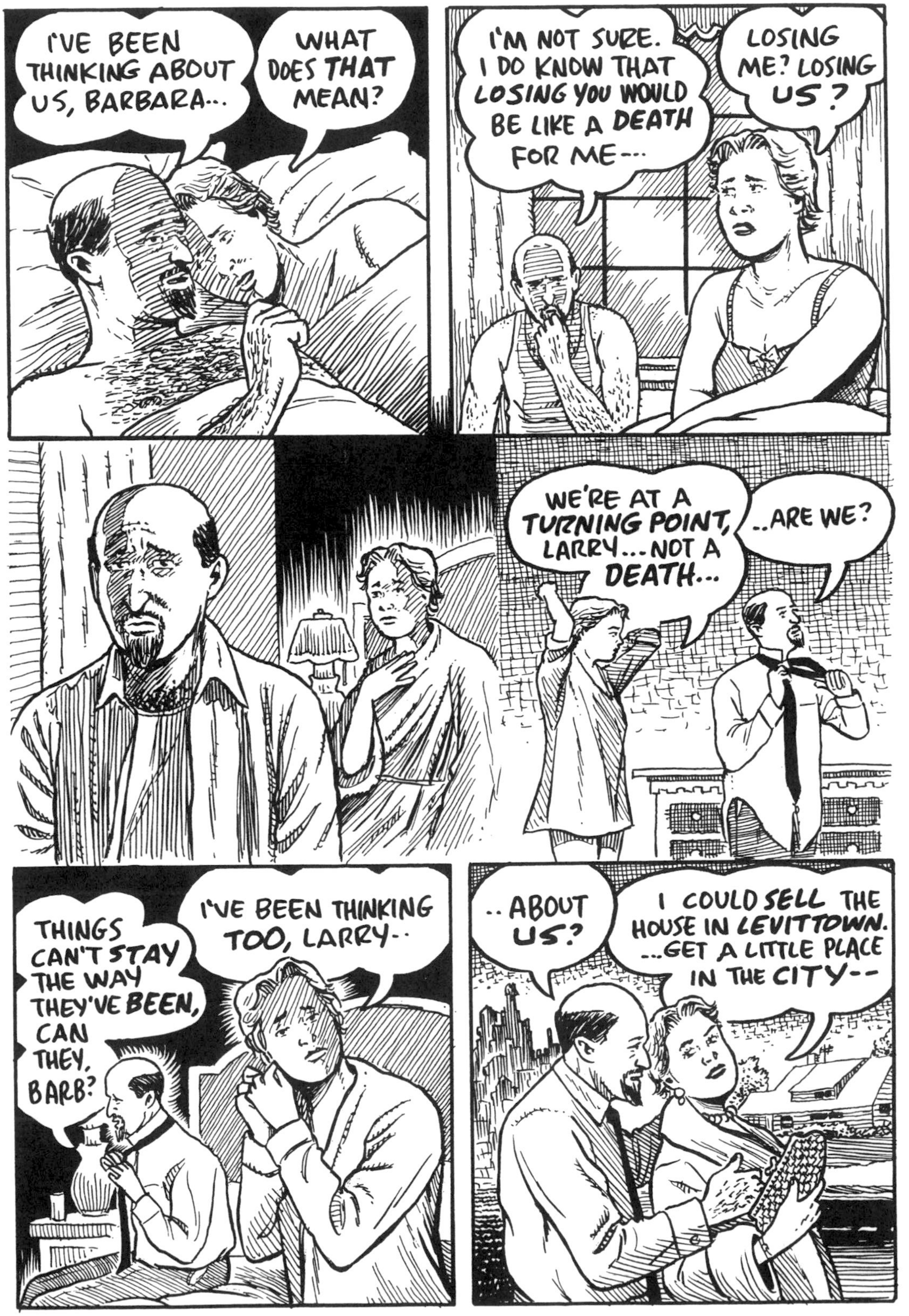
I'VE BEEN THINKING ABOUT US, BARBARA...
WHAT DOES THAT MEAN?
I'M NOT SURE. I DO KNOW THAT LOSING YOU WOULD BE LIKE A DEATH FOR ME---
LOSING ME? LOSING US?
WE'RE AT A TURNING POINT, LARRY... NOT A DEATH...
..ARE WE?
I'VE BEEN THINKING TOO, LARRY..
THINGS CAN'T STAY THE WAY THEY'VE BEEN, CAN THEY, BARB?
..ABOUT US?
I COULD SELL THE HOUSE IN LEVITTOWN. ...GET A LITTLE PLACE IN THE CITY--

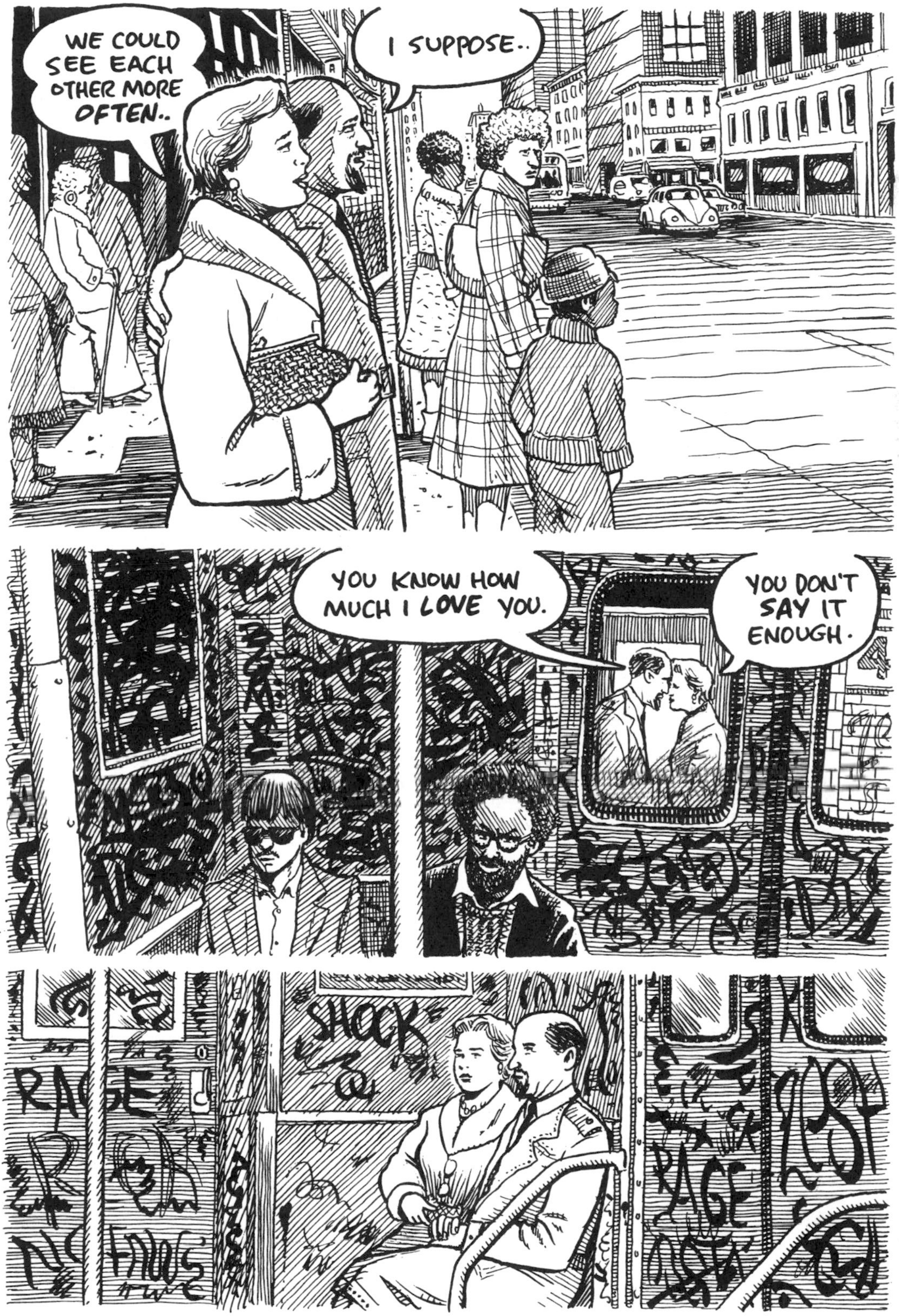
WE COULD SEE EACH OTHER MORE OFTEN..
I SUPPOSE..
YOU KNOW HOW MUCH I LOVE YOU.
YOU DON'T SAY IT ENOUGH.
SHOCK
RAGE

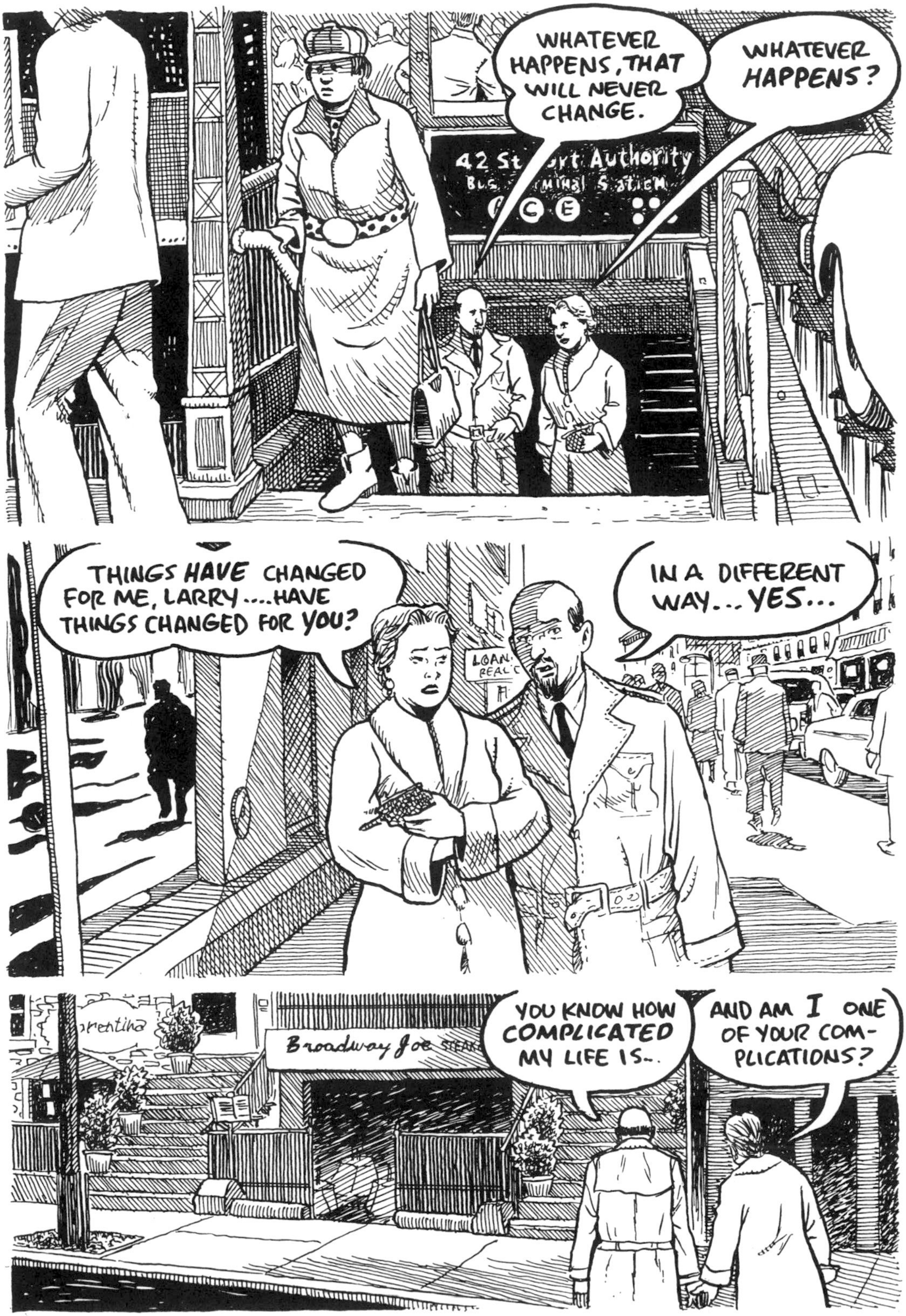
WHATEVER HAPPENS, THAT WILL NEVER CHANGE.
WHATEVER HAPPENS?
THINGS HAVE CHANGED FOR ME, LARRY....HAVE THINGS CHANGED FOR YOU?
IN A DIFFERENT WAY... YES...
Broadway Joe
YOU KNOW HOW COMPLICATED MY LIFE IS..
AND AM I ONE OF YOUR COMPLICATIONS?

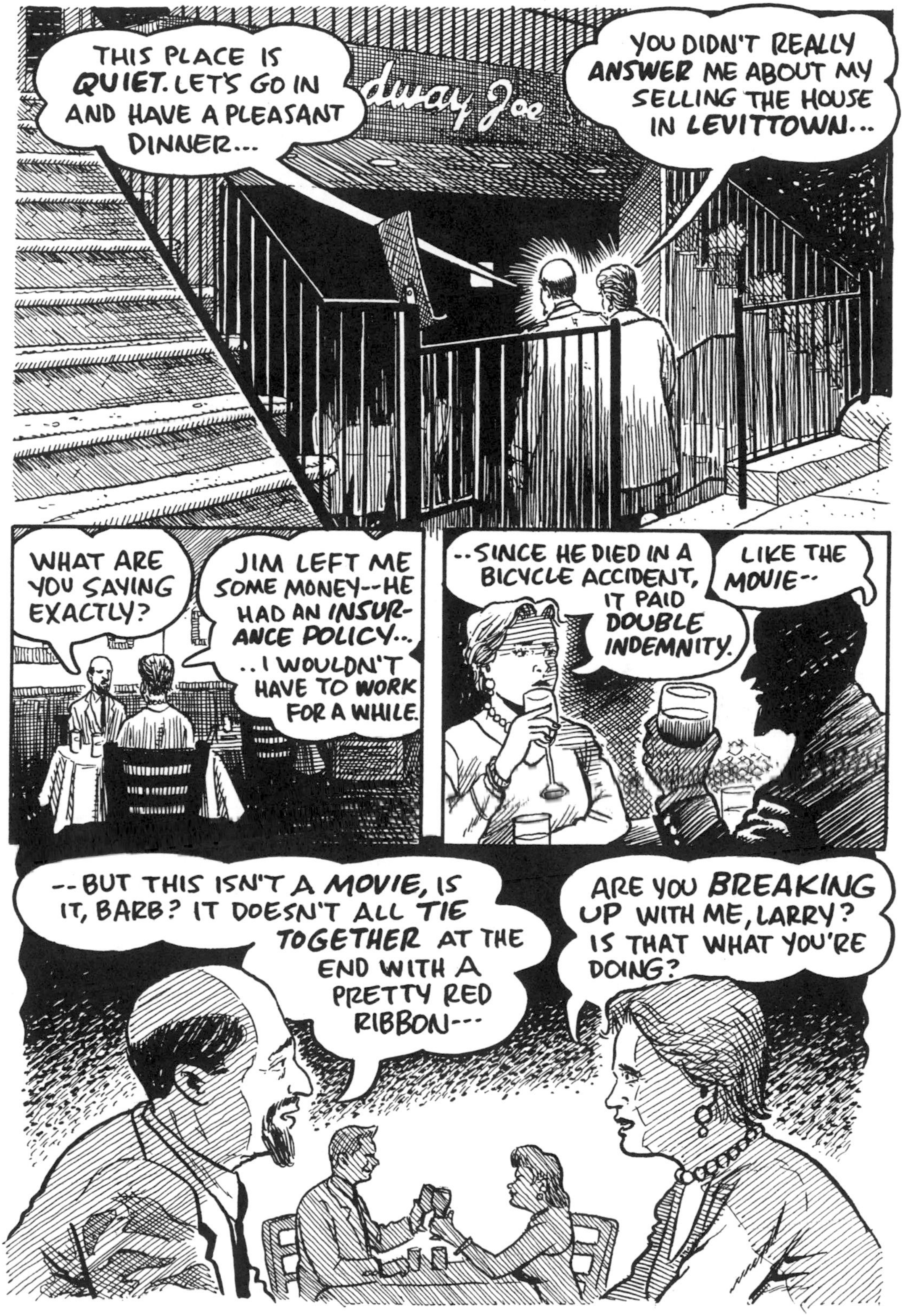
THIS PLACE IS QUIET. LET'S GO IN AND HAVE A PLEASANT DINNER...
YOU DIDN'T REALLY ANSWER ME ABOUT MY SELLING THE HOUSE IN LEVITTOWN...
WHAT ARE YOU SAYING EXACTLY?
JIM LEFT ME SOME MONEY--HE HAD AN INSURANCE POLICY...
..I WOULDN'T HAVE TO WORK FOR A WHILE.
--SINCE HE DIED IN A BICYCLE ACCIDENT, IT PAID DOUBLE INDEMNITY.
LIKE THE MOVIE--
--BUT THIS ISN'T A MOVIE, IS IT, BARB? IT DOESN'T ALL TIE TOGETHER AT THE END WITH A PRETTY RED RIBBON---
ARE YOU BREAKING UP WITH ME, LARRY? IS THAT WHAT YOU'RE DOING?

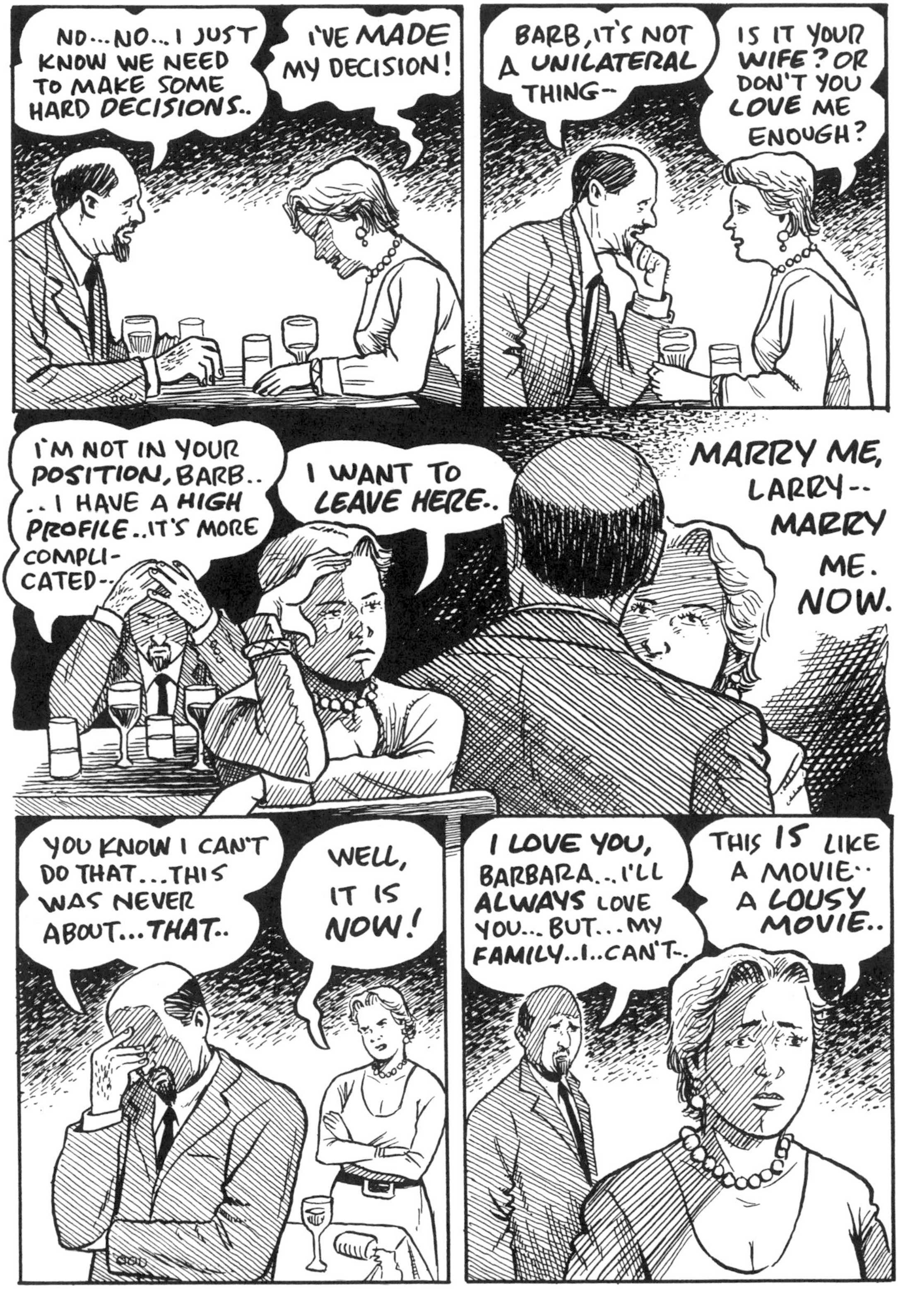
NO...NO...I JUST KNOW WE NEED TO MAKE SOME HARD DECISIONS..
I'VE MADE MY DECISION!
BARB, IT'S NOT A UNILATERAL THING--
IS IT YOUR WIFE? OR DON'T YOU LOVE ME ENOUGH?
I'M NOT IN YOUR POSITION, BARB.. ..I HAVE A HIGH PROFILE..IT'S MORE COMPLI- CATED--
I WANT TO LEAVE HERE..
MARRY ME, LARRY-- MARRY ME. NOW.
YOU KNOW I CAN'T DO THAT...THIS WAS NEVER ABOUT...THAT..
WELL, IT IS NOW!
I LOVE YOU, BARBARA...I'LL ALWAYS LOVE YOU... BUT... MY FAMILY..I..CAN'T..
THIS IS LIKE A MOVIE.. A LOUSY MOVIE..

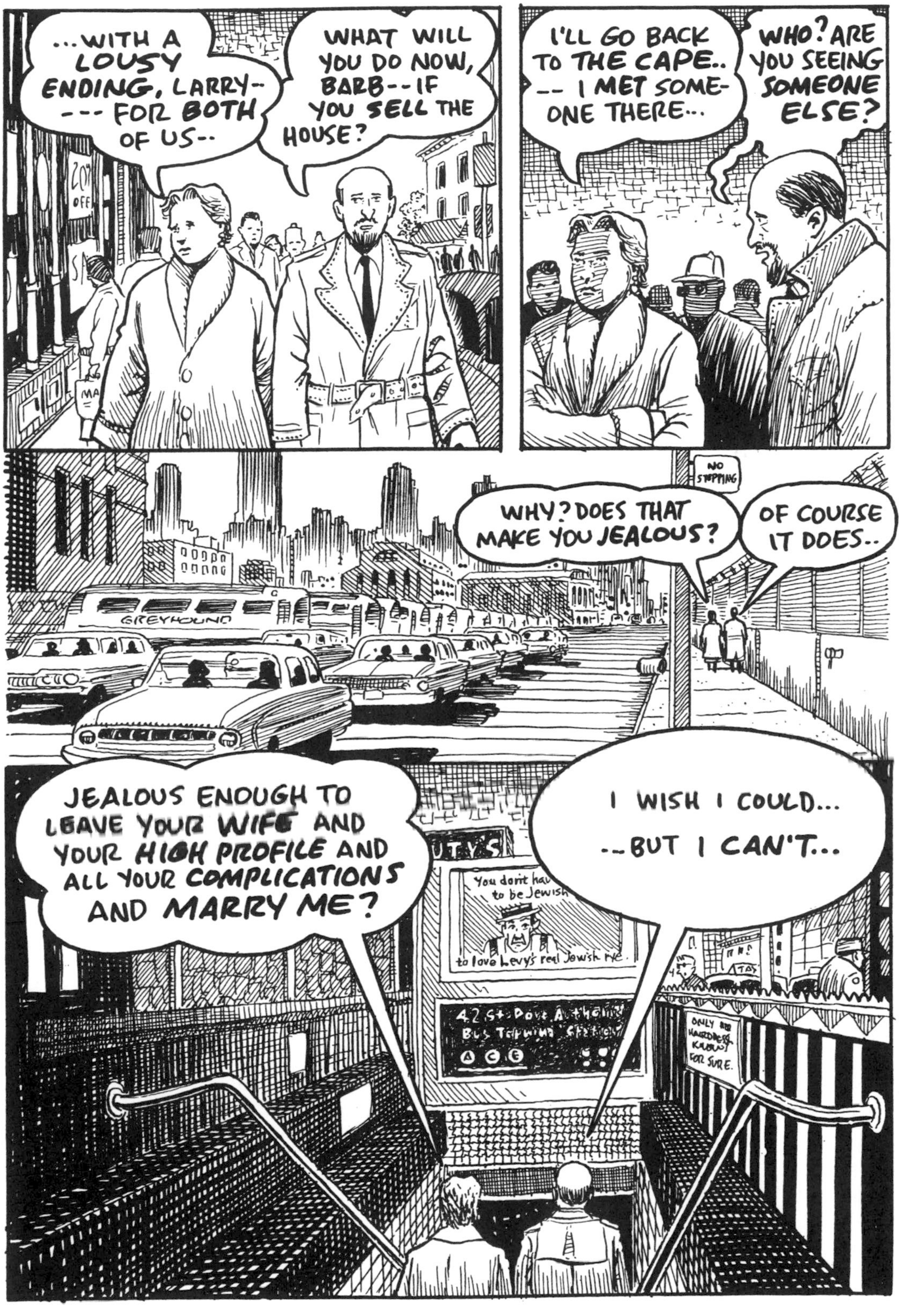
...WITH A LOUSY ENDING, LARRY-- --- FOR BOTH OF US--
WHAT WILL YOU DO NOW, BARB--IF YOU SELL THE HOUSE?
I'LL GO BACK TO THE CAPE.. -- I MET SOME-ONE THERE...
WHO? ARE YOU SEEING SOMEONE ELSE?
NO STEPPING
GREYHOUND
WHY? DOES THAT MAKE YOU JEALOUS?
OF COURSE IT DOES..
JEALOUS ENOUGH TO LEAVE YOUR WIFE AND YOUR HIGH PROFILE AND ALL YOUR COMPLICATIONS AND MARRY ME?
I WISH I COULD... --BUT I CAN'T...
to love Levy's real Jewish rye

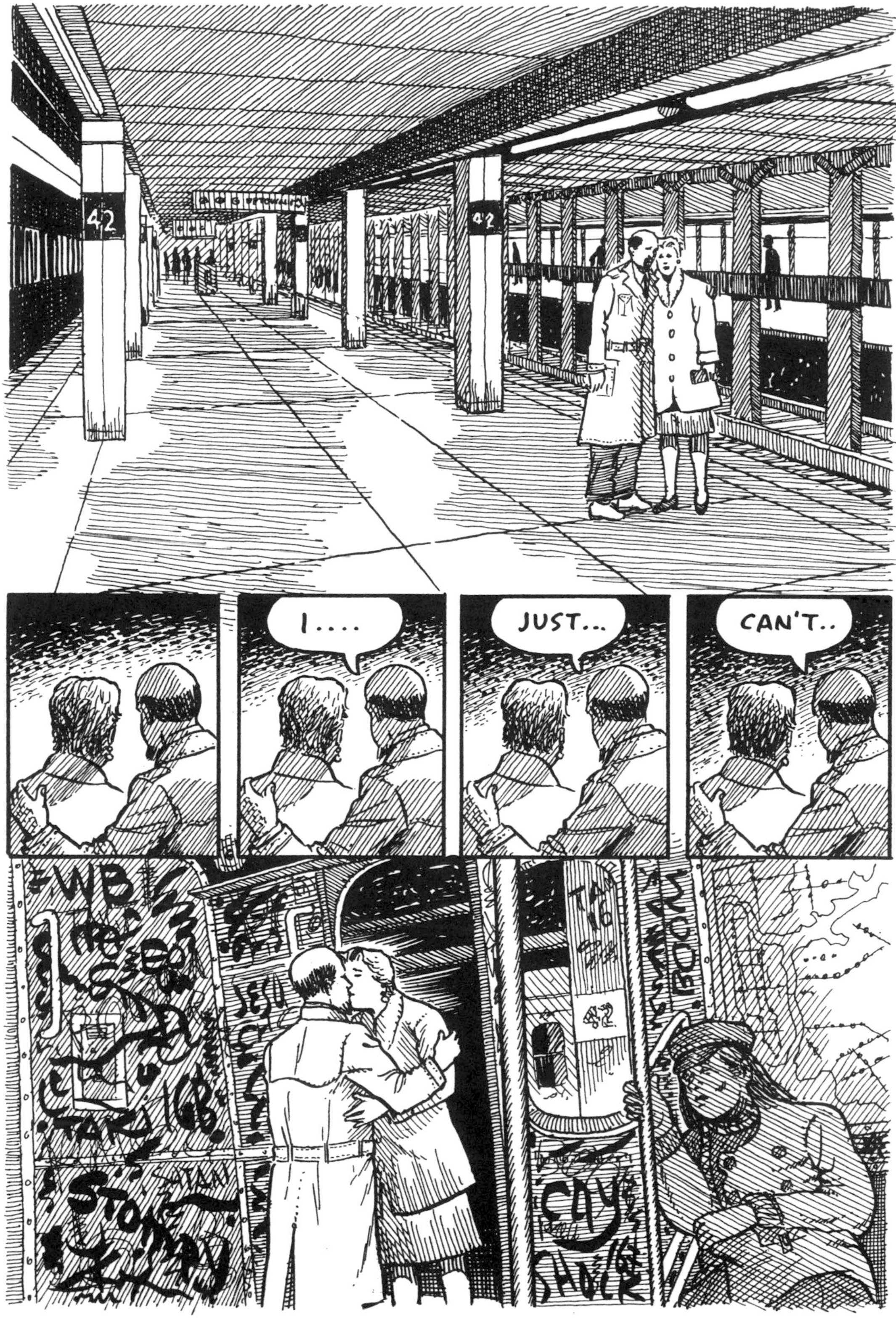
42
I....
JUST...
CAN'T..

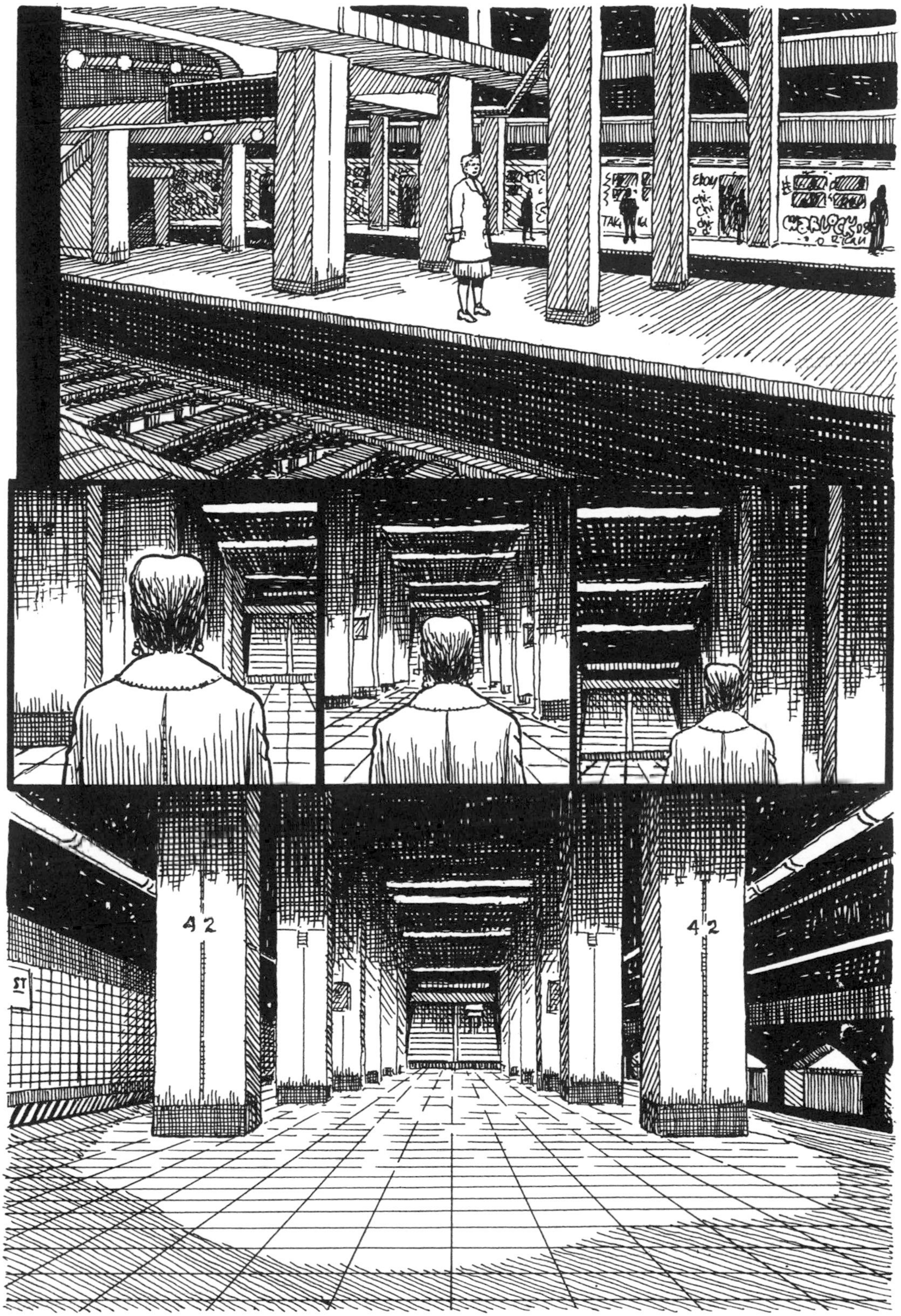
ST
42
42

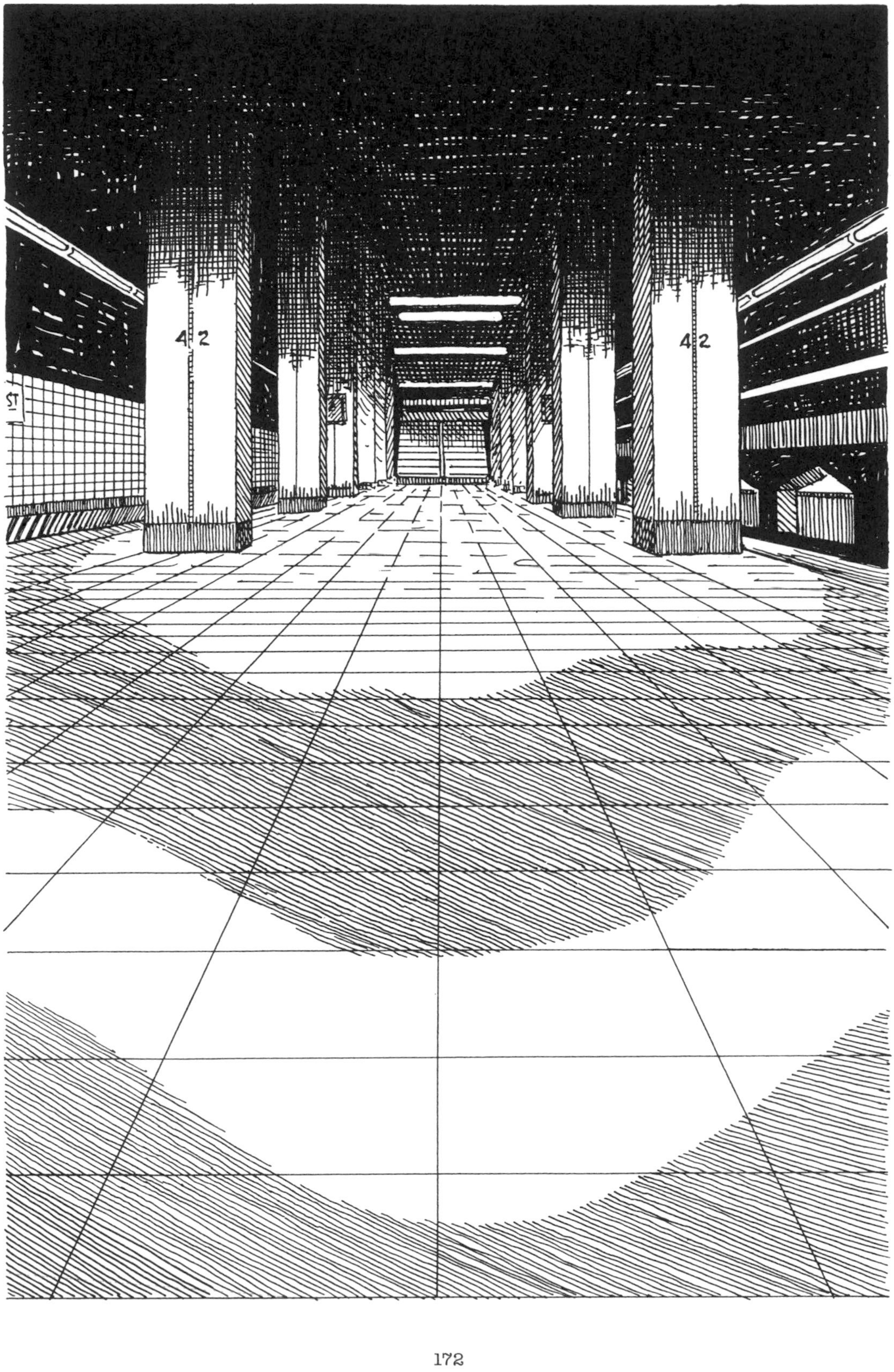

ST
42
42

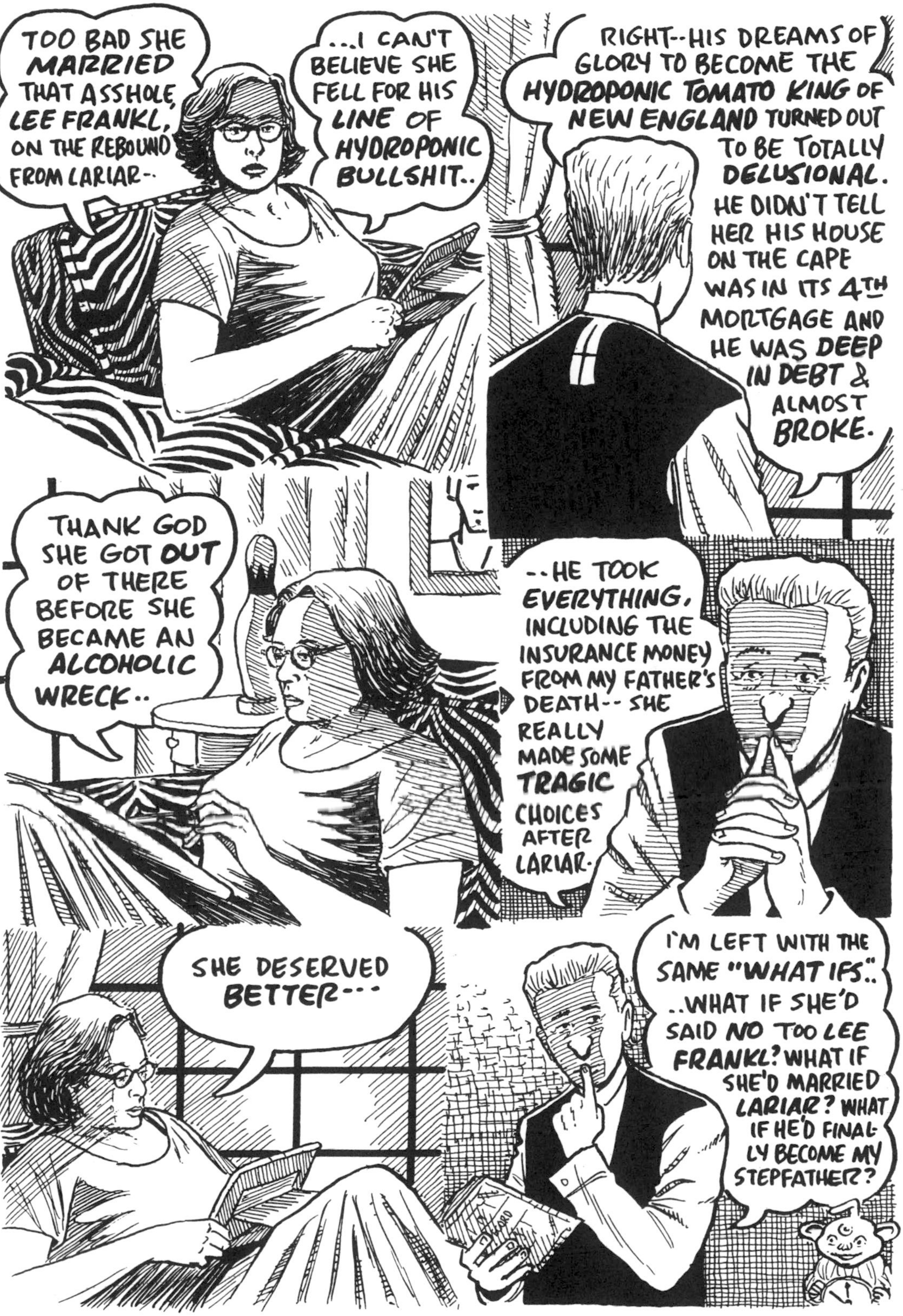
TOO BAD SHE MARRIED THAT ASSHOLE, LEE FRANKL, ON THE REBOUND FROM LARIAR--
...I CAN'T BELIEVE SHE FELL FOR HIS LINE OF HYDROPONIC BULLSHIT..
RIGHT--HIS DREAMS OF GLORY TO BECOME THE HYDROPONIC TOMATO KING OF NEW ENGLAND TURNED OUT TO BE TOTALLY DELUSIONAL. HE DIDN'T TELL HER HIS HOUSE ON THE CAPE WAS IN ITS 4TH MORTGAGE AND HE WAS DEEP IN DEBT & ALMOST BROKE.
THANK GOD SHE GOT OUT OF THERE BEFORE SHE BECAME AN ALCOHOLIC WRECK..
--HE TOOK EVERYTHING, INCLUDING THE INSURANCE MONEY FROM MY FATHER'S DEATH-- SHE REALLY MADE SOME TRAGIC CHOICES AFTER LARIAR.
SHE DESERVED BETTER---
I'M LEFT WITH THE SAME "WHAT IFS".. ..WHAT IF SHE'D SAID NO TOO LEE FRANKL? WHAT IF SHE'D MARRIED LARIAR? WHAT IF HE'D FINALLY BECOME MY STEPFATHER?

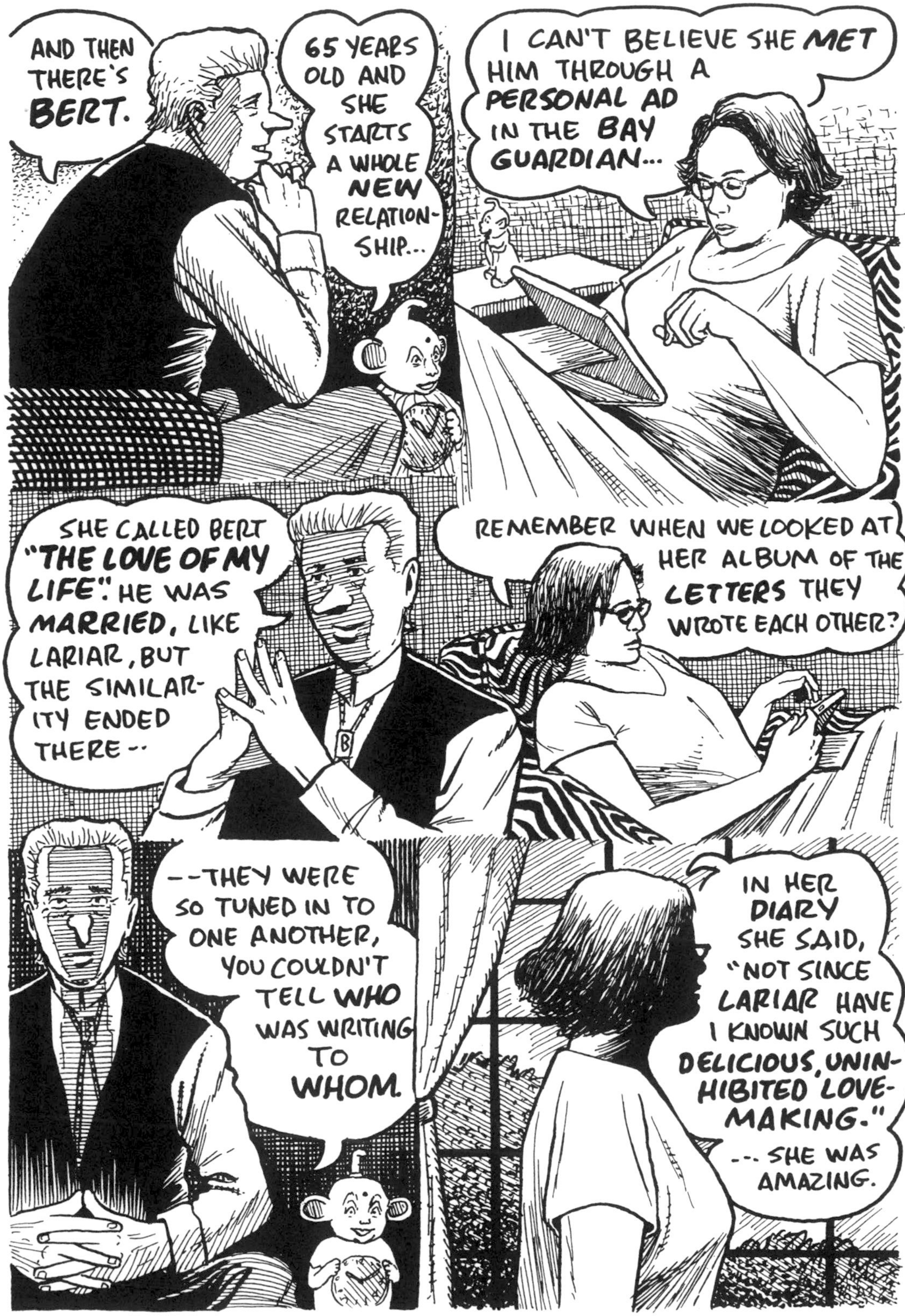
AND THEN THERE'S BERT.
65 YEARS OLD AND SHE STARTS A WHOLE NEW RELATION-SHIP...
I CAN'T BELIEVE SHE MET HIM THROUGH A PERSONAL AD IN THE BAY GUARDIAN...
SHE CALLED BERT "THE LOVE OF MY LIFE". HE WAS MARRIED, LIKE LARIAR, BUT THE SIMILAR-ITY ENDED THERE--
REMEMBER WHEN WE LOOKED AT HER ALBUM OF THE LETTERS THEY WROTE EACH OTHER?
--THEY WERE SO TUNED IN TO ONE ANOTHER, YOU COULDN'T TELL WHO WAS WRITING TO WHOM.
IN HER DIARY SHE SAID, "NOT SINCE LARIAR HAVE I KNOWN SUCH DELICIOUS, UNIN-HIBITED LOVE-MAKING."
--. SHE WAS AMAZING.

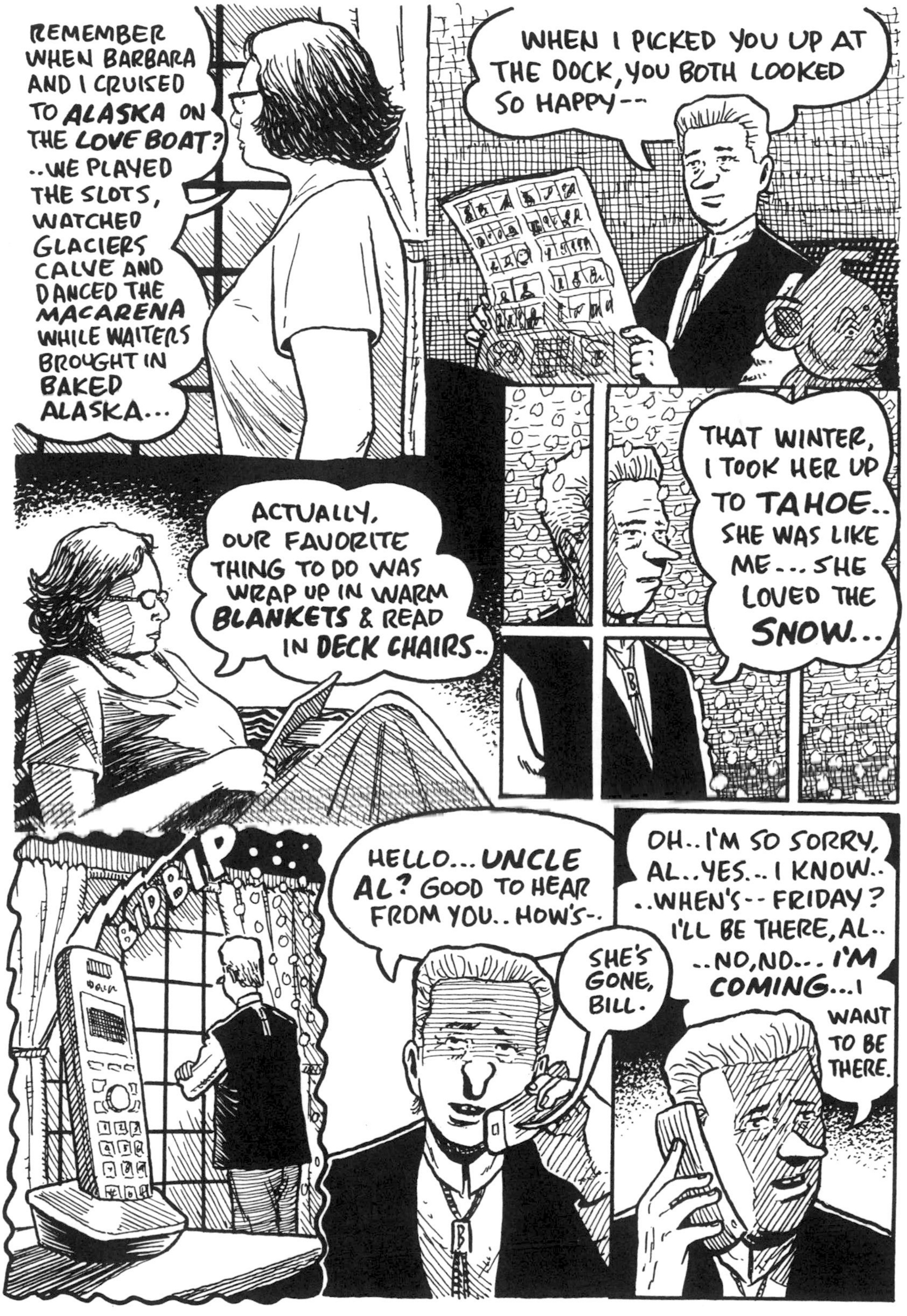
REMEMBER WHEN BARBARA AND I CRUISED TO ALASKA ON THE LOVE BOAT? ..WE PLAYED THE SLOTS, WATCHED GLACIERS CALVE AND DANCED THE MACARENA WHILE WAITERS BROUGHT IN BAKED ALASKA...
WHEN I PICKED YOU UP AT THE DOCK, YOU BOTH LOOKED SO HAPPY--
ACTUALLY, OUR FAVORITE THING TO DO WAS WRAP UP IN WARM BLANKETS & READ IN DECK CHAIRS..
THAT WINTER, I TOOK HER UP TO TAHOE.. SHE WAS LIKE ME... SHE LOVED THE SNOW...
BIPBIP
HELLO... UNCLE AL? GOOD TO HEAR FROM YOU.. HOW'S-.
SHE'S GONE, BILL.
OH..I'M SO SORRY, AL..YES...I KNOW.. ..WHEN'S-- FRIDAY? I'LL BE THERE, AL.. ..NO,NO... I'M COMING...I WANT TO BE THERE.

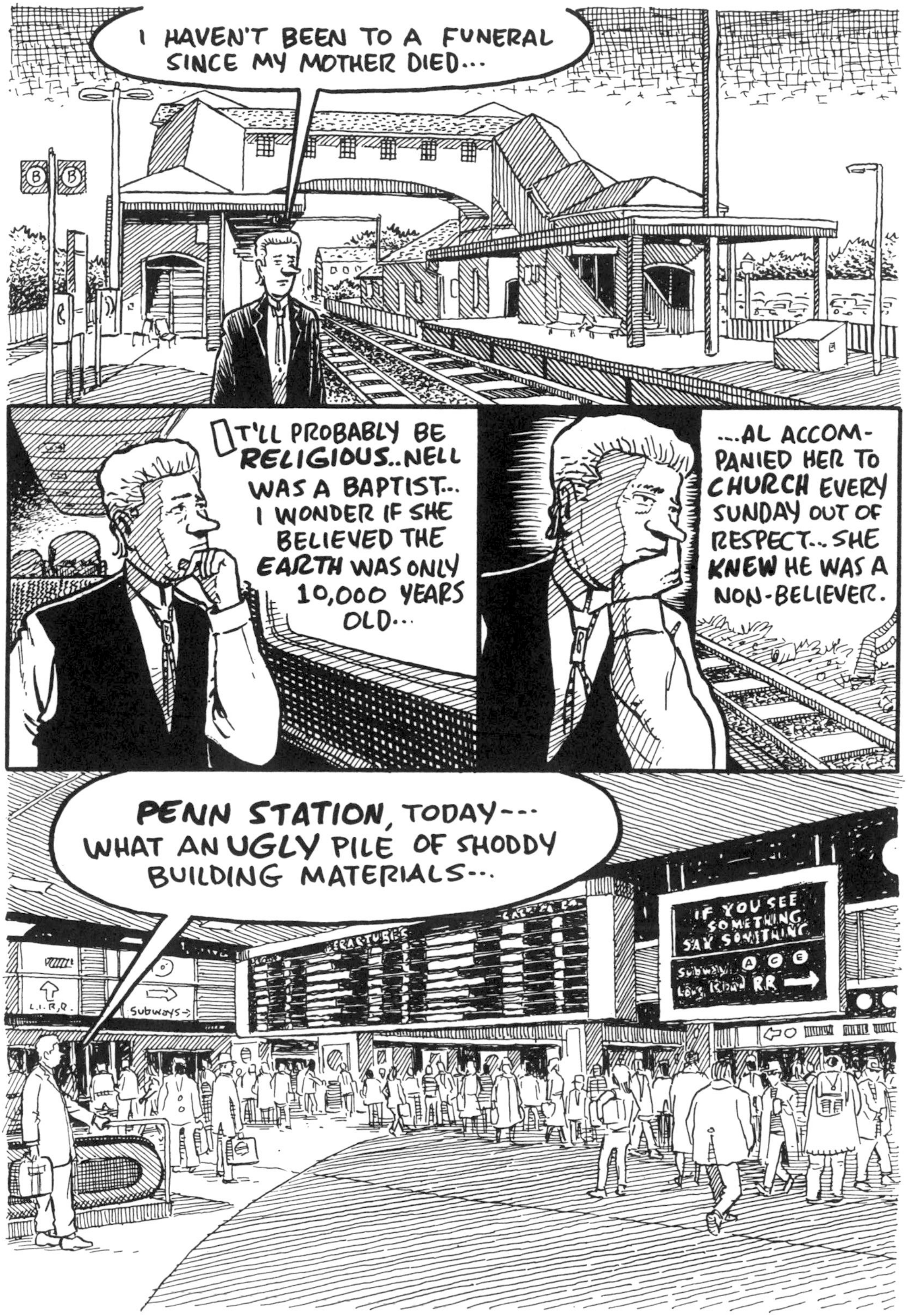
I HAVEN'T BEEN TO A FUNERAL SINCE MY MOTHER DIED...
IT'LL PROBABLY BE RELIGIOUS..NELL WAS A BAPTIST... I WONDER IF SHE BELIEVED THE EARTH WAS ONLY 10,000 YEARS OLD...
...AL ACCOMPANIED HER TO CHURCH EVERY SUNDAY OUT OF RESPECT... SHE KNEW HE WAS A NON-BELIEVER.
PENN STATION, TODAY--- WHAT AN UGLY PILE OF SHODDY BUILDING MATERIALS...
IF YOU SEE SOMETHING
L.I.R.R.
Subways

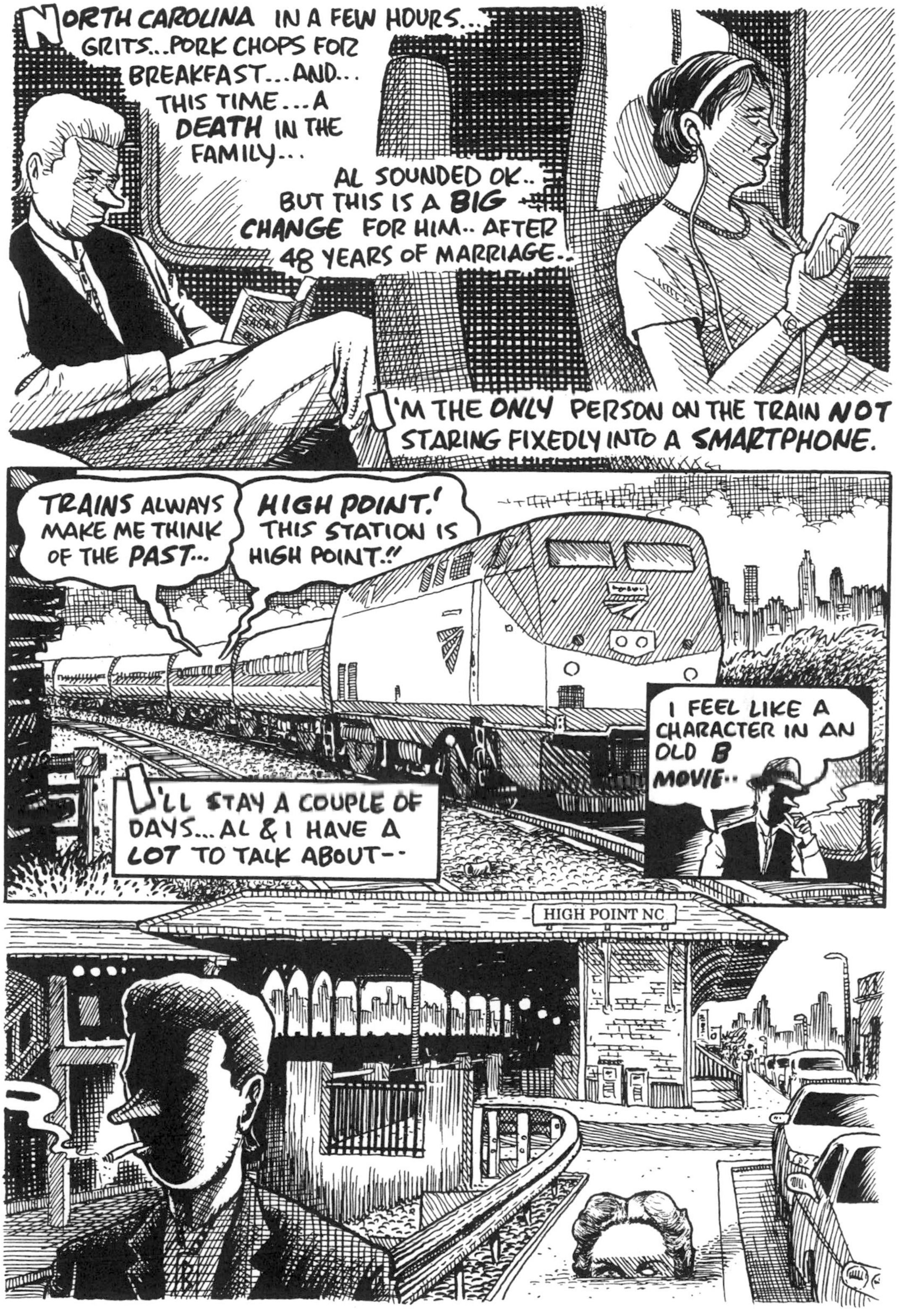
NORTH CAROLINA IN A FEW HOURS... GRITS...PORK CHOPS FOR BREAKFAST...AND... THIS TIME...A DEATH IN THE FAMILY...
AL SOUNDED OK.. BUT THIS IS A BIG CHANGE FOR HIM.. AFTER 48 YEARS OF MARRIAGE..
I'M THE ONLY PERSON ON THE TRAIN NOT STARING FIXEDLY INTO A SMARTPHONE.
TRAINS ALWAYS MAKE ME THINK OF THE PAST...
HIGH POINT! THIS STATION IS HIGH POINT!!
I FEEL LIKE A CHARACTER IN AN OLD B MOVIE..
I'LL STAY A COUPLE OF DAYS...AL & I HAVE A LOT TO TALK ABOUT--
HIGH POINT NC

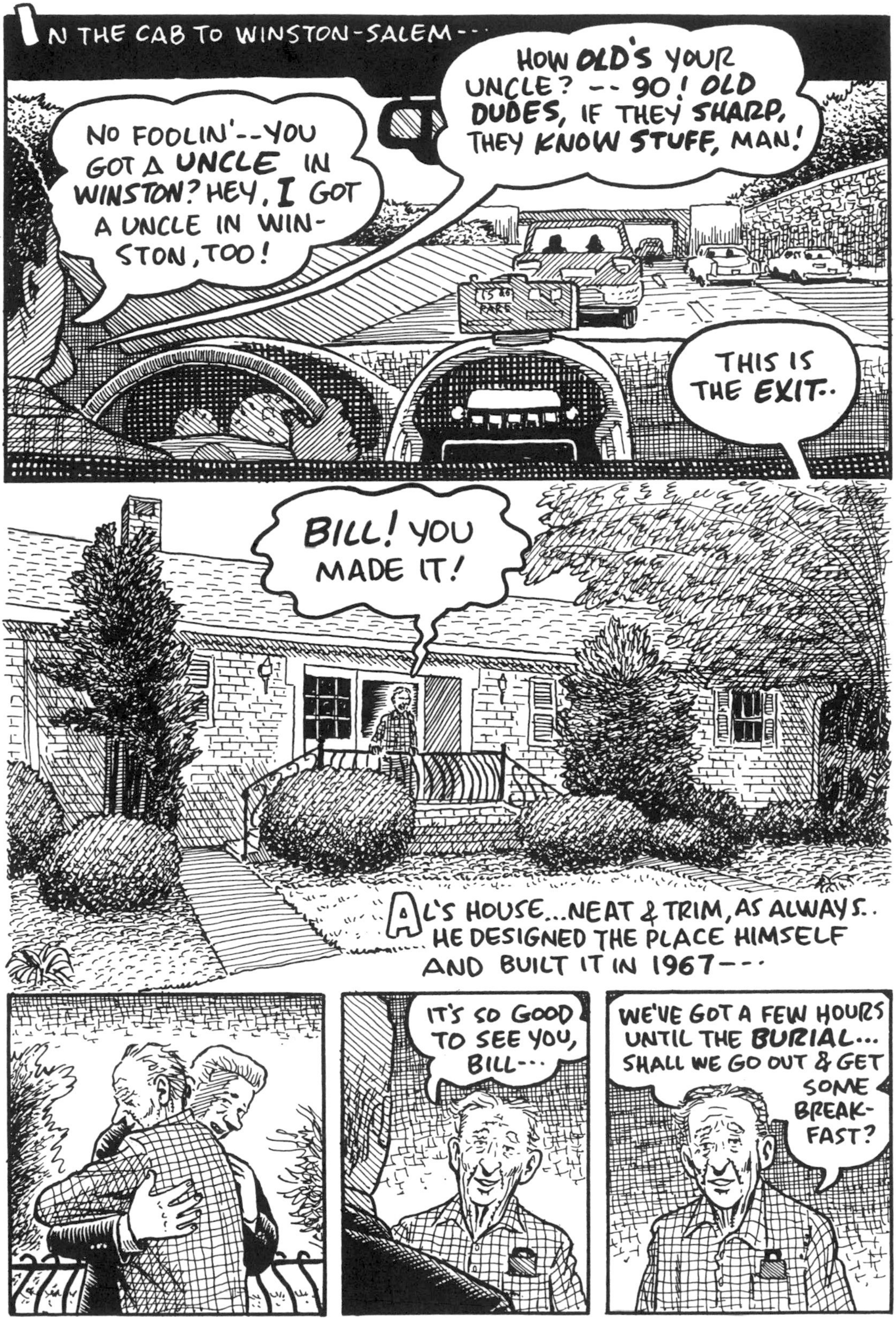
IN THE CAB TO WINSTON-SALEM---
NO FOOLIN'--YOU GOT A UNCLE IN WINSTON? HEY, I GOT A UNCLE IN WINSTON, TOO!
HOW OLD'S YOUR UNCLE? -- 90! OLD DUDES, IF THEY SHARP, THEY KNOW STUFF, MAN!
THIS IS THE EXIT..
BILL! YOU MADE IT!
AL'S HOUSE...NEAT & TRIM, AS ALWAYS.. HE DESIGNED THE PLACE HIMSELF AND BUILT IT IN 1967---
IT'S SO GOOD TO SEE YOU, BILL---
WE'VE GOT A FEW HOURS UNTIL THE BURIAL... SHALL WE GO OUT & GET SOME BREAKFAST?

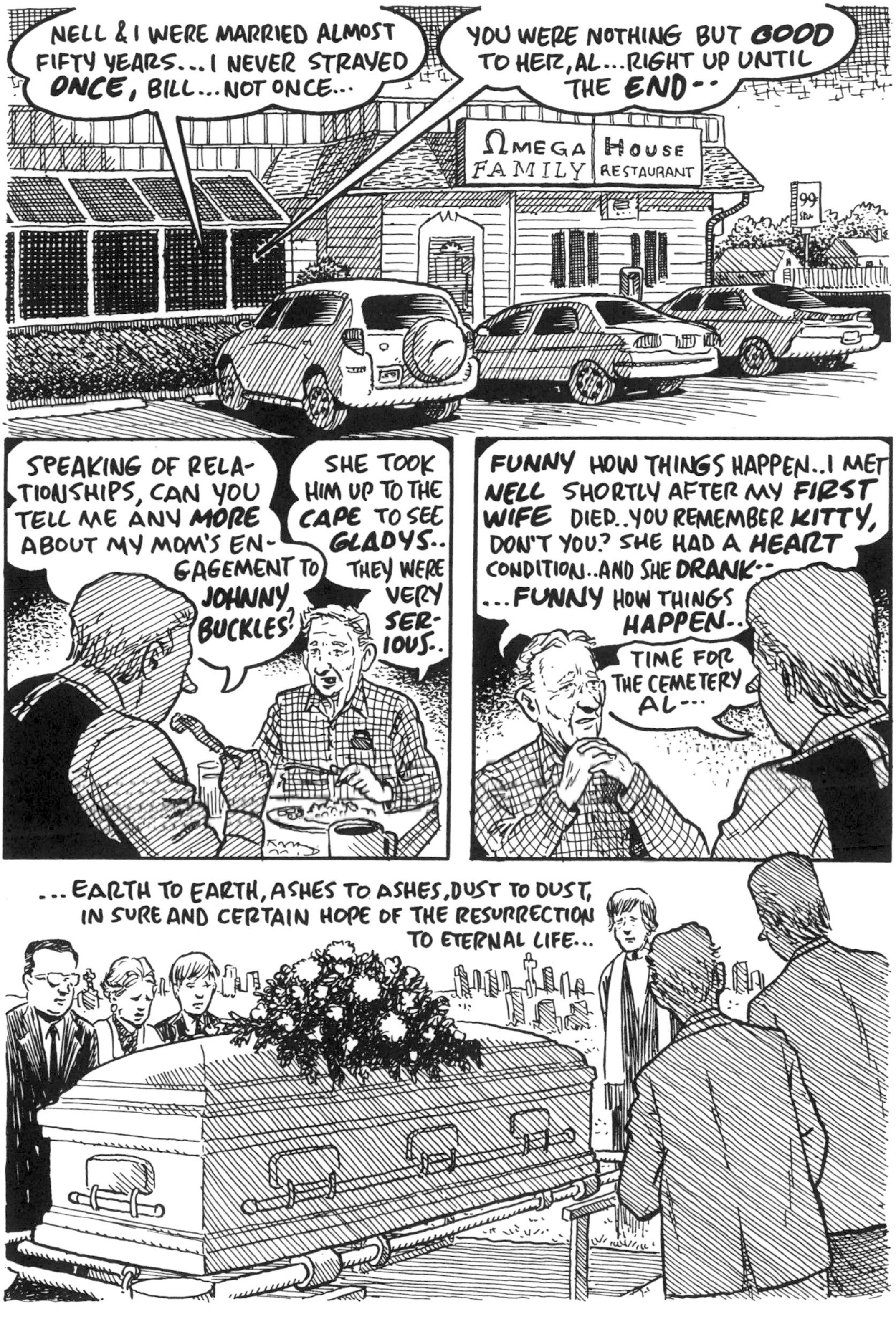
NELL & I WERE MARRIED ALMOST FIFTY YEARS... I NEVER STRAYED ONCE, BILL... NOT ONCE...
YOU WERE NOTHING BUT GOOD TO HER, AL... RIGHT UP UNTIL THE END--
ΩMEGA HOUSE FAMILY RESTAURANT
SPEAKING OF RELATIONSHIPS, CAN YOU TELL ME ANY MORE ABOUT MY MOM'S ENGAGEMENT TO JOHNNY BUCKLES?
SHE TOOK HIM UP TO THE CAPE TO SEE GLADYS.. THEY WERE VERY SERIOUS..
FUNNY HOW THINGS HAPPEN.. I MET NELL SHORTLY AFTER MY FIRST WIFE DIED.. YOU REMEMBER KITTY, DON'T YOU? SHE HAD A HEART CONDITION.. AND SHE DRANK--
...FUNNY HOW THINGS HAPPEN..
TIME FOR THE CEMETERY AL...
...EARTH TO EARTH, ASHES TO ASHES, DUST TO DUST, IN SURE AND CERTAIN HOPE OF THE RESURRECTION TO ETERNAL LIFE...

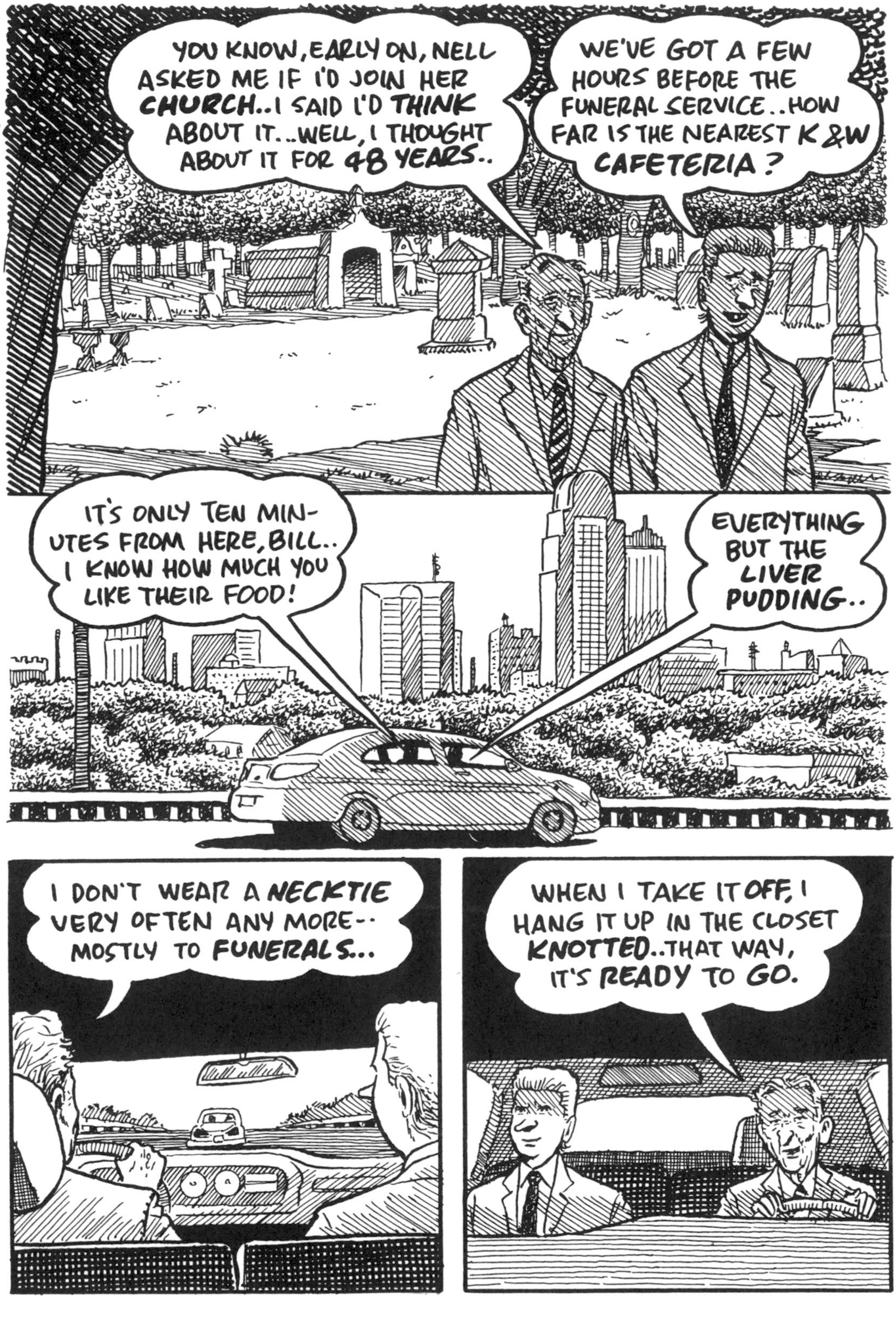
YOU KNOW, EARLY ON, NELL ASKED ME IF I'D JOIN HER CHURCH.. I SAID I'D THINK ABOUT IT... WELL, I THOUGHT ABOUT IT FOR 48 YEARS..
WE'VE GOT A FEW HOURS BEFORE THE FUNERAL SERVICE.. HOW FAR IS THE NEAREST K&W CAFETERIA?
IT'S ONLY TEN MINUTES FROM HERE, BILL.. I KNOW HOW MUCH YOU LIKE THEIR FOOD!
EVERYTHING BUT THE LIVER PUDDING..
I DON'T WEAR A NECKTIE VERY OFTEN ANY MORE-- MOSTLY TO FUNERALS...
WHEN I TAKE IT OFF, I HANG IT UP IN THE CLOSET KNOTTED.. THAT WAY, IT'S READY TO GO.

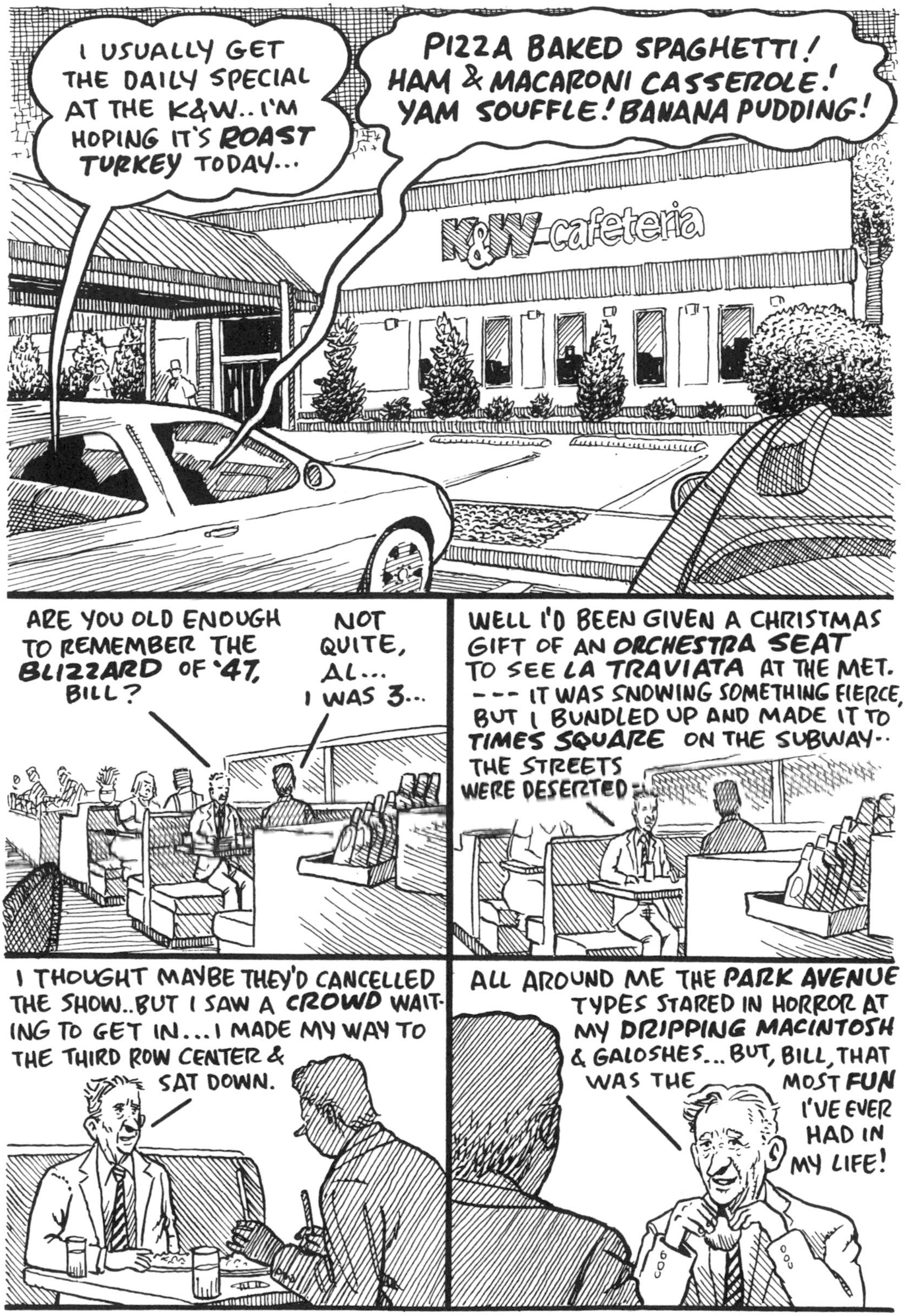
I USUALLY GET THE DAILY SPECIAL AT THE K&W.. I'M HOPING IT'S ROAST TURKEY TODAY...
PIZZA BAKED SPAGHETTI! HAM & MACARONI CASSEROLE! YAM SOUFFLE! BANANA PUDDING!
K&W cafeteria
ARE YOU OLD ENOUGH TO REMEMBER THE BLIZZARD OF '47, BILL?
NOT QUITE, AL... I WAS 3...
WELL I'D BEEN GIVEN A CHRISTMAS GIFT OF AN ORCHESTRA SEAT TO SEE LA TRAVIATA AT THE MET. --- IT WAS SNOWING SOMETHING FIERCE, BUT I BUNDLED UP AND MADE IT TO TIMES SQUARE ON THE SUBWAY.. THE STREETS WERE DESERTED-
I THOUGHT MAYBE THEY'D CANCELLED THE SHOW..BUT I SAW A CROWD WAITING TO GET IN... I MADE MY WAY TO THE THIRD ROW CENTER & SAT DOWN.
ALL AROUND ME THE PARK AVENUE TYPES STARED IN HORROR AT MY DRIPPING MACINTOSH & GALOSHES... BUT, BILL, THAT WAS THE MOST FUN I'VE EVER HAD IN MY LIFE!

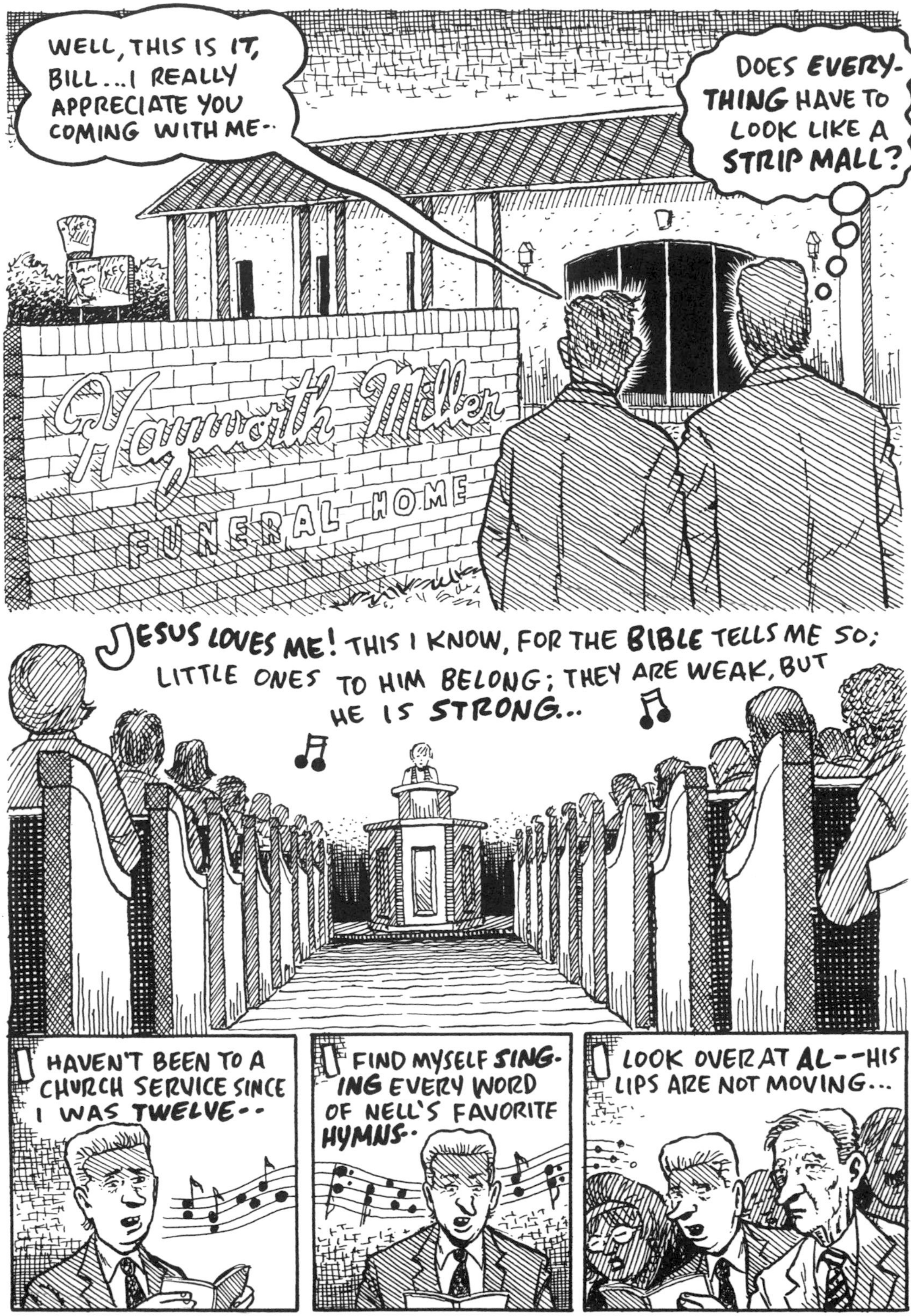
WELL, THIS IS IT, BILL...I REALLY APPRECIATE YOU COMING WITH ME..
DOES EVERYTHING HAVE TO LOOK LIKE A STRIP MALL?
Hayworth Miller
FUNERAL HOME
JESUS LOVES ME! THIS I KNOW, FOR THE BIBLE TELLS ME SO; LITTLE ONES TO HIM BELONG; THEY ARE WEAK, BUT HE IS STRONG...
I HAVEN'T BEEN TO A CHURCH SERVICE SINCE I WAS TWELVE--
I FIND MYSELF SINGING EVERY WORD OF NELL'S FAVORITE HYMNS..
I LOOK OVER AT AL--HIS LIPS ARE NOT MOVING...

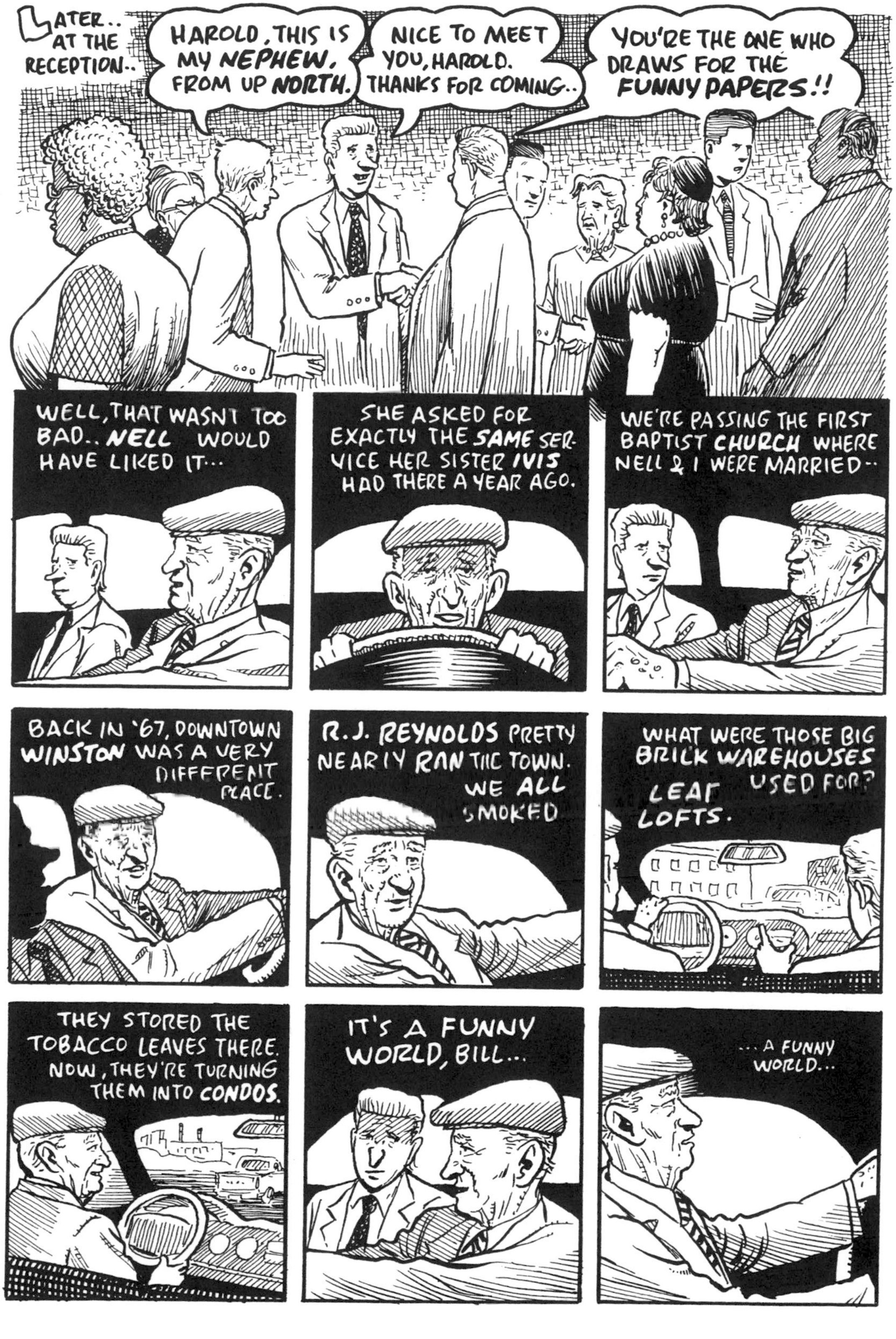
LATER.. AT THE RECEPTION..
HAROLD, THIS IS MY NEPHEW, FROM UP NORTH.
NICE TO MEET YOU, HAROLD. THANKS FOR COMING..
YOU'RE THE ONE WHO DRAWS FOR THE FUNNY PAPERS!!
WELL, THAT WASN'T TOO BAD.. NELL WOULD HAVE LIKED IT...
SHE ASKED FOR EXACTLY THE SAME SERVICE HER SISTER IVIS HAD THERE A YEAR AGO.
WE'RE PASSING THE FIRST BAPTIST CHURCH WHERE NELL & I WERE MARRIED..
BACK IN '67, DOWNTOWN WINSTON WAS A VERY DIFFERENT PLACE.
R.J. REYNOLDS PRETTY NEARLY RAN THE TOWN.
WE ALL SMOKED.
WHAT WERE THOSE BIG BRICK WAREHOUSES USED FOR?
LEAF LOFTS.
THEY STORED THE TOBACCO LEAVES THERE. NOW, THEY'RE TURNING THEM INTO CONDOS.
IT'S A FUNNY WORLD, BILL...
...A FUNNY WORLD...

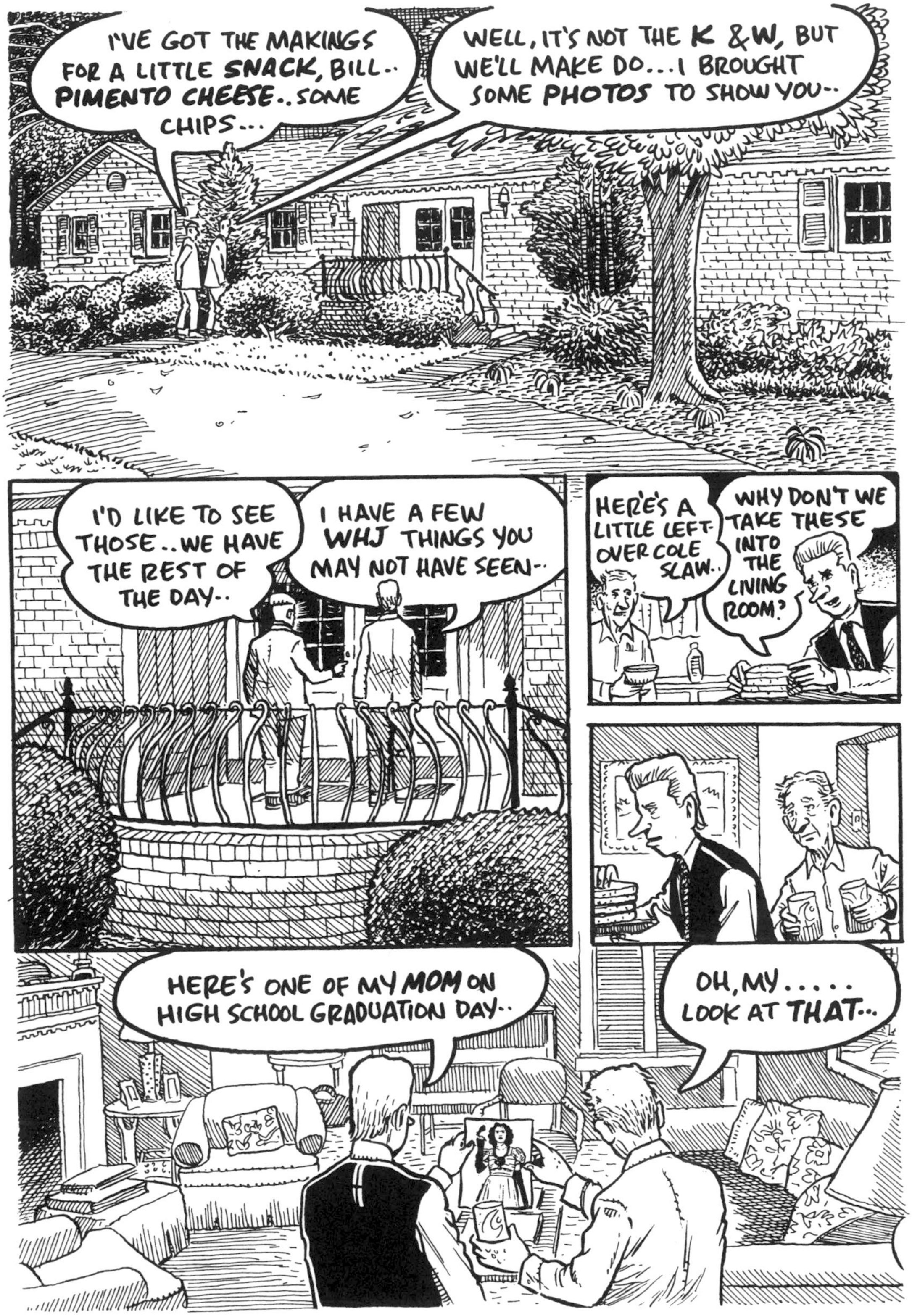
I'VE GOT THE MAKINGS FOR A LITTLE SNACK, BILL.. PIMENTO CHEESE..SOME CHIPS...
WELL, IT'S NOT THE K & W, BUT WE'LL MAKE DO...I BROUGHT SOME PHOTOS TO SHOW YOU..
I'D LIKE TO SEE THOSE..WE HAVE THE REST OF THE DAY..
I HAVE A FEW WHJ THINGS YOU MAY NOT HAVE SEEN..
HERE'S A LITTLE LEFT-OVER COLE SLAW..
WHY DON'T WE TAKE THESE INTO THE LIVING ROOM?
HERE'S ONE OF MY MOM ON HIGH SCHOOL GRADUATION DAY..
OH, MY..... LOOK AT THAT...

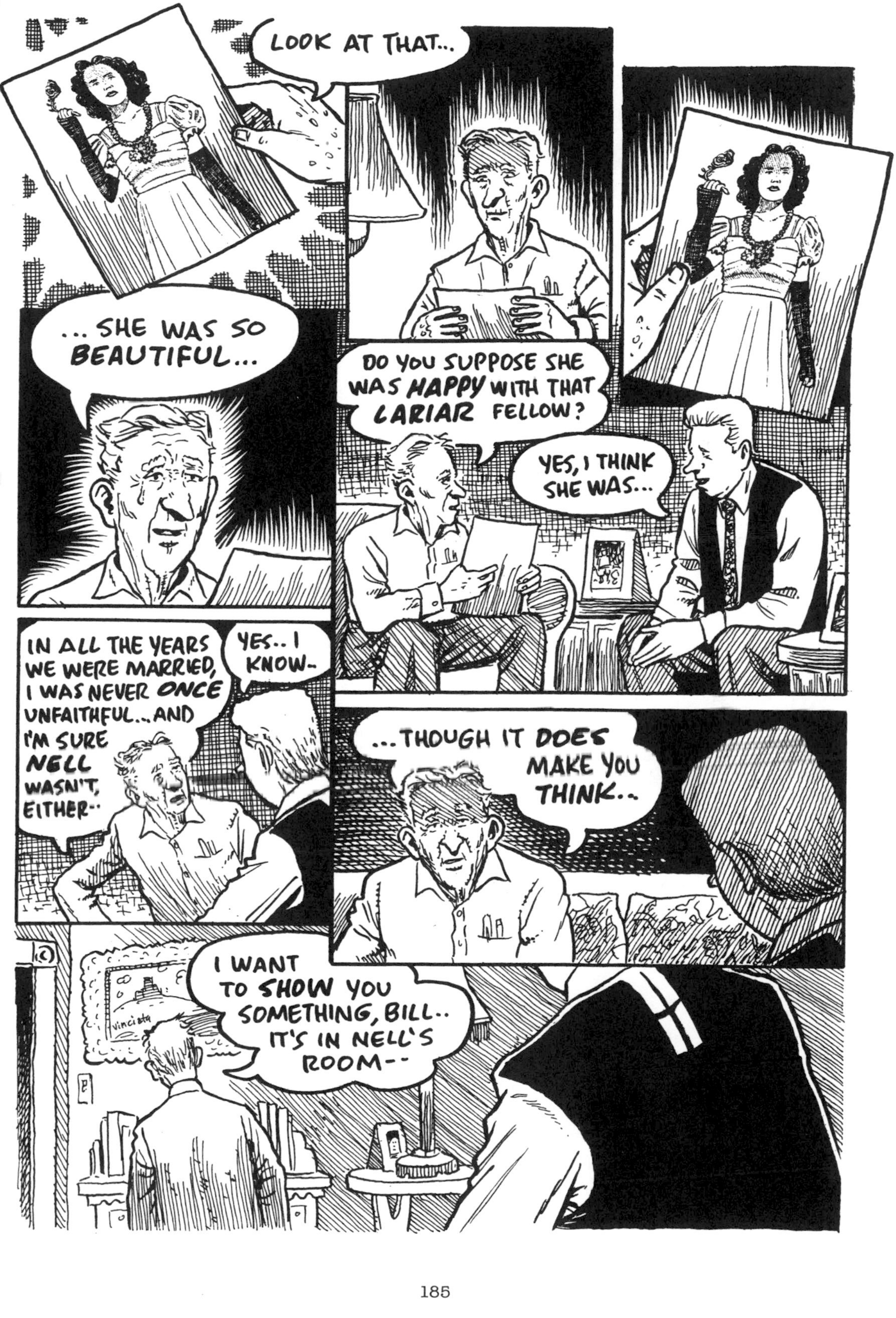
LOOK AT THAT...
... SHE WAS SO BEAUTIFUL...
DO YOU SUPPOSE SHE WAS HAPPY WITH THAT LARIAR FELLOW?
YES, I THINK SHE WAS...
IN ALL THE YEARS WE WERE MARRIED, I WAS NEVER ONCE UNFAITHFUL...AND I'M SURE NELL WASN'T, EITHER--
YES.. I KNOW..
...THOUGH IT DOES MAKE YOU THINK..
I WANT TO SHOW YOU SOMETHING, BILL.. IT'S IN NELL'S ROOM--

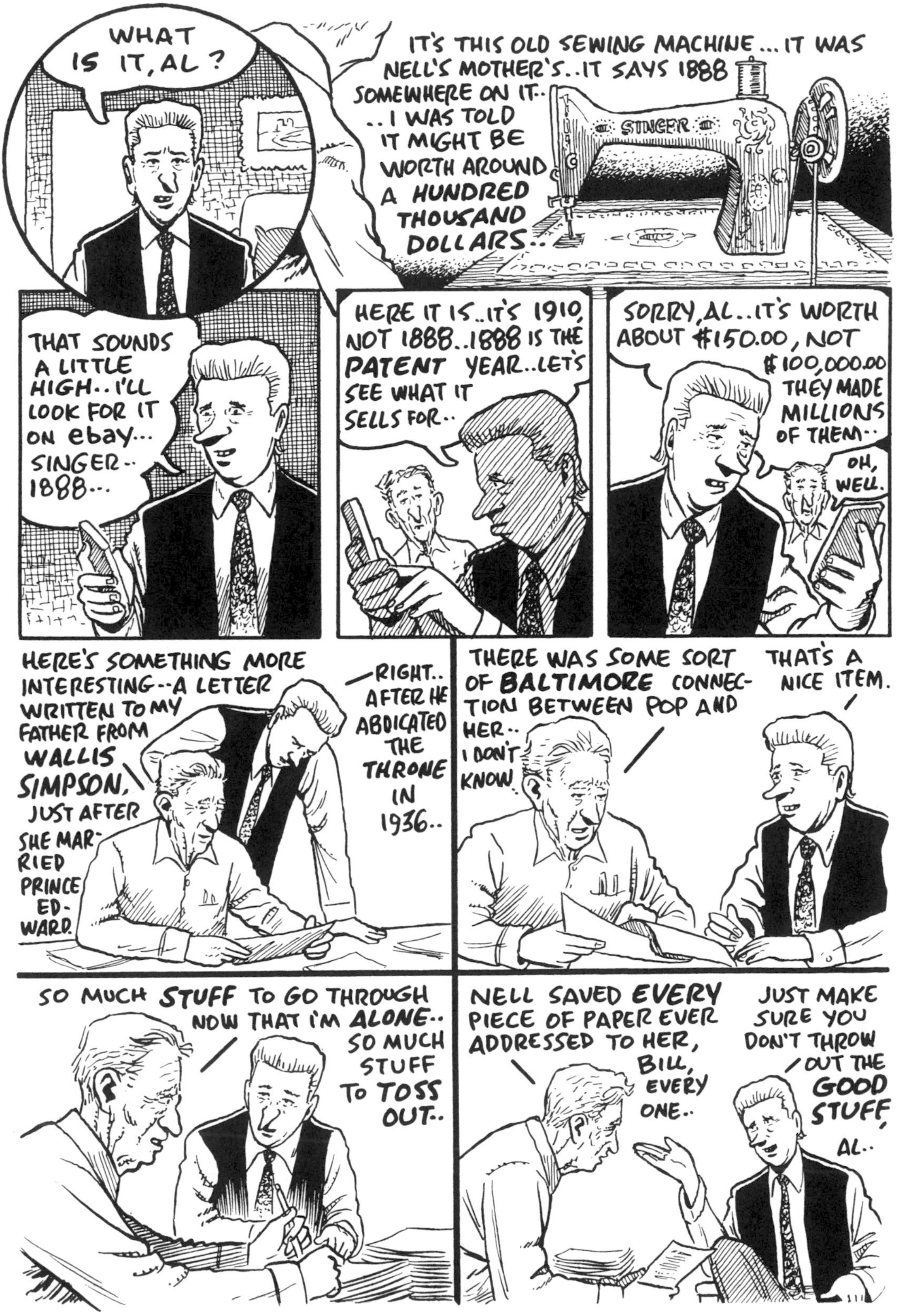
WHAT IS IT, AL?
IT'S THIS OLD SEWING MACHINE... IT WAS NELL'S MOTHER'S.. IT SAYS 1888 SOMEWHERE ON IT.. ..I WAS TOLD IT MIGHT BE WORTH AROUND A HUNDRED THOUSAND DOLLARS..
SINGER
THAT SOUNDS A LITTLE HIGH.. I'LL LOOK FOR IT ON ebay... SINGER.. 1888...
HERE IT IS..IT'S 1910, NOT 1888..1888 IS THE PATENT YEAR..LET'S SEE WHAT IT SELLS FOR..
SORRY, AL..IT'S WORTH ABOUT $150.00, NOT $100,000.00 THEY MADE MILLIONS OF THEM..
OH, WELL.
HERE'S SOMETHING MORE INTERESTING--A LETTER WRITTEN TO MY FATHER FROM WALLIS SIMPSON, JUST AFTER SHE MARRIED PRINCE EDWARD.
RIGHT.. AFTER HE ABDICATED THE THRONE IN 1936..
THERE WAS SOME SORT OF BALTIMORE CONNECTION BETWEEN POP AND HER.. I DON'T KNOW..
THAT'S A NICE ITEM.
SO MUCH STUFF TO GO THROUGH NOW THAT I'M ALONE.. SO MUCH STUFF TO TOSS OUT..
NELL SAVED EVERY PIECE OF PAPER EVER ADDRESSED TO HER, BILL, EVERY ONE..
JUST MAKE SURE YOU DON'T THROW OUT THE GOOD STUFF, AL..

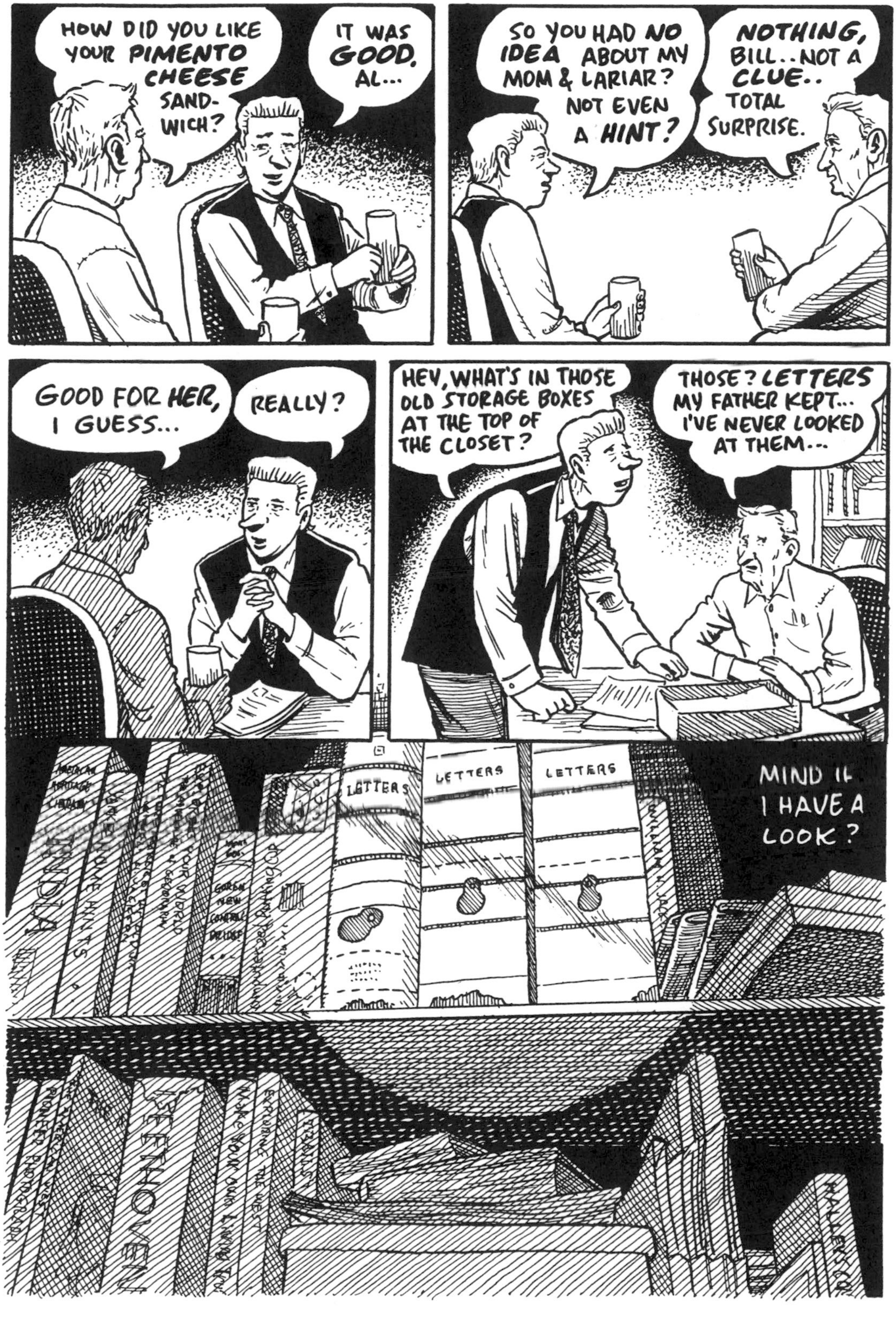
HOW DID YOU LIKE YOUR PIMENTO CHEESE SANDWICH?
IT WAS GOOD, AL...
SO YOU HAD NO IDEA ABOUT MY MOM & LARIAR? NOT EVEN A HINT?
NOTHING, BILL.. NOT A CLUE.. TOTAL SURPRISE.
GOOD FOR HER, I GUESS...
REALLY?
HEY, WHAT'S IN THOSE OLD STORAGE BOXES AT THE TOP OF THE CLOSET?
THOSE? LETTERS MY FATHER KEPT... I'VE NEVER LOOKED AT THEM...
LETTERS
LETTERS
LETTERS
MIND IF I HAVE A LOOK?
BEETHOVEN

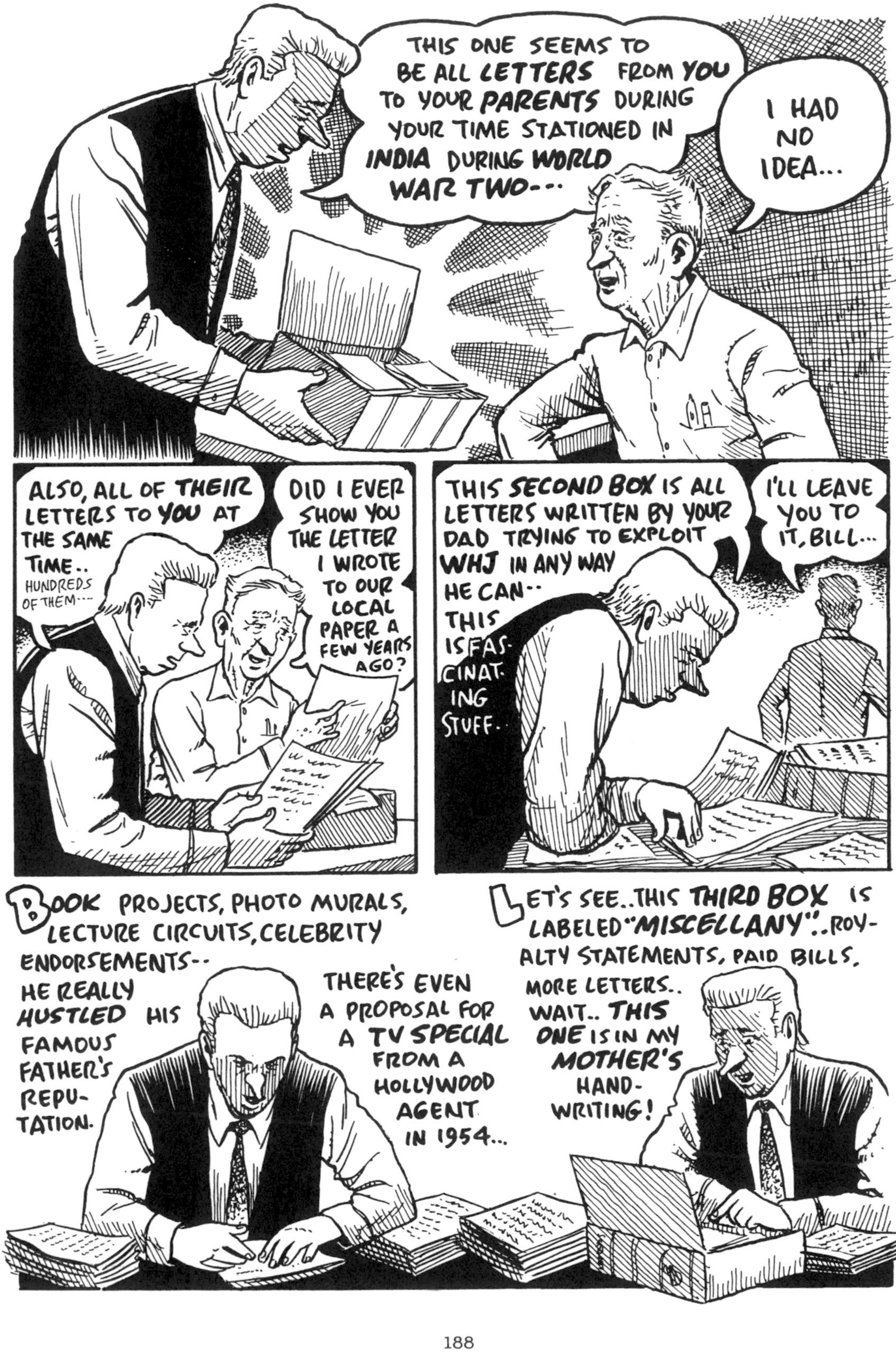

THIS ONE SEEMS TO BE ALL LETTERS FROM YOU TO YOUR PARENTS DURING YOUR TIME STATIONED IN INDIA DURING WORLD WAR TWO...
I HAD NO IDEA...
ALSO, ALL OF THEIR LETTERS TO YOU AT THE SAME TIME.. HUNDREDS OF THEM...
DID I EVER SHOW YOU THE LETTER I WROTE TO OUR LOCAL PAPER A FEW YEARS AGO?
THIS SECOND BOX IS ALL LETTERS WRITTEN BY YOUR DAD TRYING TO EXPLOIT WHJ IN ANY WAY HE CAN.. THIS IS FASCINATING STUFF..
I'LL LEAVE YOU TO IT, BILL...
BOOK PROJECTS, PHOTO MURALS, LECTURE CIRCUITS, CELEBRITY ENDORSEMENTS.. HE REALLY HUSTLED HIS FAMOUS FATHER'S REPUTATION.
THERE'S EVEN A PROPOSAL FOR A TV SPECIAL FROM A HOLLYWOOD AGENT IN 1954...
LET'S SEE.. THIS THIRD BOX IS LABELED "MISCELLANY".. ROYALTY STATEMENTS, PAID BILLS, MORE LETTERS.. WAIT.. THIS ONE IS IN MY MOTHER'S HANDWRITING!

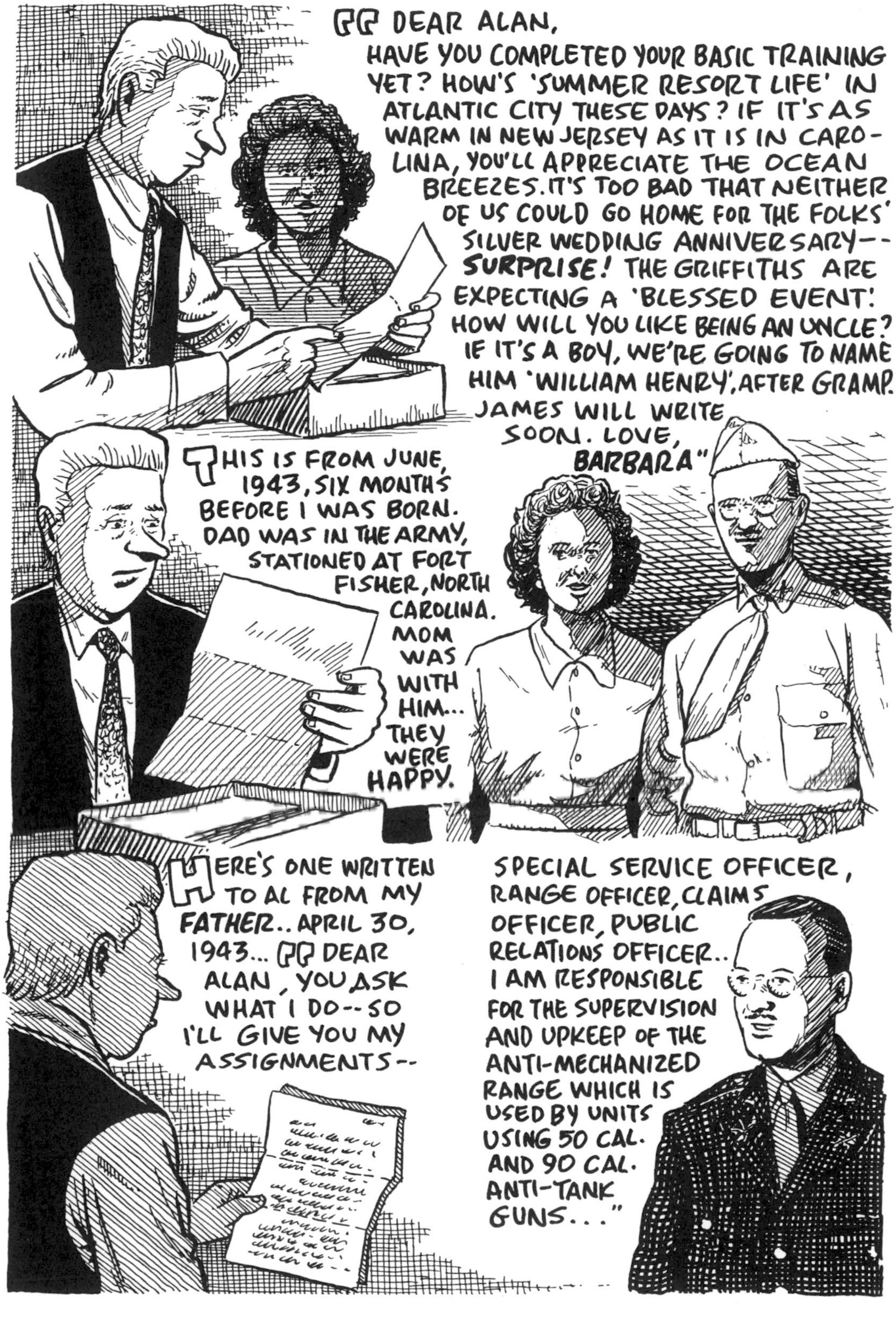
"DEAR ALAN,
HAVE YOU COMPLETED YOUR BASIC TRAINING YET? HOW'S 'SUMMER RESORT LIFE' IN ATLANTIC CITY THESE DAYS? IF IT'S AS WARM IN NEW JERSEY AS IT IS IN CAROLINA, YOU'LL APPRECIATE THE OCEAN BREEZES. IT'S TOO BAD THAT NEITHER OF US COULD GO HOME FOR THE FOLKS' SILVER WEDDING ANNIVERSARY-- **SURPRISE!** THE GRIFFITHS ARE EXPECTING A 'BLESSED EVENT'. HOW WILL YOU LIKE BEING AN UNCLE? IF IT'S A BOY, WE'RE GOING TO NAME HIM 'WILLIAM HENRY', AFTER GRAMP. JAMES WILL WRITE SOON. LOVE, **BARBARA**"
THIS IS FROM JUNE, 1943, SIX MONTHS BEFORE I WAS BORN. DAD WAS IN THE ARMY, STATIONED AT FORT FISHER, NORTH CAROLINA. MOM WAS WITH HIM... THEY WERE HAPPY.
HERE'S ONE WRITTEN TO AL FROM MY **FATHER**.. APRIL 30, 1943... "DEAR ALAN, YOU ASK WHAT I DO--SO I'LL GIVE YOU MY ASSIGNMENTS--
SPECIAL SERVICE OFFICER, RANGE OFFICER, CLAIMS OFFICER, PUBLIC RELATIONS OFFICER.. I AM RESPONSIBLE FOR THE SUPERVISION AND UPKEEP OF THE ANTI-MECHANIZED RANGE WHICH IS USED BY UNITS USING 50 CAL. AND 90 CAL. ANTI-TANK GUNS..."

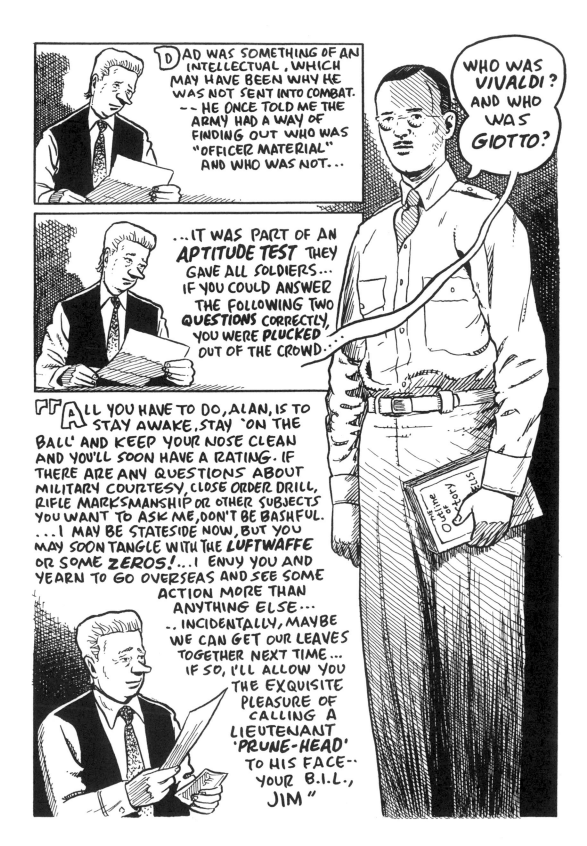

DAD WAS SOMETHING OF AN INTELLECTUAL, WHICH MAY HAVE BEEN WHY HE WAS NOT SENT INTO COMBAT. -- HE ONCE TOLD ME THE ARMY HAD A WAY OF FINDING OUT WHO WAS "OFFICER MATERIAL" AND WHO WAS NOT...

WHO WAS *VIVALDI*? AND WHO WAS *GIOTTO*?

...IT WAS PART OF AN **APTITUDE TEST** THEY GAVE ALL SOLDIERS... IF YOU COULD ANSWER THE FOLLOWING TWO QUESTIONS CORRECTLY, YOU WERE **PLUCKED** OUT OF THE CROWD...

"**A**LL YOU HAVE TO DO, ALAN, IS TO STAY AWAKE, STAY 'ON THE BALL' AND KEEP YOUR NOSE CLEAN AND YOU'LL SOON HAVE A RATING. IF THERE ARE ANY QUESTIONS ABOUT MILITARY COURTESY, CLOSE ORDER DRILL, RIFLE MARKSMANSHIP OR OTHER SUBJECTS YOU WANT TO ASK ME, DON'T BE BASHFUL. ...I MAY BE STATESIDE NOW, BUT YOU MAY SOON TANGLE WITH THE **LUFTWAFFE** OR SOME **ZEROS!**...I ENVY YOU AND YEARN TO GO OVERSEAS AND SEE SOME ACTION MORE THAN ANYTHING ELSE... ..INCIDENTALLY, MAYBE WE CAN GET OUR LEAVES TOGETHER NEXT TIME... IF SO, I'LL ALLOW YOU THE EXQUISITE PLEASURE OF CALLING A LIEUTENANT 'PRUNE-HEAD' TO HIS FACE-- YOUR B.I.L., JIM"

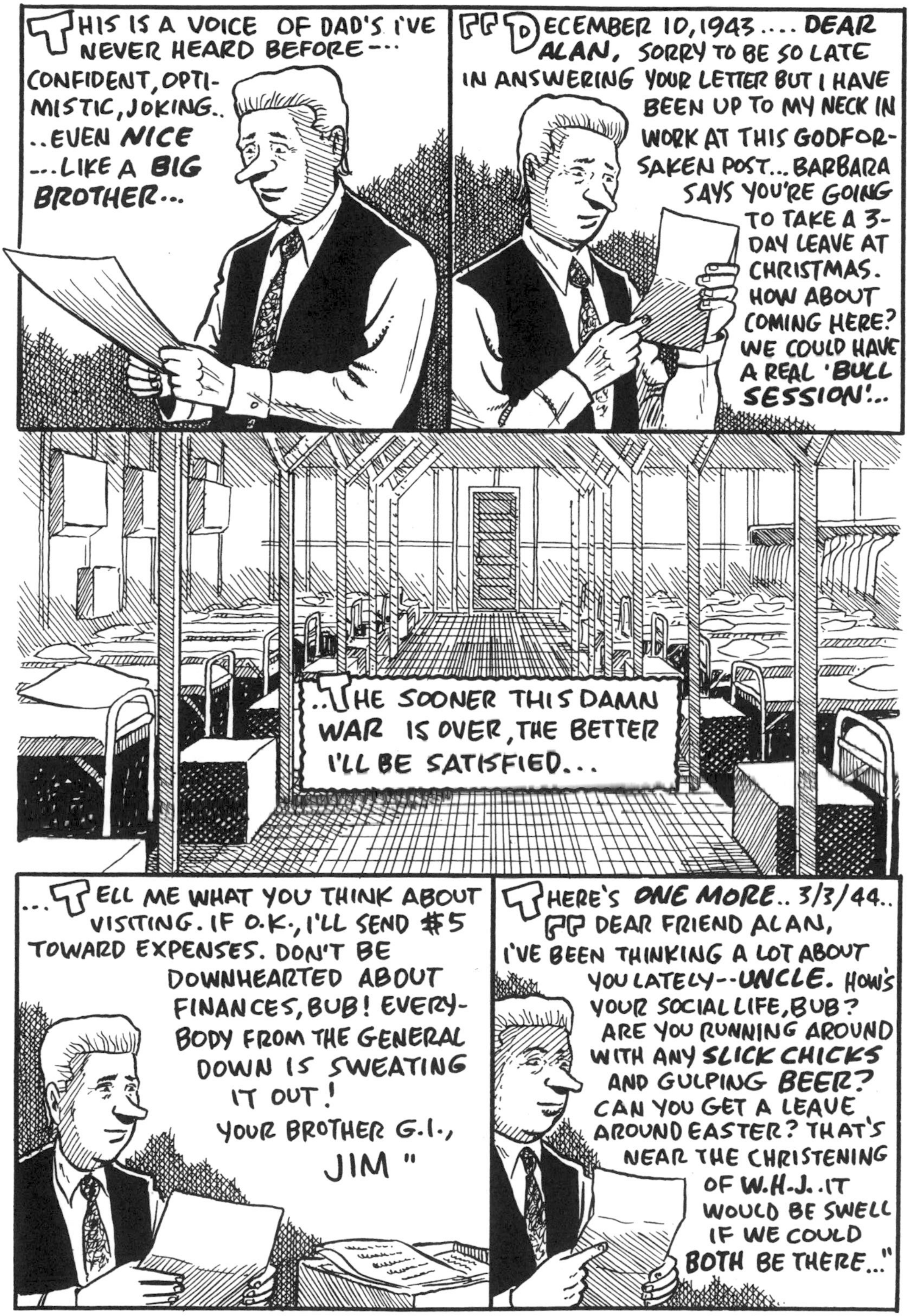
THIS IS A VOICE OF DAD'S I'VE NEVER HEARD BEFORE--- CONFIDENT, OPTIMISTIC, JOKING.. ..EVEN NICE ---LIKE A BIG BROTHER...
"DECEMBER 10, 1943.... DEAR ALAN, SORRY TO BE SO LATE IN ANSWERING YOUR LETTER BUT I HAVE BEEN UP TO MY NECK IN WORK AT THIS GODFORSAKEN POST... BARBARA SAYS YOU'RE GOING TO TAKE A 3-DAY LEAVE AT CHRISTMAS. HOW ABOUT COMING HERE? WE COULD HAVE A REAL 'BULL SESSION'...
..THE SOONER THIS DAMN WAR IS OVER, THE BETTER I'LL BE SATISFIED...
...TELL ME WHAT YOU THINK ABOUT VISITING. IF O.K., I'LL SEND #5 TOWARD EXPENSES. DON'T BE DOWNHEARTED ABOUT FINANCES, BUB! EVERYBODY FROM THE GENERAL DOWN IS SWEATING IT OUT!
YOUR BROTHER G.I.,
JIM"
THERE'S ONE MORE.. 3/3/44.. "DEAR FRIEND ALAN, I'VE BEEN THINKING A LOT ABOUT YOU LATELY--UNCLE. HOW'S YOUR SOCIAL LIFE, BUB? ARE YOU RUNNING AROUND WITH ANY SLICK CHICKS AND GULPING BEER? CAN YOU GET A LEAVE AROUND EASTER? THAT'S NEAR THE CHRISTENING OF W.H.J.. IT WOULD BE SWELL IF WE COULD BOTH BE THERE..."

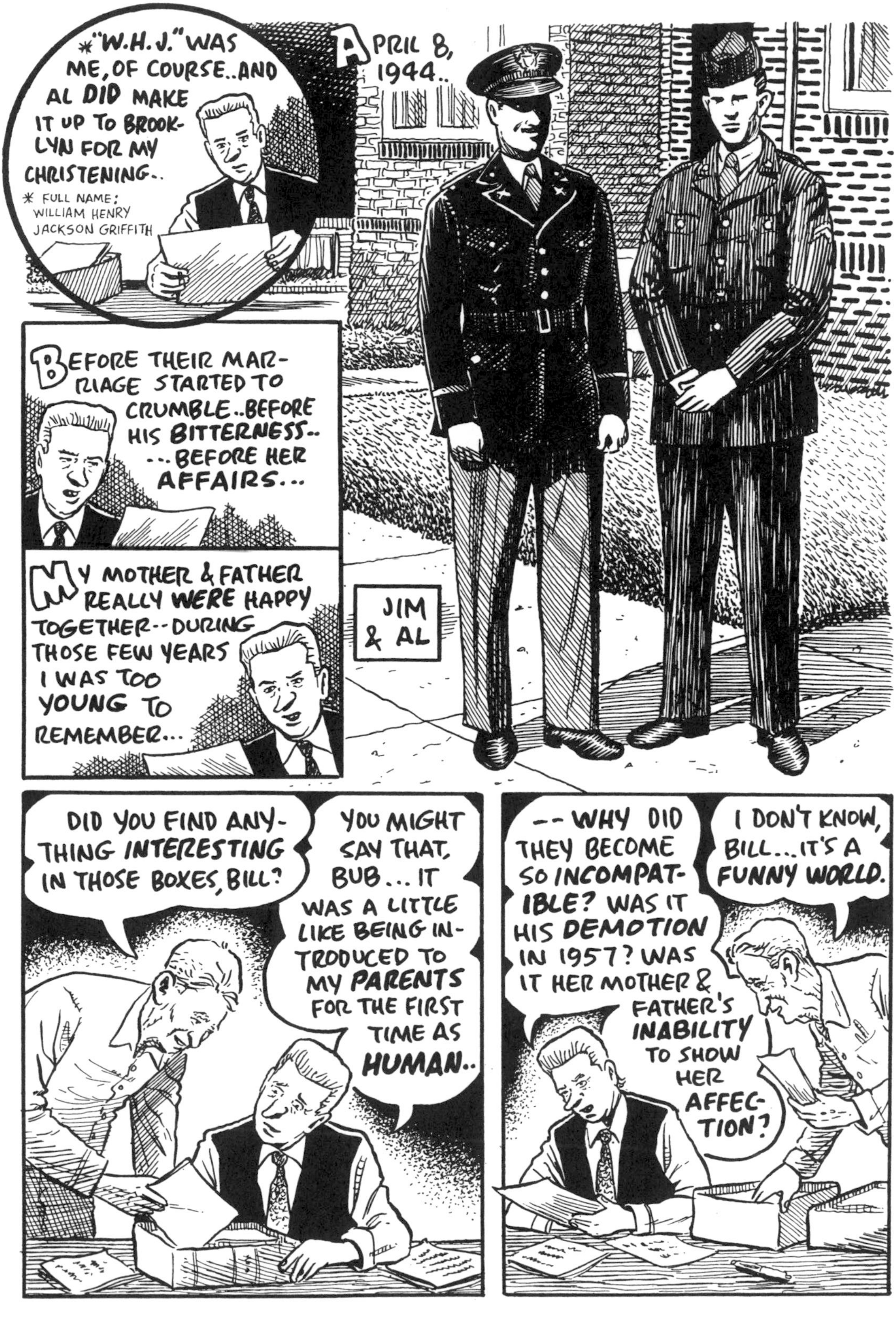
*"W.H.J." WAS ME, OF COURSE.. AND AL DID MAKE IT UP TO BROOKLYN FOR MY CHRISTENING..
* FULL NAME: WILLIAM HENRY JACKSON GRIFFITH
APRIL 8, 1944..
JIM & AL
BEFORE THEIR MARRIAGE STARTED TO CRUMBLE.. BEFORE HIS BITTERNESS.. ...BEFORE HER AFFAIRS...
MY MOTHER & FATHER REALLY WERE HAPPY TOGETHER--DURING THOSE FEW YEARS I WAS TOO YOUNG TO REMEMBER...
DID YOU FIND ANYTHING INTERESTING IN THOSE BOXES, BILL?
YOU MIGHT SAY THAT, BUB... IT WAS A LITTLE LIKE BEING INTRODUCED TO MY PARENTS FOR THE FIRST TIME AS HUMAN..
--WHY DID THEY BECOME SO INCOMPATIBLE? WAS IT HIS DEMOTION IN 1957? WAS IT HER MOTHER & FATHER'S INABILITY TO SHOW HER AFFECTION?
I DON'T KNOW, BILL... IT'S A FUNNY WORLD.

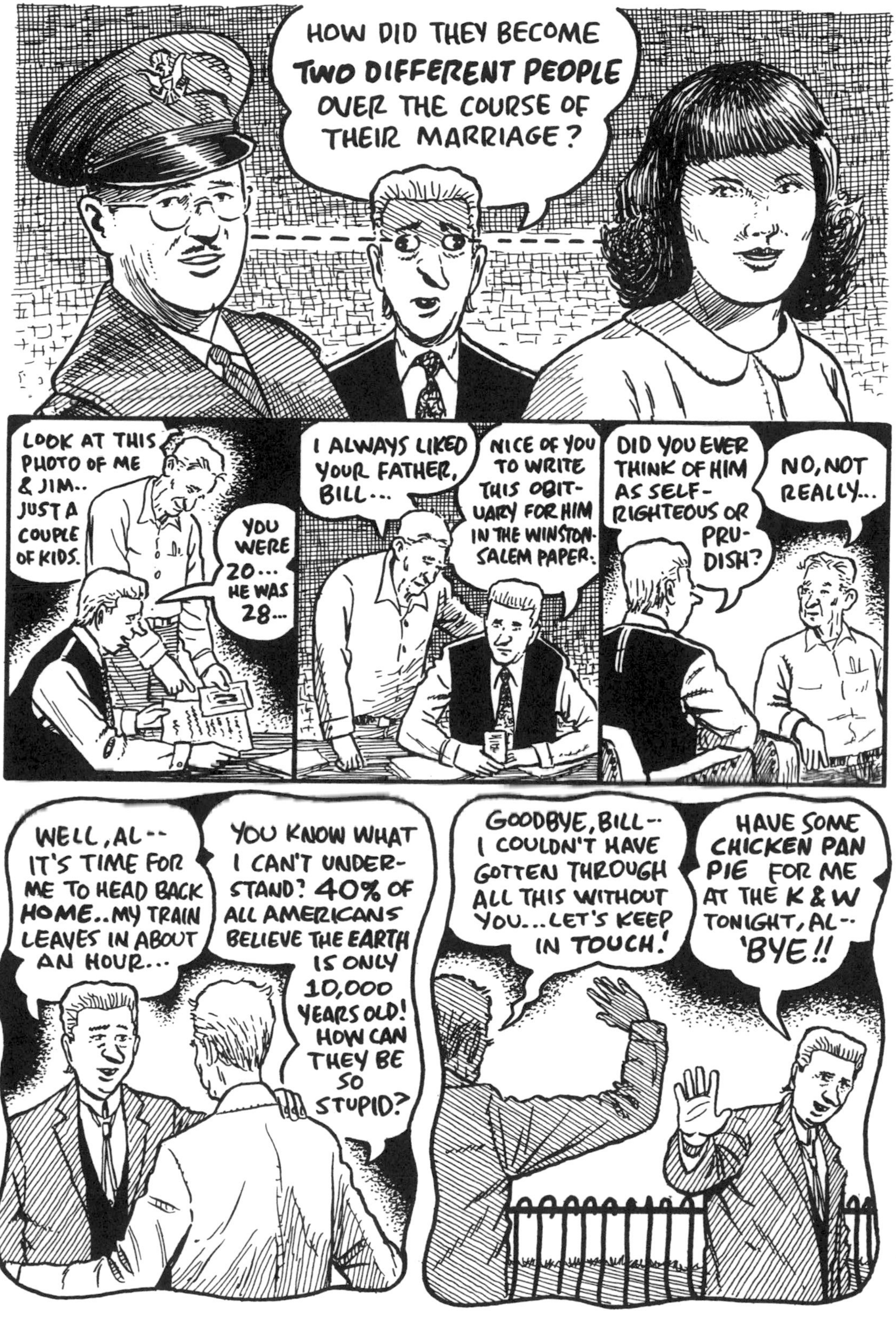
HOW DID THEY BECOME TWO DIFFERENT PEOPLE OVER THE COURSE OF THEIR MARRIAGE?
LOOK AT THIS PHOTO OF ME & JIM.. JUST A COUPLE OF KIDS.
YOU WERE 20... HE WAS 28...
I ALWAYS LIKED YOUR FATHER, BILL...
NICE OF YOU TO WRITE THIS OBITUARY FOR HIM IN THE WINSTON-SALEM PAPER.
DID YOU EVER THINK OF HIM AS SELF-RIGHTEOUS OR PRUDISH?
NO, NOT REALLY...
WELL, AL-- IT'S TIME FOR ME TO HEAD BACK HOME.. MY TRAIN LEAVES IN ABOUT AN HOUR...
YOU KNOW WHAT I CAN'T UNDERSTAND? 40% OF ALL AMERICANS BELIEVE THE EARTH IS ONLY 10,000 YEARS OLD! HOW CAN THEY BE SO STUPID?
GOODBYE, BILL-- I COULDN'T HAVE GOTTEN THROUGH ALL THIS WITHOUT YOU... LET'S KEEP IN TOUCH!
HAVE SOME CHICKEN PAN PIE FOR ME AT THE K & W TONIGHT, AL-- 'BYE!!

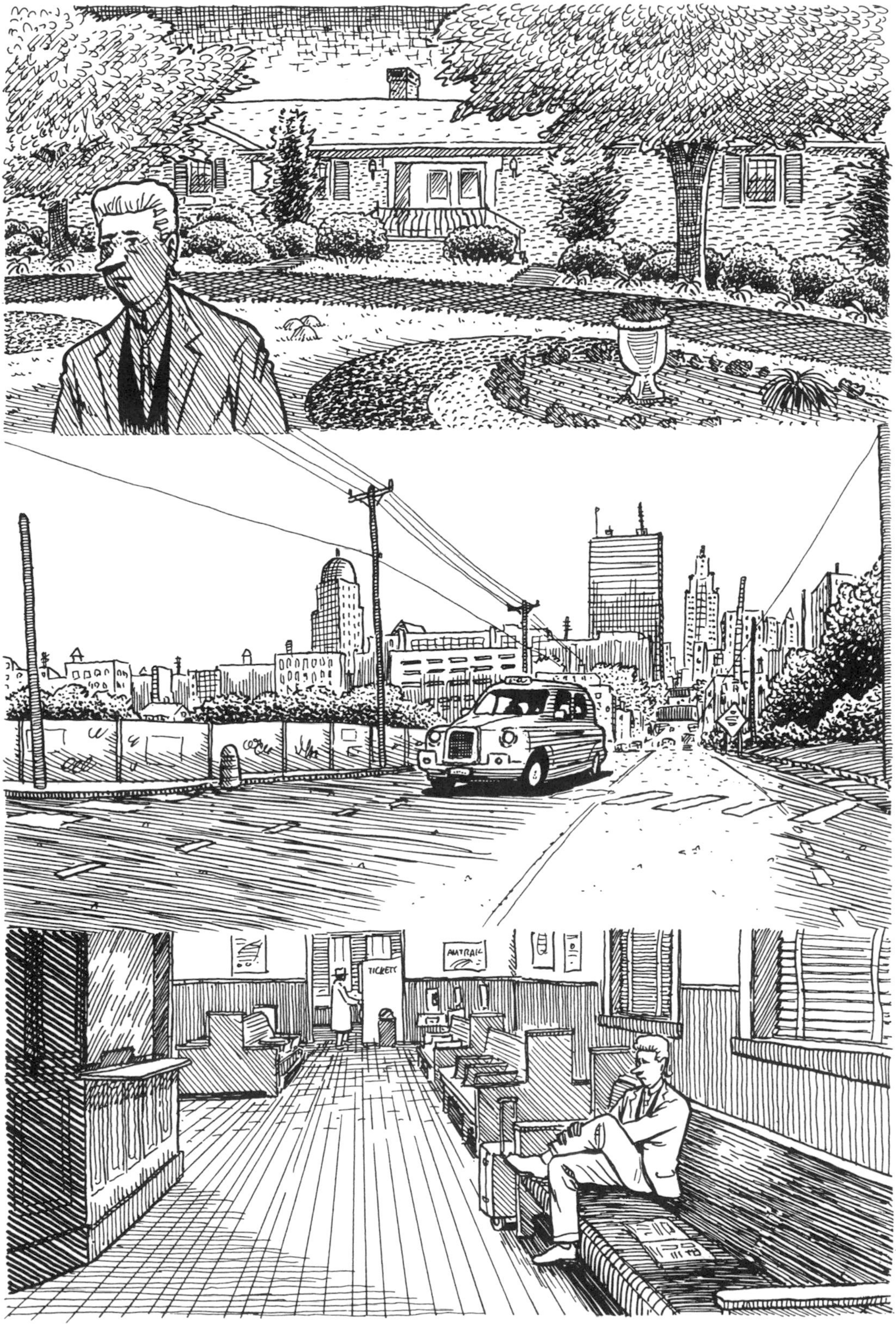
TICKETS
AMTRAK

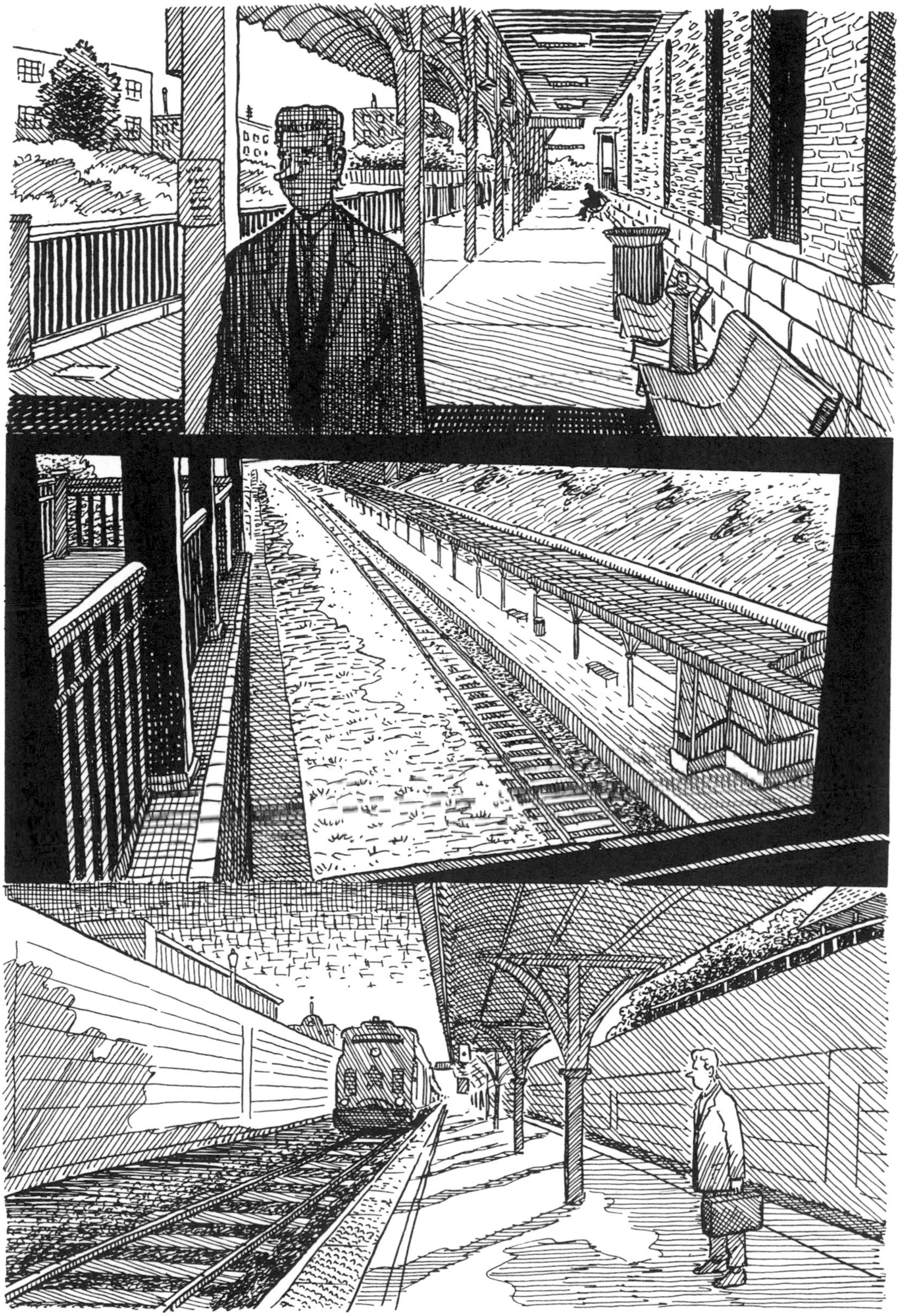

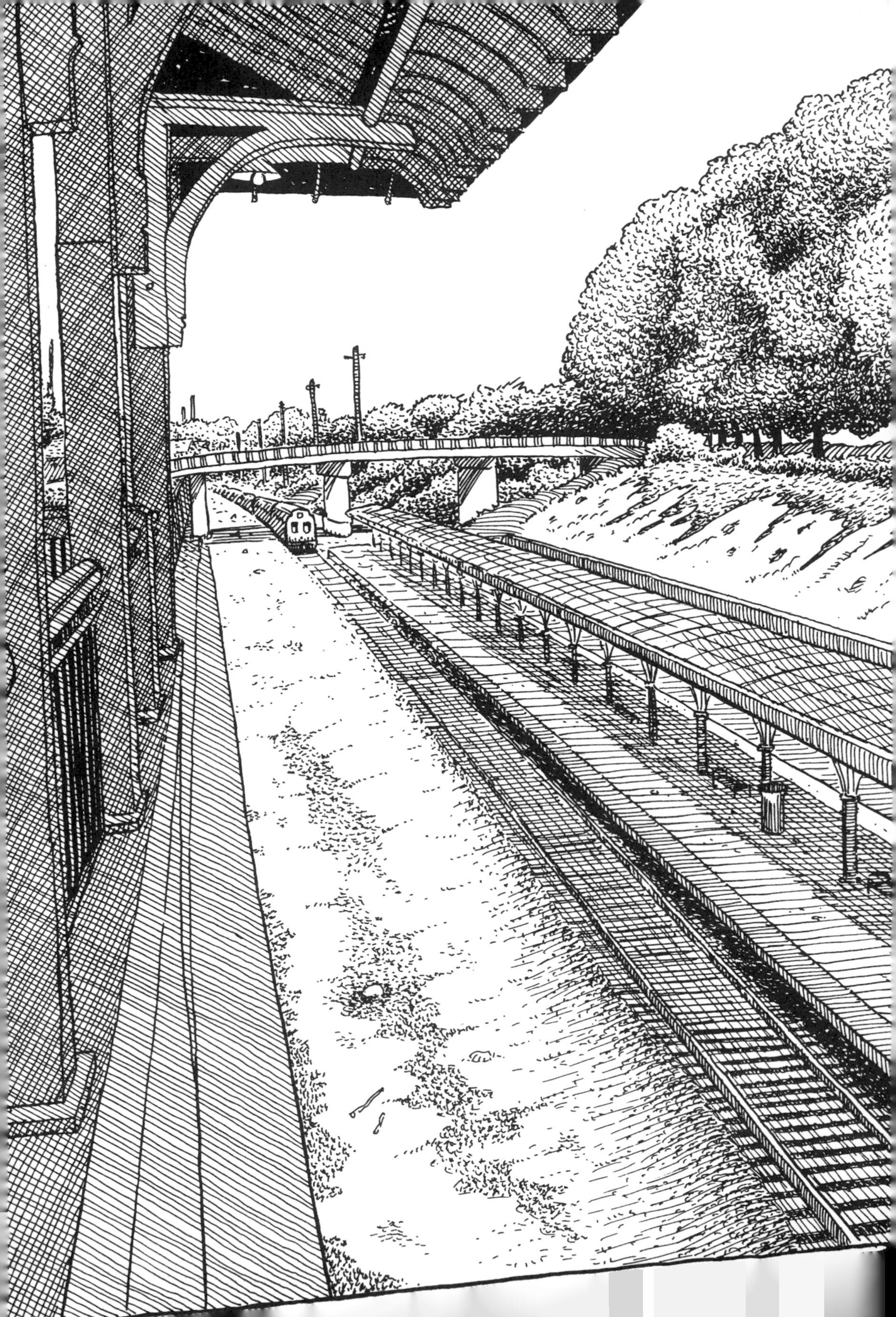

INVISIBLE INK FAMILY TREE

Includes only people mentioned in this book

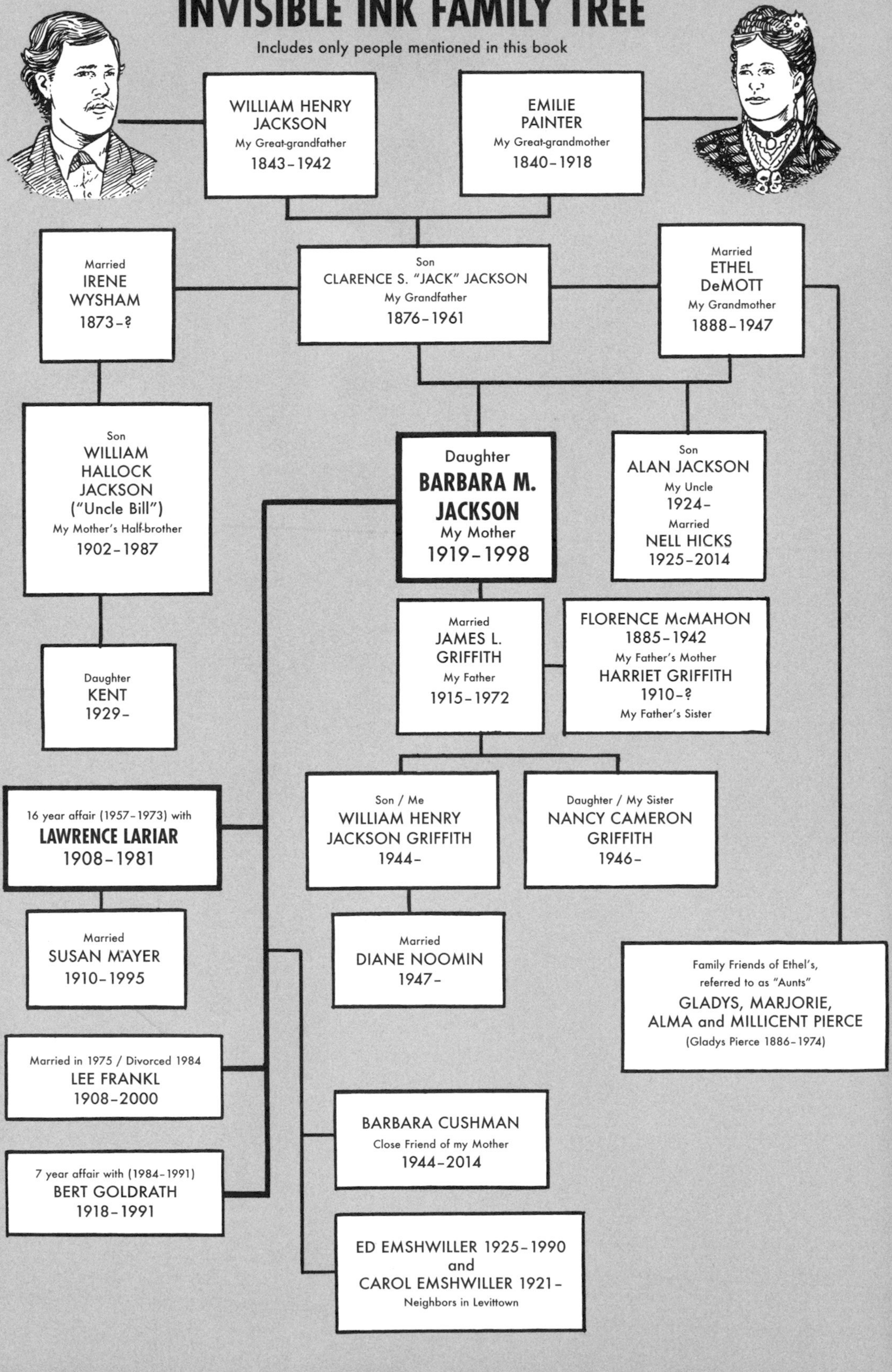

WILLIAM HENRY JACKSON
My Great-grandfather
1843–1942
EMILIE PAINTER
My Great-grandmother
1840–1918
Married
IRENE WYSHAM
1873–?
Son
CLARENCE S. "JACK" JACKSON
My Grandfather
1876–1961
Married
ETHEL DeMOTT
My Grandmother
1888–1947
Son
WILLIAM HALLOCK JACKSON
("Uncle Bill")
My Mother's Half-brother
1902–1987
Daughter
BARBARA M. JACKSON
My Mother
1919–1998
Son
ALAN JACKSON
My Uncle
1924–
Married
NELL HICKS
1925–2014
Daughter
KENT
1929–
Married
JAMES L. GRIFFITH
My Father
1915–1972
FLORENCE McMAHON
1885–1942
My Father's Mother
HARRIET GRIFFITH
1910–?
My Father's Sister
16 year affair (1957–1973) with
LAWRENCE LARIAR
1908–1981
Son / Me
WILLIAM HENRY JACKSON GRIFFITH
1944–
Daughter / My Sister
NANCY CAMERON GRIFFITH
1946–
Married
SUSAN MAYER
1910–1995
Married
DIANE NOOMIN
1947–
Family Friends of Ethel's,
referred to as "Aunts"
GLADYS, MARJORIE,
ALMA and MILLICENT PIERCE
(Gladys Pierce 1886–1974)
Married in 1975 / Divorced 1984
LEE FRANKL
1908–2000
BARBARA CUSHMAN
Close Friend of my Mother
1944–2014
7 year affair with (1984–1991)
BERT GOLDRATH
1918–1991
ED EMSHWILLER 1925–1990
and
CAROL EMSHWILLER 1921–
Neighbors in Levittown

"DEPARTED ACTS" FAMILY TREE

Principal characters from the unpublished novel by Barbara Griffith
and their equivalents in real life

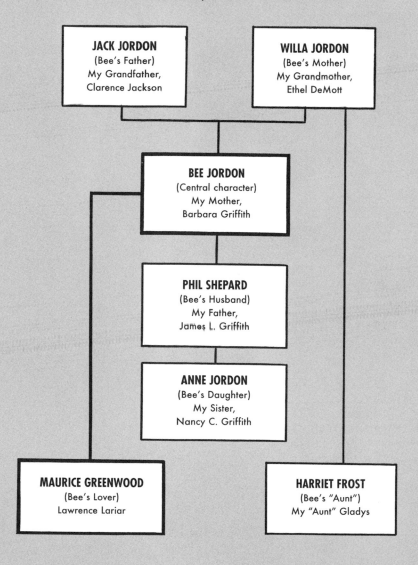

JACK JORDON
(Bee's Father)
My Grandfather,
Clarence Jackson

WILLA JORDON
(Bee's Mother)
My Grandmother,
Ethel DeMott

BEE JORDON
(Central character)
My Mother,
Barbara Griffith

PHIL SHEPARD
(Bee's Husband)
My Father,
James L. Griffith

ANNE JORDON
(Bee's Daughter)
My Sister,
Nancy C. Griffith

MAURICE GREENWOOD
(Bee's Lover)
Lawrence Lariar

HARRIET FROST
(Bee's "Aunt")
My "Aunt" Gladys